# Managing the Guest Experience
# in Hospitality

# Managing the Guest Experience
# in Hospitality

**Robert C. Ford, Ph.D.**
*University of Central Florida*

**Cherrill P. Heaton, Ph.D.**
*University of North Florida*

Africa • Australia • Canada • Denmark • Japan • Mexico • New Zealand • Philippines
Puerto Rico • Singapore • Spain • United Kingdom • United States

## NOTICE TO THE READER

Publisher does not warrant or guarantee any of the products described herein or perform any independent analysis in connection with any of the product information contained herein. Publisher does not assume, and expressly disclaims, any obligation to obtain and include information other than that provided to it by the manufacturer.

The reader is expressly warned to consider and adopt all safety precautions that might be indicated by the activities herein and to avoid all potential hazards. By following the instructions contained herein, the reader willingly assumes all risks in connection with such instructions.

The Publisher makes no representation or warranties of any kind, including but not limited to, the warranties of fitness for particular purpose or merchantability, nor are any such representations implied with respect to the material set forth herein, and the publisher takes no responsibility with respect to such material. The publisher shall not be liable for any special, consequential, or exemplary damages resulting, in whole or part, from the readers' use of, or reliance upon, this material.

**Delmar Staff:**
Business Unit Director: Susan L. Simpfenderfer
Executive Editor: Marlene McHugh Pratt
Acquisition Editor: Erin O'Connor Traylor
Editorial Assistant: Judy Roberts
Executive Production Manager: Wendy A. Troeger
Production Editor: Elaine Scull
Executive Marketing Manager: Donna Lewis
Channel Managers: Nigar Hale, Eleanor J. Murray
Cover Design: Joseph Villanova

**Library of Congress Cataloging-in-Publication Data**
Ford, Robert C. (Robert Clayton), 1945-
   Managing the guest experience in hospitality / Robert C. Ford, Cherrill P. Heaton.
      p.   cm.
   Includes bibliographical references and index.
   ISBN: 0-7668-1415-7
   1. Hospitality industry—Customer services.  I. Heaton, Cherrill P.  II. Title
TX911.3C8 F67 1999
647.94'068"—dc21                                                         99–049972

# Dedication

*This book is dedicated to
Bruce Laval,
the father of guestology*

# Contents

# Foreword

As a long-time hospitality practitioner and teacher, I have learned that hospitality is essentially a simple business: You find out what the guest wants, and you organize your resources in a way that enables you to provide that and maybe a little more. The best thing hospitality management programs can do is to be sure that these two simple concepts are firmly embedded in the thinking and actions of their graduates. Regardless of what else they learn, if our students don't understand the importance of systematically asking their guests and potential guests what they want and then managing everything and everyone in the organization so as to fulfill these guest expectations, then we have not taught the fundamental lessons of hospitality.

Several authors have written textbooks and articles that cover some aspects of the first issue very well. Most hospitality programs teach the marketing fundamentals that give students a solid awareness of the need to discover what guests really want. The rest of this equation, however, has awaited thorough coverage: how to manage a hospitality organization in a way that focuses on the guest. Although we have many fine texts and many great courses on front-desk operations, housekeeping, restaurant management, and other specific aspects of the hospitality industry, we have lacked a comprehensive book on how to manage in an industry that is uniquely different from industries covered in traditional management texts. Our business *is* different, and this book not only recognizes the differences but does so in a comprehensive way that gives us the teaching tools we all need to ensure that our students graduate with a robust appreciation of the importance of managing our businesses with the guest first and foremost in our minds and in the minds of all who work with us.

This book fills an important gap and does so extremely well. It begins and ends with the guest. It focuses on how to manage an organization in such a way that the guest's expectations are met or exceeded. A missing ingredient in many academic programs has now been supplied with this text.

The book is easy and fun to read; it is brightened by many contemporary illustrations from all parts of the industry but especially from the Walt Disney Company. The authors live in Florida and have obviously learned well from some of the hospitality industry's true leaders. The book has been reviewed by a number of hospitality executives and respected academics and field-tested in classes for over two years. This is a well-written, student-friendly, comprehensive, and reality-based text. Students will enjoy reading it, and instructors will enjoy building on the concepts and principles it contains.

I am glad to see a text that finally covers the missing half of our simple business, and you will be, too.

Robert C. Lewis, Ph.D.
University of Guelph

# Preface

## The Engineer

In 1971 the Walt Disney Company opened its brand-new Magic Kingdom in the middle of a 43-square-mile site near the quiet town of Orlando, Florida. Among the many people hired to help operate this venture was a newly graduated industrial engineer from the University of Florida. One of his first jobs was to study the capacity requirements of the monorail system that carried customers from the main parking lot to the Magic Kingdom. Because customer demand had turned out to be higher than expected, long lines of customers had to wait to be transported by monorail train into the Magic Kingdom. Customers hate to wait. The logical solution seemed to be adding more carrying capacity, and the study's original purpose was to help justify the need for and associated cost of an additional monorail train.

This young engineer had just completed his master's thesis on computer simulation, a technique enabling the analysis and optimizing of complex queuing systems. In essence, queuing theory is a mathematical technique for studying and understanding how best to serve people waiting in lines, or queues, at grocery store checkout counters, bank teller windows, and the like. The engineer saw this monorail problem as a perfect opportunity to apply computer simulation to real life. He created a computerized queuing model of the entire Magic Kingdom monorail system and simulated the average waiting time of customers at the parking-lot station wanting to go by monorail to the park entrance.

The engineer's analysis of all possible system configurations led him to a startling conclusion: The computer simulation showed that to increase the system capacity and thereby reduce customer wait times, Disney should not add another monorail train but *eliminate* an existing train. The simulation clearly showed that too many trains were on the system already and, as a result, the trains were never able to get up to full design speeds. Safety control devices on the monorail system prevented trains from getting too close to each other by automatically cutting power to any train that encroached into the zone of the preceding train. Therefore, because too many trains were on the system at a time, the trains were constantly being slowed down and often stopped while waiting for a preceding train to clear its zone. With one less train on the system, incoming trains were able to unload, load, and leave a station immediately and travel at design speed between stations without having to wait before leaving or slow down while in motion (or even stop, sit, and wait between stations), because the preceding train had not cleared its zone. Since overall monorail system capacity is a function of how quickly trains can be dispatched from stations after unloading and then reloading, enabling fewer trains to travel between stations more quickly would increase the system's carrying capacity. Or so the simulation said.

Convincing people unfamiliar with queuing theory and simulation that these results were valid was difficult. But, after much discussion, management decided to let the young engineer try out this crazy idea and agreed to conduct a test. Much to everyone's surprise, it worked. The lines did decrease and, more amazingly, the customer waiting times predicted by the simulation were accurate within thirty seconds of the actual average wait recorded during the test. Needless to say, this outcome led to some interesting career opportunities with Disney for the young college graduate, who continued to use quantitative models to describe and predict Walt Disney World Resort customer behavior.

Bruce Laval, now Executive Vice President, Operations Planning and Development, Walt Disney Attractions, was that young engineer. During his next twenty-five years with the company, he held various executive operating and planning positions, including Executive Vice President, Operations Planning and Development, Walt Disney World Resort. He and his staff were responsible for studying, measuring, and managing the service experience at Walt Disney World Resort to ensure that customers have the outstanding experience for which Disney is famous. He is the man to whom this book is dedicated.

## The Academic

In 1993 Bob Ford went to the University of Central Florida to head the Department of Hospitality Management. Dick Nunis, then President of Walt Disney World Resort, sponsored an internship for Bob with Disney, to help Bob build an academic program to train the next generation of leaders for Disney and other forward-looking hospitality organizations in the area. Bob spent time in the three theme parks (the Magic Kingdom, Epcot, and Disney-MGM Studios), several hotels and restaurants, water parks, Pleasure Island, and the central kitchen and laundry on Disney property, talking to managers and employees about what they did and why. This company is frequently cited as a leader in hospitality management, and the internship was a great way to learn more about the hospitality industry and the Disney approach to managing.

Out of many interesting experiences, the most influential for Bob occurred during the Traditions training program required of all new Disney employees. As the trainee group came out of the underground tunnel onto the square at Main Street, U.S.A., in the Magic Kingdom, the training guide asked an interesting question about the streets that branched off from the square: Could anyone see any difference between the street that went toward Tomorrowland and the street that led to Frontierland? When no one could, she pointed out that the street going off to the customer's right (to Tomorrowland) was slightly wider than the one to the left (to Frontierland); Disney researchers had studied customer behavior and had learned that when customers come to a decision point about which they are really indifferent, they tend to go in the direction of their *handedness*. In designing the park, Disney made the roads wider toward the right (since most people are right-handed) than toward the left.

This explanation excited the academic; it suggested that a rational, scientific process was used to create and manage the park. He set out to find the person behind this thinking.

He found Bruce Laval. Their continuing dialogue was one stimulation for Bob Ford to get together with Cherrill Heaton, coauthor with Bob of *Principles of Management: A Decision-Making Approach* and *Organization Theory: An Integrative Approach,* to write this book. The guest-focused approach to hospitality management, as seen at Disney and other progressive hospitality organizations, is a whole new way of managing. This book blends an explanation of this approach to hospitality management with relevant research findings about managing hospitality organizations.

During the internship, Bob made the mistake (only once!) of referring to park visitors as customers. He was quickly informed that park visitors are Disney's *guests* and are always to be treated that way. Bob heard the term *guestology* used at Disney. It seemed to mean something like "treat our park visitors as our guests. Find out what our guests want and expect from their park experience, and organize all of Walt Disney World Resort's functions, people, attractions, and activities so they provide the park experience that guests expect, and then some." Bruce Laval's monorail study and the study of handedness as it relates to guest choices at intersections are examples of the scientific approaches to discovering and meeting guest needs that Disney and other leading-edge hospitality organizations use.

Bob also met executives from other hospitality organizations and found that many of them, like Disney, also managed their businesses from the customer's or guest's point of view. The way they ran their businesses was not a mere modification of the traditional management principles long taught in business schools; Bob realized they were using principles, practices, and methods that were part of the emerging services literature plus much that was based largely on their acquired knowledge—gained through hard experience—of the differences between the service industry and smokestack industries.

## Purpose of the Book

This book is an attempt to organize and present this information, some of which comes from academic studies, some from the school of experience. It was written to meet the needs of college classes devoted to or including exploration of this exciting, undeveloped area: managing hospitality organizations. It should also be of help to executives and managers who want to implement a guest-focused service strategy in any hospitality organization that wants to compete successfully in today's customer-driven market.

The book fills a void. Up until now, instructors and students in hospitality management classes have had to use a text on general services management, with specific applications to restaurants, lodging, and other hospitality areas made by the instructor or by means of handouts and articles on serving guests in hospitality settings. *Managing the Guest Experience in Hospitality* fills that void. It joins between two covers the findings of the most significant research on services and hospitality services in particular with the best practices of leading hospitality organizations like the Walt Disney Company, Marriott, Ritz-Carlton, Darden Restaurants, Southwest Airlines, and many others.

In addition to reviews by numerous college and university instructors of hospitality, the material has been reviewed by practicing executives in many successful hospitality organizations, among them Walt Disney World Resort, Hertz Corporation, Bristol Hotels, Sodexho-Marriott, Boykin Hotel Corp., Planet Hollywood, Tishman Hotel Corporation, Darden Restaurants, Cheesecake Factory, SeaWorld of Florida, Opryland Hotel, and Hilton Hotels. These academic and practitioner reviews have assured that the text content is supported by sound theoretical underpinnings and real-world findings.

## The Hospitality Principles

*Managing the Guest Experience in Hospitality* represents theory that has passed the test of relevance. A proven principle of hospitality management keys each chapter of this book. Leading hospitality organizations have found these principles to be important, workable, and useful. They represent the key points to keep in mind when putting the book's material into practice. They can guide hospitality organizations and their managers as they seek to reach the levels of excellence achieved by the benchmark organizations.

## Systematic Sequence

Its clear structure and organization are major strengths of *Managing the Guest Experience in Hospitality*. A section is devoted to each of hospitality management's three major concerns: **Strategy, Staffing, and Systems.** Each of the fourteen chapters is keyed to a principle of successful hospitality management.

**Section 1** (The Hospitality Service Strategy) begins by explaining some of the book's major concepts: some differences between **products** and **services,** what is meant by **guestology,** meeting **customer expectations,** the three parts of the **guest experience,** and the definitions of **quality, value,** and **cost** in a guest service context. This Section then moves to a thorough coverage of the **planning** processes used to assess and meet guest expectations. Also explained are such essential planning topics as quantitative and qualitative **forecasting tools,** the importance of **demographic trends,** and the organization's service strategy origins in its **vision, purpose,** and **mission,** which themselves are based on the organization's careful assessment of guest expectations. Chapter 3 is on why the **service setting** or **environment** is crucial to service success. Many Walt Disney World Resort examples are used to illustrate the principles and best practices of creating an appropriate setting. Disney organizes its parks and attractions around fantasy **themes.** Disney's attention to detail is the benchmark against which other hospitality organizations measure the quality and effectiveness of their own service environments. Therefore we have based our discussion of service environments in general and theming in particular on Disney examples. Part 1 concludes by discussing the importance to the hospitality organization of a total **service culture** and how to achieve it.

**Section 2** (The Hospitality Service Staff) covers how to recruit and **hire** "persons who love to serve," and how to **train, motivate,** and **empower** them to provide outstanding guest service. A section that many students find particularly interesting is devoted to how the hospitality organization can, when the conditions are right, encourage and help guests to **coproduce,** or participate in providing their own experiences!

**Section 3** (The Hospitality Service Systems) shows how to glue the different parts of the guest experience together by communicating **information** to the right person at the right time. Because of its obvious importance to the successful guest experience, **service delivery** is the subject of a separate chapter. Because no organization's server/system combinations can match demand perfectly, techniques for managing the inevitable **waits** for service are covered. All organizations want to provide perfect experiences; we cover how to **avoid service failures** and problems. But because no servers and systems have yet been devised that can provide so complex a service as the guest experience perfectly every time, we also cover how to **fix service failures** when they occur. Chapter 13 presents some ways of **measuring results** in terms of service quality and guest satisfaction so organizations and servers know how they are doing.

Section 3 and the book conclude with an explanation of how the organization's people, units, and their efforts are tied together to provide remarkable guest service that delights guests; that blending of parts and people is accomplished by outstanding organizational **leadership.**

## Learning Objectives, Key Terms, and Discussion Questions

Every chapter opens with a comprehensive set of **learning objectives** addressing the chapter's main points. The list of **key terms and concepts** serves as a brief preview of the subjects and ideas in the chapter to come. These terms and concepts are boldfaced the first time they appear in the chapter. The **discussion questions** at each chapter's end are designed to provoke thought and classroom interaction about chapter content and to enable students to make self-assessments of how well they understand the material.

## Activities and Case Studies

Each chapter includes at least one **hospitality activity** to encourage students to visit local hospitality organizations and study them from the perspective of the book's ideas. Some activities suggest that students talk with guests, employees, and managers to obtain a variety of perspectives on the guest experience. Other activities suggest exploration of the Internet to visit sites established by hospitality organizations and to acquire further information on the book's concepts and ideas. **Case studies** provide an opportunity to discuss hospitality concepts and principles in terms of real (if disguised) and hypothetical hotels, restaurants, and other business types found in the hospitality industry.

## Instructor's Guide to Text

The **Instructor's Guide** provides **answers** to the end-of-chapter questions and to the discussion questions following the chapter cases, **additional field exercises** in hospitality, true-false and multiple-choice quizzes, and **additional material** to assist the instructor in preparing course outlines and lesson plans.

## To the Student

*Managing the Guest Experience in Hospitality* is designed for you. The material has been tried out in several classes of students with backgrounds similar to yours. The information presented is based on the best available research on services and hospitality services in particular, and on the best practices of leading hospitality organizations. The book should give you a thorough understanding of the principles of managing a hospitality organization; we think you will want to keep the book with you if you enter the hospitality field.

## Primary Support Staff

Once again and always, we thank our wives, Barbara Ford and Marieta Barrow Heaton, for unfailing support and for continuing to exceed our expectations; they put the *wow!* in our lives.

Robert C. Ford
Cherrill P. Heaton

# Acknowledgments

We would like to thank many people for reading our manuscript and offering suggestions for revision. Their insightful comments added great value to our project.

## Teacher-Scholars

The following teacher-scholars in the fields of management, services, and hospitality provided careful commentary on our manuscript and offered sound suggestions for revision. Thanks to their help, we are confident that our book rests on firm theoretical underpinnings and that it represents the best of current academic thought about the ideas and principles with which we deal.

John Newstrom
University of Minnesota—Duluth

Joe West
Florida International University

Abe Pizam
University of Central Florida

Robert Lewis
University of Guelph

Taylor Ellis
University of Central Florida

Frank McLaughlin
University of North Florida

Carl Riegel
Florida Atlantic University

Taylor Damonte
Coastal Carolina University

Myron Fottler
University of Central Florida

Kathryn Hashimoto and her hospitality
  management class
University of New Orleans

John Crotts and his hospitality
  management class
College of Charleston

Robin W. Turner
Delhi University

David K. Hanson
Idaho State University

William Dunham
Cuyahoga Community College

David Cohen
Bergen Community College

Special thanks to the more than 180 students at the University of Central Florida who used a draft of this book as their text and shared their reactions with us.

## Industry Professionals

We are hugely indebted to the hospitality industry professionals who made time in their busy schedules to read our book in its draft forms. We admit to feeling gratified that so many of them said something like, "Yes, you've got it right; that's how we try to run our organizations."

Bruce Laval, Walt Disney Attractions, to whom this book is dedicated

Carol Pacula
Walt Disney World Resort

Cesar Gonzales
Walt Disney World Resort

Ben Redshaw
Walt Disney World Resort

Bill McCreary
Walt Disney World Resort–Dolphin

Duncan Dickson
Hospitality Consultant

Cathy Moore
Hertz Corporation

Michael Sansbury
Loew's Hotels

Michael Terry
Bristol Hotels

George Koenig
Sodexho-Marriott

Ron Cook
Boykin Hotel Corp.

Rob Mitchell
Kessler Enterprises

Richard Maladecki
Central Florida Hotel and Motel Association

Bob Wacker
Hospitality Consultant

Bill Lombardo
Planet Hollywood

Victor Meena
Universal Studios of Florida

John Griswold
Tishman Hotel Corporation

Kent Shoemaker
Red's Market

Rick Walsh
Darden Restaurants

Dan Lyons
Darden Restaurants

Blaine Sweatt
Darden Restaurants

Bill Streitberger
Cheesecake Factory

Victor G. Abbey
Sea World of Florida

Ken Kinka
Interlachen Country Club

Emily Ellis
Opryland Hotel

Samir Shafei
Hilton Hotels

Wellington Morton
Photographer

Our thanks to Dick Nunis, the Walt Disney Company, for encouraging us to teach the course in guestology that led to the creation of this book.

We appreciate the help of the editing and production staffs at Delmar and Shepherd, Inc. Our special thanks to Editorial Assistant Judy Roberts and Production Editor Elaine Scull.

## THE PRINCIPLES
## OF
## HOSPITALITY MANAGEMENT

1. Provide the service quality and value that guests expect.

2. Focus strategy on the key drivers of guest satisfaction.

3. Provide the service setting that guests expect.

4. Define and build a total service culture.

5. Find and hire people who love to serve.

6. Train your employees, then train them some more.

7. Motivate and empower your employees.

8. Empower guests to help create their own experience.

9. Glue the guest experience elements together with information.

10. Provide seamless service delivery.

11. Manage the guest's wait.

12. Don't fail the guest twice.

13. Pursue perfection relentlessly.

14. Lead others to excel.

# Introduction

## SERVICE RULES!

The modern economy is dominated by service organizations. The service sector is 75 percent to 80 percent of the U.S. economy and growing. Roland Rust points out that even businesses dealing primarily in physical goods "now view themselves primarily as services, with the offered good being an important part of the service (rather than the service being an augmentation of the physical good)."[1] These firms have adopted such traditional services terms as *customer satisfaction, customer retention,* and *customer relationships.*

Yet, surprisingly few articles and books focus on how to manage service organizations, even fewer on how to manage hospitality organizations. The purpose of this book is to provide a comprehensive review of the best that is known about managing hospitality organizations. From the neighborhood restaurant to the resort hotel, from the small convention center to the huge theme park, the principles of managing hospitality organizations are the same. Even more importantly, they are different from the principles of managing manufacturing organizations taught in most business schools.

## HOSPITALITY *IS* DIFFERENT

Traditional bureaucratic structures and manufacturing management principles get turned on their heads in the hospitality sector. It's one thing to design, organize, and control a work process and motivate a workforce when the product is tangible and the production process takes place in a big closed brick factory with an "Employees Only" sign on the door. A totally different challenge arises when the customer is consuming your "product" while you're producing it. The challenge is often intensified by the product's intangibility: "Hospitality" is intangible, and the hospitality *experience* may not even physically exist! Designing and producing such an experience is quite different from the design and production of goods.

These "production" problems in the hospitality industry are matched or exceeded by the challenge of managing employees who must be carefully trained to provide a service whose quality and value are defined by each guest. To top it off, employees must be taught to provide this service not behind closed doors but while customers, guests, or clients are watching, asking questions, and changing their minds about what they want. They may even participate jointly with the employees in providing the guest experience itself! Manufacturing managers sometimes moan about how hard it is to teach their employees to perform the necessary manufacturing steps accurately. They should talk to their colleagues in the hospitality industry who not only have to teach their employees how to "manufacture" the product but also how to do so with the guest watching and sometimes participating. These managers know that the principles taught in smokestack management courses in traditional business schools don't seem too relevant. Managing in the hospitality industry is a very different world.

## STUDY THE BEST

Only recently have researchers and management scholars begun to study this different world as a separate field, and much of what is known is still based on anecdotal information and case-study examples. This makes perfect sense. In the early stages of inquiry into any field of business, the logical approach is to find the best organizations and study them to discover the principles that drive what they do. A review of the service management literature quickly reveals several benchmark organizations. The list includes Southwest Airlines and American Airlines, hotel chains Marriott and Ritz-Carlton, Nordstrom's Department Store, USAA Insurance Company, Shouldice Hospital, and the Walt Disney Company. These organizations learned long ago the importance of understanding what their customers expect from all parts of their service experience, and they manage their businesses around satisfying those expectations. Because they have studied their guests long and hard, they know what their guests want, what they are willing to pay for it, and how to give it to them. The *magic* of Disney and the other outstanding hospitality organizations is that they meet guest expectations, of course, and then exceed them in a thousand ways that get guests not only to say "wow!" on the first visit but to return repeatedly and say "wow!" every time. Customers, clients, patrons, and guests return to the great organizations—manufacturing or service— because they get it right and then some.

## WHY DISNEY?

Although this book provides examples from all of these organizations, more come from Disney than from any other. Disney is an easy company for us to learn about. We live and work within two hours of the Walt Disney World Resort. Many Disney employees take classes at the University of Central Florida, the local and regional Florida newspapers and magazines cover Disney activities, Disney executives make speeches in the area and are open to conversation. Disney is a storytelling organization, and the stories its leaders tell help explain the company and its approach to managing. Therefore, we don't need "inside information"; Disney cast members are proud of what they do and how they do it.

Another reason is that the Walt Disney World Resort near Orlando provides an exceptionally wide representation of the hospitality industry. Operating on the grounds are successful examples of restaurants from quick-serve to fine dining; lodging from campgrounds to upscale hotels; a transportation system that includes trains, boats, buses, and monorails; catering services, convention and meeting planning services, entertainment and night clubs, retail stores, golf courses, and (not far away) cruise ships—virtually all the major types of hospitality organizations except gaming establishments. These organizations include almost every specific job category in the hospitality field. The range of jobs for study on the Disney property—in terms of staffing, training, motivating, and job performance—is very wide. Disney itself hires and trains thousands of people annually to fill 1,100 different positions.

But the main reason for the many Disney examples is that Disney is one of the best hospitality organizations in the world. Although few organizations will ever own a major theme park and few readers will ever manage one, any hospitality organization and every hospitality manager can learn much from Disney. This book will show that the successful hospitality organizations *treat their customers like guests* and offer their guests not just goods and services but *memorable experiences*. When it comes to following those two principles, Disney is the best.

Here are two of many ways in which Disney has been a pioneer in providing outstanding guest experiences. First, organizations have learned from Disney that the most successful experiences are based on a theme, and Disney provides its "service product," family entertainment, in themed fantasy settings. For example, the Magic Kingdom is based on the fantasy theme of the Disney characters. Second, Disney learned early that the satisfaction guests receive from their experiences is a direct function of employee satisfaction in providing those experiences. Disney managers and supervisors know how to achieve and maintain the levels of employee satisfaction that motivate employees to provide outstanding, memorable guest experiences. In the emerging "experience economy," Disney did it first and no one does it better.

## FOCUS ON YOUR *GUEST*

Two fundamental concepts, based on the practices of successful hospitality organizations, will appear in one form or another throughout the book. First, *everything the organization does should focus on the guest.* Most managers think first about their organization, their production requirements, and their employee needs. They are used to starting with themselves or their employees when they design their product, create the setting or environment in which the customer interacts with the organization, and set up the system for delivering the goods or services that their customers came to the organization to buy. They manage from the inside out. This first fundamental concept requires managing from the outside in: *Start with the guests.* Study them endlessly; know what they want, need, value, and expect. Then focus everyone in the organization on figuring out how to do a better job of meeting and exceeding guest expectations in a way that allows the organization to make a profit.

## YOUR CUSTOMER IS YOUR GUEST

Here is a second fundamental concept that must be part of the hospitality organization's culture: *Treat each customer like a guest.* If appropriate to the organization (and it probably *is* appropriate in all hospitality organizations), always use the term *guest* and not *customer.* Create a guest-focused culture. Most important of all, train employees to think of the people in front of them as their guests, whom they are hosting on behalf of the organization. This is not a simple change in terminology; it is a big deal. In fact, outstanding companies like Disney think it's such a big deal that they use the term *guest* instead of *customer* for their millions of visitors. They know the importance of constantly reminding their thousands of employees to think of their customers as guests in everything they do. Disney even coined the term *guestology* to refer to the scientific study of guest behavior to learn learn more about meeting—and exceeding—the expectations of their guests.

Looking at a customer as a guest changes everything the hospitality organization and its employees do. A customer comes to the organization seeking to buy something that the organization sells, and the only obligation of the organization and its employees is to execute a commercial transaction in an effective, businesslike manner. The person comes in the door expecting to be treated like a customer, at best. But if the organization can provide a hospitable *experience* of which the actual commercial transaction is only a part, the customer will think "wow!" Creating an experience instead of merely selling a product or service is an important way to turn customers into patrons or guests. Rather than thinking of selling admission tickets or hotel rooms, the truly guest-focused organizations like Ritz-Carlton try to create a memorable event for their customers. They not only provide the commercial transaction but do so within a warm, friendly experience that brings the customer back time after time. Ritz-Carlton and all other excellent hospitality organizations know that it's cheaper to keep loyal customers than it is to recruit new ones and that repeat business is the key to long-term profitability.

To become a believer in this fundamental concept, think about the business organizations you deal with. To some, you are a component in a commercial transaction; others treat you like a guest. The difference is so clear it is unforgettable. Anyone who has been to a Disney theme park or a Hyatt-Regency hotel knows the special way they treat their guests. The idea of treating customers like guests is a lesson that any hospitality organization—in fact, any organization that seeks to compete successfully in the modern service-dominated economy—must learn. Customers are increasingly aware of who treats them right and who does not. They know more about what does and does not have value for them, and they expect more from the organizations they deal with. Even more important, the few organizations that have discovered and use the principles explained in this book are taking business away from those organizations that still don't get it. While the best keep raising the bar for each other, they are also making it increasingly difficult for the rest to understand why their customers are never satisfied with their service or product. This book organizes what the best hospitality organizations know and what the rest must learn to compete successfully, over the next millennium, in an increasingly customer-driven marketplace.

While *focus on the customer* and *treat customers like guests* sound simple enough, they are actually huge managerial challenges that the exemplars in hospitality services spend enormous amounts of time and energy to meet.

## SOME THEORETICAL UNDERPINNINGS

In addition to studying Disney and other outstanding hospitality organizations, we have also reviewed the services management and marketing literature. The concepts and principles contained in this book represent a unique combination of what the academic literature says *should* work and what the long experience of some of the most successful hospitality organizations in the world have found *does* work.

## STRATEGY, STAFF, AND SYSTEMS

We have organized the best that is known about hospitality management according to the three critical *S*s of the successful hospitality organization: *strategy, staff,* and *systems.* Each *S* organizes the material in one of the book's three major sections. Each *S* is important, and none is more important than the others in providing superior service. First comes *strategy* and the definition of what plans hospitality organizations must make to be effective. Next is the *staff.* Although every organization wants an effective staff, the hospitality organization depends completely upon its personnel to deliver the high-quality guest experience that distinguishes the excellent hospitality organization from the merely good. Finally, the third *S* represents the systems. The best hospitality staff in the world cannot succeed without an effective array of systems to back them up in delivering the service that the customer came for. An impressive mission statement and a big server smile can't make up for a burned lasagna, a dirty room, a late flight, unpredictable room service, or a broken air conditioner.

Although the hospitality organization's strategy, staff, and systems are obviously related to each other, they all have one focus—the guest—and exist for one overriding purpose: to provide *guest satisfaction.*

## STRUCTURE AND THE FOURTEEN PRINCIPLES OF HOSPITALTIY MANAGEMENT

Within this overall three-part structure, we have framed the information under fourteen principles in fourteen chapters. Here is an overview of how all this fits together.

### The Hospitality Service Strategy

1. Provide the service quality and value that guests expect.
2. Focus strategy on the key drivers of guest satisfaction.
3. Provide the service setting that guests expect.
4. Define and build a total service culture.

### The Hospitality Service Staff

5. Find and hire people who love to serve.
6. Train your employees, then train them some more.
7. Motivate and empower your employees.
8. Empower guests to help create their own experience.

### The Hospitality Service Systems

9. Glue the guest experience elements together with information.
10. Provide seamless service delivery.
11. Manage the guest's wait.
12. Don't fail the guest twice.
13. Pursue perfection relentlessly.
14. Lead others to excel.

Within this structure, we think we have captured the important aspects of managing in hospitality organizations. We hope it will be fun for readers to learn more about this fascinating business segment.

## PROVIDE THE BETTER CHOICE

Service in the hospitality industry is too often unsatisfactory. Dissatisfied guests are defecting to other organizations. Hospitality owners and managers are increasingly aware that if they want guests to keep coming back to their hotel, restaurant, sports bar, or bed and breakfast instead of going somewhere else, they'd better learn to give good service. If guests feel that they are receiving unsatisfactory service from one organization, they can probably find a similar organization just down the street, and they will go there.

Everybody sees the problems with guest service, and many people looking for answers ask, Who does it right, and how? This book, which combines the key principles of good hospitality service management with examples drawn from some of the world's most successful hospitality organizations, should help any hospitality organization or manager who wants to be of better service to guests.

## Notes

1. Roland Rust. 1998. (Editorial) What is the Domain of Service Research? *Journal of Service Research* 1(2):107.

Section

# 1

# The Hospitality Service Strategy

*If you don't have a road map, or know*
*where you are, you may be there already.*

—Norman Brinker
Former CEO, Chili's Restaurants

*Running a business without a plan*
*is like going into the forest,*
*shooting off your rifle and hoping*
*that dinner runs into the bullet.*

—Herman Cain

# Chapter 1

# The Basics of Wow!
# The Guest Knows Best

**Hospitality Principle:**

*Provide the service quality and value that guests expect.*

*Everything I do I keep a practical eye towards its appeal to the public.*

—Walt Disney

*You don't know what you aren't going to get until you don't get it.*

—Theodore Levitt

## LEARNING OBJECTIVES

After reading this chapter, you should understand:

▮ Important differences between making products and serving guests.
▮ The importance of meeting the hospitality guest's expectations.
▮ The importance of the guest experience.
▮ The components of the guest experience.
▮ The definition of service quality and service value in the hospitality field.
▮ Reasons why "it all starts with the guest."

## KEY TERMS AND CONCEPTS

benchmark organizations
cost
expectations
guest experience
guestologist
guestology
hospitality
internal customers
moment of truth
quality
service

service delivery system
service encounter
service environment
service package
service product
service quality
service setting
service value
servicescape
value

Serving guests and making products are such different activities that they require different management principles and concepts. Catching a defective tire or a paint blemish in a car finish at the final inspection stage of the assembly-line production process is one thing. Quite another is listening to irate guests tell you in no uncertain terms that your motel, restaurant, or airline has failed to deliver the service experience they expected. In the first instance, the quality inspector—one of many middlemen between the maker of the product and the final customer—can send the defect back to rework so that the customer never sees the faulty product. In the second situation, there may be no one to buffer the relationship between the person delivering the unsatisfactory service and the guest dissatisfied with it.

At its most basic, the **hospitality** industry is made up of organizations that offer guests courteous, professional food, drink, and lodging services, alone or in combination. Beyond that, the industry has been defined in many different ways. An expanded definition might also include theme park, gaming, cruise ship, trade show, fair, meeting planning, and convention organizations. Because we think the principles and practices presented in this book have wide application, we are going to use this more expanded concept of the industry. The challenge for organizations in this industry is to ensure that their personnel always offer the high level of service that guests want and expect—every time, perfectly. This book is designed to show them how to do that.

Even more challenging for those in hospitality organizations is the simple reality that **service quality** and **service value** are defined not by managers, auditors, or rating organizations but *in the mind of the guest.* No J.D. Power rates the service quality of the local Holiday Inn, Friendly Travel Agency, or Olive Garden. While *Consumer Reports* has from time to time evaluated airline, hotel, and restaurant companies, in the final analysis, *the decision about the quality and value of a hospitality experience is made anew by each individual guest in every transaction with a specific unit of a hospitality organization on a particular date with a certain service staff.* On the wrong date, for that guest the restaurant is no good, the airline inept, and the hotel a major disappointment. One unfortunate incident can negatively influence the opinion of the guest, and anyone the guest talks to, about the quality of service provided by that particular organization across the world.

Hospitality organizations are very different businesses to run from those discussed in traditional management texts. The challenge is to develop principles and guidelines for managers hoping to run these organizations well. The success or failure of the **guest experience** (to be explained shortly in detail) may depend on how a single **moment of truth** between the hospitality employee and the guest is handled. Management's responsibility is to ensure that each moment of truth has been prepared for—has been *managed*—as well as humanly possible to yield a satisfying, even outstanding, outcome for the guest.

How to achieve such outcomes is the focus of this book. Once dominated by the manufacturing sector, the economy is now overwhelmingly dominated by the service sector. This shift to a service economy requires that traditional management models and methods be reorganized and redirected if they are to meet the unique challenges and opportunities of hospitality organizations.

## GUESTOLOGY: WHAT IS IT?

In this book we organize the available knowledge about meeting these challenges and opportunities around **guestology,** a term originated by Bruce Laval of the Walt Disney Company. Guestology means in essence *treat customers like guests and manage the organization from the guest's point of view.* Customer-guests are, to the extent possible, studied scientifically (the *-ology* in guestology). Their demographic characteristics and their wants, needs, and expectations regarding the hospitality guest experience are determined. In addition, their actual behavior within the hospitality organization is carefully observed.

The findings of such study are then turned into the organizational practices that provide outstanding service. The organization's *strategy, staff,* and *systems* are aligned to meet or exceed the customer's expectations regarding the three aspects of the guest experience: *service product,* **service setting** (also called **service environment**), and *service delivery.* These aspects or elements are carefully woven together to give guests what they want and expect, plus a little bit more. "It all starts with the guest" is not just an inspirational slogan; in the service-centered hospitality organization, it is the truth and everybody accepts and lives up to it.

Guestology turns traditional management thinking on its head. Instead of focusing on organizational design, managerial hierarchy, and production systems to maximize organizational efficiency, it forces the organization to look systematically at the guest experience *from the customer's or guest's point of view.* What customers do and want are first systematically modeled, studied, and predicted. Only then can the rest of the organizational issues be addressed. The goal is to create and sustain an organization that can respond to the customer's needs and still make a profit.

## Meeting Customer Expectations

Customers come to a service provider with certain **expectations** for themselves and their families. First-time guests may have general expectations. For example, first-time guests of a major hotel expect nice beds, good mattresses, clean surroundings, satisfactory meals, and a reasonable price. Repeat guests may have more specific expectations based on past experience. Steak & Ale knows that all guests, new and repeat, expect food of good quality, fast and attentive service, cleanliness, and a pleasant atmosphere; therefore, the organization solicits comments about those characteristics on its guest comment card.

A **guestologist** seeks to understand and plan for these expectations before guests ever enter the service setting, so that everything is ready for each customer to have a successful and enjoyable experience. We explained in the Introduction why the road from the Magic Kingdom's Main Street, USA hub to Tomorrowland is wider than the road to Frontierland, in anticipation that more people will choose to go to the right. That is guestology in practice. Here is a second illustration of the concept. Disney knows that one of its greatest assets is its reputation for cleanliness. Keeping a theme park clean is a big job, so the Disney organization encourages its guests to help out by disposing of their own trash. After all, whatever people throw away themselves does not have to be cleaned up by a paid employee. In studying guest behavior, Disney learned two things. First, if cast members (the Disney term for park employees) constantly pick up even the smallest bits of trash, park guests tend to dispose of their own trash. The cast members practice and respect cleanliness, and the guests copy them. Second, people tend to throw their trash away if trash cans are convenient, easily seen, and not far apart. Disney locates the trash cans to match those criteria. Go inside the Magic Kingdom on a quiet day when the crowds are not distracting, and Main Street, U.S.A. looks like a forest of trash cans, located 25 to 27 paces apart. Understanding how guests respond to environmental cues and using that knowledge to help maintain a high standard of cleanliness is guestology in practice.

Managers of all hospitality organizations can extend the lessons learned by Disney guestologists to their own firms. If the organizational goal is to provide an outstanding experience, then the organization must understand why the guest comes to the hospitality organization, what that guest expects, and how to deliver that expectation. Many people think running a restaurant is simple: Cook good food, and everything else takes care of itself. Profitable restaurants know that guests patronize them (or get angry and leave) for a variety of reasons other than food quality. Managing the total dining experience is a much bigger job than merely executing a good recipe. Guestology involves systematically determining what those factors are, modeling them for study, measuring their impact on the guest experience, testing various strategies that might improve the quality of that experience, and then providing the combination of factors or elements that attracts guests and keeps them coming back.

### *Serving Internal Customers*

In addition to serving public consumers, the hospitality organization has within itself many **internal customers,** persons and units that depend on each other and "serve" each other. The principles for providing an outstanding service experience for external customers also apply to these many internal customers. For example, as a computer help desk serves its internal customers, it must understand and fulfill the expectations of these customers just as the organization seeks to meet and exceed the expectations of its external customers.

This logic can easily and rightfully be extended to the individual employee level. The organization must meet or exceed the expectations of employees about how they will be treated. Smart hospitality organizations know employees deserve the same care and consideration that the organization encourages employees to extend to guests. As expressed in the Southwest Airlines mission statement, "Employees will be provided the same concern, respect, and caring attitude within the organization that they are expected to share externally with every Southwest customer." Extending guest treatment to employees is so important to organizational success that much of Chapter 7, on employee motivation and empowerment, will be devoted to it.

### *Competition Increasing*

New hospitality organizations spring up every day. The competition for guest loyalty and dollars is intense and will grow more so in the future. Many hospitality organizations are relatively easy to set up, depend for early success upon the ability and motivation of the founder, and enter the market easily because of relatively low capital requirements. Of course, setting up a hospitality organization like a hotel, convention center, or airline costs a lot of money. But for thousands of restaurants, travel agencies, sports bars, and convention services organizations, the amount of start-up capital needed is comparatively small. Therefore, those organizations hoping to survive and prosper in this competitive environment need to master and practice the principles of guestology. If they don't provide the experience their guests expect, someone else will.

## Service

We have frequently spoken of **service,** a word with numerous meanings. A common way to think of service is as the intangible part of a transaction relationship between a provider organization and its customer, client, or guest.[1] Another way to think of service is strictly from the customer's point of view rather than the organization's. For example, FedEx defines service not as what the organization sells or provides but as "all actions and reactions that customers perceive they have purchased." Here is the helpful definition or description of service offered by Richard S. Lytle and colleagues: "To be of service literally means to attend to someone's needs. It involves helping, giving, sharing, and meeting needs." These authors point out that "service is always rendered ultimately to *people* (customers) and/or their property either (1) directly via person-to-person service encounters (traditional education, haircut, surgery, personal selling, counseling), (2) directly via person-to-property service encounters (lawn care, car repair, phone line repair), (3) indirectly via high-tech service devices (automated teller machine, automated fueling devices, voice mail, Internet), or (4) some combination of these."[2] Some of these relationships are depicted graphically in Figure 1-1, later in the chapter.

Most services include a tangible physical product or tangible materials and equipment in the transaction as well: At McDonald's you get a hamburger you can see, touch, eat, or take home in a box; you also get service with none of those characteristics. A cruise line will include a ship, a dining experience will provide food, and a teacher's lesson may require chalk, texts, and notes. Other service transactions, like a session with a psychiatrist or Social Security counselor, offer little but the customer-provider interaction itself.

### Service Product

Another, perhaps even more common, meaning of service refers to the entire bundle of tangibles and intangibles in a transaction with a significant service component. If you leave town for a month and pay for pet-sitting service, the organization or individual may buy and serve pet food, brush and comb pets, interact with them, bring toys, clean their litter box, and so forth. Some of what you pay for when you purchase the pet-sitting service is tangible (the cat food, for example); some is intangible. For such tangible-intangible mixtures or bundles, the term **service package** or **service product** is often used. It is used to describe pure services as well, since the pure service provided *is* the product the organization offers for sale. Although these overlapping meanings can be confusing (*service* sometimes referring to a tangible-intangible mixture, *service product* sometimes referring to a pure service with no tangible product), the way the term is used in context should make clear what we are talking about in this book. In different contexts, sometimes one term will feel appropriate, sometimes the other.

One necessary distinction is to realize that the service product does not refer specifically to the tangible items that may accompany the transaction, though it can include them. That is, if you go to Steak & Ale for dinner, the actual meal is not the service product; it is just a tangible part of the service product that Steak & Ale delivers to diners within rooms themed to resemble an eighteenth-century English inn.

A final point about the service product: Both the organization and the guest define it, and the definitions may not be the same. The organization may think its service product is the well-made tasty hamburger, reliably consistent from location to location. But the guest may be "buying" a more extended service product: a well-made, tasty, consistent hamburger delivered quickly in clean surroundings by a cheerful server. Cleanliness and cheerfulness may be as important as burger taste for many guests. Since it all starts with the guest, the hospitality organization would do well to define its service product not in terms of its own interests but in terms of what guests want and expect. Charles Revson, founder of Revlon, Inc., long ago drew this important distinction between what his organization makes and what the clientele buys: "In the factory we make cosmetics, in the store we sell hope."[3]

### Service Industries?

Just as the service product is a mixture of tangible and intangible elements, so are the entire industries that provide these products. Although some industries have traditionally been referred to as *service industries,* Theodore Levitt made an important point about service as early as 1972: "There are no such things as service industries. There are only industries whose service components are greater or less than those of other industries. *Everybody is in service.*"[4]

### Goods to Services to Experiences

A characteristic of the contemporary economy that hospitality organizations were the first to understand is that, for many consumers, receiving well-made goods or well-rendered services may no longer be sufficient. If you build a better mousetrap today, the world may or may not beat a path to your door. More and more, today's consumers want their goods and services packaged *as part of a memorable experience.* Of course, today's airlines must fly passengers from point to point on schedule, restaurants must serve tasty food, hotels must provide clean rooms—all at a fair and reasonable price. But the most successful hospitality organizations, and an ever-increasing number of organizations in many other fields, are providing carefully designed experiences that unfold over a period of time for their customers, clients, and guests.

B. Joseph Pine and James H. Gilmore maintain that just as we moved from an industrial to a service economy, we are now in transition to an experience economy.[5] If that is so, thinking in terms of providing customer experiences will become important for many organizations in varied industries; in the hospitality industry, such thinking is already considered essential to a successful competitive strategy.

### Understanding the Guest

Guests are not statistical entities, vague concepts, or abstractions to well-managed hospitality organizations. They understand that within the heterogeneous mass of people they serve or want to serve, each is an individual, each is unique; some companies use the term VIP to denote *very individual people.* Each guest brings to the guest experience a different bundle of needs, wants, and expectations. Some guests will arrive happy and excited about whatever is going to happen to them. Others will arrive unhappy, bored, or even angry. The hospitality organization must strive to satisfy each of these varied guests.

The first step in understanding how to manage the guest experience then is *to understand the guest,* to whatever extent possible. Ideally, this understanding would include not only the traditional demographic breakdowns of age, race, sex, and guests' home location, but also the psychographic breakdowns of how they feel, what their attitudes, beliefs, and values are, and what kind of experience they need, want, and expect the hospitality organization to deliver.

Meeting the expectations of a customer who arrives needing but not really wanting the service and angry at the service provider, perhaps even at the world itself, is difficult. Most dental patients coming in for a root canal will neither enter nor leave the dentist's office filled with joy. Fortunately, guests of most hospitality organizations eagerly anticipate the service and have no problems with needing it or wanting it. They are easier to keep happy than the person waiting for the dentist's drill, surgeon's knife, or divorce lawyer's advice.

Understanding and appreciating that guests and their expectations are so varied motivates the guest-focused organization to design each guest experience from each guest's point of view, to offer a personalized experience insofar as possible.

## THE GUEST EXPERIENCE

A term that will recur many times in the following pages is *the guest experience.* It is the sum total of the experience that the guest has with the service provider on a given occasion or set of occasions. If you tell your friend that last night you had a "wonderful evening of dinner theater," you are referring to the evening as a whole and are thinking of it that way; the evening of theater was your guest experience. To provide you with the different phases and aspects of the wonderful evening, however, many dinner theater organization members worked on many different activities and projects. For purposes of planning and execution, most hospitality organizations divide the total experience they offer into convenient units.

For purposes of discussing and explaining the total guest experience, we shall do the same, even though such a division is to an extent artificial. C. Lovelock and R. Young support that point: "As products are increasingly bundled with service components, the neat separation between product and interaction experience can become blurred."[6]

## Product, Setting, and Delivery

In a way, this entire book can be oversimplified into one (fairly long!) sentence: *We are going to show how the* **benchmark** *hospitality organizations use their strategy, staff, and systems to provide each guest with a seamless three-part guest experience—service product, service setting, and service delivery—each part of which will at least meet the guest's expectations and the sum total of which ideally will make the guest say, or at least think, wow!* In a simple service situation, the entire guest experience might be delivered by a single person, but for the typical guest experience, speaking of a **service delivery system** seems more accurate. That system consists of an inanimate *technology* part (including organization and information systems and techniques) and the *people* part—most importantly, the front-line server who delivers, presents, or "produces" the service to the guest. Here is the basic equation:

$$\text{Guest experience} = \text{service product} + \text{service setting} + \text{service delivery system}$$

All the moments you spent at the theater add up to the guest experience you later describe as a "wonderful evening of theater." But you probably had many, smaller service experiences during the evening. If, for example, at intermission you went to a designated area and received beverage service, that short experience consisted of service, setting, and a delivery system. The next time you spend a day at a vacation resort, you will have numerous service experiences, and you will end up with a feeling for the overall guest experience. If you spend three days or a week at the resort, as many people do, each day's individual guest experiences will add up to the overall day's experience, and the one-day experiences will add up to the overall resort experience.

### Unique, Yet Similar

Because incidents and occurrences are never exactly the same for two people, whether at a theater, a beverage bar, or a theme park, no two guest experiences are exactly alike. Even if the incidents and occurrences were exactly the same, your experience of them would be unique because the wants, needs, tastes, preferences, and expectations you bring to the experience are uniquely yours. Add in the intangibility of service itself, and the uniqueness of each guest experience cannot be questioned. That uniqueness is what provides the primary challenge to the hospitality service provider. The old saying has it that "you can't please every guest," but the hospitality organization has to try, even though everybody is different.

On the other hand, guests do respond to some experiences in similar if not identical ways. These categories of responses can be sampled, studied, and modeled to produce extremely accurate predictive models of what guests will do and how they will behave. Probabilistic statistics are a major tool in the guestologist's kit for identifying how hospitality organizations can best respond to the needs, wants, and expectations of their targeted guest markets. Good hospitality organizations spend considerable time, effort, and money studying their guests to ensure that each part of the entire guest experience adds something positive to it. They also expend significant resources fixing the inevitable mistakes as best they can.

## Components of the Guest Experience

Though the three elements that the hospitality organization has to work with often blend seamlessly into one experience, and should do so, we can for purposes of discussion break them out into the service product, environment, and delivery system. Here is a fuller description of each.

### The Service Product

The service product, sometimes called the *service package* or *service/product mix,* is why the customer, client, or guest comes to the organization in the first place. An organization's reason for being is often embodied in the name of the business: Riverside Amusement Park, Omni Convention Center, Sally's Video Arcade, Multiplex Movie Theater, Cheers Bar and Grill. The basic product can be relatively tangible, like a hotel room, or relatively intangible, like a rock concert. Most service products have both tangible and intangible elements and can range from mostly product with little service to mostly service with little if any product.

### The Service Setting

The second component of the guest experience is the **setting** or **environment** in which the experience takes place. The term **servicescape,** the landscape within which service is experienced, has been used to describe the physical aspects of the setting that contribute to the guest's overall physical "feel" of the experience. For example, the attention to detail in the physical setting clearly adds to the value of the Walt Disney World Resort experience. Elements ranging from the use of real gold leaf on the buildings, to the level of cleanliness, to the careful layout of waiting lines for the various attractions all communicate to guests that Disney wants them to have an outstanding experience. The servicescape is extremely important to the themed "eatertainment" restaurants like Hard Rock Cafe, Planet Hollywood, and Rainforest Cafe. They use the distinctive theme of the food-service setting as the primary means of distinguishing themselves from other restaurants.

### The Service-Delivery System

The third part of the guest experience is the service delivery system, including the human components (like the restaurant server who places the meal on the table or the sound engineer at the rock concert) and the physical production processes (like the kitchen facilities in the restaurant or the rock concert's sophisticated amplification system) plus the organizational and information systems and techniques that help deliver the service to the customer. Unlike a factory's assembly line system, which is generally closed to consumers, many parts of service delivery systems are open to consumers who can avail themselves of the services directly. Also, the output products of an assembly line system can be touched, physically owned, and seen; the services produced by the service delivery system are *experienced.*

While all aspects of the service delivery system are important, *the people interacting with customers or guests* are by far the most important component of the service delivery system—and the most challenging *to manage.* It is the waitstaff, the cabin crew, the desk agents, the valet parkers—their attitude, friendliness, genuine concern, and helpfulness— who largely determine both the value and the quality of the experience for the guest. At the moment or across the series of moments when the service is delivered and experienced, that one person, that single server, *is* the server's department, the entire organization, perhaps in effect the entire hospitality industry to the guest. The feeling that the guest takes away from the guest experience is largely derived from what happens during the encounters or interactions between the guest and the employee, and the less tangible the service product, the more important the server becomes in defining the quality and value of the guest experience. No wonder the leading hotels, restaurants, and other hospitality organizations spend endless hours and countless dollars finding, training, and supporting their frontline employees. If these folks fail to do it right, the guest and everyone the guest ever tells about the experience may be lost.

## Service Encounters and Moments of Truth

Although many service situations or interactions between organization and guest are now automated, the automatic teller machine being a familiar example, the term **service encounter** is often used to refer to the person-to-person interaction or series of interactions between the customer and the person delivering the service—in brief, "employee interactions with customers."[7] It is a period of time during which the organization and the guest interact. The length of a typical service encounter will vary from one service provider or organizational type to another. The purchase of a ticket is a brief service encounter; the interaction between guest and agent at a hotel front desk is usually somewhat longer, and the series of interactions between guest and server comprising a restaurant meal is a longer encounter. A day in a theme park may involve fifty to a hundred service encounters.

Special Expeditions is an organization that takes guests on adventure vacations. Len Berry says, "Whereas many service encounters last only a brief time, Special Expeditions' service lasts for a week or more. . . . This type of service—called an extended, affective, intimate service encounter by Price, Arnould, and Tierney—is extremely difficult to deliver" because the staff and the guests are so actively and intimately involved for so long a time.[8]

Service encounters or interactions, and especially certain critical moments within them, are obviously of crucial importance to the guest's evaluation of service quality; they can make or break the entire guest experience. Jan Carlzon, the former president of Scandinavian Airline Services, refers to the key moments during these interactions, and to some brief encounters or interactions themselves, as *moments of truth*.[9] Obviously, if the meal was bad, the airplane wouldn't fly, or the air conditioning in the hotel room didn't work, you won't care how pleasant the server was or how good that person made you feel. On the other hand, since most meals are similar to other meals, most plane rides are like other rides, and most hotel rooms are like other hotel rooms, the distinguishing characteristic of most guest experiences is how the people providing the service did it! Even if the meal, plane ride, or hotel room are the best of your life, a rude or careless service person can wreck your guest experience in a moment. If that happens, all of the organization's other efforts and expenditures are wasted. Little wonder that the effective hospitality organizations spend serious time and money to manage those moments.

For example, a potential passenger's first interaction with airline personnel is an obvious moment of truth; it can determine whether the potential passenger leaves your airline and goes to another, or whether a lifetime relationship with the passenger is begun. Carlzon managed the entire airline so as to provide good service at the moment of truth, "the fifteen golden seconds" during which the mammoth airline is represented to one guest by one server, because the success of the entire organization depends on that first fifteen seconds. In another type of hospitality organization, the first fifteen seconds will be important but may not be a make-or-break moment. The original definition of *moment of truth* was Carlzon's, but other writers have expanded the term to include any significant or memorable interaction point between server and guest or (if no server is present, as at an ATM machine) organization and guest.

At the moment of truth, a server or other organizational representative is typically present and attempting to provide service. Some writers include interactions with inanimate objects as potential moments of truth. Opening the door of a hotel room might be such a moment. If the guest's first impression is negative, if the organization has slipped up and forgotten to clean the room, for example, a crucial moment has not been properly managed and a guest, possibly an excellent long-term customer, may be lost for good.

The moment-of-truth concept is very important. Each guest may have only a few moments of truth during a guest experience or in a lifetime relationship with a company, but each server is involved in many make-or-break moments of truth every day.

Another term sometimes seen in the services literature is *critical incident.* Mary Jo Bitner and colleagues cite twelve types of incidents, favorable and unfavorable, that can occur during the service encounter.[10] If such an incident does occur—if, for example, a guest becomes disruptive or a service failure occurs—it would equate to Carlzon's moment of truth.

## The Nature of Services

Services and manufactured products have different characteristics. Manufactured products tend to be tangible; produced, shipped, and purchased now for consumption later; and lacking in much if any interaction between the manufacturer and the consumer. Services tend to be intangible, purchased (if not always paid for) first, then simultaneously produced and consumed, and accompanied by considerable provider-customer interaction.[11] Let's look at these characteristics more closely.

***1. Services Are Partly or Wholly Intangible.*** If the service rendered includes a tangible item (the Mickey Mouse hat, the gold filling, a good meal), then the total guest experience is the sum of the service/product mix, the environment within which it is delivered, and the service product's delivery. Because part or all of the service product is intangible, it is impossible to assess the product's quality or value accurately or objectively, to inventory it, or to repair it (although we will talk later about correcting service failures). Since the customer decides whether or not the quality is acceptable or value is present, the only way to measure either quality or value is through subjective assessment techniques, the most basic of which is to *ask the customer.*

A second implication of this intangibility characteristic is that every guest experience is unique. Even though a room at the Ritz-Carlton looks the same to everyone, the overall experience at the Ritz will be different for each guest. The less tangible the service provided, the more likely each guest will define the experience differently. The point is simple: Since every guest is unique, every guest experience will also be unique.

Another implication of intangibility is that hospitality organizations cannot keep an inventory of guest experiences. The stockpile of airline seats on today's 10 A.M. flight to New York is gone after the plane leaves. Tonight's unsold hotel rooms cannot be held over until tomorrow night, nor can tonight's rock concert. Once a convention ends, the opportunity to participate in an exciting meeting session is gone. The lack of inventory has important results for hospitality organizations. At the level of service organization design, capacity is the crucial issue. At the managerial level, because capacity is limited and guest experiences take place over periods of time, capacity must be carefully managed to meet demand. If demand exceeds capacity, then someone has to wait or doesn't get served at all. If capacity exceeds demand, then the hospitality organization's human and physical resources sit idle.

Finally, because services are intangible and therefore difficult to comprehend fully before they are delivered and experienced, organizations wanting guests to try their services rather than those of competitors must make the intangible tangible—through photographs in advertising, an Internet view of a restaurant interior, amenities on the night table, Dave Thomas of Wendy's doing his own TV advertising, elegant paneling on the hotel lobby wall, endorsements by famous people, and so forth. Such efforts to give tangible evidence of service quality help the employees as well. After all, the service is as intangible for organizations as for guests. Tangibles help organization members form a mental image of what the service should be like and what its quality level should be.

### 2. Services Are Consumed at the Moment or during the Period of Production or Delivery.
Even if the guest takes home the Mickey Mouse hat, or the gold filling, or the full stomach, or even if the luncheon was prepared an hour before the customer ate it, the service as a whole and from the customer's perspective was consumed as delivered. The customer can take the hat home but not the service. What are the important managerial implications of this characteristic for hospitality managers? Organizational systems must be carefully designed to ensure the service is reliably produced so that each guest has a high-quality experience nearly equal to that experienced by every other guest (except for differences supplied by servers in response to each guest's expression of unique needs). In addition, the experience must equal that which the same guest had in previous visits. The hospitality organization must think through the service delivery process by *working from the guest backward.*

This working backward to meet customer desires and expectations is a major difference between all hospitality organizations and the typical bureaucratic functional organization, which is often designed for the convenience and efficiency of the organizational members. In a well-designed hospitality organization, the focus is on the guest experience and those who deliver it. All the traditional organizational and managerial concepts that have been classically taught as the best way to manage are turned upside down. Instead of concentrating on managerial control systems to ensure consistency and employee predictability, hospitality organizations must concentrate on *employee empowerment.* They know managers cannot watch every guest-employee interaction. The guest experience cannot be held back until the boss checks it for errors, as would be true of a new book, tractor, or suit. The frontline service provider who cares about the service, the organization, and the guest must be trusted to deliver the guest experience as well as that person knows how. Instead of managers following the traditional model of reviewing performance after the fact, in the hospitality organization they must use new skills that help the employee know how and why the consistent delivery of a high-quality guest experience is critical to guest satisfaction and organizational success. Instead of tracing information and authority from the top down, the guest-focused organization must trace it from the bottom up.

| | Customer present | Customer not present |
|---|---|---|
| **Service provider not present** | Electric/Gas utilities, ATM, Vending machines | Answering services, TV security services |
| **Service provider present** | Hospitality, Medical, Professional | Lawn service, Watch repair |

**Figure 1-1** *Interaction Relationships between Customer/Guest/Client and Service Provider.*

***3. Services Usually Require Interaction between the Service Provider and the Customer, Client, or Guest.*** This interaction can be as short as the brief encounter between the customer and the order taker at McDonald's or as long as the lifetime relationship between the patient and the family physician. These interactions can be face-to-face, over the phone, or by mail, e-mail, or fax.

Figure 1-1 displays four different types of relationships between provider and customer, with examples of each type noted inside the respective boxes. Different service situations call for different strategies in systems, personnel, and settings by the service provider. If the provider is not going to be present in the encounter, the service system must be foolproof for all types of customers who will use it. South Florida automatic teller machines, for example, ask customers whether they want to read the instructions on the screen in English or Spanish. Some ATMs have phones for people who cannot figure out the instructions. On the other hand, if the provider is present, then the organization must focus on the customer's interactions with that provider as a major means for adding value to the product. A full-service hotel or restaurant, for example, relies extensively on its employees to deliver the value in the guest experience; the owner of vending machines does not.

Many services are delivered with customers present at some stages but not all. At car dealerships, most car repairs take place out of the customer's sight. The two points of contact occur at the customer service desk and the payment window. The appearance of both the physical setting and the people at those contact points are quite different from those back in the repair area, beyond the sight of customers. Each type of customer contact may call for a different managerial strategy, environment, and delivery system.

## GUEST EXPECTATIONS

Guests arrive with a set of expectations as to what that chosen hotel or restaurant can do and should do, how it should do it, how the people providing the service should behave, how the physical setting should appear, what the guest's role or responsibility should be, how the guest should dress and act, and what the cost and value of the successfully delivered service should be. First-time guests build this set of expectations on advertising, familiar brand names, promotional devices, their previous experiences with other hospitality organizations, their own imaginations, and stories and experiences of people they know who have already been guests. The organizational responsibility for creating guest expectations usually lies with the marketing department.

Once people have been a particular organization's guests, their own past experiences with that organization provide the primary basis for their expectations regarding future experiences.

Most hospitality organizations try to provide their guests with accurate information ahead of time so these customers come to the experience with expectations that the organization can meet or exceed. If the hospitality organization does not provide that information, then guests will obtain or infer it, accurately or inaccurately, from other sources, perhaps the organization's general reputation or experiences that friends have had with the organization or that they themselves have had with similar organizations. People going to Wendy's have well-defined expectations about the entire experience and notice quickly when the food is not up to par, the rest rooms are dirty, or something else is different from what they expected.

## Meeting Expectations

The major responsibility for fulfilling the expectations created by the marketing department and by the past experiences of repeat guests lies with the operations side of the organization. If what guests get falls short of what they have been led to expect or what they have learned to expect, they will be unhappy. They will not think back later on a delightful, carefully planned guest experience; they will remember the events surrounding the poor service as a bad experience. To preserve its reputation and customer base, *the hospitality organization must meet or exceed the expectations of its guests.* If it cannot or does not, it must either change its marketing strategy and create different guest expectations or change its service product and/or service delivery system so that it *can* meet present guest expectations. If enough people tell their friends what a terrible experience your restaurant or hotel provided, your reputation will be gone. These days, happy and unhappy guests are no longer restricted to talking with friends and neighbors over the backyard fence or on the phone. Angry customers with the technological ability are already establishing Web sites dedicated to bashing organizations they think have treated them badly. As Internet access becomes more widespread, customers will be able to convey their opinions about any hospitality organization almost instantly to thousands of strangers all over the world!

The challenge for hospitality organizations is to estimate guest expectations accurately and then meet or exceed them. The excellent organizations spend extra time and money to ensure that the experience of each guest—first time and repeater—not only matches but exceeds that guest's expectations. This is an especially big challenge when one considers the high expectations with which guests arrive at, say, a fancy cruise ship. First-time customers have received travel agency brochures and have seen cruise ships in movies and on television for years. They probably know of the cruise line's outstanding reputation. Repeat passengers arrive with high expectations based on prior cruises. The cruise line wants new and repeat customers to leave the trip wowed and spares no effort or expense to exceed each passenger's expectations.

The same is true throughout the hospitality industry. The Hops Restaurant statement of organizational intent is typical: "The Hops Way is your way—it's paying attention to all the details, exceeding your expectations and taking genuine pride in making your experience at Hops the very best possible."

If the organization cannot meet expectations, it should not say it can; it should not promise more than it can deliver. During difficult times for the airlines, no-frills Southwest

Airlines has continued to do well. One reason is superb service, but Ed Perkins, retired editor of *Consumer Reports' Travel Letter,* maintains that Southwest's success lies in not promising more than it can deliver: "They give people what they say they will give them. You go in there with realistic expectations. They don't say 'Come fly our luxurious airplanes.'"[12] The hospitality organization must assess guest expectations, assess its own competencies, decide which guest expectations it can reasonably meet, then try to meet or exceed them wholeheartedly.

## Do Not Provide More Hospitality Than Guests Want

On the other hand, the organization must be careful not to overdeliver to the point of making guests feel uncomfortable or unpleasantly surprised. If customers enter Eat 'n' Run, which looks and sounds like a fast-food restaurant, and see white linen tablecloths, they may feel that they are about to experience expensive, leisurely, "fine" dining. Most restaurant-goers enjoy fine dining, but they want to pick the occasion, not be surprised when it occurs.

Waiters are supposed to be attentive and polite. But consider a dining experience during which the waiter constantly hovers and speaks to the diners. If Mary Jones has taken her boss out for an important business discussion, or Bob Smith has come to the restaurant with his love interest in hopes of finding a quiet moment to propose marriage, the constant presence of an overly attentive waitstaff will be a major annoyance and too much service. When does enough become too much? The excellent hospitality organization will constantly ask its guests what they thought about the experience to ensure that guests receive more service value than they expect but not so much more as to detract from the experience. As former Chili's Restaurants CEO Norman Brinker said, "Listen to your customers. They'll tell you what to do."[13]

## Just What Does the Guest Expect?

Most guests have the same general expectations when they go to a hospitality organization for service. Surveys and interviews are not required to determine that most guests expect cleanliness, courtesy, responsiveness, reliability, and friendliness.

Customers complain when they do not get what they expect or when they receive negatives that they do not expect. Another way to get at what customers expect is to examine their complaints. Len Berry has listed the ten most common customer complaints. Considering what customers do not want can provide insight into what they *do* want. A common thread running through the complaints suggests that what bothers customers most is *disrespect.* Here are Berry's ten complaints; they can help us arrive at a still general but slightly more specific set of guest expectations:

1. Guest Complaint: Lying, dishonesty, unfairness.
   Guest Expectation: To be *told the truth and treated fairly.*
2. Guest Complaint: Harsh, disrespectful treatment by employees.
   Guest Expectation: To be *treated with respect.*
3. Guest Complaint: Carelessness, mistakes, broken promises.
   Guest Expectation: To receive *careful, reliable service.*
4. Guest Complaint: Employees without the desire or authority to solve problems.
   Guest Expectation: To receive *prompt solutions to problems.*
5. Guest Complaint: Waiting in line because some service lanes or counters are closed.
   Guest Expectation: To wait *as short a time as possible.*

6. Guest Complaint: Impersonal service.
   Guest Expectation: To receive *personal attention and genuine interest* from service employees.
7. Guest Complaint: Inadequate communication after problems arise.
   Guest Expectation: To be *kept informed about recovery efforts* after reporting problems or service failures.
8. Guest Complaint: Employees unwilling to make extra effort or who seem annoyed by requests for assistance.
   Guest Expectation: To receive *assistance rendered willingly by service employees.*
9. Guest Complaint: Employees who don't know what's happening.
   Guest Expectation: To receive *accurate answers from service employees to common questions.*
10. Guest Complaint: Employees who put their own interests first, conduct personal business, or chat with each other while the customers wait.
    Guest Expectation: To have ***their*** interests come first.[14]

Being aware of these common guest concerns and expectations should be part of any hospitality organization's knowledge base. As we shall see later, however, the benchmark organizations dig deeper to discover the more specific guest expectations that allow them to personalize each guest's experience as much as possible. Some organizations actually keep a record of these expectations to be sure of meeting them on the guest's next visit.

## QUALITY, VALUE, AND COST DEFINED

In the hospitality industry, the terms *quality, value,* and *cost* have specialized meanings to fit the guest-focused orientation of the benchmark firms.

### Quality

Two "equations" can help make clear what quality, value, and cost mean to the guestologist and why we say that quality and value are determined not in any absolute sense, as they might be in other situations, but by the guest.[15] The **quality** of the entire guest experience or of any part of it is defined as *the difference between the quality that the guest expects and the quality that the guest gets.* If the two are the same, then quality in this special sense is average or normal; you got what you expected and you are satisfied. If you got more than you expected, quality was positive; less than you expected, quality was negative. Let's say that on succeeding nights you stay at a Hyatt resort hotel and at a Knight's Inn. If the Hyatt did not live up to your high *quality* expectations and the Knight's Inn exceeded your somewhat lower *quality* expectations, then according to the guestologist's definition, the Knight's Inn guest experience was of higher quality for you.

The first equation that follows describes these relationships for the quality of the guest experience, Qe. It is equal to the quality of the experience as delivered, Qed, minus the quality expected, Qee. If the delivered and expected quality are about the same, quality is not zero as it would be if these were true mathematical equations but average or normal. If quality is average or above average, the guest can be described as satisfied. If quality is below average, the guest is dissatisfied.

$$Qe = Qed - Qee$$

As reflected on the right side of the equation, quality as perceived by the guest will be affected by changes in either guest expectations or organizational performance. If Qe is high enough, the guest had an exceptional, memorable, or *wow* service experience. The quality of any aspect of the service experience could be described in the same way.

Quality is independent of cost or value. Quality can be high and cost also high; quality can be high and cost low, and so forth.

## Value

The **value** of the guest experience (Ve) is equal to the quality of the experience (Qe) as "calculated" in the first equation divided by the *costs of all kinds* to the guest of obtaining the experience:

$$Ve = Qe/\text{all costs}$$

If the quality and cost of the experience are about the same, the value of the experience to the guest would be normal or about average; the guest would be satisfied by this fair value but not wowed. Low quality and low cost, and high quality and high cost, satisfy the guest about the same, because they are a good match for the guest's expectations. Organizations try to add value to the guest experience by providing additional features and amenities for guests without increasing the cost to guests.

## Cost

One **cost** to a guest eating lunch today at your restaurant rather than someone else's is, of course, the price of the meal. In addition, experienced restaurant and other hospitality managers appreciate that the guest has also incurred other, less quantifiable costs, including the so-called "opportunity costs" of missing out on alternative meals at competing restaurants and of foregoing experiences or opportunities other than eating a restaurant meal. The cost of the guest's time and the cost of any risks associated with entering into this service transaction must also enter the equation. The guest's time may not be worth an exact dollar figure per minute or hour, but it is certainly worth something to the guest, so time expenditures (time spent getting to your restaurant, waiting for a table, waiting for service) are also costly. Finally, the customer at your restaurant runs some risks, slim but real and potentially costly, like the risk that your restaurant cannot meet expectations or the risk that your service staff will embarrass that customer in front of the customer's own special guest today: her boss.

All of these tangible and intangible, financial and nonfinancial costs comprise the "all costs" denominator of the second equation's right side. They make up the total burden to the guest who chooses a given guest experience.

### *Cost of Quality*

An important concept in service organizations is the cost of quality. Interestingly enough, it is often used to serve as a reminder not of how *much* it costs the organization to provide service quality at a high level but of how *little* it costs compared to the cost of *not* providing quality. If the organization thinks about the costs of fixing errors, compensating guests for failures, lost customers, low employee morale, and negative word of mouth that can result from poor service, the cost of quality is low indeed and the cost of *not* providing quality enormous. That is why benchmark organizations expend whatever resources are necessary to accomplish two complementary goals: *exceed expectations* to deliver wow to the level of guest delight and *prevent failures.*

Because preventing and recovering from failure are so important, we devote Chapter 12 to these topics.

## Who Defines Quality and Value?

Because service is intangible and guest expectations are variable, no objective determination of quality level (and therefore of value) can be made. In some areas of business, a quality inspector might be able to define and determine the quality of a product before a customer ever sees it. In the hospitality field, *only the guest can define quality and value.* No matter how brilliantly the organization designs the service, the environment, and the delivery system, if the guest is dissatisfied with any of these elements, the organization has failed to meet the guest's expectations; it has not provided a guest experience of acceptable quality and value.

Of course, the hospitality organization may help the guest to perceive quality and value. Baymont Inns & Suites, for example, promises good value in its advertising: "More for your money. A value to stay with." It substantiates the good value being offered by listing some of the services and amenities provided. In addition to helping make an intangible service tangible, so that a potential guest can get a better sense of it, such a list can also serve as a set of easily measurable standards. The items are either available or they are not, and if not, the guest can reasonably complain that a service standard has not been met.

The Baymont organization supports its list of services with a pledge to meet the guest's expectations:

---

*BAYMONT INNS & SUITES Pledge of Perfection*
*It is our pledge that every guest is pleased*
*with BAYMONT INNS & SUITES and our services.*
*If we fail to live up to your expectations,*
*we ask that you contact the front desk*
*staff or the general manager to correct the*
*situation before leaving the inn.*
*If it is not right, we make it right.*
*That's BAYMONT INNS & SUITES' pledge to you.*
*If you do not receive full satisfaction,*
*please contact me.*
*David T. Lucas*
*President*
*BAYMONT INNS & SUITES, Inc.*

---

To meet or exceed the expectations of all the different types of guests with their different needs, wants, experiences, and moods is the fundamental and most exciting challenge of a hospitality organization. If the hospitality manager does not believe that the guest is always right (at least in the guest's mind), then the manager had better find a new career. Even when guests are wrong according to any reasonable standard, the hospitality manager must find ways to let them be wrong with dignity so that their self-esteem and satisfaction with the guest experience and the organization are not negatively affected.

## Importance of "Guestology"

While guestology is obviously most helpful in organizing knowledge about the management of hospitality businesses—like hotels and restaurants—which have traditionally spoken of their clientele as guests, it can be used to study and understand *any* situation in which people are served in some way. Even manufacturing firms have "guests" or people that they should treat like guests: their own employees, their customers, and their strategic partners. Nevertheless, the traditional management model found in typical texts tends to be oriented toward the manufacturing sector, the making of physical products. Using the manufacturing model to describe providing hospitality services is a questionable approach.

Is hospitality management different from traditional management? Do hospitality organizations face challenges different from those faced by other business organizations? Should they therefore design themselves differently and set different types of goals? Do managers of hospitality organizations face different types of problems and require different training than managers of traditional manufacturing organizations? Do hospitality employees respond best to managerial strategies different from those to which manufacturing employees respond? The young but growing literature on hospitality management and the experience of successful hospitality organizations indicate that the answer to all these questions is yes. A purpose of this book is to show why.

Why bother to consider the guest part of this guestology material seriously? Why should I think of my subordinate as a guest, the person walking into my travel agency as my guest, or the family coming off I-95 to my tourist attraction as guests? Let's look at the service situation from the other side for a moment. What hospitality organizations do you personally patronize, and what kind of restaurant or hotel would you yourself want to work for? Those that treat you like a special guest or those that make you feel like an interruption of their organizational procedures and policies?

The answers to all of these questions are plain. The hotels and restaurants you return to, the travel agent you call again and again, and the theme park you enjoy and recommend to friends and family are the ones that take the time to figure out what you seek in the guest experience, offer it to you, and then make clear in all they say and do their pleasure that you sought it out from them. If they understand you and give you what you seek in that experience, you will like them, ascribe high value to the guest experience they provide, return again when you need that service, and tell your friends and neighbors what a terrific place that hospitality organization is.

## Lessons Learned

1. Treat each customer like a guest, and always start with the guest.
2. Your guest defines the value and the quality of your service, so you had better know what your guest wants.
3. Ask, ask, ask your guests.
4. Provide memorable experiences that exceed guest expectations when possible, but know when enough is enough; deliver more than the guest expects, but not more than the guest wants.
5. Manage all three parts of the guest experience: the service product, the service environment, and the service delivery system (both the processes and the people).
6. The less tangible the guest experience, the more important are the front-line people delivering the service to the guest's perception of quality and value.
7. *Under*promise and *over*deliver.
8. The cost of providing quality is very low, compared to the potential cost of *not* providing quality.
9. **Service product + service environment + service delivery system = guest experience**

## Review Questions

1. Consider the formula presented in the chapter:

   service product + service environment + service-delivery system = guest experience

   A. Although all parts are important, do you think these three types of organization—a hotel, a restaurant, and an airline—would tend to place a different emphasis on the three parts in providing the total guest experience?
   B. If product + environment + delivery system = 100%, how would the hotel, restaurant, and airline divide up their emphasis? Or, if you prefer to compare them this way, how would these organizational types rank the three parts of the guest experience in order of emphasis?
2. Imagine that a Rolex watch, a Radio Shack watch, an Eagle Mirado #2 pencil, and a Cross fountain pen are sitting on a table in front of you. Which item is highest in quality, and which is lowest in quality?
3. These standard rooms are available in your locality: the Ritz-Carlton Hotel ($350 per night), a Holiday Inn ($100), a YMCA or YWCA ($40), and a No-Tell Motel ($29.95). Which room is highest in quality, and which is lowest in quality?
4. Consider the examples in questions 2 and 3 in terms of value. Under what circumstances can quality be high and value low? Value high and quality low?
5. A guest experience is a service, and this chapter explained that services are largely intangible. Think of a somewhat costly guest experience you have had. What tangibles did the organization use to make you feel that your intangible experience was worth the cost you paid?
6. Reflect on a recent, enjoyable guest experience and on a disappointing guest experience.
   A. What were the significant events, the moments of truth, during each experience?
   B. How did they contribute to your enjoyment or disappointment?
   C. How does all that relate to managing the guest experience in hospitality organizations?

7. This chapter makes some general statements about how people form their expectations for guest experiences.
   A. How do those statements match up with the way you personally form your expectations for a new upcoming experience?
   B. If you are going for a repeat experience, would your expectations be based totally on previous experiences?
   C. If you were a hospitality manager, what level and type of expectations would you want to create in your guests, and how would you try to create them?
   D. How would you take into account the fact that some guests are new, some are repeaters, and you may not know which are which?
8. You are probably familiar with the expression "too much of a good thing." In the hospitality setting, that would describe overdelivering the service guests have come to receive.
   A. How much service is too much service? Have you ever experienced excessive service?
   B. How does a hospitality manager ensure that guest expectations are met or exceeded without going overboard?
9. From an article in a guest services magazine: "What brings hotel guests back? A fluffy robe hanging on a padded hanger? Creamy chocolate reposing on the pillow? The jungle safari bedroom decor? Or plain vanilla, old-fashioned service?" What do you say?
10. How is *service quality* related to *guest satisfaction*?

## Activities

Many of the chapters in this book will include suggested hospitality field exercises or activities that might involve speaking to customers, employees, and managers of hospitality organizations. Your instructor will guide you on whether to do these assignments and how to go about them. You will also have assignments that ask you to report on a service failure or write a letter of complaint. You are doing these assignments to learn, not to make trouble for hospitality employees, so don't use real names in your reports unless your instructor gives permission.

Excellent sources for study are your own organization, if you are presently working, and the organizations for whom your friends may be working. Ideally, your information will come from hospitality organizations but if your personal situation does not permit that, study some other type of service organization. For some of the requested first-hand information, however, you may have to visit the organization and talk with its people. If so, be a good guest!

For the following three exercises, and all the others in this book, you will write your responses or prepare to discuss them in class, as your instructor directs.

1. Pick two service organizations, in the same service field, you have patronized recently or can visit conveniently. Compare them in terms of the service quality and value you received.
2. Think about the last business of any kind you visited or the next one you visit. What are the tangibles of its service product? What are the intangibles?
3. Divide up into groups. On the basis of the group's collective experience, what is good service? Mention some organizations that deliver good service. Compare notes with other groups.

## Case Study

### Eastern States Air Environment

*G*loria Rooney assumed the presidency of Eastern States Air in the later 1990s, after proving her ability as executive vice president with two other major airlines. Like most other surviving airlines, Eastern States Air weathered rough times during the early 1990s. But as the year 2000 neared, Rooney took over an airline that was doing well. Naturally, Rooney couldn't be satisfied with simply staying the course; she wanted to do better. And she thought she knew how.

Rooney saw that service in the airline industry had been in a state of steady decline for several years. More and more passengers were flying than ever before, but their level of satisfaction went down as their numbers went up. Crowded airports, flight delays, overbooking, the occasional disastrous accident, and other factors had all combined to raise industry complaints to all-time-high levels just when passenger flight miles were also at an all-time high.

In that atmosphere, Rooney finally had an opportunity to put into practice one of her most deeply held beliefs about running an airline: "It's not what you do; it's how you do it." She told her staff time after time: "The What is the easy part. What we do is take passengers from here to there. The way we can distinguish ourselves favorably from our competitors is in The How."

Eastern States Air became known as "the airline that put the Frills back into Flying." A small lounge was added to all planes that could accommodate one. For people not wanting to leave their seats, two complimentary drinks per passenger per flight, delivered to the seat, became the standard. An internationally known chef was hired to supervise a food-service system that produced meals as close to the gourmet level as was possible given the state of technology. Just before passengers exited each Eastern States flight, they were surveyed to see how satisfied they had been with the basics of the flight and with the frills which Eastern States had put back into flying. Early results of Rooney's campaign showed that passenger satisfaction levels were off the chart at the top. In one astonishing month, the airline received no complaints about anything. Rooney was overjoyed. "They said zero defects was an impossible standard in airline service. We proved them wrong." The passengers who raved about Eastern States Air and flew the airline as often as they could, sometimes simply for sheer pleasure, understood that there is no free lunch. Eastern States had to raise its fares considerably to provide outstanding service, but some people paid the higher prices happily.

Unfortunately, the number of passengers flying Eastern States Air took a disastrous drop. The ones who stayed loved the airline. They became evangelists for Eastern States, but there were not enough of them. Rooney realized that she had been somewhat deceived by the excellent survey results. She had been surveying only those who stayed, not those who left.

Surveying a broader cross section of passengers, former passengers, and passengers of other airlines led Rooney to change her strategy. "When you get right down to it," she said, "this is really a very simple business. Steamships used to be a mode of transportation; now they provide luxury cruises that end up where they started. But in our business, what people want is to get from here to there as inexpensively as possible. In the current market, cheap airfares are what people expect, and that's what we need to give them. But we won't forget the loyal customers who have stayed with us. If we do this right, we can appeal to both groups."

To implement the new strategy, Eastern States cut back on the number of seats in first class but increased their size, along with first-class appointments and level of service, to retain the airline guests who had been satisfied to have the frills put back into flying and were willing to pay for them. Throughout the rest of the plane, however, economy became the watchword. More seats were stuffed into each plane, the number of flight attendants was reduced, and "meals" consisted of dry finger food, mainly pretzels.

Eastern States began to make a financial comeback, but the number of complaints sky-rocketed to record levels. The following comments were typical:

"You are putting all your service into the front of the plane. What about those of us stuck in the back?"

"I've seen the animals in cattle cars treated better than this."

"I used to be able to get by a window or on the aisle; now I always seem to get stuck in the middle seat. Why is that?"

"I see that your industry is enjoying record profits. How about using some of that dough to give us a better ride?"

"I'm a little over six feet tall, and I have to twist my legs to fit in that cramped space you give me."

"Seats too narrow, too close together. Flight attendant handed me pretzels just as we were landing."

"I've had better seats and better service on the crosstown bus."

Some of these disappointed and angry passengers took out their resentment on the flight crews. Morale among the pilots and flight attendants began to drop. Rooney was baffled and disappointed. "You can't win in this business. You give people what they want, and the complaints go through the roof." She was quite concerned about the next board of directors meeting and what the board would have to say about her management of the airline.

**1.** What *is* the service product of the airline industry?
**2.** What were Rooney's mistakes?
**3.** How could they have been avoided?
**4.** What now?

## Additional Readings

Barsky, Jonathan. 1996. Building a Program for World-Class Service. *Cornell Hotel and Restaurant Administration Quarterly* 37(1):17–27.

Berry, Leonard L. 1984. The Employee as Customer, in Christopher H. Lovelock, ed., *Services Marketing* (Englewood Cliffs, NJ: Prentice Hall).

Bitran, Gabriel R., and Johannes Hoech. 1990. The Humanization of Service: Respect at the Moment of Truth. *Sloan Management Review* 31(4):89–96.

Brewer, Geoffrey. 1998. Selling an Intangible. *Sales and Marketing Management* 150(1):52–58.

Clow, Kenneth E., et al. 1997. The Antecedents of Consumer Expectations of Services: An Empirical Study Across Four Industries. *Journal of Services Marketing* 11(4 and 5):230–48.

Cohen, Barry. 1997. The "WOW" Effect: How One Restaurateur Continues to Delight Customers. *Cornell Hotel and Restaurant Administration Quarterly* 38(2):74–81.

Drew, J. H., and T. R. Fussell. 1996. Becoming Partners with Internal Customers. *Quality Progress* 29(October):52.

Fitzgerald, T. 1988. Understanding the Differences Between Services and Products to Exploit Your Competitive Advantage. *Journal of Services Marketing* 2(1):25–30.

George, William R. 1990. Internal Marketing and Organizational Behavior: A Partnership in Developing Customer-Conscious Employees at Every Level. *Journal of Business Research* (20)1:63–70.

Getty, J. M., and K. N. Thompson. 1994. A Procedure for Scaling Perceptions of Lodging Quality. *Hospitality Research Journal* 18(2):75–96.

Goodstein, Leonard D., and Howard E. Butz. 1998. Customer Value: The Linchpin of Organizational Change. *Organizational Dynamics* Summer:21–34.

Harris, Kimberley J., and Joseph J. West. 1995. Senior Savvy: Mature Diners' Restaurant Service Expectations. *FIU Hospitality Review* 13(2):35–44.

Javier, R., and B. Moores. 1995. Towards the Measurement of Internal Service Quality. *International Journal of Service Industry Management* 6(3):64–83.

King, C. A. 1995. What Is Hospitality? *International Journal of Hospitality Management* 14(3/4):219–234.

Knutson, B., et al. 1992. Consumers' Expectations for Service Quality in Economy, Mid-Price and Luxury Hotels. *Journal of Hospitality and Leisure Marketing* 1(2):27–43.

LeBlanc, G. 1992. Factors Affecting Customer Evaluation of Service Quality in Travel Agencies: An Investigation of Customer Perceptions. *Journal of Travel Research* 30(4):10–16.

Levitt, Theodore. 1980. Marketing Success through Differentiation—of Anything. *Harvard Business Review* 58(1):83–91.

Levitt, Theodore. 1981. Marketing Intangible Products and Product Intangibles. *Harvard Business Review* 59(3):94–102.

Oliver, Richard L., and Raymond Burke. 1999. Expectation Processes in Satisfaction Formation: A Field Study. *Journal of Service Research* 1(3):196–214.

Oliver, Richard L., Roland T. Rust, and Sajeev Varki. 1997. Customer Delight: Foundations, Findings, and Managerial Insight. *Journal of Retailing* 73(3): 311–336.

Parasuraman, A., V. A. Zeithaml, and L. L. Berry. 1985. A Conceptual Model of Service Quality and Its Implications for Future Research. *Journal of Marketing* 49(4):41–50.

Parasuraman, A., V. A. Zeithaml, and L. L. Berry. 1994. Reassessment of Expectations as a Comparison Standard in Measuring Service Quality: Implications for Further Research. *Journal of Marketing* 58(1):111–124.

Pitt, L. F., and B. Jeantrout. 1994. Management of Customer Expectations in Service Firms: A Study and a Checklist. *The Service Industries Journal* 14(2):170–189.

Rathmell, John M. 1966. What Is Meant By Services? *Journal of Marketing* 30(4):32–36.

Stipanik, David M. 1996. The U.S. Lodging Industry and the Environment—An Historical View. *Cornell Hotel and Restaurant Administration Quarterly* 37(5):39–45.

Verma, Rohit, Gary M. Thompson, and Jordan J. Louviere. 1999. Configuring Service Operations in Accordance with Customer Needs and Preferences. *Journal of Service Research* 1(3):262–274.

Wah, Louisa. 1999. The Almighty Customer. *Management Review* 82(2):17–22.

Zeithaml, Valarie A., et al. 1993. The Nature and Determinants of Customer Expectations of Service. *Journal of the Academy of Marketing Science* 21(1):1–12.

## *Notes*

1. For more on the intangibility of services, see Carole A. Congram and Margaret L. Friedman. 1991. The Quality-Leadership Connection in Service Businesses, in Congram and Friedman, eds., *The AMA Handbook of Marketing for the Service Industry* (American Marketing Association); pp. 3–19.

2. Richard S. Lytle, Peter W. Hom, and Michael P. Mokwa. 1998. SERV*OR: A Managerial Measure of Organizational Service-Orientation. *Journal of Retailing* 74(4):458.

3. Quoted in Theodore Levitt. 1972. Production-Line Approach to Service. *Harvard Business Review* 50(5): 50.

4. Ibid., 41.

5. B. Joseph Pine and James H. Gilmore. 1988. Welcome to the Experience Economy. *Harvard Business Review* 66(4):97–105.

6. C. Lovelock and R. Young. 1979. Look to Customers to Increase Productivity. *Harvard Business Review* 57(3):169.

7. Lytle, Hom, and Mokwa, 460.

8. Leonard L. Berry. 1999. *Discovering the Soul of Service* (New York: The Free Press), p. 82. See also Linda L. Price, Eric J. Arnould, and Patrick Tierney. 1995. Going to Extremes: Managing Service Encounters and Assessing Provider Performance. *Journal of Marketing* 59(2):83–97.

9. Jan Carlzon. 1987. *Moments of Truth* (New York: Ballinger).

10. Mary Jo Bitner, Bernard H. Booms, and Mary Stanfield Tetreault. 1990. The Service Encounter: Diagnosing Favorable and Unfavorable Incidents. *Journal of Marketing* 54(1):71–84.

11. Congram and Friedman, The Quality-Leadership Connection in Service Businesses; and Christopher H. Lovelock. 1981. Why Marketing Management Needs to Be Different for Services, in James H. Donnelly and William R. George, eds., *Marketing of Services* (Chicago: American Marketing Association), pp. 5–9.

12. Jean Marbella. 1999. Airline Passenger Complaints Soar. *The (Florida) Times-Union,* January 3: F–2.

13. Norman Brinker and Donald T. Phillips. 1996. *On the Brink: The Life and Leadership of Norman Brinker* (Arlington, TX: The Summit Publishing Group), p. 192.

14. Berry, 31.

15. Adapted from J. L. Heskett, W. E. Sasser, Jr., and C. W. L. Hart. 1990. *Service Breakthroughs: Changing the Rules of the Game* (New York: The Free Press), p. 2.

# 2

# Meeting Guest Expectations through Planning

**Hospitality Principle:**

*Focus strategy on the key drivers of guest satisfaction.*

*Give the people everything you can give them. Keep the place as clean as you can keep it. Keep it friendly, you know. Make it a real fun place to be.*

—Walt Disney

## LEARNING OBJECTIVES

After reading this chapter, you should understand:

▓ The three generic strategies for positioning products and services.
▓ The organizational planning cycle and how its different elements result in the establishment of the hospitality organization's overall strategic plan and service strategy.
▓ The basics of how organizations plan and design the guest experience.
▓ The key external and internal factors that must be examined for successful planning.
▓ The quantitative and qualitative tools used to assess the hospitality environment—external and internal.
▓ The process to determine core competencies.
▓ The importance of including the key drivers of guest satisfaction in the planning process.
▓ The importance and value of product and service branding.
▓ A planning model, showing how components are tied together and action plans developed.

## KEY TERMS AND CONCEPTS

action plans
brand image, brand name
core competency
design day
differentiate, differentiation
environmental assessment
internal audit
key driver
low-price provider
market niche
mission statement

qualitative forecasting tools:
  brainstorming
  Delphi technique
  focus group
  scenario building
quantitative forecasting tools:
  econometric models
  regression analysis
  time series and trend analyses
strategic premises
strategic plan
vision statement
yield management

When guests show up at a restaurant, hotel, or any other hospitality service provider, they expect certain things to happen and other things not to happen. To give guests what they expect takes detailed planning, forecasting, and sound intuitive judgment. Managers of excellent hospitality organizations try to mix all three together into a strategy that allows them to give guests exactly what they expect and even a bit more. Guests will return only if their experiences meet, if not exceed, their expectations. The service strategy is the organization's plan for providing the experience that guests expect.

Planning and strategy making are simple to talk about and difficult to do. In theory, all one has to do is to assess the environment within which the organization operates, assess the organization's capabilities, decide where the organization wants to go within that environment and in light of those capabilities, and then make a plan to get there. Unfortunately, the expectations of real customers change quickly, competitors eventually duplicate the firm's strategic advantage of the moment, governments pass new laws, and advances in technology require the firm to scrap its old delivery system and create a new one. In other words, people change, their needs and expectations change, the competition changes, and so does the hospitality organization itself. Finding ways to deliver what customers expect in light of the uncertainties created by such changes is a major challenge.

## THREE GENERIC STRATEGIES

A saying in business is, "Price, quality, speed—pick any two." The implication is that no organization can do it all, so no customer should expect it all; the organization must determine the basis on which it hopes to compete. McDonald's gives you speed and price; the Four Seasons Restaurant gives you quality. In addition to price, quality, and speed, the organization could compete on variety, convenience, friendliness, no-frills, uniqueness, helpfulness, or some other basis.

According to Michael Porter, an organization usually employs one or more of three different generic strategies.[1] First, it can aim to be the low-cost producer and **low-price provider** in its industry, area, or market segment. Second, it can **differentiate** its product or service from those of its competitors. Third, it can fill a particular **market niche** or need. Successful hospitality organizations establish a strategy that may include one or more of these generic strategies and stick with it.

### A Lower Price

"We will not be undersold!" The low-price provider tries to design and provide pretty much the same service that the competition sells, but at a lower price. Management tries to maximize operational or production efficiencies to minimize the organization's costs. Southwest Airlines focused on reducing the costs of running the airline (turnaround times, loading and unloading, food service, and so forth) to achieve the lowest production cost per mile in the industry. Wal-Mart focused on controlling inventory and cutting merchandise costs by mass buying. The low-price producer tries to offer the service at a price so low that competitors cannot offer the same service and value at a lower price without losing money. Red Roof Inns and Motel 6 are competing with Budgetel and Sleep Inn, not with Ritz-Carlton and Hilton. Of course, all hospitality organizations are cost conscious, but some focus on offering bargain prices to a wide market rather than focusing on differentiating their service to a wide market or meeting the special needs of a narrow market.

Companies employing this strategy must recognize that if they reduce prices to customers by reducing their own costs, the resulting deterioration in the guest experience may decrease the value of the experience to guests and drive them to competitors.

### A Different Product

All hospitality organizations practice product differentiation to an extent; all want to be perceived as offering a service product—the guest experience itself—that is different in favorable ways. Many try to attract guests by emphasizing these differences rather than by offering low prices.

Differentiating one's product in the marketplace results from creating in the customer's mind desirable differences, either real or driven by marketing and advertising, between that product and others available at about the same price. In an era of movies filled with sex and violence, everybody is familiar with the "difference" in Disney movies: They provide good, wholesome, family entertainment. Hotel companies try to differentiate themselves in the marketplace by advertising special amenities ("Free continental breakfast!" "Kids sleep free!"). They hope that the consumer looking for a place to spend the night will remember and want the amenities and drive into a Holiday Inn instead of a Ramada Inn, or vice versa, for what is essentially the same service: a clean room in which to sleep.

As an example, the Holiday Inn Family Suites Resort at Lake Buena Vista, Florida, differentiates itself from most other hotels by offering suites only. In addition, it has Kidsuites with rooms themed for children, Sweet Heart Suites for romantics, Cinemasuites with separate theater rooms featuring large-screen televisions with excellent stereo systems and dual recliners, and Fitness Suites by Nautilus with separate workout rooms.[2]

### The Brand Image

A major way to differentiate one's service from those of competitors is through the creation of a strong **brand image.** Once a strong brand preference is established, it can provide some protection against cost cutting by competitors. The strong **brand name** can also extend the company's reach into new markets. Because services are intangible—with no dress, guitar, or minivan to touch and try out before buying—brands are particularly important in both adding value to the guest experience and differentiating it from competing services. Even producers of more tangible products, like hamburgers, know the value of a brand and work hard to protect its integrity and image.

A McDonald's restaurant is a McDonald's restaurant, no matter where in the world it is located, and customers know McDonald's will consistently provide meals and service of the same quality regardless of location. The Golden Arches is a brand worth a great deal as a symbol of quality and value, and it provides McDonald's with a tremendous competitive advantage. It favorably differentiates McDonald's, in an instant, from other hamburger operations. McDonald's works hard to protect this valuable symbol and to maintain the reputation for which it stands.

Disney also has a valuable brand image that it carefully protects. Walt Disney said, "Anything that has a Disney name to it is something we feel responsible for."[3] Because the Disney name has come to differentiate Disney products and services as high-quality and family-oriented, Disney can extend its brand reach into a variety of related products and services. Parents know that the Disney Store in the local shopping mall, the Disney theater on Times Square, the new Disney movie at the local theater, and the Disney doll in Wal-Mart will all have the same wholesome, high-quality characteristics they want for their children. Because the Disney name instantly communicates wholesome value to the customer on whatever it appears, the organization carefully watches over how that name is used. A high-quality brand image enables a company like Disney, McDonald's, or Marriott to gain acceptance for anything new it brings to the marketplace. Customers will usually be willing to give the new product or service a try on the basis of the brand's reputation. Thousands of people, many of them families that had never before felt comfortable going on a cruise, booked trips on the Disney Magic even before the ship was launched. They knew that Disney would not risk hurting its brand by putting it on something inconsistent with the customer's expectation of what Disney stands for.

Having a strong brand can also be a disadvantage. Fear of hurting the brand image may unnecessarily inhibit a company from exploring new market opportunities or putting its name on a potentially profitable product or service just because it may seem inconsistent with the brand image. Compared to the advantages of instant and favorable product differentiation, this disadvantage is small, and most companies with strong brands are happy to pay this price.

## A Special Niche

Finally, the organization can try to find and fill a particular market niche or gap. It can focus on a specific part of the total market by offering a special appeal—like quality, value, location, or exceptional service—to attract customers in that market segment.

CEO Barbara Cassani of Go Airline literally wanted to fill a "Gap." She says, "I've always thought, where's the airline brand equivalent of Swatch, Ikea, or Gap? You either fly on a top-end world-class airline or on some terrible airline thinking, 'I don't really want to be here!' There's no Gap airline. Why not?" Owned by British Airways, the first low-cost Go flight took off on May 22, 1998.[4] Southwest Airlines, "the United States' only major shorthaul, low-fare, high-frequency, point-to-point carrier,"[5] believes itself to be alone in its niche. While some cruise lines have made great efforts to capture the family cruise market, Renaissance Cruises in 1999 committed itself to adult-only cruises; passengers must be at least 18 years old at the time of sailing. Surveys by Carnival Lines showed that 75 percent of their passengers did not smoke; so the new Carnival Paradise became the industry's first no-smoking ship. Passengers cannot board until they sign a statement agreeing "to refrain from smoking altogether while on board."[6]

To communicate more effectively with a deaf customer, waitress Marjorie Landale took a class in signing. As a result, the Regent Square Tavern in Pittsburgh became a gathering place for the many people with hearing impairments in the neighborhood. Says Paulette Thomas, "Ms. Landale is proof of the difference one energetic employee can make. Her attention to a single customer brought in ever-widening circles of his family members, his signing classmates, their teachers, other deaf people and their hearing and non-hearing friends."[7] After carving a niche for themselves by specializing in Sichuan hot-pot soup, some restaurants in Shanghai, China, have tried to establish a niche within a niche by adding dried seeds from the opium poppy to their soup. A police raid on 45 hot-pot restaurants found a quarter of them doping the soup.[8] More and more company cafeterias—at Hallmark Cards, John Hancock, Procter & Gamble, and Exxon among others—are competing with restaurants and grocery stores by providing take-home dinners for employees. At Foremost Insurance Company employees can e-mail in their orders by 2 P.M. for 4 P.M. pickup.[9]

As some further examples of niche marketing, in the fast-food market and budget-hotel market, the competitive strategy of a McDonald's or Day's Inn is to be the low-cost producer in the budget segment of the market. Casual dining restaurants like Olive Garden and Chili's have tried to position themselves in the dining-out market by offering price and food values at a point above fast food and below fine dining restaurants. By focusing on one particular part of the total market, they hope to distinguish themselves from other types of eating places. Other market niches that have been identified and used as a focus for organizational strategies are the healthy-eating niche in restaurants, convention hotels in lodging, and water parks in parks and attractions. In these instances, the market niche is carefully defined demographically, psychographically, or geographically, and the organization focuses on that segment. It seeks to build a top-of-mind awareness within customers in its targeted market as to how unique the experience provided by that organization is and how it uniquely meets the particular needs of the customers in that market segment. The distinction between *differentiation* and *finding a niche* is not clear cut. One way to think of it is that the organization determines the market at which it wants to aim, the niche it hopes to fill, and then uses strategies to differentiate itself from other organizations in that same market or niche. The

*Niche Restaurant: Angel's Diner Bakery. (Courtesy of Angel's Diner Bakery.)*

most common strategy is to try to differentiate its product or service from similar products or services.

The organization that concentrates on filling niches is often a market innovator seeking to meet an unfulfilled customer need (perhaps a need that customers don't recognize until they see the product that will fulfill it) by creating a new product or service: a high-priced luxury airline for rich people, a square bagel, or any other of the thousands of innovative products and services brought to the marketplace each year. This need might be identified by careful market research, serious study of population and demographic trends, a lucky guess, or some intuitive combination of all these approaches. Some researchers argue that this combination is the most likely way for managers to develop **strategic plans,** especially those plans that make a real difference in an organization's success.[10]

The differences between these three competitive strategies—lower cost, product differentiation, and finding a niche—are illustrated in these three restaurant examples. The fast-food, limited-menu restaurants like McDonald's compete on price, Red Lobster differentiates itself from other full-service restaurants by specializing in seafood, and Planet Hollywood fits into a niche, the "eatertainment" restaurant. However, the differences between the differentiation and niche strategies are not always clear. Consider the Totenko Restaurant, for example. Does its all-you-can-eat-by-the-minute gimmick differentiate it from restaurants that charge by the item, or has it found a niche in people who want to eat and run? At the Just Around the Corner Restaurant, where you pay whatever you think the meal is worth, has the restaurant differentiated itself from restaurants that tell guests what they must pay? Or has it found a niche in people who want to have the entire guest experience before deciding what it is worth and who will not abuse the privilege because they appreciate the trust placed in them?

## Combining Strategies

These strategies are not mutually exclusive. An organization can seek to differentiate its product from all others in the market (Strategy 2) by positioning the product in people's minds as the best value for the lowest cost (Strategy 1). This strategy combination requires the organization to use both effective marketing techniques that reach this best-value, lowest-cost market segment and operating efficiencies that allow it to make money at the low price. Successful theme parks seek to apply this combination by advertising a park visit as a high-value, low-cost, family-entertainment experience while keeping their costs, especially labor costs, low. At those times of the year when the tourism volume is low, Florida parks offer Florida residents special prices as a means of attracting local residents. Some parks are more effective than others at making money during these low-price times because of their operating efficiencies.

## Reinventing the Industry

Picking and following a strategy is an important decision for any hospitality manager trying to cope with present and emerging uncertainties. The strategy might be to get smaller, better, and faster. If drastic change is forecast, the organization might even have to reinvent itself and learn new **core competencies.** These are all reactive strategies, of the kinds that most organizations must employ as circumstances change. Organizational strategists Gary Hamel and C. K. Prahalad note in their book *Competing for the Future* that the organization might even need to be capable of reinventing its industry.[11]

Most companies listen to their customers and then respond to their articulated needs. But some rare, highly creative organizations can actually create the future for themselves and their industries; they can "lead customers where they want to go but don't know it yet."[12] They "do more than satisfy customers, they constantly amaze them."[13]

The creation of Disneyland Park is a great example of a visionary leader reinventing an industry by leading customers to a place they didn't know they wanted to go. Disneyland was an attempt to create within park visitors the feel of being actual participants in a motion picture. The traditional concept of an amusement park, with rides and attractions, was embellished in creative ways with new technology and the introduction of theming to become a service—the theme park—that didn't exist until Disney and his creative team imagined it and built it.

## Providing Superior Service Quality and Value

The three generic strategies—competing on price, finding a niche, and differentiating—may each work for a while, but they may also have potential shortcomings. If you compete on price, somebody is eventually going to undercut your price. Also, establishing a close and lasting relationship with guests is difficult if you stress your low price. If you find a niche and succeed there, an imitator eventually will join you in the niche, and soon it will be just another market segment. If you differentiate successfully, somebody will copy your differentiation feature. Many successful service organizations have found that the best way to succeed long term is to differentiate on the basis of superlative service quality and value. Provide better service and value than the competition does, and they can't beat you. David

Lipton, president of Sensors Quality Management Inc., puts it this way regarding competition in the hotel business: "Most hotels have decent locations, are reasonably clean, have nice beds with good mattresses, offer satisfactory meals, and have prices grouped in the same range. The big difference is in the service. Anyone wanting to differentiate a property has to do it here. It's the last frontier."[14] As Tom Peters, author of *The Circle of Innovation,* says, "You can knock off everything . . . except awesome service."[15]

## THE HOSPITALITY PLANNING CYCLE

Leading guests to where they want to go but don't know it yet is how the truly outstanding hospitality organizations become outstanding. The focus of this chapter is finding a way to give guests what they want, when they want it, even if they don't know yet exactly what they want. The organization tries to imagine what kinds of experiences guests of the future will find satisfying, then plans ways to deliver them. As one example, Walt Disney planned out a theme park that he knew would wow park visitors long before they knew what a theme park was. Disney said, "You don't build it for yourself. You know what the people want and you build it for them."[16] As a more recent example, bank customers didn't know they needed debit cards (on which expenditures are deducted directly from the customer's checking account) until banks began to offer them. Similarly, phone customers didn't recognize their need for a single telephone number that can be used anywhere and includes e-mail and paging capabilities until phone companies made them aware of how convenient such a service could be. In the late nineteenth century, travelers did not realize how much they had previously been inconvenienced by the unavailability of ready cash, or by having to carry too much cash, until American Express created the traveler's check. Hospitality organizations did not know they needed an 800 phone number until the idea was introduced.

The way to achieve this end is through the strategic planning process. The process has two basic steps: *assessment* (external and internal) and *figuring out what to do* on the basis of that assessment. The *external assessment of environmental opportunities and threats* leads to the generation of *strategic premises* about the future environment. The *internal assessment of organizational strengths and weaknesses* leads to a redefinition or reaffirmation of organizational *core competencies.*

As can be seen in Figure 2-1, hospitality planning follows an ongoing cycle that begins at the big-picture level and ends at specific **action plans,** departmental or project budgets, and individual yearly objectives. Typically, such planning is done annually and begins with management's simultaneous consideration of three elements: the external environment with its opportunities and threats, the internal organization with its strengths and weaknesses, and the relationship of these elements to the statements of organizational vision and mission. We shall talk first about the external and internal assessments, then about the vision and mission statements.

### Looking Around

The **environmental assessment,** or the long look around for opportunities and threats, in turn defines the **strategic premises.** These premises are the beliefs of the managers assessing all long-term aspects of the external environment and trying to use them to discover what customers will want in that future environment, what the **key drivers** of guest satisfaction

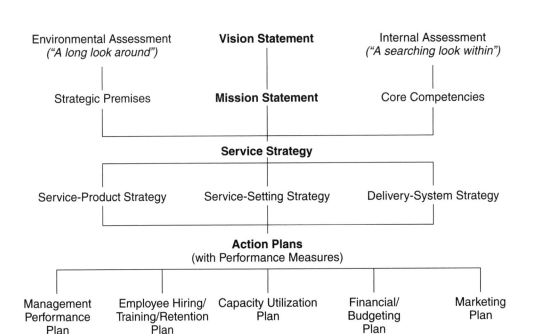

**Figure 2–1** *The Hospitality Planning Process.*

will be in the intermediate-term and longer-term future. Although guests will not always know what the key drivers of their future satisfaction will be, the guestologist will still try to find out what kinds of experiences guests *think* will be satisfying in the future.

Loew's hotels asked 36,000 guests in such categories as families with children and business travelers what items they either often forgot to pack or would like to have available in their rooms. Loew's predicted that making such items available would be a driver of guest satisfaction. In each hotel, Loew's put a "Did You Forget Closet" including the items most requested by guests: fax modems and portable computers, rain gear, handheld audio devices to use while working out, first aid kits, baby bath tubs, cat litter, and so on.[17]

## Looking Within

The internal assessment, or the searching look within for strengths and weaknesses, defines the organization's core competencies and considers the organizational strong and weak points in terms of the organization's ability to compete in the future.

### Vision and Mission Statements

The **vision statement** articulates what the organization hopes to look like and be like in the future. Rather than presenting specific principles, goals, and objectives, it presents hopes and dreams; it creates a picture of that toward which the organization aspires; it provides inspiration for the journey ahead. It depicts what the organization hopes to become, not what the organization needs to do to get there. The vision statement is used to unite and inspire

*New York-New York Hotel, Las Vegas. (Courtesy of New York-New York Hotel and Casino™.)*

employees to achieve the common ideal and to define for external stakeholders what the organization is all about.

The **mission statement** articulates the organization's purpose, the reason for which it was founded and for which it continues to exist. The mission statement defines the path to the vision, given the strategic premises and the organization's core competencies. The mission statement is a guide to determining the organization's overall service strategy that in turn drives the design of the service product, service environment, and service delivery system. These decisions lead to action plans and to the other steps and decisions that put resources in place to fulfill those plans. Some sample vision and mission statements will be presented later in the chapter.

Once the hospitality planning process is complete, the cycle should begin again in some predefined time frame. The planning process should never stop because the world in which any organization operates never stops changing.

## The Necessity for Planning

The process described in Figure 2-1 is an attempt to apply rationality to an irrational world and to predict an unpredictable future. It will therefore be accompanied by errors, wasted time, and frustration. Nevertheless, the planning process is worthwhile. Every hospitality organization needs a road map to unite and focus the efforts of the organization's members and get them prepared for the future that the organizational planners predict. Everyone makes decisions today that they must live with in the future, and most managers want to make those decisions as rationally as possible. Even though no one, including planners, knows what the future will bring, only by creating and implementing plans can we communicate to those both inside and outside the organization where we want to go, what criteria we should use to allocate our scarce resources, and which activities we should pursue or avoid.

Some time ago, an investor group was strongly convinced that over the indefinite future people would continue to be interested in going to Las Vegas and gambling. Based on that vision, they planned and built the $460 million New York-New York Hotel. The early results, reporting that over a million visitors had come to see this replica of New York City with slot machines, seemed to justify the future these investors forecasted. No organization can instantly create such a magnificent project. It must make decisions that anticipate the future as best it can. Creating and following a careful strategic plan is the best known way to do so.

## ASSESSING THE ENVIRONMENT

Figure 2-1 and the hospitality planning process start with a long look around the environment. Here the organization carefully studies the opportunities and threats the future holds for both it and its industry. Table 2-1 presents the three categories of factors that should be included in an environmental assessment: those in the overall environment, the industry environment, and the company's operating environment.

The many forecasting techniques range from the heavily **quantitative** or objective to the highly **qualitative** or subjective. The quantitative techniques include the powerful tools of statistical forecasting. The qualitative include **scenario planning,** the **Delphi technique,** and pure creative guesswork.

Most forecasting techniques are based on the idea that the future is somehow related to the past, that what has already happened has some predictable relationship to what will happen. If a restaurant's customer growth rate has been about 10 percent per year for thirty years, then forecasting that this growth rate will continue next year seems reasonable. If records show that by 10 A.M. on an average day 20 percent of all visitors who will come into a zoo for that day are already on the grounds, then the day's total attendance can probably be reliably forecasted by 10:15 A.M. On a grander scale, if the growth rate of tourists coming to a Caribbean island paradise has been 10 percent per year for the past decade, then predicting that this growth rate will continue for at least a few more years seems reasonable.

The problem with assuming that the past can be used to predict the future is that all too frequently the assumption does not hold true. In the early days of the telephone, the ratio of phones to operators was very small. If only population trends and that ratio had been used to predict the number of telephone operators to be needed in the distant future, the prediction might well have been that half the people in the United States would now be working as telephone operators. Major improvements in technology and work productivity have greatly increased the ratio of telephones to operators. Any forecast based only on the past can be thrown off by unexpected technological, economic, societal, or political changes.

When the automobile began to be commonly available, some astute human beings predicted that increasing numbers of motorists would want roadside hotels. Human beings predicted that deregulation of the airline industry would lead to new airlines, increased competition, lower fares, and more travelers. Only a Walt Disney, not a forecasting model, could have foreseen the impact of sound on movies, television on entertainment, and the interstate highway system on the theme park industry.

**Table 2-1** *Environmental Assessment Factors*

**The Overall Environment**

**The Economy.** Where is it going? Growth, inflation, interest rates, capital and credit availability, consumer purchasing power. Changes in currency valuations in a global market.

**Society and Demographics.** How will shifts in attitudes/values regarding childbearing, marriage, lifestyle, racial equality, retirement, pollution, etc., affect the organization? Population shifts, pressure groups.

**Ecology.** Natural or pollution-caused disasters ahead? Environmental legislation?

**Politics.** Government policy changes regarding antitrust activities, foreign trade, taxation, depreciation, environmental protection, and foreign trade barriers? Political or legal constraints or supports in international business?

**Technology.** Where is it going? New products, services? Technological breakthroughs?

**The Industry Environment**

**New Entrants.** Competitors? Who will they be? Will technological advances enable them to offset our present advantages (economies of scale, brand-name differentiation, availability of capital)?

**Bargaining Power of Suppliers.** How stable, reliable? Any who may become potential competitors? Substitute suppliers available? Can we supply ourselves?

**Substitute Products or Services.** Likely? Can we fight with price, advertising?

**Rivalry Among Existing Firms.** Growth slowing, competition fiercer? Excess capacity in the industry? Can our competitors withstand intensified price competition?

**The Operating Environment**

**Competitive Position.** What moves are competitors expected to make, inside and outside of the United States? Is the behavior of our competitors predictable?

**Customer Profiles and Market Changes.** Which customer needs are not being met by existing products? Are R&D efforts underway to fill these needs? What marketing and distribution channels should we use? How will demographic and population changes affect our markets? Any new market segments? What impact will the Internet have on marketing strategy?

**Supplier Relationships.** Cost increases coming because of dwindling supplies? Will sources of supply, especially of energy, be reliable? Major changes coming in cost or availability of needed suppliers? Which suppliers can we count on in a pinch?

**Creditors.** Will we have enough credit to finance growth? Will we stay worthy of credit? Do we have enough cash if we need it?

**Labor Market.** Will we have enough employees, with the right skills, when and where we need them?

Source: Adapted from John A. Pearce II and Richard B. Robinson, Jr. 1997. *Formulation, Implementation, and Control of Competitive Strategy* (Chicago: Irwin), pp. 142–143. With permission of The McGraw-Hill Companies.

**Table 2-2** *Popular Approaches to Forecasting*

| Technique | Short Description | Cost/Complexity |
|---|---|---|
| **Quantitative-Causal Models** | | |
| Econometric models | Simultaneous systems of multiple regression equations | High |
| Single and multiple regression | Variations in dependent variables are explained by variations in one or more independent variables | High/medium |
| Time series models | Linear, exponential, S-curve, or other types of projections | Medium |
| Trend extrapolation | Forecasts obtained by linear or exponential smoothing or averaging of past actual values | Medium |
| **Qualitative or Judgmental Models** | | |
| Sales force estimate | A bottom-up approach aggregating forecasts of salespersons | Low |
| Juries of executive opinion | Forecasts jointly prepared by marketing, production, finance, and purchasing executives | Low |
| Customer surveys, market research | Learning about intentions of potential customers or plans of businesses | Medium |
| Scenario development | Impacts of anticipated conditions imagined by forecasters | Low |
| Delphi method | Experts guided toward consensus | Low/medium |
| Brainstorming | Idea generation in a noncritical group situation | Low/medium |

Source: Adapted from John A. Pearce II and Richard B. Robinson, Jr. 1997. *Formulation, Implementation, and Control of Competitive Strategy* (Chicago: Irwin), p. 145. With permission of The McGraw-Hill Companies.

Forecasting techniques are useful to capture the impact of current trends on future business. However, they are only one source of input into the creative process by which thoughtful hospitality managers develop strategic plans.

Table 2-2 presents and briefly describes some popular quantitative and qualitative forecasting techniques and indicates their cost/complexity. We shall discuss some of the more important techniques.

## Quantitative Forecasting Tools

Statistical techniques used for forecasting are of several major types: econometric, regression, time series, and trend analysis. Each is based on the idea that definable and reliable relationships exist between what the organization wishes to forecast and some other variable.

### Econometric Models

**Econometric models** are elaborate mathematical descriptions of multiple and complex relationships that are statistically assembled as systems of multiple regression equations. Thus, if a chain of movie theaters in New England wishes to predict the relationship between theater attendance and the level of economic activity in New England, the chain would use a complex econometric model built to describe how New England's level of economic activity and the amount of personal discretionary income allocated to entertainment purchases relate to movie theater admissions.

### Regression Analysis

In **regression analysis,** the relationship between variables is studied so that they can be statistically associated. If statistical studies of park visitors show that in July and August visitors consumed an average of 1.5 Cokes per visit, then determining how many Cokes, cups, servers, and how much ice will be needed on a particular day is a straightforward calculation. Using regression analysis, we can further predict sales on the basis of other known numbers (probable park visitors) and the known relationships between these numbers and the variable of interest (in this case, Coke sales). If we know that a convention is bringing 15,000 visitors to a city in a certain month, we can predict through regression analysis the number of rooms a hotel is likely to sell, the number of meals that will be consumed at a restaurant, and the number of taxi rides that will be taken in that time period.

### The Design Day

A basic problem for many hospitality organizations is that demand is uncertain and capacity is fixed. An important concept in capacity planning for hospitality organizations is the **design day.** Whenever a new restaurant, hotel, theme park, or other service facility is created, management must determine how big to build it. How many people should the new physical facility be able to handle at one time? It should not be designed to accommodate demand on the slowest day of the year, because for the other 364 days its capacity will not be able to meet demand. But if the facility is designed to meet demand on the busiest day, capacity will exceed demand for the rest of the year. The idea of a design day is to decide which day of the year to assume when determining the design capacity of an attraction or facility.

As an example, a theme park could use past and predicted attendance figures to set the design day at the 50th percentile, so that overall park demand (and demand for particular rides and attractions) would exceed capacity on about half the days, and about half the time capacity would exceed demand. But a successful park does not want guests to experience excessive wait times for half the days of the year. The park designers must decide what percentile level they want to establish for their design day. The higher the percentile level chosen, the lower the number of days they will exceed their design-day wait-time standards. For example, if they choose a 75 percentile day, the park will exceed wait-time standards on 90 days of the year; if they choose a 90 percentile design day, they will exceed their wait-time standards on only 36 days per year.

The design-day percentile is a critical management decision. A higher percentile day means increasing capital investment to increase park capacity. A lower percentile day will cost less initially, but guest dissatisfaction will probably be higher; once the design-day capacity is exceeded, the quality of their experience will be diluted for some guests. This dissatisfaction will have a negative impact on repeat visitation, long-term attendance growth, and revenue. Management must balance carefully the trade-off between investment costs and guest service.

Every hospitality organization uses a method to plan its capacity. The design-day concept is one way to find the best balance between carrying the costs of excess park capacity and ensuring the quality and value of each guest's experience. Costs are associated with buildings, grounds, people, and stocking perishable products. But customers expect the service to be available to them when they want it; otherwise they are dissatisfied with the quality and value of their experience. Finding the best balance between economic realities and guest satisfaction is what guestologists do.

Consider a theme park with numerous rides and other attractions. Once the design-day decision has been made, the park management can calculate how many demand units (people per time period per attraction) will be in the park to consume or enjoy the capacity available. Thus, if the park attendance on a design day is 18,000 people and a new ride or attraction that takes 30 minutes is expected to capture 3 percent of this capacity per hour, then the capacity of the ride has to equal 270. With this capacity and assuming a continuous flow of people coming to enjoy an attraction, no one will have to wait longer than 30 minutes. As the ride or attraction begins, the first of the next 270 people wanting to enjoy it will start forming a new waiting line. As soon as the ride gets back to its starting point or the show ends, the 270 people who have been waiting for varying lengths of time will enter the ride or show, and a new waiting line will start to form. If the design-day decision includes a wait of a fixed amount of time (for example, an average of 15 minutes across all park attractions), then the actual capacity of the new attraction can be less than 270 because the capacity will assume a certain acceptable number of people waiting in line. The point is that this important capital-allocation decision—how big to build a new ride or other attraction—can be based on straightforward calculations that are themselves based on design-day decisions made long ago, which are in turn based on the organization's estimates of what quality and value customers expect.

For any hospitality organization, the original design-day decision is based on forecasts, information derived from organizational past experience, and perhaps from knowledge of similar facilities. Then, as Walt Disney said, you "say a little prayer and open it and hope it will go." Once real information can be gathered through real experience with real people, the design-day decision can be refined. Because most hospitality organizations would rather add capacity than tear down existing capacity or let it stand idle, the original design-day decision for a new facility should probably use conservative estimates.

## Yield Management

A capacity-management concept that has gained substantial favor in the airline, cruise line, convention center, and lodging industries is **yield management** (YM)—managing the sale of units of capacity to maximize the profitability of that capacity. Successful yield management involves selling the right capacity to the right customer at the most advantageous price, to maximize both capacity use and revenue. This concept is based on the idea that guest demand patterns can be predicted to some extent and those predictions can be used to allow the hospitality organization to charge different rates to different people (or groups) based on

(1) when reservations are made and (2) the capacity projected to be available at any given time. Early reservations with restrictions (e.g., airline passengers staying over Saturday or paying a high financial penalty for schedule changes) might receive the lowest prices. Guests who wait until later to make reservations, with fewer restrictions and more flexibility, can expect and are usually willing to pay more. Balancing capacity, demand, and price is the job of the computerized yield-management system.

For example, a sophisticated YM system will predict the demand pattern for reservations on a specific flight from Los Angeles to New York four months from now, then price each seat in a way that exactly meets the forecasted demand for travel on that flight. That is, the airline will know how many seats it should set aside on that flight for full-fare guests (who will book their reservations late and will expect to pay more) and how many it must sell at lower prices. Using historical data, the YM program may estimate that 20 percent of the flight's capacity should be reserved for full-fare guests who book late. It may also forecast or calculate a *pick-up rate* indicating how additional passengers will book reservations from now until the plane flies four months from now. This rate, also based on historical experience, can be a smooth curve or any other distribution that describes how guests make reservations.

The airline's goal is to sell as many seats as possible at the highest rate possible. It will start by setting aside the expected full-fare capacity and then calculate the capacities to be set aside at each successively lower rate. As every traveler knows, the farther out from the flight date the reservation is made, generally the lower the ticket price. The closer to the actual date of the flight, generally the higher the ticket price. The yield-management process is designed to set aside seats at each price level in such a way as to sell each seat at the highest possible price. The airline might set aside the 20 percent mentioned earlier at full fare, 30 percent at a 10-percent discount, 40 percent at a 20-percent discount and 10 percent at half price. If the airline's predictions are accurate, the bargain hunters will make their reservations early and fill up the half-price seats, followed by the later bargain hunters who were not willing or able to commit to the flight soon enough to fly at half price. They will be disappointed that they can't get the 50 percent off fares but are happy with a 20 percent percent discount anyway. The guests who commit even later can't get the 20 percent discount but are still relieved not to pay full price. People paying full price are those who have no choice but to travel on that particular day or business travelers who must book their flights close to the actual departure date.

The reservation process is dynamic, and an effective yield-management system will continuously compare the actual reservation rate to the forecasted rate. The number of seats set aside in each price category or the price of seats in each category can be modified based on the actual, evolving relationships between the supply of that flight's seats and the demand for those seats. If the pick-up rate prediction is incorrect, the airline can always advertise the empty remaining seats on its Web page at a substantial discount that still covers its direct costs and contributes to the flight's total revenue, or it can sell the seats to a consolidator.

A good yield-management model can maximize the revenue on every flight by filling up every seat at a price that perfectly balances seat supply and passenger demand. Yield management is an important capacity-planning device for airlines but also for other organizations that have both capacity limitations and a perishable commodity, like a room for the night or a cruise date. Because the organization's salespeople must have accurate and timely information about guest demand and available capacity, true yield management in the modern sense can hardly be accomplished without the computer.

### Time-Series and Trend Analyses

**Time-series** and **trend analyses** are simply extrapolations of the past into the future. If we know how much our market has grown every year for the last ten years, a time-series forecast will project that rate of growth into the future to tell us what our park attendance, hotel occupancy rate, or covers (the number of meals served at a restaurant) will be in a given future year. These numbers can be adjusted for fluctuations in the economy, changing assumptions about tourism and population growth rates, or what the competition is doing.

The opening of its fourth park near Orlando, Disney's Animal Kingdom, has changed the area's historical trend in a major way, so the historical time-series and trend-analysis statistical formulae have also had to change. If Orlando visitors spend five days as Disney guests (or even more if they also use the Disney Cruise Lines), then the number of Orlando visitors who go to Universal Studios, Sea World, or Gatorland will drop significantly, unless the overall tourist rate or average length of stay rises. It has become critical for the other attractions to create new strategies to market themselves and all of Orlando as a destination separate from Walt Disney World Resort. If successful, they can attract a new market of visitors who were not planning to visit Walt Disney World Resort or who have been there and done that and are looking for something new to do. The creation of the Universal Studios/Sea World/Busch Gardens/Wet'n Wild Combination Ticket and the opening of Universal Escape's second theme park, Islands of Adventure, appear to be a strategic response to the important change in the statistical relationships caused by Disney's Animal Kingdom opening that allows these other theme parks to define and attract a new market segment.

### An Example: Trends Affecting Food-Service Organizations

An interesting illustration of trend analysis is seen in the 1982 book *Megatrends* by John Naisbitt. He sought to identify major social trends, or megatrends, by content analysis of newspapers and popular magazines. Hospitality strategist Michael Olsen used a similar method to identify three major trends affecting the food-service industry: safety and security, managing chaos, and resource scarcities.[18]

*Safety and Security.* People are increasingly apprehensive about their personal safety and security. Their fears have implications for food-service organizations. Potential customers worry about whether or not a particular restaurant is a safe location for them to visit, and potential employees worry about workplace safety. People wonder increasingly if the food served to them away from home is safe to eat. Potential guests of most hospitality organizations have similar concerns about safety and security.

*Managing Chaos.* How can we manage the chaos of modern-day living? More and more, people seem to want someone to help them make sense out of the chaos, confusion, and information overload in their lives. A food-service organization understanding this trend will focus management attention on easy-to-understand menus, simple and clear interior layouts, and an atmosphere of order.

*Resource Constraints.* A third trend is resource constraints. Qualified employees, investment capital for expansion, and natural resources such as clean water are limited as to availability for food-service and most other hospitality firms. Organizations need to stay aware of major social trends and take them into account as they plan strategy.

While the Olsen study was directed at food-service organizations, these same trends have relevance to any service organization, especially those in the hospitality field.

## Qualitative Forecasting Tools

Other forecasting tools are used to make more qualitative or subjective projections. Among them are brainstorming, the Delphi technique, focus groups, and scenario building or war gaming.

### Brainstorming

Walt Disney said, "We get in there and toss ideas around. And we throw them in and put all the minds together and come up with something. . . ."[19] The old strategy of asking a group of people to ponder the future and what it may mean, based on what they already know, is called **brainstorming.** Brainstorming can be formal and structured, requiring participation from everyone, or very informal and unstructured. As a forecasting tool, it assumes that everyone has some degree of creativity, that people will voluntarily contribute their best ideas in an open group discussion, that the sharing of those ideas will spark the generation of good new ideas, and that the sum total of those ideas will be a more accurate forecast than the forecast of any one person. Unfortunately, these premises do not always hold up, and participants encouraged or forced to brainstorm often view the time spent as wasted. On the other hand, Disney's successful use of "imagineering" in its creative planning department shows that placing creative people in discussion sessions like brainstorming can provoke new ideas or ways of looking at things.

### The Delphi Technique

The Delphi technique is a more formal way than brainstorming of tapping the forecasting skills of experts. If a cruise line wants to know what percent of overall ship capacity will be filled at this time next year, the Delphi technique would be a good tool to use. A group of industry experts would make individual estimates for next year, and the estimates would be combined or averaged. If that average estimate is not sufficient for organizational purposes, the average might be shared with the experts, along with the individual estimates and the thinking that went into them. The experts would then be asked to consider this new information and make a second round of estimates.

Even though this process cannot guarantee a precise forecast of such future unknowables as how many Kiwanis Club members will attend a national convention or how many meals will be eaten away from home next year, combining expert estimates can yield the best composite estimate available.

### Focus Groups

Focus groups are asked to concentrate on an issue and discuss their thoughts about it with a trained group-discussion leader. Focus groups, which will be discussed in more detail in a later chapter, are perhaps most frequently used in assessing the quality of service already rendered. They can also be helpful in forecasting what people are apt to like and not like about a service experience. If an organization has an innovation in mind, it can form a focus group that is demographically and psychographically representative of its target market and see how the group reacts to the innovation. For example, groups of young teens living in trend-setting areas are frequently used to predict clothing fashion trends that retailers use to order clothing inventories.

### Scenarios

**Scenario building,** or war gaming, has become a fairly popular subjective forecasting technique. We assume a certain future situation or scenario, then try to assess its implications for our organization. If a hospitality organization has a major investment in Florida and California theme parks, a future scenario of concern might be the rapid developments that are occurring in virtual-reality technology. If this scenario occurs, making quick and easy access to virtual theme parks possible for millions of people, what will its impact be on the willingness of people to travel to distant, fixed-site locations for theme park experiences?

Organizations must be careful not to be ruminating at the scenario stage while the competition is actually building facilities. The virtual-reality scenario above is no longer merely hypothetical. Sega and Lockheed have formed a joint venture to build simulated theme-park rides in areas across the world that are too sparsely populated or out of the way to justify a full-scale theme park. Disney opened the $30 million DisneyQuest in Orlando, to test the VR concept. You can ride over waterfalls and rapids, and paddle through jungles on the Virtual Jungle Cruise; you can design and ride your own roller coaster and float over an ancient city on Aladdin's Magic Carpet. At other, non-Disney VR centers, customers can take virtual rides on roller coasters that go to the center or top of the earth, through space to other worlds, undersea, into beehives or through swarms of bees, through computers or the human body, down an Alpine avalanche, or on a runaway train down mountain tracks. Many of these motion theaters and simulators are capable of creating new rides by simply putting different programs into the equipment. Some simulators offer as many as 100 different rides.

*DisneyQuest. (Used by permission from Disney Enterprises, Inc.)*

A real amusement park must expend large sums on real estate and construction just to provide one more ride. A likely scenario session for a theme park might focus on the impact of virtual theme parks on future attendance at large, fixed-site destinations. Another scenario session should probably be devoted to what the *next* major development beyond virtual-reality technology will be.

Similarly, convention centers might try to forecast their future by creating scenarios that embody technological advances in teleconferencing. If people can sit in their own offices and experience the "feel" of being in a crowded meeting at a distant location, will market opportunities for convention centers and planners continue to exist on the present scale?

Scenario builders often need to act quickly. Aggressive changes are taking place in information technology and simulation. The scenario builder is in danger of looking up from the scenario or simulation being created to find that the scenario is already here.

## WHAT THE FUTURE MAY HOLD

The organization must try to assess the uncertain future in terms of potential changes in demographics, technology, social expectations, economic forces, competitors, other relevant groups (suppliers of resources, capital, and labor), and surprise factors.

### Changing Demographics

Assessing future demographic trends and their effects may require both qualitative and quantitative forecasts. Hospitality organizations already know a lot about their future guests since so many of them are already here. In 1998, 62 million consumers were over age fifty, and that number is expected to double over the next thirty years. The fifty-plus group had a combined annual income of more than $900 billion and accounted for 80 percent of the nation's savings. Americans over fifty outnumbered teenagers in 1998, and they will be active twenty to thirty years longer than seniors a generation or two ago. The aging baby boomers retiring early with substantial discretionary income will continue to be a prime market target of the hospitality industry. These people have the time, money, and physical ability to travel and participate in many guest experiences unimaginable to their parents at comparable times in their lives.

### *Generations X and Y*

Many future market opportunities can be identified by reviewing information already known about baby boomers and the Generation X and Generation Y segments of the population. "Generation X is the 46 million Americans aged 18–29."[20] According to *Business Week* in 1992, Members of Generation Y, now in grade school, will be the "youthquake" in the early twenty-first century. The group includes the approximately 4 million children born each year between 1989 and 1993. The roughly 57 million American children under the age of fifteen represent a significant demographic category. Although smaller than the group produced by the postwar baby boom, which lasted nearly 20 years and resulted in a generation of some 78 million children, Generation Y will obviously become a force of its own as it matures. By 2006, the teenage population will reach 30 million, the highest number in this age grouping since 1975.[21]

This generation will be different because the world it has to deal with is quite different from the one its parents faced. Of these children under the age of six, nearly 60 percent have mothers working outside the home compared with 18 percent in 1960. Around 61 percent of U.S. children aged three to five are attending preschool compared to 38 percent in 1970; nearly 60 percent of households with children aged seven or younger have personal computers; and more than one-third of elementary school students are black or Hispanic compared to 22 percent in 1974. Fifteen percent of U.S. births are to foreign-born mothers whose backgrounds are so diverse that the school systems of New York, Los Angeles, Chicago, and other large city systems report more than 100 languages spoken. One-quarter of children under six live in poverty. As the twentieth-century ended, one in three births was to an unwed mother, and one in three marriages ended in divorce. These final statistics mean more children are being brought up in single-parent homes where the parent is working. They also mean that the children are socialized at younger ages, learn to read earlier, spend longer days at school or day care, and must rely on someone other than a parent for much of their early childhood care.[22]

### Demographic Implications

These statistics have several implications for all organizations serving the public; some of them will have special impact on the labor-intensive hospitality industry. With dollars for education under pressure as aging baby boomers press for allocation of more government dollars to their growing health-care and retirement needs, agile hospitality companies can define themselves as white knights to schools and their students by finding innovative ways to promote their products and services while helping schools achieve their educational mission. The production of support lesson plans, videos, "edutainment," and electronic media will represent prime opportunities for companies to do good things for school systems while doing well for themselves. Those organizations that have a fundamental appeal to children, like theme parks or makers of children's products, can seize these opportunities in education as a cost-efficient and focused marketing strategy for reaching this estimated $100 billion-per-year market.

### Generation Y in the Workforce

The characteristics of Generation Y also have important implications for managing the workforce of hospitality organizations. The divergence between the haves and the have-nots in this Information Age is already wide among today's school children, who will be the workers of tomorrow. It can be seen even at the elementary-school level where those children who have access to computers are educationally outstripping those who don't.[23] Today's children will be the eighteen- to twenty-one-year-old workers of 2008 and 2010. Those who enter the workforce without the requisite basic skills will represent a major training and development challenge for the many hospitality organizations that depend upon young, eager, capable employees to provide and ensure guest satisfaction. The challenge will be to keep this new group of employees, especially the have-nots, competitive with the rapidly emerging, highly educated workforce of the Asian rim countries who are now investing heavily in education and training. The workforce is rapidly becoming global, and workers from many nations are competing for the same jobs. Advances in technology and communication make where a person is located less important than what the person can do.

These new workers will be different in other ways as well. As the first generation to have easy access to worldwide communication through the Internet, Generation Y will define their friends and their interests globally instead of in the neighborhood. This trend will be both good and bad as the power of neighborhood and community over individual beliefs, values, and behavior will decline while at the same time these people will be more inclined to have a global perspective and the diversity of thinking that such a perspective creates.

### *Limiting Creativity?*

This is the video generation. First graders now average twenty-three hours of TV per week. Parents remember how they used to play outside with neighborhood friends, but today 60 percent of children live in households with two working parents concerned about drugs, AIDS, and random crime in the streets. They can buy safe, supervised activities for their children, but free play time, during which earlier generations had to use imagination and creativity to find something to do, has decreased considerably.[24] Today children have soccer teams, tennis lessons, and judo. They go to Discovery Zone for structured play in the little time left to them after their working parents pick them up from after-school day care. Their opportunities to work things out for themselves or to be creative on their own are increasingly limited. When one has a Game Boy or computer with fantastic games and graphics, the motivation to stretch and grow one's own imagination and creativity is limited. The impact of such trends on both the future customer and on employee creativity and ability to develop new ideas may be profound.

## Changing Technology

Several developments, other than the population trends that are changing the workforce and customer base, will affect the strategies of hospitality organizations. Dramatic changes in technology will continue to have a major influence on both individual organizations and entire industries. Many demographic trends shift slowly. Because changes in technology, especially information technology, occur so rapidly, they and their impact are difficult to forecast.

The communications and computing power now found in a laptop computer were unthinkable only ten years ago. Today anyone with a laptop computer and Internet access can search for the lowest airfare to a destination, make a plane reservation, book a hotel room, and reserve a rental car. Yesterday's comic-strip fantasy was Dick Tracy's two-way wrist radio. Seiko has already produced a wristwatch personal computer that can download text and pictures from other computers. A wristband personal communicator with a built-in, artificial-intelligence-based personal management system is already being test marketed. The unit enables a person to communicate anywhere at any time with anyone similarly equipped. The day is soon coming when this wrist-mounted technology will be linked to a personal computer system with individualized decision-making capability. On that day, a guest will speak into a personal communicator and ask a computerized personal decision maker to find and book a hotel room, in a distant location, that the computer knows will suit the guest's needs and expectations. The implications of such a capability for travel agents, hotels controlling their room inventory, and other existing (and yet to be created) parts of the travel, tourism, and other hospitality markets are enormous.

Other aspects of technological change will be equally important to managing the hospitality organization. The need to blend innovative high-tech solutions into high-touch service situations will be increasingly recognized as a competitive strategy and, if done successfully,

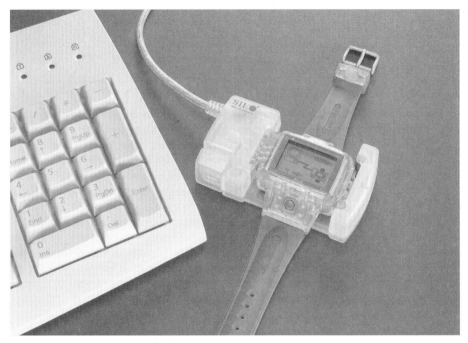

*Seiko Wrist Computer. (Courtesy of Seiko Instruments, Inc.)*

rewarded by the marketplace. Hotels, restaurants, and other guest service organizations will find new ways to substitute technology for people, to reduce their dependence on this expensive and increasingly scarce resource. At the same time, these same organizations will need to find ways to maintain the high level of personal contact that defines a positive guest experience. The challenge is to substitute technology for labor in ways that the guest perceives as either a positive increase in service quality and value or does not perceive at all.

Phone mail in hotels is an example of technology with which guests feel increasingly comfortable. While most luxury hotels still take messages for guests wanting this personal service, they also offer the technology for those who prefer the convenience of receiving a voice message. Voice mail is more convenient for everyone, takes less time, and is considerably cheaper for the hotel than staffing up to take messages manually. In this instance, the substitution of technology for people increases the guest's perception of service quality and value. In contrast, most people are annoyed when they call an organization wanting to talk to a person and are not allowed to do so until after punching several phone keys, if then. In those instances, technology has decreased the customer's perception of service quality and value rendered by the organization.

## Changing Social Expectations

Another factor in the long look around is society's changing expectations for all its institutions, including those in the hospitality industry. Some expectations wind up in the political process and result in new laws, rules, or regulations. Others are expressed through trade associations that monitor industry behavior and activist groups that identify and oversee industry practices.

Because they deal directly with the public, hospitality organizations must confront and respond to an array of government rules. When government regulators began requiring that food handlers stop using their bare hands and start using gloves or tongs to handle ready-to-eat food, the impact on many food-service organizations was considerable. They not only incurred the costs of gloves they didn't have to buy before, but they had to train food handlers in this new procedure. With the high levels of employee turnover in many areas of the food-service industry, accommodating the numerous extra costs created by this rule was a challenge to their strategy, product-market focus, delivery system, and service environment.

As another instance of government's impact, the Internal Revenue Service has been cracking down on the unreported tip income of servers. The IRS program requiring restaurants to keep track of employee tips has caused numerous restaurants to institute a "service charge" in place of tips. Many customers and most servers don't like that system, and the best servers won't work at restaurants using it, which leads to staffing problems.

Another major change in social expectations can be seen in certain emerging social trends and institutional changes. Casual dining did not exist as a food-service category until recently. Changing demographic trends led to this new category as more dual-income families sought an experience in between fast food and fine dining. A recent concept is the take-out family meal, pioneered by Boston Market, enabling the busy parent to stop in on the way home from work and get a full meal "like mom used to make" to feed the family. An even newer idea is the "grocerant," which combines a grocery store and a restaurant.

Changes in the social expectations of interest groups, and in the steps they are willing to take to exert influence, have affected hospitality organizations. One example is the increasing use of political action by religious groups. If a hospitality organization starts offering health and other benefits to same-sex partners of its employees, certain religious groups opposing same-sex relationships may well ask their members to boycott the organization. Because they are so dependent on maintaining a good relationship with the public, hospitality organizations are especially vulnerable to attacks by interest groups that disagree with management policies or business decisions. If a hospitality organization has any thoughts of building a major facility in a historically significant area, it can expect that groups wanting to preserve the area in its present state will generate negative publicity. Even if constructing the facility is a good business decision, public opposition may make it a bad customer-relations decision. Any hospitality organization dependent on a broad customer base has a real challenge when every action it takes is so visible to its guests.

At a minimum, planners should try to stay aware of shifting social expectations. Including input from social groups can sometimes enhance the strategic planning process greatly. When planning began for Disney's Animal Kingdom theme park, the organization invited representatives of environmental and animal-rights groups to help in the development process. By working with them, Disney was able to develop a park consonant with their ideals.

## Changing Economic Forces

Many environmental factors already covered have an economic aspect. Economics is such an important issue, however, that it deserves special discussion. The organization must consider the effects of governmental economic policies on its suppliers of capital, the ability of its customers to buy the service, and competitors' ability to compete. It must also consider in its strategic planning process numerous other economic factors as well.

One important consideration is the future direction of the local, regional, national, and even international economies and how these directions will influence the demand for hospitality services. Consider foreign currency exchange rates as an example. If Spain's growth rate is lower than that of the United States and therefore its currency is less valuable in foreign exchange than this country's, foreign tourists will consider going to Spain rather than coming to the United States. In the labor-intensive service sector, the influence of inflation on competitiveness is especially important. If inflation rates move up or down, then the organization's cost of capital—its ability to expand the business, buy new equipment, and keep up with rising wage expectations—will be affected. Other economic factors would include productivity growth, income distribution, and stage in the business cycle. Most hospitality organizations are more sensitive to variations in general economic health than organizations making and selling necessities. When the economy is in a downward cycle, so too is the travel and tourism industry. People must buy groceries and clothing; they don't have to take vacations.

## Changing Competitors

An organization has existing competitors, potential competitors, and indirect competitors that offer customers a substitute or alternative service. These competitors can be local, national, or even international.

Existing competitors have an established position in your market niche. If you are a small corner restaurant, your competitors are all those other restaurants in the same market area. Since most people go to restaurants within a short drive of their home, these competitors are easy to identify. Potential competitors are those who are likely to enter your market area. The sign may be up, the building begun, and the "buy one, get one free" coupons already printed to mark the existence of a potential competitor to your restaurant. The alternative or substitute providers include anyone who sells food. They can range from Weight Watchers, which provides its own branded food products to dieters, to the local grocery store, to a food-delivery service. Anyone who can fill the same basic need with an alternative product is a competitor.

In the theme park industry, a competitor is anyone who can encourage customers to spend money at their attraction rather than in your theme park. Because Orlando visitors can spend money in a wide variety of alternative ways, Orlando theme parks are especially sensitive to this competitive market reality. And of course people can choose not to come to Orlando at all; they can go to competitive attractions at other destinations like Las Vegas, Spain, or Branson, Missouri. The in-market competition includes other theme parks, dinner theaters, civic museums, art galleries, and factory-outlet stores. It even includes noncustomers who stay away from parks entirely and watch videos at home or in a motel room. One response of a theme park organization to such an array of competition is to use all the principles of guestology to provide park visitors with an ultimate, irresistible guest experience. The guestologist would also try to find out how guests want to spend their time and money, other than on the basic guest experience that the theme park offers, and if possible provide those options rather than letting customers go to competitors.

## Changes in Other Relevant Groups

In addition to the various factors and groups we have already discussed, several other groups in the organization's external environment must be included in any environmental forecast: the suppliers of resources, capital, and labor.

*Red Lobster. (Courtesy of Darden Restaurants.)*

### Resource Suppliers

One important group is the resource suppliers of raw material, capital, and labor. When Red Lobster adds a new seafood item to its menu, it must first check to be sure its demand doesn't exhaust the world's supply of that item. Because Red Lobster has so many restaurants, adding or removing a menu item can have a major impact on the supply of that product. If a certain type of shrimp now retails for $7.99 per pound, how much will the price change if Red Lobster buys up half of the world's supply next year? Obviously, the planning process needs to take such supply-related issues into consideration.

### Capital Suppliers

A second major interested group is the suppliers of capital. As the capital market becomes more global and the availability of electronic transfers makes movement of capital easier and quicker, the organization may need to spend more time forecasting the availability of capital for its business and industry. If capital availability is driven by the next quarter's financial report, the impact on the organization's decision-making and planning horizon will be considerable. If Wall Street demands a certain short-run return on investment, finding the extra resources to develop a new service or to take a chance on a new concept or location may be difficult. Once the tax advantages of building hotels were eliminated by the Tax Reform Act of 1986, the number of new hotels under construction dropped dramatically. The previous tax laws had made the financial returns attractive enough to justify new hotel construction. Without these tax advantages, however, the returns on investment were sharply reduced, and the availability of new money for hotel construction dried up. The restaurant industry undergoes a periodic devaluation of its stock prices as the capital market expresses its opinion about the industry's overcapacity problems and how much it will hurt to fix them. No matter how good a strategy an organization has, if it can't convince the capital market, the strategy may be worthless.

### The Labor Supply

A third supplier of a crucial resource is the labor market. It is so important that we devote Chapter 5 on Staffing to it.

## Surprises

The final external issue to address in this long look around at the environment is the potential for surprise. While one cannot often predict stock market crashes, wars, or natural disasters, thoughtful planners consider these possibilities. If most customers have to drive long distances to get to your service setting, your planners should keep in mind the problems that intensifying instability in the chief oil-producing nations might create. If your airline serves or your hotel chain is located in an area that seems subject to terrorist attacks, you need to have a contingency plan. If you are Marineland located in a small northeast Florida county full of pine trees, and you are already on the financial ropes because highway tourists get on the interstate and go directly to newer, bigger Central Florida attractions, you need to consider what will happen to your organization if uncontrollable forest fires cause the entire county to be evacuated, as occurred in 1998. That is an actual example: Marineland closed its doors after the fires. While hoping and planning for the best, strategic planners must realize that any number of unpredictable future events can have a severe impact on how many customers want or need the service the organization offers.

## The Impact of Change on Strategic Premises

All these changes will have varying effects on the organization. But not all factors are equal in either their impact on the organization or in terms of our ability to forecast them fully. Some are predictable and simple, such as the estimate of teenagers available for work in ten years. Since they have all been born already, predicting the number available in ten years is a straightforward calculation. Some other factors are simple but unpredictable. Using demographics again, estimating the number of skilled and trained employees who will be available in Orlando, Florida, in twenty years is a simple number to calculate, but the calculations rest on unpredictable information such as unknown changes in family formation, net migration into the Central Florida area, and other factors.

As was true of simple future elements, complex future elements are either predictable or unpredictable. Once a certain number of people are in a destination market, a relatively predictable percentage will come to any given tourist attraction on any given day. Calculating the number of people who will be in the market, however, is a complex process; it depends on airline routes and fares, propensity to travel by people all over the world, the price of gasoline, the level of economic activity, consumer confidence, and a variety of other factors.

The complex and unpredictable outcomes are, of course, the hardest to forecast. An example would be changes in technology. If technology develops to the point that the experience of going to a major attraction can be duplicated through virtual reality, then people won't have to go to the trouble and expense of coming to the site of the attraction to rent cars, stay in hotels, and buy admissions. If this happens, the entire area surrounding the attraction will suffer a severe economic decline. Predicting whether it will happen and, if it does, how severe the decline will be is a major challenge for both hospitality and civic forecasters.

Some forecasts are easy, because the elements comprising them (which are themselves forecasts) are predictable and the calculations simple, and others are difficult. Guestologists must try to make the forecasts relevant to their futures, regardless of ease or difficulty, and include them in their strategic planning processes. Since things that can be counted are often more comfortable to deal with than those that can't, managers are sometimes tempted to emphasize those factors that are numerical while ignoring those that cannot be easily measured. Unfortunately for those managers, in real life the crucial factors are usually those to which we can't apply numbers.

## Strategic Premises

The hospitality organization draws conclusions about the future of its industry and market from its environmental assessment, then uses them to make the assumptions, called *strategic premises,* on which the service plan is based. Premises are educated guesses. The organization may guess wrong; even if it guesses right, it may devise the wrong strategy. But not to guess at all means reacting day to day to whatever seems to be going on, without a plan or a focus for organizational activities.

Dave Thomas, founder of Wendy's, tells how his environmental assessment led to certain premises on which his corporate strategy was based. In 1969, he identified five trends he thought offered him a market opportunity that he had the competence to meet:

1. *People wanted choices.* They were tired of living in a prepackaged world; they wanted some influence over the products they were buying in the marketplace, and they wanted something new.
2. *People were fed up with poor quality.* He saw a big interest in things that were fresh and natural.
3. *People were trying to adjust to a newer, more complicated way of life.* Older people were looking for relief from the many social and political changes occurring during the 1960s, and young people were looking for changes that they could handle. Thomas notes, "In a funny way, the old fashioned decor and the Tiffany lamps provided a novelty for the young adults and nostalgia for the older generation at the same time."[25]
4. *People were on the move.* Any business had to accommodate this restless mobility.
5. *People were ready for an upscale hamburger place.* He felt that many people had grown up loving hamburgers but were not satisfied with the product generally available at fast-food outlets.

Thomas writes, "Knowing these five trends allowed Wendy's to focus on the right market. My bet is that if you looked at any successful business, you would find factors very much like these behind that business's success. If you're going to bet your bankroll on a business concept, you had better be able to understand those forces. If you can't describe them, you had better feel them so clearly in your gut that you know you're right."[26]

## Strategic Premises: Theme Parks

*At the Park,* a major theme park industry journal, offers several interesting forecasts. Any theme park organization believing them to be accurate could use them as premises on which to base strategic plans.

1. There will be more parks, but they will be smaller. These will be niche parks appealing to specific market segments, close to population centers, and they may well include sophisticated, high-technology entertainment attractions. Economic trends will create niches for expensive, exclusive, upscale parks that will appeal to a large and growing number of affluent customers.

2. Immigration trends will create more demand for ethnic-themed parks. Foreign-born Americans represented 8 percent of population in 1990 but will constitute 14 percent by 2045. One out of three new Americans is of Asian or Hispanic descent. Parks will be themed so as to appeal to these important new markets.

3. More competition and more investment opportunities will be outside the United States. Tourists from all over the world visit our theme parks. The theme park idea has global potential; its appeal has hardly been met anywhere except in the United States. Theme parks and water parks have been started in Tokyo, Paris, the Netherlands, the Philippines, Korea, and China, and these are only the beginning.

4. The customer base will get progressively older. The median age of Americans in 1996 was 33. In 2005 it will be 36.3, and in 2010 it will be 44.3. Theme parks like Sea World and Epcot are great destinations for older tourists because they provide rides of the mind rather than the body. Future theme parks must take into account the shifting expectations and abilities that accompany advancing age. These customers will have older bodies with less stamina and more physiological limitations such as less acute eyesight and hearing, weaker bones, and a less reliable sense of balance. They won't want to be jarred in physically demanding rides or attractions or risk heart attacks in roller coasters or loop-the-loops. This customer group will have more disposable income and time. They will often be accompanied by the young children of their own working children and will look for attractions that appeal both to themselves and these children. Both they and the children accompanying them will have shorter attention spans than the average present-day customer. They will value time and nutrition, will be healthier and more worldly than their parents were, and will demand service experiences that are novel, interesting, and reaffirming of their values.

5. Cultural attractions such as museums, historical sites, aquariums, and symphony orchestras will either learn how to enter the entertainment business to compete or lose their public support and funding. Like the Boston Pops, these attractions will have to provide a "show" along with high-quality substance. As people focus on government costs and demand more for their tax dollar, the need to attract more customers will drive publicly owned organizations into stronger competition with commercial theme parks and attractions.

6. The growth and availability of virtual-reality technology will change the experiences that customers seek and expect from attractions. As people get used to the availability of virtual

experiences that make them feel as if they are actually *there,* the appeal and value of amusement parks will be more directly tied to the shared experience of being with other people and the energy of being part of a real crowd of people.

7. More emphasis will be placed on personal safety and security, because customers will expect and demand it.

8. The role of theme parks in affirming and teaching our cultural heritage, beliefs, and values will continue to expand. Theme parks define a view of culture and to some extent teach guests what the culture is all about. In the future, theme parks will continue to serve as places where cultural values are reaffirmed; they will espouse positive, conservative, universally shared human values. In America, theme parks will continue to tell stories and display themes that have universal appeal; they will try to represent the best of the culture's values, beliefs, ideals, and themes. Sea World, for example, promotes the themes of environmental and animal respect, and Disney's Animal Kingdom does the same. The themes of successful parks reflect what is good about our culture; they teach, reinforce, and reaffirm those cultural values we all share.

9. Technology will continue to change the way in which the theme park experience is enjoyed, but the fundamental premise of a theme park or any service organization will not change. As *At the Park* puts it, "You still need to make them laugh, charm them, dazzle them, take them somewhere new and different, give them a chance to be part of a crowd, to see and be seen, feed them well, take great care of them and make them feel better about themselves and the world."

Source: *At the Park,* 1996, Issue 36:55–56.

## ASSESSING THE ORGANIZATION ITSELF: THE INTERNAL AUDIT

On the right side of our planning model in Figure 2-1, opposite the long look around, is the internal audit, or the searching look within. The hospitality organization cannot plan with any confidence until it admits its weaknesses and identifies its central strengths, frequently termed its core competencies.

### Core Competencies

The definition given by Hamel and Prahalad is helpful: an organization's **core competence** is the bundle of skills and technologies (often called, confusingly enough, competencies) that gives the organization an important difference in providing customer benefits and perceived value.[27] Chrysler's core competence is the ability to make cars. The core competence of the Walt Disney Company is the ability to manage family entertainment facilities. The core competence of most Disney properties is the ability to entertain people. Knowing its areas of competence will enable an organization to make a key strategic decision: What shall we *not* do?

If a company has proven it has the ability and technology to combine the merchandising of consumer goods, entertainment, and an eating experience in a striking setting, then it can do what Rainforest Cafe and most other theme restaurants have done: seek to expand the variety of consumer goods it sells alongside its restaurant operations. In contrast, after Disney bought ABC/Capital Cities, it decided to retain parts of the new business that fit its core competence and eliminate those that did not. It sold off some businesses, acquired as part of the ABC package, such as magazine publishing and other nonentertainment business units. The point is that every successful organization has developed a core competence, an ability to do something very well. As long as it sticks to activities appropriate to that core competence, it will probably continue to succeed. When it strays from its core competence, it may find itself pitting its weaknesses against the strengths of other organizations.

Successful managers must have two skills or qualities: management ability and expertise in a specific industry or functional area. They know, just as successful organizations know, that they should focus on developing their management ability and industry expertise, which as a bundle comprise their core competence. A factory manager and a hotel manager may have many of the same managerial skills. But the successful factory manager may fail as a hotel manager. The core competence leading to success, for managers and for organizations, will be different in the two industries.

The internal audit tells the hospitality organization where it stands now, what new strengths it must develop, and what weaknesses it must eliminate to build the core competence it will need to succeed in the future industry it foresees. If an organization accurately perceives itself to be the dominant force in entertainment and foresees the future of entertainment in electronic media, then that company should probably set its sights on dominating any electronic medium that develops and delivers entertainment. Such reasoning is, of course, what made Wall Street applaud Disney when it bought ABC and criticize Westinghouse when it bought CBS at about the same time. For Disney, the fit with its core competence and industry vision was perfect. Wall Street perceived the Westinghouse purchase as a venture into a new and unknown area, outside its proven core competence, and so did Westinghouse! As a result of an internal audit and long look around, the company decided its core competencies could no longer make money, so it abandoned them, got rid of its old lines of business, changed its name, rewrote its mission statement, and adopted instead the core competencies of CBS. Rarely do the internal and external audits lead to such dramatic decisions.

## Internal Assets

An **internal audit** includes an assessment of all the organization's internal assets. Each organization has a reputation, a pool of human capital (its employees), managerial capabilities, resources in place, and competitive advantages based on its technology, patents, **brand names,** copyrights, and customer loyalty that help define its core competencies.

Disney, for example, is generally considered to be one of the world's most able hospitality organizations. It knows what it should do to sustain its core competence of providing service excellence in the family entertainment field. It has a unique, well-established, loyal customer base, a committed pool of employees, well-trained management, a strong brand image, and a well-maintained capital base. In an assessment of its own internal strengths and weaknesses, Disney builds upon its core abilities—not only by acknowledging them as an organizational strength but also by incorporating them into its business plan as a marketable product, to be shared with others through seminars offered at the Disney Institute on how to manage service organizations.

Marriott Hotels understands that one role of planning based on a knowledge of core competencies is to keep the organization out of businesses it should not be in. If a company

*Market Segmentation: Marriott Brands. (Courtesy of Marriott International, Inc.)*

achieves great success and finds itself with a lot of cash on its hands, as Marriott did around 1980, it might be tempted to try new lines of business just because it can afford to. What Marriott did as the decade moved on was to sell two businesses—airline catering and restaurants—that it had operated successfully for sixty years. Marriott forecasts in those areas were not promising, so Marriott left those businesses. At about the same time, the organization realized that the market for its core competence—running large, full-service Marriott hotels—was limited. The company decided to capitalize on its name and core abilities by moving into other segments of the lodging market: Marriott Suites, small-sized, medium-priced Courtyard by Marriott, economy-priced Fairfield Inn by Marriott, and extended-stay Marriott Residence Inn. It also acquired the Renaissance, Ramada, and new World chains.[28]

An unsatisfactory bottom line will motivate a company to take a searching look within. For years McDonald's sold precooked hamburgers kept warm under heat lamps. Falling sales and the public's obvious desire for made-to-order hot food prepared "their way" convinced the company that it had to change the way it executed its core competence: making and selling hamburgers quickly. Its new slogan? "Made For You . . . At the Speed of McDonald's." The company totally revamped its production and delivery system to provide customers with hotter, fresher food served faster. In 1998 and 1999, the new cooking technology was installed in 12,000 McDonald's stores. The service standard of the new food-preparation technology? To serve hot, made-to-order meals, juicy meat on hot buns, to customers no more than 3.5 minutes after they walk in, no matter how many customers are already waiting in line.[29]

Marriott also serves as an example of how a careful internal audit found a deficiency in what Marriott had thought was a competency: having a sufficient number of dedicated, able employees. In 1996 an internal assessment revealed that the company needed to address certain characteristics of the lower-paid end of its workforce if it wished to use this employee group effectively. According to *Business Week,* identified problems included "lack of education, poor work habits, inability to speak English, culture clashes, financial woes, inadequate child care, and domestic violence, for starters. People don't show up when they should; they leave without explanation."[30] Marriott recognized that although these employees were available for relatively low pay, they were costly in other ways and required an excessive commitment of management time. The company established a program to train these employees in dealing with the many life and work challenges they faced.

## Vision and Mission Statements

In the middle of the model in Figure 2-1 are the organization's vision and mission statements. Most organizations spend a great deal of time trying to articulate these concepts, and the reason is clear: If you don't know what you want to do, how can you decide how to do it? Most companies wind up writing mission and vision statements—and other statements such as credos, beliefs, and values—but not all need to; some know what they are doing and where they are heading without writing it down. Vision and mission statements vary from the simple to the complex, and the simpler the better.

### *The Vision Statement*

The vision statement describes what the organization should look like in the future and what significant contributions it expects to make. Former Chili's CEO Norman Brinker said, "When it comes right down to it, I do one thing: I have a vision, then I create an atmosphere that involves the people in that vision."[31] Though *mission* and *vision* are to an extent overlapping terms, the corporate vision is the really big picture of hopes for the future. Hamel and Prahalad call this vision definition the "quest for industry foresight" as the organization defines what its future could be and works backward to what it must do today to make that future happen. The real creative imagination of management and the entire organization needs to be focused on articulating the vision and how to achieve it. Hamel and Prahalad describe the difficulties involved in getting from here to there, from today to tomorrow:

> Although potentially useful, technology forecasting, market research, scenario planning, and competitor analysis won't necessarily yield industry foresight. None of these tools compels senior management to preconceive the corporation and the industries in which it competes. Only by changing the lens through which the corporation is viewed (looking at core competencies versus focusing on only strategic business units), only by changing the lens through which markets are viewed (functionalities versus products), only by broadening the angle of the lens (becoming more inquisitive), only by cleaning off the accumulated grime on the lens (seeing with a child's eyes), and only by occasionally disbelieving what one sees (challenging price-performance conventions, thinking like a contrarian) can the future be anticipated. The quest for industry foresight is the quest to visceralize what doesn't yet exist. . . . Having imagined the future, a company must find a path that leads from today to tomorrow.[32]

Sometimes an organization is created to fulfill a personal vision. Walt Disney wanted to build his theme park, Disneyland, so badly that he was willing to borrow against his insurance policy to begin it. He had a vision to fulfill. Selling others on the same vision was a difficult challenge. After all, who else could imagine a theme park built on 182 acres of citrus grove in the middle of then-undeveloped Anaheim, California? The park would wind up costing $17 million to build, far exceeding the original estimates. While Disneyland was a visionary project, it pales in comparison with the vision required to conceive Walt Disney World Resort and bring the park into being. Disney bought nearly 28,000 acres, mostly citrus groves, near the quiet town of Orlando, Florida, on which to build his dream. It included not only an expanded version of his Disneyland theme park but also hotels, restaurants, and even Epcot, the city of the future. Epcot was originally envisioned as a complete, self-contained city with its own schools, apartments, and shopping facilities. The development in 1996 of the Celebration community has brought to fruition this final part of Walt Disney's grand vision.[33]

Here are the vision, mission, and values of the Walt Disney World Dolphin at Walt Disney World Resort:

Our Vision: The Walt Disney World Dolphin provides an experience as unique as its setting and, through cast commitment to "WOW" service, will be the most unique hotel in the world!

Our Mission: The Cast of the Walt Disney World Dolphin will achieve our vision by attracting and serving guests in the group and leisure market segments through the

*WDW Dolphin. (Used by permission from Disney Enterprises, Inc.)*

**WELCOME TO
NORDSTROM**

We're glad to have you with
our Company.

Our number one goal is to provide
outstanding customer service.

Set both your personal and
professional goals high.
We have great confidence in your
ability to achieve them.

Nordstrom Rules:

Rule #1: Use your good
judgment in all situations.

There will be no additional rules.

Please feel free to ask
your department manager,
store manager or division general
manager any question
at any time.

# NORDSTROM

**Figure 2-2** *Mission, Creed, Values: Nordstrom. (Used with permission.)*

implementation of total Customer Satisfaction and attracting, retaining, and motivating the best Cast Members Possible.

Our Values: Integrity, Creativity, Open Communication, Passion for Excellence, Commitment to Continuous Improvement, Perseverance, Vision, Commitment to Empowerment, Commitment to do the Right Thing, Enthusiasm for our Business, Compassion, Commitment to Teamwork, Commitment to Being the Hotel Leader.

Other statements of company mission, creed, or values appear in Figures 2-2 and 2-3: a page from the Nordstrom employee handbook and a card carried by Extended StayAmerica Efficiency Studios managers.

The Nordstrom statement includes the company's one-sentence "policy manual": "Use your good judgment in all situations." The reverse side of the Extended StayAmerica card reminds managers of the "2-Minute Rule": Spend two minutes a day with each employee, taking an interest in that person's life.

EXTENDEDSTAYAMERICA.
EFFICIENCY STUDIOS

### Creed

**Treat each guest as you would want to be treated.**

**Treat fellow employees with the respect they deserve.**

**Be a good steward of all that is entrusted to you.**

**Use good judgement at all times.**

EXTENDEDSTAYAMERICA.
EFFICIENCY STUDIOS

### "2-Minute Rule"

Your employees are special – they have families, outside interests, goals, etc. – just like you! It's important to all of them that their personal life is respected and that we as leaders demonstrate a genuine interest in each person.

If you spend just 2 minutes a day with each employee, taking an interest in their life, you'll gain greater trust, commitment, and a better working relationship. It's critical to let your employees know they are important to *you* and to the continued success of Extended Stay America.

. . . just 2 minutes a day . . . try it!

**People**
**Produce**
**Profits . . . let's not forget!**

**Figure 2-3** *Extended Stay America Creed and "2-Minute Rule." (Used with permission.)*

### The Mission Statement

The organization's mission statement expresses the reason for which the organization was created and exists. It guides managers as they allocate resources, focuses organizational marketing efforts, and defines for all employees how they should deal with guests and customers. An example would be the simple but elegant motto statement of The Ritz-Carlton Hotel Company, L.L.C., winner of a Malcolm Baldrige Quality Award: "We are Ladies and Gentlemen serving Ladies and Gentlemen." The motto is printed on a pocket-sized laminated card, presented as Figure 2-4, carried by every employee. Also printed on that card are the company's credo, its three steps of service, and its twenty basic service standards—all of these being known collectively as the company's Gold Standards. Of the card, President and Chief Operating Officer Horst Schulze says, "Every employee has the business plan of The Ritz-Carlton in his or her pocket, constantly reinforcing that guest satisfaction is our highest mission."[34]

Red Lobster, part of Darden Restaurants, couches its vision and mission in terms of its passion, dream, and goals: "Our *passion* is hospitality, over-the-top performance, and creating a legacy of greatness that endures and prospers for generations to come. Our *dream* is to be a world-class company of restaurants that our stakeholders—customers and guests, crew, suppliers, communities, and Darden Restaurants—are proud of. Our *goals* are to earn a sterling reputation for measured excellence in everything that we do and to retain the loyalty of our stakeholders for life."[35] These somewhat general statements are made specific in the

```
┌─────────────────────────┐
│   Three Steps           │
│   Of Service            │
│                         │
│        1                │
│ A warm and sincere      │
│     greeting.           │
│ Use the guest name,     │
│ if and when possible.   │
│                         │
│        2                │
│ Anticipation and        │
│   compliance            │
│ with guest needs        │
│                         │
│        3                │
│ Fond farewell. Give     │
│ them a warm good-bye    │
│ and use their names,    │
│ if and when possible.   │
└─────────────────────────┘
```

## *"We Are Ladies and Gentlemen Serving Ladies and Gentlemen"*

```
┌─────────────────────────┐
│   The Ritz-Carlton®     │
│                         │
│       Credo             │
│                         │
│ The Ritz-Carlton Hotel  │
│ is a place where the    │
│ genuine care and        │
│ comfort of our guests   │
│ is our highest mission. │
│ We pledge to provide    │
│ the finest personal     │
│ service and facilities  │
│ for our guests who will │
│ always enjoy a warm,    │
│ relaxed yet refined     │
│ ambience.               │
│ The Ritz-Carlton        │
│ experience enlivens the │
│ senses, instills well-  │
│ being, and fulfills     │
│ even the unexpressed    │
│ wishes and needs of     │
│ our guests.             │
└─────────────────────────┘
```

## The Ritz-Carlton® Basics

1 The Credo will be known, owned and energized by all employees.

2 Our motto is: "We are Ladies and Gentlemen serving Ladies and Gentlemen." Practice teamwork and "lateral" service" to create a positive work environment.

3 The three steps of service shall be practiced by all employees.

4 All employees will successfully complete Training Certification to ensure they understand how to perform to The Ritz-Carlton standards in their position.

5 Each employee will understand their work area and Hotel goals as established in each strategic plan.

6 All employees will know the needs of their internal and external customers (guests and employees) so that we may deliver the products and services they expect. Use guest preference pads to record specific needs.

7 Each employee will continuously identify defects (Mr. BIV) throughout the Hotel.

8 Any employee who receives a customer complaint "owns" the complaint.

9 React quickly to correct the problem immediately. Follow up with a telephone call within twenty minutes to verify the problem has been resolved to the customer's satisfaction. Do everything you possibly can to never lose a guest.

10 Guest incident action forms are used to record and communicate every incident of guest dissatisfaction. Every employee is empowered to resolve the problem and to prevent a repeat occurrence.

11 Uncompromising levels of cleanliness are the responsibility of every employee.

12 "Smile--We are on stage." Always maintain positive eye contact. Use the proper vocabulary with our guests. (Use words like--"Good Morning," "Certainly," "I'll be happy to," and "My pleasure").

13 Be an ambassador of your Hotel in and outside of the work place. Always talk positively. No negative comments.

14 Escort guests rather than pointing out directions to another area of the Hotel.

15 Be knowledgeable of Hotel information (hours of operation, etc.) to answer guest inquiries. Always recommend the Hotel's retail and food and beverage outlets prior to outside facilities.

16 Use proper telephone etiquette. Answer within three rings and with a "smile." When necessary, ask the caller, "May I place you on hold?" Do not screen calls. Eliminate call transfers when possible.

17 Uniforms are to be immaculate. Wear proper and safe footware (clean and polished), and your correct name tag. Take pride and care in your personal appearance (adhering to all grooming standards).

18 Ensure all employees know their roles during emergency situations and are aware of fire and life safety response processes.

19 Notify your supervisor immediately of hazards, injuries, equipment or assistance that you need. Practice energy conservation and proper maintenance and repair of Hotel property and equipment.

20 Protecting the assets of a Ritz-Carlton Hotel is the responsibility of every employee.

**Figure 2-4** *Ritz-Carlton Credo Card. (Used with permission of The Ritz-Carlton Hotel Company, L.L.C.)*

eight principles tied to them under these headings: Hospitality, Fairness, Caring, Respect, Fun, Quality, Zip, and Balance.

The Olive Garden Restaurants (another Darden organization) have a seven-point vision statement and also a simple four-point statement that provides guidance for employees:

1. Hot food hot
2. Cold food cold
3. Know your product
4. Clean rest rooms
5. Money in our bank

These points provide focused and clear guides to employee decisions.

The organization's statement of mission often includes its core values. Wal-Mart founder Sam Walton combined mission and values when he said, "We put the customer ahead of everything else. . . . If you're not serving the customer, or supporting the folks who do, we don't need you."[36] All of these organizations recognize the importance of providing straightforward guidance to all employees as to how the organization expects them to act in their jobs.

Southwest Airlines started out in 1971 with this mission: "Get your passengers to their destinations when they want to get there, on time, at the lowest possible fares, and make darn sure they have a good time doing it."[37] Here is the Southwest mission statement of today:

> Southwest Airline is dedicated to the highest quality of Customer Service delivered with a sense of warmth, friendliness, individual pride, and Company Spirit.
>
> We are committed to provide our Employees a stable work environment with equal opportunity for learning and personal growth. Creativity and innovation are encouraged for improving the effectiveness of Southwest Airlines. Above all, Employees will be provided the same concern, respect, and caring attitude within the organization that they are expected to share externally with every Southwest Customer.

## DEVELOPING THE SERVICE STRATEGY

Once the external and internal assessment factors have been examined in light of the corporate vision and mission, the hospitality organization is ready to define its *service strategy*. This strategy is critical to any service organization's success because it provides guidance in how to make every organizational decision, from capital budgeting to handling a customer complaint. Defining and creating the service strategy are as much art as science. The organization must now define its market, craft its service product to meet that market's needs, create the appropriate service environment, and design the service systems to reach the target market. In Chapter 1 we discussed these key components of the hospitality organization, and this is the place where the strategy must be translated into specific actions. If the company mission is to deliver a service product to an upscale, educated, retired socioeconomic group, then the service delivery system should be high touch, and the service environment should be elegant and congruent with what an upscale market wants. Knowing what any market wants takes us back to an important point from the first chapter: *Ask the customer.*

### Asking Customers What They Want

The best way to know what your customers want or expect is to ask them. The organization should not only look inside to evaluate its core competencies but must also ask its customers to find out what the key drivers of customer satisfaction are. Only customers can tell the organization what they really value, and these values should drive the decision process on resource allocations. The customers will tell the organization if its core competencies are important to providing customer value and satisfaction, and excellent hospitality organizations measure these key drivers carefully and frequently.

As a true believer in identifying key drivers, Disney surveys its guests constantly. On one such survey, Walt Disney World Resort guests were asked a variety of questions about their experiences and how those experiences related to both their intention to return to the parks and their overall satisfaction with Walt Disney World Resort. Fast food in the parks and the park transportation system received relatively low ratings. However, analysis of the data revealed only a weak statistical relationship between these low ratings and both intention to return and overall satisfaction with Walt Disney World Resort. The quality of the fast food and the transportation system did not seem to matter all that much. On the other hand, ratings of hours of operation and fireworks were strongly related to both the return intention and the satisfaction measure.

Guided by the survey results, Disney decided to invest available funds in extending park hours and expanding the fireworks displays. Although the organization felt competent to improve fast food and the transportation system, it allocated scarce resources to improving areas of key importance to guests. The strategic planning process did not just involve managers introspectively looking at organizational core competencies. It incorporated the wishes and expectations of guests into these decisions. Most other guest-focused organizations do the same. They find out what key factors drive the experiences of organizational guests, and they work hard to ensure that the organization has or develops the core competencies to provide and enhance those key drivers.

## The Excellent Service Strategy

Service expert Len Berry suggests that an excellent service strategy has four characteristics.[38]

### Quality and Value

First, the excellent strategy emphasizes *quality*. Without a commitment to quality, nothing else matters. Any hospitality organization can write a mission statement, but those truly committed to excellence start by committing the organization to providing the customer with a guest experience of high quality. Second, an excellent service strategy emphasizes *value*. It commits the organization to providing customers with more benefits from the guest experience than their costs.

Recall that value and cost cannot be defined solely in monetary terms. If "time is money," organizations can provide value by saving time for customers. Organizations doing so fill a significant market niche. The many people who pay extra for personal shoppers in retail stores believe they receive good value in time saved for the money they spend on having someone shop for them. Home-delivered pizza is even a better value; you save time, and you pay no more than if you had gone to the restaurant. Organizations must budget funds for measuring the perceived value of their services to customers. No matter what the service costs, customers must believe that they are getting significant value for their money.

### Service and Achievement

The third characteristic of an excellent service strategy is that it focuses the entire organizational effort on *service*. This strategy commits the organization to hiring people who believe in service, employee training programs emphasize the commitment to service quality, resources are allocated to serving the customer, the performance and reward systems carefully reinforce the entire workforce's commitment to service, and all action plans support the service mission. The service strategy should ensure that everyone in the organization walks the service-quality walk by constantly reflecting total commitment to service excellence.

Finally, the service strategy should foster among employees a sense of *genuine achievement.* It should stretch and push every employee to grow and develop so that the employee group stretches and develops the entire organization to do things no one thought were possible. Taco Bell found a way to stretch its employees so it could operate 90 percent of its company-owned restaurants without a full-time manager. According to Berry, "These locations are team managed by their mostly younger person crews who order inventory, schedule work hours, and recruit and train, among other functions."[39]

### Supporting Strategies: Service Product, Environment, and Delivery System

Once the service strategy has been defined, it provides the basis for determining what the organization's service product should be, what the service environment in which the service product is provided or delivered should look and feel like, and how the service delivery system makes the service product available to the guest.

If the organizational mission, for example, is to create and sustain a low-cost airline to serve the budget market in the Western United States, then the service product must be designed to meet that market's expectations, the environment must be designed to fit the product and match or exceed the guest's expectation of how this type of airline experience should look and feel, and the service delivery system must be designed to ensure that the service product is provided to the guest in a way that is congruent with how the guest expects to experience that service. The joint consideration of these three guest-experience components leads to the short-run action plans that can support and implement the components and thereby achieve the organization's mission.

## ACTION PLANS

Once this point in the hospitality planning process is reached, action plans can be developed because the organization now has a clear idea of what and where it is, where it wants to go, and how it intends to get there. The action plans represent the leadership's decisions on how to best implement the service strategy in specific terms that will motivate and guide the rest of the organization's members toward accomplishing the overall service strategy and organizational mission. These plans lay out the specifics of how the organization will operate and what everyone needs to do in the next time period, usually a year.

### Key Action-Plan Areas

The bottom tier of Figure 2-1 indicates the five key areas in which action plans should be established: Management, Staffing, Capacity Utilization, Finance, and Marketing. Benchmark organizations not only develop plans in each of these areas but also make sure each area has an appropriate means for measuring the degree to which those plans were achieved. Not only must employees understand the direction in which everyone is supposed to go; everyone must also know what getting there looks like. The measures ensure that the right things are done, the right goals are achieved, and the employees can see how well they're doing as they work toward achieving the action plan goals. Good plans are accompanied by good measures of achievement so everyone knows how the plan is working.

All action plans need to be considered as a whole and individually. No marketing plan or capacity utilization plan, for example, should be set without also taking into account the financial/budgeting plan. Similarly no managerial performance plan can be set without carefully planning for the necessary resources that will allow managers to reach their targeted goals. Just as it makes no sense to put a lot of resources into a marketing plan that will draw many customers without considering the capacity decisions, it also makes little sense to develop performance targets for managers without also considering what physical, financial, marketing, and human resources they will need to reach their targets.

* * *

This process defines hospitality service planning. The plan lays out the necessary steps and identifies the mileposts along the path which the organization must follow to fulfill its mission, to achieve its vision. If the organization foresees the wrong future, misdiagnoses its core competencies, poorly defines its mission, or chooses the wrong service strategy, then it will soon lose its competitive stature.

## THE UNCERTAIN FUTURE

Of course, unforeseen developments may disrupt or overturn even the best laid plans. Good plans attempt to bring rationality and stability to the organization's operations and efforts, but organizations seldom operate in purely rational or stable situations. Indeed, the very plans that made a firm competitive under one set of circumstances may make it uncompetitive if managers get so wedded to the plans that they ignore or don't see changes in the marketplace.

The strategic planning model in Figure 2-1 is neat and orderly. But the world is not a neat and orderly place. The cycle of planning may be deftly tied to a yearly calendar and duly placed on everyone's time management screen. But the plans laid out in August may be totally turned upside down in September by such external events as competitors' innovations or technological developments or an organizational disaster such as the illness or death of a CEO, a prolonged strike, or an unfavorable judgment in a lawsuit. If such events occur, the organization cannot wait until next August to revise its plan.

Plans are designed to be flexible guides along the path between today and tomorrow, not the final word on everything. Effective hospitality organizations stay nimble in responding to the many uncertainties that can affect their operations and the services they provide. Many create contingency plans which offer alternative strategies to meet changed circumstances. But since no one can anticipate everything that may happen to an organization, contingency planning can go only so far.

## INVOLVING EMPLOYEES IN PLANNING

In late 1997 US Airways called together two dozen employees—mechanics, luggage carriers, aircraft cleaners, ramp supervisors, flight attendants, dispatchers, and reservation agents—and asked them not to fill out employee comment cards or organize a company picnic but to plan a new low-fare airline. The planning team spent four months putting together recommendations on every aspect of the new "airline-within-an-airline": how fast to fly, whether to have first-class cabins (they decided on all-coach), whether to keep blankets in the cabin, how to board passengers, and who should take tickets. A steering group of US Air senior executives and union leaders accepted almost every recommendation. The first planes of the new Metro Jet Airline, planned by employees, took off in mid-1998.[40]

The need to plan for the probable, and to be nimble enough to react quickly and appropriately if the improbable occurs, brings up another important point. Increasingly, hospitality organizations are including their employees in the planning processes. They have learned that good things come from widespread employee participation. First, the frontline employees know more about guests than anyone else does. They understand what makes guests happy and what doesn't. They also have ideas about what products or services the organization could add, redesign, or delete to add value to the guest's experience or to reduce costs. Second, to implement any strategic plan means that everyone must understand it and accept its logic. What better way to gain understanding and obtain employee buy-in than to have the employees help to develop the plan? After all, if they understand the need to plan and how the plan will help the organization solve problems and reach the future, why wouldn't they support it and try to implement it? Most managers have learned the hard way that the best plan in the world is worthless unless those who have to make it work *want* to make it work.

A Wal-Mart store in Louisiana had a shoplifting problem so the manager stationed an elderly man at the door to "greet" customers as they entered and left. Potential shoplifters learned that someone would be observing them directly as they left, but even more significantly, honest customers were impressed by this friendly touch. The idea spread to other stores, and Wal-Mart has become known for its friendly greeters.

Was this company success the product of strategic planning, or any planning? A Wal-Mart executive of that time said, "We live by the motto, 'Do it. Fix it. Try it.' If you try something and it works, you keep it. If it doesn't work, you fix it or try something else."[41] The Louisiana manager tried it, and it worked far better than the manager thought it would, so the whole company kept it.

That's one way to run an organization, and Sam Walton built a hugely successful company. Hospitality organizations can learn from Wal-Mart's use of employee ideas. When everyone is responsible for thinking strategically about how to fulfill the organization's mission, the power of individual creativity can be unleashed in very positive ways. A planning process should include the people who must make the plans become reality or the effort will be at least partly wasted. The best plan in the world is worthless without implementation, and the benchmark organizations have learned the power of employee participation in planning to achieve implementation more smoothly and efficiently.

## Lessons Learned

1. Strategy starts with the guest. Know what key factors drive the guest's determination of quality and value.
2. Try to understand the future environment and what it might do to you and your future guests.
3. Use appropriate, powerful forecasting tools, but don't let them replace managerial judgment.
4. Know your core competencies, why they are your core, and why you are competent in them.
5. Know which core competencies you need to build for the future.

6. Use your vision to define your mission.
7. Prepare for the unexpected.
8. Involve employees in planning.
9. Compete on value, not on price.

## Review Questions

1. You are about to start your own restaurant. Think of five key decisions you need to make, and tell how you will make them.
2. List a few necessary core competencies for successfully operating a fast-food restaurant versus a fine dining restaurant versus a casual dining restaurant.
   A. Why are these competencies *core?*
   B. Why do they differ from one type of restaurant to another?
3. How does the design-day concept help a manager meet guest expectations in a guest experience?
4. Think about kids in junior high school today; they will be part of tomorrow's workforce and customer base. What management and guest-service changes will hospitality organizations have to make if they want to succeed with these future employees and customers?
5. Think of a hospitality organization that you are familiar with.
   A. What seem to be the key drivers of the guests in its target market?
   B. How do these key drivers influence how the organization operates?
   C. How *should* they influence how that organization operates?
6. Think of a product, service, or brand to which you are loyal. Why are you loyal to that product, service, or brand? What did the organization do to acquire your loyalty, and what has it done to maintain it? Based on the reasons for your loyalty, what one piece of advice would you give to future hospitality managers?
7. What is service anyway? What are the components of good and bad service? Which components of bad service are something that you expect or want but don't get? Get but don't expect or want?
8. If an organization like an airline uses yield-management techniques, guests end up paying different prices for what is essentially the same service. What are the implications of that difference, if any, for guest expectations, service quality, value, and guest satisfaction?
9. Consider the expression "Price, quality, speed—pick any two." Do you think a company strategic planner said it, or a customer? Is the expression fair and accurate in today's business world?

## Activities

1. Four qualitative techniques that can be used for forecasting are brainstorming, the Delphi technique, focus groups, and scenario building. Divide up into groups and, as your instructor directs, come up with a forecasting problem that a local hospitality organization might face and try to arrive at a conclusion about it by using one or more of the techniques. Different groups might use different techniques for the same problem to see if they come up with the same conclusion or problem solution.

2. Find a hospitality organization that uses forecasting techniques. How does the organization use them: to predict its staffing and product supply needs, or for other purposes? How does the organization gather data? Does it use prediction models and statistical techniques, or is forecasting done mainly by the seat of someone's pants?

3. This chapter suggests that an organization should focus on its core competencies, not spread itself into areas in which it may not be competent. Some competency pairings are generally accepted, like "bar and grill." Others might reflect an organizational intention to operate in unrelated areas, like "college and fish camp" or "blacksmith and nail care." Look for unusual competency pairings in business names you come across and report them back to the class.

## Case Studies

### Profit? Growth? Survival? Service? Customers? Environment?

Six hospitality administration students were having a discussion at the Student Center about the primary goal of hospitality organizations.

Jim said emphatically, "Large hospitality corporations are in business to make as much money as they can. No matter if it's food, lodging, or gaming, profit maximization is their primary goal, and everything else is secondary. Businesses exist to make a profit."

Will agreed, up to a point: "If the hospitality organization is a public corporation, profits are a necessity, but the primary goal of any business is to grow. No business wants to stay small and unimportant. Company officials and stockholders want growth, for the feeling of progress and accomplishment it brings and for the profits that will eventually accompany growth."

Jane said, "There's something to what you both say. Any company needs profits, and any company would like to grow. But survival is the primary goal, because without it you can't have profit or growth."

Sally said, "Any hospitality organization's goal had better be to give good guest service. If the organization achieves that goal, all if the rest will fall into place. If they don't, they have no chance anyway."

Spiro said, "My dad owns a restaurant, and he agrees with my professor who said that the main goal of any business is to get and keep customers. No customers, no nothing. I agree with my dad."

Betty said, "No matter what you learned in class, you are all kidding yourselves. Primary goals are just for looks anyway. No matter how specific an organization's goals, no matter how carefully it plans, no matter how hard it works to meet those goals, the environment within which the organization markets its product or service will determine the organization's destiny. Organizations react to environmental forces, regardless of goals. To succeed, a business organization doesn't need to establish goals; it needs to be lucky enough to be in the right place at the right time and take advantage of the opportunities presented to it."

\* \* \*

1. With whose position would the company's stockholders most likely agree?
2. The CEO? The employees? The guests?
3. Where do you stand on the issue?

## Economy Airlines

*M*inor Hamblin had a humanistic dream: to found a company in which every employee would be an owner/manager, a company in which people really would work together. Hamblin started the revolutionary low-fare, no-frills Economy Airlines. Within a few years, Economy was the fifth-largest U.S. passenger carrier. The company had no unions. New employees had to buy and hold 100 shares of Economy common stock, offered at a 70 percent discount. Profit sharing regularly added substantial amounts to their paychecks. Hamblin believed that participatory management was the style that best suited contemporary employees. One university professor wrote that Economy Airlines was "the most comprehensive and self-conscious effort to fit a business to the capabilities and attitudes of today's workforce. Economy Airlines is doing everything right."

Economy had a flat structure with only three management levels. In terms of the organization chart, pilots and flight attendants were on the same level and had the same clout. The company had no secretaries; managers did their own typing and answered their own phones.

The company rapidly expanded its routes and schedules. Unfortunately, traffic growth failed to keep up with expansion. Other airlines adopted the low-fare, no-frills approach and even attacked Economy directly in their advertising campaigns. Economy's stock plunged from over 100 to 8. One employee observed, "When stock prices were high, profit sharing and stock ownership were great. Now they aren't so great." The Air Line Pilots Association began a drive to unionize Economy's pilots. New government regulations made Minor Hamblin wonder if he could even keep Economy's flying certificate.

Hamblin had a renewed realization that a company can't always control its own destiny. "That professor said I was doing everything right. Now I'm in danger of going belly-up." He wondered if he should convert Economy over to a more traditional structure, with more management layers, a clearly defined chain of command, and specialized employee tasks. Or perhaps he should sell out.

\* \* \*

1. What caused Economy's problems?
2. Do you see any way that Economy could have avoided those problems?
3. What steps should Economy Airlines take now?

## The Diamondback Plaza Hotel

*D*wight Robinson owns The Diamondback Plaza, a large hotel in a popular vacation area. Robinson tries to maintain a reputation of casual elegance for his hotel and is known among local hoteliers for his dignified advertising and for sticking to the "rack rate." He feels that to do otherwise is not fair to guests paying full price. Robinson is happy about all aspects of his hotel operation except his average nightly occupancy rate of 68 percent. The average for his geographic area is 78 percent.

*In an attempt to improve his results, Robinson has hired a consultant who, after studying the situation, has presented the following recommendation:*

*Mr. Robinson, your rooms are not yielding the income that they might because you establish one price for your rooms and then sit back hoping people will stay with you. In today's market that strategy won't work; you have to manage your situation to improve your yield per room.*

*You need to use all available means to lure travelers into your hotel. When you see at a certain time in the evening that your hotel is not going to be full, you have to cut prices until you sell out. You may not be able to sell every room every night, but don't be satisfied until your occupancy rate is over 95 percent. Follow this principle: Don't go to sleep yourself until you get people to sleep in all your rooms.*

*Your debt relative to your property value is low; you don't have high interest charges to cover. So you can offer lower room prices than your competitors and still make a profit.*

*Put a big flashing sign outside your hotel. If people aren't checking in and you foresee vacancies, start that sign flashing at $39.95. If you can't fill up at that figure, drop it to $29.95 or even $19.95. Anything is better than nothing.*

*First thing every morning, check the previous night's records. If the Diamondback wasn't sold out, ask your night manager why! She'll soon get the message.*

*Sure, your average daily room rate will drop, but so what? That's just a prestige number to brag about when you get together with other local hotel owners. By managing the yield on each unit, you'll maximize your profits, and isn't that why you're in business?*

\* \* \*

Should Dwight Robinson take the consultant's advice?

## Additional Readings

Badinelli, R. D., and M. D. Olsen. 1990. Hotel Yield Management Using Optimal Decision Rules. *Journal of the International Academy of Hospitality Research* 26(November):1–35.

Baker, M., and M. Riley. 1994. New Perspectives on Productivity in Hotels: Some Advances and New Directions. *International Journal of Hospitality Management* 13(4):297–311.

Becker, G. S. 1991. A Note on Restaurant Pricing and Other Examples of Social Influence on Price. *Journal of Political Economy* 99(5):1109–1116.

Bendapudi, Neeli, and Leonard L. Berry. 1997. Customers' Motivations for Maintaining Relationships with Service Providers. *Journal of Retailing* 73(1):15–38.

Bitran, G. R., and S. V. Mondschein. 1995. An Application of Yield Management to the Hotel Industry Considering Multiple Day Stays. *Operations Research* 43(3):427–443.

Booms, Bernard H., and Mary Jo Bitner. 1981. Marketing Strategies and Organizational Structures for Service Firms, in James H. Donnelly and William R. George, eds., *Marketing of Services* (Chicago: American Marketing Association), pp. 47–51.

Boone, Juliette M. 1997. Hotel-Restaurant Co-Branding—A Preliminary Study. *Cornell Hotel and Restaurant Administration Quarterly* 38(5):34–43.

Bull, A. O. 1994. Pricing a Motel's Location. *International Journal of Contemporary Hospitality Management* 6(6):10–15.

Burgess, C., A. Hampton, and A. Roper. 1995. International Hotel Groups: What Makes Them Successful? *International Journal of Contemporary Hospitality Management,* 7(2/3):74–80.

Canas, J. 1982. Strategic Corporate Planning, in A. Pizam, R. C. Lewis, and P. Manning, eds., *The Practice of Hospitality Management* (Westport, CT: AVI Publishing), pp. 31–36.

Chambers, John, Satinder Mullick, and Donald Smith. 1971. How to Choose the Right Forecasting Technique. *Harvard Business Review* 49(4):45–74.

Corgel, J. B., and J. A. deRoos. 1992. Pure Price Changes of Lodging Properties. *Cornell Hotel and Restaurant Administration Quarterly* 33(2):70–77.

Cranage, D. A., and W. P. Andrew. 1992. A Comparison of Time Series and Econometric Models for Forecasting Restaurant Sales. *International Journal of Hospitality Management* 11(2):129–142.

Cross, Robert C. 1997. Launching the Revenue Rocket: How Revenue Management Can Work for Your Business. *Cornell Hotel and Restaurant Administration Quarterly* 38(2):32–43.

Damonte, L., et al. 1997. Brand Affiliation and Property Size Effects on Measures of Performance in Lodging Properties. *Hospitality Research Journal* 20(3):1–16.

Desiraju, Ramaro, and Steven M. Shugan. 1999. Strategic Service Pricing and Yield Management. *Journal of Marketing* 63(1):44–55.

Dev, C., and S. Klein. 1993. Strategic Alliances in the Hotel Industry. *Cornell Hotel and Restaurant Administration Quarterly* 34(1):42–45.

Dev, C., and M. D. Olsen. 1989. Environmental Uncertainty, Business Strategy and Financial Performance: An Empirical Study of the U.S. Lodging Industry. *Hospitality Education and Research Journal* 13(3):171–186.

Donaghy, Kevin, Una McMahon, and David McDowell. 1995. Yield Management: An Overview. *International Journal of Hospitality Management* 14(2):139–150.

Ellwood-Williams, C., and C. Y. Tse. 1995. The Relationship Between Strategy and Entrepreneurship: The U.S. Restaurant Sector. *International Journal of Contemporary Hospitality Management* 7(1):22–26.

Escoffier, Maurice R. 1997. Yield Management: Where We've Been, Where We Are, Where We're Going. *FIU Hospitality Review* 15(1):47–56.

Fisher, Douglas P. 1997. Location, Location, Location: Ensuring a Franchisee's Success. *FIU Hospitality Review* 15(1):37.

Germain, Richard, and M. Bixby Cooper. 1990. How a Customer Mission Statement Affects Company Performance. *Industrial Marketing Management* (19)1:47–54.

Griffin, Robert K. 1996. Factors of Successful Lodging Yield Management Systems. *Hospitality Research Journal* 19(4):17–30.

Hayes, D. K., and L. M. Huffman. 1995. Value Pricing: How Low Can You Go? *Cornell Hotel and Restaurant Administration Quarterly* 36(1):51–56.

Hemmasi, M., K. C. Strong, and S. A. Taylor. 1994. Measuring Service Quality for Strategic Planning and Analysis in Service Firms. *Journal of Applied Business Research* 10(4):24–34.

Jauncey, S., I. Mitchell, and P. Slamet. 1995. The Meaning and Management of Yield in Hotels. *International Journal of Contemporary Hospitality Management* 7(4):23–26.

Kiefer, N. M., T. J. Kelly, and K. Burdett. 1994. Menu Pricing—An Experimental Approach. *Journal of Business Economics and Statistics* 12(3):329–337.

Kimes, Sheryl E., et al. 1998. Restaurant Revenue Management: Applying Yield Management to the Restaurant Industry. *Cornell Hotel and Restaurant Administration Quarterly* 39(3):32–41.

Langton, B. D., C. Bottorff, and M. D. Olsen. 1992. The Strategy, Structure, Environment Co-Alignment, in R. Teare and M. D. Olsen, eds., *International Hospitality Management* (London: Pitman Publishing), pp. 31–35.

Lombardi, Dennis. 1996. Trends and Directions in the Chain-Restaurant Industry. *Cornell Hotel and Restaurant Administration Quarterly* 37(3):14–17.

Mintzberg, H. 1992. Five Ps for Strategy, in H. Mintzberg and J. B. Quinn, eds., *The Strategy Process: Concepts and Contexts* (London: Prentice-Hall), pp. 12–19.

Moon, Mark A., et al. 1998. Seven Keys to Better Forecasting. *Business Horizons* 41(5):44–52.

Morey, Richard C., and David A. Dittman. 1997. An Aid in Selecting the Brand, Size, and Other Strategic Choices for a Hotel. *Journal of Hospitality and Tourism Research* 21(1):71–99.

Nebel, E., and J. D. Schaffer. 1992. Hotel Strategic Planning at the Business and Unit Level in the USA, in R. Teare and M. D. Olsen, eds., *International Hospitality Management* (London: Pitman Publishing), pp. 228–254.

Norman, Ellis D., and Karl J. Mayer. 1997. Yield Management in Las Vegas Casino Hotels. *Cornell Hotel and Restaurant Administration Quarterly* 38(5):28–33.

Olsen, M. D. 1991. Structural Changes: The International Hospitality Industry and Firm. *International Journal of Contemporary Hospitality Management* 3(4):21–24.

Olsen, M. D. 1993. International Growth Strategies of Major U.S. Hotel Companies. *Travel and Tourism Analyst* 2(3):51–64.

Olsen, M. D., B. Murthy, and R. Teare. 1994. CEO Perspectives on Scanning the Global Hotel Business Environment. *International Journal of Contemporary Hospitality Management* 6(4):3–9.

Olsen, M. D., and A. DeNoble. 1981. Strategic Planning in a Dynamic Environment. *Cornell Hotel Restaurant and Administration Quarterly* 22(4):75–80.

Park, C. W., B. Jaworski, and D. MacInnis. 1986. Strategic Brand Concept-Image Management. *Journal of Marketing* 50(4):135–145.

Pasumarty, Kishore, et al. 1996. Consumer Behavior and Marketing Strategy: A Multinational Study of Children's Involvement in the Purchase of Hospitality Services. *Hospitality Research Journal* 19(4):87–112.

Radas, Sonja, and Steven M. Shugan. 1998. Managing Service Demand: Shifting and Bundling. *Journal of Service Research* 1(1):47–64.

Reichel, A. 1982. Competition and Barriers to Entry in Service Industries: The Case of the American Lodging Industry, in A. Pizam, R. C. Lewis, and P. Manning, eds., *The Practice of Hospitality Management: State of the Art and Future Prospects* (Westport, CT: AVI Publishing), pp. 79–89.

Reichel, A. 1986. Corporate Strategic Planning for the Hospitality Industry: A Contingency Approach, in R. C. Lewis et al., eds., *The Practice of Hospitality Management II: Profitability in a Changing Environment* (Westport, CT: AVI Publishing), pp. 49–63.

Reid, R., and M. D. Olsen. 1981. A Strategic Planning Model for Independent Food Service Operators. *Journal of Hospitality Education* 6(1):11–24.

Roberts, Chris, and Linda Shea. 1996. Core Capabilities in the Hotel Industry. *Hospitality Research Journal* 19(4):141–154.

Schaffer, J. D. 1987. Competitive Strategies in the Lodging Industry. *International Journal of Hospitality Management* 6(1):33–42.

Schmelzer, C., and M. D. Olsen. 1994. A Data-Based Strategy Implementation Framework for Companies in the Restaurant Industry. *International Journal of Hospitality Management* 13(4):347–359.

Sheel, A. 1995. Monte Carlo Simulations and Scenario Analysis. *Cornell Hotel and Restaurant Administration Quarterly* 36(5):18–26.

Shostack, G. Lynn. 1987. Service Positioning Through Structural Change. *Journal of Marketing* 51(1):34–43.

Slattery, P., and A. Boer. 1991. Strategic Developments for the 1990s: Implications for Hotel Companies, in R. Teare and A. Boer, eds., *Strategic Hospitality Management* (London: Cassell Educational Limited), pp. 161–165.

Smith, Barry C., John F. Leimkuhler, and Ross M. Darrow. 1992. Yield Management at American Airlines. *Interfaces* 22(1):8–31.

Strate, Robert W., and Clinton L. Rappole. 1997. Strategic Alliances Between Hotels and Restaurants. *Cornell Hotel and Restaurant Administration Quarterly* 38(3):50–61.

Thomas, Dan R. E. 1978. Strategy Is Different in Service Businesses. *Harvard Business Review* 56(4):158–65.

Tse, E., and M. D. Olsen. 1990. Business Strategy and Organizational Structure: A Case of US Restaurant Firms. *International Journal of Contemporary Hospitality Management* 1(3):17–23.

Tse, E., and J. West. 1992. Development Strategies for International Markets, in R. Teare and M. D. Olsen, eds., *International Hospitality Management* (London: Pitman Publishing), pp. 118–134.

Tulgan, Bruce. 1996. Common Misconceptions about Generation X. *Cornell Hotel and Restaurant Administration Quarterly* 37(6):46–55.

Vishwanath, Vijay, and Jonathan Mark. 1997. Your Brand's Best Strategy. *Harvard Business Review* 75(3):123–131.

West, J., and M. D. Olsen. 1989. Competitive Strategies in Food Service: Are High Performers Different? *Cornell Hotel Restaurant and Administration Quarterly* 30(1):68–71.

West, J., and M. D. Olsen. 1990. Grand Strategy: Making Your Restaurant a Winner. *Cornell Hotel Restaurant and Administration Quarterly* 31(2):72–75.

## *Notes*

1. Michael E. Porter. 1980. *Competitive Strategy: Techniques for Analyzing Industries and Competitors* (New York: The Free Press), pp. 40–41.
2. Tim Barket. 1999. Holiday Inn Has a Suite Idea. *Orlando Sentinel,* January 8:B-1.
3. *Walt Disney: Famous Quotes.* 1994. Printed for Walt Disney Theme Parks and Resorts, 83.
4. *Princeton Alumni Weekly,* January 27, 1999:55.
5. http://www.iflyswa.com/info/airborne.html (May 1999).
6. Thomas Goetz. 1998. On Board the Carnival Paradise, Don't Sing "Smoke on the Water." *Wall Street Journal,* December 28:B-1.
7. Paulette Thomas. 1999. A Tavern's Fame Spreads Hand to Hand. *Wall Street Journal,* March 2:B-1.

8. Craig S. Smith. 1999. In China, a Bowl of Hot-Pot Soup May Keep You Wanting More. *Wall Street Journal,* March 2:B-1.

9. Richard Gibson. 1999. Company Cafeterias Create Dinners to Go. *Wall Street Journal,* January 13:B-1.

10. Henry Mintzberg. 1994. *The Rise and Fall of Strategic Planning* (New York: The Free Press):324–331.

11. Gary Hamel and C. K. Prahalad. 1994. *Competing for the Future* (Boston: Harvard Business School Press, p. 16.

12. Ibid., 109.

13. Ibid.

14. Lou Cook. 1998. Mystery Shoppers: Can They Help Hotels Head Off Major Quality Problems? *Lodging* 23(8):76.

15. Tom Peters. 1997. *The Circle of Innovation* (New York: Alfred A. Knopf), p. 457.

16. *Walt Disney: Famous Quotes,* 81.

17. *Florida Hotel & Motel Journal,* July 1998:11.

18. Presentation to the Hospitality Management faculty at the University of Central Florida, March 1997.

19. *Walt Disney: Famous Quotes,* 63.

20. *Business Week,* December 14, 1992.

21. *Wall Street Journal,* February 5, 1997:B-1.

22. *Wall Street Journal,* February 3, 1997:B-1.

23. *Wall Street Journal,* February 5, 1997:B-1.

24. *Wall Street Journal,* February 4, 1997:B-2.

25. Dave Thomas. 1992. *Dave's Way* (New York: Berkeley Books), p. 94.

26. Ibid.

27. Hamel and Prahalad, 221–222.

28. J. W. Marriott, Jr., and Kathy Ann Brown. 1997. *The Spirit to Serve: Marriott's Way* (New York: Harper Business), pp. 88–95.

29. Bruce Horovitz. 1998. Re-inventing McDonald's. *USA Today,* February 20:1–2B.

30. *Business Week,* November 11, 1996:109.

31. Norman Brinker and Donald T. Phillips. 1996. *On the Brink: The Life and Leadership of Norman Brinker* (Arlington, TX: The Summit Publishing Group), p. 191.

32. Hamel and Prahalad, 114–115.

33. Ron Grover. 1991. *The Disney Touch: How a Daring Management Team Revived an Entertainment Empire* (Homewood, IL: Richard D. Irwin), pp. 8–9.

34. http://www.ritzcarlton.com/corporate/commitment.htm (May 1999).

35. *Our Compass,* company publication, n.d.

36. James C. Collins and Jerry I. Porras. 1994. *Built to Last: Successful Habits of Visionary Companies.* (New York: Harper-Collins), p. 74.

37. http://www.iflyswa.com/info/airborne.html (May 1999).

38. Berry, 65–68.

39. Ibid., 67.

40. Susan Carey. 1998. US Air 'Peon' Team Pilots Start-Up of Low-Fare Airline. *Wall Street Journal,* March 24:B–1, B–6.

41. Quoted in Collins and Porras, 98.

# Chapter 3

# Setting the Scene
# for the Guest Experience

## Hospitality Principle:

Provide the service setting that guests expect.

*I don't want the public to see the world they live in while they're in the Park. I want them to feel they're in another world.*

—Walt Disney

## LEARNING OBJECTIVES

After reading this chapter, you should understand:

■ Why the service setting or service environment is important.
■ How the service environment affects guests and employees.
■ Which elements of the service environment need to be managed.
■ How service environment factors moderate or affect the responses of guests, according to the Bitner model.
■ Why providing a service environment in which guests feel safe and secure is critical.
■ How theming the service setting pays off.

## KEY TERMS AND CONCEPTS

Disney "show"
eatertainment
lean environment
rich environment

service environment
service setting
servicescape
theming

In the first chapter, we defined the guest experience as consisting of three component elements: the service itself, the service environment, and the service delivery system (the people and the processes that provide the service to the guest). This chapter focuses on the **service environment** or **setting** in which the guest experience takes place. For a restaurant, the environment can be a Rainforest or a Planet Hollywood where the physical structure is an integral part of the guest experience, or it can be a Denny's with simple booths. The difference between these two types of restaurants is something more than just the food. The **eatertainment** restaurants such as Planet Hollywood, All-Star Cafe, and Hard Rock Cafe create environments that enhance the eating experience well beyond the meals they serve. They deliver a high-quality meal, but they also add a show for their customers that differentiates their restaurant from others. Although all service organizations give some thought to the service setting, its importance to the customer experience has been most thoroughly understood by those who view and treat their customers as guests—the hospitality industry. Perhaps no one in this industry devotes more time and energy to making the service environment fit customer expectations than the Walt Disney Company. This chapter will focus on why managing the setting for the hospitality experience is so important and how benchmark organizations like Disney do it so well.

*Planet Hollywood, Beverly Hills, Calif., Interior. (Courtesy of Planet Hollywood International, Inc.)*

## THE DISNEY "SHOW"

Disney refers to everyone and everything that interfaces with guests as **"the show."** Although employees and other customers are part of any guest service organization's "show" or environment in the larger sense, this chapter will focus on the physical aspects of the service setting.

Without question, the setting can influence the guest's determination of the quality and value of a guest experience. Perhaps more than any other organization, Disney understands that its guests have extraordinary experiences largely because of the attention Disney pays to creating the show. Walt Disney originated the idea that *a guest experience can be unified and enhanced if it is based on a theme.* Disney spends endless time and effort ensuring that the environment and the cast members/employees within it—the show—are as consistently and accurately themed as possible.

For some experiences offered to guests, the environment is in effect the setting for a dramatic production or play in which the guest is a participant. Occasionally the environment is so significant to the successful enjoyment of the fantasy that it should perhaps be considered as a part of the service itself. Much of Walt Disney's early success with his theme park ventures resulted from his insight that many guests would enjoy feeling like participants in a drama or play rather than simply observing. In making movies, Walt had learned to present stories that offered viewers the opportunity to experience fantasy vicariously. Why not set up parks and rides with characters and fantastic settings within which guests could move

*Bahama Breeze. (Courtesy of Darden Restaurants.)*

and participate as if they were in a movie? For an organization offering such a "product," the service setting is critical to success.

## The Fantasy Theme

To see the many Disney cartoons and movies is to see a fantasy. Walt Disney's vision for his theme parks was to take guests out of the real world and transport them into a world of make-believe. To visit a Disney theme park is to experience a series of fantasies. That's what guests want and expect. The details of the park's environment and cast are carefully themed—organized and presented around a unifying idea, often a fantasy idea—to create the feeling within the guest that every park area is an accurate representation of what the guest might reasonably expect to see if the fantasy were to come true.

In the Disneyland Park Town Square, for example, Disney not only provides detailed period costumes for the cast members working there; it also sought out and purchased actual cannons used by the French army in the nineteenth century and 150 antique street lamps for Main Street, U.S.A., to ensure an authentic look. Other parts of Disneyland Park are as elaborately and authentically themed as Town Square. The Penny Arcade's nickelodeons and the hand-cranked mutascopes are authentic turn-of-the-century amusement equipment. The Carousel horses are hand-painted, hand-carved originals about 100 years old.[1] On Main Street, U.S.A., every detail of the setting "magically" conveys the guest back to the turn of the century. To create and maintain the fantasy requires that the details of the setting be consistent and authentic.

Likewise, the fantasy of a five-star restaurant, or Rainforest Cafe or Bahama Breeze Restaurant, is to take guests out of the real world and serve them a memorable meal. The setting within which the meal is presented needs to be consistent with that vision, but it may serve only as a part of an eating experience. Many hospitality organizations have achieved fantasy through **theming** have learned the value of a setting that enhances and contributes to the total guest experience. Other hospitality organizations can learn from them.

## To Theme or Not to Theme?

Theming is a way to add value to the guest experience. If used effectively, a theme can enhance the total experience. For a Rainforest Cafe, Dolphin Hotel, or Disney theme park, the theming contributes to maintenance of the fantasy, enhanced visual stimulation, and finding one's way around. It gives guests something to talk about after they've gone home; it reinforces their remembrance of what they've done and provides additional confirmation of the experience's value. Theming is an opportunity for the organization to add wow to the experience by providing more than guests expect.

Consider a five-star restaurant. It is a kind of fantasyland. It takes guests out of the real world and serves them a memorable meal in compatible surroundings. The setting is of consistently high quality, and it enhances and contributes to the total guest experience, but the memorable part is intended to be the world-class meal and the way it is served.

Contrast the fantasy created by the five-star restaurant with the fantasy created by a Rainforest Cafe, Hard Rock Cafe, Fantasea Reef restaurant, or any good ethnic restaurant you can name. These restaurants and many other organizations within and outside the hospitality industry—Disney being the prime example—have created consistency of service setting through theming. They realize that blending the sights, sounds, and even the tastes and smells of the service setting to fit in with an overall theme can enhance the guest's experience and make it more memorable. Restaurants have been themed for many years, but at such totally themed restaurants as Planet Hollywood and House of Blues, the food becomes a secondary aspect of the overall themed guest experience. The customers of yesterday lived in cabins or on farms, told stories or played games for entertainment, and shopped at the country store or via the Sears, Roebuck catalog. Today's customers have become accustomed to enriched environments in their homes, offices, entertainment sites, and automobiles. Organizing the experience around a theme is one way for hospitality organizations to meet guest expectations of an enriched service setting.

Numerous other industries have followed the hospitality industry's lead in conceiving of the services they offer as experiences that take place over time in a themed setting. A Long Island nursing home has provided a 1930s-themed environment for residents, to take them in fantasy back to their youthful days (and perhaps to assure their relatives that the home is not such a bad place to be). Photographs of Clark Gable and Lana Turner and murals of 1930s New York adorn the walls. A replica of a stall at New York City's Fulton Fish Market has a tank containing live fish. Airports, hospitals, and banks have themed their interiors to represent colorful locales.[2] As the author of an article on this subject says, organizations are learning that they must "Disney-fy or Die."

These varied businesses are providing themed service settings because customers want them. We have become accustomed to richer environments in all aspects of life.

A themed environment is not always appropriate, and theming has its risks. By definition, theming places limits on what the organization can offer in terms of service, setting, and delivery system. Compared to an all-purpose non-themed restaurant, a themed restaurant will generally have a narrower range of menu offerings. Patrons of Lone Star Steakhouse and Saloon want and expect to find steak, ribs, chicken, barbecue, and chili on the menu, and a hot sauce on the table. Only if the market for those offerings continues to be strong, despite a more health-conscious dining public, will Lone Star continue to succeed.

Few organizations are fortunate or insightful enough to develop themes with as much universal appeal as Disney's. Hooters, a Florida-based limited-menu restaurant chain whose waitresses dress in tight orange shorts and skimpy, figure-hugging t-shirts, attracts young white males, not older customers and other ethnic groups. The more specialized the theme, the more it will appeal to customers who already liked that theme anyway, but the narrower will the market be. This appeal to a relatively narrow market can succeed. No hospitality organization can be all things to all guests. Hard Rock Cafe is no place for small children, and rock fans are not the key customers whose expectations Chuck E. Cheese is trying to meet. Even organizations whose themes appeal to almost everybody—like Planet Hollywood and its movie stars—must find ways to refresh the guest experience by changing the exhibits and varying menu items. Otherwise, guests will come a few times for the novelty, then seek other experiences. People become tired even of superstars and Hollywood memorabilia.

The organization must provide a service setting consistent with the guest's expectations for the overall guest experience. Theming is one approach toward that consistency. All aspects of the physical setting—layout of physical objects, lighting, colors, appointments, signs, employee uniforms, materials—must complement and support each other and give a feeling of integrated design.

## Control and Focus

The principles used to organize the theme parks reflect Disney's cinematic heritage. The consummate storyteller, Walt Disney arranged the layout of the parks to tell stories. Describing Disneyland Park, Stephen Fjellman says, "Attractions, lands, and worlds are put together in acts and scenes. We are led step by step through Disneyland stories, whether in single attractions or in larger areas of the park. Even in the most extended presentations—those that seem most like theater—the scenes are cinematically short."[3] As is true of any good story, the theme park stories are controlled and focused; we see what the storyteller wants us to see. We are pointed by the visual cues, the positioning of the cars on the ride, the use of light and dark, and other elements of the environment to have the experience that the storyteller envisioned for us. Rides are designed to give guests the feeling of moving through a story. Fjellman says, "Rides are the most constrictive attractions. We are strapped into a conveyance and sent passively around a story. The cars or boats move past tableaux that often surround us. We face forward or look to the side. Many cars have high backs and eye-restricting sides. They spin and turn, point us to the next scene and away from anything that might spoil the illusion. They frame our view as we ride past in the dark."[4]

## The Architecture

The same idea, having the attention of guests focused as they move through an experience or a story, is carried forward in the architectural theming of the resort hotels on the Disney property. Architect Michael Graves designed the Walt Disney World Dolphin Resort to create in guests a feeling of movement toward a central dreamscape: the huge and spectacular Rotunda Lobby. At the main entrance (Portico) to the Dolphin, one enters the Starlight Foyer with a waterfall cascading down its walls. Above, in the ceiling of the Foyer, fiber-optic stars twinkle. The various abstract visual motifs—the stars, squiggles, banana leaves—that are first seen on the outside walls of the building are carried forward in a variety of designs as one moves inside the building to give the guest the sensation of moving through a continuous experience. As the guest moves through the Foyer, the relaxing and peaceful sound of the waterfall diminishes, to blend in—as the guest continues on—with the sound of the large fountain in the Rotunda Lobby. Visual sensations complement the sounds. Along the way to the Lobby, the sound of the waterfall on the hotel's exterior carries the water theme forward. The water sounds in the entry area focus our attention on the sound so we pick it up again as we enter the Rotunda Lobby, and it focuses us on the central fountain. It is a relaxing and peaceful sound but less pronounced as one approaches the Lobby's large fountain so that the interior and exterior sounds will not be in competition. While the activity in which the guest is engaged is walking, the environmental setting turns the walk into a fantasy experience in a relaxing tropical forest.

Some settings can be experienced from a single location. Most architectural structures—environments that often cost millions of dollars to create—can best be experienced by moving through them to perceive the intersecting planes, spaces, and shapes of which architec-

*WDW Dolphin Rotunda Lobby and Fountain. (Used by permission from Disney Enterprises, Inc.)*

ture is made. Whether you shop your way through the various plazas of Adventureland, stroll through the lobby of the Polynesian Resort, or loiter by the lagoon at the Yacht and Beach Club Resort, the architecture throughout the Walt Disney World Resort intentionally situates you in a theme and a narrative story that depend upon procession, an ability to move through it.[5]

The creation of a movie-type of experience in both Disneyland Park and the Magic Kingdom is most evident in the rides, but it is also an important element in the overall architecture of the park. A walk down Main Street, U.S.A., in the Magic Kingdom, for instance, opens up carefully planned and themed vistas, with Cinderella Castle always looming in the distance. The Castle appears at first to be far away, as if this symbol of childhood fantasy is only a distant memory, a part of a small middle-American town's collective memory. As guests move toward the Castle, they see it more distinctly, and they can eventually reexperience the fantasy by entering the Castle.

The "Casting Center" building used for interviewing and hiring is themed in a way that introduces potential employees into the Disney culture. Applicants walk up a long incline to

*WDW Casting Center Doorknobs: "One Good Turn Deserves Another." (Used by permission from Disney Enterprises, Inc.)*

a reception desk. The art and architecture along the way portray important Disney images and symbols. The intent of the design is to communicate to prospective cast members some of the Disney culture and a feeling of an open invitation to join the Disney family. In the reception Lobby are statues of fifteen famous Disney characters. Even the knobs on the building's front door are designed in the shapes of Tweedle Dum and Tweedle Dee, cartoon characters from *Alice in Wonderland.*

## Sights and Sounds

Sound is often an important service-setting element. Music is a particularly potent environmental factor. A convenience store that was plagued by some teenagers hanging out at the store and bothering patrons began playing "elevator" music through its sound system. Unable to take the music, the troublemakers moved on.

The basic principle, of course, is that environmental sounds should serve a purpose. In general, the sounds (most often music) should complement the experience which the organization is trying to provide to its target guests. Again in general, but with many exceptions, louder, faster music in the service setting appeals to younger guests; softer, slower music appeals to older guests. The sounds of music can also affect guest behavior. Studies have shown that bar patrons finish their drinks faster or slower depending on the tempo and subject matter of the country music on the jukebox. People tend to eat faster and drink more (and leave sooner, meaning that more tables are typically turned) if the music is fast and loud. Slow music encourages people to dine in a leisurely fashion. A study revealed that Fairfield University cafeteria diners chewed an average of 4.4 bites a minute to fast music, 3.83 bites a minute to slow music.[6]

Lighting is an important feature of most service settings. Some guest experiences are best delivered in bright lights, some in dim. Glare and lights at eye level are unpleasant in any setting. If you enter a service setting and don't notice the lighting, it is probably well done. In a Rainforest Cafe, you see not the lighting but what is lit. Lights should be selected, turned on, and directed not just to avoid darkness. Like every other aspect of the setting, the lighting should be an element of a greater design with the purpose of enhancing the guest experience.

At the Walt Disney World Resort careful attention is paid to the meshing of visual and auditory effects to enhance the guest's experience. Music and spoken words are carefully integrated into the design of individual rides so that the guest has a continuing, seamless experience while moving on the ride or through a park area. As the guest moves away from one room or segment area to another of the Haunted Mansion, Pirates of the Caribbean, or It's A Small World, the sounds and visual effects merge, with no sense of overlap, to provide a smooth transition from one phase of the experience to the next.[7]

### The ECS

The entertainment control system (ECS) at the Magic Kingdom is designed to maximize each guest's experience by managing the visual and auditory aspects of the setting. For parades covering the wide geographic area of the Magic Kingdom, the visual and musical effects could easily clash. Since the floats move and the guests stand still, Disney has found a way to accompany each float with appropriate lighting and music as it moves through the twenty-four zones of the parade route. Disney uses two different technological solutions. The first is a series of remote interface cabinets linked together through fiber optic cable to

*Rainforest Cafe. (Courtesy of Rainforest Cafe.)*

the ECS. As the different parade floats pass by the buried antennae, the ECS reads a code associated with each float and then creates appropriate lights and music, from hidden loudspeakers, near the float. Each float carries an FM wireless receiver, audio amplifier, and speaker system. Each float is designed to carry one channel of the audio signal sent by the ECS and play it through its own sound system. The result is that each guest experiences the same light-and-sound show, part of which emanates from the float and part from the hidden light and sound sources in each zone, all of these media synchronized by the ECS.

## Special Effects

Ours is an era of incredible special effects; properly used, they can add wow to the service environment. Although simple sights and sounds are appropriate for some service settings, others require the expertise of the special-effects team. Here are just a few of the special effects—created with lasers, mirrors, lights, gas discharges, and fiber optics—in the arsenal of Bill Novey, who created Disney's special-effects department in 1976: steam, smoke clouds, drifting fog, erupting volcano with flowing lava, lightning flashes, waterfalls, spinning galaxies, comets, rotating space stations, meteor showers, shooting stars, moons and planets, floating images (the Witch's apple in the Snow White's Adventures dark ride), crackling neon, magic pixie dust, twinkling gems, and beams from ray guns. Most hospitality organizations will not want to enhance the service setting with holograms, jellyfish fountains, and ray-gun beams, but the technology is available to create almost any effect that the hospitality manager can dream up, and pay for.[8]

## WHY IS THE ENVIRONMENT IMPORTANT?

Hospitality managers must pay attention to the environment for several major reasons. It influences guest expectations, sets and maintains the mood, and has positive effects on employees. Some service environments, such as those in theme restaurants and parks, are such a major part of the experience that they can almost be viewed as part of the service itself. Finally, the environment serves several functional purposes.

### Expectations

First, the environment influences the guest's expectations, even before the service is delivered. If the outside of the restaurant is dirty, guests will enter with negative expectations, if they enter at all. Objectively, the number of cigarette butts on the ground next to the front door has nothing to do with the chef's ability to prepare a high-quality meal and the staff's ability to present it, but guests do not view the environment objectively. If the restaurant doesn't care enough to clean up outside its building, the guest may conclude that it does not clean up its kitchen either and probably doesn't care about how it prepares the meal. Many guests evaluate a restaurant by using the rest room test, to see how much the restaurant cares about cleanliness. Good restaurant managers make sure that procedures are in place to keep the rest rooms clean.

### Guest Mood

Second, the environment sets and maintains the mood after the guest begins the guest experience. Once the guest enters the Magic Kingdom, the entire focus is on establishing the fantasy and maintaining the "magic." One way to do so is to maintain the consistency between what the guest expects to see and what the guest actually sees. Guests expect the cast members in Disney costumes to stay in character, and they do. They are not allowed to speak because if they did, Mickey would probably not sound the way he does in the cartoons. Better to make guests wonder than to disappoint their expectations. If the characters were allowed to take off their heads or any other part of their costumes while in public view, they might destroy the magic of the illusion. A Disney rule requires that character costumes must be transported in black bags to ensure that no child will accidentally see a lifeless Mickey or other beloved character being hauled in the back of a van. Another component of maintaining the mood is the detailed costuming of all cast members, even those not portraying Disney characters. The quest for authenticity goes so far in Epcot that Disney has set up a Cultural Representation Program that brings students from around the world to staff the various World Showcase Pavilions. The program ensures that all on-stage positions are staffed by people who can accurately represent each country's culture and heritage.

In a similar effort to use the environment to set the mood, Disney spends considerable money on ensuring that the park grounds are clean, the lawns carefully manicured, and the flowers always in bloom. The company has learned through studies of guests that people associate "clean and orderly" with "safe and high in quality." They know that everyone has been to a typical amusement park and seen the dirt and debris scattered all over the grounds. Disney wants to differentiate its parks from traditional amusement parks, and cleanliness is one way to do so. Walt Disney's wife said, "Why do you want to build an amusement park? They're so dirty." His answer: "I told her that was just the point—mine wouldn't be."[9] The real world is not always a clean place, so providing a sparkling-clean park is yet another way to enable guests to leave the outside world behind and enter the fantasy enjoyment that Disney is trying to create.

### Main Street, U.S.A.

As the example of the Dolphin Resort suggested, even the architecture is used to enhance the mood that the theme park strives to create and maintain. Every guest at Disneyland Park or the Magic Kingdom must pass through Main Street, U.S.A., to enter the park. The Main Street buildings are constructed to enhance the feeling of being not in a huge and spectacular park but in a cozy, friendly place. The architectural technique called *forced perspective* led to designing the first floors of the buildings along Main Street, U.S.A., in Disneyland Park at 9/10th scale, the second floors at 7/8 and the third floors at 5/8 scale. According to David Koenig in *Mouse Tales,*

> The decreasing heights make the shops appear taller than they are, yet still cozy. The Sleeping Beauty Castle uses the same effect, its stones large at the base and increasingly smaller up high. On the Matterhorn, trees and shrubs halfway up are smaller than those at the base. The Mark Twain [steamboat], Disneyland Railroad, and Main Street vehicles are all 5/8 scale and other structures were built in various scales based on what looked most effective to the designers.[10]

While this old production technique to save space and costs in building movie sets came naturally to Disney, it is also an effective means for creating an environment that reinforces the feeling that Disneyland Park seeks to create

Disney consciously conceives and creates all aspects of the service environment, from building architecture to doorknobs, to set and maintain whatever mood is appropriate to each fantasy in the series of fantasies comprising the overall guest experience of a Disney theme park. Other organizations use their physical structures and settings to do the same. A doctor hangs her diplomas on the wall to reassure patients that she has the training necessary to provide high-quality medical care. A checklist of how often the bathrooms have been cleaned is posted on the bathroom door for all McDonald's customers to see. Good hoteliers are constantly stopping to pick up pieces of paper and other debris in their hallways and other public spaces, to serve as a role model for others to emulate and to keep the hotel spotless. They, like Disney, know the degree to which guests associate cleanliness with overall quality.

## Employee Satisfaction

A third contribution of the service setting is its effect on a group of people who do not even use the service: the employees who deliver it. Nobody wants to work in a dangerous or dirty environment. In his book *Customers for Life,* Carl Sewell relates the story of a service technician complaining about Sewell's Cadillac dealership employee rest room. The employee asked Sewell if he thought the employees lived that way at home and, if not, then why he didn't show a level of respect for them by providing a clean, nice-looking rest room. Sewell says, "That was humbling. A week later we had a carpenter crew in there, and we tore it out and rebuilt it and did it right."[11]

Although the environment is designed primarily to enhance the guest's experience, it should insofar as possible be supportive of and compatible with the employee's experience as well. Employees spend a lot more time in the service setting than guests do, and a well-designed environment can promote employee satisfaction, which is highly correlated with guest satisfaction. Employee satisfaction is so important to the success of McDonald's new hotter-fresher-faster cooking technology that a large sign at the research facility developing the new technology read:

> ### CORE
>
> ### Customer-Oriented Restaurant Experience
> ### Crew-Oriented Restaurant Environment

McDonald's knows that a crew-oriented restaurant environment will encourage the crew to provide a customer-oriented restaurant experience.

Care and attention to environmental details show employees that the organization is committed to guest satisfaction and service quality. Disney employees know that anyone who spends the amount of time and energy Disney does on the details of the park, even on those details that most guests will never notice, must really care about the quality of the guest experience. The impact of this caring on the cast members is immeasurable; in ways large and small, it shows employees the commitment that the company expects from itself and from them.

## Setting as a Part of Service

The environment may serve merely as a neutral backdrop for some guest experiences. But for others, the environment is so significant to the success of the experience that it has a fourth major importance to hospitality managers: The setting for such guest experiences should almost be considered a part of the service itself. The hospitality service setting may represent a major part of what the guest is paying for and seeking from the guest experience. No one wants to go to a fine dining restaurant and sit on plastic seats, to eat a gourmet meal served on disposable "china" by a waiter dressed in blue jeans and t-shirt who is trying to turn the table in forty-five minutes. No matter how good the meal, the quality of the food, or the presentation on the paper plates, the guest will be dissatisfied with the fine dining experience in such an environment. Not only must the meal be good; the decor, ambiance, tablecloth, attire of the servers, number and attitude of other guests, and place setting must all be consistent with what the guest expects in a fine dining experience.

The quality of the environmental context within which the guest's experience occurs affects the quality of the experience itself and also the guest's opinion of the hospitality organization's overall quality. An example of the care given to environmental detail is the Main Street, U.S.A., painters at the Magic Kingdom. Their only responsibility, all year long, is to start at one end of Main Street, U.S.A., and paint all the buildings and other structures until they get to the end, and then they start all over again. They come to work, paint Main Street, U.S.A., and then go home. Each painted rail is completely stripped down to the metal and repainted five times a year. The fantasy part of the guest experience requires a clean, freshly painted park, and the guest who finds the paint chipped or soiled will define the quality of the experience in a less favorable way than the guest who finds everything freshly painted and clean.

## The Functional Value of the Setting

Finally, the environment is important for several pragmatic, functional reasons. The guest relies on the hospitality organization to create an environment that is safe and easy to use and understand. Environmental features must be such that the guest can easily and safely enter, experience, and then leave without getting lost, hurt, or disoriented.

For the modern hospitality organization, the issue of safety and security has become more important than ever before. People worry increasingly about whether they will be safe from harm or injury when they go to a restaurant, bank, or theme park or leave home for any reason. Guests must perceive that service settings have a high level of safety and security. Light, open space, smiling employees making eye contact with guests, and cleanliness make guests feel secure. Such environmental elements as well-lit parking lots and pathways, low-cut hedges that no one can hide behind, and the presence of uniformed employees are appropriate and reassuring in just about any service situation. Banks hire guards to give their customers a feeling of security as they enter and leave the bank; hotels train their employees to emphasize their presence by looking at guests, making eye contact, and speaking to them; and theme parks have vehicles cruising the well-lit parking lots to reassure guests that they are about to enter a crime-free world.

Most hospitality organizations want guests to relax and enjoy the guest experience. Because guests cannot relax if they fear for their safety, managers must provide a safe and secure environment. It's as simple as that.

## A MODEL: HOW THE SERVICE ENVIRONMENT AFFECTS THE GUEST

The hospitality manager seeking to provide an excellent and memorable experience should give as much attention to managing the setting as to the service itself and the service delivery system. The rest of this chapter will be based on Figure 3-1, which shows how environmental influences operate on the guest to determine the guest's reaction to the service setting. The combination of elements can cause the guest to want to approach the setting and remain in it or to avoid or leave the setting.

As seen in Figure 3-1, which is to be read from left to right, five environmental components comprise the service setting as perceived by guests: ambient conditions; spatial use; functional congruence; signs, symbols and artifacts; and other people, including employees and other guests.[12] No guest will be aware of all environmental elements. Consciously and subconsciously, each guest selects the combination of elements that comprises, for that guest, the perceived service landscape, or **servicescape,** as a whole. Each guest will respond differently to the elements of that servicescape, depending on the guest's individual characteristics. The responses will not only be different, but they may be different within any or a combination of three general response types: physiological, cognitive, or emotional. Finally, the guest's overall response to the setting will cause the guest to want to approach the setting again, or to avoid it.

Each element in the setting is capable of infinite variation. These infinitely variable elements can be combined in an infinite variety of ways. Thus, each guest's experience of the setting is unique.

Now, let's look at the Bitner model in Figure 3-1 in more detail.

### Ambient Conditions

Ambient conditions in the environment—the ergonomic factors such as temperature, humidity, air quality, smells, sounds, physical comfort, and light—affect the nature of the guest experience. The effect on a guest of a dark, humid, quiet tunnel with intermittent noises and cool air blowing is different from the effect of a light, airy, music-filled shopping mall. The first setting feels ominous and scary, the second warm and positive. The whole category of "dark" theme park rides and attractions, like Disney's Haunted Mansion, Pirates of the Caribbean, and The Twilight Zone Tower of Terror, is designed around the concept that darkness has an element of suspense, surprise, and potential terror that light doesn't have. On the other hand, the romantic feel of dimly lit restaurants is also due to the careful management of ambient conditions.

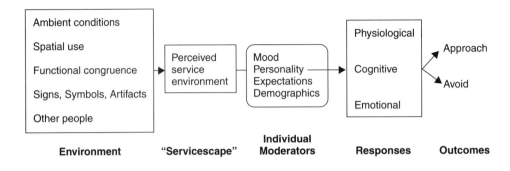

**Figure 3-1** *Guest Responses to Environmental Influences. (Source: Adapted from Mary Jo Bitner. 1992. Servicescapes: The Impact of Physical Surroundings on Customers and Employees.* Journal of Marketing *56(2):60. Reprinted with permission of the American Marketing Association.)*

## Space

The second environmental category is the use of space. It refers to how the equipment and furnishings are arranged in the hospitality service setting, the size and shape of those objects, their accessibility to the customers, and the spatial relationships among them.

The nature of the guest experience is also affected by the organization's use of space. Depending on how the waiting space is designed, waiting lines can feel open and friendly or they can make a customer feel closed in and alone. How paths are laid out to get from one part of a park, whether a theme park or a community park, to another also influences the feeling of openness or closedness that the guest experiences. Closed spaces and areas with a lot of open space or green evoke different feelings. The basic decision about space is how to use it to lay out the service setting so as to enhance the guest's experience.

Space must be used wisely. A restaurant with too many tables and seats or a hotel with too many rooms within its available space may both be unattractive to guests. An organization that attempts to increase the revenue-producing space within which it provides guest experiences at the expense of essential but non-revenue-producing space (for offices, kitchens, supplies, and utilities, for example) may have a memorable service environment, but its delivery system cannot reliably provide the service product required for a memorable guest experience.

The space layout should also help people to know where they are. As Disney said, "Have a single entrance through which all the traffic would flow, then a hub off which the various areas were situated. That gives people a sense of orientation—they know where they are at all times. And it saves a lot of walking."[13] Logical, easy-to-follow pathways lead people in the Magic Kingdom from one attraction to another. The big circular path around the World Showcase in Epcot makes it easy for guests to go from one attraction to another in an orderly way, and the lake in the middle of everything provides a superb orientation for the guest at any point around the circle. Cinderella Castle in the Magic Kingdom, the Twilight Zone Tower of Terror in Disney/MGM Studios, and the Spaceship Earth in Epcot are other landmarks that provide constant points of orientation. Guests know where they are in the park and can see how to get to other locations.

Within specific Walt Disney World Resort areas, many visual and audio aids help to orient the guest. The cast members in each location are costumed consistently. Key structures

*Enchanted Tiki Room. (Used by permission from Disney Enterprises, Inc.)*

help identify where in the Magic Kingdom one is. The Carousel in Fantasyland, the Mark Twain Paddlewheeler in Frontierland, and the Enchanted Tiki Bird Room-Under New Management in Adventureland are examples of key attractions that by location, size, and sounds help guests identify where in the Magic Kingdom they are. The challenge is to ensure that the physical environment consistently reinforces the feeling of being in a particular section of the park by blocking out the sight of other areas, while providing landmarks that let guests know how to get to other park areas. The need to prevent guests from seeing anything that would make them think that they are anywhere else but in Frontierland, for example, is carefully balanced against the need to provide clear and easy guidance to other park locations.

All service settings have this same problem. Hospitality managers must maintain the environmental feel of the setting while also providing orientation devices to help guests locate rest rooms, public phones, meeting rooms, and exits. Circus legend P.T. Barnum set

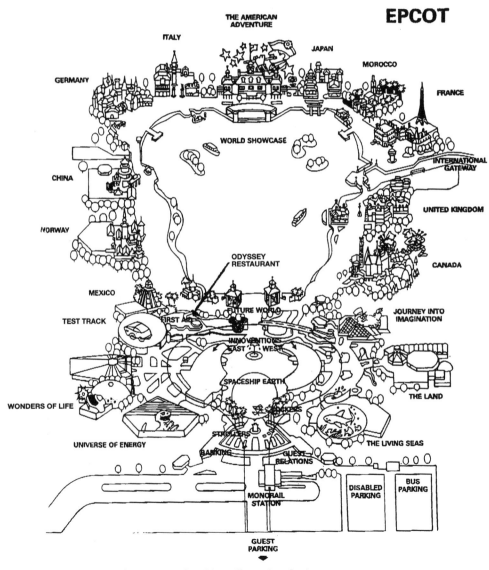

*Map of Epcot. (Used by permission from Disney Enterprises, Inc.)*

up his exhibits and signage to guide customers from start to finish. It is said that just beyond the last exhibit was a door labeled "This way to the egress." Circus patrons going through the door and hoping to view a rare animal or bird found themselves passing smoothly and effortlessly into the alley outside the building.

Hospitality settings should be designed to ensure smooth flow for both guest and employee. Guests must feel they are moving smoothly and effortlessly through the service setting. Employees must have sufficient space, traffic routes, and sufficiently short distances to travel to provide timely service to guests. In a restaurant, if waiters entering and leaving the kitchen use the same door, collisions and dropped trays (which do not enhance the diner's experience) are inevitable. If the kitchen is too far from the dining area, food temperatures will suffer. If tables are too close together, servers cannot move smoothly through the room, and the guest experience suffers.

Restaurants offer a nice example of how the placement of facilities within a space is related to the level and character of the guest experience provided. In a casual dining restaurant, guests accept a distance of only two to three feet between tables (plus their chairs). In an upscale restaurant, tables must be at least four feet apart. If they are closer together, guests may not be able to put a finger on just what is wrong, but the service environment will not suit their expectations.

## Functional Congruence

Functional congruence refers to how well something with a functional purpose fits into the environment in which it serves that purpose. The functioning of the equipment, layout of the physical landscape, and entire design of the service environment must be congruent with what the guest expects to find in that environment. In a self-service environment, items and equipment necessary to the experience must be easy to use, or someone had better be available to help guests figure out how to "serve themselves." If customers must perform complicated or unfamiliar tasks, like figure out how to operate a multistep ATM or a sophisticated video game or virtual-reality machine, the instructions had better be clear. Self-service pumps at gas stations, ATM machines, and self-service restaurants require more focus on spatial design clarity and layout than would service experiences accompanied by a gas attendant, bank teller, or waiter.

The functional congruence of environmental elements is given great consideration in a well-designed service environment so that whatever physical or environmental element the guest requires for maximum enjoyment of the experience is provided when needed. As the Magic Kingdom guest enters Main Street, U.S.A, stores on the right-hand side sell items useful inside the park like film, sun screen, and snacks. Disney carefully places theme park eating places where guests can find them, often just after a ride or attraction. Retail shops are located at the exit points of rides for guests wanting a souvenir of the experience they have just enjoyed. As guests leave the park, retail outlets on the right side sell souvenirs. Disney knows that most guests will be looking and walking on the right-hand side of the street, so they make sure that shops on the right sell those things that guests will be looking for at that stage of their park visit.

## Signs and Symbols

The fourth component of the environment is the signs, symbols, and artifacts that communicate information to the guest. Carl Sewell states that signs serve one or more of only three purposes: to name the business (Nordstrom's Department Store, Ramada Inn, Shula's Steak

House), to describe the product or service (Rooms for Rent, Hot Dogs, Rest Rooms), and to give direction (Entrance, Do Not Enter, Pay Here, No Smoking, Employees Only, Wrong Way, You Are Here).[14]

*Signs* are explicit physical representations of information that the organization thinks guests might want, need, or expect to find. Signs must be easy to read, clear, and located in obvious places where they can direct and teach people how to use the service easily. Tourist cities wanting international visitors to come back again know that, to encourage returns, they must stimulate positive emotional and cognitive responses within visitors from many different countries. Taking the national origins and cultural backgrounds (called *demographic moderators* in Figure 3-1) into account, they go to great effort and expense to create not small signs in English (which would cause negative cognitive and emotional responses in non-English-speaking visitors) but large, easy-to-see street and directional signs with universal symbols on them to make it easy for all tourists to get where they want to go. Even such an apparently small and easy a job as making a sign must be done from the guest's point of view, rather than the organization's. For example, hotels, airports, and other tourist locations often use "You Are Here" signs to help orient customers within the service environment. If these signs are not done carefully, and from the perspective of a total stranger to the environment, they can cause more confusion than if there was no sign in the first place. Then the customer is not only still lost or disoriented but also feels stupid, and customers do not continue to patronize organizations that make them feel stupid.

Signs convey their messages through the use of *symbols,* often language itself. Some signs contain not words but other symbols, such as representational icons that can replace any specific language. These signs, of course, are especially important in travel and tourism settings to which customers come from many different nations, cultures, and linguistic backgrounds. If the customer must remember the information on the sign, a symbol often works best. The Magic Kingdom uses Disney characters to represent sections in the parking lot. At the end of the day, people can more easily remember that the car is in the Chip 'n' Dale section than in Section 17A or Section 31D.

*Artifacts,* as Bitner uses the term, are physical objects that represent something beyond their functional use. As such, they are a type of symbol. Disney frequently uses artifacts in creating story settings. A chair is for sitting, but a Frontierland chair that was once actually situated in a wild-west saloon is both for sitting and for transporting a guest into a fantasy world.

## Other People

The last component of the environment is the other people in it: employees, other guests, or perhaps even Audio-Animatronics creations that guests come to think of as real people. Guests often want to see other guests. If they are alone, they wonder why; are they foolish to be there? No one likes to eat in an empty restaurant; you can eat alone at home. A positive eating experience generally requires the presence of other diners enjoying their meals. Guests of many hospitality organizations expect to see other people also enjoying the experience. Happiness and satisfaction are contagious. Many service settings would feel depressing and lonely without other people.

Employees are environmentally important even before they deliver the anticipated service. A restaurant that employs well-dressed, well-groomed people will have an atmosphere very different from that of a place where everyone is wearing ragged dungarees and tank tops. Most guest-service activities have standards of dress for employees and guests. The dress and

*SeaWorld Entrance, Orlando. (Courtesy of SeaWorld Adventure Parks.)*

personal-appearance code for most hospitality employees and guests is structured and specific. Employees must dress in keeping with the expectations of guests, most of whom view clean, neat, appropriate attire as a mark of respect for guests. Few hospitality organizations cater to guests who want and expect unshaven, overly made-up, or haphazardly attired employees. Though society's standards of dress are more casual than they once were, that market niche is still fairly small. Guests also arrive in some service settings with expectations for each other. Although patrons of a fancy restaurant may not expect those around them to dress up to employee standards, most people are less enthusiastic about paying fine dining prices when some guests are sitting around in cut-off shorts and halter tops. An open-air lakeside restaurant would have a more relaxed dress code for both employees and guests.

Although Figure 3-1 includes *other people* as part of the environment, and clearly they often are, they sometimes seem almost like part of the service itself. If you go to a baseball camp, dude ranch, or on an Outward Bound team-building trip through the wilderness, other people are not just wallflowers or scenery; they are necessary to the experience, and you may even participate in or coproduce it with them. However, even though the other customers may be an important or even a necessary part of a guest experience, and in fact can sometimes make it or break it, their presence is only rarely the reason why you sought out the experience. So they are usually best thought of as part of the environment within which the service is delivered, rather than as part of the service itself, though the distinction is not always clear.

## The Servicescape

Temperature, humidity, sounds, lights, signs, furnishings, green space, open space, other people—although no guest ever singles out or even notices all of the elements within the environment, they do combine to create an overall, unified impression of that environment. In the model seen in Figure 3-1, we use the term *perceived service environment* for the general perception or picture that the guest draws from the countless individual environmental factors. Bitner calls this overall perception the *servicescape;* it is what the individual environmental factors add up to for each guest.

Because each guest perceives different environmental elements, each guest's servicescape is a little bit different. Making even more difficult what might have seemed an easy task—providing a setting within which to deliver the service—the hospitality service provider must realize that each guest's reaction to the perceived servicescape is affected or "moderated" by the guest's mood, personality, expectations, and demographic characteristics. Even if they perceive the servicescape similarly, a shy seventy-year-old female entering a wild disco bar by mistake is going to have a reaction different from that of a twenty-four-year-old male accustomed to spending most evenings there. Service experience designers and hospitality managers must realize that the guest whose perception of the servicescape has been moderated by that guest's individual differences from all other guests is going to respond to the servicescape in one, or perhaps more likely in some combination, of three ways: physiologically, emotionally, and cognitively. We shall talk about each of these in a moment.

## Factors That Moderate Individual Responses

Not only do different guests respond differently to the same physical environment but even the same guest may respond differently from day to day or even hour to hour. Although the hospitality organization usually provides the same servicescape elements for everyone, it should always remember the uniqueness of guests.

We label as *moderators* the individual, personal factors that cause guests to respond to the service setting in different ways. Guests bring a particular day's moods, purposes, demographic characteristics, and personality traits to a particular day's guest experience. These factors affect or moderate each guest's response to the servicescape.

Some people like to be alone and object to standing in long, crowded lines. Other people love to be around crowds and view rubbing elbows and sharing gripes with people in line as part of the fun. Some customers arrive in a happy mood while others are angry or upset. Some older people have a hard time walking longer distances while most young children love it. Some parents don't like to get wet on a ride while most teens think it's great.

*Cultural values and beliefs* also influence how guests respond to the servicescape. Some cultures find red a happy color, and others find it threatening; some find handshakes a positive gesture, and others are offended. Each culture produces an infinity of cultural nuances, and hospitality managers can only do their best to recognize the individual variations that these differences create and design an environment that will offer a guest experience of high quality and value to most people.

Moderators include the *individual moods* that people bring to the servicescape. When people are upset or angry, they may not be able to perceive any environment as positive or fun. Every restaurant server dreads the arrival of an unhappy diner. Regardless of how good the service, fine the dinner, or exciting and pleasant the environment, the diner is likely to leave as unhappy (and unmotivated to leave a generous tip) as when that person arrived.

People arriving either in a neutral mood or unfamiliar with the experience awaiting them will be most influenced by environmental cues. The wonderful smell of freshly popped popcorn or baking cinnamon buns will influence the neutral guest, and every other guest, to consider purchasing the food product. Smart retailers make sure these familiar odors are fanned out into the wandering crowd to encourage product awareness and interest. The Disney Smellitzer machine, which can produce artificial, environmentally appropriate aromas, reproduces the aroma of freshly baking chocolate-chip cookies and projects it out to the crowds walking down Main Street, U.S.A., in the Magic Kingdom. Why an artificial aroma? Disney knows that blowing air across real cookies would dry them out. The machine creates the aroma of fresh cookies without affecting cookie quality.

## RESPONDING TO THE SERVICESCAPE

A guest can respond to a service setting in one or more of three ways: physiologically, emotionally, and cognitively. The moderating factors discussed in the previous section will affect the nature of the response.

### Physiological Responses

***The senses.*** A physiological response results primarily from the servicescape's effects on the guest's senses. Another look at Figure 3-1 will suggest that most physiological responses to the environment are responses to such ambient conditions as temperature, humidity, air quality, smells, sounds, and light.

***Information processing.*** A second type of physiological response to the environment is the information-processing activity of the brain. A well-known study of how much unfamiliar information a human brain could process at any one time found that the capacity was seven (plus or minus two) random pieces of information, such as random numbers. The study was done for the phone company, which wanted to know how long a telephone number people could remember. The study results led to using combinations of words and numbers (like REpublic 7-5914) to help people overcome their physiological limitations by combining a familiar word with five unfamiliar numbers. We can see variations on this method today in the word-based phone numbers used by organizations competing for our business with easy-to-remember numbers such as 1-800-I-FLY-SWA, 1-800-HOLIDAY, 1-800-HILTONS.

The importance of this concept to those managing the service environment is to recognize that random information will quickly overtax the capacity of the human mind to comprehend the environment and enjoy the service experience. It doesn't take much unconnected information—a lengthy menu in an unfamiliar restaurant, for example, or a vast assortment of machines in a self-serve photocopy center—to confuse a customer, and many service operations are unfamiliar territory for their customers. Organizations must respect the information-processing limitations that we all share; customers become frustrated when confused, lost, or overwhelmed with too much information or too many options.

*Rich and lean environments.* Environments can be made **rich** with information or **lean.** Obviously, they should be relatively lean when guests are expected to be unfamiliar with the setting, or when they have to process a lot of information, and can be rich when guests are familiar with the setting or have few choices or decisions to make. The directional or instructional parts of the environment must be kept lean enough in information content to make sure that guests can figure out what they are supposed to do; the richer or more elaborate environments can be used when guests have no responsibility for figuring anything out. Thus, a themed restaurant can be rich in detail and content because the guest only has to sit, observe, and eat. If customers must make decisions about where they are or what to do next, as in a major medical complex, the setting should be kept relatively simple and familiar. This point ties in well with the cognitive aspects of the environmental experience.

## Cognitive Responses

*Expectations and the servicescape.* The cognitive impact depends on the knowledge we bring to the experience. We enter every experience with a set of expectations based on what we have seen and done before. The human tendency is to seek points of similarity between what we have done, seen, or experienced before and the new situation. These prior experiences build expectations as to what ought to be seen, which obviously influences what we actually see. If we expect to see a whole television picture on our screen, then we don't bother to look closely at the picture to see the thousands of little dots that collectively make it up. Likewise, if we enter a cafeteria similar to one we have visited before, then we have our behavior scripted to perform the tasks necessary to eat by the familiar cues in the environment (the arrow pointing to the beginning of the line, the arrangement of the trays, the rack for the silverware, and the bars upon which our tray should slide as we review the food items available).

Indeed, one advantage of chain or branded restaurants is that we know what to expect because we have been there before. We know that the environment in one Morrison's is pretty much like the environment in another, and so we know immediately how to get our food selections after a quick scan of the physical facility to confirm that it is set up the same as every other Morrison's. Imagine, in contrast, the customer who has never seen a cafeteria before and has had no similar experience. Or worse, what if Morrison's managers were authorized to lay out the restaurants however they wished, as a cafeteria, a typical restaurant, or otherwise? Without any previously scripted behavior patterns to rely on, customers new to each location would be quite confused and would require employee time and assistance to navigate this unfamiliar experience.

The point is that hospitality organizations should recognize the information-processing limitations of their guests and seek to introduce the environmental cues necessary to ensure that the present experience ties into some previously built and familiar guest script. The more familiar the organization can make the experience to the guest, the less confusion, frustration, and unhappiness the guest will have. As noted earlier, theming is used extensively to simplify the ability of guests to orient themselves to a location inside the Magic Kingdom. If you are in Frontierland, all the streets, decorations, cast-member costumes, and even the trash cans are themed to provide the multiple cues that help guests quickly determine where in the park they are.

***Nonverbal communication.***   Those aspects of the environmental setting that evoke a cognitive response can be viewed as a form of nonverbal communication whereby the designers of the guest experience communicate what the experience is and teach the guest how to enjoy it. If patrons see a white linen tablecloth in a restaurant, they link that information back to what they have learned previously about the relationship of white linen to restaurant type and price range. In other words, servicescape layout and content tell the guest something about what to expect from the experience. These informational cues tap into previous knowledge and form the beliefs about what the experience should be like. If diners find that the white-linen-tablecloth restaurant also has inexpensive menu prices and excellent food, they will be *wowed* about what a great deal the experience represents because they have been cued to expect a big bill. Conversely, if the same diners see disposable china on plastic tables and are then handed menus filled with twenty-dollar entrees, they will be upset.

*Former Lake Buena Vista Travelodge. (Courtesy of Best Western Lake Buena Vista Resort Hotel.)*

Guests bring a lifetime of history to the guest experience that influences what they expect to find. Whether or not their expectations are met obviously bears on their satisfaction with the experience, so physical cues—like all other aspects of the experience—must be carefully constructed and managed to be consistent with the expected experience. Guests don't want inconsistencies—they don't expect them or like them—or negative surprises. If you are going to offer surprises, make them pleasant ones. Travelodge is a budget hotel chain. The former Travelodge Hotel in Lake Buena Vista, Florida (now a Best Western hotel) was an exceptional Travelodge. When guests walked in expecting the typical Travelodge, certainly adequate and serviceable but not outstanding, and found a very nice hotel, they were impressed. The hotel's high level of guest-satisfaction ratings was helped by the fact that guests got more than they expected based on their prior knowledge of Travelodges.

Olive Garden originally placed machines making pasta in the front of their restaurants, providing a nonverbal cue to their guests that the pasta was fresh. Since people waiting for a table could watch an employee making pasta right then, the product had to be fresh, suggesting nonverbally to guests that Olive Garden cared enough to use fresh ingredients.

## Emotional Responses

Finally, the customer may react emotionally to the servicescape. Old grads get choked up when they return for reunions at their college campuses. Children and adults alike are emotionally touched by holiday decorations. The flags flying, the breeze blowing, and the majesty of the presidential speakers have strong emotional impact on many American visitors to Disney's American Adventure. Little children have the same emotional reaction when Mickey Mouse walks by. It not only represents an individual physical act but also builds an emotional tie to the entire park experience that many children never forget.

Emotional responses have two distinct elements of interest to the hospitality organization. The first is the degree of *arousal,* and the second is the amount or degree of *pleasure/ displeasure* that the experience represents. The emotional response that the hospitality organization seeks to create should have elements of arousal and pleasure to gain the emotional interest of its guests. People want to spend time and money in pleasurable environments; they avoid unpleasant environments. Those that create high levels of arousal are viewed positively unless the arousal is unpleasurable. A sudden explosion that creates loud noise, confusion, and overstimulation would be high on arousal but might be low on pleasure, except on the Fourth of July. Most customers avoid explosive settings.

On the other hand, some people seek out high levels of arousal and pleasure, in such activities as sky diving, ultra-light plane flying, playing or watching contact sports, stock car racing, or deep-sea fishing. A trip on a roller coaster is a scary but not terrifying ride that yields high levels of pleasant experience combined with high levels of arousal. In activities like these, a little fear stimulates a positive experience for the customer. Arousal can also be obtained in other ways, such as the appeal to patriotism in Fourth of July celebrations or the familiar music accompanying the Main Street, U.S.A., parades.

Good hospitality managers have learned to use arousal cues effectively. For example, in the morning when guests are flooding into a theme park, they might hear upbeat, up-tempo music; employees would greet guests in strong, enthusiastic voices to sustain the positive feelings and high level of energy that guests bring into the park. When guests are leaving at the end of the day, both the music and the final comments of employees should probably be sedate and restrained, to be consonant with the lower arousal level of the tired guests.

## The Bottom Line: Come and Stay, or Stay Away

These three response factors—physiological, cognitive, and emotional—operating together lead the guest to make one of two choices—approach or avoid—about the guest experience (see far right of Figure 3-1). Leaving the service and its delivery out of the equation, the guest can decide that the experience of the service environment was, on balance, positive or negative. Servicescape perceptions can encourage the guest to stay longer and come again, or go away and stay away. Hospitality organizations must work hard to create environments that encourage the longer stays and repeat visits that result in increased revenues.

The model in Figure 3-1 should help hospitality managers to choose and arrange environmental factors so as to provide servicescapes that enhance the service and its delivery and that guests, in their infinite variety, will generally respond to in a positive way

## Lessons Learned

1. Envision and create the service setting from the guest's point of view, not your own.
2. Make it easy for guests to go where they want to go and to know where they are.
3. Supply rich environments when and where guests have time to appreciate and enjoy them; use lean environments when and where guests are trying to figure out what they should do or where they should go.
4. Do not overload the environment with information; recognize that most people can process only small amounts of unfamiliar information at one time.
5. Know and manage the cognitive, physiological, and emotional impact of your environment on guests.
6. Manage the environment to maintain the guest's feeling of safety and security.

## Review Questions

1. Consider how theming a guest experience adds value or improves the quality of the guest experience. Compare two similar experiences you have had, such as one restaurant that offered a themed experience and another that did not. What differences did you note between the quality and value of the two experiences?
2. Why should managers pay attention to the environmental setting in which the guest experience occurs?
3. Reflect on the service environments of two different hospitality organizations, one that "felt good" to you and one that "felt uncomfortable." Use the factors in the model in Figure 3-1 to determine why they felt different.
4. Imagine yourself as a first-time visitor to your town or your campus.
   A. How hard or how easy would it be to direct yourself to the location where you are right now?
   B. How could you make finding this location easier for an unfamiliar visitor, using the ideas suggested in this chapter?
5. Think about the environmental and "people" factors that make you feel safe and secure in the location where you live.
   A. To what extent are these same factors applicable to hospitality environments?

B. Have you ever been in a hospitality setting in which you did not feel safe and secure? What more could or should the organization have done to enhance your feelings of safety and security?

6. Consider the places you go as a guest or customer.
    A. Are these environments too rich or too lean with information, and why do you make that judgment?
    B. How would you change those environments to make the amount of information in those environments "just right" for achieving whatever it is you need to do when you are in that particular situation?

## Activities

1. The hospitality service product is largely intangible. Observe and report how one or more hospitality organizations with which you are familiar use environmental design cues to give some tangibility to this intangible service product.

2. Using Figure 3-1 as your reference, go to a hospitality organization and take note of as many environmental factors as you can. Which ones seem to have been "managed" by someone? Which factors can and cannot be managed by the local manager? Which ones seem managed well and which ones do not?

## Case Studies

### Safety at the Downtown Hotel

*It is 1975. Faramarz has recently purchased the Downtown Hotel, a 125-unit facility in downtown Central City, a very large city in the northeast. The Downtown Hotel was originally a Holiday Inn, built in the early 1960s and owned by the Holiday Inn parent company rather than a franchisee. Prior to that time, the strategy of Holiday Inns was to build only on the outskirts of town. But as the number of inns multiplied, the company decided that inns in downtown areas could be profitable. When the Central City Holiday Inn was built, it was located near the bustling central business district but in a neighborhood that was typical of the older northeast working-class ethnic neighborhoods. Although most Holiday Inns built in or near central business districts at that time were many stories tall, a zoning peculiarity on this site restricted the building to two levels.*

*At the turn of the decade, the Holiday Inn company began to suffer heavy losses and sold many units in its chain, including the hotel in Central City. By 1975 the neighborhood in which the hotel was located had become more dangerous, the inner-city central district was less desirable to businesses, and the hotel building had begun to look dated. Faramarz knew these facts but bought the property anyway; the price was right, and he anticipated that he could revitalize it. The building was still structurally sound and located next to an interstate highway. It still had a 50 percent occupancy rate, although the rate had been gradually falling over the past few years. Faramarz attributed the falling occupancy rate to poor management and facility deterioration; he thought he could do better.*

*Faramarz spent considerable money refurbishing the interior. When he was finished, the rooms were nicely decorated, the amenities appropriate for the market segment, and the exterior pleasant to look at.*

*The design of the hotel was typical of 1960s construction: two levels of rooms facing the street with exterior entrances to rooms on both levels, the guests on the second level entering their rooms from an open balcony facing the street. Guests parked their cars in front of the rooms in an unfenced lot. The original bushes and trees that were planted years ago were now fully mature and, in combination with the two-level building structure, gave the property a shaded country feel.*

*Now that he had enhanced the attractiveness of his building and its rooms, Faramarz wanted to develop a strategy to improve the Downtown Hotel's occupancy rate. His basic information source was guest comment cards and mystery shoppers. The common theme of their feedback was that while they appreciated the modernization and the country feel of the place, they somehow felt very unsafe here. Many guests said that they did not intend to return to the hotel on future visits to Central City. Faramarz could see that he had a problem but didn't know quite how to solve it.*

\* \* \*

Based on what the chapter and your own common sense tell you (and any interviews you might obtain with hotel personnel), develop a strategy for making Faramarz's guests feel safer at the Downtown Hotel.

## *Fine Dining at the Silver Slipper*

*A*fter profitable careers in the stock brokerage industry, Fred and Song Yi attended Chef Elmo's School of Culinary Arts. When they graduated, they fulfilled their dream of many years: They opened their own fine dining restaurant, The Silver Slipper.

*They found a building in what they concluded was an excellent location. It had originally been a Denny's Restaurant. The next owner, Bella Starr, had converted the family restaurant into a steakhouse, the Tombstone Restaurant and Saloon. She left most of the Denny's decor intact but superimposed on the interior the rough timbers and boards that Americans have come to expect in their western steakhouses.*

*Buying the Tombstone Restaurant and Saloon used up a large chunk of Fred and Song Yi's available capital. They decided that since their focus was to be excellent food, they would invest the rest of their funds in an upgrade of the kitchen. They patterned their kitchen after the model fine dining kitchens at Chef Elmo's School. The couple realized that the dining area needed refurbishing and upgrading, but they couldn't do everything at once. They decided to struggle along with the vinyl upholstery, plastic furnishings, and rough-hewn timbers and boards until their superb meals had generated some profits. After all, guests came to a fine dining restaurant for fine dining, not for the decor. They knew that some of Europe's finest restaurants, with the highest prices, were simple and basic almost to the point of bareness. They had graduated*

(Continued)

*at the top of their culinary class, had served apprenticeships at excellent restaurants, and knew they could provide tastier culinary creations than any other chefs in town.*

*The big night came; Fred and Song Yi were open for business! Their reputations as trained chefs had preceded them, and many guests arrived in response to the excitement created by the new fine dining opportunity. Fred and Song Yi received many compliments on the excellence of the food. But more than a few guest comment cards also referred to how expensive the meals were.*

*Although comments on the food continued to be highly favorable, the crowds of diners began to dwindle as the initial excitement wore off. Within a few weeks, though the small numbers of diners still willing to pay premium prices continued to rave about the food, Fred and Song Yi saw that they had to do something or they weren't going to make it. Song Yi even had to begin selling mutual funds on the side.*

*Fred wrote a letter to Chef Elmo asking him for advice. Chef Elmo offered to "help out in the kitchen" for a weekend, after which he would give his frank opinion as to how Fred and Song Yi should proceed.*

\* \* \*

What do you think Chef Elmo will tell Fred and Song Yi is wrong with their new business endeavor? What advice do you think he will give them?

## Additional Readings

Arnould, E. J., L. L. Price, and P. Tierney. 1996. The Wilderness Servicescape. *Proceedings of the 4th International Research Seminar on Service Management* (Aix-en-Provence, France), pp. 599–619.

Bach, Susan, and Abraham Pizam. 1996. Crimes in Hotels. *Hospitality Research Journal* 20(1):59–76.

Bitner, M. J. Evaluating Service Encounters: The Effect of Physical Surroundings and Employee Responses. 1990. *Journal of Marketing* 54(2):69–82.

Booms, Bernard H., and Mary J. Bitner. 1982. Marketing Services by Managing the Environment. *Cornell Hotel and Restaurant Administration Quarterly* 23(2):35–39.

Compeau, Larry D., Dhruv Grewal, and Kent B. Monroe. 1998. Role of Prior Affect and Sensory Cues on Consumers' Affective and Cognitive Responses and Overall Perceptions of Quality. *Journal of Business Research* 42(3):295–308.

Grove, Stephen J., and Raymond P. Fisk. 1997. The Impact of Other Customers on Service Experiences: A Critical Incident Examination of "Getting Along." *Journal of Retailing* 73(1):63–85.

Hopkins, Jeffrey. 1994. Orchestrating an Indoor City: Ambient Noise Inside a Mega-Mall. *Environment and Behavior* 26(6):785–812.

Hui, Michael K., Laurette Dube, and Jean-Charles Chebat. 1997. The Impact of Music on Consumers' Reactions to Waiting for Services. *Journal of Retailing* 73(1):87–104.

Klein, Hans-Joachim. 1993. Tracking Visitor Circulation in Museum Settings. *Environment and Behavior* 25(6):782–800.

Kotler, Philip. 1973. Atmospherics as a Marketing Tool. *Journal of Retailing* 49(4):48–64.

Sherry, John F., ed. 1997. *Servicescapes: The Concept of Place in Contemporary Markets.* Lincolnwood, IL: NTC Business Books.

Sirakaya, Ercan, Anthony G. Sheppard, and Robert W. McLellan. 1997. Assessment of the Relationship Between Perceived Safety at a Vacation Site and Destination Choice Decisions: Extending the Behavioral Decision-Making Model. *Journal of Hospitality and Tourism Research* 21(2):1–10.

## Notes

1. David Koenig. 1994. *Mouse Tales: A Behind-the-Ears Look at Disneyland* (Irvine, CA: Bonaventure Press), pp. 42–43.
2. Examples taken from Leslie Kaufman, Our New Theme Song, *Newsweek,* June 22, 1998, pp. 46–47.
3. Stephen M. Fjellman. 1992. *Vinyl Leaves: Walt Disney World and America* (Boulder, CO: Westview Press), p. 257.
4. Ibid., 258.
5. Shelton Waldrep. 1995. Monuments to Walt, in *Inside the Mouse: Work and Play at Disney World* (Durham, NC: Duke University Press), p. 201.
6. Andrea Peterson. Restaurants Bring In da Noise to Keep Out da Nerds. *Wall Street Journal,* December 30, 1997, B-1.
7. Waldrep, 212–213.
8. For further information about Bill Tovey and special effects at Disney, see Judith Rubin. 1997. Art and Technology: The Story of Modern Special Effects. *At the Park,* Issue 41, 48–57.
9. *Walt Disney: Famous Quotes.* 1994. Printed for Walt Disney Theme Parks and Resorts, p. 29.
10. Koenig, 42–43.
11. Carl Sewell and Paul B. Brown. 1990. *Customers for Life* (New York: Pocket Books), p. 22.
12. The structure of the following discussion is adapted from Mary Jo Bitner. 1992. Servicescapes: The Impact of Physical Surroundings on Customers and Employees. *Journal of Marketing* 56(2):57–71.
13. *Walt Disney: Famous Quotes,* 34.
14. Sewell and Brown, 124.

# Developing the Hospitality Culture: Everyone Serves!

### Hospitality Principle:

> Define and build a total service culture.

*Work together with employees to develop a "can-do" culture
of honesty, integrity, energy, and initiative.*

—Norman Brinker, Former CEO, Chili's Restaurants

*My role? Well you know I was stumped one day when a little boy asked, "Do you draw
Mickey Mouse?" I had to admit I do not draw anymore. "Then you think up all the jokes
and ideas?" "No," I said, "I don't do that." Finally, he looked up at me and said,
"Mr. Disney, just what do you do?" "Well," I said, "sometimes I think of myself
as a little bee. I go from one area of the studio to another and gather pollen and sort
of stimulate everyone. I guess that's the job I do."*

—Walt Disney

## LEARNING OBJECTIVES

After reading this chapter, you should understand:

▧ Why a hospitality organization's culture is so important to service success.
▧ Why the organization's leaders are so important to defining, developing, teaching, and maintaining its culture.
▧ What essential roles the organization's beliefs, values, and norms play.
▧ How the organization communicates its culture to its employees—through laws, language, stories, legends, heroes, symbols, and rituals.
▧ How the organization can accomplish the difficult task of changing its culture, if that becomes necessary.
▧ What research reveals about organizational cultures.

## KEY TERMS AND CONCEPTS

| | |
|---|---|
| beliefs | ritual |
| norms | symbol |
| organizational culture | values |

When you go to the Walt Disney World Resort, fly on Southwest Airlines, shop at Nordstrom's, or stay at a Marriott hotel, you can sense something special about the organization and the people who work there. If customers of these organizations are asked about the experience, they invariably describe it as better than they expected. What's even more amazing is that their employees will also tell you that the organizations are different. The Disney cast members talk about their commitment to the quality of the "show" they produce for park visitors. Marriott and Nordstrom employees talk about the commitment to guest service, and Southwest Airlines employees talk about their commitment to providing a unique and pleasurable flying experience. Not only do employees talk about these corporate values; they believe in them and show the customer their commitment in a thousand different ways every day. The hospitality manager seeking excellence can learn a great deal by examining how these organizations create and sustain their culture of service excellence.

## THE IMPORTANCE OF THE LEADERS

Getting everyone in the organization committed to high levels of guest service is a daunting challenge. Not only did Walt Disney, Herb Kelleher of Southwest Airlines, and Bill Marriott spend the personal time and energy necessary to create and sustain the **organizational culture** that defines the corporate values for which their organizations are famous; they also got their employees and managers to believe in the culture as well. They knew that as leaders, they were responsible for defining the culture. They all had a strong commitment to excellent service, and they communicated it—through their words and deeds—clearly and consistently to those inside and outside the organization.

Can managers who are not the presidents or founders of organizations have the same kind of influence on the culture that these famous leaders have had? They certainly can, and they must, although managers and supervisors serve more as translators than as definers of culture. The most important influence on any organizational culture is *the behavior of the organization's leader.* Viewing this influence from the bottom of the organizational chart, employees try to behave as their supervisors do, supervisors are influenced by the behavior of their managers, the role models for managers are their own managers, and so on until top-level managers, and especially the organization's leader, become the role models for the whole organization and the ultimate definers of each organization's cultural values.

Supervisory personnel at all levels, then, must realize how important they are as cultural keepers and translators. If they do not perform this function well, then service delivery will suffer. Managers must not only walk the walk and talk the talk of excellent service; they must consistently remind all employees that they supervise to do the same. Disney referred to ". . . never letting your personnel get sloppy . . . never let them be unfriendly."[1] If a manager moving through the service environment sees an employee doing something inconsistent with the culture and ignores it, that manager sends a message to all employees that such behavior is a legitimate option, that not everybody has to focus on guest service all the time. After a few instances of managers saying one thing but rewarding or not punishing another, everyone knows what the real level of service commitment is.

Not only must all the public and private statements support the idea that *everyone serves;* the organizational reward system, training programs, and measures of achievement must also support and reinforce this message. When managers publicly and loudly celebrate the service achievements of their employees, they send a very strong message to everyone else about what the organization believes in and what its culture values.

## Culture and Reputation

A company's culture, like a person's character, drives its reputation. Companies whose cultures honor customers, employees, and shareholders usually have excellent reputations. These organizations recognize the importance of a strong culture in the competitive marketplace, a strong culture that everyone believes in, understands, and supports. All organizations have a culture, whether or not anyone spends any time worrying about it, shaping it, or teaching it. Managers of effective hospitality organizations understand the value of a strong culture and do whatever they can to reaffirm and support what the organization values. If the culture supports excellent service, then the members learn that providing excellent service is what they are supposed to do. The stronger this cultural norm is and the more the members accept and believe in it, the more likely it is that they will try to do whatever they can to create and sustain service excellence.

Unfortunately, many managers don't understand their responsibilities in managing the culture to get this level of employee commitment, and both their employees and customers can tell. Successful hospitality managers spend enormous amounts of time and energy on training new employees in the culture, reminding their existing employees of the cultural values, and rewarding and reinforcing these values at every opportunity. While there are always other things to do, these managers make the time to reinforce culture.

Disney is an outstanding example of an organization that has worked very hard to define and sustain its culture. Corporate culture is so important to Disney that it is included and defined in the employee handbook. But in addition to being words in a book, the Disney culture is real and important for cast members. After interviewing Disney employees, Jane Kuenz concluded about the people she met:

These are frequently people who have migrated to Orlando specifically to work at Disney, often with exceedingly high, perhaps naive, expectations about the park. While these expectations are sometimes vague notions that Disney must be "the epitome of the fun place to work," at other times they reflect a high level of personal investment with the park and with its power to raise the innocuous or mundane lives of average people into the fantastical and magical existence of the Disney cast member.[2]

In other words, many people believe so strongly in Disney's ability to create a magical experience for its guests that they want to become a part of it. Whatever cultural training Disney provides after these people become employed is icing on the cake; they arrive already believing in the Disney standards of excellence. Few hospitality organizations have this head start in getting employees to understand and participate enthusiastically in the organizational culture. It is, however, a model worth pursuing.

## The Manager's Most Important Responsibility

This chapter will present the concept of corporate culture, why and how excellent managers communicate culture to employees, how to change it, and how managers can work with their culture to ensure that it supports the organizational mission of service excellence. Everyone has been in an organization that feels warm, friendly, and helpful, perhaps for reasons they can't quite explain. Similarly, everyone has been in an organization that feels cold, aloof, uncaring, and impersonal. While most people can readily give examples of organizations that fit the two types, few can really explain what makes the two types different.

Making culture different in the right ways is the hospitality manager's responsibility. Len Berry says, "Sustained performance of quality service depends on organizational values that truly guide and inspire employees. And how does an organization get such values? It gets them from its leaders who view the infusion and cultivation of values within the organization as a primary responsibility."[3] Indeed, some leading writers go so far as to maintain that it is every manager's most important responsibility.

## THE IMPORTANCE OF CULTURE

In Chapter 2, we talked about defining a service strategy. That strategy is no more than a paper reality. Implementing it is impossible without a supporting culture. No matter how brilliant and well thought out the strategy is, it will fail if it doesn't fit with the organization's culture.

### Strategy and Employee Commitment

The firm's competitive strategy provides the basis for such critical decisions as how the organization will be structured, what type of service it wants to deliver, what market niche it seeks to fill, what production and service delivery system it will use, who it will hire, and how it will train, reward, promote, and evaluate those people. But only employee commitment to implementing all those critical decisions can turn plans into actions. All the plans in the world are useless without employee understanding, commitment, and support.

Hospitality organizations require an especially high level of commitment and understanding. Because the guest experience is to an extent intangible and each moment during the experience is so critical to determining guest satisfaction with the experience, employees must have extensive knowledge of both the service itself and the guests they serve and an ability to respond quickly to the many variations in guest expectations. But knowledge is not enough. Employees must also have high levels of motivation to deliver the hospitality experience consistently, in the way it should be done. Consequently, a strong and focused organizational culture becomes an especially important managerial emphasis in hospitality organizations. At Disney theme parks, a "magical moment" for a guest is hard to define but easy to see in practice. The motivation of employees to create magical moments whenever they can results directly from their understanding of and commitment to the Disney culture.

## Culture as a Competitive Advantage

The organization's culture can be a significant competitive advantage if it has value to its members, is unique, and cannot be easily copied by others. If an organization has a thriving culture that others cannot readily duplicate, it can use that culture to attract both customers and employees. A good strategy for other organizations is to identify organizations in their industries with successful cultures and try to imitate their cultures as well as they can.[4]

Southwest Airlines has a thriving culture that others can use as a benchmark for their own. The "Southwest Spirit"

> is the twinkle in your eye, the skip in your step; it is letting that childlike spirit escape and be heard. To know what really makes Southwest Spirit, you have to look beyond the machines and things because running a fun and productive airline defies science; it is an art that comes from working hard with feeling.[5]

Working in a culture where the employees truly have the "spirit" is very different from working in a typical nine-to-five job. More importantly, being a customer who encounters this type of culture is unique and fun. The Southwest culture represents a competitive advantage for them over other airlines.

## Management by Culture!

The stronger the culture, the less necessary it is to rely on the typical bureaucratic management controls—policies, procedures, managerial directives—found in traditional industrial organizations. If the culture can effectively substitute for such expensive control mechanisms, that in itself is a pretty good reason for the hospitality organization to spend money on building its culture. Since hospitality organizations must find ways to delegate more decision-making responsibility to their employees, especially their guest-contact employees, they must rely on strong cultural values to ensure that their people do the right things for their guests. Also, guests are not passive; they frequently participate in providing their own hospitality experience under the guidance of employees. A strong culture can help employees guide guests properly even when the manager is not nearby. Unlike a manufacturing organization where the production process is fairly predictable, the process of providing a hospitality experience is subject to incredible variation; as many different things can happen as there are different types of people. Since defining all the possibilities is impossible, the hospitality organization must rely on its employees to understand what is expected and deliver it to the guest every time. The more uncertain the task, the more employees must depend on corporate values instead of managerial instructions, formal policies, and established procedures to guide their behavior.[6]

## An Example: The Chef

The culture of the professional chef is particularly strong. While much of any culinary program is devoted to teaching the principles of cooking, implicit in all of the training is the cultural value of preparing a consistent fine dining experience. Regardless of program or type of culinary training, one central value stands out: The chef must strive for flawless production of a fine dining experience for every guest every time. Indeed, some casual dining chains have sent their cooks to culinary courses not so much to learn how to cook, since the chain's recipes are standardized, but to learn how to respect the culinary cultural values of product quality and consistency so that the diner at a Chili's or Olive Garden, like the diner at a five-star Parisian restaurant, will have a consistently prepared meal.

## Culture as a Competency

If an organization's culture is strong, it becomes another core competency. As would be true for other core competencies, the organization that seeks to do something incompatible with its culture is likely to fail. If, for example, the organization's culture is accustomed to providing a high-value service experience, any manager trying to implement a cost-saving move that somehow jeopardizes that experience will meet resistance.

The basic principle is simple. If the organization is committed to a strategy of service excellence, then its culture must support service excellence. Otherwise, excellence will not happen.

*The Chef.*

## Culture Defined

An organization's culture is a way of behaving, thinking, and acting that is learned and shared by the organization's members. One definition might be: the shared philosophies, ideologies, values, assumptions, beliefs, attitudes, and norms that knit a community together. All of these interrelated qualities reveal a group's agreement, implicit or explicit, on how its members should approach decisions and problems. In other words, culture is the way people in the organization act and think as they go about doing their jobs. "It's the way we do things around here." Any culture is also dynamic and constantly changing as anyone who has followed the changes in teen music and dress for the past decade can readily confirm. A culture both influences its members and in turn is influenced by its members. The interaction between members over time as they deal with changing circumstances means that cultures too will change.

## Culture and the Outside World

Culture helps an organization's members deal with two core issues that all organizations must resolve: how to relate to the world outside of the organization and how the organization's members should relate to one another. Ed Schein calls culture a "pattern of basic assumptions—invented, discovered, or developed by a given group as it learns to cope with its problems of external adaptation and internal interaction—that has worked well enough to be considered valid and, therefore, to be taught to new members as the correct way to perceive, think, and feel in relation to those problems."[7]

Some managers define how their organizations should deal with the outside world by taking a closed or negative view of the outside environment and encouraging an us-versus-them cultural mind-set. Members of such a culture are unreceptive to new ideas from the outside; they tend to discard or downplay common industry practices or innovations and are generally secretive about what their organization is doing and protective of its "proprietary knowledge." On the other hand, managers trying to create an open-culture organization constantly encourage their people to grow and develop by interacting with others in the industry, to benchmark against best-practice organizations wherever they can be found, and to consider ideas and innovations developed outside the organizational boundaries. Not surprisingly, people in these learning organizations adapt more quickly to changes in customer expectations and respond better to customer needs.

## Culture and the Internal Organization: X and Y

Relating to the outside world refers to how the members of the organization see the world, what assumptions they make about the organization's relationship to that world, and how members are supposed to respond to external events. Relating to one another inside the culture refers to how the members see their collective mission, the ways they interact or interrelate with each other to accomplish that mission, and the assumptions they should use in making decisions about those things they control—their functional areas, interpersonal relationships, and attitudes toward change and adaptation. With regard to internal interaction, a culture can be democratic, supportive, friendly, informal, and participatory in its decision making, or it can be formal, rigid, bureaucratic, and autocratic, allowing only those at the top of the organization to make decisions. These two extremes reflect the classic distinction made by Douglas McGregor in his discussion of Theory X and Theory Y management styles. In life, of course, most organizations fall somewhere between the extremes. These two theories represent two very different sets of assumptions about how people behave. Theory Y assumes that people like to work, derive real satisfaction from their work, and want to do a good job. Theory X assumes that people will work only as hard as they are made to work. People entering one culture type from another quickly learn that the behaviors and actions rewarded and respected in their former organization may not be respected or rewarded in the new one. Indeed, part of the employee hiring process should include an indoctrination into the new culture.

## Teaching the New Values

Since everyone brings to a new job the cultural assumptions of past experiences, managers of excellent hospitality organizations know they must start teaching new cultural values to employees from day one. The Traditions training program at Disney is a good illustration of how to teach new employees about the organization's cultural values and beliefs. On the first day of employment, new employees go to a classroom at Disney University where they learn about the traditions, history, and core beliefs of the Disney organization. This experience gives everyone a common cultural background and also communicates the importance and meaning of the Disney culture. If it wasn't important, why would the company spend an entire day teaching it to *every* new cast member, regardless of the job? No matter what function they may later perform inside the organization, the glue that binds cast members together is the belief that they are all participating in the Disney culture, and they know exactly what that means. Disney teaches its employees four company values, in the order of their importance: *safety, courtesy, show,* and *efficiency.* When employees encounter unfamiliar situations in which they have to take some action, these four values provide guidance.

## Culture Fills the Gaps

These cultural teachings become beliefs about how things should be, values of what has worth, and norms of behavior. They provide guidance to the culture's members as they interact with each other and their customers. In Schein's terms, they guide the members in how they should perceive the world about them, feel about the events they face, and think about what they do and don't do within their jobs. Many bureaucratic organizations believe that the best way to make sure employees do the right thing in their jobs is to establish extensive rules and regulations to cover every possible contingency. Ideally, there would be a rule for every possibility. Excellent hospitality organizations, knowing that rules and procedures cannot cover everything, spend their time defining and teaching the culture so that their employees will know how they should act in treating their guests and one another. These organizations teach their employees as much as they can, then rely on culture to fill in the inevitable gaps between what can be predicted and what actually happens when guests enter the service setting.

# BELIEFS, VALUES, AND NORMS

Culture-driven organizations seek to define the beliefs, values, and norms of the organization through what they do and say, and what they reward, rather than through rules and regulations. Let's take a closer look at what we mean by beliefs, values, and norms.[8]

## Beliefs

**Beliefs** form the ideological core of the culture. A belief is how people in organizations make sense of their relationships with the external world and its influence on the internal organization. If culture is a set of assumptions about how things operate, then beliefs are formed to help the people inside the organization make sense of how those assumptions influence what they do inside the organization. Beliefs define the relationships between causes and effects for the organizational members.

As a simple illustration, if the people in an organization assume that the marketplace rewards with profits those organizations that provide good service and punishes those that don't, then the importance of providing good customer service becomes a cultural belief. It's something that everyone believes in. Obviously, most beliefs are more complex than this; a multitude of assumptions about how the environment operates may translate into a whole system of sense-making beliefs. The point here is that every organization's members make a number of assumptions about the world and develop beliefs that reflect how they will respond as an organization to those assumptions. The management of an organization that understands the importance of these beliefs will take an active role in defining both the assumptions and the beliefs that those assumptions create.

## Values

**Values** are preferences for certain behaviors or certain outcomes over others. Values define for the members what is right and wrong, preferred and not preferred, desirable behavior and undesirable behavior. Obviously, values can be a strong influence on employee behavior within an organizational culture. If management sends a clear signal to all employees that providing good customer service is an important value to the organization, then the employees know they should adopt this value. They are more likely, consequently, to behave in ways that ensure that the customer has a good service experience.

## Norms

**Norms** are standards of behavior that define how people are expected to act while part of the organization. The typical organization has an intricate set of norms. Some are immediately obvious, and some require the advice and counsel of veteran employees who have learned the norms over time by watching what works and what doesn't work, what gets rewarded and what gets punished.

Most outstanding hospitality organizations have norms of greeting a guest warmly, smiling, and making eye contact to show interest in the guest. Some use "the fifteen-foot rule." Once guests are within fifteen feet of employees—window washers, engineers, and grounds crew, as well as guest-contact persons—the behavior norm is to make positive contact with the guest. Within this "hospitality zone," employees are expected to make eye contact, smile, and briefly engage the guest in conversation. Some organizations print the service norms on cards, supplied to every employee to serve as the guidelines for service.

Cultural norms are defined and shaped for the hospitality employee not only by fellow employees and supervisors but also by guests who make their expectations plain. Such guests are an advantage that hospitality organizations have over manufacturing organizations as guests become potent assistants to the managers in monitoring, reinforcing, and shaping employee behavior. At Disney, the guest service guidelines are so well established that even the guests often know them. If a ride operator in the Magic Kingdom fails to make

---

*Disney Guidelines for Guest Service*

1. Make Eye Contact and Smile
2. Greet Each and Every Guest
3. Seek Out Guest Contact
4. Provide Immediate Service Recovery
5. Display Appropriate Body Language at All Times
6. Preserve the "Magical" Guest Experience
7. Thank Each and Every Guest

---

eye contact or doesn't smile, a park patron may comment about the deviation from the service norm ("What's the matter? Did Goofy step on your toe?") or offer a reminder. Ride operators learn quickly what is expected of them by the constant hints, looks, glares, and comments guests make. Guest expectations of normal behavior help shape employee behavior. As with many organizations that make sure their guests know their commitment to service excellence, Disney's guests help reinforce the norms of behavior; they demand that Disney cast members live up to their reputation for providing a high-quality Disney experience.

### Norms in Advertising

Many hospitality organizations use advertising as a means to sell their services, to show the guest visually what the guest experience should look like. Since the employees see the same ads, they also learn the norms of behavior that guests expect, and this advertising serves to train them just as it informs prospective guests. The guest arrives with predefined expectations, and the hospitality employees had better meet or exceed the expected standard or the guest will be unhappy and dissatisfied.

### Norms of Appearance

In addition to the norms of behavior, most hospitality organizations also have norms of appearance and standards of personal grooming. For example, employees may not be allowed to have hair that extends below a certain length, only women may have pierced ears and all earrings must be smaller than a certain size, fingernails may not be excessively long or colored in unusual ways, no necklaces, bracelets, beards, moustaches, visible tattoos, and so forth. Although such norms can lead to criticism about restrictions on personal freedom of expression regarding appearance, hospitality organizations must meet guest expectations in this as in all areas of service. If Ritz-Carlton guests expect to see clean-cut employees greeting them upon check-in, then the Ritz-Carlton had better hire clean-cut employees. Disney wants its employees to have a conventional appearance; anything other than the "Disney Look" would detract from the guest's experience of the Disney show. On the other hand, the Disney Look would probably not be appropriate at a Hard Rock Cafe, Harley Davidson Cafe, or Jekyll and Hyde Club. While organizations that don't serve external customers can ignore such personal-appearance concerns, the hospitality organization cannot. It must carefully define and enforce its norms of appearance to ensure that employees have the look guests expect.

We have seen that advertising can help predefine guest expectations. Here is an example of how an appearance norm at a southern resort hotel affected the appearance and expectations of the hotel's convention clientele. Traditionally, this hotel had required that the men on its management team be dressed in blazers and ties, the women in blazers and skirts. Whenever meeting planners visited the hotel to discuss potential convention business, they could see by the outfits of the hotel managers that the culture was clearly somewhat formal. When these meeting planners went back to their organizations, they reported to their members that the attire for the convention, even though it was to be held in the sunny south, would be jackets and ties, and jackets/skirts or dresses. Now that the hotel's management has quit wearing jackets and instead wears short-sleeve shirts with collars, or skirts and blouses, the entire atmosphere of the meetings held in the hotel has changed. Meeting planners, adopting the new appearance norm, now report to their convention attendees that the meeting attire will be informal and relaxed.

### Folkways and Mores

*Folkways* are the customary, habitual ways in which organizational members act or think, without reflecting upon them. Shaking hands (or not shaking hands), addressing everyone by first or last name, and wearing or not wearing a tie would all be examples of folkways. In a restaurant, a folkway might be to roll silverware when there is nothing else to do in the quiet times between crowds. An organization's *mores* are folkways that go beyond being polite. These are customary behaviors that must be followed to preserve the organization's efficient operation and survival. Mores require certain acts and forbid others. By indicating what is right and wrong, they form the basis of the organization's code of ethics and accepted behaviors.

## CULTURE AND THE ENVIRONMENT

The organization's culture, then, represents a shared learning process that continues over time as the people inside the organization change, grow, and develop while responding to a world that does the same. The world external to the organization (consisting of the physical, technological, and cultural environment) defines the activities and patterns of interactions for the organization's members who have to deal with that external world. Ed Schein says,

> One must never forget that the environment initially determines the possibilities, options, and constraints for a group, and thus forces the group to specify its primary task or function if it is to survive at all. The environment thus initially influences the formation of culture, but once the culture is present in the form of shared assumptions, those assumptions, in turn, influence what will be perceived and defined as the environment.[9]

### Learning the Culture, Learning from the Culture

As new people join the organization, they learn the culture from both formal company practices such as training and reward systems and informal social interaction with fellow employees, supervisors, and subordinates. They learn the right way and the wrong way to do things in that particular culture. The point is that culture is an important influence on how people inside organizations behave in their job performance, how they make decisions, how they relate to others, and how they handle new situations.

The guidance that culture can give in handling unusual situations becomes especially meaningful in hospitality organizations. Unlike manufacturing organizations, where much of the job can be defined in advance through engineering methods and bureaucratic control mechanisms, the hospitality industry is full of unusual events. People ask unbelievably odd questions, make the most outrageous requests, and behave in unpredictable ways. Without a cultural value system to guide them, employees in hospitality organizations would frequently fail the guest because they would not know how their organization wants them to respond. While most manufacturers of products can focus on teaching employees only the hows of producing the product, the hospitality organization must also teach its employees the whys. Developing, reinforcing, and communicating clear cultural norms about what is and is not the right way to deal with customers is a very effective way to teach those whys. A sign frequently seen in customer-focused organizations says:

---

**Rule 1:** The customer is always right.
**Rule 2:** If you think the customer is wrong, re-read Rule 1.

---

While no organization believes that all customers are always right in all situations, the two principles are a good guide to behavior in those organizations that want to remind their employees of the organization's fundamental value structure. This sign is a strong symbolic reminder of this important cultural value.

Like everybody else, employees need to make sense out of their environment and how to behave within it. Culture helps them do so. When people collectively make assumptions about how the world outside the organization operates, they form beliefs that help them make sense of those assumptions, collectively decide upon what is valued, and then define norms that enforce and carry forward those values in the day-to-day behavior of the members.

It sounds more complicated than it is. Essentially, managers who recognize these concepts and their worth to the organization spend considerable time and effort clarifying and articulating the assumptions, shaping the belief system, and making clear the organizational values to all the members. Members of every culture want to make sense of what's happening inside and outside the organization and will find a way to do so with or without management help. Hospitality organizations wanting to ensure that the primary cultural value is service excellence will continually emphasize and define that critical value for the entire organization.

## Subcultures

Cultures often split into subcultures. Usually, the more people involved in the culture and the harder it is for them to stay in communication with one another, the more likely it is that the organization will see some subcultures form. They can be good or bad, supportive or destructive, and consistent with or contrary to the larger corporate culture. Since culture relies on interaction to sustain itself, people who work together may well create a subculture of their own, especially if they don't interact much with other organizational units. Organizations that depend greatly on part-time employees are especially susceptible to subculture formation; the part-timers may not spend enough hours in the greater organization to absorb its culture. The organization will want to do what it can to ensure that the subcultures are mainly consistent with the overall cultural values even if their behaviors, beliefs, and norms do vary somewhat from them. Communication is the key to sustaining the overall culture.

The authors of *Inside the Mouse* show how the large size of the entire Walt Disney World Resort operation has led to the development of subcultures. The categorizing and subdividing of employees by place (Tomorrowland versus Frontierland), type (food and beverage versus attractions operator), shift (weekend versus weekday), and amount of work (full-time versus part-time) have the effect of forming many different and clearly identifiable subcul-

*Jungle Cruise Entrance. (Used by permission from Disney Enterprises, Inc.)*

tures. Cast members tend to associate with others like themselves who are doing things like what they do in areas where they are likely to meet one another frequently. After all, a culture is a shared experience, and the more it is shared, the more definable it becomes for those sharing it. Pirates of the Caribbean people tend to hang out with other Pirates of the Caribbean people, Haunted Mansion people hang out with other Haunted Mansion people, and so forth.

The subcultures forming within the overall culture can be a managerial challenge if they operate in ways that do not support the overall corporate culture. The Jungle Cruise operators have a tendency to see themselves as excellent stand-up comedians and compete against one another for the best comedy routine during a Jungle Cruise ride. Although some humor can enhance the "show" for guests, this subcultural competition promotes values that, if carried to an extreme, could directly conflict with the overall Disney culture. Gross deviations from the accepted scripts might become so outlandish as to violate the overall cultural value of providing a wholesome and nonoffensive family entertainment experience. While the worst comedians eventually get caught, the damage to the overall Disney experience for some guests may by then be irreparable. The larger culture must be strong enough to override the subcultures on issues important to the organization's survival. While some cultural variation may be tolerated, the overall culture has to be defined and reinforced by management in ways sufficiently strong that the central values of the organization come through in the customer experience.

## COMMUNICATING THE CULTURE

While the substance of culture is a set of assumptions that lead to beliefs, values, and norms, culture is communicated to those inside and outside the organization in a variety of ways, including laws, language, stories, legends, heroes, symbols, and rituals. In these ways people can express, affirm, and communicate their shared beliefs, values, and norms to each other and to those outside the organization. Each form is important in helping the members learn, implement, teach, and reinforce the culture that the members share. They should be used together and become part of an overall message to members of what the culture stands for. The more these communications support each other in sending a single clear message to the organizational membership, the stronger the impact of that message will be.

Leading hospitality organizations know the importance of these elements in defining the organizational culture. They manage these cultural mechanisms in a holistic way to reinforce, clearly and consistently, those organizational values which they expect all employees to have in mind when they meet, greet, and serve customers. Learning the culture becomes part of the training for all new employees. Managers and other experienced employees, internal communications media, and organizational reward structures all continue to teach, reinforce, and celebrate the corporate culture thereafter.

### Laws

The laws of an organization are its rules, policies, and regulations—the norms that are so important that they need to be written down so everyone knows exactly what they are. They tell the members what behaviors are expected within that culture and also detail the consequences of violating the norm.

Two norms are so important to Disney that they are corporate policies—in effect, laws. One, a cast member in costume must not walk in an area where the costume is inappropriate.

An employee in the futuristic Tomorrowland cannot go to Frontierland. Nor may an Epcot World Showcase member of the China Pavilion be found in costume in the Moroccan Pavilion. A cast member violating either norm can be fired. Another strict policy is that cast members portraying Disney characters must stay completely *in* character; they must maintain and fulfill the character expectations of Disney guests. They cannot speak, be seen out of costume, take off any part of the costume in public, or do anything else that might destroy the sense of fantasy for the children (of all ages). Indeed, a policy forbids transporting any character costume in a public area unless it is in a black bag that completely covers all its parts so no child (of any age) will see a favorite fantasy character "in pieces."

## Language

In addition to the common language of the larger social culture, each organization develops a language of its own, which is frequently incomprehensible to outsiders. The special language is an important vehicle for both communicating the common cultural elements to which the language refers and in reaffirming the identity with the culture that those who speak this language share. Terms an insider uses to talk with another insider communicate an important concept quickly and also distinguish that person from an outsider.

For example, everyone at Disney uses certain important terms which carry strong cultural messages. All employees, recruited by *casting,* are called *cast members.* This term sends two important messages. First, everyone is equally part of the overall cast of the organization, a concept reinforced by the use of first names only on all name tags. Second, the term reminds cast members that they are playing "roles" that help make up the Disney "show." This show concept is reinforced by the use of other terms such as "on stage" to define all situations and areas where cast members are in front of their customers and "back stage" to define areas the customers cannot see. Law enforcement staff are called *security hosts,* and everyone's uniforms are *costumes* which are checked out daily from *wardrobe.* In other words, the language of the culture is carefully constructed to ensure that cast members constantly think of themselves as participants in an ongoing stage production designed to create a magical fantasy experience. So effective is this training in language that Smith and Eisenberg report that no Disneyland Park employee they talked to during their 35 half-hour interviews used any of the traditional terms *uniforms, customers,* or *amusement park,* instead using *costumes, guests,* and *property.*[10]

## Stories, Legends, and Heroes

Stories, legends, and heroes are another way of transmitting cultural beliefs, values, and norms. They communicate proper behaviors and the right and wrong way to do things. The cultural belief the Magic Kingdom has magical qualities that create a positive fantasy experience for children of all ages is reinforced by stories about people who work there. There are the stories about the busy corporate executive from another organization who makes time to work at the Magic Kingdom for a few days every month, and the heiress who jets over from her own private island to ladle punch at Aunt Polly's landing. While the stories may or may not be completely accurate, they represent a central belief by employees in the culture that "Walt Disney World is the place where truck drivers' daughters work alongside corporate executives in their common mission of producing magic."[11] In other words, being a part of the Disney experience is so positive that it draws in everyone regardless of social status or position, and, while in the park, all cast members are united in doing the same thing: providing a magical experience for guests. Numerous powerful stories teach this cultural belief.

Many tales are told about Walt Disney and his attention to detail, service excellence, and the future direction of the parks. It is reported that when he died in 1966, he left behind a series of films in which he conducted staff meetings to an empty conference room with the intention, and apparently the result, that they be shown monthly to his senior staff after his death. As one observer reported, he held conferences into at least the 1970s in which he would make statements like, "Bob, this is October, 1976. You remember we were going to do this or that. Are you sure it's underway now?"[12] Such attention to detail and commitment to service quality left an important legacy behind. Indeed, for years after Disney's death, many decisions were reportedly made by trying to figure out "what Walt would have done" or "what Walt would have wanted." This thinking so permeated the culture that the organization continued for many years to work as if the brilliant leader were still somehow nearby and able to guide the new leadership's thinking.

Few organizations can access the vast array of heroes that Disney has available to it. Through the many fictional characters seen in its motion pictures, management can teach, perpetuate, and model desired behaviors and core values. The Lion King was such an inspirational movie to one Disney hotelier that he used it as the basis for teaching the "Circle of Service." Instead of the Circle of Life used in the movie, he used the movie's characters and songs to bring a strong message to his employees about the value and importance of the guest service commitment in which he wanted them to believe. The movie was a dramatic medium for bringing this message home in a powerful way. Other resort hotel managers have used the "Be Our Guest" song from *Beauty and the Beast* to build similarly inspirational stories about providing excellent guest service. These are only two examples of the many powerful symbols that Disney managers have available to them.

### American Express: Great Performers

American Express calls those employees who have provided exceptional service to customers Great Performers. Two customer service people in Florida got money to a woman in a foreign war zone and helped her get a ship out of the country; travel agents in Columbus, Georgia, paid a French tourist's bail so he could get out of jail; an employee drove through a blizzard to take food and blankets to stranded travelers at Kennedy Airport; an employee got up in the middle of the night to take an Amex card to a customer stranded at Boston's Logan Airport. Any hospitality organization has its heroes—employees who have gone above and beyond the call of duty—and their stories should be preserved and shared. American Express distributes its Great Performers booklets to all employees worldwide.

### Larry's Chair

The Olive Garden restaurant also uses stories to teach employees the cultural value of service it hopes to communicate. At all new store openings when the corporate culture is being taught to new employees, the opening manager will usually tell a story about a customer named Larry. It seems that Larry came to an Olive Garden and found the armchairs uncomfortable for his significantly above-average weight. He wrote the company president a letter praising the food and complaining about the chairs. In response, the Olive Garden ordered and placed in each restaurant two Larry Chairs that have no arms. These chairs are discreetly substituted for the normal chairs whenever a person of extra girth comes into the restaurant. Needless to say, telling the Larry Chair story at an opening reveals a great deal about the company's service values and sends a strong message to the new employees about how far the restaurant (and they) should go to respond to and meet a customer's needs.

All organizations need stories, heroes, myths, and legends to help teach the culture, to communicate the values and behaviors that the organization seeks from its employees in their job performance, and to serve as role models for new situations. Most people love stories. It's so much easier to hear a story of what a hero did than to listen to someone lecturing about "customer responsiveness" in a formal training class. Not only are stories more memorable than some five arbitrary points listed on a classroom overhead, but the tales can be embellished in the retelling and the culture thereby made more alive. Tales of "old Joe" and what wondrous things he did while serving customers teach desired responses to customer concerns and reaffirm the organization's cultural values at the same time. Every hospitality organization should capture and preserve the stories and tales of its people who do amazing things, create magical moments, to wow guests. The effort will yield a wonderful array of inspiring stories for all employees and send a strong message about what the organization values and desires in its employees.

## Symbols

A **symbol** is a physical object that has significance beyond itself, a sign that communicates an unspoken message. Cultural symbols are everywhere in organizations. A window office, an office on the top floor, or a desk and office in a particular location communicate information about the status level and organizational power of the person within that transcends the mere physical objects involved. At Walt Disney World Resort, the Mouse Ears are everywhere. The plants are grown in mouse-ear shapes, the anniversary service pins are mouse ears, the souvenir balloons are ear shaped, the entrance to Team Disney is framed by ears, and Disney-MGM Studios landmark water tower ("The Earful Tower") has mouse ears on it. Mouse ears are subtly hidden everywhere around the property and serve as a constant symbolic reminder of where Disney began. Not even the employees know where all the mouse ears are, and a Web site is devoted to "Hidden Ears." Other symbols are evident as well, to communicate parts of the culture. The executive offices are in a building called "Team Disney" to represent the corporate value placed on the team concept.

## Rituals

**Rituals** are symbolic acts that people perform to gain and maintain membership or identity within an organization. At most hospitality organizations, all employees go through a similar training program. It is mainly informational; new employees learn the organizational basics and cultural heritage. But, like military boot camp or initiation into a sorority, it also has ritualistic significance because *everyone* goes through the experience upon entry into the company to learn and share the common culture. Most hospitality organizations develop elaborate ritual celebrations of service excellence. These can range from a simple event like a departmental pizza party to honor all those receiving positive comments on customer comment cards, to very elaborate Employee of the Year award ceremonies that resemble a major gala. The point

*Team Disney Administration Building. (Used by permission from Disney Enterprises, Inc.)*

is that what the organization celebrates ritualistically and how much effort it makes to celebrate tell the members a lot about what the culture believes in and holds valuable.

## Leaders Teach the Culture

Managers of effective hospitality organizations constantly teach the culture to their employees, reinforcing the values, mores, and laws. Strong cultures are reinforced by a strong commitment by top management to the cultural values. Ed Schein suggests that the *only thing* of real importance that leaders do is to create and maintain the organization's culture.[13] Davidow and Uttal make a similar point: "Leaders who take culture seriously are bears for internal marketing, selling their points of view to the organization much as they would sell a product or service to the public, with slogans, advertisements, promotions, and public relations campaigns. The largest single chunk of their time is spent communicating values."[14]

These leaders worship at the altar of the customer every day, and they do it visibly. They are personally involved in service activities. They back up slogans with dramatic, often costly actions. To instill values, they stress two-way communications, opening their doors to all employees and using weekly work-group meetings to inform, inspire, and solve service problems. They put values into action by treating employees exactly as they want employees to treat their customers.[15] They use rituals to recognize and reward the behaviors that the culture values, and they praise the heroes whose actions have reflected worthy cultural values. Other employees can use these hero stories as models for their own actions.

Ed Schein offers further insights about how leaders can embed the culture, especially at the time the organization is being formed.[16] In the beginning, the leader defines and articulates a set of beliefs and assumptions about how the organization will operate. According to Schein, "At this stage the leader needs both vision and the ability to articulate it and enforce it."[17] Since new members join the organization with mixed assumptions and beliefs, the leader must carefully and comprehensively define the new organization's culture. Schein says, "It is intrinsic to the leadership role to create order out of chaos, and leaders are expected to provide their own assumptions as an initial road map into an uncertain future."[18] This process creates the definition of the corporate culture, embeds it in the organization's consciousness, and shows what behaviors are reinforced. Whatever the leader responds to emotionally or with great passion becomes a powerful signal to which subordinates also respond. Thus, during the period of an organization's creation, the leader must spend some thoughtful time defining what is important, how the organization's members should interpret the world they face, and what principles should guide their actions. Once the organization's culture is in place, the leader constantly adjusts and fine-tunes it as markets, operating environment, and personnel change.

Schein suggests that leaders can use five primary mechanisms to define and strengthen the organization's culture: "(1) what leaders pay attention to, measure, and control; (2) leader reactions to critical incidents and organizational crises; (3) deliberate role modeling, teaching, and coaching by leaders; (4) criteria for allocation of rewards and status; (5) criteria for recruitment, selection, promotion, retirement, and excommunication."[19]

### Setting the Example

Bill Marriott, Jr., provides a good example of how a leader can help to sustain the culture. He is a constant teacher, preacher, and reinforcer of the Marriott cultural values of guest service. He believes in staying visible. He flies more than 200,000 miles every year to visit his many operations and to carry the Marriott message visibly and personally to as many people as he can.[20] He is famous for dropping in at a hotel and chatting with everyone he sees. He has been known to get up early in the morning and wander into the Marriott kitchens to make sure the pancakes are being cooked properly. This intense commitment to personal contact with each and every Marriott employee and visible interest in the details of his operations have become so well known among the Marriott organization that his mere presence on any Marriott property serves as a reminder of the Marriott commitment to service quality.

Southwest Airlines is also famous for this hands-on commitment to service. Herb Kelleher was the premier example of quite literally walking the walk through airports, planes, and service areas to show employees his concern for the quality of each customer's experience.

Even today this tradition lives on as all Southwest managers are expected to spend time in customer-contact areas, both observing and working in customer-service jobs. These actions send a strong message to all employees that everyone is responsible for maintaining the high quality of the Southwest experience. This same modeling behavior can be seen in the many hotel managers who visibly and consistently stop to pick up small scraps of paper and debris on the floors as they walk through their properties. Employees see and emulate this care and attention to detail.

Xerox has established a Customer Care Day for forty executives, including the CEO. One or two days a month, each executive becomes the "duty officer," personally handling and resolving any customer complaints coming into headquarters that day. These executives keep in touch with real customer problems and show by example the level of company concern with customers.[21]

A leading hotelier in Orlando has earned a reputation among his employees and fellow hoteliers alike as a can-do manager. A story is told about how he took a chance and bought a bankrupt hotel with very little money and a whole lot of courage. When he was seen mowing his own property's lawn, a legend was born that here was a guy who would do what it took to get the work accomplished. He reinforced the message by his attire. His typical working outfit was blue jeans and a polo shirt. His employees learned, by reputation and by deed, that this owner was ready to work at any job that needed doing. Since he also had a big sign on the interstate which could advertise different room rates for each night, he earned a further reputation as a relentless competitor. His strategy was to fill his rooms at rates that would allow him to capture his variable costs plus whatever else the market could bear. His flexibility in room rates and his nightly phone calls to his front-desk manager, asking about the percentage of rooms sold rather than revenues, sent a powerful message to his organization that its goal was *to fill the rooms every night.* By his own actions, dress, and style, he has been extraordinarily effective in teaching his employees at all organizational levels the cultural values and norms that he wants for his organization.

Hospitality managers must stay close to both their employees and their guests. Only in walking around can they see for themselves that the quality of guest experiences is high, that concerns of guests and employees are being met, and that everyone remains focused on the guest. Unlike the manufacturing industry, which can rely on statistical reports to tell managers how things are going on the production line, hospitality managers inform themselves about how things are going by staying as close to the point where the service experience is produced as possible. As Norman Brinker puts it, "There's no substitute for spending time with people in their own environment. You not only meet everybody personally, you are able to see and hear for yourself what's going on."[22] Many restaurant managers are told to meet every guest and to make as many table visits as possible to talk to them; hotel managers wander the lobbies to observe the reactions of guests; and retail-store managers monitor the looks on customers' faces to make sure the shopping experience is going well. All these strategies are based on the simple idea that the reason for the organization's existence and basis for its success is the customer. For good organizations, being out with the customer is an important organizational value and not just a company slogan, and managers from the top down must set the example. As most of them know, the pressures of day-to-day administrative responsibilities can easily push aside this fundamental ingredient in service success, so they build customer contact time into their schedules.

## Guests Teach the Culture

Hospitality organizations often have the added help of guests in teaching and reinforcing the values, beliefs, and norms expected of the employees. As Van Maanen reports from his observations of Disneyland Park,

> Ride operators learn how different categories of customers respond to them and the parts they are playing on stage. For example, infants and small children are generally timid, if not frightened, in their presence. School age children are somewhat curious, aware that the operator is at work playing a role but sometimes in awe of the role itself. Nonetheless, the children can be quite critical of any flaw in the operator's performance. Teenagers, especially males in groups, present problems because they sometimes go to great lengths to embarrass, challenge, ridicule, or outwit an operator. . . . The point here is that ride operators learn what the public (or at least their idealized version of the public) expects of their role and find it easier to conform to such expectations than not. Moreover, they discover that when they are bright and lively, others respond to them in like ways.[23]

## Culture and the Chart

Schein suggests that a leader can use other, secondary mechanisms to reinforce or define the organization's culture.[24] A leader can define the value of a functional area by placing that area at the bottom or near the top of the organizational chart. Placing the quality-assurance function near the top of the chart and requiring its manager to report to a high-level executive tells the organization that the leader values quality. The way in which the leader designs the organizational systems and procedures will also tell everyone in the organization a great deal about what is valued. McDonald's sends a strong value message through its quality checklist and by the procedures it uses to maintain its standards of cleanliness and to guarantee its customers the freshness of each hamburger it sells. McDonald's spends a great deal of money sending quality-control people out to individual restaurants to check on these key items, to let restaurant managers know what is important, and to make sure that customers get what they expect. All McDonald's employees know what's on the quality checklist and how seriously the organization takes these inspections, so the checklist helps to define the cultural values of cleanliness and quality.

## Culture and Physical Space

The layout of physical space is another secondary mechanism that can send a cultural message. For example, office size and location are traditional symbols of status and prestige. By putting the executive chef in the big office out front, the leader tells the rest of the organization that the chef plays an important role in the organizational culture and that producing food of high quality is an important organizational function. Finally, the formal, published statements of mission, purpose, and vision teach employees the philosophy, creeds, and beliefs by which the organization lives. Although some organizations may not say what they really mean in these public statements, the excellent hospitality organization will do so clearly, concisely, and consistently.

## Culture and Leadership Skills

The success with which leaders use these mechanisms to convey cultural values is a good measure of their leadership skills. When they concentrate on using them together in a holistic way, they can ensure that all mechanisms convey to employees a consistent set of cultural beliefs, values, and norms. Consistency is important as a powerful reinforcer of the culture. The more consistently used all these mechanisms are, the more powerfully reinforced the culture will be. Leaders must take care about what they say to ensure that the messages they send are intentional and explicit. What the leader gets angry or excited about tells everyone what is important. A leader who expresses outrage over a service failure caused by a careless employee sends a strong message to all the employees that good service matters. A story is told of how Bill Marriott, Sr., fired an employee on the spot for insulting a guest. When this story got around the organization, there was no question in anyone's mind of the guest orientation that Marriott valued.

### *At Southwest: Teaching Each Other*

Truly outstanding hospitality organizations also engage all their members in teaching each other the organization's culture. Good managers create the opportunities for this teaching/learning to happen. For example, Herb Kelleher and Southwest Airlines created a Culture Committee whose responsibility was perpetuating the Southwest Spirit:

> The Culture Committee was created to pull together people who exemplify Southwest's culture. Most of the original committee had ten or so years at Southwest and embraced Southwest's maverick, caring, irreverent way of doing things. They were all great in their individual jobs and were hand-picked for their creativity, expertise, energy, enthusiasm, and most importantly, Southwest Spirit. For the two years they serve on the committee, they engage in leadership activities that protect the company's unique and highly valued culture. Committee members have been known to visit stations with equipment and paint in hand to remodel a break room. Others have gone to one of Southwest's maintenance facilities to serve pizza and ice cream to maintenance employees. Still others simply show up periodically at various field locations to lend a helping hand.
>
> Their labor is really a labor of love; their payoffs are the relationships they build with other workers, the knowledge that they have sparked worthwhile and fun endeavors, and most importantly, the satisfaction of having been a vital part of keeping the Southwest Spirit alive.[25]

Another Southwest effort to promote the culture and the Southwest Spirit was the Walk a Mile in My Shoes program which encouraged people to use a day off without pay to shadow another employee doing another job. The program helped employees understand how their jobs fit together in making the organization work. They also created a Helping Hands program to get people to spend some time helping employees at other locations where the growth in traffic was overwhelming. All of these programs had multiple positive effects for the organization and its employees. They reinforced the togetherness of the "extended family" that Southwest believed was an important part of its cultural value system, allowed members to teach each other the culture norms of helping, caring, and having fun at work, and provided a strong visible expression of the cultural values that all employees were encouraged to share.[26]

## CHANGING THE CULTURE

The world changes and the people inside the organization change. The culture too must evolve to help members cope with the new realities which the organization faces. Even a culture that starts out with a strong customer orientation may change over time as the managers, customers, and employees change. No matter how good a job the founder did in defining the culture and getting everyone to buy into it, the next generation of managers must work, perhaps even harder, to sustain those cultural values that should endure while changing those that need changing. They have available, of course, all the tools discussed in this chapter to do this. The communication tools of symbols, legends, language, stories, heroes, and rituals need constant attention to sustain the cultural values in the face of changing circumstances.

### Storyboarding at Disney

Disney chairman Michael Eisner built on the strong cultural values that Walt Disney had created, while responding to his own different needs as a leader. Eisner affirmed the important cultural values and beliefs that should last while being willing to change behavioral norms, even those established by Disney himself, to accommodate new situations. One illustration of how he adjusted past procedures can be seen in his handling of *storyboarding*. Storyboards had for many years been the normal way of planning out all Disney projects. Walt Disney used storyboards to organize everything he did, from cartoons to theme park attractions. Basically, storyboarding is arranging a series of cartoon drawings, service experiences, or theme park attraction plans to tell the story of the movie, attraction, or whatever Walt was designing.

When Eisner first encountered the storyboarding technique, it frustrated him. He recognized that he comprehended the story line of a movie or a park attraction not by looking at pictures but by reading written scripts. Since the storyboarding format was visual, he had a hard time following it. But the creative culture of Disney Imagineers was based on storyboarding everything. Eisner felt he had to change a deeply ingrained norm of creative production without destroying the creative culture that Walt Disney had left behind.

Eisner tells how he modified the cultural norm without changing the underlying cultural beliefs, values, or Disney's legacy:

> I couldn't follow it [the storyboarding]. I'd go down there and they'd go through the storyboards. And you go through one storyboard and they'd bring in another storyboard. And I'd sit there for hours and I couldn't remember what was in the first storyboard. And it was a hard process for me to deal with. I'd been used to working in the script area.
>
> And I was a little critical of some of our animated films that had been done before Walt died. Because I think there were great scenes but a lot of scenes put together. But sometimes the art of the story [as he motions his hands back and forth in an arc in the air] didn't follow the way I was used to thinking about stories, or what I had learned in school about the construction of—the stories and all that. And I'd keep thinking about this.
>
> And every time I'd say: "How was it done in the past?" And I'd hear about Walt. He'd just be there and he'd jump up and down and he'd go back and forth between things and so forth. And Roy Disney [Jr.] told me a story about how he [Walt] sat on

his bed when he had the flu or the mumps or something and told the entire story of Pinocchio in the bed. *And I finally discovered they did have a script!*

And the script was in Walt Disney's head. We didn't have Walt Disney. And therefore we didn't have a single mind, tracking the entire movie. We had a committee of minds. And that was the problem. And now we do scripts.[27]

Eisner recognized and affirmed Walt Disney's creative brilliance; Disney could keep the entire story in his head and show it to others by storyboarding. But Eisner had to make a change that was important for him. He had the insight and skill to retain and build on the good parts of the culture while changing those which needed to change to accommodate the new circumstances and people.

## Carlzon and SAS

The most difficult task of all is changing an entire culture that is not service oriented. When Jan Carlzon took over Scandinavian Airline Services, he was confronted with tough labor unions, disheartened management, a stagnant market, and an obsolete corporate strategy. He knew that the only chance of survival was to change SAS into a customer-focused organization:

The change in employee attitudes was one of the most significant results of the SAS turnaround strategy. By stating that we would turn a profit by becoming a service oriented airline, we ignited radical change in the culture at SAS. Traditionally, executives dealt with investments, management, and administration. Service was of secondary importance—the province of employees located way out on the periphery of the company. Now the *entire* company—from the executive suite to the most remote check-in terminal—was focused on service.

. . . .

Beyond the attention to service, we were also able to stir new energy simply by ensuring that everyone connected with SAS—from board members to reservation clerks—knew about and understood our overall vision. As soon as we received approval from the board, we distributed a little red book entitled "Let's Get in There and Fight" to every one of our 20,000 employees. The book gave the staff, in very concise terms, the same information about the company's vision and goal that the board and top management already had. We wanted everyone in the company to understand the goal; we couldn't risk our message becoming distorted as it worked its way through the company.[28]

Carlzon had learned his lesson about the power of getting employees involved directly in the change process during his earlier experience at Linjeflyg, the Swedish domestic airline. His first official act after being appointed president of that airline was to call all the staff together in one airline hangar. He climbed a 15-foot stepladder and told them,

This company is not doing well. It's losing money and suffering from many problems. As the new president, I don't know a thing about Linjeflyg. I can't save this company alone. The only chance for Linjeflyg to survive is if you help me—assume responsibility yourselves, share your ideas and experiences so we have more to work with. I have ideas of my own, and we'll probably be able to use them. But most important, *you* are the ones who must help *me,* not the other way around.[29]

People left the meeting with a new spirit of enthusiasm and commitment.

Whether the culture was established by another leader and needs to be updated to accommodate new circumstances and new realities, or the culture is negative and needs to be recreated, the organizational leadership must use all available communication tools to make those changes. Or, if the culture is healthy and thriving, the leaders use the tools to keep it that way. As we noted at the beginning of the chapter, the most important job of the leader may be to frame the culture's beliefs, define its values, reinforce the appropriate norms of behavior, recognize and tell stories about those who personify what the culture should mean for the customer, and find every possible occasion to celebrate when the members make good things happen for their customers. If peerless service is important to the leadership and they tell the members so, clearly and without equivocation, the members who believe in that culture will do the right things to make excellent customer service happen.

## WHAT WE KNOW ABOUT CULTURE

Here are some principles about organizational culture that seem to hold generally true.

- *Leaders* define the culture (or redefine it if necessary), teach it, and sustain it. Doing so may be their biggest responsibility in the organization. Kelleher and Bartlett of Southwest Airlines believe that culture is one of the most precious things a company has, so leaders must work harder at it than anything else.[30]
- An organizational culture that emphasizes *interpersonal relationships* is uniformly more attractive to professionals than a culture that focuses on work tasks.[31]
- Strong cultures are worth building; they can provide employee guidance in uncertain situations where company policies or procedures are unavailable or unwritten.
- *Subcultures* will form in larger organizations. A strong culture will increase the likelihood of keeping the subculture consistent with the overall culture values in important areas.
- Sustaining the culture requires constant attention to *the means of communicating culture* so that they all consistently reinforce and teach the organization's beliefs, values, and norms of behavior to all employees.
- Excellent hospitality organizations *hire and retain employees who fit their culture and get rid of those who do not.* The fit between the individual and the culture is strongly related to turnover, commitment, and satisfaction.[32]

## *Lessons Learned*

1. Leaders define the culture for everyone by what they say and do every day, and by what they reward.
2. Culture fills in the gaps for employees between what they've been taught and what they must do to satisfy the guest.
3. To create a culture of success, celebrate success—publicly.

4. Leaders think carefully about how every corporate action ties into supporting the cultural values of guest service.
5. Leaders find heroes, tell stories, and repeat legends to reinforce the important cultural values.

## Review Questions

1. Recall any organization in which you were heavily involved as an employee or as a student.
   A. How would you describe the culture of that organization?
   B. What did the managers or leaders do or not do to cause the culture to be as you described it?
   C. What ideas in this chapter could the managers or leaders have used to improve the organizational culture?
   D. How does all that relate to managing the guest experience in hospitality organizations?
2. Why is culture such an important concept to guest service organizations? How does culture influence the guest experience?
3. What is the difference between a strong and a weak culture? What can a manager do to create a strong culture?
4. Does a culture exist whether a manager does anything about it or not?
5. Why is storytelling important to building and sustaining a strong culture?
   A. Give examples of stories you have heard that helped teach cultural values.
   B. How does all that relate to managing the guest experience in hospitality organizations?
6. "Walking the walk" is an expression that one hears in hospitality organizations in connection with the leaders. What are some possible meanings of the concept in the hospitality context?
7. See how many key terms and concepts in the first four chapters you can relate to Larry's Chair, starting in this chapter and working backward.

## Activities

1. Divide into groups. Come up with a list of what factors or aspects make up an *organizational culture*. Which characteristics are the most important?
2. Find a hospitality organization that has a strong, clearly defined service culture. You may work for one yourself or have friends who do. How does the organization create and sustain that culture? What training methods, incentives for managers and employees, and communications techniques are used to create and define the culture? If you know of an organization that has a weak, muddled, unfocused culture, talk about that organization, too.

## Case Study

### Doug's Fried Chicken

*W*ithin four years of assuming the presidency, Judy Hart brought Doug's Fried Chicken from a 2 percent market share to 20 percent. She was a risk-taking, innovative entrepreneur. She increased the chain from 400 outlets to 1,743 and rapidly expanded into 27 countries. "I've got to be involved in a continual go-go growth cycle. Because of my successful track record, the franchisees and the board go along with any programs I propose," Hart believed. Hart was flamboyant and sensational. She shifted the annual franchisee convention from Des Moines, Iowa, to New York. She moved headquarters from a converted post office into a new $5.8 million building.

Then one Friday afternoon, Doug's board of directors dismissed Hart from the presidency. "Judy," said chairman Doug Jones, "for a while we liked your 'full-steam-ahead' attitude. But you can't seem to slow down. You're trying to change too many things too fast."

The board elevated John Davis, vice president for finance, to the position of president. Davis was a conservative, accommodating executive who watched budgets closely and believed in rigorously controlled expansion. He emphasized fiscal responsibility. Davis set up a centralized purchasing system (which Judy Hart had always opposed). Board Chairman Doug Jones was pleased; he considered Davis to be "in tune with the mood of the board and the franchisees at this point in time."

Judy Hart was unemployed over the weekend. Then she was enthusiastically hired by Berger's Burgers, a company that had achieved financial stability only in the last couple of years. Now they were in a strong cash position. "Judy," said Horace Berger, chairman of the board, "we think we're ready to take off. We want to triple the number of Berger's Burgers outlets within three years. Can you do it?"

"Can do, Mr. Berger," said Judy happily. "But first we've got to refurbish this tacky headquarters building and change the site of the annual convention. I envision a truly spectacular party for the franchisees in Las Vegas. . . ."

\* \* \*

1. How do you explain Judy Hart's unceremonious dumping from Doug's and her warm welcome at Berger's?

## Additional Readings

Denison, Daniel R. 1996. What *Is* the Difference Between Organizational Culture and Organizational Climate? A Native's Point of View on a Decade of Paradigm Wars. *Academy of Management Review* 21(3):619–654.

Goffee, Rob, and Gareth Jones. 1996. What Holds the Modern Company Together? *Harvard Business Review* 74(6):133–148.

Lundberg, C., and R. Woods. 1991. Modifying Restaurant Culture: Managers as Cultural Leaders. *International Journal of Contemporary Hospitality Management* 2(2):4–12.

Schneider, B. 1980. The Service Organization: Climate Is Crucial. *Organizational Dynamics* 8(3): 52–65.

Van Maanen, John. 1992. Displacing Disney: Some Notes on the Flow of Culture. *Qualitative Sociology* 15(1):5–35.

## Notes

1. *Walt Disney: Famous Quotes.* 1994. Printed for Walt Disney Theme Parks and Resorts, 80.
2. Jane Kuenz. 1995. Working at the Rat, in *Inside the Mouse: Work and Play at Disney World* (Durham, NC: Duke University Press), pp. 108–109.
3. Leonard L. Berry. 1999. *Discovering the Soul of Service* (New York: The Free Press), p. 38.
4. For further information on adapting the culture ideas of other organizations, see Jennifer A. Chatman and Karen A. Jehn. 1994. Assessing the Relationship Between Industry Characteristics and Organizational Culture: How Different Can You Be? *Academy of Management Journal* 37(3):522–553.
5. Kevin Freiberg and Jackie Freiberg. 1996. *Nuts! Southwest Airlines' Crazy Recipe for Business and Personal Success* (Austin, TX: Bard Press), p. 154.
6. For more information on this point, see William H. Davidow and Bro Uttal. 1989. *Total Customer Service* (New York: Harper), pp. 96–97.
7. Edgar H. Schein. 1985. *Organizational Culture and Leadership: A Dynamic View* (San Francisco: Jossey-Bass), p. 9.
8. The definitions in this section are indebted to Harrison M. Trice and Janice M. Beyer. 1993. *The Cultures of Work Organizations* (Englewood Cliffs, NJ: Prentice Hall), pp. 33–34.
9. Schein, 51.
10. John Van Maanen. 1989. The Smile Factory: Work at Disneyland, in Peter J. Frost et al., eds., *Reframing Organizational Culture* (Newbury Park, CA: Sage Publications), p. 66.
11. *Inside the Mouse,* 143.
12. Ibid., 133.
13. Schein, 2.
14. Davidow and Uttal, 48.
15. Ibid., 107.

16.  Schein, 317–320.
17.  Ibid., 317.
18.  Ibid., 318.
19.  Ibid., 224–225.
20.  Karl Albrecht. 1988. *At America's Service: How Your Company Can Join the Customer Service Revolution* (New York: Warner Books), p. 130.
21.  Alan G. Robinson and Sam Stern. 1997. *Corporate Creativity: How Innovation and Improvement Actually Happen* (San Francisco: Berrett-Koehler Publishers), p. 209.
22.  Norman Brinker and Donald T. Phillips. 1996. *On the Brink: The Life and Leadership of Norman Brinker* (Arlington, TX: Summit Publishing Group), p. 191.
23.  Van Maanen, 70–71.
24.  The discussion of secondary mechanisms is indebted to Schein, 237–242.
25.  Freiberg and Freiberg, 165–166.
26.  Ibid., 166–172.
27.  David M. Boje. 1995. Stories of the Storytelling Organization: A Postmodern Analysis of Disney as '*Tamara*-land.' *Academy of Management Journal* 38(4):1023.
28.  Jan Carlzon. 1987. *Moments of Truth* (New York: Ballinger), pp. 26–27.
29.  Ibid., 11.
30.  Freiberg and Freiberg, 145.
31.  John E. Sheridan. 1992. Organizational Culture and Employee Retention. *Academy of Management Journal* 35(5):1052.
32.  Charles A. O'Reilley III, Jennifer Chatman, and David F. Caldwell. 1991. People and Organizational Culture: A Profile Comparison Approach to Assessing Person-Organization Fit. *Academy of Management Journal* 34(3):487–516.

*There is something unique about a person who loves to serve others.*

# Staffing for Service

**Hospitality Principle:**

Find and hire people who love to serve.

*If someone isn't smiling during the interview, what in the world would make you think they will be smiling when faced with a line of customers all in a hurry for service, service, service?*

—T. Scott Gross, *Positively Outrageous Service*

*You don't need specific qualifications to work here. You just need to be customer-focused.*

—Go Airline receptionist,
fielding calls from prospective employees

## LEARNING OBJECTIVES

After reading this chapter, you should understand:

▓ The process of recruiting employees who will give excellent guest service.
▓ Internal and external recruitment strategies organizations use.
▓ Standard approaches and techniques for screening and interviewing job candidates.
▓ Employee skills, traits, and general abilities that have been found to lead to guest service success.
▓ The importance of a service orientation for *all* organizational employees, not just those on the front line serving guests.
▓ The importance of a diversified workforce to hospitality organizations.

## KEY TERMS AND CONCEPTS

| | |
|---|---|
| KSAs | selection |
| recruitment | structured interview |

A young family was visiting the Magic Kingdom. They had saved for some time to come to Orlando from their home in the Midwest and had planned carefully to make this trip truly memorable. They were spending the week in the Grand Floridian Resort, the most expensive resort on the property, and were enjoying their trip fully. One day, toward the end of their visit, they were in the Haunted Mansion attraction, and the little boy in the family lost his Mickey

*The Haunted Mansion. (Used by permission from Disney Enterprises, Inc.)*

ears during the ride. At the exit, the father displayed his obviously distraught son and asked the ride operator to look through the cars to see if the ears might be there. These weren't just a hat to this little boy; these were his prized possession, purchased on the first day of the visit and worn faithfully ever since. The ride operator looked. The ears were nowhere to be found, and the operator watched as hope died in the little boy's face and the father's concern grew.

The ride operator seized the moment, went across the walkway to a souvenir stand, took two Mickey hats, put one on dad's head and one, triumphantly, on the boy's. Management got a letter of thanks a few weeks later. The family spent a lot of time and money at the theme parks, but this one simple act by a truly committed hospitality employee made the trip memorable for this family.

## INTERACTING WITH GUESTS

In Chapter 3 we discussed how the service setting or environment helps create the "show" part of the guest experience. This ride operator illustrates the role of the hospitality employee in creating the show. Scott Gross devotes a significant part of his book *Positively Outrageous Service* to the importance of hiring and training people who can create the show. He believes a touch of spontaneous, unrehearsed showmanship can sometimes provide the margin of difference between a hospitality experience that merely meets the guest's expectations and one that is truly memorable. Hospitality "showpeople" engage guests in their performances and enable guests to capture their memories of the experience. Whether it is the waiter who bursts into unexpected song during a restaurant meal, the Avis bus driver who delivers a comedic monologue in the ride to an off-airport rental location, or the Disney employee who spontaneously turns a bad experience into a good show, the point is the same.

*Service With a Smile! (Courtesy of Darden Restaurants.)*

Employees who are recruited, hired, and trained to create a good show for the guests add value to the guest experience in important ways. First, they make the experience memorable and help keep the hospitality organization in the top of the guest's mind, increasing the likelihood of return or repurchase. Second, employing servers who interact with guests in this way creates a competitive advantage since no competitor can design into its service experience the same feeling of a unique and personalized show for the guest that the well-selected, well-trained employee can. Finally, the opportunity to provide a show for the guest is for the properly selected employee a terrific opportunity. An organization that encourages its employees to take every opportunity to be creative and individualistic with guests, play with guests, and use their showmanship tells employees that it appreciates their skills and trusts them to do the right thing with customers. For servers who sought the job partly for the opportunity to demonstrate their creativity and originality, this is a fun part of the job.

The people part of the show, however, hinges on recruiting and selecting employees who are willing and able to create these memorable moments and to engage guests in a unique way that enhances rather than detracts from the guest experience. Of course, not every employee is comfortable in a showmanship role, and not every employee need be. Many employees can be creative and original in more conventional ways, and every hospitality organization needs them as well.

## LOVING TO SERVE

There really is something different about outstanding hospitality employees like the Haunted Mansion ride operator. In his book *Positively Outrageous Service,* Scott Gross calls these people "lovers" because they love to provide great service. These are the employees who can provide their guests with a "feel good" level of service. It feels good because the server somehow connects with the guest in a way that builds a relationship. Though very brief, this relationship somehow makes the guest feel good about that guest experience and believe that something is special and memorable about it. The challenge for hospitality organizations seeking excellence is to find and hire these people.

Gross estimates that people who love to serve represent only one in ten of the available workforce. As he states, "Ten percent can't get enough of their customers. Five percent want to be left alone. When it comes to customers, the vast majority can take 'em or leave 'em."[1] If Gross's percentages are accurate, he raises two major challenges for hospitality managers. First, they need to work hard at developing a process that will systematically find, recruit, and select those ten percent who are truly committed to providing excellent service. Second, they must work even harder to develop an effective process for showing the rest how to provide the same quality of service that the naturals do naturally. Because naturally talented people are so rare in the labor pool, the organization must identify what skills are lacking in the people they do hire and train them in those skills.

Given the challenges of recruiting and hiring good employees in the hospitality industry, some organizations are tempted to place the "lovers" in the guest-contact jobs and hire the rest for support jobs that don't have direct contact with the guest. Since not all jobs in hospitality organizations require extensive guest contact, putting people not naturally good at service in these behind-the-scenes jobs might seem like a way out. The truly excellent organizations, however, recognize the fallacy of this reasoning. They know that all employees are somehow involved in serving either external paying guests or internal fellow workers. Knowing that service effectiveness depends on everyone throughout the organization taking service responsibility seriously, these outstanding organizations try not to hire anyone unwilling or unable to provide outstanding service. There is simply no longer a place to hide the "trolls" who may be outstanding technically but have no service skills.

Though many hospitality organizations try to "select the best and train the rest," those at the top have gained a competitive edge by developing recruitment, training, and placement programs that motivate all employees to provide outstanding service for customers, both external and internal. It all begins with recruitment and selection. If the organization can somehow attract and select the best potential employees, then it will gain a significant advantage over those organizations that do not systematically seek out and find these guest-focused people. This chapter covers recruitment and selection. Chapter 6 will address training and development.

## EMPLOYEE RECRUITMENT

### Hiring Internal Candidates

Jobs can be filled either from inside the organization or outside. If suitable internal candidates are available, most organizations prefer inside recruitment for several reasons.

#### The Known Quantity

First, the internal candidate is a known quantity. That person's performance has been available for observation and evaluation every day, and the person's strengths and weaknesses are known. Some people interview well and some poorly, so organizations can make mistakes about outsiders. But the good and bad qualities of a person observed every day become evident. Perhaps even more importantly, the present employee has shown loyalty to the organization by staying on and seeking higher levels of responsibility and challenge. For these reasons, most organizations usually prefer a known person over an outsider. Because customer relationships are so important in hospitality organizations, promoting current employees who have proven successful in their job performance and are also familiar with the organization's customers makes even more sense.

#### Internal Equity

The second reason for internal hiring is internal equity. Many hospitality organizations employ people from varied backgrounds and with different levels of training and education. All new employees except those in technical or highly specialized areas start at the same entry-level point and then prove their commitment to service excellence if they wish to get promoted. These employees learn that commitment to service and mastery of the job earn promotions, not where you went to school or what degree you earned. At a hotel front desk, you might find a recent college graduate, an older person changing careers, and a person with a high school or technical school degree—all working side by side and all trying to impress the front-desk manager with their merits for promotion. If an outsider gets the vacancy at a higher level, these hard-working employees will not feel fairly treated. They helped the organization get to this point; now they aren't allowed to share the rewards.

Ritz-Carlton employees can see examples all around them that career advancement is a real possibility. The hotel chain wants its front-desk agents, servers, and bellmen to move up. Says human resources director Kevin Richeson (who started with the Ritz-Carlton as a server in 1990), "Hiring people to stay in those jobs doesn't make sense for the best quality of service. We hire people who can move up and be examples to others."[2]

### Experience

Another reason for giving the job to an insider is that the outsider may lack the service-related experience and understanding that entry-level jobs in the hospitality industry demand. The entry-level positions most often and most directly deal with guests. Since organizational success is based on service success, everyone starts at the bottom. This hiring strategy makes many hospitality jobs uncompetitive and unattractive for college graduates who have not acquired such experience through co-op or intern programs. While most graduates appreciate the need to take the entry-level jobs as an opportunity to prove themselves, many are unwilling to accept the relatively low starting salaries that hospitality organizations offer. The hospitality industry has, consequently, relied on growing its own from non-college talent or finding college students who are so committed to the industry that they will pay any price to enter it. In a tight labor market, this belief in the need to start everyone at the entry level has caused the industry some difficulty. Bright college graduates interested in the hospitality industry often have better options even in other service industries. The entry-level approach makes attracting MBAs and other advanced-degree holders especially difficult. In short, the hospitality industry has not yet discovered how to make itself really attractive to entry-level college graduates; these young people are not often willing to make the heavy financial sacrifice that the industry asks of them.

If the job to be filled is at the managerial or supervisory level, another experience-related point in favor of hiring internally is the belief that you cannot manage someone doing something you've never done. The core technology of hospitality organizations is providing service, and unless you have had experience in providing service, felt the pressure of guests in your face, and found ways to resolve guest problems on the spot, you don't really know what it's like. You are in the business of providing an outstanding guest experience and, as a manager, of establishing and sustaining a guest-focused culture within the organization, so you need to have real examples from your own real experience that help you tell your employees how to provide excellent guest service. Although hospitality experience and real-life examples can be acquired in one company and brought to another, the most relevant experience and examples are obviously those that are acquired internally, within the organization you work for.

### Knowing the Culture

Organizations like to hire or promote from within because much of the training in the organizational culture has already been done. Internal candidates already know the company's beliefs and values and have proven themselves comfortable in that culture. The cultural learning curve for new hires is substantially reduced when the organization promotes its own people as they already know the office political structure, the real corporate goals, and the real way things get done inside the organization. It takes time for new hires to figure out what the company really expects from them while internal candidates already know what management really believes in and rewards. As Len Berry puts it, excellent companies "hire entry-level people who share the company's values and, based on performance and leadership potential, promote them into positions of greater responsibility."[3]

## Internal Search Strategies

A pool of internal candidates can be created in several ways. Many organizations use job-posting services, hot lines, newsletters, or other communication means to let eligible employees know about job opportunities throughout the organization. Marriott has created an electronic version of the traditional job-posting service. It has built a comprehensive database of jobs and employees looking for jobs. When a Marriott hotel in Boston has a vacancy for a pastry chef, the manager can advertise for internal applicants through this on-line job-vacancy service. All present employees looking for new opportunities within Marriott can list themselves and their qualifications in this service. The Boston hotel manager can advertise for a pastry chef who is geographically nearby, has five years of experience, and is a graduate of a recognized culinary program. The computer program then produces a list of the top eligible and available candidates ranked according to the manager's criteria. The manager then contacts the leading candidates and explores the employment relationship further.

Such on-line, real-time job hot lines are quickly growing even more sophisticated. Some systems can now interface with college and university placement services, governmental employment services, and industry hot lines, permitting candidates to identify job opportunities with one stop on the Internet. The Internet has job banks where people can post their resumes and organizations can post job openings. The Marriott program, which began as an internal job posting and referral system for the thousands of Marriott employees across the world, is rapidly crossing the line into being an open listing available to both internal and external candidates interested in all open Marriott jobs.

## Hiring External Candidates

Not every job can be filled by an internal candidate nor do organizations always want to promote only from within. External candidates are desirable when the particular ability needed in a particular job is unavailable among existing employees or when an external viewpoint might help change a corporate culture that has become too inbred to consider new ideas. Many hospitality organizations must look outward for information systems skills that are not generally acquired through the experientially based internal-development career paths. While they would like to promote internal candidates, the technological revolution has happened so fast that the traditional in-house training processes have not been able to keep up. The hospitality industry increasingly looks to the more technologically advanced industries for potential employees.

The same phenomenon has occurred in finance where the increasing need to have employees skilled in asset-management and capital-budgeting techniques means that the traditional approach of growing the necessary skills internally doesn't work well enough or fast enough to keep up with the rapid pace of change. When a leading hotelier looks not to another hotel but to the blue jeans textile company Millican as his benchmark for an organization that knows how to produce a high-quality product, it suggests that the traditional internal strategy of "start at the bottom and grow your way to the top by watching others do it the way we've always done it" is becoming increasingly outdated.

## External Search Strategies

Several major external-search strategies are listed in Figure 5-1. In large hospitality organizations and in cities and towns where the tourism and hospitality industries dominate, all of

### Advertising

A message containing general information about the job and the organization is placed in various media, e.g., newspapers, radio, television. These media can have a local, regional, or national audience and can serve the general public or a specific segment of population.

### Associations and Unions

Many occupations have state, regional, or national associations that hold meetings, publish newsletters, and represent the interests of the occupation. Such associations frequently have job-placement units.

### Colleges and Secondary Schools

Organization members are sent to schools to meet with individuals or groups of students to provide specific information about the organization or the job and to answer any questions. They may also perform the first review of applicants.

### Employee Referral Programs

A word-of-mouth technique in which employees are provided with information about job openings and asked to refer individuals to the company. Often the employee is given a bonus if the individual who is referred is employed. Should the applicant be rejected, the employee is given a brief explanation.

### Employment Agencies

Contact is made with organizations whose main purpose is to locate job seekers. The company provides information to the agency about the job, which is then passed along by the agency to its clients. Clients can be either employed or unemployed. Agencies can be either public or private. Fees may be charged to either or both the client seeking a job and the company seeking applicants.

### Walk-Ins

Unsolicited individuals initiate contact with the organization. The number depends on such factors as the level of the positions open, the image of the company, the frequency of job openings, and the physical proximity of the labor market.

### Employment Events, Job Fairs, Career Fairs

A specially organized event to attract a large number of potential candidates to a specific location on a certain day to talk about and interview for jobs. These events can be held in conjunction with other organizations and may be in one's own labor market or in a distant location where unemployment is high. Job fairs are also increasingly being held in central business-district locations where any potential employee can talk to recruiters from sponsoring organizations.

**Figure 5-1** *Recruitment: External Sources. (Source: Figure adapted from* Human Resource Selection *Second Edition by Robert D. Gatewood and Hubert S. Field, copyright © 1990 by The Dryden Press, reproduced by permission of the publisher.)*

these strategies are important to provide the tremendous number of people that the hospitality industry needs. The smart hospitality organizations go where the growth is; that growth plus replacement needs add up to a big recruitment job. A major challenge for these hospitality organizations is how to build a qualified labor pool when the competition for employees is strong.

How can organizations provide outstanding service quality under such competitive conditions? They must make creative use of all the available external recruitment strategies to build a large and talented pool of applicants.

### Public Advertising

In addition to the typical newspaper help-wanted ads and the less typical ads in magazines and weeklies targeted to potential employees, aggressive recruiters use more creative means to reach people who may not read the want-ads, may not be thinking about changing jobs, or may not even be thinking about working. Just as marketers segment their markets to find likely candidates for their products and services, employment managers increasingly segment their markets to reach and attract job candidates. As seen in Figure 5-1, many recruitment sources may be useful to help find the employee segment that the organization hopes to reach. Disney, for example, put up local billboards and ran TV and radio ads suggesting that work in the parks might be just the thing for a retired person or unemployed mother not willing or able to work full time.

This type of public advertising can also attract interest from employees who are currently working for someone else. These people might not have thought about working for the advertising organization until they happen to see or hear the ad, which suggests an intriguing opportunity. If these people are at all dissatisfied with their current jobs, the possibility of interesting them in your organization becomes even greater. Even though they weren't looking for a job, the billboard or the television or radio ad can capture their interest.

Such public advertising can create problems. For example, having a sign in the front of a fast-food restaurant may be an efficient way to advertise for new employees, but it also sends a negative message to potential customers: We don't have enough employees, so our fast-food experience may be a lot slower today.

### Niches

Targeting specific segments of the labor market to identify potential employees is another strategy. Some organizations target high schools, minorities, handicapped associations, homeless people, or senior citizens. They structure the job opportunities and marketing to appeal to the needs and limitations of that particular segment of the employment pool. For example, many hospitality organizations find that some of their best employees are older, retired people, so they target that group. Retired seniors are often lonely, bored, and looking for something to do that will bring them into positive contact with other people. Many guest–contact jobs can provide this opportunity for them. Organizations that originally recruited older people because of labor shortages have often found to their pleasant surprise that their older employees bring an enthusiasm for helping and interacting with guests that makes them great employees.

### Professional Networks and Placement Services

Most hospitality organizations actively join professional organizations both to find good employees and to find good ideas about how to find good employees. The amount of movement back and forth across hospitality organizations causes these networks and services to be strong, accurate, and informative.

### Student Recruiting

An important strategy for finding the many people the hospitality industry needs is student recruiting. A number of different programs develop pools of potential employees among

**AT UNIVERSAL STUDIOS ESCAPE℠**

Want some dinosaur-deafening, bone-jarring, side-splitting, egg-scrambling, gamma ray-boosting fun in your life? Get a job at **Universal Studios Islands of Adventure℠, UNIVERSAL STUDIOS ESCAPE**'s amazing new theme park. There's nothing like it in Florida — the country — the world! Built around five fabulous islands, it is the theme park for the 21st century, with thrills that are beyond belief.

**Seuss Landing℠ • The Lost Continent℠ • Jurassic Park®
Toon Lagoon℠ • Marvel Super Hero Island℠**

**The Adventure Continues...**
# Job Fair
**Friday, March 5 • 4pm-8pm
Saturday, March 6 • 10am-4pm**

—— *Can't attend our Job Fair?* ——
**Apply in person Mon.-Sat. • 9am-6pm**

**UNIVERSAL STUDIOS ESCAPE**
Human Resources Building, 1000 Universal Studios Plaza, Orlando
(Take Turkey Lake Road, turn at Universal Studios Plaza)

You must be at least 16 years of age to apply for the following full-time, part-time and seasonal positions. Positions are also available at Universal Studios Florida®, the No. 1 Movie Studio and Theme Park in the World.

★ Culinary     ★ Admissions     ★ Parking & Transportation
★ Travel Reservationists     ★ Ride & Show     ★ Merchandise/Games
★ Tour Guides     ★ Park Services/Custodial     ★ Food & Beverage
(Day & Night Cleaners)

# JOB HOTLINE 407-363-8080
## www.uescape.com

**It's a big universe. Where do you fit in?**

*Hospitality Ad. (Courtesy of Universal Studios Escape.)*

young people who are either still in school or who have recently graduated. Being young, full of energy, and enthusiastic, students are often ideal hospitality employees. In addition, they come to the job with the anticipation of learning and growing and are therefore quite comfortable with structured work requirements and extensive training. The most common recruiting strategy here is the traditional campus visit by a company recruiter. The placement office schedules eligible students to meet with the recruiter and provides an interview space on campus. The recruiter may interview graduating senior applicants for full-time jobs or undergraduates for part-time jobs. A variation on this idea is the "Job Fair" where many employers come to the campus on the same date and set up booths where they can talk to potential employees.

Organizations can sometimes get students to work for them as part of a required school experience, such as co-op, internship, or work-experience programs. Most schools of business, some other academic majors, and many high schools and junior colleges encourage their students to get some real-world work experience while they are taking academic course work. The student not only makes some money to help cover education costs but benefits from seeing the practical application of classroom theory in the real world. This relevant work experience can add value to a college student's resume or high school student's college application.

The company also benefits from these programs as it gains access to an eager, young, energetic labor pool that does not expect a permanent employment commitment. The smart organizations, however, keep a close eye on these student employees and make sure that impressive student workers know of the company's interest. They offer them scholarships or put them in special work experiences that prepare them to be fully trained employees upon graduation. Unfortunately, not all organizations use these programs well, and they can work to the student's and the industry's disadvantage. Some short-sighted organizations place young, part-time students only in simple, quickly learned, highly repetitive, and monotonous jobs that provide little learning experience and even less personal growth. The fast-food industry has burned out many students in this way. Putting students in these jobs not only keeps turnover high but more importantly has discouraged many bright young people from seeking careers in the food-service industry. These companies have unfortunately taught many young people that the industry is full of jobs suitable only for "burger flippers."

Enlightened organizations, taking a longer view of the need to get and keep young people interested in the hospitality industry, have designed their work-experience programs to provide some real learning opportunities and growth challenges. The point is that student-recruitment programs can be designed and used not only to get good employees who learn, earn, and contribute to the business today but also employees who will be eager to stay in the industry tomorrow upon graduation. The best organizations know how to use these work-experience programs to identify the better students and keep them after they graduate. Since many of these same organizations also place a high premium on "dues paying," these programs give the students the opportunity to pay their dues in these entry-level jobs while they are still in school and put themselves in a better position for promotion to higher-level and better-paying jobs by the time they graduate.

The Disney College Program is probably the most widely known illustration of such a work-experience or intern program.[4] Recruiters from Walt Disney World Resort go around the globe to interview and recruit college students who wish to spend a semester working and learning at Disney. Every year several thousand students from over 130 different colleges and universities across the world participate in this program. It is run in cooperation with the participating schools so students frequently earn academic credit from their home institutions during their semester in Orlando. They are provided housing, a working role to play as a Disney cast member, and a classroom-based educational experience, including course work in Disney management techniques and marketing strategies. Students are awarded a "Ducktorate" upon completion of the semester. The experience is positive for both Disney and the student. Disney wins as the student works in the parks to help alleviate a chronic labor shortage for qualified people at peak times, and the student wins by gaining the opportunity to learn how to create magic in an internationally acclaimed hospitality organization. The students have fun and get valuable work experience to put on their resumes.

Other versions of college recruiting are available through co-op, intern, and other work experiences that many colleges and universities require of their students. Helped by the current federal funding emphasis on school-to-work programs, the hospitality industry has found these programs to be an effective way to provide opportunities to attract and interest the large number of new employees required by this industry's growth rate while reducing the immediate challenge of finding enough employees. Many colleges, junior colleges, and high schools offer hospitality programs that include a required work experience, and many organizations have been quite successful in recruiting these students. They are young, full of energy, and enthusiastic; they make ideal hospitality employees.

### Employee Referrals

Another large source of employees for many hospitality organizations is referrals by current employees. The easiest way to get the kind of new employees you want is to ask your star employees to find them. Your good employees know what your organization is like, perform well in it, obviously like working for you, and can therefore be your best recruiters and spokespersons in the labor market. A bonus of this strategy is that existing employees who bring in their friends feel responsible for them and their performance. They exert positive peer pressure and encourage the new employees they sponsored to do well, to the organization's benefit. Some organizations pay a bounty to their existing employees if they bring in a job candidate who is hired and stays through a probationary period. The reward might be monetary, or it could be something else that has value to employees such as a free weekend trip to a nice resort area, dinner at a special place, or some other inducement.

### Employers of Choice

A company's reputation can also aid in recruitment. As Benjamin Schneider and David Bowen note, employers who have a positive image in the community and a satisfied and motivated workforce have a deep applicant pool from which they can pick the best.[5] These "employers of choice," as Berry calls them, are good neighbors to the community and have established their reputation for hiring and developing people for the long term. Their mentality is to "recruit and hire well, offer a viable, expandable job, and expect most people to be productive, long-term employees. Invest in these people rather than save on those who leave."[6] In other words, hold out for the best employees, invest in those people so they grow and develop, keep them challenged and motivated in their current jobs, and offer them future opportunities with the organization. Selling an employment opportunity is like selling the guest experience itself. If the company is known for offering its people high-quality job and career opportunities, it will attract high-quality applicants and build a pool of people who prefer to work for it rather than the competition.

Southwest Airlines provides an excellent example of how a company can establish an exceptional community reputation. In addition to providing multiple educational programs and opportunities that have earned it the reputation for growing and developing its people, Southwest has spent much time and money making itself into a good neighbor. It strongly supports United Fund drives, gives to community organizations, and encourages its employees to be community volunteers. It employs many people who derive great satisfaction out of working for the company and enthusiastically tell their friends. Even when the labor market is tight, Southwest still has a rich labor pool. Being a good neighbor enhances the company's positive reputation among potential employees, and motivated and satisfied employees tell their friends that this is a great place to work

### Walk-Ins

Some hospitality organizations also rely extensively on walk-ins. Here, they have a significant advantage over the manufacturing and industrial sector. A prospective employee curious about what goes on cannot casually walk into the General Motors assembly plant in Doraville, Georgia, to see and feel what it is like. Almost anyone can casually walk into a hotel or restaurant and get a pretty good idea of what it might be like to work there. Indeed, many Disney employees are people who fell in love with the place after visiting with family or friends. One employee said that, after visiting the Magic Kingdom with her family, she had planned for twenty years to work there. When her husband died and her children grew up, she sold her home and moved to Orlando to work in the parks because she wanted to be one of the people who made other people happy. Students in hospitality management programs tell similar tales of a great experience in a hotel, restaurant, or other hospitality organization that excited them about the industry. As a result of that experience, they found out what they wanted to do when they grew up. This type of experience-based enthusiasm is rarely seen or possible to acquire in the manufacturing sector.

Walt Disney World Resort intentionally located its uniquely designed Casting Center so as to be visible from Interstate 4. Drive-bys become walk-in job applicants. The triangles on its exterior are said to represent Walt's fondness for argyle socks. While no statistics are available, having a high-visibility building whose purpose is hiring people has obviously been an advantage

### Check the Competition

Scott Gross adds another strategy: Seek out excellent employees in similar service jobs elsewhere. Again, unlike the manufacturing sector where a potential employer is not going to be able to walk in and watch the best workers on the assembly line, watching customer-contact employees do their jobs in the hospitality industry is easy. Every time you receive service or watch someone receiving service, you can evaluate the server as a potential employee in your own organization. Gross hands his business card to those who really impress him and tells them to come see him if they are interested in another job. Hiring people because you saw them working well elsewhere has the additional advantage of starting off the new relationship on excellent terms. New employees found in this way will be flattered that you sought them out and asked. Everyone likes to be recognized, and if, by asking people to consider a job opportunity, you do a better job of recognizing them than their boss has done, you may very well land some excellent candidates. A variation on this strategy is to ask good people, whether they work for you or not, if they know about good people. A surprisingly

*Walt Disney World Casting Center. (Used by permission from Disney Enterprises, Inc.)*

large part of the existing workforce is networked with people who are like themselves or have similar jobs. Using the network to build a candidate pool can be a rewarding strategy. Carl Sewell's philosophy is similar. The people he wants to hire are not out of work; they already have jobs. He seeks them out by getting their friends to refer them to his Cadillac dealership because he believes that people who are truly good at providing outstanding service are probably friends of those who are also good.

### Call-Back File

This is a strategy whereby those who have entered the recruitment process but dropped out before they could be interviewed or screened are called back several months later to see if they are still interested. Many times people drop out because they have found another job. If the position has not turned out to be what they hoped for, they might now be interested. The feeling is that they were once interested and might be again.

## EMPLOYEE SELECTION

### Screening and Interviewing Applicants

#### The Application Form

Application forms are the first screen an employer should use in deciding who to hire. A typical application form will include the applicant's past employment history, education level, possible conviction record, and similar demographic questions. The form should provide enough information to permit reasonable decisions about who to keep in the pool and who to drop. Obviously, a major trade-off is involved here. The recruitment strategy should be designed to bring in as many legitimate candidates as possible. The advertising should state what qualifications, work experience, or training are minimum requirements for employment. The application form serves as a preliminary check on whether or not the candidates do in fact have bona fide occupational qualifications. They should really be bona fide to ensure that they do not lead unfairly to discriminatory hiring practices.

Sometimes the application form can be built into a telephone application system. Applicants are encouraged to call a job hotline to find out about job openings and apply for those that interest them. A telephone application-and-screening process collects basic information about the candidate. If the information matches the organization's predetermined criteria, the automated interview ends with a request for a faxed or mailed resume. Sophisticated optical character recognition (OCR) systems can even scan the resumes, evaluate each candidate's suitability for the job, and have the summarized information ready for the employment manager the next time that person looks. These systems allow the employment function to operate twenty-four hours a day, seven days a week; they guarantee that any applicant at any time will have an opportunity to be heard by the organization. Increasing numbers of people are working nontraditional hours. These "24/7" automated recruiting systems, just a phone call away from all potential applicants and particularly useful for people who may not be able to call during the usual work day, are a comparative advantage for those firms using them.

### The Interview

If the applicant passes the initial screen, the organization will most often schedule an interview to determine if the information on the application checks out, if the applicant seems to fit the organization, and to tell the candidate what the job actually is to weed out applicants who do not really want to do this type of work.

Disney has set up the entire interviewing process at Walt Disney World Resort in the same way they would design an attraction. To enter the Casting Center, the applicant goes up a ramp similar to those that handle lines inside the park; in fact, the ramp is designed to handle as many as 1,000 applicants per day. Candidates are shown into a room where they watch a twelve-minute film, which serves as the pre-show of the actual interview. This film is designed to provide candidates with a realistic preview of the jobs they are likely to have and also to make sure that the candidates are exposed to some basic employment information such as pay, attendance requirements, transportation, and personal appearance and grooming norms. If, after seeing the film, the candidate is still interested in a job, an interviewer will further explain Disney job opportunities and work expectations, while trying at the same time to ascertain if the candidate would be a likely fit for the organization. If not interested, as is true of 10 to 15 percent of applicants, the candidates will self-select themselves out, thereby saving interviewer time and company money.

Hospitality organizations should try to maintain good relationships with all applicants. They may need them in the future and, after all, they are potential future guests as well.

### The Background Check

Once a candidate gets to the point of hiring, a police or background check will generally be conducted. Most hospitality organizations do these checks routinely to protect themselves and their guests. Obviously, a hotel's baby-sitting service must avoid hiring convicted child molesters. Indeed, no organization that sends its employees out unsupervised to provide a service can afford to assign someone who has not been thoroughly checked out. Even if services are provided on the organization's premises, a background check is critical because employees are dealing directly with customers, with *people*. The hospitality industry is quite different from the manufacturing sector in this regard. A car doesn't care if a former car thief is part of the assembly team, but a hotel guest will care a great deal if the bellman or housekeeper is a former professional thief. Learning that you've hired a person who could do damage to your organization is not only embarrassing; much worse are the legal cases that can arise if a customer sues you for not exercising due diligence in your hiring practices.

### Sewell's Approach

Although training and education are important, prior work experience may be more so. Cadillac dealer and author Carl Sewell always finds out how well people have performed on the job, figuring that if they've performed well in the past, they'll probably perform well in the future. His rule of thumb is to interview twenty-five people to find the one he wants to hire. He would really like to interview 100 people to find the truly exceptional employee, but that would take too much time. But if he has not talked to twenty-five applicants, he feels he has not interviewed hard enough. In a competitive labor market, a more realistic rule of thumb is interviewing four people to find one good entry-level candidate.

In his interviews, Sewell seeks to measure candidates on five different dimensions: history of success, intelligence, energy (he likes people who fidget and move around a lot in the interview, who were athletes, or who have active hobbies), character (he checks references, requires drug exams, and does a credit check), and fit (he wants people who can get along with his other employees).[7] Others believe it is too hard to measure energy and personality in an interview and focus instead on less subjective characteristics.

### Servers Are Different

The reality is that the successful hospitality employee is different from the successful traditional manufacturing employee, and the selection interview must take the difference into account. The manufacturing employee needs certain job skills, so the interview will focus on identifying the ability to do that task. Frontline hospitality employees must be able to do the task, but they also need interpersonal skills to relate to the guests and creativity skills to fix service problems when they occur. The manufacturing employee can be quite confident that each car on the assembly line is essentially the same as every other car when it reaches the work station. The assembly-line worker can also rely on the quality-control inspector to catch any errors before the car is shipped to a dealership. Hospitality employees deal not with fairly identical products but with all types of guests who have all types of personalities, expectations, and needs. They and their guests serve jointly as their own quality-control inspectors. Employees must respond quickly, appropriately, and creatively when the organization fails the guest in some way. The nature and critical importance of each aspect of service delivery make it essential to assess the applicant's attitude and personality before that person is hired and put out in front of guests.

## The Structured Interview

Most writers believe that interviewing should follow a structured pattern. **Structured interviews** increase the likelihood that interviewers will assess all candidates according to the same criteria. When large numbers of interviewers interview large numbers of candidates, consistency becomes both organizationally and legally important. A structured array of questions ensures that the interviewer collects the necessary personal and job-related data. Probing questions (e.g., "Tell me about yourself and why you're interested or qualified for this job") can sometimes add valuable information. They can also yield information that differs in quality and amount from candidate to candidate because of interviewer differences in ability to ask and interpret appropriate questions.

A properly designed and administered structured interview ensures that the questions are job related, consistently scored, and asked of all candidates. Research shows that such an interview can be a valid predictor of job performance.[8] Typically, a structured interview will include questions that address critical incidents, work competencies, and willingness to do the job as designed.

### Critical Incidents

A potential restaurant employee might have to respond to a hypothetical guest who asks, "What is that fly doing in my soup?" For a hotel job candidate, the situation might be that a guest has arrived late on a night when the hotel is only half full. The interviewer might ask how the prospect would answer the question, "How much is a room?" Since most hotels give desk agents some latitude in this situation, based on such factors as how full the hotel is or the time of day or night, the candidate's answer would be a good test of how well the candidate understands the hotel business.

Scott Gross gives his prospective employees "Scott's No Fail 10-Percent Finder" test. He asks the people he interviews, "How many times in the past six months have you felt it necessary to get tough with a customer? Tell me about the worst incident."[9] He believes the three basic answers can tell him whether his potential employee is one of the 10 percent who love to serve, one of the 85 percent who is average, or one of the 5 percent who doesn't have any interest in giving good service. If the candidate says something like, "About twice a month, a customer tries to push me around, and I tell the blankety-blank off," he crosses that person off his list. If the candidate says, "I try to keep in mind that the customer is always right, but every now and then you get somebody who tries to take advantage and you have to throw this rule out the window," he knows he is dealing with a member of the great majority. If the candidate tells Gross, "I've learned never to get tough with a customer. The customer is always our guest, and even if the customer is wrong, I try to smooth the situation over," he knows he has found a member of the special 10 percent.[10]

### Work Competencies

The second group of questions that should be included in a structured interview are those related to work competencies. The interviewer would assess the competence of an applicant for a hotel front-desk position by asking specific questions about check-in and checkout procedures and processes. While hotels use different software systems and vary the routine somewhat, the steps of checking guests in and out are basically the same across all hotels. This part of the interview can be objectively scored, based on the candidate's correct and incorrect responses to job-related questions.

### As Designed

The third type of question in a structured interview should focus on the candidate's willingness to do the job as it is designed. The interviewer asks questions about such things as the applicant's willingness to work overtime, long shifts, or weekends. Many hospitality workers have to work when others do not. If candidates can't or won't be available when needed, then they are probably not a good fit.

## Choosing the Right People

Once the recruitment and interview processes have taken place, selecting the right people from the applicants attracted to the organization becomes the next critical step in ensuring that the organization gets the employees who will provide the level of service the organization expects. Ben Schneider and Dave Bowen note in their book *Winning the Service Game* that companies truly striving for service excellence need to seek out and hire people who have the motivation and interpersonal competence demanded by the market, who have or can learn the skills needed to be competent at the technical aspects of the job, who can effectively cope with the emotional strains associated with personal-contact service work, and who can package these motivations and capabilities in ways that reveal a seamlessness to their behavior when performing their work.[11]

In other words, the people hired should be able to offer the quality of service that guests expect. They should be able to handle the stress of providing service, especially when a service failure occurs. They must handle failure smoothly and successfully enough to satisfy the guest. Finally, they must act in such a way that each and every guest feels specially treated, safe, and secure.

## KSAs

Recruiting and selecting only those people who meet all these requirements is not easy. In fact, selecting the best person for the job should begin by first looking not at the applicants but at the job itself, to determine what employee abilities and characteristics it requires. A careful, thorough job analysis allows the organization to identify the exact job specifications and required competencies for each job classification and type. A job analysis will tell you if you need physically strong people to assist park visitors into a ride, skilled lifeguards to keep people safe in the water parks, or multilingual people to speak to foreign customers.

---

### *Online Advertisement for Casino Server with KSAs*

*Job Description:* Responsible for coordinating entire section and communicating with front- and back-of-the-house personnel to provide a dining experience that meets or exceeds guest expectations. Processes guest orders to ensure that all items are prepared properly and on a timely basis.

*Qualifications:* Must be able to speak and understand English; must be able to perform simple numerical calculations; willingness to learn proper operation of microcomputer.

*Physical:* Must have ability to stand and exert fast-paced mobility for periods of up to eight hours in length; must have good sense of balance, be able to bend, kneel, and stoop and have the ability to lift bus pans and trays frequently weighing up to 25 pounds.

Studying the job enables the organization to deduce the necessary **knowledge, skills and abilities (KSAs)** necessary to perform the job. Many organizations have spent considerable sums of money identifying the KSAs associated with each major job or job category and then have developed measurements to test applicants on the degree to which they have these KSAs. A carefully developed measurement process ensures that the tests are both valid and reliable to provide an effective and legally defensible means for putting the right candidates in the right jobs. Further, a careful job analysis to develop accurate selection measurements has the added benefit of identifying training needs and building reward structures that are directly related to the critical knowledge, skills, and abilities closely linked with job performance.

While the KSA approach is the most widely used strategy for selection in industrial organizations, using it in the hospitality organization is difficult because of service intangibility and the variability in guest expectations. Measuring the strength, height, and manual dexterity competencies necessary to build an automobile is far easier than measuring friendliness, ability to stay calm under guest criticism, integrity, and willingness to help—all necessary to provide excellent guest service. For this reason, many hospitality organizations follow this staffing principle: Hire for attitude and values; train for skill. From the guest's perspective, another way of expressing this idea is found in the hospitality saying, "Guests don't care how much you know until they know how much you care."

## Study the Best

The intangibility of the guest experience and the uniqueness of what each guest expects from it have frequently led hospitality organizations to use a secondary strategy for identifying good candidates: study the organization's best performers and identify the personal traits, tendencies, talents, and personality characteristics that enable them to serve guests successfully.

This approach attempts to define the necessary knowledge, skills, and abilities of successful people, instead of identifying the KSAs particular jobs seem to require. The logic of defining the KSAs in terms of the person instead of the job is that many parts of the hospitality job defy precise measurement or definition. Putting together a meaningful and useful job-driven KSA for a hotel general manager, a master chef, or an events coordinator would be difficult. If the job defies definition and proper measurement, then the best alternative is to study the people who have been successful in the organization and seek to determine the knowledge, skills, and abilities that allowed these people to become good at whatever organizational role they play. If these people succeeded through a hospitality career across all types of jobs, then perhaps there are some universal KSAs, competencies, personality characteristics, or innate talents that can be identified and accurately (and scientifically) measured. If so, then the successful job performers in each job category can serve as templates for hiring new people for those jobs.

In essence this is benchmarking against your own very best practitioners of the job. If you hire only employees who have traits, skills, abilities, tendencies, talents, and personality characteristics that are similar to those found in the current strong job performers, then they should be more successful than new employees who don't have those same characteristics. If you want to find a successful new job performer, find an existing successful job performer and hire someone as nearly like that person as possible. The trick, of course, is to discern the distinguishing characteristics that make strong performers succeed.

### Developing Talent Profiles

Many organizations have followed this strategy based on work by the Gallup Corporation, S.R.I., J.D. Power, and other similar organizations. They look at an organization's strong performers and, based on their talents, develop talent profiles for each major job category. Then they use these benchmark profiles to screen new applicants. For example, theme park ticket sellers have traditionally been hired and rewarded on their ability to handle large sums of money quickly and accurately. Careful analysis has shown that the best ticket sellers have additional talents. In effect, the ticket seller is the first point of contact between a theme park and its guests. Newly arriving guests are not typically knowledgeable about the many ticket package options and need to talk to a person who can quickly and easily identify what guests really want to do and then sell the most appropriate ticket package. The talents required of the employee who can do this well include having very good empathetic listening, interpersonal, and coaching skills in addition to the ability to handle large sums of money rapidly and carefully. The successful ticket seller is really something of a vacation planner. Once the talent profile of successful ticket sellers is identified, a reassessment of both the selection process and the reward structure for this job can be done.

The use of this approach could even be extended to looking at the mix of talents in entire departments. If an analysis of a particular department shows that the current composition of people does not include some vital talent for departmental success, the selection process can ensure that the person next hired will have an ample supply of the missing ingredient.

Marriott has used this basic approach to identify the competencies associated with success in its organization. The company defines competencies as the groups of knowledge, skills, and abilities that are needed to achieve the company's strategic vision. By reviewing existing high performers, Marriott identified seventeen competencies that are associated with high performance in the organization. Among them are the ability or skill to be an activator, developer, planner, innovator, and team builder, and having a service orientation.

### Competency-Based Approaches: Disadvantages

Competency-based approaches to selection have a few drawbacks. Designing them for a single job or single job category can be quite expensive unless the organization has a lot of people doing that job. While Marriott employs so many hotel assistant managers that developing a competency profile becomes worthwhile, an individual hotel may not believe that the considerable expense of having a professional survey organization come in to do this work can be recaptured in any selection efficiencies gained. Further, competency models often become outdated when technology and/or job expectations change. As the necessary competencies change, so too must the selection measures. Finally, many individual job-category competency measures are not interlinked with models in other parts of the organization. As Richard Mansfield says, it may be "difficult to compare the competency requirements of one job to the requirements of another job or an individual's competency assessments in one job to the requirements in another job."[12] Like Marriott, some organizations have developed a more generic competency measure, and that seems to avoid some limitations of the single-job measures.

Nonetheless, all competency measures are essentially anchored on the successful practitioners in the current organization. If the organization's success factors change over time, then the measures may become irrelevant. Finally, if the organization wants diversity in opinion, talents, and personalities to promote change and organizational growth, the use of existing executives to establish the norms for who should be hired in the future may impede the acquisition of diversity's benefits. To avoid these potential problems, competency measures should be considered as only one tool in the selection process.

## Other Approaches to Identifying Talented Employees

Regardless of KSAs, competencies, job analyses, and the rest, employees who are actually serving customers, clients, or guests should have certain general abilities.

### General Abilities

First, they must have an enthusiastic approach to life. Enthusiasm is contagious, and guests come to most hospitality organizations expecting to be served by employees who are enthusiastic about the service itself, the organization, and the opportunity to provide service. Most guests want and expect a feel-good guest experience that only enthusiastic employees can deliver.

The second ability is the control of one's emotions. Hospitality jobs require a heavy emotional commitment by the service providers. It is up to them to be upbeat, cheerful, enthusiastic, and genuinely interested in serving the guest, even when the guest is not reciprocally positive and even when they themselves don't feel upbeat or positive. Putting on a happy face when you yourself are having a bad day is difficult. Not everyone, no matter how service oriented, can make this heavy emotional commitment consistently. All hospitality employees have had guests who push to the limits their genuine commitment to providing service. Some positions require listening to complaining guests all day, and for most employees a point comes when they can endure it no longer. It may take a day, a week, or years, but this type of negative experience eventually exacts its toll on the employee and results in burnout. Sometimes it doesn't even take negative experience. Some employees burn out because they tire of doing the same job in the same way every day. Watch a fast-food server greet everyone with the same smile and the same affected cheery greeting and wonder how long that person has performed this same ritual. At some point most people switch into an automatic-pilot mode because they have lost the emotional commitment to treat guests with sincerity. Bowen and Schneider term this emotional commitment a *passion for service,* and they have developed a questionnaire for measuring it. More importantly, their research reports that a passion for service is highly correlated with positive service outcomes.

The third characteristic is that the hospitality employee should be polite, considerate, and willing to make a genuine effort to help other people.[13]

To put these three general abilities together would lead to selecting someone who can put on a consistent "show" in front of the guests, who cares about the quality of the performance and the guest's reaction to it, and who does it all with positive gusto.

### Psychological Tests

Psychologists have developed a variety of tests to distinguish one person from another along different dimensions. Tests of mental ability measure logical reasoning, intelligence, conceptual foresight, semantic relationships, spatial organization, memory span, and a number of other cognitive factors. Tests of mechanical ability, physical ability, and personality are also available. Organizations have used these tests with mixed results. Some measures of personality traits and behavioral predispositions have also been developed and validated for use in the selection process. One group of researchers reports that a service orientation is associated with gregarious and outgoing personalities who make a conscientious effort to help others.

Physical and mechanical ability tests are more easily shown to be valid predictors of later job success than mental or cognitive tests. Proving that an excellent typist must have the mechanical skill to use a typewriter and the eye-hand coordination necessary to type at an acceptable speed is easier than proving that a smart person is usually a better customer-contact employee than a dumb one. Personality and other mental measures are much harder to validate against successful job performance. What you really need to know to be a successful manager, or what personality type makes a more effective leader in a particular situation, are difficult questions to answer and even more difficult to prove. How much intelligence is required to be successful is even harder to specify. Even so, Norman Brinker says, "Look for people . . . who are smart. Remember, sinners can repent, but stupidity is forever."[14]

### Personality Traits

Recent research has indicated that personality can be reliably measured and summarized along five dimensions. They are:

1. *Extroversion*—the degree to which someone is talkative, sociable, active, aggressive, and excitable.
2. *Agreeableness*—the degree to which someone is trusting, amiable, generous, tolerant, honest, cooperative, and flexible.
3. *Conscientiousness*—the degree to which someone is dependable and organized, conforms to the needs of the job, and perseveres on tasks.
4. *Emotional Stability*—the degree to which someone is secure, calm, independent, and autonomous.
5. *Openness to Experience*—the degree to which someone is intellectual, philosophical, insightful, creative, artistic, and curious.

Of these five, *conscientiousness* is generally considered to be the most valid predictor of job performance.[15] In studies investigating the relationship between these five traits and service-industry success, three dimensions showed some important correlation: agreeableness, conscientiousness, and emotional stability. Employees high in customer orientation are friendly, stable, and dependable.[16] While these findings seem somewhat obvious, the implication of this research is that measures *do* exist which organizations can use to gain an indication of a potential employee's orientation to serve. Although more complete studies need to be done before any claim can be made about total reliability and validity for these measures, the fact that certain measurable and definable personality constructs are statistically associated with a tendency toward service orientation is useful information and confirms with research what the popular writers on services management have been saying. Some work has been done to identify personality characteristics of those who have a propensity to provide service. Specifically, Hogan, Hogan and Busch [17] and Frei and McDaniel [18] have proposed measures for identifying a service orientation in people.

Other types of psychological tests have been proposed as ways to assess job candidate characteristics. The key to their use is that they must be demonstrably related to job performance. Both Wet Seal and Burger King corporations have succeeded to a degree in using psychological tests to identify the more motivated candidates in the available labor pool. Others, particularly banks, have had some success using paper-and-pencil psychological tests to screen out people who are prone to stealing on the job. Nonetheless, these types of tests can be difficult to link directly with job performance, and the key criterion of any measure used to screen potential employees is that it discriminates on the right characteristics and does not discriminate on the wrong. By law, selection strategies may not unfairly disfavor those protected by antidiscrimination legislation.

## The Advantages of a Diversified Workforce

Beyond the legal and moral need to comply with antidiscrimination laws, however, contemporary hospitality organizations have three other very good reasons to foster diversity in their staff. First, thanks to advances in transportation and communication, a general state of economic prosperity, and the breaking down of many cultural and racial barriers, increasing numbers of their guests are from diverse cultural and demographic populations. In some service settings, these diverse guests expect that service providers will be similar to themselves or will at least understand the expectations of people like themselves. They want servers who "speak their language," figuratively and perhaps literally. Many large airlines try to hire multilingual flight attendants and reimburse attendants for taking language lessons or classes. United Airlines offers classes for flight attendants in "Air Spanish," "Air Portuguese," and "Air Japanese." They learn the 40 or so words necessary to greet, board, and serve native speakers of these languages and use a smile and hand gestures for everything else.[19] When the Opryland Hotel was preparing to host a large international meeting, it gave its 7,000 employees special training in international guest service. The grand training finale was an all-day international marketplace; employees won prizes by participating in post-test games while dining on international foods.[20]

Although no workforce will be as diverse as the broad cultural range of guests, staffing strategies should be designed to hire guest-contact employees sufficiently insightful to read cues indicating the expectations of guests from different cultures and backgrounds and flexible enough to meet those varied expectations.

A second reason for interest in diversity is that the hospitality organization's workforce may well be quite diverse without organizational attempts to diversify it. According to the Census Bureau, better than one in four people living in the United States are now racial or ethnic minorities. By 2015 the figure will be one-third. There is no longer a typical hospitality employee for whom the organization can design one-size-fits-all selection, training, and reward systems. Dual-career couples, same-sex relationships, single mothers with child care responsibilities, grown children with elder care responsibilities—all these and many others are apt to be represented in the hospitality organization's workforce. The manager of the modern hospitality organization must be sensitive to the needs of employees from these varied backgrounds and lifestyles.

The third reason is that employing a diversified workforce by tapping all available segments of the general labor pool will result in the best workforce. In a competitive environment like the hospitality industry, all organizations must hire the best employees, regardless of background, cultural heritage, or other differences. Finding qualified, talented, motivated employees is not easy; recognizing the factors that make effective employees and ignoring those unrelated to employee performance is imperative.

Some business organizations still do not fully appreciate the underutilized talent in many segments of the population. The best organizations gain a competitive advantage by seeking out and recruiting talent wherever it may be found. Recognizing and appreciating diversity can be a stimulus to developing innovative ways to recruit. Knowing that Orlando, Florida, has a large Moroccan population, a hotelier seeks them out. Since few other hospitality organizations recognize this group's size or bother to understand their proud cultural heritage, this hotel has gained a unique and valuable advantage by recruiting from this relatively untapped resource.

No matter how diverse the hospitality organization's workforce, the fact remains that guest-contact personnel will be different in most ways from the guests they serve. For example, most restaurant servers are younger than the patrons. The organization must hire people who are adept at interacting with the great variety of guests, who can take a reading of guest expectations during the first few moments of the service encounter, and who enjoy the challenge of providing personalized service to today's multicultural hospitality clientele.

## The Perfect Combination

While finding and hiring the right person is challenging for all organizations, it is especially difficult for those in the hospitality industry. Although many jobs require definable skills that can be identified, measured, and tested, the hospitality industry has the extra challenge of ensuring that the guest-contact employees they hire are not only competent in the task skills but also have the interpersonal skills necessary to interact successfully with the guests and the creative skills to fix the inevitable service failures. The difference between a good and great guest experience is so often the indefinable extra that the employee adds to the experience. Finding, hiring, training, and rewarding the employee who happily and naturally gives that extra is one of the biggest challenges for hospitality organizations.

## Lessons Learned

1. Find the best people; train the rest.
2. Recruit creatively; use the major search strategies, but try to think of others.
3. Build a large candidate pool; it will improve the odds of finding good people.
4. Carefully check applicants; are they the people you want serving your guests?
5. Know and hire the knowledge, skills, and abilities necessary to provide outstanding service.
6. Look for technical competence, strong interpersonal skills, and creative problem-solving ability.

## Review Questions

1. Why are hiring and promoting from within so popular in the hospitality industry? What are the disadvantages of that strategy?
2. Assume that you are in a tight labor market for entry-level employees.
   A. Do any of the recruitment strategies described in the chapter seem more or less appropriate under those circumstances?
   B. What innovative ideas do you have that might improve your ability to recruit outstanding entry-level employees?
3. Recruiting applicants is only half the task.
   A. Indicate several techniques you would use to select those you want to hire.
   B. Assume that you are hiring a server for a casual dining restaurant. What KSAs would you look for?
   C. Assume that you are hiring a hotel front-desk agent. What KSAs would you look for here?
   D. Are the front-desk agent KSAs different from those for the restaurant server?
   E. What problem-solving skills would you look for in either type of candidate?
4. Assume you are interviewing candidates for a position that involves selling your hotel to groups as a convention site.
   A. What questions would you ask of the candidates?
   B. What questions are you not legally permitted to ask? Why?
5. Do certain personality traits seem to be typical of the best hospitality employees who have served you as a guest? How do these traits compare with those mentioned in the chapter?
6. When Scott Gross meets good employees in other hospitality organizations, he gives them his business card as a means of suggesting that they might want to give him a call for a job interview.
   A. Do you have any problems with the ethics of this method, which is not uncommon in the business world?
   B. If a competitor sent someone into your employee parking lot to put job-interview invitations under the windshields, would you view that situation differently? Why or why not?
7. When Lone Star Steakhouse & Saloon needs staff, they print a large announcement on guest checks: NOW HIRING ENERGETIC OUTGOING SERVERS! What do you think of this technique?

## Activity

Find a hospitality organization that will tell you about its employee selection processes and procedures. How does the organization determine which recruits are likely to succeed as hospitality employees? What selection devices, if any, do they use? How well are the organization's predictors of employee success working?

## Case Studies

### Choosing a Manager

*T*he director of management development for the Long Stay Suites was faced with the necessity of recommending someone for a high-level management position in the company. Careful screening of all present employees narrowed the selection to two men: John Jarvis and Satya Patel. After lengthy interviews the following information was accumulated.

John Jarvis had a tenure with the company of three years. He was very seldom absent from work and had obtained a college degree in hospitality administration by taking evening courses. His superiors rated his management potential as promising. The one complaint voiced against him was that he appeared impatient and overly ambitious. During his interview with the director of management development, Jarvis indicated that promotions had not come along fast enough for him and that unless he received this promotion he would seek employment with another major hospitality organization. He hinted that he had received offers.

Satya Patel was several years older than Jarvis. He had been with the company since graduation from a nearby university six years previously. He was rated by his superiors as a steady, dependable employee, apparently very intelligent, but he had been given little opportunity to display his talent. Three years ago he had turned down a more responsible position at one of the organization's branches in another city. He said he didn't want to relocate, and the job required some traveling. Since that time he had not been given another opportunity to move upward in the organization.

In considering the recommendation he would make, the director of managerial development recalled a comment Patel had made during his interview: "I'm confident that you will recognize the importance of seniority when you make your final recommendation."

\* \* \*

1. Weigh the pros and cons of promoting Jarvis or Patel.
2. Which one would you recommend for the position, and why?
3. Ideally, what additional information would you like to have before making a recommendation?

### Regal Five-Star Hotel

*D*uring her first year as personnel manager of the Regal Five-Star Hotel, Margarita Gonzalez became increasingly aware of a possible morale problem among the housekeeping staff. Employee absenteeism and tardiness were rising. Coffee breaks were being extended beyond the allowed fifteen minutes. According to the grapevine, employees were not happy with working conditions or with the workload.

Although Gonzalez was aware that turnover had been rising, she was surprised to receive data indicating that it had exceeded 50 percent among the housekeeping staff over the past year. She reviewed the year's resignations. They accounted for 95 percent of the turnover. The other 5 percent were workers who had been terminated as unsatisfactory. Approximately

*25 percent of the resignations were women whose stated reasons for resigning were: "husband being transferred to another city" and "leaving to devote more time to home and family." Gonzalez viewed these resignations as beyond the hotel's control and ignored them. The remaining resignations occurred for four reasons, in the following frequency of occurrence: (1) left to get salary increase, (2) left to get greater opportunity for advancement, (3) left to get different type of work, (4) personal reasons.*

*Margarita Gonzalez reviewed the criteria for hiring housekeepers, from desirable to undesirable in the hotel's view: under 25; single or newly married without children; husband in armed forces or for other reasons temporarily in the area; divorced with children; early twenties to early thirties; family fully established; husband permanently employed in the area; children fully grown. The hiring policy was obviously designed to appeal to women who seriously needed an income but who did not need a high income.*

\* \* \*

**1.** How should Gonzalez change the Regal Five-Star Hotel hiring policies, if at all?

## Cruising Travel Agency

*Ho-Chien Lee is a manager at a travel agency that specializes in cruises. Among his other administrative duties at Cruising Travel Agency, he hires and trains entry-level employees.*

*The typical agency job applicant is fresh out of college, excited about the future of travel, and confident that some of the world's problems can be relieved if hard-working people have a chance to relax on a cruise. Most applicants understand that first travel-agency jobs are at the entry level. In return for these ideals and this ambition, the agency offers minimal training, little chance for advancement, considerable job security, low pay, and long hours at night and on weekends.*

*For several years, job applicants have been plentiful. In recent months, the number of applications has dwindled.*

*Lee recently expressed his concern to Mary Ammerman, sitting at the next desk. "Where are we going to get fresh new employees? How can we keep the good people we have at the lower levels? I can't for the life of me see why so many stay on at Cruising Travel. Of course, the best ones go somewhere else for more money and faster promotions. But I'm surprised that any of them at all stay. I wonder what they get out of it. And how can we help them to get more out of their jobs?"*

*Mary Ammerman said she didn't know. As a matter of fact, she thought to herself, she wasn't getting all that much out of her own job.*

\* \* \*

**1.** How would you describe the staffing situation at Cruising Travel Agency?
**2.** Do you think hospitality-related organizations like this agency make a mistake in hiring college graduates at the entry level?

## Additional Readings

Aston, Michael C. 1998. Personality and Job Performance: The Importance of Narrow Traits. *Journal of Organizational Behavior* 19(3):289–304.

Babin, Barry J., and James S. Boles. 1998. Employee Behavior in a Service Environment: A Model and Test of Potential Differences Between Men and Women. *Journal of Marketing* 62(2): 77–91.

Baum, T. 1996. Unskilled Work and the Hospitality Industry: Myth or Reality? *International Journal of Hospitality Management* 15(3):207–210.

Behling, Orlando. 1998. Employee Selection: Will Intelligence and Conscientiousness Do the Job? *Academy of Management Executive* 12(1):77–86.

Bell, Chip R., and Kristin Anderson. 1992. Selecting Super Service People. *HRMagazine* (February):52–54.

Berger, Florence, and Ajay Ghei. 1995. Employment Tests: A Facet of Hospitality Hiring. *Cornell Hotel and Restaurant Administration Quarterly* 36(6):36–42.

Boles, James S., Lawrence E. Ross, and Julie T. Johnson. 1995. Reducing Employee Turnover Through the Use of Preemployment Application Demographics: An Exploratory Study. *Hospitality Research Journal* 19(2):19–30.

Bonn, M., and L. Forbringer. 1992. Reducing Turnover in the Hospitality Industry: An Overview of Recruitment, Selection and Retention. *International Journal of Hospitality Management* 11(1):47–63.

Charles, Reuben O., and Kerr B. McCleary. 1997. Recruitment and Retention of African-American Managers. *Cornell Hotel and Restaurant Administration Quarterly* 38(1):24–29.

Cowling, A., and K. Newman. 1995. Banking on People: TQM, Service Quality and Human Resources. *Personnel Review* 24(7):25–40

Crafts, Dan, and Loanna Thompson. 1995. Career Advancement Obstacles for Women in the Foodservice Industry. *Journal of College and University Foodservice* 2(3):5–14.

Fischer, Eileen, Brenda Gainer, and Julia Bristor. 1997. The Sex of the Service Provider: Does It Influence Perceptions of Service Quality? *Journal of Retailing* 73(3):361–382.

Griffin, Robert K. 1995. Personality Characteristics and Their Relationship to Foodserver Performance. *Journal of College and University Foodservice* 2(3):31–42.

Guerrier, Yvonne, and Margaret Deery. 1998. Research in Hospitality Human Resource Management and Organizational Behaviour. *International Journal of Hospitality Management* 17(2):145–160.

Harrison, David A., and Joseph J. Martocchio. 1998. Time for Absenteeism: A 20-Year Review of Origins, Offshoots, and Outcomes. *Journal of Management* 24(3):305–350.

Kossek, Ellen Ernst, Melissa Huber-Yoder, and Domini Castellino. 1997. The Working Poor: Locked out of Careers and the Organizational Mainstream? *Academy of Management Executive* 11(1):76–92.

Ladki, Said M., and John J. Beasley. 1996. The Restaurant Industry: A Force for Diversity and Civil Rights. *Hospitality and Tourism Educator* 8(1):65–67.

LaLopa, Joseph M. 1997. Commitment and Turnover in Resort Jobs. *Journal of Hospitality and Tourism Research* 21(2):11–26.

MacHatton, Michael T., and Virginia C. Owens. 1995. Hospitality Internships: Opportunities and Obligations. *Hospitality and Tourism Educator* 7(3):31–36.

Morris, J. Andrew, and Daniel C. Feldman. 1996. The Dimensions, Antecedents, and Consequences of Emotional Labor. *Academy of Management Review* 21(4):986–1010.

Muller, Christopher C., and Douglas F. Campbell. 1995. The Attributes and Attitudes of Multiunit Managers in a National Quick-Service Restaurant Firm. *Hospitality Research Journal* 19(2):3–18.

Partlow, Charles G. 1996. Human Resources Practices of TQM Hotels. *Cornell Hotel and Restaurant Administration Quarterly* 37(5):67–77.

Samenfink, W. H. 1994. A Quantitative Analysis of Certain Interpersonal Skills Required in the Service Encounter. *Hospitality Research Journal* 17(2):3–16.

Schneider, B., and D. Bowen. 1993. The Service Organization: Human Resources Is Critical. *Organizational Dynamics* 21(4):39–52.

Simons, Tony. 1995. Interviewing Job Applicants—How to Get Beyond First Impressions. *Cornell Hotel and Restaurant Administration Quarterly* 36(6):21–27.

Siu, Vickie. 1998. Managing by Competencies—A Study on the Managerial Competencies of Hotel Middle Managers in Hong Kong. *International Journal of Hospitality Management* 17(3):253–274.

Sparrowe, Raymond T., and Pamela A. Popielarz. 1995. Getting Ahead in the Hospitality Industry: An Event History Analysis of Promotions Among Hotel and Restaurant Employees. *Hospitality Research Journal* 19(3):99–117.

Von Hippel, Courtney, et al. 1997. Temporary Employment: Can Organizations and Employees Both Win? *Academy of Management Executive* 11(1):93–104.

## Notes

1. T. Scott Gross. 1991. *Positively Outrageous Service* (New York: Warner Books), p. 159.
2. Robert Johnson. 1998. Who Says Service Jobs Are Dead Ends? *Wall Street Journal,* November 18:F-1.
3. Leonard L. Berry. 1999. *Discovering the Soul of Service: The Nine Drivers of Sustainable Business Success* (New York: The Free Press), p. 45.
4. For further information about the Disney internship program, see Pamela Roush, Duncan R. Dickson, and Stephen M. LeBruto. 1996. Disney's Internship Program: More Than Hands-On Experience. *FIU Hospitality Review* 14(1):27–35.
5. Benjamin Schneider and David E. Bowen. 1995. *Winning the Service Game* (Boston: Harvard Business School Press), p. 115.
6. Leonard L. Berry. 1995. *On Great Service: A Framework for Action* (New York: The Free Press), p. 171.
7. Carl Sewell and Paul B. Brown. *Customers for Life* (New York: Pocket Books), pp. 68–69.
8. Luis R. Gomez-Mejia, et al. 1996. *Managing Human Resources* (Englewood Cliffs, NJ: Prentice Hall), p. 212.
9. Gross, 164–165.
10. Ibid., 165–166.
11. Schneider and Bowen, 112.
12. Richard S. Mansfield. 1996. Building Competency Models: Approaches for HR Professionals. *Human Resource Management* 35(1):10.
13. Shawn M. Carraher, et al. 1995. The Assessment of Service-Orientation with Biodata. *Proceedings: Southern Management Association* (Valdosta, GA: Southern Management Association):172. This article confirms empirically what common sense would suggest: politeness and helpfulness are good predictors of success in the hospitality field.

14. Norman Brinker and Donald T. Phillips. 1996. *On the Brink: The Life and Leadership of Norman Brinker* (Arlington, TX: The Summit Publishing Group), p. 191.

15. Gomez-Mejia, et al., 210.

16. D.S. Ones and C. Viswesvaran. 1996. What Do Pre-Employment Customer-Service Scales Measure? Explorations in Construct Validity and Implications for Personnel Selection. Paper presented at the 11th annual conference of the Society of Industrial and Organizational Psychology, San Diego, CA.

17. Joyce Hogan, Robert Hogan, and Catherine M. Busch. 1984. How to Measure Service Orientation. *Journal of Applied Psychology* 69(1):167–173.

18. Richard L. Frei and Michael A. McDaniel. 1996. Validity of Customer Service Measures in Personnel Selection: A Review of Criterion and Construct Evidence. Unpublished manuscript.

19. Susan Carey. 1998. Flight Attendants Master Airplane Spanish (40 Words). *Wall Street Journal,* November 23:B-1.

20. Guest Relations—Individual Property. 1998. *Lodging* 23(8):117.

# Chapter 6

# Training for Service

### Hospitality Principle:

Train your employees, then train them some more.

*The how and why of every operation may be clear as day to you, but it's clear as mud to a brand new employee. You wouldn't believe the number of employees who say "I never could figure out exactly what they wanted me to do." They usually say that on their way out the door.*

—T. Scott Gross, *Positively Outrageous Service*

## LEARNING OBJECTIVES

After reading this chapter, you should understand:

▦ The importance of training and development to hospitality organizations.
▦ The principles and methods used by hospitality organizations to train and develop their employees.
▦ Methods used by hospitality organizations use to measure the effectiveness of training.

## KEY TERMS AND CONCEPTS

| | |
|---|---|
| employee development | internal training |
| external training | training methods |

Heskett, Sasser, and Hart tell the story about a bellman at a Sheraton Hotel who when confronted with an unusual problem implemented an ingenious solution.[1] A departing guest had locked his car keys in his trunk while checking out. The car was parked in the middle of the driveway that handled all the arriving and departing traffic and, if not immediately moved, would bring the entire check-in/checkout process to a halt. The bellman called for a floor jack which he had had the foresight to store away nearby, jacked the car up, and rolled it away from the middle of the driveway. He told the guest he had called for a locksmith, estimated how long it would take for the locksmith to arrive, and promised to keep the guest informed as events unfolded. The traffic problem was solved, the guest's car problem was promptly addressed, and the guest was spared the embarrassment of being the cause of everyone else's delay.

Teaching such resourcefulness to new employees is difficult, but every new employee in the area learned from the bellman's example what a Sheraton employee is expected to do to solve a guest's problem. The bellman had the big picture: he knew that a creative solution was expected of him, and he delivered one.

Len Berry has identified five key factors customers use to judge the overall quality of service.[2] Of these five, four are directly related to the ability of the service employee to deliver service in the way the customer expects, and the fifth, *tangibles,* includes the appearance of the service employee. The other four are *reliability* (the ability of the organization and its employees to deliver service consistently, reliably, and accurately), *responsiveness* (the willingness of the organization's employees to provide prompt service and help customers), *assurance* (the employee's knowledge, courtesy, and ability to convey trust), and *empathy* (the employee's willingness to provide caring and individualized attention to each customer).

While the hospitality organization's service, environment, and nonhuman component of the delivery system are clearly important in forming the guest's impression of the guest experience, guestologists know that the individual hospitality employee delivering the service can make or break the organization's relationship with the guest in each and every encounter, or moment of truth. Mary Jo Bitner sums up the research on this subject: "First and foremost, customer satisfaction depends directly and most immediately on the management and monitoring of individual service encounters."[3] Everyone remembers a truly bad service experience that was caused by an indifferent, uncaring, discourteous, or ignorant employee. One awful experience can overshadow the rest of the outstanding experiences that the customer may have had with the organization. The customer may never return to the organization and, even worse, may tell others about the one bad experience so no friends will come either. Disney estimates that each guest has *74 service encounters* in a single visit to its theme parks.[4] Disney managers know how important it is to manage every one of these encounters by getting the right people selected and trained to provide the consistent quality of guest service that customers expect.

The impact of a negative experience on the organization's reputation can be devastating. The disappointed guest won't come back and will spread the bad word. Excellent hospitality organizations recognize the value of investing time and money on employee training and development to prevent service disasters. Engineers can design an efficient service delivery system and the human resources department can select the right people, but those efforts are not enough. Companies that consistently deliver high-quality guest experiences also extensively and continuously train their people.

## EMPLOYEE TRAINING

Although the average company that trains spends an amount equal to 1.5 percent of its payroll on training-related efforts, the best organizations spend a lot more. The Ritz-Carlton Hotel Company, for example, provides at least 120 hours of training per employee each year.[5] The Ritz-Carlton knows the value of ensuring that employees have the ability, skills, and knowledge to deliver the high-quality service their customers expect. A commonly accepted rule of thumb is that each training dollar yields $30 in productivity gains in the next three years,[6] and outstanding service providers are willing to make the investment to reap these productivity outcomes. Federal Express spends nearly 4.5 percent of its payroll on training annually. It invested nearly $70 million to build a totally automated education-certificate system that provides training to 40,000 couriers and agents in 700 locations. Holiday Inns Worldwide spends more than twice as much on training as most other hotel companies. The return on that training investment is a drop in guest complaints in some hotels from 200 per month to two or three with a simultaneous revenue increase of 15 percent.[7]

Hospitality organizations face the special challenge of training not only the required job or task skills; they must also teach the server how to interact positively with guests and how to solve inevitable problems creatively. A car going down the assembly line doesn't care if the auto worker has a bad attitude. The customer facing the bartender at a private club, the front-desk agent at the Marriott, or the ticket seller at a Broadway play certainly does. Guest service employees must be trained to do the required job task consistently for each guest in real time, with many different types of people looking over their shoulders and with a sense of positive caring. This is a major training task. It goes far beyond the simple requirements of training someone to mix a martini, check in a guest to the proper hotel room, or receive money and make change.

## Training at Disney

Disney uses an extensive training program to teach new employees how to do their assigned jobs and how to deal with guests in a manner consistent with guest expectations about what the Disney experience should be and how employees who deliver it should act. Visitors to Walt Disney World Resort assume employees will be competent at the technical aspects of their jobs, but they also arrive with high expectations about the level of employee caring, consistency, and enthusiasm. A street cleaner inside the Magic Kingdom can quickly learn the mechanics of operating a pickup broom and dustpan. Learning the rest of the job, however, can be an enormous challenge. The street sweeper is to many guests the always-handy expert on where everything is, the available extra person to snap a group photo, or the symbol of continuing reassurance that the park is clean, safe, and friendly for all. To prepare that person properly for those multiple roles is an essential training task.

Disney's innovative Traditions training program is required for all new employees. The program teaches them the company's history, achievements, quality standards, and philosophy, details the responsibilities of new cast members in creating the Disney "show," and provides a tour of the property. It becomes the first exposure for new employees to the culture that unites all Disney cast members in a common bond. Here they are taught the four parts of the Disney mission in their order of importance: safety, courtesy, show, and efficiency. They also receive an introduction to company policies and procedures, a summary of recreational and social benefits available, and an introduction and orientation to each cast member's new work area. Above all, and regardless of their job assignments, cast members learn that Job #1 is creating happiness in guests. A supervisor/mentor then teaches the new employee the necessary job skills. The Traditions training is a combination of classroom experiences, with both instructors and interactive videos at Disney University, and on-the-job training. After a set period of time, employees are evaluated to ensure that the training provided was sufficient to teach new cast members the Disney way and their individual job responsibilities.

## Wall-to-Wall Training at SAS

Other organizations also appreciate the value of including every employee in a training program. When Jan Carlzon took over the ailing Scandinavian Airline Services in 1980, he immediately recognized the deficiencies in the airline's strategy and its employees' understanding of the airline's mission. He launched a service quality training program for all 20,000 employees that eventually cost several million dollars at a time when SAS was losing $17 million a year. Because it involved training every employee throughout the airline, this concept became known as *wall-to-wall training.* Karl Albrecht, the author of *At America's Service,* says, "He wanted the message [of service quality importance] presented in its original, compelling, unfiltered, undiminished form to every SAS employee."[8] Albrecht suggests this was the first time a major corporation used a 100 percent training process to help create a cultural change in an organization. Every employee from shop workers to top managers went through a two-day workshop entitled "The New SAS."

This program was so successful in creating a total organizational enthusiasm for service excellence that Carlzon initiated a second program in 1983. This follow-up was designed to teach everyone in the organization how to read the company's financial statements. Carlzon believed that if everyone could understand these statements, they would better understand where the revenues came from, where the money went, how much it cost to run the company, and how much each employee could influence profit. The success of these wall-to-wall training efforts at SAS encouraged other organizations to train their entire workforce, including British Airways, which trained all of its 37,000 employees.[9]

Hospitality service providers should not only be trained in the skills necessary to deliver the service expected; they should also be taught the company's values, practices, strategies, products, and policies. This knowledge helps them figure out how to fix a problem when a customer is unhappy. Unless they understand the corporate values and beliefs, they cannot know what the company expects them to do. Because the guest defines the quality and value of the guest experience, hospitality service providers should also learn about their customers' expectations, competitors' services and strategies, industry trends and developments, and the general business environment.[10] Even a cab driver needs to know more than how to drive a car to meet the service expectations of the rider in the back seat.

## Berry's Five Training Principles

Len Berry recommends that service companies, including hospitality organizations, should follow five key principles in developing an effective training strategy:[11]

1. Focus on critical skills and knowledge.
2. Start strong and teach the big picture.
3. Formalize learning as a process.
4. Use multiple learning approaches.
5. Seek continuous improvement.

We shall discuss each of these in turn.

### Critical Skills

Critical skills are those that service employees simply must have. A hospitality organization can identify critical skills through a systematic analysis of the service, delivery systems, and staff and also by asking its guests and employees. The guests can tell you what employee skills are related to their own satisfaction, and employees can be trained to ask them. The organization can survey regular customers who know the business well. Employees should become involved in the design of training as they have a pretty good idea of what training is needed for their positions even if they may not know how to offer it. Ask the best service providers in the organization. Study the servers who do things well to understand what everyone else needs to learn. Study what the best do and what they know.

### The Big Picture

Teaching the big picture is teaching employees the organization's overall values, purposes, and culture, and how what they do helps the organization succeed. This is what Jan Carlzon did with SAS, and it paid handsome dividends for this organization. Once he told the people what things they did that helped and what they did that hurt the organization, they could understand for themselves how their performance and skills added to the airline's success. New employees in any organization are usually eager to learn the organization's core values and what the company is all about so they can see how their jobs fit into the big picture. When an employee is later confronted with a problem situation that doesn't exist in a handbook or a training manual, the core values learned and accepted during training should lead that employee to do the right thing for the customer. Since so many situations in services are unplanned and unplannable, teaching the big picture and core values is especially critical. People who are taught the values and beliefs from the first day are far more likely to make the right choice for the customer and the organization when the situation calls for decisive action.

### Formalized Learning

Formalizing learning means to build learning into the job, make learning mandatory for everyone, and institutionalize that expectation. Send employees to learning opportunities, and do it on company time. By putting their money where their values are, organizations can send a strong message to employees that learning is vital to the organization and that everyone must participate. Motorola, an organization that has made a commitment to lifelong learning programs for its employees, has linked training programs to the company's strategic objectives. For example, it set an objective of reducing product development time and offered a course to teach its key people how to achieve the objective.[12]

### Varied Approaches

Using a variety of learning approaches is also important. Berry recommends leaving no opportunity unexplored. In addition to traditional methods, he suggests that organizations sponsor book clubs, send employees out to observe exceptional organizations in the service industry to benchmark against the best, and constantly practice the necessary skills through a variety of means.

### Continuous Improvement

A commitment to continuous improvement is essential. The initial training provides the KSAs that enable employees to begin doing their jobs. But training shouldn't stop there. Good service organizations and good employees both want continuing employee improvement through on-the-job training and supervision, special training sessions, video demonstrations, on-line courses, and the full range of training methods available to modern organizations.

## MEASURING TRAINING EFFECTIVENESS

If you don't know what your training is or is not accomplishing now, you cannot know how to improve it. Obviously what you hope to learn is whether or not the content of the training has somehow been transferred from trainer to trainee. Four basic measurement methods are available. They range in expense and degree of accuracy in measuring training effectiveness.

## Participant Feedback

The first, cheapest, and most commonly used measure of assessing training effectiveness is asking the participants. They fill out a questionnaire on some general evaluation criteria. Since these questionnaires tend to reflect the entertainment value of the training rather than its effectiveness, they have relatively little usefulness for accurate program evaluation. At least they tell you if the participants enjoyed the training.

## Content Mastery

A second, more sophisticated measure is to test for content mastery. After all, if the point of the training was to learn some specific skill, competency, or content area, then it should be possible to design a test to determine whether participants learned what they were supposed to learn. These measures can be as simple as paper-and-pencil tests similar to academic exams or as elaborate as on-the-job demonstrations of how well participants mastered the skill.

## Behavioral Change

A third and more advanced level of measurement is to assess the behavioral change in the participant. Many people quickly forget what they learned in classroom settings, especially if they don't apply it. "Use it or lose it," as the saying goes. College students often say they learn a subject well enough to get through the final exam and then flush all the information out of their brains. To be effective in any meaningful way, training must be followed by real and lasting behavioral changes when the employee returns to the job. If the training is well designed and anchored to mastering specific service-related competencies or skills and if the behaviors are reinforced by positive results or what happens on the job, then positive, measurable behavioral change should result.

## Organizational Performance

The final and most sophisticated level of evaluating the effectiveness of training is to watch what happens to the measures of overall organizational performance. The training may be well received, the employees may remember most of it upon completion, and they may continue to use it on the job, but the training is useless unless it eventually contributes to overall organizational effectiveness in some tangible way. To maintain the organization's competitive position, the training objectives and the training program require constant monitoring to make sure they continue to prepare employees to provide the level of service expected by an ever-changing customer.

# DEVELOPING A TRAINING PROGRAM

## What Do We Need?

Training should always be preceded by a needs assessment to determine if perceived organizational problems or weaknesses are related to training or something else. What do we need? Will training give it to us? For example, a service problem might be initially identified as a training issue, to be solved by offering servers a short training session. Upon closer examination, however, the issue might turn out to be a fault in the nonhuman part of the service delivery system. Constant guest complaints about slow beverage service at a local restaurant might seem at first to require training for the servers. But maybe the coolers in the beverage service area are too small. All the server training in the world can not correct a flaw in some other part of the service delivery system.

Needs assessment takes place at three levels: organizational, task, and individual. The *organizational* analysis seeks to identify which skills and competencies the organization needs and whether or not it has them already. If, for example, the organizational analysis reveals a need for several new restaurant managers in the Boston market and people to fill that need are not available, the organization would initiate a training program to prepare either existing employees or new entrants to be restaurant managers in that market. The second level of analysis is the *task*. What tasks need to be performed? Are they being done well, or is training needed? Most training in the hospitality industry is at the task level, either to prepare new or newly promoted employees to perform the necessary job tasks or to retrain existing employees when existing task requirements change. At the third or *individual* level, the organization reviews the performance of people doing tasks to determine if they are performing up to job standards. Once the organization's needs at these three levels have been assessed, training programs can be set up to meet them.

## Solving the Guest's Problem

This needs assessment also leads to identifying the objectives of training. If the needs analysis reveals a lack of some important employee skill, then the training objective would be to ensure that each employee needing that specific skill to perform effectively has it. If, for example, guest comment cards show general dissatisfaction with the effectiveness of a hotel's front-desk agents in checking guests in and out, then the training objective would be to improve their mastery of the check-in and checkout procedures. The point is that training works best if tied to solving a service problem that can be identified, measured, and remedied through training.

Guest feedback about service problems or failures should serve as an important trigger for training. If the guests perceive a problem with employee performance, you have a problem with employee training, regardless of what you think you've already done. You have a need, whether your needs assessment has revealed it or not. The effective hospitality organizations are constantly measuring and monitoring the performance of their people, systems, and services to identify problems. Many problems in delivering the guest experience are caused by the people part of the delivery system. If managers learn about these problems quickly, either from guests or their own observation, they can quickly institute corrective training to get things right before other guests have the same problems.

## External Training

Training can be provided by persons inside or outside the organization. Many organizations are not large enough to afford their own internal training departments. Unless the owner/operators of these smaller organizations are willing to do the training themselves, they generally turn to training consultants or to independent training organizations. These **external training** companies range from small organizations with an expertise and reputation in training within some specialized area of a particular industry, to large multinationals that offer training programs on just about any skill, area, or topic imaginable. Universities and colleges are also important sources of training as their faculty members frequently have job or industry expertise and the teaching experience and ability to convey it. The easiest way to learn what expertise is available in a community is to call the local educational institution and ask about the availability of courses in the area where training is needed. Most universities, for example, have banking and finance departments, retail marketing expertise, or even hotel and restaurant management programs. The people teaching the material to college students can also teach your employees.

While many companies contract with training organizations that develop and deliver customized, on-site training, others send their employees to more generic, often less expensive external programs. If the required training is in some highly specialized area or if only a few people need it, a company-specific program would probably not be worth the expenditure, so employees needing training are sent outside to get it. Advanced techniques of financial management, information systems design and use, computer skills, and new marketing strategies are examples of specialized programs frequently offered through universities and other organizations that provide generic training for the general public. These programs can make up for their lack of specific application to the industry or firm by being relatively inexpensive.

Training in even more general topics such as supervision, human relations, and services orientation is frequently available through these same organizations. Universities offer similar programs through their executive development and continuing education programs. These programs can be a fairly inexpensive way to send one or two key people to get some important training if producing a specially tailored in-house program would cost too much. Frequently, trade associations also offer programs that focus on topics of interest to their members, such as working with unions, new purchasing techniques, sanitation in food-service organizations, and the rules and regulations in the Americans with Disabilities Act. The common interest of the membership means that the organizations can collectively hire an expert consultant, or use someone from a member organization who has mastered the topic, to educate and train others in the industry. Trade associations also frequently offer certification programs in topic areas of interest to their membership. The American Hotel and Motel Association, National Restaurant Association, and the Professional Convention Management Association have all developed training products for their members.

## Internal Training

In-house training departments are widely found in larger hospitality organizations. Every major company has an **internal training** unit that provides programs to its employees. Hyatt, Marriott, McDonald's, Holiday Inn Worldwide, Darden Restaurants, and Disney are all multiunit organizations that have internal training departments. Some companies have even set up their own "universities," such as Hamburger University for McDonald's, Quality University for American Express (one course: How to Treat the Customer 101), and Suits U for Hart, Schaffner, & Marx. Some companies sponsor "virtual" universities that can be brought to any site where employee training is needed. Holiday Inns Worldwide provides a great example of how to use this virtual type of educational strategy. The corporation shut down its Memphis campus in 1990 and replaced it with sixteen training teams, each with a customized van, laptop computers, and all the materials needed to take training to individual hotels throughout the Holiday Inn market. The program, called Road Scholars, was so successful that it led to another training-delivery concept called Project Darwin. This project created thirty-three training regions, each with a full-time service delivery consultant who works with the thirty to thirty-five hotels in that region to help them discover ways to improve their revenue and service levels through training.[13]

## Training Costs

Although some organizations keep all training in-house to preserve the organizational security and culture, the usual determinant of whether to use in-house or outside training is cost. Cost is determined by the number and location of employees who need training and the level of expertise they need to acquire. If only a few employees need highly technical training, the training will be expensive for the organization to deliver itself; if the employees are scattered at multiple locations, the training will cost even more. But if those employees need only some basic skills training, the organization will probably offer it internally. If many employees at a single location need training, the organization will probably find a way to do its own training. The high employee turnover that is a basic problem for many hospitality organizations can influence the decision. An organization of 1,000 employees with an annual employee turnover rate of 200 percent has the same basic training requirements for new employees as an organization of 20,000 employees with a 10 percent turnover. Likewise, the level of expertise that the training must develop in these new employees has an important impact on the training cost. If considerable employee expertise will be required, training costs will be high. Offering 100 training hours to 10 new employees who will be responsible for operating a sophisticated point-of-sale electronic system as ticket sellers in a theme park might cost about as much as offering ten training hours to 1,000 employees hired to work at a fast-food drive-through window.

## The Cost of Turnover

When the training costs associated with turnover are analyzed, as new people must be trained in skills that departing people had already acquired, the importance of developing a managerial strategy that minimizes turnover and maximizes retention becomes apparent. These turnover and training-cost numbers show why organizations are frequently torn between designing a job task in a way that makes it challenging, complicated, and interesting (to reduce turnover) and designing the task to be quickly learned and easy to do (to reduce training costs). In the former situation, if the strategy does not reduce the turnover typically found in the hospitality industry, the organization will be constantly investing heavily in new employees who won't stay long enough to justify the cost of training. On the other hand, the simple, boring, and repetitive jobs are the ones that tend to have high levels of turnover. Obviously, this is something of a chicken-and-egg problem: more interesting jobs might lead to lower turnover, but most organizations are unwilling to pay the costs to find out.

Unrelated to training is one more cost of turnover: the cost of disappointed customers. Guests frequently build relationships with servers, and being served again and again by the same person is part of the value they receive from an organization's guest experience. If turnover is high, these relationships are destroyed or don't get built at all, and a powerful means for retaining repeat guests—the familiar face—is lost. As the "Cheers" TV theme song reminded us, "You want to go where everybody knows your name."

# TRAINING METHODS

The most common **training methods** are classroom presentations, video (either live or taped), one-on-one supervised experiences, home study, and computerized presentations (on-line, interactive, or programmed). Many training programs use a combination of presentation techniques with increasing emphasis on the computerized training and multimedia methods as computers become more widely available and people become more comfortable with them.

## Training in the Classroom

Classroom presentations can follow a variety of formats. The most common is the lecture presentation. A knowledgeable expert talks to employees in the hope that they can learn the necessary skill or knowledge in the available lecture time. The approach is based on the assumption that an expert can train the uninformed by speaking to them. The degree to which this assumption has been disproved by research on learning doesn't seem to deter its continued use. The method has advantages: It's cheap, time efficient, and to the point. If one of the top performers in the company stands up and tells you what she knows, she may not feel the need to develop elaborate visual aids, computerized instructional screens, or anything else that takes time and money to produce. Since she has been there, done that, and done it well, she is obviously worth listening to and will have great credibility with employees. Sometimes, these assumptions may even prove accurate. This strategy is combined with on-the-job training and mentoring to help reinforce the important points made in the classroom presentation.

Another basic classroom technique is the interactive case study. Here, the organization provides learners with some case material for discussion. Perhaps the material is related to the skill they need to learn, or it may be broader material to teach the more general skills of decision making or problem solving. More recently, with the increasing emphasis in organizations on teams and team leadership, team-based training is becoming popular. Leaderless groups may be given a problem to solve or an issue to address, and they are supposed to form themselves into collaborative problem-solving teams. People learn to work together, but they also learn about discovering and sharing the tremendous amount of knowledge that often exists within a team. Smart managers take advantage of team knowledge; most managers never discover its power.

An interesting variation on learning to work together and using team knowledge is wilderness training. The great outdoors becomes the classroom, and the team is given problems to solve. The team members learn to trust each other and become aware of how vitally important each team member is to the group's (and the organization's) effectiveness. This type of training was popularized when the Saturn Car Company used it to build teams that could produce high-quality cars. Even in highly specialized training areas, teams can often teach each other specific skills more efficiently than a single instructor can, partly because the sum total of knowledge available in the group can fill in the gaps regarding how the skill is supposed to be performed. Teams also learn to monitor each other's ongoing performance, which should continue after the training program itself ends.[14]

## Training Videos

A second major training technique is videos. They are frequently used in conjunction with a live presentation as a way to bring in new material beyond the expertise of the classroom presenter or to add variety to the presentation. For many hospitality organizations, videos are a cost-effective strategy. A centralized training department can make or buy video presentations and then ship them to individual units, all over the world if need be. Smaller, independent hospitality organizations can obtain a wealth of video instruction through either commercial retailers or their trade associations. Larger organizations usually make their own videos. Holiday Inns has a series of instructional videos on all the basics of innkeeping. The company contends that sending out a professional-looking video that captures and holds employee attention is more effective and cheaper than sending training experts to the many hotel locations. In addition, with the high turnover in the hotel industry, an instantly available video is useful and practical. New employees can watch it by themselves and learn the basics of how housekeeping, as one example, is to be performed in a Holiday Inn. Darden

Restaurants uses a series of videos to educate new employees in its many Red Lobster and Olive Garden locations across the United States. New servers learn how the different menu items are to be prepared and served, how the guest is to be greeted, and how the waitstaff is supposed to do its job. Darden's goal for its standardized training is to teach its people to provide the same high-quality restaurant experience in every facility throughout the entire chain.

Indeed, one of video's many advantages is to standardize the presentation of the material so that everyone learns the same information and learns how to do the required tasks in the same way. Being able to offer the same high-quality experience every time in every location is quite important for a multiunit operation like a chain or franchised restaurant or hotel where guests have standardized expectations about what the organization is supposed to do, how it provides its service, and what it looks like.

Videos are also relatively cost effective when organizational locations are numerous and widely dispersed. The cost and logistics for Hard Rock Cafe to send a corporate trainer to every location every time a new employee is hired would be prohibitive. But sending training videos to every part of the world to teach new employees how Hard Rock Cafe operates is easy. A well-designed and well-produced video can do an excellent job of holding the new employee's attention, portraying outstanding role models of expected service behavior, and stressing important points. With professional actors in a video showing the correct means of providing guest service, a new employee can see far more easily what the expected behavior is than if an instructor talked for several hours. Truly, a picture is worth a thousand words when it comes to training in service. The making of videos can itself be used as a training technique. The organization can call upon its best employees in the video subject area and have them create and produce the video. Such a "home-made" video lets the participants see that the organization appreciates the quality of their job performance, gives them ownership in the training role, and provides live role models for the new employees to follow. Making a video is an enjoyable and status-enhancing recognition reward for service jobs well done.

Live video is often available to organizations willing to pay for the broadcast time or satellite downlink. The classroom may be in one location, and the students may be at several other locations. They are hooked together through a live satellite feed or via a telephone line. The more elaborate versions of this technique have hook-ups that allow both sending and receiving of video and audio so that the learners and the instructor can talk back and forth, no matter where they are. The cost of live productions is still quite steep, so these training presentations are usually limited to important new information, or information that requires a high level of security, that must be sent to many people at the same time. A new menu item that will be the cornerstone of next month's promotional campaign may be an appropriate subject for live video. Employees need to know, and the restaurant organization may believe it can gain considerable advantage by keeping the information away from its competitors as long as possible. The increasing availability of teleconference facilities, advances in Internet technology, and the escalating costs of sending people to central training locations may make taped and live video presentations an increasingly desirable training option, especially when employees and service units are geographically dispersed.

Videos come quite close to providing the just-in-time education and training that many organizations need in industries like hospitality where the organization, the guest, the technology, and the employees change rapidly.

## Training at Home

Home study is another major training method. Here, a trade association or private training organization produces materials that people can receive in their homes and study at their own learning pace. When they have gone through the materials, they take an exam, at home or at a central location. The American Hotel and Motel Association uses home-study material extensively. The home study is ideally backed up with classroom experience, but the geographic dispersion of hotels makes offering classes difficult except in cities where a lot of hotels are clustered together. Home-study courses work well in this industry; they provide skill and knowledge training in topics unique to the hotel business at times and locations convenient for employees—after hours and at home.

## One-on-One Training

One-on-one supervised experiences are a typical on-the-job training method. The trainee may attend a short classroom introduction and then be sent to a work station where a supervisor or trainer demonstrates, observes, corrects, and reviews the employee performing the required tasks. This classic learning-by-doing strategy is by far the most commonly used training technique in the hospitality industry; the skills required to do a job are often unique, so the only cost-effective training method is to put new employees in the live job and let

*Service Training. (Courtesy of Marriott International, Inc.)*

them learn it by doing it, under close supervision. The traditional culinary training program is a good illustration of this approach. After a brief classroom experience, future chefs work in real restaurants preparing food for real guests under the watchful eye of a master chef. The one-on-one technique is extensively used in large hospitality organizations because the many tasks to be performed are so varied. Experienced waiters help new ones; the apprentice bartender prepares beverages under the supervision of a master mixologist. Even if some hospitality tasks are quickly learned and readily mastered, the variation among them is so great that putting together a classroom experience or a training video to teach what is essentially a unique skill makes little sense. Many a small organization, like Ralph's Restaurant on the corner, does the same thing. If Ralph can't hire the experience he needs for one of the restaurant's many jobs, then the most efficient and cost-effective training method is for Ralph to teach the new employee "Ralph's Way" of washing dishes, making spaghetti, or serving meals.

Southwest Airlines matches new people with employees who know how to give good service. According to Kevin Freiberg and Jackie Freiberg,

> New customer relations representatives, for example, go through a four-week learning-by-example process. To start, they get first-hand experience in ground operations. They spend time with the customer service agents selling tickets, issuing boarding passes, tagging bags—doing all the things involved in customer service at the airport. When the new reps return to the Customer Relations Department, they don't just read some standard training manual cover to cover; instead, they team up with senior reps for the next phase of watching and doing. The first week, they listen to the senior people talk on the phone and watch them use the computer system for online research necessary to assist customers. The next week they start learning the computer while they continue to listen to the more experienced reps handle incoming calls. Finally, the employee team reverses roles.[15]

## Training at the Computer

Computers are an increasingly commonplace presentation technique. This training method could turn out to be the most exciting and valuable of all. Computers can be used for training in two ways. The simplest is to use a stand-alone machine to teach a specific skill or body of knowledge by means of a preprogrammed presentation. To teach eye-hand coordination skills, perhaps something as simple as a video game could be used to let employees practice the relationships between seeing something and responding appropriately by pressing a trigger to kill a space invader on a computer monitor. "Edutainment" software programs have shown considerable promise in the American educational system and hold even greater promise for the future training and development needs of business. Training that is both fun and educational will reshape the nature of many corporate training efforts, dramatically improve the ability of organizations to teach all types of employees, and accommodate the wide cultural and linguistic variety of our increasingly diverse workforce. Computers never get frustrated with a slow learner and will stay with the student until the educational goal is achieved.[16]

Some skills can be taught by simulating on the computer the real situations that the new employee is expected to face. A restaurant could teach employees how to handle guest complaints by using a computerized simulation with an interactive videodisc or a CD-ROM. The video could display an irate guest and then lead the employee through the complaint-resolution process by letting the trainee take steps to resolve the complaint and then showing the trainee the outcomes of these decisions. A hotel could simulate its front-desk operations so trainees could practice using the front-desk equipment and responding to questions and requests from guests. After the trainee chooses a response by touching the screen at the designated decision point, the video would show what happened after that choice had been made. The organization is using the simulation to show its commitment to guest service, so it will develop the decision outcomes to show what personal and organizational rewards the employee can gain by giving good service. For example, if a guest in the simulation asks the way to a meeting room, the simulation can be set up to reward a highly service-oriented trainee response, such as personally escorting the guest to the meeting room. Each option chosen in the simulated encounter could be rewarded (or not rewarded) by both guest and organization in a different way.

Federal Express uses 1,225 videodiscs, updated monthly, in more than 700 locations as the core of its automated educational certification system.[17] Using this system, it can offer skill-upgrade training for any employees who need it. They are given four hours of company-paid study and preparation time and two hours of self-administered tests. Airlines use sophisticated flight simulators to teach their pilots how to fly different airplanes into different airports and how to prepare for emergency situations. They create a "virtual" airplane with all the controls, physical layout of a cockpit, and simulated motions so that pilots flying the simulator feels like they really are flying an aircraft. Arcades offer simulations of driving cars, flying planes, and similar experiences on a lesser scale that nonetheless develop an appreciation for how to drive or fly without actually putting oneself at risk. Learning to do something without putting oneself or the organization's reputation at risk is the key advantage of a simulated experience. The more advanced simulations allow the employee to practice repeatedly until the performance meets desired standards and can be done in real life on the employee's own.

Even more exciting than virtual-reality simulations and the increasing power of stand-alone computers to deliver useful and focused training are the new interactive training opportunities available through networked computers, mainly via the Internet. With the increased commercialization of the Internet have come new applications that the original research scientists and college-professor users of the Internet could only dream about. Now live pictures and voice can both be sent over the Internet; these capabilities allow interaction between instructor and learner across the world. Expertise can be delivered anytime, any-place, to anyone who is on line. On-line access is becoming increasingly available to every-one through many commercial providers.

As the sophistication and quality of this type of training develop, it will increasingly challenge the monopoly of libraries as repositories of knowledge. Once on the Internet, the user can tap into the knowledge in any major library anywhere, or if that is not sufficient, can tap into just about any expertise anywhere. A university business student had a project due on a case study of a brewery in Western Canada. The student logged on to a beer inter-est group chat room on the Internet and asked if anyone knew anything about this company. Within three days, he had responses from several people, including the wife of the brewery comptroller and the person who had written the case. Needless to say, this student's interest in traditional forms of research, which require plowing through library reference materials, was not heightened by this experience. He learned that he could get the specific information he needed faster and more efficiently through the Internet.

The more sophisticated applications of Internet technology mean that colleges and universities no longer have a monopoly on education in their geographical areas. These developments are a boon to the hospitality industry, as many organizations are multiunit and geographically dispersed. Getting their people to an educational center or a centralized training program is difficult, often impossible. Getting these same people to log onto the Internet is comparatively easy, and the amount of information, knowledge, and even training they can obtain through this medium is enormous. Internet capabilities make just-in-time education a reality as the people needing training can log on to the appropriate site at exactly the time they need it.

## Further Approaches to Training

Training can be very specific or somewhat general. The specific is typically used for new entrants who must quickly start performing a job skill well to justify their salary. Consequently, the major training costs tend to be for skills training. It can cover a wide variety of topics ranging from literacy to operating complex electronic systems. Some restaurateurs even find it necessary to teach employees basic bathroom usage and hygiene, including teaching food handlers how to wash their hands.

Marriott has had considerable success with its "Pathways to Independence" program, a company class on basic work skills for former welfare recipients at hotels in fifteen cities. They learn business basics such as showing up on time and life lessons such as personal financial management.[18]

We will touch on several other types of training. For example, *retraining* is often made available to employees who have burned out, have become unable to perform their current jobs because of technological developments, or whose jobs have been eliminated. Disney has operated a retraining program for many years that tries to "sprinkle Pixie Dust" on employees who have become disenchanted with their present jobs or otherwise lost their enthusiasm. In the program, they can retrain for new jobs that might recapture their enthusiasm or rethink why they are unhappy with their existing jobs, to regain the spirit of doing it the way the guests expect.

*Cross-functional training* enlarges the workforce's capabilities to do different jobs. The Opryland Hotel cross-trains its front-desk personnel and telephone-reservation operators so that each can help out the other if need be. The front desk often needs help when a number of people wish to check in or check out within a short period of time. The hotel has set up a separate registration desk in the lobby, and when the lines at the front desk start to reach unacceptable limits, these cross-trained operators are called to the separate desk to help serve guests. Since all hospitality organizations have such variable demand patterns, cross-training is often necessary to handle the sudden bulges in guests at different points in the service delivery system. At the same time, it provides task variety and higher interest level for employees, which has significant benefits in employee motivation and morale. Cross-training is clearly a win-win-win situation for guests, hospitality organizations, and employees.

To encourage employees to be more effective and responsive to guests, outstanding hospitality organizations offer *training in special competencies,* such as working as a team, creative problem solving, communications, relationships, and guest service orientation. These organizations realize that having the job skills is only part of the service requirement for their employees. They know they must also show their employees how to handle the many types of relationships that their guests will expect of them and how to solve the many problems that inevitably occur when different guests bring their different expectations to the guest experience.

Companies have learned that *diversity training, attitudinal training,* and other efforts to change how people look at other people can have significant payoffs in changing the way their service employees interact with each other and with the many types of guests who come through the entrance.

### The Message: Guest Service

One positive benefit of any training is that it reminds the employees of what management thinks is important. Sending people to a training program that focuses attention on service, no matter how effective or ineffective the actual training is, sends a powerful message to all employees that management cares enough about this topic and these people to invest real time and money in them. Any training tends to make employees feel more positively about the area covered, because they recognize the training as a visible show of organizational commitment to improving the area. An added benefit of training is to let trainees know that *they* are important and that management cares enough about *them* to invest time and money in their training.

## PROBLEMS AND PITFALLS OF TRAINING

Some possible problems with training are a failure to establish training objectives, measure results, and analyze training costs and benefits.

### Know Your Training Objectives

Training programs can run into trouble if the precise nature and objective of the training are unknown or imperfectly defined, or if the outcome expected of the training is hard to define or measure. Such programs are hard to justify or defend when senior management reviews the training budgets. Typical examples of areas in which the effectiveness of training is difficult to measure are "human relations" and "supervisory skills." Since these terms are vague and situationally defined, knowing what and how much training to offer to improve trainees in these areas, and how to measure results, is difficult. Hospitality organizations quite naturally want their employees to have a "service orientation," but the concept is hard to define as is knowing whether the training has resulted in such an outcome. Such training is important, without question. What exactly that training should be and whether it is effective are much more difficult to determine.

### Before and After Training

Even so, organizations should try. One measure of change in guest service orientation might be the number of guest complaints before and after training. Or an organization could use paid mystery shoppers to sample the level of service both before and after the training. The point of any such technique is to measure the value added by any training. With no "before" measurement, the organization has little way to know if the measurement after the training represents any improvement. Here, larger organizations have an advantage as they can use different parts of the organization to test different types of training and statistically determine whether or not one training type is more effective than another in terms of reducing guest complaints or increasing positive comments. Another strategy might be for the organization to measure the attitudes of its own employees toward guests both before and after the training. Since we know that the relationship between the attitudes of the guest and the attitudes of hospitality employees is positive, employee attitude may indicate how guests perceive the service level.

## Getting Good Value from Training

Training programs have obvious direct costs, but they involve indirect or opportunity costs as well; all the time that trainees spend away from their regular jobs costs money. Training is too expensive for the organization to train everybody in everything, so it must try to get the best value for its money by using those training programs that can be shown to give the greatest positive result in guest satisfaction for the training dollar expended. Too many organizations are at the mercy of consultants selling programs of unproven usefulness and value. Organizations should make the effort to ascertain the value of each training program, whether internal or external, in terms of whether it results in greater guest satisfaction.

## EMPLOYEE DEVELOPMENT

Norman Brinker of Chili's said, "People either shrivel or grow. Commit to helping people help themselves."[19]

Training typically focuses on teaching people how to do new jobs for which they have been hired or to overcome deficiencies they may have in performing their current jobs. **Employee development,** on the other hand, is typically focused on getting people ready for their future. Training tends to look backward to identify and correct employee deficiencies in performing the job today. Development looks forward to identify the skills, competencies, and areas of knowledge that the employee will need to be successful tomorrow. The problem with employee development is that knowing what the future will bring is so hard. Therefore, employee development programs tend to be more general, so measuring them and evaluating their effectiveness is harder.

### Tuition Refunds

A good example is the traditional employee tuition-refund policy that many organizations use to encourage employee development. Is the organization doing the right thing for itself or its employees if it pays a tuition refund only for those courses that are directly related to the employee's existing job, or is it doing a better job if it pays for any legitimate course at any legitimate educational institution? In the first case, the policy looks quite practical as it underwrites courses that directly enhance the employee's ability to do a current job. On the other hand, paying for any course regardless of field expands the total pool of knowledge available to the organization. Consider a group of people who are studying different topics in different majors and then bring them together in a quality circle or problem-solving group session to work on an organizational matter. This group's total knowledge will obviously be greater than if everyone had gone through the same educational program or had majored in the same subject. A variety of learning experiences expands the creative potential of both the employee and the organization and therefore increases the possibility of finding new and innovative ways to perform existing jobs and prepare for the future.

### *Supporting General Education*

Supporting any legitimate employee effort to improve, grow, and learn is in the employer's interest. Such support sends a message to employees that the organization values their potential as much as it values their current contributions; it is also a relatively inexpensive employee and organizational development strategy. Even more important is that it supports a learning environment. An organization that actively promotes learning of all kinds sends a powerful message to its employees that it believes the only way it will stay competitive is to learn continuously. These learning organizations promote the active seeking of new knowledge that not only benefits the individual but the entire organization by building its total pool of knowledge. No matter how irrelevant the material may seem, the creative employee will use it to make organizational connections.

The organization will eventually benefit from whatever creativity the educational experience spurred and from the increased loyalty and feeling of support that any employee gets from working for an organization that supports employee education. Forward-looking organizations understand that most of their profits in ten years will be from products or services they don't even know about today. Restricting educational reimbursement programs to those courses the organization thinks are important today may be as silly as trying to predict which products will be around ten years from now.

### *Supporting Career Development*

A good employee development program should also include career development. Very few people picture themselves doing the same thing in the future that they are doing today. An organization that thinks of its own development should also pay careful attention to its current employee development so that the people who are helping the organization succeed today are prepared to help it succeed in the future. Employees tend to believe that the longer a person is with a company, the more that person is worth to the company. Many organizations support that belief by celebrating anniversary dates with parties and pins to show that the organization recognizes and appreciates the employee's commitment to the organization.

Pins and parties are not enough, however, and the outstanding service organizations recognize that the individual's need for personal growth and development must also be satisfied in a well-designed career development path. The hotel housekeeper should be able to see a path to the top of the organization that can be successfully traveled with hard work, dedication, and effort. Too many organizations typecast their employees, and these people know that no one expects them to go very far. Indeed, many employees lack the ability, training, or desire to go very far and don't mind. Trying to convince a successful bellman at a resort hotel to abandon his tip money and "move up" to front-desk manager is a tough sell because many bellmen don't care to give up their higher income (much of it in tips) for the lower salary of an entry-level manager.

On the other hand, the American Dream lives on in the minds of many lower-paid, entry-level employees in the service sector; even if presently content, they know that they may need to do something different some day. The outstanding organizations provide career paths that give talented people the opportunity to realize their dreams. The opportunity is symbolically important, even if employees don't choose to take it.

## Get In, Move Up: The Total Development Package

Walt Disney said, "Get in. Be part of it and then move up."[20] CEOs of the best hospitality organizations would agree. They provide many opportunities for employees to grow and develop, and they promote from the ranks. In many hospitality organizations, just about everyone starts at the entry level and works their way up through their individual efforts. Employee growth can be facilitated by means of the many techniques covered in this chapter. Organizations should make it possible for employees with ambition, ability, and a willingness to expend the effort, to rise as far as they want to. Career paths should be made available and visible. The current leaders of many hospitality organizations took advantage of the educational opportunities and the promotional paths available and worked their way to the top. When each entry-level employee can see the same possibility, it provides a general feeling of opportunity for all. The desire to learn, the encouragement of learning, and the assumption that learning can lead to advancement should be an important part of the organization's culture.

## The Competition Is Looking

Too many organizations don't offer development programs, and their employees feel permanently stuck where they are. While such organizations may think that keeping their best service employees at the guest contact level is smart, other organizations seek out the stuck people and invite them to join an opportunity to grow and develop.

### At Outback

A good example is Outback Steakhouses, which recruits the best restaurant operators it can find. It offers them something most corporate restaurants do not: a chance to participate financially in their own restaurant. Many restaurant operators share a common dream of running their own restaurant. They will tell you that they are working for someone else only until they can save up enough money to buy their own. Outback has recognized this dream and has invited the best operators to run Outback restaurants with an ownership interest. This part-ownership gives them a direct payoff for their ability to run their restaurants well through sharing in the profits that they help to generate. It is a true win-win for both Outback and the operator. Outback gains excellent restaurant operators, and for a relatively small financial commitment, the operators gain an equity interest in an excellent restaurant.

### They Want Your Best

Your competitors will always seek to hire your best people and not your worst. Scott Gross is out in your restaurant or resort right now, handing his business card to your best employees. Ignoring the needs of the employee to grow and develop may be an inexpensive short-run strategy, but it will be a long-run expense. Not giving the employees opportunities to grow means that the hospitality organization itself may not grow and develop as rapidly. The best employees you need for your future can always find opportunities elsewhere to use their talents if you don't give them the chance. The key idea behind organization development is that everyone must continue to grow and develop. Skill and knowledge development is a continuous process. It must be ongoing to meet the ongoing changes in the guest's expectations. It is a never-ending journey.

## Lessons Learned

1. Teach employees not only job-related skills but also interpersonal skills and creative problem-solving techniques.
2. Do not train to be training; know what outcomes you expect from your training dollars, and measure your training results to be sure you get them.
3. Before training people, check the delivery system technology; the problem may lie there.
4. Develop your people for your organization's future.
5. Do more than just believe in your people; champion their training and development.
6. Reward behaviors learned through training to keep them alive.

## Review Questions

1. Virtually all organizations give their employees some training.
   A. "Training front-line employees is more important to hospitality organizations than to manufacturing organizations, because hospitality employees are dealing with people, not widgets." Agree or disagree? Discuss.
   B. How can organizations try to find out if the training they provided was effective? Can they ever be sure?
2. This chapter presents Berry's five principles of training. How would you set up a training program to apply these principles to restaurant servers?
3. How should a training program for fine dining and casual dining waitstaff be different?
4. The chapter presents several types of training. Match several of those training types to employee types and job types. For example, which techniques described in the chapter might be most effective with restaurant servers? Ride operators at a theme park? Clerks at an information booth on a cruise ship?
   A. How do you like to be trained or instructed? Which method or methods work best for you, and why?
   B. If the class shares responses to that last question, how do you account for the differences among students?
   C. How does all that relate to managing the guest experience in hospitality organizations?
5. What does it mean to "develop" employees anyway? Why is it particularly important to develop employees in hospitality organizations?
6. Some types of hospitality organizations typically experience (and accept) a high rate of entry-level employee turnover. Do you think these organizations should develop their entry-level employees to reduce turnover? Or would they simply be spending money to develop employees who will be moving on anyway, possibly to competitors?

## Activities

1. Interview three friends who have held jobs. Find out which of the chapter's training methods were used to train them. To what extent were any of your friends "developed" as well?
2. Divide into groups. For the group members who have held jobs, make a list of the different training methods that their organizations used. How are they similar to or different from the methods described in the text?
3. The next few times you visit a service provider, take particular notice of your servers. Although you did not see the training they received, do they seem to be conforming to some training and doing the job as it was designed to be done? If not, where are they going wrong, and why?
4. Interview four employees at a restaurant or hotel to discuss their training. Report your findings back to the class.

## Case Studies

### Hot Pants at Mideast Airlines

*I*n the early 1970s, the "Somebody Else Up There Loves You" airline called its planes Love Birds, drinks Love Potions ("Love Potion Number Nine" was a popular song of the time), peanuts Love Bites, and drink coupons Love Stamps. Tickets came from Love Machines. A special kind of stewardess was needed to turn every trip into a love affair.

Each of the forty original Mideast Airlines stewardesses or hostesses was chosen for "her own special sparkle." As one executive recalled, "A cute girl without a great personality was not good enough." Mideast hired a chic design boutique to design uniforms for "its long-legged beauties." Applicants had been asked to come to their interviews wearing hot pants to show off their legs; the uniform featured hot pants and high boots.

Mideast's president "believes the uniform attracted a special kind of personality." On graduation day from flight-attendant class, the forty were lined up in their hot pants and boots. The president said, "How many of you were cheerleaders, majorettes, or baton twirlers in high school or college?" More than thirty raised their hands. Said the president, "The uniform attracted the right kind of person. They were extroverts who loved to get out there and perform. They're in the people business."

\* \* \*

Discuss.

### Hiring for Attitude at Mideast Airlines

*M*ideast Airlines, according to a brochure, "hires for attitude and trains for skills. First and foremost, Mideast Airlines looks for a sense of humor." Mideast's CEO, referred to by Fortune magazine as "The High Priest of Ha Ha," said, "We look for attitudes—people with a sense of humor who don't take themselves too seriously. We'll train you on whatever it is you have to do, but the one thing Mideast cannot change in people is inherent attitudes."

*During interviews, potential employees might be asked, "Tell me how you recently used your sense of humor in a work environment. Tell me how you have used humor to defuse a difficult situation." The hiring department also looks for humor as prospects interact with each other during group interviews.*

\* \* \*

Discuss.

## The Beef and Reef Mystery Guest

*S*ally Salkind has worked for two years as a server at the Beef and Reef Restaurant while getting her degree in hospitality management. As a national restaurant chain, the Beef and Reef has specific written standards about how guest service should be provided and posts those standards in the kitchen where all employees can see them. The chain also allows local managers considerable latitude in training employees and providing service, so long as unit financial results are satisfactory. Most of the servers go "by the book" in serving guests, figuring that the company knows best and that they can't go wrong in following company standards. But Sally has developed her own very successful way of opening the service encounter and delivering service thereafter. Since manager Bill Gordy has had nothing but good things to say about her performance, she has continued to serve guests in her own style. Apparently the guests like it; her tips are among the highest and her average check the highest in the restaurant.

Early one evening, Bill Gordy informed the servers of a rumor he had heard at a national meeting: corporate headquarters intended to use more mystery shoppers in the following month. He said, "I know you all do the best job possible, and I appreciate it, but next month, let's all lift our service to a new level." About two weeks later, as Sally Salkind started to walk to greet a couple who had just been seated, Bill Gordy whispered to her, "Mystery shoppers. I can tell them a mile away. Do it by the book, Sally, and you'll be fine."

Sally tried to do it by the book: "Good evening. I'm Sally and I'm going to be your server tonight." But then Sally got tongue-tied. She couldn't remember if procedure called for her to solicit a beverage order, recite the specials, or encourage the party to choose an appetizer. The rest of the meal went the same way. The party of two had to ask for information that Sally usually related in her comfortable, natural way. But when called upon to do it by the numbers, she couldn't remember what the numbers were. She had never been so happy to see two people leave.

Several days later, Bill Gordy called Sally into his office and reprimanded her for not following standard serving procedures at the very time when following procedures was most important.

"Sally, I had been considering promoting you to head server, but I can't promote somebody who can't follow simple instructions."

Sally went quickly from surprise, to shock, to anger. She asked Bill Gordy why, if the procedures posted on the kitchen wall were so important, he had never said anything about them in her two years with the restaurant.

(Continued)

*"I'm not dumb, Bill. I can learn as well as anyone. But you never told me that I had to learn that stuff, much less taught me how to do it. You threw me in the water, and fortunately I could swim. I did darn well on my own, plus some things I learned in my hospitality courses. How can you expect me to change my whole way of doing things with 20 seconds notice?"*

*Bill Gordy didn't have an answer for Sally's question. He simply reiterated his criticism, told her that she had embarrassed him and the restaurant in front of "a big shot from headquarters," and sent her back to her station.*

*Sally had been thinking of trying to get a permanent position with the Beef and Reef organization after she finished her studies, but she decided that she didn't want to work for an outfit that gave her little training in how to do the job, complimented her for the way she did it, then criticized her because she didn't follow formal procedures and memorize the silly little phrases. She would stick around for now because the tip income was good, but she would be looking.*

* * *

1. What went wrong? Who was at fault?
2. Discuss the pros and cons of a strict set of serving standards for everybody.

## Flint Hill Beef and Lamb

*J*ust before graduating with a degree in hospitality management, Sally Salkind interviewed with several hospitality organizations. She was most impressed with Beef and Lamb, a medium-sized restaurant chain founded by Bob Beef and Larry Lamb. She was particularly impressed that Bob and Larry had come to campus to do the interviewing themselves.

Sally got along well with Bob and Larry. They invited her to corporate headquarters for further interviews, and the impression she made on other Beef and Lamb executives was exceeded only by the impression that they made on her. On the second day of her interview series, she was surprised to be offered a selection of several assistant manager positions in different cities. She had relatives and friends in central North Carolina so she picked Flint Hill, NC, a growing community near Charlotte. The week after her college graduation, she headed for Flint Hill exuberant with optimism.

Smith Hamilton, manager of the Flint Hill Beef and Lamb, had only the day before been told that he was being sent an assistant manager. When Sally entered the restaurant, eager to begin the career that she had trained for, make a good impression, and justify the faith that Larry and Bob had shown in her, Smith Hamilton barely gave her the time of day. He told her he was busy but said that she should "make herself useful." Sally was quite surprised to receive such a reception at the local level, since she had been treated so beautifully by the company founders, but she resolved not to be down about it.

Sally spent her first day walking around in the restaurant, meeting people, taking notes, asking questions of employees and guests, and generally getting the lay of the land. Since Smith Hamilton was too busy to talk to her on the second day, she spent it in much the same *way. By the end of the week, with no help from Hamilton, Sally had gathered valuable information, given it much thought, and saw numerous ways in which the already successful operation of the restaurant could be improved.*

*The next day, she made her presentation to manager Smith Hamilton. She was too excited to notice that he kept looking at his watch. When she finished, he said:*

*"Young lady, I have made money with this Beef and Lamb restaurant every year since I have been here. I have 18 years of experience in the business, and I've got this restaurant set up just like I want it. Sure, I never went to college, but I know the food business. All you have is book learning. These ideas of yours might look good on a homework assignment, but they will not work in Flint Hill, North Carolina. I don't want all these 'point of sale' machines you talk about; they aren't worth the money. Neither are any of your other ideas. Maybe you ought to interview with Beef and Reef; your high-faluting college notions might be just what that outfit needs. Or you can stick with me and learn something about the restaurant business."*

\* \* \*

1. How did things go so wrong?
2. Should Sally bear any part of the blame? Should the institution where she received her training in hospitality bear some blame?
3. If you were Sally, what would you say to Smith Hamilton, and what would you do? Would you "stick with him and learn something about the restaurant business"?

## Additional Readings

Breiter, Deborah, and Robert H. Woods. 1997. An Analysis of Training Budgets and Training Needs Assessments in Mid-Sized Hotels in the United States. *Journal of Hospitality and Tourism Research* 21(2):86–97.

Conrade, G., R. Woods, and J. Ninemeier. 1994. Training in the U.S. Lodging Industry: Perception and Reality. *Cornell Hotel and Restaurant Administration Quarterly* 35(5):16–21.

Donnellan, Laurel. 1996. Lessons in Staff Development. *Cornell Hotel and Restaurant Administration Quarterly* 37(6):42–45.

Harris, Kimberley J., and Debra Cannon. 1995. Opinions of Training Methods Used in the Hospitality Industry: A Call for Review. *International Journal of Hospitality Management* 14(1):79–96.

Lundberg, Craig C., and Cheri A. Young. 1997. Newcomer Socialization: Critical Incidents in Hospitality Organizations. *Journal of Hospitality and Tourism Research* 21(2):58–74.

McColgan, Ellyn A. 1997. How Fidelity Invests in Service Professionals. *Harvard Business Review* 75(1):137–143.

Ninemeier, Jack. 1995. Training Strategies in World-Class Asian Hotels: Relevance to the United States Lodging Industry. *Hospitality and Tourism Educator* 7(4):21–24.

Scandura, Terri A. 1998. Dysfunctional Mentoring Relationships and Outcomes. *Journal of Management* 24(3):449–467.

Tracey, J. Bruce, and Michael J. Tews. 1995. Training Effectiveness: Accounting for Individual Characteristics and the Work Environment. *Cornell Hotel and Restaurant Administration Quarterly* 36(6):36–42.

Young, Cheri A., and Craig C. Lundberg. 1996. Creating a Good First Day on the Job—Allaying Newcomers' Anxiety with Positive Messages. *Cornell Hotel and Restaurant Administration Quarterly* 37(6):26–33.

# Notes

1. J. L. Heskett, W. E. Sasser, Jr., and C. W. L. Hart. 1990. *Service Breakthroughs: Changing the Rules of the Game* (New York: The Free Press), p. 109.
2. Leonard L. Berry. 1995. *On Great Service: A Framework for Action* (New York: The Free Press), pp. 78–79.
3. Mary Jo Bitner. 1990. Evaluating Service Encounters: The Effects of Physical Surroundings and Employee Responses. *Journal of Marketing* 54(2):69.
4. Mary Jo Bitner. 1995. Building Service Relationships: It's All About Promises. *Academy of Marketing Science* 23(4):248.
5. http://www.ritzcarlton.com/corporate/commitment.htm (May 1999)
6. *Business Week,* March 28, 1994:163.
7. Stanley Davis and Jim Botkin. 1994. *The Monster Under the Bed: How Business Is Mastering the Opportunity of Knowledge for Profit* (New York: Simon & Schuster), p. 97.
8. Karl Albrecht. 1988. *At America's Service: How Your Company Can Join the Customer Service Revolution* (New York: Warner Books), p. 185.
9. Ibid.
10. Berry, 188.
11. Ibid., 191.
12. *Business Week,* March 28, 1994:159.
13. Davis and Botkin, 98–99.
14. Ibid.
15. Kevin Freiberg and Jackie Freiberg. 1996. *Nuts! Southwest Airlines' Crazy Recipe for Business and Personal Success* (Austin, TX: Bard Press), p. 287.
16. *Business Week,* February. 28, 1994:81.
17. Davis and Botkin, 96.
18. *Business Week,* November 11, 1996:116.
19. Norman Brinker and Donald T. Phillips. 1996. *On the Brink: The Life and Leadership of Norman Brinker* (Arlington, TX: The Summit Publishing Group), p. 194.
20. *Walt Disney: Famous Quotes.* 1994. Printed for Walt Disney Theme Parks and Resorts, 55.

*Chapter*

**7**

# Serving with a Smile: Motivation and Empowerment

### Hospitality Principle:

Motivate and empower your employees.

*A happy employee will stick with the company, give better service to the customer, and recommend company products to others.*

—Sears Roebuck study of employee attitudes

*A smile costs nothing—and in the hospitality industry, it means everything.*

—Bryan D. Langton, Chairman & CEO, Holiday Inns Worldwide

*It takes happy employees to make happy customers.*

—J. Willard. Marriott, Jr., Chairman & CEO, Marriott International, Inc.

*Leaders think about empowerment, not control.*

—Warren Bennis

## LEARNING OBJECTIVES

After reading this chapter, you should understand:

- How hospitality organizations motivate their employees to provide outstanding guest service.
- How organizations reinforce and reward guest-centered employees.
- How outstanding hospitality organizations fulfill employee needs.
- What characterizes successful work teams.
- What team decision making can and cannot accomplish.
- How role playing can enhance guest service.
- How modern hospitality organizations enhance guest service by empowering employees.
- What role authority plays in organizations and why employees accept authority.

## KEY TERMS AND CONCEPTS

| | |
|---|---|
| authority-acceptance theory | positive reinforcement |
| eager factors | role theory |
| empowerment | work groups and work teams |
| job content/job context | work team characteristics |
| motivation | |

The environment is superb, and the mechanical and back-of-the-house aspects of the delivery system are flawless—so far, so good. Now it's up to the frontline employee. In almost all guest experiences, the employee can make the difference between a satisfied guest and a dissatisfied guest. The employee can also turn satisfaction to *wow*. In the manufacturing sector, the tire or automobile on the assembly line doesn't really care about the scowl on the employee's face, the sarcastic comments, or the bad attitude. But people who come to the guest experience are very aware of how employees treat them. If the hotel gift-shop clerk makes a comment that offends a guest, the guest is angry at the employee and also at the hotel that hired and "trained" the employee. Because the guest service employee is so important in the guest's determination of value and quality, hospitality organizations that strive for "positively outrageous service" take great care, as we have seen in previous chapters, in the hiring, training, development, and retention of their employees.

This chapter focuses on *motivating and empowering* the hospitality employee to provide a high-quality guest experience. Since quality is defined by the guest, the employee who provides the guest experience must be not only well trained but highly motivated to meet the guest's expectations and to do so consistently. If the role of the hospitality service provider is this important to the organization, the role of the hospitality manager—whose leadership and managerial skills can influence employee attitudes and behaviors greatly—is vital.

## MOTIVATING EMPLOYEES

A family was checking in at the Hyatt Grand Cypress on a busy night. The hotel was full, the family's reservation had not been properly handled, and the husband, wife, and three tired children were upset. The front-desk employee assessed the situation and acted promptly. She took some quarters out of the petty cash drawer and gave them to the kids to go and play the video games and gave the parents chits for a drink in the lobby bar, while she went to find a manager to straighten out the problem. The parents were happy, the kids were happy, and the front-desk person had defused a tense situation.

At the Imperial Hotel in Tokyo, a waiter overheard two guests talking about their college reunion. In Japan, college reunions occur yearly and usually have a good turnout. The waiter realized that college reunions were an untapped source of business for the hotel. He brought the idea up at the weekly meeting of his work group. Not long after, the hotel introduced this new service. It was a huge success, bringing in $600,000 in revenue in the first two months.[1]

The Hyatt employee didn't take a creative path to solving a guest problem because she had to but because she wanted to. Something or someone **motivated** the Imperial Hotel employee to see the creative possibilities in a new idea and pass it along for development. The challenge for hospitality managers is to discover what makes employees not only do their jobs efficiently and competently but also want to go the extra mile.

Hospitality organizations have learned the importance of using their employees from the neck up as well as from the neck down. Every guest experience is unique, and any manager who believes it possible to predefine policy and procedures for handling any and all guest experiences is mistaken. Employees should know that they are encouraged, expected, and trusted to handle all the many and varied situations that come up in the guest service areas for which they are responsible. If they were properly selected and trained in the first place, management must make it possible for them do their jobs with responsibility, skill, enthusiasm, and fun. But how?

## The Power of Positive Reinforcement

The answer is simple. Implementing the answer, however, is the challenge facing every manager. The answer is based on the well-accepted psychological principle that behavior which is rewarded tends to be repeated, and behavior which is not rewarded tends not to be repeated. The way to keep employees at high levels of performance, then, is to provide rewards for behaviors that are associated with high levels of guest satisfaction and not to reward behaviors that are not.

**Positive reinforcement** is no simple task. Employees are as varied as guests. Just as guests differ in what they expect, employees have different definitions of what they expect in terms of rewards from their organizational relationships. In a sense, employees are the manager's customers. They define the value and quality of the employment relationship just as the customer defines the value and quality of the customer experience. Bob Jones and Mary Smith each define what is and is not a reward for them. The managerial challenge is to discover and then provide rewards in types and amounts that each employee believes are equitable and appropriate. To make rewarding good performance even harder for the manager, employees have changing expectations, moods, and valuations of the employment relationship.

## Wanted: Fun, Fair, Interesting Jobs

For the most part, however, the employees of hospitality organizations look for three things in a job. It must be *fun, fair,* and *interesting.* Walt Disney said, "You don't work for a dollar—you work to create and have fun."[2] Chili's Norman Brinker said, "If you have fun at what you do, you'll never work a day in your life. Make work like play—and play like hell."[3] The key to managing and retaining these employees, then, is to create job situations and provide rewards that the employees perceive as fun, fair, and interesting. If the organization can successfully build these elements into the job situation, employees will be motivated to work hard and follow direction. The trick is that everyone's definition of fun, fair, and interesting is different.

## Employee Satisfaction and Guest Satisfaction: A Direct Relationship

According to Disney managers Craig Taylor and Cindy Wheatley-Lovoy, "Leaders motivate people, develop their talents, and provide proper resources and rewards to them to succeed."[4] If hospitality managers and supervisors offer appropriate incentives and fulfill employee needs, then employees will find their jobs to be fun, fair, and interesting; they will be satisfied in their work. If employees are satisfied, then they are much more likely to try to satisfy the guests they serve. Guest satisfaction obviously translates into repeat business and bottom-line profitability. This series of relationships—the importance of leaders to employee satisfaction, and the importance of employee satisfaction to guest satisfaction—makes intuitive sense and is supported by research.

Valarie Zeithaml and Mary Jo Bitner support the relationship between employee satisfaction and guest satisfaction: "There is concrete evidence that satisfied employees make for satisfied customers (and satisfied customers can in turn reinforce employees' sense of satisfaction in their jobs). Some have even gone so far as to suggest that unless service employees are happy in their jobs, customer satisfaction will be difficult to achieve."[5]

How do you find out if guests are satisfied? Chapter 13 is largely devoted to different ways of determining guest satisfaction, and the best way may be to ask them. How do you find out if employees are satisfied? In the same way. MCI Communications surveys its employees several times a year on job aspects that typically lead to job satisfaction or dissatisfaction, such as employee relationships with their bosses, their feelings about their pay, and opinions about working conditions. The human resources director says, "We know employee satisfaction does increase customer satisfaction, as well as productivity, for us."[6]

Sears Roebuck studied attitudes of employees in 800 stores and found that attitudes about such job aspects as workload and how their bosses treated them had, according to Sue Shellenbarger, "a measurable effect on customer satisfaction and revenue. Basically, a happy employee will stick with the company, give better service to the customer, and recommend company products to others."[7] If employee attitude improved by 5 percent, customer satisfaction improved by 1.3 percent, and revenue improved by 0.5 percent. If Sears executives "knew nothing about a store except that employee attitudes had improved 5%, they could reliably predict a revenue rise of .5% over what it would otherwise have been."[8] The Sears study supports other evidence that a happy employee gives better service to the customer.

## Rewarding the Desired Behavior

Most managers attend to the problem people and ignore those who perform at their normal, competent level. Employees learn that the "squeaky wheel gets the grease."

Rewarding the wrong behavior is as big a mistake as not rewarding the right behavior. The organization's reward system needs constant and careful review to ensure that the behaviors being rewarded are the behaviors that the organization wants. For example, Guest-

First Hotels tells its employees they should make every effort to satisfy the guest. But Guest-First evaluates and rewards employee performance only according to the budget numbers. This practice has been called "rewarding A while hoping for B." Most employees will naturally focus on the numbers and not on the guest-satisfaction ratings. Similarly, if GuestFirst tells its employees how important team performance is but rewards its employees only as individuals, employees will see that team effort does not matter that much.

### At the Buffet

A popular buffet restaurant decided to add a greeter position to welcome guests as they entered the restaurant. The manager told the newly hired employee explicitly that his primary responsibility was to greet and welcome the guests. However, as time went on, to keep the employee busy when guests were not entering the restaurant, the manager added responsibilities to the position—such as checking periodically to make sure there were enough trays or making sure that the butter dish was always full. The greeter quickly realized that the manager never complimented him for properly greeting the guests, nor did he ever say anything to him when he missed a guest because he was too busy with his other duties. But if he ever let the buffet line run out of trays or butter, he was strongly reprimanded. Therefore, by her actions or lack of action, the manager had redefined the job description. The manager made her real priorities clear, and the employee adjusted his actions accordingly.

### Identifying the Rewards

The first step in satisfying the employees who must satisfy the guests is to identify the rewards desired by employees. Most employees begin new jobs with energy and enthusiasm. They want to do well. But this fast start can't last forever without encouragement and help. The expectations that they will receive desired rewards for performance are what keep people energized, enthused, and working hard on behalf of organizations. Effective employee performance is a result of ensuring that the right people are in the right jobs for their talents, properly trained to do the job the way it should be done to provide the hospitality experience that guests expect. They must be kept energized to perform those jobs with efficiency and enthusiasm.

### Necessary Managerial Skills

Managers must have certain skills to support and motivate employees. *Administrative skills* are the ability to take care of the routine. Managers must be able to handle the paperwork, administrative procedures, and policies that directly influence each employee's ability to perform the job. A manager who forgets to submit the proper payroll or who schedules too few people to work on a Saturday evening creates situations in which the most enthused, energetic employee can't succeed. Managers must attend to the basic job-related requirements of employees.

*Leadership skills* include the ability to identify and provide those rewards that the individual employee wants from membership in the organization. While fear and the threat of punishment may be powerful short-run motivators, the ability of the organization to fulfill employee needs is what yields energetic commitment to organizational goals in the long run. Other chapters have discussed the way to find the right people and to train them properly. This chapter focuses on the leadership skills that are necessary to energize people.

Employee needs must be identified and satisfied if we want employees to give us their enthusiasm, commitment, and effective job performance. What we offer in return for these employee contributions are the inducements that they consider rewards. These are the factors that make the job fun, establish the fairness of how the rewards are distributed, and make the job interesting. We'll call these the **eager factors.**

## The Eager Factors

What made the employee eager to join the organization in the first place? People join organizations to fulfill their needs. Though individual needs are infinitely varied, they usually include the need for financial security, the need to belong to an organization that matches and enhances one's self-image, the need to associate with people who think and feel the same way, and the need to grow and develop as a person and as an employee. A manager who can satisfy these needs within the workplace will have highly motivated people who want to stay with the organization. While every organization will have its misfits, most people work hard at doing what they love to do because the job satisfies their needs.

## Financial Needs

People cannot concentrate on their jobs when they are hungry, worried about financial crises, or otherwise focused on money. Managers can diminish or eliminate these concerns in several ways. The most obvious is a pay scale ensuring that all employees are paid well enough to meet their basic needs. Managers must attend to the financial details that concern employees, especially the minimum-wage and entry-level people at the bottom of the pay scale for whom every dollar matters. These financially related details include scheduling enough hours to meet people's needs, scheduling around day-care or elder-care needs when possible, making employee discounts available, and providing information about economical health-benefit plans if the company does not provide or subsidize coverage. These and similar efforts can help fulfill the basic needs of employees who must watch their finances closely. Many guest-contact employees are at the minimum-wage level or a little above, and these financial needs frequently are primary concerns to these people who are responsible for success or failure in the moment of truth.

Organizations can help fulfill the longer-term financial needs of employees and motivate them at the same time by giving them stock or stock options, or selling them these instruments on favorable terms. Providing people with an opportunity to achieve an actual ownership interest in the company, as is done by Outback Steakhouses, Cracker Barrel, and other hospitality organizations, can be a powerful motivational tool. When people see a relationship between their own efforts and the success of "their" company's stock and their own personal wealth, the motivational impact can be strong.

## Belonging Needs

Most people, especially younger people like teenagers, enjoy being a part of a group or team. Well-designed work groups can be helpful in managing employee direction and behavior in the workplace. Indeed, as studies at the Hawthorne Plant of the Western Electric Company showed many years ago, the sense of belonging or not belonging greatly influences what people will do or won't do in the workplace. The managerial focus here should be to work in harmony with the group to support each employee's effort to achieve the group goal, which will help achieve the organizational goal. The first managerial challenge in

*Outback Steakhouse. (Courtesy of Outback Steakhouses, Inc.)*

meeting employee belonging needs, then, is to identify those groups to which employees belong (not always obvious); the next is to identify group goals.

Most groups are formed to satisfy or fulfill some type of member need. A church group forms to provide for religious needs, a health group to provide for health needs, and a social group to provide for social needs. Social groups in the workplace form for a variety of reasons. People who work together tend to have things in common: what they do and who they do it with. They not only work together on the job but also tend to associate off the job. They have things in common to talk about, shared experiences and continuing reminders of their common basis for acquaintance by continual on-the-job relationships. Since the modern hospitality organization uses careful hiring criteria, these people also tend to share even more commonalities that bind them together as a group. They frequently are young, share similar values and beliefs, and have many personality traits in common. When you take similar people and put them together in a work setting, you have the basis for forming both a work group and a friendship group.

### Sharing

Another reason the group forms is the benefit that the group provides. Having the opportunity to share the dreams, ambitions, challenges, joys, and problems of life with someone else is important to most people. Groups give the individual a sympathetic ear, reassurance of self-worth, and help and assistance in times of individual challenge. Members look to their groups to affirm their worth, acknowledge their successes, and respect their achievements. Organizations that help groups do these things benefit by finding ways to incorporate the group goals into the organizational goals.

### Achieving through the Group

If, in addition, groups offer members the opportunity to achieve something greater than themselves by being a part of the group, then the value of the group becomes greater than merely satisfying belonging needs. Membership in organizations with strong corporate cultures, whose purposes are respected by the society as a whole, is valuable to both group and individual. Asking the group to help accomplish the valued, respected organizational purpose becomes a powerful motivational tool for the organization and a primary means for keeping the individual and the group positively involved in the organization.

## WORKING AS A TEAM

Magic Kingdom employees often say they want to work for Disney because they can bring such great joy to children of all ages. These cast members are committed to their work group and to the organization because they realize they can't do this wonderful social good alone. They believe they can create this magic for guests only through their participation in this work setting. If Disney calls a group of these people together and asks them to serve as a quality team to identify service quality problems and opportunities, they will work hard on behalf of that group's goal because they are so committed to the purpose of the organization.

The point is simple. People join groups to satisfy needs, and the group can satisfy some of each other's needs without any organizational help. But if the organization enables the group to satisfy additional or even higher-level needs, then the organization is going to get the support of the group and its members. While this sounds easy to do, it is not. Most organizations make no attempt to understand the relationships among the goals of the individual, the group, and the overall organization. Nor do most organizations know what they can do or stop doing to enhance the positive benefits of these relationships.

### Groups and Teams

Table 7-1 sums up what **work team characteristics** are required to support a collection of people—a group—to function successfully as a **work team.** The hospitality manager can use these characteristics to help weak work teams be successful and improve the performance of adequate teams.

### The Benefits of Teams

Building strong work teams is worth the effort. Organizations reap many benefits from supportive and productive teams.

### Good Ideas

The organization gains access to the many good ideas that a team can generate by discussing and resolving problems affecting the team and the organization. Hospitality managers do not know everything nor are they capable of identifying the best answers to every guest's problem. Using team problem-solving processes provides a wealth of new ideas and frequently a better perspective than the manager alone might have. After all, those who deal with the guest and the problems that serving the guest may create know the details of those problems better than does the manager with multiple responsibilities.

**Table 7-1** *Successful Work Team Characteristics*

1. Has a meaningful team purpose that inspires and focuses the members' efforts.
2. Has goals and objectives that are measurable, specific, realistic, and easy to understand with defined areas of authority.
3. Is small enough to act as a true team (5–15 members).
4. Has members with the necessary skills to operate as a team (functional/technical skills appropriate for the decision area, problem-solving/decision-making skills, interpersonal/team skills).
5. Has clear, well-organized work procedures and rules of behavior that are enforced by the team.
6. Has a cultural value of mutual accountability where only the team can fail or be a hero, and not any one team member.
7. Is led by a team-building coach who builds a performance culture.
8. Has enough group time to allow members to interact and learn how to care about one another.
9. Understands the extent of its authority.
10. Is supported by the organization's reward and information systems and other resources necessary to succeed.

Work Team. (Digital Imagery® Copyright 1999 PhotoDisc, Inc.)

### Monitoring Member Behavior

Teams can also assist in the supervisory role of management by providing an ongoing monitoring of each team member's behavior and productivity. If the team has a common performance objective, then the team can better monitor and oversee each member's relative contribution than management itself can. The group and the group's approval will likely have a more important influence on the individual employee's behavior than will the supervisor.

### Everybody Learns

Another important benefit for the organization using groups is helping everybody to learn more about the organization and what it does. By involving teams in solving problems and making decisions, the organization learns more about what it wants to do and how to do it, and the individual learns more about the job, why the job is done the way it is, what other team members contribute to the job's accomplishment, and the relationship of the job to the overall organizational purposes. Involving groups in decision making also forces the manager to understand clearly what the problem or issue is. After all, if you don't know what you're trying to do or why a particular issue is important, you can't explain it to anyone else very well. Furthermore, what better way is there to teach employees the reasons the jobs are done the way they are, the way those jobs relate to others across the organization, and how those jobs help achieve the organizational purpose than by involving the employees who do the jobs in the job-related decisions? Using team decision making helps the organization and its leadership to understand their own purposes, procedures, and reasons for doing things while it teaches the employees how to be more involved and accountable for their own work.

### It's Our Decision

Team decision making leads to one more important benefit. When the team makes decisions for itself, *it owns them*. It *understands* them. It becomes responsible for making the decisions work and monitoring the outcomes. If the quality team at the hotel decides that too many dishes are breaking on the food-service carts while running over the tiled floor, it puts itself in the position of identifying the best solution and then making it work. In this example, the problem was caused by stacking the trays for food on top of one another without spacers. The team came up with rubber spacers between the trays and solved the problem. Since the team and not management came up with the solution, the team members, who were also the people pushing the carts, made sure they used the rubber bumpers and proved to themselves their solution worked. Such problems are too frequently "solved" by an industrial engineer who comes up with an elegant solution that nobody uses. The problem continues, and frustrated managers wonder what to do with uncooperative employees.

### Other Potential Benefits

The use of teams sends all employees the message that they are trusted. Employee morale improves, absenteeism decreases, and organizational recruitment efforts are enhanced.

## Possible Problems with Teams

Potential problems with teams are that they do not always work as fast as individuals do, they require new attitudes and leadership behaviors on the part of managers, and they cost money and time. In addition, teams should be limited to certain problems, situations, and tasks that lend themselves to team effort.

### Takes More Time

Team decision making is not always the solution, and it can have disadvantages. Without question, team or group decision making takes more time than an experienced manager would take to decide how to solve a problem. Most people do not intuitively know either how to make decisions systematically nor how to collaborate in a team setting. Teaching people how to do these things adds more time to the time required to solve the problem. It takes time to teach group members what the problems are, why they occur, and how to work as a team to solve them. The team meetings themselves take time.

### Mixed Messages for Managers

The second major challenge created by work-teams for decision making organizations is that managers and supervisors have to learn brand-new behaviors. Most were promoted because they were the best at doing whatever job they now supervise. The best salesperson becomes a sales manager, the best server becomes the head server, and so forth. If the organization tells Ellen Brown she is being made a manager because she is the best at doing her job, Ellen may be confused when the organization now tells her to coach a group that is going to make the decision instead of her. After all, she may wonder, why did the organization promote me if it didn't want me to make the decision? The message here is mixed, and many managers have a difficult time shifting gears to be coaches instead of doers.

The other aspect of this problem is based on fear. Managers wonder what their own futures will be when they see employees being empowered to make decisions. If the job of the manager is to oversee people working and to make decisions about how that work should be done, what happens to the manager's job once the team is empowered to make its own decisions and to oversee its own members? Many empowerment programs have not worked because middle managers, as a simple issue of job survival, have found ways to sabotage them.

### Not Worth the Expense?

The third major problem with team decision making is that teams are neither cheap to use nor always effective. Taking people out of their jobs to make decisions has a cost associated with it. Furthermore, teams are incapable of making or making well entire categories of decisions. A team has a difficult time making decisions about issues beyond its group's concerns or knowledge. A group of casino croupiers, for example, would have a hard time making a good corporate strategic policy decision or a decision that has an impact on another group or unit within the organization because even if the croupiers had received some training in grasping the big picture, they probably would not know about or be able to see all the ramifications of the issues involved. Similarly, decisions that require technical expertise beyond that typically available to the involved employees will not likely be successful.

### Other Potential Problems

"If our ideas are so good, why don't you pay us more?" Team members may get an inflated sense of their value to the organization and of their decision-making capability. "If our ideas are so good, why don't you use all of them?" Employees not on a team may feel left out and become resentful. Some team members may become freeloaders and not bear their part of the job. Finally, not everyone can work successfully in a team format, nor is every problem appropriate for a team solution.

## When to Use Work Teams

An organization needs to determine the answers to four critical questions before it uses team-based decision making.

First, is management comfortable letting employees make decisions about their job responsibilities? While this sounds easy to answer, it is not. Many managers are uncomfortable letting go of their managerial prerogatives. Second, is management ready to let teams be accountable for their efforts and decisions? Since most managers are evaluated on the basis of their unit's performance, this is another hard step. If the manager is accountable for the decision, how can the manager be comfortable with the group making the decision that might come back to haunt the manager if it turns out poorly? Most people believe that if they have to be accountable for the results, they might as well make the decision themselves, and they have a hard time trusting someone or some group to make those decisions.

Third, is management ready to share the benefits of the decisions? If the group makes good decisions and saves the organization money, will management share the rewards with the group? In a related way, will management share the glory and other benefits that result from high levels of performance in an organization? If the team makes the decision that wins the boss the big bonus and the trip to Hawaii, will they ever work that hard on behalf of the organization (or that manager) again unless they too benefit in a meaningful way?

Finally, management must decide who learns and who gets promoted. If the group and its members don't get the opportunity to grow and develop, but they see management getting these opportunities as a result of the group's efforts, they will lose their interest in and enthusiasm for the team decision process. Management that wishes to use team decision making successfully must be ready to let the team and its membership participate in growth and development opportunities and organizational rewards. Managers must be willing to trust teams with the authority and responsibility for decision making.

While work teams provide an important benefit to the employee by providing a sense of belonging, effective work teams do more for their members. They provide a sense of self-worth, the opportunity to grow and develop, a means to recognize and share achievements and failures, and a way to reinforce member's values and beliefs. In brief, they help satisfy each group member's need to grow and develop as a person and as an employee.

## Role Theory

**Role theory** is a way to explain how the group or team influences the behavior of its members. People behave in the roles they play in fairly predictable patterns that are influenced by others. A student behaves, for the most part, as a student is expected to, and a Hard Rock Cafe employee usually behaves as a Hard Rock Cafe employee is expected to. Roles are the parts we play in the social and work groups to which we belong. Employees play a variety of roles. A person may be a church member, a student, a parent, and a civic-group member as well as an employee. Each role has different expectations of the person and, while playing the role, the person is continuously influenced by the others watching the person behave. Guests or other employees may give a funny look or make a comment to a frowning hotel desk agent or receptionist. Anyone observing a mother ignoring her child in danger will scowl or even speak up. People continually tell us by word, facial expression, or deed how they think we should be behaving in a particular situation.

As seen in Figure 7-1, the playing of a role has two major elements: *role senders* and the *role receiver* or focal person. Role senders are all those who let us know what role we are

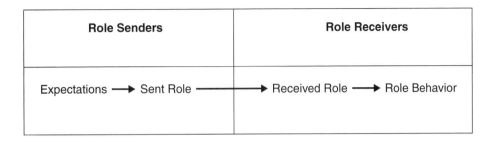

**Figure 7-1**  *Role Episode Model. (Source: Daniel M. Katz and Robert L. Kahn. 1966.* The Social Psychology of Organizations, *p. 182. Reprinted by permission of John Wiley & Sons, Inc.)*

to play and then try to tell us how to behave in performing the role. The instruction and training the boss sends, the verbal and nonverbal cues the coworkers and guests send, and the social norms that our society sends all help define the guest service role. The role receiver or focal person is us. We observe and receive all the expectations people are sending us and interpret them into the behavior we think people want from us. We then decide to comply or not with those expectations and act or don't act accordingly.

## Role Conflicts

This continual process is full of potential and real conflicts. A person who is sent different role expectations by different people will feel conflict and confusion. If the guest expects one thing and the company policy requires another, the employee faces the difficult choice of determining which way to go, which role to play. Conflict can also occur when the supervisor sends out conflicting role expectations, when the role expectations conflict with the focal person's fundamental values or beliefs, and when the roles themselves come into conflict. If Sally's husband tells her to come home early for the children's birthday party and Sally's boss asks her to work an extra shift tonight, Sally will have a role conflict.

## The Cast Member Role

Disney uses the concept of role in a unique way to enhance the nature of the job. By using the term *cast member* for all employees, Disney emphasizes the idea that everyone in the organizational cast is playing a role in a public performance. The terms *on stage* and *off stage* are also used to reinforce this notion in the minds of all employees. The idea that employees comprise a cast putting on a show has many organizational benefits, but perhaps the biggest is to get people to think of their jobs as roles and of what they are asked to do in those roles as part of a performance for their guests or audience. This mind-set gives new and greater importance to every job throughout the organization. Now, instead of thinking "I am merely a street sweeper," which may demean the employee's many years of education and experience, the street-sweeping *cast member* can look at the task as the playing of a role. In a theatrical production, nothing is demeaning or lowly about playing the role of a street sweeper. After all, you're not really a street sweeper but rather a cast member/actor doing an excellent job of *playing* a street sweeper. This attitude helps eliminate role conflicts. The distinction between the real you and what you're capable of doing or being in real life, on the one hand, and your skillful performance of the street sweeper's role is clear.

### Staying "Up" through Role Playing

Role playing helps solve another major personal challenge that people involved in delivering services to guests face: how to stay "up" all the time. People who deal with people have to be good at performing what has been termed *emotional labor.* They need the skills and knowledge to perform the service, which may require some physical labor, but they also need whatever it takes to perform the service in a certain way. Hardly anyone smiles naturally all the time nor can anyone's natural response to a guest's needs always be sympathetic. But thinking of the job as playing a "role" in a theatrical performance can help decrease the personal wear and tear of this emotional labor. Instead of actually paying the emotional price of getting personally involved in every guest's needs, the employee can display the emotional response that would be required of someone in an acting job. The emotional labor expended in genuinely feeling the emotions that might seem appropriate to the many needs and problems of guests would wear anybody out long before a work day at the racquet club or convention hall or work night at the restaurant or motel was over. Thinking of the job as performing a role makes it possible for hospitality employees to perform well without becoming emotional wrecks.

The research on this topic suggests that role playing is actually better for the employee and the organization than genuine emotional involvement. According to Ashforth and Humphrey, "Given the repetitive and scripted nature of many service roles, one may develop habitual routines for . . . acting such that emotional labor becomes relatively effortless."[9] Individuals who strongly identify with their organizational roles are apt to feel more authentic when they are conforming to role expectations, even if they are only acting to display rather than actually feeling the emotional involvement required of the role.[10] Further, acting like a certain type of person tends to commit one to becoming that type of person, especially if one volunteers to play the role to a public audience.[11]

The emphasis on being a cast member also encourages people to think of themselves as being on stage even when they are feeling low or distracted by other role expectations in their lives. If you come to work bothered by the fight you had with your significant other that morning, once you go "on stage" you can usually get into the role and leave your nonwork problems behind.

### Clarifying the Role

Obviously managers need to spend time and energy in minimizing role conflict and maximizing role clarity. People like to know what is expected of them. When the organization and its leadership don't spend the necessary time clarifying the role expectations for the employee, the potential for conflict is great. Effective hospitality training programs clearly define their roles for employees and thereby minimize the conflicts they will have to face. When they have finished training and begin to serve guests, they should know their roles thoroughly. For example, when Disney cast members go "on stage" to perform, they know that the priority of the elements in the roles they play is safety, courtesy, show, and efficiency. Safety is never to be compromised. If a cast member has a choice of two actions, one safer and the other more showy, the cast member feels no role conflict in taking the safe action.

## EMPOWERING EMPLOYEES

Teams need to grow and develop, but so do individuals. One great asset that a team provides to its members is the opportunity to grow within the group setting. But the organization must provide additional opportunities for its members to satisfy this important need. The most widely discussed strategy for doing so is **empowerment.** Although becoming empowered may add to the fun of the job for employees, and they may think it only fair that they be given some responsibility for making decisions related to their own work, the main benefit of empowerment is that the job offering opportunity for growth and development though empowerment is a more interesting job. The organization also benefits from interested, empowered employees. As Norman Brinker said, "You can achieve so much more by empowering people to achieve on their own. Don't be too hands-on."[12] The empowered server can personalize the service experience to meet or exceed each guest's expectations and can take whatever steps are necessary to prevent or recover from service failure. On those complementary ends can hinge organizational success or failure.

### What Is Empowerment?

Empowerment is the assignment of decision-making responsibility to the individual.[13] It requires sharing information and organizational knowledge that enables the empowered employees to understand and contribute to organizational performance, rewarding them based on the organization's performance, and giving them the authority to make decisions that influence organizational outcomes.[14] Empowerment is broader than the traditional concepts of delegation, decentralization, and participatory management. Empowerment can stretch decision responsibility beyond a specific decision area to include decision responsibility for the entire job and for knowing how the performance of that job fits within the organizational purpose and mission.

Some organizations talk the talk of employee decision input without giving employees any real power and authority to implement decisions. The purpose of employee empowerment is not only to ensure that effective decisions are made by the right employees but to provide a mechanism by which responsibility for job-related decisions is vested either in individuals or in work teams.[15] Empowerment also means that management is willing to share relevant information about and control over factors that impinge upon effective job performance.

### How Much Empowerment?

Empowerment is not an absolute; it has degrees. Managers may find that more is not necessarily better. For example, a manager could choose to provide higher degrees of empowerment for some individuals and teams doing certain tasks than for others. Indeed, even within a given individual's job or a given group's task responsibilities, different decision areas could be empowered to different degrees. A restaurant chain, for example, may wish to empower its individual restaurant managers with complete authority to negotiate prices within a certain level of variation to meet competition. However, the same organization might not be willing to let the same managers make even minor modifications in the menu.

## The Job Content/Context Grid

Managers may need help in seeing how to use this concept in their own organizations. They may also need help in managing the delicate balance between giving employees control over their own work processes while retaining some supervisory control over what employees do. What would happen, for example, if management empowered a work group by assigning both authority and responsibility over the job and the employees decided not do anything at all related to the organization's goals or even the goals of the work group next to it? Obviously, empowerment must occur within some limits, and where to place them becomes a major challenge in implementing any empowerment strategy.

An organization wanting to empower its employees must first analyze its jobs. All jobs have two dimensions: content and context. **Job content** represents the tasks and procedures necessary for doing that job. **Job context** is much broader. It is why the organization needs that job done, how one job interacts with related jobs, and how the job fits into the overall organizational mission, goals, objectives, and job setting.

### *Empowerment in Stages*

Managers trying to use empowerment will also find it helpful to view decision making not simply as an act of making a choice among alternatives but instead as a five-stage process: identifying the problem, discovering alternative solutions, evaluating the pros and cons of those alternatives, making the choice, and, finally, implementing and following up on the impact of that choice. Employees can be empowered to participate in one, some, or all of these stages.

Figure 7-2 shows a grid with the context of the job on the vertical axis and the content of the job on the horizontal. The horizontal axis shows the way in which the employee's or team's decision-making responsibility over job content progressively increases in relationship to the decision-making process. For example, at the far left of the figure in the first step of the decision-making process, employees have little responsibility, but as one moves to the right, the level of responsibility and decision involvement increases. Similarly, as one moves up the vertical axis, responsibility and involvement over decisions related to job context increase. A manager seeking to empower employees may wish to increase decision responsibility over job content, job context, or both. The five points identified on the grid allow a better understanding of varying strategies for empowerment available to managers.

*Point A* (No Discretion) represents the traditional assembly-line type of highly routine and repetitive job. This is the classic fast-food job, designed by someone other than the worker and monitored by someone else. No decision-making responsibility is associated with this job in terms of either job content or job context. The employee is used from the neck down. J. B. Schor has noted that the most stressful workplaces are electronic sweatshops and assembly lines where a demanding pace is coupled with virtually no individual discretion.[16] A good hospitality illustration would be the loaders on a high-volume ride like a famous roller coaster. The job is highly routinized, repetitive, and boring. It has no variety, and loaders have no discretion about how to do it. The contact with the customer is so brief that loaders don't have enough time to interact with customers in any meaningful way to break up the task performance.

*Point B* (Task Setting) represents the essence of many empowerment programs used today. Here the worker is given a great deal of decision responsibility for the job content and little for the context. The worker is empowered to make decisions about the best way to get the assigned task accomplished. In these cases, management defines the mission and goals,

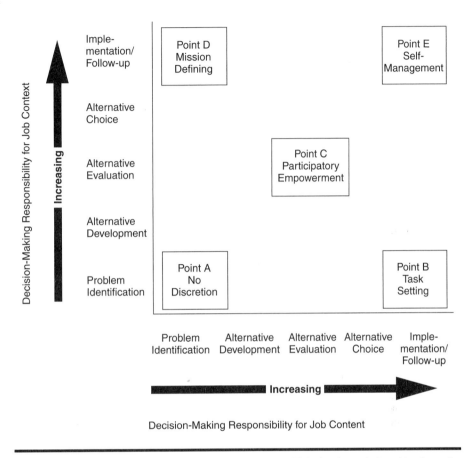

**Figure 7-2**   *The Employee Empowerment Grid. (Source: Republished with permission of Academy of Management, P.O. Box 3020, Briar Cliff Manor, NY 10510. Empowerment: A Matter of Degree, R. C. Ford & M. D. Fottler, Academy of Management Executive, 1995, Vol. 9, No. 3, p. 24. Reproduced by permission of the publisher via Copyright Clearance Center.)*

and the worker is empowered to find the best way to reach them. Management hopes that the empowered workers will apply their job knowledge and intellect to discover ways to improve what they do in their jobs. Many hospitality jobs are in this category; the guest service employee must do the job as designed but has flexibility to do it in a variety of ways to meet the needs and expectations of varied guests. Even if the same meal comes out of the kitchen for 100 different diners, the way in which that meal is served and the interaction patterns that take place between the server and the diner make each occasion somewhat different and potentially interesting. Since tipped positions are guest contact jobs, like waiting tables in a restaurant, the power of guests to reward or not to reward is always an additional incentive to provide an excellent delivery that meets each guest's unique requirements.

Point B represents a significant departure from Point A because employees are totally involved in making decisions about job content. Jobs at Point B can be redesigned by employees or even teams of employees. They may redesign their tasks to add more content or develop a variety of new employee skills. In addition, they are now energized and free to decide how to do their work, get more feedback, and understand their jobs more fully. Many Point B employees find such enriched jobs more motivating and satisfying, leading them to do higher-quality work. Even when management confines empowerment to job-content decisions, employee motivation may be enhanced for those who strongly value feelings of accomplishment and growth.[17] The success of the Point B strategy, however, will partly depend on factors beyond employee control, such as service delivery system design and organizational structure, guest expectations, reward systems, and top-management support.

More will be said about Point B and the hospitality industry in a moment.

*Point C* (Participatory Empowerment) represents an area more typical of autonomous work groups that are given some decision-making involvement in both job content and job context. Such groups usually participate in problem identification, alternative search and analysis, and recommending the best alternative in job content. They participate similarly in job-context decisions. While research is sparse, some evidence suggests higher job satisfaction and productivity in such groups. The best-known Point C American success story is the Saturn plant of General Motors in Spring Hill, Tennessee, where autonomous work teams have been established to emphasize teamwork, efficient use of resources, and a continuing effort to improve quality. The teams at Saturn operate at the mid-range of the decision-making process along both the job content and job context dimensions.

In the early 1990s, the Ritz-Carlton hotels set a goal: "the revolution/transformation of hotel operations through the implementation of Self-Directed Work Teams (SDWTs)."[18] The organization felt that SDWTs could improve processes, increase efficiency, and heighten guest and employee satisfaction. After a two-year pilot project, SDWTs were instituted in Ritz-Carlton hotels and resorts all over the world.

As described by the Ritz-Carlton, an SDWT is a group of employees who are responsible for a complete work process, including:

- sharing various management or leadership functions
- planning and improving work processes
- developing team goals and mission
- scheduling and payroll
- reviewing team performance
- coaching and training fellow team members
- ordering and purchasing of supplies and maintenance of inventories

The Ritz-Carlton believes that

SDWTs give true authority and accountability for the success of the business to the people who run the business. They take responsibility for the quality of their products and services. . . . SDWTs liberate and unleash the creative potential and entrepreneurial abilities of employees. The result is an improvement in quality and subsequent rise in guest, owner and employee job satisfaction.

In addition, SDWTs free managers from the day-to-day operational aspects of a hotel or work area. Rather than working in the system, managers will work on the system, providing vision and direction.

The Ritz-Carlton Hotel Company is service-driven and therefore, employee-driven. SDWTs create a work force of multi-skilled individuals performing broad duties rather than unskilled, easily replaceable people in narrowly defined jobs.

*Point D* (Mission Defining) represents an unusual situation and one seldom discussed in the literature of empowerment. Here employees are empowered to decide on job context but not the content. An example might be a team in a unionized maintenance operation that is given the task of deciding whether or not an outside vendor might do a particular task more effectively than current employees. This decision to outsource would alter the mission of the unit dramatically. The union contract or the current technology may mandate the continuation of current job content and specify which occupational categories should perform subtasks if the task is retained in-house. If management assures the union employees of continued employment, an empowerment strategy to maximize employee control of the job context might well be an effective way to implement such a dramatic change.

*Point E* (Self-Management) represents an area in which employees are given total decision-making authority for both job content and job context. Giving employees this much authority requires considerable faith in their ability to use their new-found empowerment in ways that will contribute to the organization's effectiveness. It requires extensive employee involvement in the development of the organization's mission and goals, and confidence that employees are ready, willing, and able to make decisions about their work that will result in wise, intelligent, and appropriate contributions to the organization's objectives. Empowering a person to make both job content and context decisions that optimally respond to changing environmental conditions, technological innovations, and competitive challenges is the ultimate expression of trust. For obvious reasons, few companies are comfortable permitting many people, other than those in the top-management suite or high-level salespeople, to operate at the self-management level.

### Point E Benefits

The few available illustrations of the Point E empowerment level credit it with many positive benefits, including higher productivity, better attendance, less turnover, and improvements in both product and service quality and employee work-life quality. One example is Chaparral Steel where supervisors have responsibility for hiring, training, and assigning of their own new employees.[19] Chaparral employees are asked how their jobs can be redesigned to "add more value." Self-management teaches employees to compare their outputs to their goals and to administer their own reinforcement to sustain commitment and performance.

Self-management may be achieved with or without formally designated work teams. A good example of the latter is W. L. Gore and Associates, manufacturers of Goretex. This company exists without titles, hierarchy, or any of the conventional structures usually associated with a company of its size and sales of approximately $1 billion a year. The company has been highly successful and profitable for more than 30 years. Growth has been financed without debt. Empowerment at Gore is nearly total since employees have decision-making authority and responsibility for both job context and content. The culture and norms of the organization support employee empowerment. There is no fixed, assigned authority, and associates work without structure or management.

### Potential Point E Situations

Self-management may not be the appropriate level of empowerment for most organizations or even most employees. An incremental process may be more appropriate. When asked whether companies other than his could use self-management, Bll Gore, president of

W. L. Gore and Associates, stated that it works best when "put in place by a dynamic entrepreneur or a start-up company."[20] Established companies might find it very difficult to use self-management because too many hierarchies would be destroyed. When you remove titles and positions and allow people to follow whoever they want, they may want to follow someone other than the person who has been in charge. Gore's success in implementation illustrates the importance of the organizational structure in making empowerment strategies succeed. The Gore company culture emphasizes teamwork, mutual support, freedom, motivation, independent effort, and commitment to the overall system.

## Point B and the Hospitality Industry

Point B empowerment perfectly suits many hospitality organizations and many hospitality employees. The organizations design the jobs and expect employees to do the jobs as designed. Some organizations—perhaps especially in the fast-food area—expect employees to do the job strictly by the numbers. But the benchmark organizations empower employees to provide service in a variety of ways, to meet the needs and expectations of varied guests. Even if the same meal comes out of the kitchen for 100 different diners, the way in which that meal is served and the interaction patterns that take place between the server and the diner at the moments of truth can produce a so-so experience or a wow experience.

Here is how Point B empowerment works at Southwest Airlines. CEO Herb Kelleher says, "I can't anticipate all of the situations that will arise at the stations across our system. So what we tell our people is, 'Hey, we can't anticipate all these things; *you* handle them the best way possible. *You* make a judgment and use your discretion; we trust you'll do the right thing. If we think you've done something erroneous, we'll let you know—without criticism, without backbiting.' "[21]

All in all, it can be said that a Point B empowerment level is the most suitable for many frontline jobs in the hospitality industry. It gives servers the flexibility to meet and exceed the guest's expectations and to prevent and recover from service failures.

## Empowerment Implementation

Successful implementation of an empowerment program requires knowledge of appropriate strategies and key ingredients, and of situations and people who can benefit from empowerment's potential.

### Strategies

Implementation of empowerment should begin by focusing on decisions related to job content, then gradually moving through the various decision-making stages from problem identification through implementation/follow-up. Later, after employees and managers become comfortable with empowerment in job content, increasing levels of empowerment in job context could similarly be added by raising the level of decision-making authority from problem identification up through implementation and follow-up. At each step, management could determine what difficulties were created, how they should be addressed, and whether or not the individuals or teams were ready, able, and trained to move on to the next stage of decision involvement and responsibility. Alternatively, a company might empower employees to address problem identification and development of alternatives simultaneously for both job content and job context, much as was done at the Saturn plant.

For either of these approaches or any other mid-range strategies, management needs to determine first where it would like to be on the grid and then develop a plan to move its employees gradually toward that point. The grid simply illustrates the stages of employee empowerment, which allows managers to decide what level of empowerment their organization is ready for and what can be done to implement that desired degree of involvement in making job-related decisions.

### Key Ingredients

The four key ingredients to any successful empowerment program are:

1. *Training* in knowledge areas, training in decision making, and, if empowering a group (see work team discussion earlier), training in group interaction.
2. *Measurable goals or standards,* so empowered employees themselves have a means to test whether or not the decisions they make are good or bad.
3. *Methods of measuring progress toward goals,* so empowered employees can tell if what they're doing is heading in the direction of the job goal. Empowered employees need yardsticks so they can tell by themselves if what they're doing is heading toward the goal or away from it.
4. *An incentive system* to reward the employees for making good decisions and to make it worth their while, both financially and in terms of other eager factors, to take on decision responsibility.

### Limitations and Potentials

Of course, there are some organizational limitations. Employee empowerment may be less appropriate if (1) the basic business strategy emphasizes low-cost, high-volume operations, (2) the tie to most customers is short term, (3) technology is simple and routine, (4) the business environment is highly predictable, and (5) employees have low growth needs, low social needs, and weak interpersonal skills. Alternatively, employee empowerment can be highly successful and rewarding under the following circumstances, and note how many of them characterize the hospitality industry! If (1) service is customized or personalized, (2) customer relationships are long term, (3) technology is complex, (4) the environment is unpredictable, and (5) employees have high growth needs, social needs, and strong interpersonal skills, the potential gains from employee empowerment can be significant.[22] Except perhaps for complex technology, and assuming (with respect to point 5) that employees are chosen with care, most guest contact situations in hospitality would seem ripe to enjoy the benefits of employee empowerment.

### Empowerment: Not for All

Within all organizations, including hospitality organizations, some departments, employees, or jobs may be better suited for employee empowerment than others. Managers hoping to gain empowerment's benefits could initially implement a limited form of empowerment in areas where the match appears potentially fruitful. From here, problems could be worked out and the empowerment process gradually expanded. Indeed, those companies engaged in total quality management (TQM) efforts, organizational reengineering, or attempts to reenergize their corporate culture's commitment to service through the introduction of more participatory management styles may all find the incremental strategy useful.

Since the workforce is so diverse, some employees will be better suited for empowerment than others. Part-time employees or contract (temporary) employees may not be interested enough in the goals of the organization or their long-term relationship with the organization to be good candidates for involvement programs. The art of good management is to determine what degree of empowerment to extend to different employees. The grid is a useful first step in thinking about designing and implementing employee empowerment processes, which will always be a matter of degree.

Finally, empowerment can lead to problems if empowered employees make decisions that are disadvantageous to other employees. For example, if a desk agent allows guests to check out two hours late, the housekeeping staff may have difficulty in preparing the room for the next guest, especially if another empowered desk agent allows the next guest to check in early. Empowering one employee must not be allowed to affect other employees negatively in the performance of their jobs.

### Motivation, Empowerment, and Retention

The successful hospitality manager knows the vital importance of motivation and empowerment, if the organization is going to retain the employees it worked so hard to recruit and train. Excellent employees sometimes build strong relationships with long-time repeat guests. These relationships motivate guests to come back again and again; seeing those familiar employee faces adds value to their guest experience. If the hospitality organization cannot retain these excellent employees, the experience of repeat guests, so important to organizational success, is diminished.

## EMPLOYEE ACCEPTANCE OF MANAGERIAL DIRECTION

The final important idea that managers should understand with regard to motivating job performance involves authority or direction. Managers who wish others to work for them have to understand why people follow orders and do what managers ask them to do. To many managers, authority is the power to yell at someone because you are the boss. These managers are comfortable with the historically accepted idea that the boss tells subordinates to jump and lets them ask how high on the way up. These managers are less comfortable with the fact that many times they get little or no cooperation, high turnover, low morale, and a hostile work environment.

Because the research is so convincing that the employee's attitude directly influences the guest's attitude, hospitality organizations have no place for this type of manager. An unhappy worker creates an unhappy customer. While a happy worker may not single-handedly be able to ensure a positive guest experience, an enthusiastic, concerned, and happy employee does make any guest experience better. How, then, does the hospitality manager or supervisor get people to accept direction and work hard on behalf of the organization?

### Authority-Acceptance Theory

According to classic management writer Chester Barnard's **authority-acceptance theory,** authority is the quality of an order that causes someone else to accept the order and to do as ordered.[23] If someone gives you an order to bring a keg of beer from the cooler and you do it, that order has authority for you. If you do not do it, that order does not have authority for you. So, whether an order has authority or not is determined by the order *receiver,* not the sender or "person in authority." In much the same way that value is defined by the guest and rewards by the employee, authority is always accepted by the employee or there is no authority.

The factors influencing the acceptance of managerial direction lie in the nature of the sender and receiver, their relationships to the organization and to each other, and in the nature of the communication itself. The manager must understand and pay attention to these factors that influence employee acceptance of direction. Just as many governments must rely on the consent of the governed, so too must hospitality organizations.

## Conditions for Accepting Direction

Four preconditions must be met before an employee will accept managerial direction. Even if the preconditions are met, the employee may still not accept the order. But if they are not met, the employee either will not or cannot accept the order.

*1. The employee must understand the order.* Otherwise, compliance with the order is impossible. Many employees have listened carefully and then later wondered what the boss was talking about or what the boss wanted done. Many employees have thought they understood an order and then found that they did not, because the order was too confusing or too general. Area Regional Supervisor Jones tells Store Manager Smith, "Get rid of the trouble with the refrigerator at the Garden Grill Restaurant." Smith removes the troublesome refrigerator, scraps it, and replaces it with a new one, when Jones really wanted the old one repaired. The two employees had different meanings for "Get rid of the trouble." Even though they both "understood" the order, their understandings were different. A manager who has not checked to see if the communication was understood has not exercised authority. Employees who are supposed to comply with the order cannot do what they do not understand.

*2. The employee must believe that the order is consistent with the organization's goals.* An airline flight attendant notices that the exit to a plane has oil on the floor, which might endanger the safety of deplaning passengers. The pilot tells the attendant to allow the passengers off the plane anyway. Because so many training sessions have stressed the primary importance of passenger safety, the attendant may well ignore the pilot. Without some reasonable explanation for departing from safety standards, the attendant would not see the order as consistent with the organization's goals. All experienced managers know employees will not usually follow such orders. If an order appears to conflict with an organizational goal, accepted policy, tradition, or past practice, the manager must spend a moment to explain why this time is different.

A special violation of this precondition is the role conflict caused by conflicting orders from two or more different managers. Both orders are sent down, but they cannot both support the organization's effort. The employee will either accept one order and reject the other, or do nothing.

**3. The employee must believe that the order is consistent with the employee's own goals.** This precondition is related to whatever reasons the employee had for affiliating with the organization in the first place. If carrying out the order will result in the organization's becoming less attractive to the employee, the order will be disobeyed or (more usually) evaded. Such orders are inconsistent with the employee's personal motives, which are the basis for accepting any orders at all. If the order is totally inconsistent with goals or principles that are important to the employee, and the order cannot be ignored or avoided, the employee will probably resign. Accepting or rejecting managerial or supervisory direction is a result of the employee carefully weighing the balance between the inducements offered and the contributions expected in return. If inducements offered are equal to or more than the contributions expected, orders will be accepted. If required contributions outweigh inducements, orders will not be carried out.

Although each employee may have some unique goals, most employees want a job that is fun, fair, and interesting. To whatever extent organizational leaders can provide these inducements, and build them into the job situation, the organization will promote the willing acceptance of managerial direction by employees.

**4. The employee must be able, physically and mentally, to carry out the order.** This precondition may seem too obvious to mention. Yet we are sometimes asked to do the impossible. A woman with a bad back is told to carry heavy cases of liquor. An employee allergic to detergent is told to take a temporary assignment in the hotel laundry. The manager who gives orders without knowing each employee's capabilities soon finds out that if it can't be done, it won't.

## Securing Compliance with Orders

Once the preconditions to the acceptance of authority have been met, how do managers actually secure compliance with orders meeting the preconditions? The compliance necessary for a smoothly functioning organization comes about for three reasons.

**1. Effective managers issue orders that comply with the four preconditions.** The effective executive issues orders that are accepted. Orders that do not comply with the preconditions are not obeyed. Poor managers ignore the preconditions primarily for one reason: They don't know any better. They think their formal organizational positions give them the right to issue commands of all types. Many managers believe they have absolute authority over their subordinates. This belief is confirmed by many organizational experiences in which their subordinates do indeed comply with their orders.

However, effective managers soon learn that "absolute" authority is absolute only as long as the four preconditions are not violated. If managers meet the preconditions, employees allow them to be authoritarian and autocratic. Once the manager begins to ignore the preconditions, employees begin to ignore the orders.

**2. People joining an organization expect to do job-related tasks.** They expect to be given directions, instructions, and sometimes commands regarding certain aspects of their behavior in the organization. They obey orders within these "zones of acceptance" without question. Orders fall into three classes: clearly acceptable, clearly unacceptable, and questionable.

If Lois Evans tells her secretary, Bill Elliot, to come into her office and take some dictation, the order would fall within Elliot's zone of acceptance. Elliot knew when he took the job that Evans might tell him to take dictation. On the other hand, if Evans asks Elliot to come over to her apartment for drinks and dictation, Elliot would probably refuse. He would not consider such overtime work outside the office to be an acceptable part of the job.

Many orders fall into a third area: the questionable zone. If Evans asks Elliot to make the coffee, or get a birthday card for Mr. Evans, or some other task that is not part of the job but is not really outrageous, Elliot may be unsure about whether to follow the order and might have to think about it.

The width of the acceptance zone depends on the extent to which the organization fulfills the member's needs. A fanatical member of a cult might be willing to do anything the cult asked. There may be literally nothing that the fanatic would not do to advance the organization's cause. Most organizational members, however loyal and hard working they may be, are not nearly so fanatical. The essential point here is that the greater the benefits or inducements that the organization provides to its members, the more willing they are to accept orders from the organizational leadership.

Tales of Disney's early days report employees who worked incredibly long hours with energy and enthusiasm because they were so committed to what the organization was trying to accomplish. The story of one employee is illustrative:

> Everyone wanted so badly for Walt's wonderland to work, they gave it their all. "I ran my ass off," says one veteran. "I lost fifteen pounds in the first sixty days. You never walked; you got behind the scenes and ran. There was always a fire to put out. I went fourteen months straight without a day off."[24]

Employees this enthused and committed may be ready to accept even the most unreasonable requests. When the orders fall into the doubtful zone, they usually give the organization the benefit of the doubt. Effective managers find ways to keep the inducements/contributions balance tilted heavily in favor of the employee. They know what inducements are available, try to identify those that are important to the employee, and provide that array of inducements.

### 3. Most group members want "their" organization to run smoothly.
If it does, they can gain the benefits that they anticipated when they joined. Therefore, group members will bring social pressure to bear on any member unwilling to accept authority. Employees realize they cannot achieve their own personal goals if the organization fails. An organization cannot succeed if its members will not accept authority and take orders. Therefore, any member who denies an order or will not cooperate represents a threat to those members who identify with and work toward organizational goals for their own reasons. Accordingly, the group takes an active interest in maintaining every member's compliance with organizational commands.

The informal organization plays this important enforcement role in support of the formal organization's authority structure. If the informal organization wants a decision implemented, it is usually implemented. If a decision is not agreeable to the informal organization, its members can find many effective ways of holding up implementation.

The individual gives the manager *authority;* the organization gives managers *power.* Organizations promote their best and most expert employees and give them control over resources, put them in key positions where they control information (a key resource), and give them titles to remind everyone who is higher ranking. The more important the rewards which a manager controls are to an employee, the more power that manager will have to get that employee to accept authority. All employees seek certain types and amounts of inducements from their organizations; that's why they signed on. The manager able to provide those inducements can elicit effort, productivity, enthusiasm, and other contributions that the hospitality organization seeks from all employees. Determining the resources that are important to an individual or a group of individuals is a key responsibility of the manager seeking to retain the enthusiastic commitment of the people who work in that manager's area of responsibility. Making it possible for the employees to meet their financial, belonging, and growth needs while working for the organization is one key way.

## Lessons Learned

1. Set clear, measurable standards that define expectations for job performance. Constantly reinforce these standards by setting examples; let employees know that the standards are important; reward employees when they meet them.
2. Walk the talk; set the example. Employees respond more to what you do than to what you say.
3. Make all tasks and goals measurable; people like to know how well they're doing.
4. Pay attention to communication; people can't do what they don't know about or understand.
5. Be fair, ethical, and equitable. People need to feel they are being treated equitably. If you don't show people why differentials are made between employees, they will assume the worst.
6. Reward behaviors you want, and don't reward behaviors you don't want.
7. Praise, praise, praise. Look for reasons to reinforce people doing the right things. Privately re-educate and coach those doing the wrong things.
8. Show employees the relationships between their personal goals, group goals, and organizational goals. Find "win-win-wins."
9. People give you the right to lead them. Know how to earn that right.
10. Don't just support your frontline employees; trust them as well.
11. Give people a chance to grow and get better, and then reward them for it.
12. Your frontline employees are heroes; make their jobs fun, fair, and interesting.

## Review Questions

1. If you were employed in the past, what did you want from your jobs other than a paycheck, if anything?
   A. If you are employed now, have your job expectations changed from those of the past?
   B. What are your job expectations from the position you hope to hold in ten years?

    C. How if at all do your responses to these questions match up with what hospitality employees typically want from their jobs?

2. If you have been employed, can you recall times when you were doing a good job and were ignored by your boss because that person was giving complete attention to another employee who was complaining or doing a bad job? If so, what managerial lesson does this teach you? How would you use that lesson to determine or change your own managerial style?

3. What does it mean to be empowered? Give some situations in which you were empowered.
    A. How did you handle it? How did you feel?
    B. Compare those situations to a few in which you were not empowered. How did you handle those, and how did you feel?
    C. If you were a hotel or restaurant manager, can you think of some job functions that you would hesitate to empower your employees to perform?
    D. Why is it particularly important to empower the frontline people who interact with hospitality guests? Or is it?

4. Give examples of effective and ineffective teams of which you have been a part. What made them different? How were the leader characteristics related to team effectiveness or ineffectiveness?

5. Consider a restaurant meal, in which much of the service is provided one-on-one, server to guest. How important is teamwork to the success of the guest experience?

6. The authority-acceptance theory suggests that people must *accept* authority or it does not really exist. Do you agree or disagree?
    A. Give examples of situations you have been in where people did not follow direct orders. Was the refusal because the conditions for authority acceptance detailed in the chapter were not met, or for other reasons?
    B. What do managers need to know to ensure that their authority is accepted?
    C. How does all that relate to managing the guest experience in hospitality organizations?
    D. Does authority-acceptance theory seem to you to have more or less relevance to the hospitality industry as compared to most industries?

## *Activities*

1. Find a hospitality organization that seems to have succeeded in motivating its frontline employees in guest service to give outstanding service. How do they do it? If you or your friends work for organizations that do not sufficiently motivate you, what are they doing or not doing that causes you to be unmotivated?

2. Find an organization that seems to try to make its hospitality jobs fun and interesting. What do they do, and how well does it work? If you or your friends have jobs that do not provide fun and are not interesting, why is that so? Does the organization seem to care whether you are interested and having fun? Why or why not?

3. Interview three line employees from two different hospitality organizations and find out what motivates them.

# Case Studies

## Hartsell Hotels

*W*hile he was still in college, Bill Hartsell decided that he wanted to build and own hotels When he graduated, he borrowed some money, bought a bankrupt property, and created the first Hartsell Hotel. The hotel presented constant problems, but Bill was highly motivated and worked twelve to sixteen hours a day, six or seven days a week. He did as much of the work as he could himself, from making beds to preparing light meals in the hotel coffee shop.

The hard work paid off. Bill succeeded with his original hotel, bought two more, and increased his staff accordingly. He made a determined effort to hire young people, old people, women, minorities, and the handicapped, and he paid them as well as he could. Bill felt a genuine sense of responsibility to his employees and to the community. After five years, Bill had 300 employees.

Bill hired three recent hospitality graduates, intending to move them into responsible management positions after a training period. At his first meeting with them, Bill made his position plain: "No one at Hartsell Hotels works harder than I do. I'm the first to arrive and the last to leave. I work most weekends. I'm paying you well. I'm offering you a chance for rapid advancement. But don't think in terms of a 40-hour work week. I want you to work as hard as I do and act as if this business were your own. Is that clear?" In unison the three responded, "Yes, sir, Mr. Hartsell."

Three months later they had all left and taken jobs with Marriott, Radisson, and Ritz-Carlton.

\* \* \*

1. What, if anything, was wrong with Mr. Hartsell's approach?
2. Were his expectations for his new employees unrealistic? If so, why?
3. What inconsistencies, if any, do you see between the goals of the three new employees and Mr. Hartsell's goals?
4. Could those inconsistencies have been resolved? How?

## Farney Spa and Fish Camp

*F*arney Spa and Fish Camp has found its niche; it caters to women who want to combine the facilities of a luxury spa with fishing opportunities. Sally Blade, supervisor in charge of fishing guides at Farney Spa and Fish Camp, has a problem with one of the fishing guides. All guides are supposed to be at work by 5:30 A.M. They must have their skiffs ready for operation by 6:30 A.M. But Mary Lou Day is almost always late for work. She arrives any time between 5:40 and 6:15 A.M. Once she gets to work, she is excellent. She is easily the best guide in the camp and always gets her boat prepared early, even after arriving late. She is qualified for a promotion except that she has not been in her present position long enough. She understands and accepts that situation, but she hopes to move up into management some day.

Day's frequent tardiness is causing problems. Other guides, without Day's willingness or ability, are using Day's lateness to justify their own. Sally Blade feels she cannot crack down on the other guides without cracking down on Day as well. Sally has had several talks with Mary Lou. She always promises to do better, but she never does. Sally has even suggested a different reporting and leaving time for Mary Lou, to accommodate fishing parties that don't like to head out onto the lake so early, but Mary Lou does not like the idea of being treated differently. "After all," she says, "I always get my skiff ready on time, my guests like the service I provide, and I always get my boat back and cleaned up by quitting time, don't I?" Mary Lou *has even suggested that she may quit if the organization cannot be "flexible enough to let one good employee be a few minutes late every so often, without bugging me about it. There are other fish camps on this lake, you know."*

\* \* \*

1. Mary Lou Day is Sally Blade's best fishing guide. Is Mary Lou justified in asking that Sally "cut her some slack"? Should Sally comply?
2. If you think Mary Lou should meet the same work requirements that are imposed on the other guides, how would you motivate her to do so?

## Jubilee Hotels Corp.

*In the mid-1990s, Jubilee Hotels Corp. was having problems with negative worker attitudes and low productivity at its Hartwell, Alabama, hotel. To turn things around, JHC decided to change the operation of the Hartwell hotel completely. The hotel would be run with a minimum of supervision. The employees themselves would take over such traditional management prerogatives as making job assignments, scheduling coffee breaks, interviewing prospective employees, and even deciding on pay raises.*

*The new system eliminated several layers of management and supervisory personnel and assigned three primary areas of responsibility—front desk, housekeeping, and office duties—to self-managing teams of 7 to 14 workers per shift. The former middle managers, divided among the primary areas, retained some supervisory authority but had not nearly as much as before. The workers rotated between the dull and the interesting jobs. The teams made all necessary management decisions.*

*The new system was a success in many ways. Unit costs of 10 percent less than under the old system translated into a savings of $2 million per year. Turnover was only 5 percent, and the hotel went two years, eight months under this new approach. From the humanistic standpoint, quality of work life and economic results were good.*

*Notwithstanding the plan's success, by 1999 the hotel began the transition back to a traditional organizational and management system, as an accompaniment to a major expansion. JHC introduced more specialized job classifications and more supervisors, and reduced opportunities for employee participation. The company added seven management positions to the hotel, including controller, engineering manager, and services manager. Management took back the right to make decisions about pay raises.*

*Professor Andrew Stubbs analyzed what had happened at Hartwell for his hospitality class: "The basic problem was that in this functional organization, many managers became nervous about what functions they would keep after the hotel workers themselves were given so many responsibilities. In addition, they resented being left out of things; upper-level management's enthusiasm for enriching the jobs of the workers didn't take into account the feelings of the middle managers. Where was their enrichment?"*

\* \* \*

1. Do you agree with the professor's assessment of what went wrong?
2. What does the Jubilee Hotel experience tell you about applying work team, enrichment, and incentives principles in real life?

## Additional Readings

Bettencourt, Lance A., and Stephen W. Brown. 1997. Contact Employees: Relationships Among Workplace Fairness, Job Satisfaction and Prosocial Behaviors. *Journal of Retailing* 73(1):39–61.

Borchgrevink, Carl P. 1997. Leader-Member Exchange: Paying Attention to Immediate Subordinate Pays Off. *FIU Hospitality Review* 15(1):97–102.

Bowen, David E., and Edward E. Lawler, III. 1995. Empowering Service Employees. *Sloan Management Review* 36(4):73–84.

Brymer, R. A. 1991. Employee Empowerment: A Guest-Driven Leadership Strategy. *Cornell Hotel and Restaurant Administration Quarterly* 32(May):58–68.

Dover, Kyle. 1999. Avoiding Empowerment Traps. *Management Review* 88(1):51–55.

Groves, Jim, Mary B. Gregoire, and Ronald Downey. 1995. Relationship Between the Service Orientation of Employees and Operational Indicators in a Multi-unit Restaurant Corporation. *Hospitality Research Journal* 19(3):33–44.

Haskins, Mark E., Jeanne Liedtk, and John Rosenblum. 1998. Beyond Teams: Toward an Ethic of Collaboration. *Organizational Dynamics* 26(4):34–50.

Lashley, C. 1995. Towards an Understanding of Employee Empowerment in Hospitality Services. *International Journal of Contemporary Hospitality Management* 7(1):27–32.

Mohr, L. A. and Bitner M. J. 1995. The Role of Employee Effort in Satisfaction with Service Transactions. *Journal of Business Research* 32(3):239–252.

Quinn, Robert E., and Gretchen M. Spreitzer. 1997. The Road to Empowerment: Seven Questions Every Leader Should Consider. *Organizational Dynamics* 26(2):37–49.

Schlesinger, Leonard A., and James L. Heskett. 1991. Enfranchisement of Service Workers. *California Management Review* 33(4):83–100.

Sparks, Beverly, and Graham Bradley. 1997. Antecedents and Consequences of Perceived Service Provider Effort in the Hospitality Industry. *Hospitality Research Journal* 20(3):17–34.

Sparrowe, R. 1994. Empowerment in the Hospitality Industry: An Exploration of Antecedents and Outcomes. *Hospitality Research Journal* 17(3):51–74.

Swan, John E., and Michael R. Bowers. 1998. Services Quality and Satisfaction: The Process of People Doing Things Together. *Journal of Services Marketing* 12(1):59–72.

Tannenbaum, Scott I., Rebecca L. Beard, and Hal G. Gueutal. 1998. Moving to a Service-Focused, Managed Growth Culture: A Follow-up on the Case of CDPHP. *Organizational Dynamics* 27(1):75–77.

Wageman, Ruth. 1997. Case Study: Critical Success Factors for Creating Superb Self-Managing Teams at Xerox. *Compensation and Benefits Review* 29(5):31–41.

## Notes

1. Alan G. Robinson and Sam Stern. 1997. *Corporate Creativity: How Innovation and Improvement Actually Happen* (San Francisco: Berrett-Koehler Publishers), pp. 206–207.
2. *Walt Disney: Famous Quotes.* 1994. Printed for Walt Disney Theme Parks and Resorts, 36.
3. Norman Brinker and Donald T. Phillips. 1996. *On the Brink: The Life and Leadership of Norman Brinker.* (Arlington, TX: The Summit Publishing Group), p. 195.

4. Craig R. Taylor and Cindy Wheatley-Lovoy. 1998. Leadership: Lessons From the Magic Kingdom. *Training and Development* (July):24.

5. V. A. Zeithaml and M. J. Bitner. 1996. *Services Marketing* (New York: McGraw-Hill), p. 76.

6. Quoted in Sue Shellenbarger. 1998. Companies Are Finding It Really Pays to Be Nice to Employees. *Wall Street Journal,* July 27:B-1.

7. Ibid.

8. Ibid. A compelling discussion of the employee satisfaction-customer satisfaction link can be found in: Benjamin Schneider and David E. Bowen. 1993. The Service Organization: Human Resources Management Is Crucial. *Organizational Dynamics* 21(2):39–52. See also: Benjamin Schneider and David E. Bowen. 1995. *Winning the Service Game* (Boston: Harvard Business School Press).

9. Blake E. Ashforth and Ronald H. Humphrey. 1993. Emotional Labor in Service Roles. *Academy of Management Review* 18(1):94.

10. Ibid., 98.

11. Ibid., 102.

12. Brinker and Phillips, 192.

13. This discussion of empowerment is based on Robert C. Ford and Myron D. Fottler. 1995. Empowerment: A Matter of Degree. *Academy of Management Executive* 9(3):21–28.

14. D. E. Bowen and E. E. Lawler. 1992. The Empowerment of Service Workers: What, Why, How, and When. *Sloan Management Review* 33(1):31–39.

15. L. C. Plunkett and R. Fournier. 1991. *Participative Management: Implementing Empowerment* (New York: John Wiley & Sons): 5.

16. J. B. Schor. 1991. *The Overworked American* (New York: Bagle Books), p. 11.

17. A classic book on this subject is J. R. Hackman and G. P. Oldham. 1980. *Work Design* (Reading, MA: Addison-Wesley).

18. http://ritzcarlton.com/corporate/SDWT.htm (May 1999).

19. B. Dumaine. 1990. "Who Needs a Boss?" *Fortune,* May 7:52–60.

20. F. Shipper and C. C. Manz. 1992. Employee Self-Management Without Formally Designated Teams: An Alternative Road to Empowerment. *Organizational Dynamics* 20(3):59. See also 48–61.

21. Kevin Freiberg and Jackie Freiberg. 1996. *Nuts! Southwest Airlines' Crazy Recipe for Business and Personal Success* (Austin, TX: Bard Press), p. 289.

22. See Bowen and Lawler, 31–39.

23. See Chester I. Barnard. 1968. *The Functions of the Executive* (Cambridge, MA: Harvard University Press), Chapter 12.

24. David Koenig. 1994. *Mouse Tales: A Behind-the-Ears Look at Disneyland* (Irvine, CA: Bonaventure Press), p. 27.

# Involving the Guest: Coproduction

**Hospitality Principle:**

Empower guests to help create their own experience.

*If you can't get it for yourself, who's going to get it for you?*

—Fritz Perls, father of Gestalt Psychology

## LEARNING OBJECTIVES

After reading this chapter, you should understand:

▓ How, when, and why hospitality organizations encourage or empower guests to help provide their own guest experiences.
▓ Which strategies most effectively involve the guest in the experience.
▓ What the advantages and disadvantages of guest involvement are for the organization and the guest.
▓ Why hospitality organizations must sometimes "fire the guest" and how to do it.

## KEY TERMS AND CONCEPTS

coproduction                                                        guest participation
firing the guest

## THE GUEST CAN HELP!

In the traditional manufacturing organization, the people involved in the core production tasks are insulated from external interruptions by layers of strategic planners and middle managers. The people providing many hospitality services, on the other hand, are right out in the open where the guests can see them. In some circumstances, the guests can even become involved in producing the service themselves. Obvious examples in the hospitality industry are salad bars in restaurants and coffee equipment in hotel rooms. Other obvious examples are automatic teller machines and self-serve gas pumps.

The implications for hospitality organizations of having the guest involved in the production process as either observer or participant are many. First, the organization must remain constantly aware that the server is the point of contact between the organization and the guest. Instead of a highly paid, experienced, and loyal executive or well-trained sales representative serving as the point of contact with customers and the outside world, the hospitality organization must rely on its frontline servers to represent the company. They embody the moment of truth for the guest's contact with the organization. Each year, for millions of Disney park visitors, Southwest Airlines passengers, Olive Garden Restaurant diners, and Marriott hotel guests, the visible, frontline employees answer questions, solve problems, provide services, and keep their organizations operating smoothly and efficiently. These employees not only produce the magic that guests expect, but they do it while the guests are watching, participating, and asking a million questions about everything. Unlike the automobile assembly-line production employee who can work undistracted in a controlled and structured environment, these employees must produce the guest experience consistently and flawlessly while coping with the many uncertainties that interacting constantly with guests can create.

### Guests as Quasi-Employees

Hospitality organizations know they must help manage the confusion and uncertainty guests can create for their employees while they are doing their jobs. One way is by training the employees in both job skills and guest relations. Another effective strategy for managing this confusion is to think of guests as quasi-employees and "manage" them accordingly.[1] This means organizations should design the service product, environment, and delivery system to take advantage of the skills, talents, knowledge, and abilities that these extra "employees" bring to the organization. If it is to the advantage of both guests and organization to involve guests in the experience, then the organization must take on the responsibility of figuring out how best to enable these quasi-employees to do their jobs within the experience.

Benjamin Schneider and David Bowen recommend a three-step strategy for managing these quasi-employees:

1. Define the roles you want guests to play, carefully and completely. In effect, do a job analysis similar to that developed in Chapter 5 for employees. Define the knowledge, skills, and abilities required to perform the jobs identified as desirable and appropriate for guests.
2. Make sure that guests know exactly what you expect them to do and that they are physically able, mentally prepared, and sufficiently skilled to do those tasks. Show guests that performing the tasks is to their benefit. Give them a reason to do the tasks well.
3. Once task performance is underway, evaluate the guest's ability and willingness to perform well. In effect, conduct a performance appraisal on the guest to ensure that the experience being coproduced is meeting expectations. If it is not, identify what needs fixing. Does the guest need further training? Is something about the setting or delivery system impeding the guest's success?[2]

Of course, the customer should not coproduce the experience if learning the necessary skills is too dangerous, time consuming, or difficult. Airline passengers don't help fly the plane. By assessing the entire guest experience carefully, the hospitality provider can identify those parts of it that might be designed to discourage, encourage, or even require **guest participation.** A restaurant could set up a self-service salad bar, an airline might offer self-ticketing, or a hotel might provide self-service check-in. In each of these instances, customers can choose to have an employee serve them or they can produce their own salads, plane tickets, or access to their hotel rooms.

## The Organization Decides

Some hospitality organizations do not offer the guest any choice; they either make guest participation impossible, or they structure the experience so that the guest must participate to some extent to have it. A quick-serve restaurant is quick-serve and inexpensive because it requires customers to serve as their own order-takers, servers, and table clearers. Without the cost of servers bustling about taking a variety of customized orders, filling glasses, and picking up dirty dishes, McDonald's and Burger King can save money and offer a quick, cheaper food product than a fine dining restaurant can. In the fast-food service setting, the customer must participate somewhat but cannot be allowed to take over completely. The efficiency of the quick-serve process is based on a carefully engineered food-production system that ensures a consistent quality and safe food product. Allowing customers to cook their own burgers and fries would significantly interfere with production efficiency while creating substantial food safety and sanitation problems. The quick-serve restaurant gains efficiency by letting the customers serve themselves in the part of the service delivery system that takes place in front of the counter but not allowing them behind the counter where they can slow down the production process or jeopardize food safety.

Organizations need to think through when to let guests coproduce their own experience and how much of it. Sometimes guest participation makes sense for the organization and the guest, sometimes not. The challenge is to identify which situation is which.

## STRATEGIES FOR INVOLVING THE GUEST

A guest can be involved with a hospitality organization in several ways: as a *consultant* or source of expert information, as part of the *environment* for other guests, as *coproducer* of the experience, or as *manager* of the service providers and systems. Some of these involvements may sound unlikely, but they are all common.

### Guests as Unpaid Consultants

Guests often serve as unpaid consultants. When the hospitality organization asks its guests what they like or dislike about the guest experience, they become consultants. Since their input regarding their experiences will become part of the information management uses to review and adjust its service, environment, and delivery system, the guests are acting as expert consultants in giving this important feedback to the organization. Using outsiders in this way is not unique to hospitality firms; many other types of organizations invite their suppliers, customers, and even communities to provide systematic feedback about how they are doing. Southwest Airlines extends the consulting role to include the hiring process. It invites its frequent flyers to participate in interviewing prospective flight attendants.[3] After all, who better to judge whether a person has the qualifications to be an effective flight attendant than the most intense users of the airline? Organizations also frequently invite customers to participate as members of focus groups. As discussed in a later chapter on assessing service quality, these groups are designed to give expert feedback about the service experience to the service provider, and no one should be more expert on that experience than the customers themselves.

### Guests as Part of Each Other's Experience

If you enjoy simply watching other guests, you may think of them as part of the service environment. If other guests are especially important to your enjoyment of your experience, you might even consider them a part of the service product itself. The line is not always clear. As a simple example, most people don't like to go to an empty restaurant or movie; enjoying the experience along with other people, even strangers, is part of the package. Going to an amusement park when it is comfortably full and when it is almost empty are very different experiences. Amusement parks, like many other service situations where the emphasis is on "having fun," rely to some extent on other customers being part of the fun. Thus, many people get great enjoyment out of watching other people, ordinary folks just like themselves, act as bit players in a Universal or Disney-MGM Studios' film-making demonstration. For those doing the acting, the guest experience obviously includes the opportunity to participate in the movie simulation. For observers, however, those customers doing something unusual are perhaps best considered as part of the service environment. Though interesting, unusual, or amusing, they are not really why you came to the theme park, water park, or gaming casino.

This principle of encouraging customers to watch other customers in action is as new as "Funniest Home Videos" and as old as the famous Coney Island, where one of its earliest amusement parks, Steeplechase, had a stadium set up next to a rotating Barrel of Love so that the customers could watch others fall down in a tangle with complete strangers and look foolish. For them, the opportunity to watch other people falling down awkwardly was an important part of the amusement experience. Indeed, the founder of Steeplechase Park early in the twentieth century, George Tilyou, was one of the first to recognize that a successful amusement park provided its customers with the opportunity to observe the most entertaining experience of all: other people. In his park the visitors were the main show. According to amusement parks authority Gary Kyriazi, "Tilyou felt that people will pay any price in order to provide their own entertainment."[4]

After couples had finished the Steeplechase ride, they would walk down a corridor and then find themselves on a brightly lit stage called the Insanitarium. Unknown to them, crowds of people would be sitting in bleachers watching them. As Kyriazi describes the scene, "Suddenly, strong air jets would lift the women's dresses (exposed ankles were rare

*Guests Observing Guests at George Tilyou's Steeplechase Park, Coney Island. The Human Roulette Wheel (top). The Hoop-La (bottom). (Courtesy of Seth Kaufman, Whirl-i-gig. Used with permission.)*

at the time) and blow the men's hats off. A clown would prod the man with an electric stinger. When they tried to escape, piles of barrels on either side of the exit gangway would begin to sway and appear to tumble down on them as they made their escape." They could then join the crowd beyond the glare of the stage lights and laugh at others going through what Kyriazi calls "the same light, humorous torment."[5]

Although standards have changed, and modern hospitality organizations do not see torment, even if "light and humorous," as a service they want to provide, the principle that guests enjoy watching guests is as true today as it was then. Successful operators make sure to offer plenty of opportunities for park attendees to observe each other in a variety of amusing situations.

Although a case can be made for considering other guests as part of the service itself under certain circumstances, they are most often a part of the service environment. Like any other environmental element, they can be a neutral influence, they can damage the experience for others, or they can enhance it. Movies, concerts, and Broadway plays all rely on the audience to help create the mood. All these entertainments are more enjoyable with a full house than they are when empty. The laughter and other reactions of the people surrounding the customer become an important part of the customer's environment as well. Indeed, some attractions rely on paid professionals or electronically created artificial cues to generate applause, laughter, or other emotional responses that create the right setting for the service experience. At the other extreme, everyone has had an experience ruined by a crying baby, a public family squabble, or a thoughtless bunch of loud talkers. For better or worse, other guests are part of the hospitality servicescape and therefore need to be managed like any other environmental element.

## Guests as Coproducers

Perhaps the most important way in which guests can participate, other than simply being there, is as active coproducers of the guest experience. They can actually become part of the production and delivery system. This participation can be as simple as having guests serve themselves at a fast-food restaurant as substitutes for a paid waitstaff, preparing their own salads at the salad bar, or carrying their own bags at the golf course. The value of guest **coproduction** can be substantial for the organization. Every time guests serve themselves or produce their own products, they are replacing labor that the organization would otherwise have to pay to do the same thing, while often improving the quality of their own experience.

Alaska Airlines is developing computerized receivers in airport kiosks that can read information encoded on a passenger's "proximity card" containing a computer chip, microwave transmitter, and battery. Passengers insert the card in the receiver, go to the departure gate, merely show their identification, and take a seat that has been assigned since they informed the airline of their proximity to the gate. The airline also hopes to institute self-check-in of luggage. Passengers would get computer-generated luggage tags at the proximity card kiosks, attach them to the luggage, and place bags on a conveyor, where they would be scanned and sent to the correct flight. Airline agents would always be available for passengers needing or wanting assistance with coproduction of their flight experience.

### Advantages of Coproduction for the Organization

The organization gains several advantages by having the guests coproduce their experience. First, coproduction can reduce employee costs. The more guests do for themselves, the fewer employees the organization needs to employ. In addition to being an obvious labor-saving strategy, guest coproduction allows the organization to use the talents of its employees better.

If guests are allowed, encouraged, or forced to take care of some of their own basic require-ments, employees are freed up to do more elaborate or complicated tasks that the guests would not enjoy or do successfully, and tasks that would simply not be suitable for guests. For example, at some Epcot restaurants, patrons are allowed to make their own reservations by touch-screen television. Maitre d's take fewer reservation phone calls, which permits them to spend more time responding to the needs of guests who need information or advice. In effect, the quality of the restaurant service goes up with no increase in costs by letting the guests schedule themselves through the computer.

In a similar fashion, the strategy of offering buffets at lunch is an effective way for restau-rants to stay open at lunch time without overextending the waitstaff. Many servers are unhappy working at lunch time, because the check sizes (and tips) are lower. People tired out from working at lunch cannot work as efficiently at the dinner hour. A buffet provides meals with a minimal use of waitstaff, the diner gets a good price on the meal, the restau-rant provides a better work situation for its servers, and the service at night may be better than if servers had also worked at lunch time.

### Advantages of Coproduction for the Guest

For the guest, coproduction has a number of advantages. First it can decrease the opportu-nity for service failure while increasing the perception, and perhaps the actuality, of service quality. Since the guests themselves define value and quality, handling production them-selves means they can produce exactly what they want. If guests fix their own salads at the salad bar in exactly the way they want them, how can they complain if the salads aren't per-fect? Guests can pile on their favorite salad items in their favorite quantities and avoid the items they dislike. They end up feeling they got the very salad they wanted. This opportu-nity creates the perception of real value.

*Piccadilly Buffet. (Courtesy of Piccadilly Cafeterias, Inc.)*

Second, the opportunity for self-service typically reduces the time required for service. A simple example is the customer at the bank who chooses to use the ATM instead of going inside the bank and standing in line for a teller. Fast-food restaurants make their reputation and define their market niche on the basis of saving time for their customers who are too busy to eat in a traditional restaurant.

Third, self-service reduces the risk of unpleasant surprises for guests. If diners walk through a cafeteria's buffet line, they can see exactly what the food products are, instead of ordering off a menu and hoping for the best. While not everything tastes as good as it looks, choosing one's own meal from a cafeteria line or buffet seems to reduce the perception of risk in comparison with ordering sight unseen from a menu.

### Disadvantages of Coproduction for the Organization

Permitting or requiring guest participation may also have disadvantages for both the organization and the guest. First, in this litigious society, participation exposes the organization to legal risk. Having a guest handle a hot pot in a cook-your-own fondue restaurant can lead to a major burn and lawsuit. Second, the organization may have to spend extra money to train the service delivery employees so that they can add to their usual serving jobs the task of communicating effectively and easily about what the guest is supposed to do. These employees are responsible for instructing the guests in how to provide the service for themselves and for monitoring the experience to prevent the guests from creating any disasters. Every guest is different, comes to the guest experience with different skills, knowledge, and abilities, and has different expectations for the service itself; thus, servers who train and oversee guests must be alert, observant, and well trained in how to coach guests through the experience. Hiring and training people to perform the necessary job skills at, say, a modern copy center is one thing, but to allow or encourage self-service, the organization must go beyond basic job skills to hire and train people who can successfully teach customers to use computers, scanners, and copy machines.

If guests coproduce their own experience, the service delivery system must be user friendly. If the organization wants the guest to follow a predetermined sequence of operations to create the desired experience, it must either have people to guide them, excellent directional signs, or a layout that is intuitively obvious to people from varied cultures. Only then can the organization be reasonably sure that all types of guests will do what they are supposed to do when and where they are supposed to do it. Signs in a self-serve cafeteria must indicate clearly where the entry point is, where the trays, silverware, and napkins are, and how the diner is supposed to proceed through the food selection and payment procedure. Someone unfamiliar with a cafeteria restaurant might have no idea how to navigate this service delivery process. The cafeteria workers must be alert to confused-looking people wandering around looking for signs, directions, and instructions on how to participate successfully in this food delivery process.

Involving guests in the service delivery system also has an impact on the cost and layout of the environment. As usual, the organization must spend time and energy ensuring that the traditional front-of-the-house areas that guests see meet their expectations in terms of appearance and quality. But involving guests in the service delivery system means that some back-of-the-house areas must meet their expectations as well. Making the back of the house a part of the "show" has an obvious impact on how the equipment is laid out, what it looks like, how shiny it is kept, how the personnel are dressed, and what skills they must have to work alongside the guests in service production. Instead of having not particularly articulate cooks in greasy aprons producing meals in an out-of-sight kitchen, involvement of the guest in a food-production system means that the organization must hire employees who can communicate easily with diners, look trim and neat in appearance, and ensure that the kitchen and other visible food preparation areas are always clean and healthy looking to meet the guest's expectations. All this is expensive as the costs of the uniforms, the extra interpersonal skills required of the employees, and the rearrangement of the food-production area to allow the guest to be involved in the food-production process will add to the costs of the production system.

Guest involvement changes the role of the guest-contact employee. Now the employee must have the skills and abilities to be a coach, trainer, teacher, standard setter, and manager of the guest flow through the delivery system. Hospitality employees must know how to get guests engaged in coproduction and also how to get them to disengage. If guests enjoy coproduction and are reluctant to disengage, the organization that does not want to prod its guests along may have to add extra capacity.

Clearly, when guests become coproducers, the traditional role of server in the guest experience needs redefinition, and servers need additional training in the new roles they must now play if coproduction is to work to the organization's advantage.

### Disadvantages of Coproduction for the Guest

From the guest's perspective, coproduction also may have disadvantages. The most obvious one is that paying guests may resent having to produce any part of that for which they are paying. Some task-oriented guests don't particularly want much guest-server interaction; they just want, say, a good meal. A production-line approach suits them just fine. Other guests insist and thrive on close personal attention and are willing to pay for it. If shifting part of the guest-experience production to guests themselves results in less TLC, some guests will be dissatisfied. Another possible disadvantageous outcome is failure to coproduce the service or any associated product properly. If you find that the items you assembled from the salad bar don't taste as good as you thought they would, or if your experiment with some new food selections from the buffet was not a success, you will not have coproduced a *wow* for yourself. And you can't even blame the service provider for the unsatisfactory experience. Hospitality organizations try to protect guests against self-service failures; as much as you do, they want you to have the satisfying experience you expected when you chose them rather than a competitor. They may let you try again or offer to help. The risk is nonetheless present that the guest will coproduce an unsatisfactory experience.

### The High Cost of Failure

While unsatisfactory or unsuccessful coproduction can be a minor annoyance to a restaurant patron, it can be disastrous if the cost of failure is great. If you run a dude ranch and let inexperienced riders go off alone on horseback, the result may be humiliation, broken bones, or worse—plus a law suit. Or imagine a situation in which you coproduce a meal in front of a peer, boss, or significant other—and fail. Good hospitality organizations make every effort to ensure that guests succeed as coproducers, but the risk of failure is always there. If the costs of failure would be too high, then the organization must tactfully intervene to keep the guest from failing. The server must be sensitive and aware enough to recognize when a guest is about to fail, must take over before the failure occurs, and must be able to do so with sufficient grace that the guest is not embarrassed by failing when others all around are succeeding. Those requirements add up to a tall order.

## Know-How and Motivation

Guests can safely participate when they have the necessary knowledge, skills, and abilities. Guests are motivated to participate when they must participate to have the experience at all or when they can see some benefits in participation. Some experiences can be completed only if coproduced. Psychiatric treatment will fail if the patient refuses to be involved. In any large geographically spread service setting—like a zoo, museum, food court, cruise ship, or national park—customers who want a particular array of experiences must schedule them for themselves. If customers don't plan out their time and physically move themselves around, they don't enjoy the experience as much.

Many guests are motivated to participate because of their personalities or their familiarity with the experience being offered, or they are simply looking for something to do while waiting for the other parts of the guest experience to take place. Some guests just want to be a part of whatever it is they're involved in at the moment, no matter what, and constantly look for such opportunities. Some people always park their own cars, carry their own luggage, or walk up the stairs because they like to demonstrate for themselves (and anyone else who cares to watch) that they are physically fit enough to do these things. Others like to show how mentally fit or technically adept they are by doing things for themselves—whether it be by making their own on-line travel reservations or baiting their own hooks on a deep-sea fishing trip.

Finally, some people just like to be the center of attention and seek opportunities to be "on stage." In a simple situation, Joe wants to show his friends how well known he is at Ralph's Restaurant, so he goes and gets his own coffee or refills his partner's ice water instead of waiting for the server. Even more on stage is the person who volunteers to sing in a karaoke bar or to be drenched by Shamu in the SeaWorld demonstration. Many people enjoy showing off, and hospitality organizations should try to provide appropriate opportunities for them somewhere in the service delivery system.

## The Guest as a Substitute for Management

Guests can even serve in a quasi-managerial role as unofficial supervisors and motivators of employees; they can even train other guests. How and when do they supervise employees?

### Guests as Supervisors

Guests have more contact with the service personnel, talk to them more often, and see more of their job performance than the organization's own supervisors do. Guests have the opportunity and the motivation to act as supervisors and provide immediate feedback as to whether an employee is making them happy or unhappy. After all, the guest is paying for the service and is therefore motivated to tell the server (who to the guest receiving the service *is* the organization) what the guest thinks about the service, the server, and the organization. Hospitality employees are trying to produce magical guest experiences; the guests themselves will let the employees know how well they have succeeded. The more familiar guests are with the organization, the more they know about what level of service should be provided and the more qualified they are to provide technical feedback. All of these guest activities and functions are in a sense supervisory because the guests are observing, guiding, and motivating the behavior of employees, then "paying" them for good or poor service with a large or small tip.

Everyone has watched an unhappy guest tell an employee that the employee is not providing the service properly. That guest is in effect performing a supervisory function: providing feedback to the employee. Anyone watching characters in the Magic Kingdom interact with the

*Guests Can Be Supervisors. (Photograph by Michael Dzamen.)*

children will soon see that the children are supervising the actions and behavior of the characters better than any supervisor ever could. The children will immediately respond to any deviation from character or any flaw in the character performance. They give constant feedback to cast members to let them know if they are not doing something right. Although supervisors also monitor the behavior of cast members as they perform their character roles, their job is, in a sense, much simpler than that of supervisors in the manufacturing sector. The typical auto assembly-line worker never has a car talk to him, smile at him when he installs the brakes correctly, or complain when he doesn't. The assembly-line supervisor must do all these things. In the hospitality organization, guests talk, smile, give directions, and complain. They assess the performance of servers and, through tips, compensate them accordingly. Having guests constantly monitoring and responding to the employee's job performance is a substantial aid to the supervisory responsibility.

### Guests As Motivators

Having guests participate in supervision can be highly motivating to employees when guests tell them in both verbal and nonverbal ways what a good job they are doing. Most hospitality employees find great enjoyment in meeting and exceeding the expectations of guests. Chefs love to be challenged by others who are also knowledgeable about the culinary arts. Hospitality employees usually enjoy the opportunity to be challenged by a guest who shares an interest or expertise in the subject of the experience. College professors often find the students who ask the most difficult questions to be the most fun to have in class. Most hospitality employees are constantly tested by the variety in guest expectations and ability to perform their responsibilities in the service delivery process. The challenge of making *all* children happy by responding to their unique needs and personalities makes the job of playing a Disney character a high-status and highly sought-after job inside the Magic Kingdom. It's fun to show off what you can really do when you have an appreciative audience.

### Guests Train Guests

Guests can also train each other. Learning how to stand in line seems like an obvious skill until one encounters people from other cultures who do not believe in standing in line. Someone has to train the untrained to stand in line in an orderly way, and the people already in line will do that. Watch the customers already standing in line the next time you see someone break into a line and you'll witness a training session in line standing. Most guests of hospitality organizations, like most employees, are anxious to fulfill their responsibilities and do their jobs well. They can be seen watching other people to learn what their own behavior should be in the various tasks of the production process. We all learn from watching others, and with so many people in most hospitality situations on a typical day or occasion, we can learn what we're supposed to do to enjoy the experience by observing others. The first-time guest at a basketball game learns from others when to chant "airball" and enjoys the game all the more for chanting.

The organization can also use videos of experienced guests to show waiting guests what they are supposed to do. At most amusement parks, television monitors are set up so waiting guests can see what role will be expected of them when their turn comes to participate in the attraction or get on the ride. Waiting lines are frequently located to allow guests not being served to observe guests who are being served; by the time the guests in line get to the server, they know pretty much what they are supposed to do.

If the organization can use its guests to train at least some of the other guests, it can save itself the cost of those employees who would have been required to train those guests and minimize the time spent explaining to the next guest what the last guest just did. The cost and time savings can be substantial.

## DETERMINING WHEN PARTICIPATION MAKES SENSE

Sometimes both the organization and the guest benefit from guest participation and sometimes not. Distinguishing when, where, and how much the guest should or should not be involved in any part of the guest experience depends on a variety of factors. Generally speaking, participating in the service is in the interest of guests when they can gain value, reduce risk, or improve the quality of the experience. Participation is in the organization's interest when it can save money, increase production efficiency, or differentiate its service from those of competitors in some key way. Each opportunity for guest participation should be assessed on these criteria and designed into the hospitality organization when the factors are favorable and designed out when they are not.

### Enriching the Wait

Other situations encouraging guest participation sometimes evolve when guests are required to wait for service. Organizations should try to decrease the feeling that the wait is too long by giving guests something to do, ideally something that will enrich the overall experience. A good example is getting a group of people sitting on a delayed flight to participate in a singalong, a technique frequently attributed to Southwest Airlines. Passengers get the opportunity to keep active while they are waiting for their flight to take off, and the singing may even enhance the experience by providing a pleasant way to pass the time.

## Adding Value

While some hospitality situations require participation and some guests look for opportunities to participate no matter what, almost everyone is happy to coproduce if it adds value to their experience. By definition, value can be added by reducing costs (for the same quality), increasing quality (for the same costs), or both. Costs include not only the price but also the other costs incurred by being involved in the guest experience. For example, if a potential guest sees a long line outside her favorite restaurant, the time cost of waiting for the next available table may be so great that she willingly goes to a nearby cafeteria or fast-food restaurant—to minimize the time cost of getting a meal. The guest may experience a decrease in quality but expects the greater decrease in overall cost to compensate for it. Similarly, guests who want to be sure of service quality may want to participate in providing service. Those guests derive additional value from knowing that they are getting the service "their way." Home Depot has made a lot of money serving customers who want to ensure the quality and value of their home repair by doing it themselves. Customers look to Home Depot not only to provide a fair price on the building products but also to give the necessary instruction or help to do the job correctly.

Another cost of coproduction for the guest is risk, the risk that the service may not meet expectations. Guests who provide or coproduce their own experiences minimize the risk that a hospitality employee will not provide exactly what is wanted. Many people now surf the Internet looking for both hotel accommodations and flight reservations. They believe that the travel agent or airline they contact may be more interested in selling them a travel package than in finding the best price.

## Key Factors: Time and Control

Several dimensions of providing service can help us distinguish between situations when guests can beneficially be involved and when they should not. The research suggests, surprisingly, that only two factors are important: *time* and *control*. Each of these is of two kinds: *real* and *perceived*.[6]

With respect to time, the feeling of how long something takes is as important to the guest as how long it actually takes. In Chapter 11 on waiting lines, these real and perceived factors are discussed in detail. The same is true for control. The amount of control over the quality, value, risk, or efficiency of the experience that guests think they acquire by participating is as important in determining the value of participation as the actual control guests have. As an example, Disney boat captains are at the steering wheels on the Jungle Cruise boats at Walt Disney World Resort. Boat passengers are comforted by the illusion that they can influence or control the captain who controls the boat, when in reality the boats run on an underwater track.

## Cutting Costs, Increasing Capacity

From the organization's point of view, the most obvious reason to incorporate the guest into the guest experience is to save money. As noted earlier, whenever the guest produces or coproduces the service, the guest is providing labor the organization would otherwise have to hire. The second reason is to increase production efficiency or increase capacity utilization. If a restaurant offers a buffet at lunch, it provides a meal product at a time of day when waitstaff are sometimes unavailable or unwilling to work. The restaurant still has the opportunity to derive income from its physical plant and food-production capacity without overusing its human resources. In a similar sense, many other organizations can add self-service capacity to handle surges or unevenness in guest demand. A hotel can offer its check-in and checkout guests an automated option if they don't want to wait in line, or a rental-car agency can offer automated check-in, checkout service for its regular customers. In this way the organization can maintain a constant staffing level while still being able to accommodate the variability in customer demand for this service. Letting customers coproduce this part of the service experience increases the number of customers who can be handled without increasing labor costs.

## As a Differentiation Strategy

Organizations can also use guest participation as part of a *product differentiation strategy.* The obvious example is the cook-your-own restaurant that sells the experience of doing it yourself to distinguish itself from other restaurants. Other examples abound from self-service gas stations to car-rental agencies, cafeterias, and financial services. Boston Market offers a take-home product but no delivery service. This combination distinguishes it from both the quick-serve drive-through and home-delivery restaurants. Having the customer come inside gives Boston Market the opportunity to sell more products than it could if the customer was ordering over the phone or reading off the menu at the drive-through window, while still positioning itself as a quick and convenient stop for busy people.

## Building Commitment

A final reason for letting guests participate is to build guest commitment and repeat business. If a guest feels the organization trusts her enough to let her provide her own service, then the guest feels a bond and a commitment to this place where everybody knows her name. Getting the guest involved in the guest experience is a positive way for the guest to feel ownership in that experience and a loyalty to the organization that provides this opportunity.[7] Pouring one's own coffee at the coffee shop may be a way of getting a coffee cup filled fast, but it also may be a way for that guest and the organization to express their tie to each other. Many organizations try hard to build such relationships because they recognize the lifetime value of a loyal repeat customer. Frequent-flyer and frequent-guest programs are both designed to build this attachment so that customers come back time after time to the organization that "knows" them.

## The Bottom Line: Costs vs. Benefits

The key to deciding when to offer the guest the opportunity to participate is to do a simple cost/benefit analysis, by using material like that presented in Table 8-1. The organization

**Table 8-1** *Advantages and Disadvantages of Guests Coproducing the Service*

| For Guest | | For Organization | |
|---|---|---|---|
| **Advantages** | **Disadvantages** | **Advantages** | **Disadvantages** |
| reduces service costs | may frustrate guest | reduces labor costs | increases liability risk |
| increases interest | may diminish service level | improves quality | guest training costs |
| saves service time | may not have needed KSAs | reduces service failures | increases employee costs |
| improves quality | learning curve | new market niche | increases design costs |
| reduces risk | | enriches employee jobs | interferes with other units |
| chance to show off | | | variability in guests |

needs to be sure, for both itself and the guest, that the benefits of participation outweigh the costs. The organization will want to look closely at the costs to itself: the costs of extra training or more elaborate skill requirements for employees, extra or simpler equipment necessary for guest use, and extra effort to lay out the service delivery system in a way that is user friendly. In essence these are the costs of training a guest to be a quasi-employee.

### *Help Wanted: Coproducer*

As it would in assessing any job position it wants to fill, the organization must ask itself the following questions: What are the KSAs necessary to perform successfully as a guest quasi-employee? Are we likely to find them in our job candidates/guests? What is the motivation of guests to participate, and how do we appeal to that motivation? What are the training requirements for successful performance in the guest/employee role, and do we have the time and personnel necessary to train guests in the proper performance of that role? Will guests come back and use that skill again if we spend the time and money to train them? If so, the expenditure of time and money may be worthwhile. Is it cheaper, faster, more efficient for the organization to provide the service or to allow the guest to do it? Are role models (especially other guests) available to help with the training, and how can we physically structure the service environment to use these models? Are there interactions with other guests or other parts of the organization that letting guests provide their own experience will interfere with or harm?

To employ guests effectively in the guest experience, they must have the motivation and ability to participate and the knowledge of how to participate. Since the guests left home and came to your place to receive some service, they must see a reason to do something for themselves. They must have the training and KSAs to do what the organization wishes them to do, and the role they must perform in the guest experience must be clearly defined.[8] In addition, some guests just want to do things for themselves and will do so if given the opportunity. These people get satisfaction out of serving themselves and being in control of the situation. Some people, on the other hand, do not want to do anything to help provide their own experience. If they are paying for it, why should they provide it? Organizations that see mutual benefits to coproduction and try to encourage it must always have a backup plan to accommodate the fact that some guests will and some guests won't want to participate in the experience. Those organizations that find ways of using guests as much as possible will, however, decrease their costs and increase the value and quality of the service for those guests who do participate.

## Inviting Guests to Participate: Guidelines

The basic point is that some but not all situations lend themselves to using self-service or guest participation for all guests. Two strategies are available to the hospitality organization contemplating how to gain the advantages of using guest participation while not incurring the disadvantages. First, they can let their market segment know that everyone entering the service setting must provide some of the service themselves. No one goes into a McDonald's expecting table service. The second strategy is to segment the service process so that guests entering the service setting can choose to participate or not. One can order off the menu or choose from the buffet at some restaurants that have learned that some guests wish to gain the advantages of serving themselves while others come to the restaurant expecting service and are willing to pay for it.

**Table 8-2** *Guidelines for Inviting Guests to Participate*

1. Are there peaks and valleys in the demand for the service? Can guests be used as substitutes for employees to smooth out the work flow for your employees?
2. While they are waiting for service, do guests have time on their hands that could be used to speed up the delivery of that service if they could deliver some of it for themselves?
3. Are your employees doing mechanical, repetitive, easy-to-learn tasks that could be done by guests themselves or through the use of specialized, guest-friendly equipment?
4. Are you needlessly bombarding your guests with repetitive requests for the same information which they could just as easily provide, once, via a self-serve data-entry terminal?
5. Do guests show a high level of interest in or knowledge of your service delivery system, suggesting that they might be willing to participate if asked or allowed?
6. Do guests tie up personnel asking questions that they could easily answer for themselves if you posted some signs or offered some self-serve information technology?
7. Are your guests trying to bypass your service personnel (to avoid giving tips, perhaps) in any way that offers an opportunity for self-service?
8. Are guests required to meet face to face with your service personnel when the encounters could be done through some other means such as telephone, mail, or computer?
9. Do your guests derive value from doing it themselves?

Source: Reprinted by permission of *Harvard Business Review.* "Identifying Opportunities for Improving Productivity." Adapted from Christopher H. Lovelock and Robert F. Young. Look to Consumers to Increase Productivity. *Harvard Business Review* 57(3):176. Copyright©1979 by the President and Fellows of Harvard College; all rights reserved. Lovelock's work in the area of customer coproduction is classic.

Other ideas about when to include the guest in the experience are suggested in Table 8-2. It describes several situations in which both the guest and the organization may benefit. Obviously the ideal is when both benefit in some meaningful way so that the experience is at least what the guest expected, and perhaps more.

## ONE LAST POINT: FIRING THE GUEST

In a sense, all guests coproduce—or have the potential to coproduce—the hospitality experience for others simply by being in each other's company. If a well-mannered, well-dressed guest sits quietly and passively within the service setting, that guest may be no more than a minor enhancement, an adornment, to the experience of other guests. Unfortunately, despite the old saying that the customer is always right, all organizations know that the customer is sometimes wrong by any reasonable standard; certain extreme behaviors are unacceptable in any hospitality setting. Guests get drunk, become verbally and physically abusive, refuse to comply with reasonable organizational rules and policies, and make outrageous demands.

Not all employees work out; not all guests work out. Sometimes the guest's "job performance" as a coproducing quasi-employee is so unsatisfactory that the organization must—as a last resort and employing clearly defined procedures—**"fire" the guest.** For example, if a client is rude on the phone to employees of Rosenbluth Travel, Hal Rosenbluth asks the client to find another agency. Says Rosenbluth, "I think it's terrible to ask one of our associates to talk with someone who's rude to them every fifteen minutes."[9]

## Firing Airline Passengers

Referring to customers who treat Southwest Airlines customers badly, Herb Kelleher says, "When we encounter a customer like that, we say to him, 'We don't want to see you again because of the way you treat our people.' " Kelleher says firmly that the customer is not always right. If a passenger is abusive to a Southwest employee, Kelleher may call the passenger on the phone. Customer complaints to management are common; management complaints to customers are unusual. Employees appreciate this kind of support.[10]

The airlines in particular are having trouble with guests. In 1997 over 1,000 incidents occurred on airplanes and in terminals under U.S. jurisdiction, including passengers becoming angry at flight crews, punching attendants, trying to open an emergency door, head butting a copilot, and trying to break into the cockpit. Some airlines now equip each plane with a set of plastic handcuffs. According to Captain Stephen Luckey of the Air Line Pilots Association, "Passenger interference is the most pervasive security problem facing airlines."[11] After a drunk passenger struck one of his flight attendants on the head with a bottle, the chairman of Virgin Atlantic Airways was able to achieve a British lifetime air-travel ban on the perpetrator. In the fall of 1998, British Airways began giving "warning cards" to passengers who seemed to be losing control. Northwest Airlines has permanently fired three passengers known to be violent. Some causes of these incidents seem to be the record numbers of people wanting to fly, more passengers per plane with less room to stretch and move around, free liquor in first and business class, and the smoking ban. Some passengers think the airlines have to an extent brought the unpleasant incidents upon themselves. Hal Salfen of the International Airline Passengers Association said, "Flights are full, there are fewer flight attendants, and there's a general indifference toward the passenger."[12]

## Abrupt Firings

The termination of the hospitality relationship must occasionally be dramatic and abrupt, perhaps even implemented by a security guard, large person wearing an "Events Staff" t-shirt, or "bouncer." Dramatic "firings" should occur when customers threaten the well-being or safety of other customers, employees, or themselves. No organization should tolerate a customer who is threatening, excessively rude or loud, or dangerous to others or self. If any customer threatens or endangers the physical and mental health of an employee, that employee should be empowered to tell the offender to go elsewhere for the service, as this organization is unable to continue rendering it.

## Subtle Firings

Customers can also be fired subtly. Everyone realizes that organizations place their advertising so that their target markets will see it; beer commercials accompany televised athletic events. But organizational advertising can also be carefully placed so that some customers never see the ads for a service, never get promotional mailings, or are never offered premiums for using the service. Sometimes this strategy is even more overt, such as a cruise line's refusal to allow unaccompanied children under 18 to book passage, or a resort hotel's unwillingness to book a convention of ex-convicts, or a sign in a gift shop "No Shoes, No Shirt, No Service."

### Maintaining Guest Dignity

Not even hospitality organizations are required to extend unlimited hospitality. They should of course give guests the benefit of the doubt, but for those few guests who are demonstrably unable to participate appropriately in the experience that all have come to the hospitality provider to enjoy, the organization should not hesitate to hand them their hats and show them the exit. If at all possible, however, the dismissal should be accomplished with minimal harm to the guest's physical or mental well-being and dignity. The guest who feels unfairly treated, who is really angry about being dismissed or "fired," can become a source of long-term negative publicity and bad-mouthing.

Although the firing of a guest is a response to a guest failure of some kind, the organization must realize that it has also failed in some way. The rude, troublesome guest had expectations—whether reasonable and realistic or not—and the organization failed to meet them.

## Lessons Learned

1. Train your service personnel to coach, monitor, and supervise the coproduction of guests, and hire people who enjoy this kind of activity.
2. Train your guests to participate before you let them; be sure they have the KSAs.
3. Motivate guests who derive value and quality from participation to coproduce.
4. Encourage guests to help monitor the service behavior of your employees.
5. Structure guest experiences in ways that encourage other guests to train your guests; provide preshow videos or otherwise prepare your guests to engage in the experience.
6. The more guests do for themselves, the less you have to do for them.
7. Guest involvement can improve efficiency and capacity utilization, especially at peak demand times.
8. If you have to fire a guest, try to preserve the guest's dignity.

## Review Questions

1. Name some ways or situations in which guest involvement in the coproduction of a restaurant experience can be useful to the organization.
   A. Name some ways in which it can be useful to the restaurant guest.
   B. What KSAs should restaurant guests have to be successful coproducers?
   C. "Train them if they need it; motivate them if they need it; and keep it simple, stupid." Would that formula promote successful guest coproduction?
2. Name some ways or situations in which guest involvement in the coproduction of a restaurant experience would not be useful or might be harmful to the organization.
   A. When might restaurant coproduction not be useful to guests? When might it be harmful?
   B. What can the organization do to discourage coproduction in those situations?
3. Suggest some ways in which a restaurant, a hotel, a theme park, a tour bus, and a travel agent might achieve a higher level of guest coproduction that would benefit both the

organization and the guest. Was it more difficult to apply the co-production idea to some of those hospitality or hospitality-related organizations than to others, and if so, why?

4. Under what circumstances do you think the organization is justified in "firing" a guest? Think of a hospitality situation in which you would almost but not quite fire a guest. See whether your classmates agree with you or whether they would fire the guest.

5. Some hospitality authors suggest that guests should be managed as if they were quasi-employees.
   A. Who do you suppose these authors think should do this managing?
   B. Whoever these managers are, should they be selected differently for their jobs because they will have some "management responsibilities"?
   C. Should they be trained differently?

## Activity

1. Find a hospitality situation in which the guest is required to coproduce the service experience. Try to find something more challenging than a salad bar or receptacle labeled "Trash." Describe and evaluate how the organization prepares its employees and its guests for successful guest participation. How effective is the coproduction strategy? What incentives were offered to guests to encourage their participation? In what ways is this guest participation beneficial for the guest, the organization, or both?

2. Interview a manager or supervisor within a hospitality organization to find out what the organization will and will not let guests do regarding coproducing the guest experience. Try to get some examples of guests coproducing excessively—trying to do more for themselves than the organization wants them to—and find out how the manager, supervisor, or server handled those situations. Report your findings to the class.

3. Interview a teacher who seems to believe in classroom "coproduction," even if not under that term, and find out why the teacher does so and how the teacher got that way. Bring back your findings for discussion in groups. Discuss the extent to which you are required or invited to coproduce your own education, and how you feel about it.

## Case Study

### Over the Bounding Main

*L*uke Dwyer and Sue Mayes met when they were both crewing on a yacht in a round-the-world sailing race. They married, started a software business on a shoestring, came up with several innovative ideas that enabled them to attain financial security, and then started looking for a way of life that would be more fun if perhaps not as profitable. Running a bed and breakfast was one possibility, but it seemed rather tame.

Then Sue saw an article in a shipping magazine about the Shingo Maru, a small 1920s-vintage freighter for sale. Luke and Sue sent off for a set of the freighter's plans, looked them over with a maritime architect, and decided to convert the ship into a kind of floating wilderness experience. They figured that a certain part of the cruise clientele must be tired of the *typical big-boat cruise, where all you did was sit around on deck or by the pool all day, eat huge fattening meals, and drink all night while watching bad entertainment and waiting for the midnight buffet. They would give guests an opportunity not to be pampered but to take part in an experience they would remember for the rest of their lives: helping to sail a ship around the world or, for the less committed, some part of it.*

*About a million dollars and four years later, the conversion was complete, and Sue was breaking a bottle of champagne against the prow of the now-christened Windenwaves, a classic square-rigged, three-masted sailing ship with a top mast five stories high. The ports of call on its maiden voyage were going to be romantic-sounding, faraway places that most people experienced only through the novels of Joseph Conrad and Robert Louis Stevenson: Bali, Zanzibar, Bora Bora, Fiji, the Galapagos Islands, Tahiti, Samoa, Barbados, and Antigua. About half the time would be spent sightseeing in these ports and about half the time at sea. The hired crew of twelve, all of them veteran sailors, would help the three dozen paying guests learn to climb the masts, stand proper watch, navigate by the stars, steer, repair sails, and all the other standard shipboard activities. For the privilege of coproducing their own sailing experience, the guests were to pay anywhere from $2,500 for a one-month onboard stay to $40,000 for the full 18-month round-the-world trip.*

*After about six months, approximately half of the passenger/guests had experienced the thrill of a lifetime. The other half wanted their money back. They didn't enjoy sleeping in bunks in one big dorm-type room, getting seasick, using a hose for a shower, being without TV, eating canned and dried foods (the ship had no refrigeration), and having little privacy. Some guests just couldn't "learn the ropes," and the experienced sailors among the crew didn't seem to be able to teach them how. One guest, who later claimed that he had been forced to climb the five-story mainmast, curled up into a paralyzed ball and had to be airlifted by helicopter to shore. He later sued the Dwyers and Windenwaves Partners Ltd. for $400,000 and won; the Dwyers had not thought to get insurance protection against such an action.*

*The delighted guests thought their trip on the Windenwaves was a high point in their lives, and not just because of the climb up that five-story mast. Said one, "Everybody who's been on a sailboat dreams of a trip like this. We saw places and things we would never get to see in any other way." The disappointed guests were really disappointed. They saw no reason why they should pay so much money and have to do so much of the work themselves. Said one, "I wanted a relaxing cruise. They treated me like a common sailor; made me scrub the decks and empty the slop. At those prices, who needs it? Next time, I'm going on the Disney Magic."*

\* \* \*

1. Which dangers of coproduction became realities for Luke and Sue?
2. How might they have headed off those dangers by planning more thoroughly?

## Additional Readings

Bateson, J. E. G. 1985. The Self-Service Customer—Empirical Findings, in Leonard L. Berry, Lynn G. Shostack, and Gregory D. Upah, eds., *Emerging Perspectives on Services Marketing* (Chicago: American Marketing Association), pp. 5–53.

Bettencourt, Lance A. 1997. Customer Voluntary Performance: Customers as Partners in Service Delivery. *Journal of Retailing* 73(3):383–406.

Chase, R. 1978. Where Does the Customer Fit in a Service Operation? *Harvard Business Review* 56(6):137–142.

Goodwin, Cathy F. 1990. "I Can Do It Myself": Training the Service Consumer to Contribute to Service Productivity. *Journal of Services Marketing* 2(4):71–78.

Kelley, Scott W., James H. Donnelly, Jr., and Steven J. Skinner. 1990. Customer Participation in Service Production and Delivery. *Journal of Retailing* 66(3):315–335.

Lovelock, C., and R. Young. 1979. Look to Customers to Increase Productivity. *Harvard Business Review* 57(3):168–178.

## Notes

1. For an excellent article on this subject, see David E. Bowen. 1986. Managing Customers as Human Resources in Service Organizations. *Human Resource Management* 25(3):371–383.
2. Benjamin Schneider and David E. Bowen. 1995. *Winning the Service Game* (Boston: Harvard Business School Press), pp. 88–89.
3. James L. Heskett et al. 1994. Putting the Service-Profit Chain to Work. *Harvard Business Review* 72(2):172.
4. Gary Kyriazi. 1976. *The Great American Amusement Parks: A Pictorial History* (Secaucus, NJ: Citadel Press), p. 82.
5. Ibid., 87.
6. J. E. G. Bateson. 1985. Self-Service Consumer: An Exploratory Study. *Journal of Retailing* 61(3):49–76.
7. For further discussion and examples of this point, see Neeli Bendapudi and Leonard L. Berry. 1997. Customers' Motivations for Maintaining Relationships with Service Providers. *Journal of Retailing* 73(1):15–37.
8. Scott W. Kelley, Steven J. Skinner, and James H. Donnelly, Jr. 1992. Organizational Socialization of Service Customers. *Journal of Business Research* 25(3):197–214.
9. James L. Heskett, W. Earl Sasser, Jr., and Leonard A. Schlesinger. 1997. *The Service Profit Chain: How Leading Companies Link Profit and Growth to Loyalty, Satisfaction, and Value* (New York: John Wiley & Sons), p. 125.
10. Ibid., 238.
11. Acting Up in the Air. *Time,* December 21, 1998: 40.
12. Ibid.

# Section

# 3

# The Hospitality Service Systems

*Design systems that allow you to do the job right the first time.*

# Chapter 9

# Communicating for Service

**Hospitality Principle:**

Glue the guest-experience elements together with information.

*Communicate everything you can to your associates.
The more they know, the more they care.*

—Sam Walton
Founder of Wal-Mart

## LEARNING OBJECTIVES

After reading this chapter, you should understand:

▥ The importance and uses of information to hospitality organizations.
▥ Ways in which information enhances the service product, setting, and delivery system.
▥ The sophisticated information systems that hospitality organizations are now using and their advantages and disadvantages.
▥ The hospitality organization itself as a large information-processing system.

## KEY TERMS AND CONCEPTS

| | |
|---|---|
| advanced information system | expert system |
| artificial intelligence | information overload |
| cross-sell | information system |
| daily count | integrated information system |
| decision system | managing information |
| economic ordering quantity (EOQ) | organization as an information system |

## THE CHALLENGE OF MANAGING INFORMATION

A traveler was waiting for her breakfast to be served at a business hotel. Within a reasonable time, the waiter brought her eggs and bacon. She looked at the bacon and realized it was too undercooked to eat. She moved it to the side and proceeded to eat the rest of her meal. During a normal visit to the tables, the manager asked how the breakfast was. All right, she said, except the bacon was not cooked properly. The manager apologized and went on to another table. A short time later, the waiter appeared and asked the same question. The second time the traveler was angry. Not only did the restaurant do nothing about the poorly cooked bacon; the manager didn't even share the information with the waiter so that he would know of a problem with one of his customers.

At Innoventions in Epcot is a big display by a major electronic game maker. Many different types of games are available to show the wonders of the technology and the exciting games that this company has developed. A visitor walking through the display picked up the controls of a game. After mashing every button in an effort to make the game work, the visitor walked away in frustration, unable to figure it out and without any information available to educate him.

Both situations illustrate the challenge of **managing information.** In the first case, the manager did not communicate important information to the waiter to alert him about a possible problem with one of his customers that he should know about. The manager had the information but did not communicate it so the waiter was unable to make the dining experience better. In the second illustration, the Epcot visitor was surrounded with information technology of the most advanced kind but because information was lacking, he could not use any of it.

Creating a system that manages information effectively is one of the most important and challenging issues facing any hospitality organization. Information is data that informs, and an **information system** is a method to get that which informs to those who need to be informed. A well-designed information system gets the right information to the right person in the right format at the right time so that it adds value to that person's decisions. The right person in hospitality organizations could be the employee, the guest, or both. Information that does not provide value to either the guest or the organization is useless. Informing a guest standing in line waiting for a table at Ralph's Restaurant that they had plenty of empty tables last night is not only useless; it is infuriating. Similarly, receiving a free-beverage coupon in the mail the day after the offer expires does not enhance the potential guest's fondness for the sending organization.

## Informing the Guest

Since service is by definition intangible, the information that the hospitality organization provides to help the guest make the intangible tangible is a critical concern of the information system. What information should the organization provide, in what format and in what quantity, to help create the experience that the customer expects? If the experience is a formal dinner, then the restaurant should organize all the information it provides to the patron to cue the perception that this is a formal dining environment and an excellent one at that. The restaurant should be set up to look like a formal dining experience should look. The chef should have the clean white coat and chef's hat that announce, "I am a chef, not a mere cook; I create a fine dining experience, not merely cook food." The silverware and plates should be elegant, and the rest of the environment should communicate the message "fine dining experience." Since some patrons do not have the refined taste buds necessary to identify an outstanding dining experience from the food alone, the restaurant must manage the many bits of information that the guest tastes, touches, hears, sees, and smells to be sure that each one somehow contributes to helping that guest define the intangible elegance of a fine dining experience in the way that the restaurant wants the guest to define it.

### Cues Communicate

Regardless of the hospitality experience being offered, all informational cues in the service setting should be carefully thought out to communicate what the organization wants to communicate to the guest about the quality and value of the experience. If the experience is themed, all cues should support the theme and none should contradict or detract from it. The less tangible the service, the more important this communication will be. By recognizing that information can glue together the service product, the service environment, and the delivery system to make a "whole" experience for the guest, the organization can use information to make the guest experience itself seamless. The organization can manage its information and use the available information technology to tie together all the elements of the guest experience to ensure that the guest enjoys it and will want to come back. Similarly, an organization that looks at each manager and employee as a customer for its information can design the organization's information system to facilitate the optimal flow of useful information to those people.

## Adding Quality and Value through Information

Information can be used in many ways by organizations to add quality and value to the service experience. Occasionally, information technology becomes so important that it can even transform the organization itself.

Information can enable *personalizing* the service to make each customer, client, or guest feel special. For example, having Caller ID to allow the service representative to address the customer by name when answering the customer's phone call adds a special touch to the experience. Information and information technology can improve the service itself. While a bar code on a retail product provides the basis for recording the transaction, it also provides a wealth of other information that enhances the service experience for both organization and customer. Having a real-time record of which products are selling so the store can order more in a timely (or even automatic) way ensures that customers will find the product available when they want more. Even more interesting is the opportunity to keep track of what types of products the customer is buying so that others can be suggested or offered as an enhanced service. If you buy a book on-line from Amazon.com, the electronic bookstore may let you know about new books on the same subject the next time you visit the Web site. Cross-selling between organizations is even possible. If you use your Internet browser to do an on-line search for information on a certain topic, an option will appear that enables you to see what books on that topic are available at Amazon. com.

Finally, the information technology can transform an organization or even an industry. On-line bookstores and travel agencies, customized book publishers, and e-mail are all transforming their respective industries in amazing ways. The easier, cheaper, and faster providing of information and services for customers made possible by advancing information technology is rapidly changing the dynamics of many industries.

## Getting Information Where It Needs to Go

Our concern, then, is to gather the data that can inform, organize the data into information, and distribute that information to the people—both customers and employees—who need it just when they need it. The whole challenge of information systems is to figure out exactly how to do this. Hospitality organizations that are effective in getting information where it needs to go recognize that providing information is in itself a service to guests, often as important as the primary service itself, and a necessity for employees. They must therefore identify the information needs of both guest and hospitality employee in regard to all three components of the guest experience: the service product itself, the environment, and the delivery system. Let's talk about information as it relates to each of these elements.

## INFORMATION AND THE SERVICE PRODUCT

Information about services offered is usually found within the environment rather than as part of the service itself. Chapter 3 showed the many different ways in which the hospitality organization can plant cues or information in the service setting. Such "tangibilizing" leads guests to favorable judgments about the quality and value of the guest experience. Just as doctors hang diplomas on the wall, restaurants hang food reviews and hotels hang American Automobile Association ratings, all in the effort to say to guests, "This experience will definitely be good and may be wow." Similarly, sensory information can communicate a message about the guest experience. The smell of bread baking, fresh flowers, or even antiseptic will communicate information to guests that can help make an intangible experience tangible. We shall presently speak in more detail about information in the environment.

### Information as Product: Red's Market

A good illustration of a sophisticated system properly used is that developed by Red's Market. Red's sells more fresh fruits and vegetables to Central Florida restaurants, hotels, theme parks, and other hospitality customers than all of its competition combined. Red's has so developed its information system that it can accurately predict what all of the customers will need and when they will need it. In effect, Red's has moved beyond the business of fruits

*Red's Market Truck. (Courtesy of Red's Market, Inc., and Kent Shoemaker.)*

and vegetables into the business of managing customer inventories. The computer models are so powerful that Red's Produce frequently knows better than its customers what they need and when. Fruits and vegetables are extremely perishable. Having this information system allows Red's to maintain the freshness of products that restaurants serve to their customers because Red's manages the inventory carefully.

Through the capabilities of this information system, Red's has in effect become responsible for the freshness and adequacy of fresh fruits and vegetables for its restaurant customers. In a pilot program, the purchasers at one large restaurant operation no longer even place their orders with Red's. Orders are generated automatically via EDI (Electronic Data Interchange) on one day, and Red's has the needed produce to the restaurant on the following day. This restaurant's purchasing department intends to have over 50 percent of its inventory vendor managed in the near future, and Red's is helping it to accomplish that goal.

## Informing the Employee-as-Customer

For the employee-as-customer, the service provided is often the delivery of the information that the employee needs for making decisions about how to serve external customers. This information-as-product is provided to the employee-as-customer by an employee or employee unit acting as an internal "hospitality organization." This concept is perhaps easier illustrated than explained in the abstract. Consider a health-club manager who must decide whether to revitalize or replace a room full of weight machines that have become obsolete or that for whatever reasons are no longer used at the expected rate. The manager will need such data as customer counts and use rates, wait times, customer surveys, and forecasts of future demand for weight training. Each of these pieces of information is the end product of some other employee's or unit's information production and delivery system.

Providing information is the service activity for many internal employees/customers, and all hospitality organizations seek to provide it as effectively and efficiently as they can.

Indeed, the entire movement toward frontline employee empowerment that characterizes benchmark hospitality organizations depends upon employees having easy access to information. Without some systematic way to provide it, empowerment would be impossible. Managers and empowered employees alike must have information to make good decisions and to measure the results of their decision-making activity.

## INFORMATION AND THE SERVICE SETTING

The service setting and its features and aspects can provide several kinds of useful information for guests.

### The Environment and the Service

First, the service setting can be a source of information related to the service itself, and that information must be efficiently and effectively provided. If the tangible product in the guest experience is a quick-service meal, then the patron needs to know how to get quick service, which quick-service meals are available, and when the meal is ready. Signs are therefore placed in the service environment to facilitate quick customer access to the order taker, menus are posted in easy-to-find places to aid the diner in selecting the meal, a picture of what the meal looks like may be located next to each menu item so that the diner knows what the menu item is, and the customer order number may be displayed on an overhead video screen to let the customer know as soon as the order is ready.

Many hotels have attractive graphics of the setting at their Web sites, showing room interiors or even views from a hotel room window. These graphical renditions of the setting help to make the service tangible for potential guests.

### The Environment as Information System

In a larger sense, the environment itself can be thought of as an information system of sorts by the way it is themed and laid out. The information provided in the environment can help or detract from the service experience. This information ranges from a simple orientation map

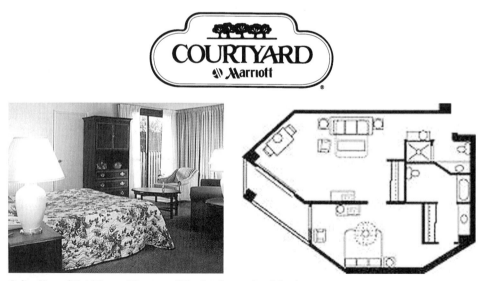

*Online View of Hotel Room. (Courtesy of Marriott International, Inc.)*

that tells customers where they are to more elaborate interactive computer systems that allow customers to obtain the information they need to enjoy the service experience most fully. At Epcot, for example, monitors in Innoventions allow guests to check on the availability of dinner reservations at the park's many dining locations. By going through a menu of options, a park visitor can learn if the Mexican or French or Moroccan restaurants have available seating capacity at the desired time; if so, the visitor can electronically make a reservation for that time. Epcot also has a WorldKey Information Service designed to answer frequently asked questions about the park.[1] This environmental feature provides specific information about the park's different services; in addition, it serves as an example or symbol of the advanced technology which the entire Epcot setting or environment is designed to portray and illustrate.

### MACS and ECS

Two other Epcot information systems that literally help create the environment are the Monitoring and Control System (MACS) and the Environmental Control System (ECS). The MACS checks the park's crucial maintenance and operating factors such as security alarms, critical bearing temperatures on various attractions, operational status of refrigerators and freezers, and wastewater lift station operations.[2] The ECS is the park's central nervous system. It receives information from the environment and sends instructions to the environment to change or maintain it. This computerized system also runs the lights and sound for all nontheater shows. Through Remote Interface Cabinets (RICs) the ECS also controls lighting, dimmers, and illuminations for special events.[3] Both the ECS and the MACS are completely integrated computerized systems that monitor all elements of the park environment, the condition of the rides and attractions, and the proper working of all mechanical aspects of the park. The continual monitoring allows any problems or malfunctions to be identified immediately and fixed. Also, the shows or special productions can be completely integrated with appropriate light and sound effects. Finally, the safety of each attraction and mechanical device can be enhanced. While MACS and ECS add up to a totally integrated information system, one part of that system is responsible for maintaining the quality of the park's environment.

## INFORMATION AND THE DELIVERY SYSTEM

Finally, and perhaps most obviously, information is required to make the service delivery system work. That system includes both people and the processes by which the service and any accompanying tangible product are delivered to the customer. Here again the nature of the service product and the delivery system unique to that product will determine what the ideal information system should be. If the end result of the service is a properly prepared hotel room, the information system needs to be set up in a way that communicates to the front-desk agent that the room is properly serviced and ready for a new guest. Such an information system could be as simple as having the housekeeper bring the room key back to the front desk only after the room has been cleaned. In this way, no guest could be checked into a dirty, unprepared room because the key wouldn't be at the desk.

### At the Ritz-Carlton

Many hotels seek to provide more than just a simple clean room, and their information systems are designed to provide this extra level of guest service. The Ritz-Carlton hotels, for example, offer an excellent guest experience partly because their service delivery systems provide their guests with more than a clean room. Their definition of a properly prepared room includes having service providers check the information system to review items that today's incoming guests have indicated in previous stays are important to them. They know from retained information that certain guests expect to find extra pillows, hot chocolate, or specific magazines in the room when they arrive. The Ritz-Carlton database tells the hotel exactly what preferences its guests have so the hotel can be sure that the desired items are in the room when the guests arrive.

Ritz-Carlton also asks employees to provide information related to service delivery. Employees are asked to listen for and record in the database any relevant guest-related information that might assist the Ritz-Carlton in adding value and quality to the guest's experience. For example, if a floor sweeper overhears guests talking about celebrating their anniversary, the sweeper is supposed to pass the information along so that the hotel can take some notice of this special event. The employees help deliver the *wow* Ritz-Carlton experience by inputting useful information into the organizational information system.

Along with all other hotels, the Ritz-Carlton knows that an important part of its service is to provide a safe and secure room. The information-system requirement in this case includes the ability to deliver this safety and security by using the information technology available in modern door locks. These electronic locks record all entries into and exits from all rooms by name of keyholder. In this way, the hotel can record who has been in each room and at what time so that any security problems related to such entries can be tracked and the people involved identified.

## Delivering Freshness

In restaurants, the information system can improve service delivery by including information about the freshness of the food products used to prepare the meals. Labels with date of production or purchase on food products, "day dots" on fresh-food items, and sophisticated inventory systems are all examples of how an information system can be designed to ensure that the chefs have the information they need to make the right decisions about using or not using the available ingredients to produce the fresh meals they are responsible for preparing. Though the information is related to the product—the ingredients—and to the service delivery system, its primary purpose is to ensure that product delivery is "just-in-time."

## Information on Service Quality

Perhaps one of the more important uses of service delivery information systems is in the systematic gathering of information on service quality. Acquiring this information, organizing it into a usable form, and disseminating it to managers and service providers is critical to ensure that service delivery and other problems are identified and resolved. Getting the fact into the information system that guests are annoyed and frustrated by a hotel's automatic telephone-answering system is a first step, but it is worthless unless the manager and other employees responsible for guest satisfaction get the same information promptly. Finally, the information system must be designed to insure that someone *follows up* on such service quality problems.

## Information to the People

In regard to the people side of the service delivery process, the information system can be used to ensure that all the people involved in delivering the service have the information they need to do their jobs in the best possible way. Here is where the most powerful applications of modern information technology have been developed. Providing the hospitality employee with the information necessary to satisfy and even *wow* the guest is an effective way to add value to the guest experience.

### At the Ritz-Carlton

Every employee phone at the Ritz-Carlton hotels has a Caller ID system that allows any employee to greet the caller by name when answering the phone. To a hotel manager, this information "allows the guest to experience a higher level of guest satisfaction and find greater value in the hotel's service." To the guest, it's "a nice personal touch." The technology provides information that was unavailable until technology made it so; it gives the service delivery employee the opportunity to add quality and value to the guest experience. The system should be designed to accommodate multiple users who want the same information at the same time. If a telephone operator is attempting to find a particular guest for a telephone caller, the front-desk agent is trying to find the name of the same guest on the database, and the restaurant is trying to bill the same guest for tonight's meal, all at the same time, the need for multiple access to databases becomes obvious.

### High Tech Becomes High Touch

In many other situations, information systems make it possible for the employee to provide service to customers quickly and efficiently. Indeed, this is the area in which the hospitality industry has worked the hardest to capture the benefits and economies of technology without losing the human contact that is so vital to the guest experience. It's a high-tech world but because technology has taken over so many functions previously performed by people, guests value a high-touch experience even more than before. Len Berry says, "Most great service companies are high touch and high tech, not one or the other."[4] Hospitality organizations therefore try to use as much technology behind the scenes as they can, primarily to save on back-of-the-house labor costs, so that they can afford enough front-of-the-house people to offer the personal contacts and touches that *wow* guests.

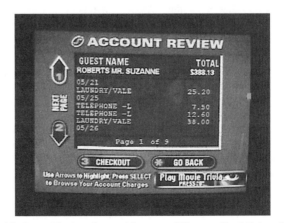

*Hotel In-Room Checkout Screen. (Courtesy of Sheraton Hotel Gainesville.)*

## Technology for Expertise

In many ways, information technology now allows the hospitality organization to provide expert skills without paying experts to provide them. A concierge who knows every good restaurant in town, or how to get last-minute tickets to a sold-out play or a couple of seats at the weekend football game, is a valuable hotel asset and generally paid accordingly. Acquiring this level of expertise takes time and experience, and the organization and the guest pay for that expertise. On the other hand, if this knowledge is on-line through a guest-room Internet connection or available through a touch-screen device in the lobby or even through an employee who can easily access a computerized database, the cost to the guest and the organization of providing that information is reduced while the quality of the information and the ease of access are increased. Clearly, this is a good illustration of using information and information technology to enhance the hospitality organization's ability to provide a valuable service and provide easy use for the guest as well.

## Centralized Reservations at Marriott

Like most hotel chains, Marriott has a centralized reservation system that all callers reach when calling in for rooms. The reservationists have access to the entire inventory of rooms available on all brands that Marriott owns and can help the caller find a room that best matches the desired price point and time when the caller wants to come. Instead of calling each hotel, the person needing a room calls the centralized reservation system and talks to a reservationist who offers complete information about how best to meet that person's lodging needs.

## Cross-Selling

Even better, from an organizational perspective, having the delivery system set up in this manner allows the organization to **cross-sell** its other products and services. A potential guest calling the Marriott reservation number for a hotel room can also be offered a room upgrade or other available products or services. The net result of this integrated reservation information system is to ensure that the guest becomes aware of the many options that Marriott can provide. The reservationist can not only sell a room in one location for one hotel but can offer hotel rooms for every night at every location the traveler will visit. Travel agents do the same type of cross-selling when they offer to book hotel rooms, arrange for rental cars, and offer other services when people call in to make airplane reservations.

## The Front and the Back of the House

Another major part of the hospitality service delivery information system ties together the front of the house, or those people and operations serving the guest, with the back of the house, or those people and operations who serve those who serve the guest. Coordination between these two geographically separate parts of the service delivery system is critical in providing a seamless experience for the guest. The guest does not care that the communications system between the cook and the server is faulty. The guest cares only about the quality of the overall restaurant experience, and the organization is responsible for serving the ordered food in a timely and appropriate manner.

## Point-of-Sale Systems

Point-of-sale (POS) systems have been developed to help managers, servers, and cooks do their jobs better. The server enters the order on a keyboard or touch screen, and it is transmitted back to the cook station for preparation. Capabilities beyond that depend on the system's sophistica-

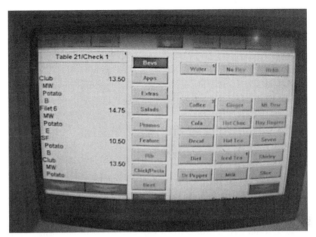

*Steak & Ale Point of Sale Unit. (Courtesy of Steak & Ale Restaurants.)*

tion level. All POS systems ensure that the orders are entered in the proper sequence so that the hot foods are served hot and the cold foods are served cold and not the other way around. The information system follows a predetermined protocol that gets the hot orders to the hot-order cook with sufficient lead time so that their completion will coincide with the preparation of the cold food on the same order. More sophisticated systems provide the order to the cook at the proper time and in the proper sequence and also display the recipe and a picture of the final plated meal so the cook can verify the meal being produced against the ideal standard. This extra informational feature lets cooks self-monitor their work; they can review the proper preparation procedures for the meals they are producing to assure a consistent, high-quality meal.

Of great interest to managers is the large amount of other useful information that these systems can quickly and easily provide. They can tell, for example, what servers are getting higher check averages and what they are selling, what times guests are coming in and how long they are staying, what combinations of food items they are ordering, and which menu items are gaining in popularity and which are losing out. Other profit, sales-volume, and revenue-related information is also available.

## The Daily Count

A good illustration of how an information system can improve experiences for customers and results for the company is a **daily count** system, like the one used at Disney. Every guest entering the park is counted and added to the total in the park at that time. Based upon their extensive attendance database and knowledge of arrival-rate distributions, Disney can accurately predict after the first hour of operation how many guests will come into the park during the whole day. This information can then be used to inform the food and beverage people how much food needs to be taken from central storage facilities and brought into the park's various restaurant and food-service locations, and how many salads, soups, and other preprepared food items need to be on hand.

Further, the same data is made available to human resources managers to ensure that the proper number of employees are scheduled to handle the total number of guests Disney now knows will be coming into the park that day. Similarly, the supervisors and area managers of the various attractions can access this data to know how many cars, boats, and trains need to be available for their attractions. The first-hour guest count can be translated into a number of important decision areas to ensure that the park is prepared to serve all of the day's guests with the level of service quality that Disney strives to provide. This one data source flowing through the information system can be used simultaneously to improve the quality of the service delivery system, the service environment, and the service itself. The information generated by the system will make countless guest experiences that day of higher quality than they would otherwise have been and will enable Disney to deliver them with high efficiency.

## The Information Flow between Levels

The last major requirement of the information system as it relates to the service delivery system is providing for information flows between organizational levels. This level-to-level flow can be as simple as an employee newsletter or a routing slip, or as complicated as an on-line, real-time, data-retrieval, and decision system. This type of information can also be provided through a centralized database or intranet of information that is available through computer terminals to all employees, so they can all access the specific information they need to interpret corporate policy, identify the dates and places of training opportunities, or the availability of alternative jobs.

All of these methods, whether on paper or electronic, are additional ways in which hospitality managers can reinforce the cultural traditions, motivate employees, and educate them to enhance the guest experience. Of course, many other communication channels flow up and down between management and employees. Employee-of-the-month programs, for example, allow the organization to communicate to all employees by example what types of behavior are desired and rewarded. Employee suggestion programs are another way for management to pick up new ideas and other types of information from their employees that let it quickly identify problem areas in the service delivery system.

Building an information system into the design, structure, and operation of the hospitality organization is vital to gather and distribute the necessary information in a timely way to manage and monitor the contribution of all parts of the organization to each guest's experience.

## ADVANCED INFORMATION SYSTEMS

Two types of systems that do more than simply provide information are decision systems and expert systems. They respond to information and choose between alternatives. Decision systems are particularly useful to organizations that want to establish lasting relationships with guests. Advanced forms of expert systems are sometimes called artificial intelligence.

### Decision Systems

More advanced systems that go beyond getting information to the right person at the right time are called **decision systems.**

#### Rules Built In

Built into these systems are decision rules that either help a decision maker make a decision or, in some cases, replace the decision maker altogether. An example of a decision system that aids a decision maker would be an automatic warning that signals a manager when an inventory level of a critical product gets low, or a computer icon that flashes on a computer screen to warn a cruise-ship engineer that a piece of equipment is heating up or malfunctioning. A decision system can even replace a decision maker when real-life situations can be accurately modeled. In these cases the information system provides a flow of information to a decision model that is programmed to respond when the monitored information indicates that a predetermined response is required.

Models can be built because the organization has learned that certain relationships are always or nearly always true. If a pressure sensor in a Tunnel of Love ride registers a certain amount of weight, the ride makes the "decision" to shut down because past experience has shown that someone has probably left the car and started walking on the track. Since this behavior is very dangerous, the information system is programmed to check the weight sensor constantly to ensure that no person is walking where that person shouldn't be. If someone is out of place, the system "decides" to shut the ride down until the operator can check. Other illustrations of automatic decision making can be seen in inventory reorders of low-merchandise stock levels, recommended staffing and prepreparation levels of certain food items based on statistical projections, and sending out a search team for an overdue airplane.

### Modeling Decisions

These decisions can all be modeled because the environment in which they occur is generally predictable. Since these decisions also recur frequently, it is worth the organization's time and trouble to develop a mathematical model describing the situation and to discover the appropriate decision rule. Thus, to keep track of the canned-food inventory, any restaurant chain should consider building a model that automatically recognizes when canned-food inventory falls to the reorder point, uses the **economic ordering quantity (EOQ) model** to determine the optimum number of units to reorder, and then sends an electronic reorder to the supplier. Such a model ensures that the canned-food inventory is maintained at the optimum level to serve guests while minimizing order and holding costs. The model may show that canned tomatoes, for example, should be reordered whenever the stock on hand falls below ten cases and that the optimal reorder quantity is fifty cases at a time. When the stock on hand falls below ten cases, the information-and-decision system automatically sends out a reorder to the supplier for another fifty cases of tomatoes. All this can occur without any human intervention and based solely on the data gathered and organized by the information system.

Not every decision has to made immediately. For example, an inventory system might have a built-in, preprogrammed reordering capability that would ensure the continuous provision of necessary ingredients for producing a menu item without overordering. The challenge is to ensure that the system collects the data necessary to measure the depletion of inventory, that the chefs using the ingredients can define their usage rate in a fairly accurate way so that they know how much of each ingredient they need to keep on hand, and that the ordering system can predict accurately how long it takes to reorder and receive the necessary products. A system can be designed to collect and analyze this information to ensure that the proper quantity of each necessary ingredient is maintained in inventory.

As is true of any procedure designed to improve service to customers, the organization needs to assess the relationship between the value and the cost of the information before it establishes such a system. Because professional chefs are artists and not accountants, they may not get around to gathering and organizing data about ingredient supplies often enough to justify the expense and sophistication of an on-line system. If the input of data is haphazard, the value of the frequently out-of-date information would be low and the expense of installing a sophisticated system unwarranted.

### Relationship Marketing

The increased emphasis in services on *relationship marketing,* or the "market-segment-of-one" concept, has been made possible through the increasing power of computers to store, digest, and interpret large quantities of information. The idea is to find out so much about customers that the organization can treat each person as a separate "market." When customers return warranty cards on products, fill out the information on cents-off coupons, or send in for free premiums such as t-shirts and company-logo coffee mugs, they provide information that companies use to gain a better understanding of their customers and their unique needs.

American Express may have taken this approach as far as anyone. In addition to putting basic demographic information about its customers into a database, the company also stores information about every customer transaction. The company has dedicated seventy workstations at their American Express Decision Sciences Center in Phoenix to scan mountains of data on millions of AmEx cardholders. The company knows which stores the cardholders shopped in, the restaurants where they dined, the places they visited, and the airlines they flew. It knows how often they went and how much they spent when they got there. AmEx can infer from the data what is likely to appeal to each customer in the future and, to encourage them to use their credit cards more, can target specific promotions like weekend getaways on their favorite airline to their favorite city to stay at their favorite hotel. AmEx figured in 1994 that the personalized marketing strategy made possible by this relationship-based information system increased member spending by 15 to 20 percent in the markets where it was used.[5]

Individual companies have information about you, based on what you did while interacting with them. In addition, organizations like National Demographics and Lifestyles make a business of collecting and providing such data. Even the state driver-license bureaus are making money by selling information about their licensed drivers. The quantity and quality of information about consumers available in various databases is staggering. General Motors has information on its 12 million credit card holders, Blockbuster Video's database is built on 36 million households, and even Harley-Davidson Motorcycles has a database on its owners that it uses to encourage them to ride their bikes more often and buy Harley products specifically tailored for them. The more a company knows about its customer, the better it can target its marketing toward satisfying that customer's unique needs and the more it can increase the company's value to that customer.

Hospitality organizations able to offer relationship marketing make it tough for their competitors that cannot provide their guests with similar value through such personalized service. Information systems and the powerful advances in information technology make it happen, and many hospitality organizations now have access to the power of building personalized relationships with their present customers and offering such relationships to their future customers.

### Severing Relationships

Organizations try to establish close relationships with their best guests. At the other extreme, companies can use information technology to weed out guests with whom they do *not* want to continue a relationship. Instead of taking a "come one, come all" approach to customers and guests, more and more organizations are severing relationships with unprofitable customers or charging them higher rates. Technology has developed to the point that organizations can identify some profitable and unprofitable customers and customer groups. If the top 20 percent of an organization's customers generate most of the profit and the lowest 20 percent of customers actually detract from the bottom line by costing more to serve than the income they generate, the organization will probably take steps to intensify its relationship with the top group and sever its relationship with the bottom. It might even reorganize itself so as to serve *only* that top 20 percent by means of contracts and other agreements. The danger, of course, is that the organization may be cutting loose presently unprofitable customers who might generate large future profits or who might, if treated well, recommend the organization to potentially profitable friends.

### Firefly

An Internet-based program even allows customers to make information about themselves available. A program called Firefly organizes and categorizes your judgments with those of people like yourself in a single database. The program knows what you like, what you like to do, and what you're likely to do in the future. It can then act as your personal *intelligence agent*. Firefly builds vivid profiles of the people that use its World Wide Web site, and then it sorts them to recommend new products and services based on what people like themselves are doing. In effect it allows the powerful influence of informal word-of-mouth marketing to be used even with strangers whose recommendations you've never heard before.[6]

## Expert Systems

Decision systems are preprogrammed to handle situations that do not require judgment. When banana inventory at Ralph's Restaurant drops to a certain level, Red's decision system automatically orders and ships a predetermined quantity of bananas. Systems can also be set up to make decisions that require choosing between alternatives when the correct decision is *not* clear cut. These are generally classified as **expert systems.** They seek to duplicate the decision process used by an expert who gathers data, organizes it in some way, applies a body of expertise to interpreting the information, and makes a decision that reflects the application of that expertise.

### The Expert and the System

An expert system, then, is built by finding out what information an expert uses, how that expert organizes it, and what decision rules that expert uses to make decisions based on the information. Once these pieces of information are collected, usually through extensive interviewing of an expert or a group of experts, a series of decision rules can be written to duplicate the decision-making process of the expert. As an example, if the organization wanted to determine what computer system it should order for each person requesting one, it could design an expert system that would ask any person wanting equipment a series of questions and, based on the answers, apply a set of decision rules that would determine what computer equipment that person needs. An advanced system would even order the equipment and schedule its delivery.

### Decisions Requiring Judgment

Expert systems can be developed to make decisions for use in a wide variety of recurring situations requiring judgment. They can schedule personnel for times and days to ensure proper staffing levels or keep track of a hotel's room inventory to ensure the maximum yield for each night's inventory of available rooms. They can be used in similar areas where there is a straightforward algorithm or mathematical formula that can calculate the best or optimal answer. In these types of expert systems, the optimal answer can be determined once the data is gathered.

The key to using expert systems is to find experts, identify the criteria they use in making decisions, program their decision rules in a logical sequence, then apply the program to problems that lend themselves to computerized analysis. The net result is to create a category of decisions that can be made twenty-four hours a day for any person having access to the system. For example, an employee wanting to find out about available retirement benefits can call up the system, perhaps even from a remote terminal, and ask the system to generate that analysis.

## Decision and Expert Systems: Advantages and Disadvantages

Decision systems and expert systems have advantages and disadvantages. As Table 9-1 shows, there are several good reasons to use them, such as the fact that they give users instantaneous access to a decision maker that makes quick, consistent decisions. These systems also have disadvantages such as the user's inability to ask further questions if the problem or question is not quite what the model expects. People do have unique needs, and even expert systems have to be designed from the customer's point of view if they are to be truly useful in problem solving within the organization. Obviously, with the potential problems they can have, expert systems should not be used for trivial, unimportant, or infrequent decision situations. They are simply too expensive.

## Artificial Intelligence (AI)

More advanced applications of expert systems open the way to using artificial intelligence. AI is used for situations where some decision rules are available but they are incomplete because part of the decision process is unknown or too unpredictable to model accurately.

**Table 9-1** *Decision and Expert Systems: Advantages and Problems*

| Advantages | Problems |
|---|---|
| • Makes consistent and impartial decisions | • May make bad decisions if problem is not routine |
| • Makes decisions quickly | • Expensive to create |
| • Rapidly sorts through large amounts of information | • Eliminates human participation in decision |
| • Frees up experts from making routine decisions | • Assumes experts will reveal decision-making secrets and rules |
| • Allows instantaneous 24-hour access to a decision maker | • Some decision processes are too obscure to duplicate in expert systems |
| • Retains expertise forever | • Legal issue of who owns decision rules |
| | • Circumstances may change too quickly for system to keep up |
| | • May frustrate users whose problems don't exactly fit system parameters |

## *Systems That Learn*

**Artificial intelligence** programs are designed to allow the computer to learn from successes and failures by ensuring that all decisions made by the AI program have a feedback loop allowing the result of implementing the decision to be fed back and tested against predetermined evaluative criteria to find out whether the decision was good or bad. If the outcome was good, the logic of the decision process used is affirmed. If not, the feedback allows the computer to learn not to make the same mistake the next time it faces the same situation. The simplest and classic illustration is a chess-playing program. A computer can be programmed to behave like an expert chess player who knows all the rules and the traditional chess gambits. As it plays games against various opponents, however, the computer learns which moves lead to bad outcomes and which moves lead to good outcomes. Over time, this knowledge accumulates to improve the computer's decision-making capabilities just as the accumulated knowledge would improve the capability of a human expert.

Adding a learning capability moves an expert system's sophistication level up to that of an AI application. Obviously, the use of AI is still limited because of the cost and time required to develop this learning capability and the cost of errors while the learning takes place.

## **Problems with Information Systems**

Although no hospitality organization is going to give up its information system, these systems have potential and actual problems associated with them. One is **information overload,** the tendency of the system to produce and transmit too much data. Since these systems produce such apparently accurate numbers, managers tend to focus on the numbers instead of on less definite but often more important qualitative and human factors. Another problem is that an information system can produce bad information that looks good. The organization has crucial and sometimes proprietary information within its system, so maintaining security is an issue. Finally, the costs of installing and learning the system must be matched against the benefits that the system can confer. These points will be discussed in turn.

### *Information Overload*

Information systems are helpful and revolutionary but far from perfect. The most obvious problem in the hospitality industry is the possibility of creating information overload for both guests and employees. Too much information is as bad as not enough. While sophisticated systems are designed to provide only the right information to the right person when that person needs it, many information systems provide a lot of raw data and then simply hope that recipients can discover whatever information they need in the pile. Indeed, many systems are designed by having systems planners ask users what information they need. Human nature being what it is, most users will ask for as much information as they can get, instead of only as much as they really need. Most people believe having too much is better than not having enough; their proof is that they have seen people disciplined for having too little information but never for having too much. A second aspect of this same issue is that when asked, most people indicate that they use many different informational data sources, instead of mentioning the one or two they actually use. Not wanting to admit ignorance or own up to how little information they use, they ask for a lot and then get lost in the pile.

### Focusing on the Numbers

A second problem with information systems is the tendency to get tied up in numbers. Since computers excel in transmitting, organizing, and analyzing numbers, much computer information is in numeric form. While this form aids in accurate conversion of data into information, it does tend to focus attention on only those things that can be quantified or somehow expressed in numerical terms. Much of a manager's job focuses on subjective, qualitative data, not quantitative. The availability of numerical information creates an overemphasis in decision making on such information and an underemphasis on qualitative information.

### Bad Information

Problem two, the tendency to fall in love with numbers, assumed that the numbers were accurate. A third problem is that the information may not be accurate. The old saying that garbage in leads to garbage out is quite true. A sophisticated information system can quickly get a lot of bad data to a lot of people; if that bad data gets into the organization's decision-making structure, as it will with a sophisticated information system, then the data will be plugged in to multiple calculations used in many decision situations. The results can be worse than garbage; they can be catastrophic. In brief, bad information leads to bad decisions. Bad information widely circulated by means of a sophisticated information and decision system can lead to disaster.

### Maintaining Security

A fourth potential problem with information systems is security, or maintaining the integrity of the database. Information systems must be protected so that one organization cannot access confidential or proprietary data from another. In this era of telecommuting and managers working at home connected to the information system by modem, protecting the integrity of the database from unauthorized or inappropriate access is an important concern. If hackers can get into the Defense Department and CIA computers, as they have, then competitors may well be able to get into your database. Protecting against such unauthorized entry is a big problem and big expense for organizations. The problem exists even internally, as database managers need to ensure that unauthorized persons cannot obtain confidential employee data. Outsiders and company insiders need to be prevented from snooping around in your database.

### Value vs. Cost

Another problem is determining the true value and true cost of the information. Information is not free. Buying data terminals and computers, hiring programmers, running a data network, and building an information system are hugely expensive. On the other side of the expense are the largely intangible benefits of the information system. How does one measure the value of instantaneous access to a guest database so that the guest is identified by name, the information the guest wants is immediately available, and the guest's unique requirements can be identified in advance and supplied? Obviously, the difference in price between a hotel room at the Ritz-Carlton and the Econolodge is one way to estimate the presumed value of these services to a guest. If guests didn't think these amenities were worth the price, they wouldn't select the Ritz-Carlton. Since many guests do, they must place a value on these services, but their exact value in relation to their cost is usually impossible to establish. Deciding how much better a decision was because the manager had the right information available is all but impossible. Yet, most organizations believe their systems are worth the cost. The problem is that when budget time comes and paybacks on investments are calculated, defending information system upgrades and improvements is difficult because evaluating the contribution of the system is difficult.

Though determining costs and benefits is difficult, companies can make estimates. Consider a service that FedEx offers its customers through the World Wide Web. The package delivery company offers its customers a direct access or window into the status of their part of the 2.4 million pieces FedEx moves each day. By calling up the Web page, customers can click through the menu to find out exactly where their packages are in the system, instead of talking to a human operator. Each day, 12,000 customers do so. FedEx figures its saves about $2 million a year in not having to pay people to answer the phones and check on the status of packages. The company has also improved the quality and value of its service to customers, though no one can calculate exactly how much.[7]

### *Learning the System*

The final problem with information systems is the cost of learning how to use the new system, the computer equipment, and the information highway. People who are at decision-making responsibility levels are the very group who need to learn how to use this information technology. At the same time, they are also the very people who are most uncomfortable and unfamiliar with it. Worse yet, given the problems in quantifying the value of the technology, these are the same people who make the decisions about buying the equipment and investing in the system. Obviously, a lot of learning has to take place before those who are uneasy talking about megahertz, bits, and bytes are totally comfortable in using the new information systems, which they must learn in order to make the high-quality decisions these tools allow them to make. Even though the increasingly user-friendly software makes it easier for these managers to learn and use the powerful technology available to them, the challenge for them will be that as soon as they master one technology, a newer and more powerful one will come along and they will need to learn that one. Managers cannot learn about information systems once and then forget about them. The rapid changes in what computers can do in managing information will require managers to change as fast.

## THE HOSPITALITY ORGANIZATION AS AN INFORMATION SYSTEM

Perhaps the easiest way to understand how information ties the hospitality organization together is by considering the **organization itself as a big information system.** The main purpose of the information network is to provide each person with whatever information that person needs to serve the customer when that person needs it. Looking at the organization in that way, everyone becomes a transmission point on the organizational network—gathering, sending, and processing information into a decision-friendly format. Those responsible for designing the organization as an information system must consider how all these network participants are linked together and what each participant's information needs are. If a Continental Airlines customer service representative is responsible for telling an inquiring customer exactly how to get from Arrival Gate #72 to the limousine service phones by Baggage Carousel #1, then the information system had better be designed to obtain and provide that information to the representative when the phone rings. The Continental system design will therefore require communication linkages, across all parts of the organization, that provide access to all information needed by the customer service rep so that person can solve customer problems. Reengineering the organization and its information system around the customer's needs is almost a necessity in our present-day competitive marketplace.

## Integrated Systems

Retail shops illustrate how organizations can design their entire physical and record-keeping setup around an **integrated information system.** The system has structure and, to gain the full benefit of the information system and its database, the organization designs its other functions to accommodate the requirements of that structure. Here's how it might work at a Cracker Barrel gift shop. The shop's POS system uses bar codes on the items similarly to the way in which restaurants use their POS systems. When a customer brings an item to the counter to pay for it, the employee responsible for registering the sale runs a scanner wand over it to register the price and quantity information. At the same time, the inventory of that product is adjusted to reflect the sale of one unit, and the customer payment is added to the daily sales cash or credit ledger, the gift shop's daily profit-and-loss figures, the particular salesperson's record of sales for the day, and other corporate databases that collect information about how the shop's operations are doing. This simple act of running scanners over product bar codes again and again builds a wealth of useful information that tells Cracker Barrel management how the product is selling, how the store is doing, and how the salespersons are producing.

## Managing by Exception

These sophisticated systems make so much information available on line that management can operate *by exception,* which means that it needs to spend its time and attention on only those stores, products, and employees that are not performing up to a predetermined budget or par. More sophisticated systems, like the one used by Wal-Mart, will take this informational resource even farther by automatically registering the data in a corporate database that keeps track of daily profit and loss for the entire operation, reorders products and arranges for payment to and shipping from suppliers for those items that have reached predetermined reorder levels, recalculates the statistics used for sales forecasts by product type, and even reassigns shelf space on the basis of product sales-volume popularity. These more extensive, probably expert or AI level, decision systems use economic ordering quantity (EOQ) determinations, sophisticated statistical forecasting techniques, and automatic reorder points to ensure that the necessary quantity of product is available to support predicted sales levels. In a real sense, the same process is used in managing hotel-room inventory, food-service items available for sale, and the ride capacity of an individual theme park attraction available on a particular day.

## The Primacy of Information

The logic of organizing around the flow of information changes the way in which jobs are organized and tasks are performed; it may drive changes in the sequence of operations and the organization of departmental units. The organization should be designed in a way that responds to information requirements. Jobs and departments dealing with uncertain, ever-changing, ambiguous situations require a lot of information flow to ensure that the managers responsible for decisions in those units can get all the information they need to make them. Job or units that are relatively insulated from uncertainty, ambiguity, and changing circumstance may not require the same volume or quality of information; they can anticipate that whatever happened or was true yesterday will pretty much be the same today and tomorrow.

Organizational units facing uncertainty need to add the information capacity that will allow the necessary information to be gathered, or they must find ways to reduce the need for that information. Both strategies involve integrating the organizational design into the information system and vice versa. We shall now take a more detailed look at these two strategies.

### Increasing Capacity

When the organization must increase its information-handling capacity, its system designers must consider the ways in which information is transmitted across the organization. They will probably have to build an expert-level system with the capability to screen out unnecessary information while conveying necessary information. Furthermore, the system will have to create *redundant* sources of critical information. Information that a decision maker absolutely must not miss should be provided in more than one channel of communication to ensure that the manager has it when it is needed. That way, if one channel breaks down or fails to get the information to the person needing it, it can be provided through another means. A simple example would be sending someone an e-mail, followed by a fax, followed by a mailed hard copy, with the same information in all three communications. Building in this redundancy obviously creates additional demand upon the information system, and organizations should carefully consider what information is so important that it needs to be sent in more than one way.

### Reducing Need

An alternative to building additional information-processing capacity into the organization is reducing the need to handle information. One major way to do this is to create self-contained decision-making units that are empowered and enabled to make decisions about their areas of responsibility. By increasing the number of decisions made at the point where the information is generated, the usage of the information channels is reduced. This is the classic strategy of decentralized decision making or, in the more current literature, the trend toward individual or group empowerment. The idea here is that with proper training in asking for job-related data and turning it into information used for decision making, the individual employee or department can make many decisions that would otherwise have been routed up the administrative chain of command. The time and effort it takes to check with a supervisor or higher-level organizational unit can use up information channel capacity, but even worse for a hospitality organization, it also slows down the response to the problem. If a furious guest is standing in front of the employee, that guest does not want to wait until someone upstairs gives approval for resolving a problem.

### Everybody On-Line

The most effective strategy for increasing the information flow is to put everyone on-line with immediate and easy access to the corporate database. Increasingly, rather than sending masses of information through the communication channels, the trend is to put information on-line so that any employee with a computer terminal can ask for it. Many organizations have an internal e-mail or intranet capability that allows any employee to ask any manager any relevant question over the e-mail system. The flow of information back and forth across all levels of the organization is incredibly enhanced by this technique. The recent move by many organizations into external linkages with the amazing databases and informational resources available on the Internet means that even more information is available to anyone who needs it whenever they need it. Frontline employees now have access to much the same information that their bosses do and, with proper education about corporate goals and training in decision making, can make decisions in specified job-related areas of the same quality that their bosses could in previous eras.

## Implications for Service

The impact that these communication systems have on empowering frontline employees to do their jobs better, faster, and cheaper is astonishing now and will grow even more so in the future. The implications of these changes for middle managers, who historically were responsible for transmitting information from senior managers to frontline employees, is also important to consider in managing the hospitality organization. The impact that these technological trends have on organizational design, frontline employee responsibilities, and need for middle managers is profound. This technology will change the way organizations are managed and organized; it will also change in a fundamental way the nature and role of hospitality employees who are concerned with delivering high-quality guest experiences.

The information systems of hospitality organizations ought to be aware of all three components of the guest experience, and the best system would integrate all three. Such a total information system would simultaneously be providing information to guests, management, guest-contact servers, and back-of-the-house staff, just when they need it. Achieving this end requires the system designer to pay close attention to the needs of users, their capabilities, and their willingness to use information. It would do no good to provide thirty pages of statistical output to a person who doesn't understand statistics or who doesn't have the time to sort through the data to find the necessary information. If you're out of food in your restaurant, you don't want to review statistical predictions of how much food you were supposed to use this week, the sales forecast for next week, or the summary data for last week, until somebody gets some more food to you. You need all that other information, but not right now. When you're in the weeds, you don't care what the chemical composition of the weed killer is, as long as you have some. The list of chemicals may be data, but it is not information.

## Lessons Learned

1. Know the unique informational needs of each internal and external customer, and satisfy them.
2. Know the value of information to each customer, internal and external.
3. Know the cost of providing that information.
4. Make information available in a format that each customer expects, can use, and will use.

5. Ensure access to information to all in the organization who need it, and exclude access to those who do not.
6. Put organizational information on-line.

## Review Questions

1. What is the difference between providing a guest with information and actually communicating with that guest? Give an example of each. How can hospitality organizations know if information has been communicated effectively to both guests and employees?
2. How is this chapter on communications related to meeting or exceeding the expectations of guests? Is an effective organizational information system more important for providing quality to guests, providing value, or both equally, and why?
3. Think about a restaurant you go to frequently. The server probably listened to you place your order and then wrote the information down on a pad or entered it into a POS terminal. What decisions and activities might this order then trigger or affect throughout the entire restaurant organization? (Clue: Think about immediate, on-the-spot matters, but also about inventory, staffing, menu selection, profit and loss calculations, etc.)
4. Think of several different hospitality organizations with which you are familiar.
   A. What are some significant decisions that those organizations must make?
   B. Which of those decisions should perhaps be made by expert systems and which by a well-informed manager?
   C. What differences do you note between the two types of decisions?
5. Some think of organizations as big information systems. According to that idea, the only function and responsibility of a hospitality organization is getting the right information to the right person at the right time so people can make the right decisions that will enable the providing of outstanding guest service.
   A. To what extent does that kind of thinking make sense to you?
   B. Does this idea of the organization as information system correspond to what you yourself have actually experienced in organizations?

## Activities

1. Interview a local hospitality manager. Find out what information technologies at that hospitality location are the most advanced and most basic. Does the manager want any technology that is not available? Find out which technology the manager thinks the organization could least afford to do without. Report back to the class.
2. Interview service employees at four different levels within an organization. Ask them how they learn what's going on in the organization. What communication devices, channels, and sources do they use or have access to? Then compare the differences between information sources of the different levels. If any of the employees don't seem to be getting the adequate, timely information that they need or want, what strategies or devices could be used to improve the information flow?

# Case Studies

## At the Country Club

*W*hile waiting to tee off at the country club, Lillian Hollowell and Sarah Dinsmore were arguing about computers. Hollowell, president of Conglomerate Restaurants, spoke this way:

"Sarah, I don't know how I got along before our restaurants purchased point-of-sale units. I got them to improve communication between the servers and the kitchen, but they have really made my job easier, too. I can combine company info with outside databases. I can convert reams of numbers into colorful charts and graphs that my managers can easily understand. These units have enabled me to get more useful information, make decisions, and have more time for golf. I don't have to depend any longer on summary reports from the branch restaurants. I have instant access to my company's database, so I can call up info on current and past performance of any of my units, along with comparative industry and economic information from outside databases. If I see something out of the ordinary, I can get right to the restaurant manager responsible and check it out, or hold a teleconference with several managers."

Sarah Dinsmore was president of International Restaurants. Although the chain had 1,400 units, they specialized in friendly, personal attention. Sarah thought of her organization as high touch, as opposed to her high-tech rival.

"I want no part of those POS units. You don't see the fine restaurants in Europe cluttered up with those machines. The blasted things churn out a ton of data, but I still can't get much information. I've tried three different POS systems and I despised them all. If you want to do anything beyond the simplest operation, you need to be very familiar with the system. I don't have the time to gain that familiarity, so I've turned my link in our current system over to my executive assistant. She knows how to run it and so I don't think I'll ever need to learn. Besides, when I go to a restaurant with POS terminals, the servers as often as not try to memorize my order, run to the unit, and punch it in. I think they make more mistakes than if they wrote the order down on a pad, as we instruct our servers to do."

\* \* \*

1. Will Sarah Dinsmore be able to function effectively for very long with this attitude, or will she eventually have to learn how to use the data that the POS units make available?
2. How can she gain the advantages of high tech without losing the high touch she believes is a differentiating hallmark of her restaurants? Or is this a trade-off situation in which you can't do both?

## Fine Family Motels

*T*he reservation agents at the 105 units of the Fine Family Motels chain worked hard, but the chain's occupancy rate seemed to keep drifting lower. When that rate hit 58 percent, management realized that something had to be done.

While most locations had an acceptable occupancy rate, a few low-occupancy locations pulled down the overall rate. Unfortunately, the low-occupancy properties seemed to shift around from month to month. The local reservation agents, travel agents, and airline reservation networks weren't aware of the low-occupancy areas until the problem became acute. The company was willing to offer discounts of up to 50 percent in the low-occupancy properties to fill rooms, if it could identify them promptly and get the information out to tour organizations, travel wholesalers, and other client sources.

\* \* \*

1. What technological changes would benefit Fine Family Motels?
2. What structural changes might they make necessary?
3. How might Fine Family Motels use the World Wide Web to improve its occupancy rates?

## Additional Readings

Archdale G. 1993. Computer Reservation Systems and Public Tourist Offices. *Tourism Management* 14(1):3–14.

Berry, Leonard L., and A. Parasuraman. 1997. Listening to the Customer—The Concept of a Service-Quality Information System. *Sloan Management Review* 38(3):65–76.

Brownell, J. 1992. Hospitality Managers' Communication Practices. *International Journal of Hospitality Management* (2):111–128.

Chervenak, L. 1993. Hotel Technology at the Start of the Millennium. *Hospitality Research Journal* 17(1):113–120.

Cho, W., and D. J. Connolly. 1996. The Impact of Information Technology as an Enabler on the Hospitality Industry. *International Journal of Contemporary Hospitality Management* 8(1):33–36.

Cho, Wonae, Daniel J. Connolly, and Eliza C. Tse. 1995. Cyberspace Hospitality: Is the Industry Ready? *Hospitality and Tourism Educator* 7(4):37–40.

Cho, Wonae, Robert D. Sumichrast, and Michael D. Olsen. 1996. Expert-System Technology for Hotels: Concierge Application. *Cornell Hotel and Restaurant Administration Quarterly* 37(1):54–60.

Collins, Galen. 1995. Information Technology Trends: Impact on Hotel Corporations. *FIU Hospitality Review* 13(1):81–91.

Davenport, Thomas H., and Philip Klahr. 1998. Managing Customer Support Knowledge. *California Management Review* 40(3):195–208.

David, Julie Smith, Severin Grabski, and Michael Kasavana. 1996. The Productivity Paradox of Hotel-Industry Technology. *Cornell Hotel and Restaurant Administration Quarterly* 37(2):64–70.

Davin, Katie. 1997. Effects of Computer Support on Group Decisions. *Journal of Hospitality and Tourism Research* 21(2):44–57.

Durocher, J. F., and N. B. Niman. 1993. Information Technology: Management Effectiveness and Guest Services. *Hospitality Research Journal* 17(1):121–131.

Ford, Loren, Robert C. Ford, and Stephen M. LeBruto. 1995. Is Your Hotel MISing Technology? *FIU Hospitality Review* 13(2):53–65.

Howey, Richard M., and Savage, Kathryn S. 1995. Information Processing: Coordination and Control in Large Hotels. *FIU Hospitality Review* 13(1):51–62.

Kasavana, Michael. 1993. High Touch Club Computing. *Club Management Magazine* (January/February): 108–128.

Kasavana, M. L. 1995. PC-Based Registers: The Next Generation of Point-of-Sale Technology. *Cornell Hotel and Restaurant Administration Quarterly* 36(2):50–55.

Kavanaugh, R., and J. Ninemeier. 1991. Interactive Video Instruction: A Training Tool Whose Time Has Come. *FIU Hospitality Review* 9(2):1–6.

Kirk, David, and Ray Pine. 1998. Research in Hospitality Systems and Technology. *International Journal of Hospitality Management* 17(2):203–211.

Kluge, E. Alan. 1996. A Literature Review of Information Technology in the Hospitality Curriculum. *Hospitality Research Journal* 19(4):45–64.

Mandelbaum, Robert. 1997. Hotel Sales-and-Marketing Management—A Snapshot of Current Practice and Technology Use. *Cornell Hotel and Restaurant Administration Quarterly* 38(6):46–51.

Moore, R. G., and S. Wilkinson. 1993. Communications Technology. *Hospitality Research Journal* 17(1):133–144.

Murphy, Jamie, Edward G. Forrest, and C. Edward Wotring. 1996. Restaurant Marketing on the Worldwide Web. *Cornell Hotel and Restaurant Administration Quarterly* 37(1):61–71.

Murphy, Jamie, et al. 1996. Hotel Management and Marketing on the Internet: An Analysis of Sites and Features. *Cornell Hotel and Restaurant Administration Quarterly* 37(3):70–77.

Nikolich, M. A., and B. A. Sparks. 1995. The Hospitality Service Encounter: The Role of Communication. *Hospitality Research Journal* 19(2):43–56.

Palmer, J., M. L. Kasavana, and R. McPherson. 1993. Creating a Technological Circle of Service. *Cornell Hotel and Restaurant Administration Quarterly* 34(1):81–87.

Pitt, Leyland, Pierre Berthon, and Richard T. Watson. 1999. Cyberservice: Taming Service Marketing Problems with the World Wide Web. *Business Horizons* 42(1):11–18.

Pollock, Ann. 1995. Information Technology and the Emergence of a New Tourism. *Australian Journal of Hospitality Management* 2(2):49–64.

Price, R. 1992. Technology Transfer in the Hotel Industry. *International Journal of Hospitality Management* 11(1):3–24.

Roberts, Karen, Ellen Ernst Kossek, and Cynthia Ozeki. 1998. Managing Knowledge in Global Service Firms: Centers of Excellence. *Academy of Management Executive* 12(4):81–92.

Sparks, B. A. 1994. Communicative Aspects of the Service Encounter. *Hospitality Research Journal* 17(2):39–50.

Van Hoof, Hubert B., Marja J. Verbeeten, and Thomas E. Combrink. 1996. Information Technology Revisited—International Lodging-Industry Technology Needs and Perceptions: A Comparative Study. *Cornell Hotel and Restaurant Administration Quarterly* 37(6):86–91.

Van Hoof, Hubert B, et al. 1995. Technology Needs and Perceptions. *Cornell Hotel and Restaurant Administration Quarterly* 36(5):64–69.

Wardell, D. 1987. Hotel Technology and Reservation Systems: Challenges Facing the Lodging Industry. *Travel and Tourism Analyst* 2(June):33–47.

## *Notes*

1. Stephen M. Fjellman. 1992. *Vinyl Leaves: Walt Disney World and America* (Boulder, CO: Westview Press), p. 377.
2. Ibid., 380.
3. Ibid., 386.
4. Leonard L. Berry. 1999. *Discovering the Soul of Service: The Nine Drivers of Sustainable Business Success* (New York: The Free Press), p. 189.
5. *Business Week,* September 5, 1994:61.
6. *Business Week,* October 7, 1996:100.
7. *Business Week,* February 26, 1996:76.

# Chapter 10

# Delivering the Service

**Hospitality Principle:**

Provide seamless service delivery.

*Being nice to people is just 20% of providing good customer service. The important part is designing systems that allow you to do the job right the first time.*

—Carl Sewell, *Customers for Life*

## LEARNING OBJECTIVES

After reading this chapter, you should understand:

▓ The process to plan, design, analyze, and check the hospitality organization's service delivery system.

▓ Several methods for designing a delivery system, such as flow charting, blueprinting, using the Universal Service Map, and PERT/CPM.

▓ A method for locating the source of problems, to prevent their reoccurrence: fishbone analysis.

▓ The advantages and disadvantages for service delivery of cross-functional organizations.

## KEY TERMS AND CONCEPTS

| | |
|---|---|
| blueprinting | Pareto analysis |
| critical path | PERT/CPM |
| cross-functional organization | PERT/CPM chart |
| fishbone analysis | simulation |
| fishbone diagram | Universal Service Map |
| Juran's Trilogy | |

## CHECK THE SYSTEM FIRST

### At the Ritz-Carlton

Horst Schulze, chief operating officer of the Ritz-Carlton Hotels, tells the story about how one hotel manager solved the problem of room-service breakfasts arriving late. After several guests complained to the manager about their breakfasts being brought to the rooms both slow and cold, the manager knew it was time to investigate. The traditional managerial solution to the problem would have been to call in the offending room-service manager and loudly criticize that person for technical incompetence and poor supervisory skills, along with whatever other comments might seem appropriate to dressing down the offending manager. The then properly disciplined manager would return to the kitchen, gather the room-service staff around, and yell at them. After all, in most organizations, blame rolls down hill to the lowest-level employee.

Schulze likes the example because it lets him illustrate a different problem-solving approach. The manager organized a team of room-service people and asked them to study the problem, find out why the meals were not getting to guests within a reasonable time, and suggest ways to solve whatever problem they found. The team did exactly that. They studied the problem at great length and found out that the cause was the unavailability of elevators needed by the room-service people to get the meals quickly to their guests. They studied why the elevators were so slow and even had a room-service employee spend an entire morning in an elevator with a stopwatch to see where the elevators were, what they were being used for, and why they weren't available when the room-service people needed them.

### *Short-Sheeted*

What they found astonished Schulze and the manager. The whole problem could be traced to a faulty management decision about how many bed sheets each floor was allowed to stock (called the "par") for the housekeepers. The decision had left some floors with too few sheets, and the housekeepers were using the elevators to hunt for extra sheets to finish cleaning the rooms on their floors. The elevators were therefore unavailable to the room-service delivery people when they needed them, cold meals intended to be hot were delivered late, and the guests got angry. Because a manager trying to save on the cost of sheets had stocked too few, the rest of the system was disrupted. This cost-saving move drove up the costs of room service (because the hotel did not charge for meals when guests complained) and housekeeping labor (because housekeepers were spending their time in elevators instead of making beds). Trying to solve a problem in one part of the service delivery system created problems for another part. The total impact was to drive up costs and increase guest dissatisfaction.

### *Lessons Learned*

As Schulze tells the story, the point is clear. What manager would ever have thought to solve the late-breakfast problem by adding more bed sheets to the available supply on each floor? He draws three lessons from this story. First, managers aren't smart enough, or don't have enough time or information, to figure out the best solutions to all the problems by themselves. Therefore, they tend to find the simplest, quickest solution, which is usually that a subordinate isn't sufficiently motivated, trained, or supervised. These managers rely on the traditional theory that "if you correct the person, you correct the problem." Second, employees may have a better chance of finding the root causes of a problem than the manager does. After all, those in the middle of the situation often know more about what is really going on than the manager does. According to Schulze, not using the talents, intelligence, and job-related knowledge of these people is worse than dumb. Finally, the most important lesson is that every problem should be addressed first from the perspective of the entire service delivery system. Although one person may end up being the cause of a service failure, Schulze believes that the fault is frequently in the system and not the person. Simply putting out one small fire ("we are spending too much money on sheets") without thinking about the system can cause big problems elsewhere.

In a similar example, Marriott's managers thought that some available funds should be spent on small television sets for bathrooms. By keeping track of requests for ironing boards, time spent delivering the short supply of ironing boards, and guest complaints when ironing boards were not available, the housekeeping department was able to show that the funds should be spent for ironing boards.[1]

## Designing and Checking the System

Stephen Tax and Ian Stuart maintain that "service design is among the least studied and understood topics in services marketing."[2] Yet it is a crucially important topic. Achieving guest delight and avoiding service failure can both be greatly affected by delivery system design. Every hospitality organization should spend whatever time and energy in studying and planning the system it takes to get it right. The total quality management movement, which emphasized that everyone is responsible for quality, not just the quality control department, has taught organizational leaders several important lessons. One is that everyone is responsible for delivering and monitoring quality; everyone is responsible for the quality of the guest experience. Another is to check the system for problems before you start blaming the people. As Schulze notes, you can have all the characteristics and features of a high-quality hotel, but the system can still fail from time to time. His goal is to use the people and the system designers to create what he terms a "self-healing system" in which the employees can override the system and fix guest problems when it fails. In addition, the employees in a self-healing system are responsible for telling management where the system has failed so that together they can fix it. Just as everyone is responsible for providing and maintaining quality, everyone is responsible for avoiding and fixing service failures.

The focus of this chapter is on properly designing the service delivery system or process to make sure that the guest experience is what the hospitality organization hoped it would be when they created it. We have said all along that the service delivery system includes both people and the systems that those people use to create and deliver the guest experience. This chapter builds on the earlier discussions of staffing to get service managers to think about the entire system that delivers the service to the guest. Having well-trained, motivated, enthusiastic employees facing your guests is necessary, but it is not sufficient. What really matters is making sure that the entire delivery system, the process by which the service is delivered to the guest, is working the way it is supposed to work.

Too many times hospitality managers assume that the employee has made an error when in reality the fault lies in a bad system that makes it difficult, if not impossible, to deliver the service with the excellence that the organization, the employee, and the guest would like. Talk with frontline servers at hotels, restaurants, and theme parks, and they will tell you how frustrated they become when the service systems can't help them do the jobs they are hired and paid to do, and which they really want to do well. When the service delivery system fails, everyone loses. The guest is unhappy, the employee is frustrated, and the organization loses a guest and all the profits the guest's future business represents.

### *Wiring Money Home*

A man we'll call Jim Jones taught a summer course at a university away from his home state. Because he was then going overseas before returning home, he went to a branch of the bank that had issued his summer paycheck and told a clerk he wanted to wire his check to his home bank account.

The clerk told him the bank could not wire the money until the check cleared. Jones pointed out that the bank could check its own records to see if funds were available to cover the check. After getting a manager's approval, the clerk agreed to wire the money, but only if Jones had an account with the bank.

Jones and the clerk went through the process of filling out the forms to open the account. Jones said he wanted no checks, ATM card, bank credit card, or any other bank service. He deposited his paycheck to open the account, asked the bank to transfer the entire balance to his home bank account, then Jones and the clerk filled out the forms necessary to close the account. The clerk merely observed that no one had ever done that before.[3]

The clerk and the system both failed Jim Jones. The bank procedures were not designed to handle the somewhat unusual request properly, the clerk had been taught to follow the inadequate procedures, and the manager approved the wire transfer but did not get sufficiently involved to find out what was really going on. The bank's system failed Jim Jones, but if the bank's employees had been sufficiently empowered and motivated, the failure might have been avoided.

### Stuck in the Snow

Contrast the clerk's customer service with that of the motivated, empowered SAS purser in the following example. A planeload of SAS passengers was stuck at an airport because of snow. Because the purser knew that the SAS philosophy was to do whatever necessary to satisfy the customers, or at least try to, she decided to offer them free coffee and biscuits. She went to the catering supervisor, a middle manager who outranked her, and asked for forty extra servings. Because each flight was allocated only so many cups of coffee and biscuits, the catering supervisor refused the request.

The purser could have let the system defeat her, but she noticed that the plane at the next gate belonged to Finnair, an airline that purchased food and drink from the SAS catering department. The SAS purser asked the Finnair purser to order the coffee and biscuits, the catering supervisor was required by SAS regulations to fill the order, the SAS purser bought the coffee and biscuits from the Finnair purser with petty cash, and the stranded customers received a welcome snack.[4]

The purser solved a problem by finding a way around regulations and the catering supervisor; through the empowered purser, the system "healed itself," in Schulze's term, to achieve the airline's primary goal: customer satisfaction. Everybody was happy—except the angry, confused, bypassed catering supervisor. The system failed once when it could not accommodate the purser's desire to satisfy the customers, but it snatched success from the jaws of failure by giving the frontline purser the autonomy to solve the customer problems, then failed again in not telling a middle manager how to deal with the autonomy that had been granted to a subordinate.

### The Message

The message here is quite simple: Study your system in intimate detail, design accurate early-warning measures for each of the many possible failure points, engage everyone in the organization in watching those measures, and follow up on everything. If failures occur repeatedly at certain points, change the system design. If the organization has a service guarantee, which should promise to provide those guest experience elements that lead to guest satisfaction and wow, be sure that the delivery system can meet and exceed the guarantee on those elements. Excellent hospitality managers know they must keep a careful eye on all the places where the system might fail, and they do their best to keep these failures from happening. Design systems that ensure success and avoid failure on the key drivers of guest satisfaction.

### No Perfect Systems

Providing a service is not like making a totally tangible refrigerator on an assembly line where you can see the product and bring in an industrial engineer to study the production process that makes the refrigerator. While parts of most guest experiences are produced by a tangible production system, like a kitchen in a restaurant that produces food, the product that the guest experiences is only partially produced by a physical production process. The rest of the product is intangible. Add to this intangibility the fact that the product's value and quality are determined by the guest at the moment or over the period of consumption and you see why all the methods engineers in the world cannot build a 100 percent reliable, dependable service system. The guest sees, experiences, and evaluates the service. The guest

*Tangible Production System: Restaurant Kitchen.*

decides what the experience was worth, whether it was worth returning for, whether to tell friends and neighbors that it was great or poor, and whether the the overall experience was satisfactory or not. To succeed under these circumstances, any service delivery system has to be as nearly perfect as thoughtful planners can make it.

### The Goal

The hospitality manager must spend the extra time and effort to plan and organize the service delivery system to get it right every time. Since the goal should be *to fail no guest,* the importance of planning the entire guest experience (the cycle of service) and focusing on an effective delivery system becomes critical. While we don't want to downplay the contributions of production management techniques and the useful solutions industrial engineers find for manufacturing organizations, they cannot guarantee the success of any hospitality organization's service delivery system because the guest is always the ultimate judge of the quality and value of the guest experience. Service delivery system designers must therefore ensure that they design the experience from the guest's point of view and not their own. Although the system should be user-friendly for employees, too many organizations design their service production processes for employee convenience. The outstanding hospitality provider organizes the production around the guest's needs, expectations, and capabilities. Service delivery should always be smooth, seamless, easy, and transparent from the guest's point of view.

## ANALYZING THE DELIVERY SYSTEM

Analyzing the service delivery system has three major components: *planning, measuring* or *controlling,* and *improving.* In the quality improvement literature, these components are known as **Juran's Trilogy,** or the *quality trilogy.*

## Planning the System

Any good delivery system must begin with *careful planning.* Years of experience in a restaurant may give a new restaurateur a good head start in designing a kitchen as the production part of the delivery system, but a careful analysis and detailing of every step in the entire service delivery process will make the difference between having it mostly right and reaching the level of excellence that the very best service organizations deliver.

## Measuring the System

The second component is *measuring for control.* We have said before that you can't manage what you don't measure, and this is especially true of service delivery systems. Industrial engineers in manufacturing have taken methods measurement to the level of a fine science. The service industry in general and guest services in particular have lagged behind in understanding how to apply measurements to the largely intangible services. The need for measuring what is happening to the guest in every step of the service delivery system is critical in understanding where the problems are and how one can tell when the solutions being tried are actually fixing the problem. Saying to a server, "I want you to do a better job of satisfying guests because guests at your tables seem unhappy" is easy but probably useless. To explain to a server exactly what level of excellence that person achieved last month, what level is being achieved now, and what the target level is can be extremely helpful. Indeed, in the best circumstances when the measures are clear, fair, and completely understood by the employees whose performance is being measured, *they will be able to measure themselves.* Self-management through self-measurement is a fundamental premise for the W. Edwards Deming quality circle movement that anchored the quality improvement literature and efforts in total quality management.

If you teach employees what is important to their individual job success and then train them to measure how they are performing on those critical factors, you have the beginnings of a *self-managing workforce.* Ideally, the measures could permit employees to monitor their own delivery effectiveness while actually delivering the service. If Bob Smith knows that the organizational maximum for answering his phone is three rings, and a computerized device displays a running record of how many average rings it takes Bob to answer a call, Bob knows at all times where he stands in relation to the company standard.

## Improving the System

After developing the measurements comes the last step in the analysis of the service delivery system: *improvement.* Information about what is actually occurring drives system improvement. If you can identify the failures, you can figure out where to fix the system. Once the plan is clearly laid out and the results of implementing that plan adequately measured to yield insights into how well the system is operating, then both management and employees have the information needed to redesign the system or fix the problems to yield continuing improvement in the guest experience.

### The Yellow and Black Tags

People on the front line are often the first to notice or be informed of system faults or failures. If they have been properly selected and motivated, they will report the need for system improvement just as the server at the Imperial Hotel in Tokyo reported a potential business opportunity in serving college reunions. A British Airways baggage handler at London's

Heathrow Airport noticed in 1993 that passengers waiting for their luggage at the carousel were asking him a strange question: How can I get a yellow and black tag for my bags? The passengers had noticed that bags with those tags arrived first, so they wanted the special tags. The baggage handler realized that because the passengers asking him the question were the first ones to arrive at the carousel, they had to be first-class passengers, who deplaned first. And yet they had to wait twenty minutes on average for their bags, while some other passengers were getting first-class luggage service. First-class passengers are highly profitable to airlines, and something was wrong with the service being provided to them.

The baggage handler's inquiries revealed that the passengers perhaps least deserving of "first-class" luggage service, those flying on stand-by, were getting it. Since they were the last to board, their luggage was loaded last and unloaded first. The baggage handler made a simple suggestion: load first-class luggage last. Although the idea was simple and had obvious merit, implementing it meant that BA had to change its luggage-handling procedures in airports all over the world, and that took time. But it was done, and the average time of getting first-class luggage from plane to carousel dropped from twenty minutes to less than ten worldwide, and under seven minutes on some routes.[5]

A dedicated, motivated, observant employee saw a way to improve the system and got it done. He had no idea he was going to receive a service award of $18,000 and two round-trip tickets to the United States on the Concorde.

## The Cycle Goes On

The cycle of planning, measurement for control, and improvement should never stop. The plan lays out what you think your service delivery system should be doing, the control measures tell you if what you planned is in fact happening, and the commitment to improvement focuses everyone's attention on analyzing and fixing the problems and moving toward a flawless guest experience.

The point is that the design for any service delivery system should incorporate all three elements. A good plan should include a way to measure how well the plan is being implemented at every step of the service delivery process and how the overall plan is succeeding. The measures should trigger an analysis of "exceptions," variations from the plan. A well-designed service system will include a way to measure every critical part of the guest experience and the entire, overall experience. Most guests respond to their stay in the guest experience as a whole. They are often unable to identify how any one part of the experience influenced their determination of the experience's value and their sense of satisfaction. They can, however, give an overall impression of service quality that can trigger managerial investigation. The guest may be unhappy with the dining experience at the restaurant, but until management sits down and carefully analyzes the data measuring each step in the entire guest experience, it may not recognize that the dissatisfaction was caused by a dirty bathroom, a cold appetizer, or a messy entrance littered with cigarette butts. Knowing the system and having the measures can trigger the necessary corrective actions.

### *Preview*

The rest of this chapter is on planning. Chapter 11 examines how to plan an important part of the guest experience that guests don't like but that organizations find necessary: waiting in line. Chapter 12 discusses improving the system by gathering and analyzing feedback about service failures and using this information to improve the system. Chapter 13 discusses measuring the system's effectiveness by assessing the overall guest experience from the guest's perspective.

## PLANNING TECHNIQUES

The first step in this quality-driven approach to service delivery system design is planning out the steps and processes in the entire system. Planning techniques focus on a thoroughly detailed step-by-step description of what the service delivery process involves. Planning always starts with the guest and frequently begins with the moment when the guest becomes aware of your organization's ability to satisfy some need. The guest's expectations begin to build from that moment, long before the guest ever arrives at your front door. Since we know that what the guest expects is the basis or criterion for determining how well the experience satisfies the guest, understanding what those expectations are becomes the first step in providing any guest experience and the beginning of the delivery system analysis.

Four basic techniques are commonly used to develop a detailed plan for delivering the guest experience. Managers can also use these techniques to focus on any part that guest feedback indicates is a problem area. These tools are especially useful because they can readily incorporate the measurements necessary for control and analysis of problems that may appear in the system. These tools are blueprinting, fishbone analysis, PERT/CPM, and simulation. Each has its own advantages, but all are premised on the idea that a detailed written plan leads to a better system for managing the people, organization, and production processes that deliver the total guest experience. If effort and care are devoted to the plan, failures should be minimized. If situations regularly get to the point where problem-solving and failure-recovery techniques become necessary, some guests will inevitably be lost to competitors.

### Blueprinting

Detailing the delivery system through a **blueprint** or service process diagram has several immediate benefits to managers seeking to fail-safe the delivery of their service. First, by writing it down, they can see on paper or on a computer screen, in a flowchart form that is easy to understand and study, how all parts of it work. Second, they can easily use the diagram to show the plan to others. A picture of what the service involves is truly worth a thousands words. A simple flowchart of activities associated with a restaurant experience appears in Figure 10-1. All activities head toward and center on "food service," the meal itself. Activities under the restaurant's control must be successfully planned, designed, and managed, if the guest experience is to succeed.

The most commonly discussed type of service diagramming is blueprinting. The entire service delivery process and its subprocesses are described in blueprint format just as if one were building a house and needed a plan of what went where. In effect, a good blueprint defines every component part and activity not just of the delivery system but of the entire guest experience, from the moment when the guest sees the front door or greeting sign to the time that the guest departs and moves out of sight. Every event that is scheduled to happen in between is laid out on a blueprint, as is every contingency that can be reasonably projected. Those points at which service failure is most likely to occur can be identified and early-warning mechanisms included. The blueprint should present not just the activities and processes involved in providing the service but should attach times to them and to the entire guest experience. If an excellent service product in a compatible

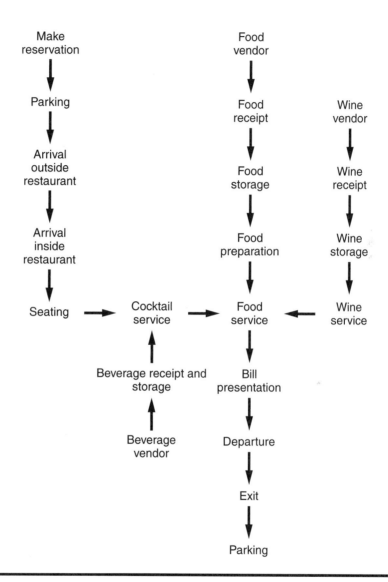

**Figure 10-1**  *Typical Restaurant Activities Flowchart. (Source: D. Daryl Wyckoff. 1984. New Tools for Achieving Service Quality. Cornell Hotel and Restaurant Administration Quarterly 25(3):155. Reprinted with permission of The Cornell Hotel and Restaurant Administration Quarterly. © Cornell University. All rights reserved.)*

environment is provided in twenty minutes, a guest may feel rushed; if in an hour, satisfied; if in two hours, the guest may never return. Finally, the benefit of blueprinting is not only to satisfy the guest but also the organization's profit goal; providing the service according to a well-designed blueprint will permit the organization to show a profit while maximizing guest experience quality and value.

Figures 10-2 and 10-3 show both a simple and a more elaborate general purpose blueprint of a service delivery system. The first should give the reader a good idea of what a blueprint of the service delivery system includes, and the second shows a more elaborate illustration that may be used to describe most guest experiences. While a specific service is not identified in the Figure 10-3 schematic, it would be relatively simple to plug in a foodservice operation, lodging experience, or convention and trace through the individual elements that describe the entire service experience of that specific application.

### The Hot Dog Stand

Figure 10-2 details the complete service cycle for a street vendor's hot dog stand.[6] As diagrammed in the figure, the service begins with the vendor greeting the potential customer. The vendor takes the order, assembles a heated dog-and-bun combination, applies condiments and dressings, delivers the hot dog to the guest, and finally collects payment. The blueprint of the service also shows an arrow dropping from the application-of-condiments step to represent a potential area of failure where the vendor might incorrectly select and use the wrong condiment—kraut instead of relish, for example. If this happens, the next step shown in the figure is for the server to fix the problem by cleaning off the wrong condiment and returning to the application-of-condiments step. The blueprint also has some other useful information in it. It provides time estimates for each step so that the total time of the service experience can be calculated. It separates the events that the customer can see from those that can't be seen by a *line of visibility.* Finally, it shows the customer tolerance time of the entire cycle.

The work cycle times are calculated from carefully studying the process. The customer time tolerance is calculated from carefully studying the customers. The entire finished schematic shows clearly the planned sequence of activities, the measures for each step in the cycle of service, and provides an easily communicated picture for analysis of the entire ser-

*Hot Dog Stand. (Courtesy of Grandad's Hotdogs.)*

vice cycle. Obviously, this example is both simple and incomplete. The excellent regional manager or staff guestologist for a string of hot dog stands would want to extend this schematic to include the events that happen before the hungry customer arrives. The manager should start at the point where the overall strategy for the hot dog stand was established in the first place. Doing so would allow the manager to see all the other influences that have an impact on the total hot dog purchase experience, from establishing the nature and appearance of the sign that initially attracts the customer to the hot dog stand, to the many other intangible and tangible aspects of the actual hot dog experience. Smart managers start off their planning of the service delivery system by surveying their customers to determine the key elements of the experience from the customer's perspective. Once those keys are determined, the delivery system can be designed to ensure that the customer's expectations regarding those key factors are met or exceeded. *The customer drives system design.*

One final factor necessary to a complete delivery system plan is the points at which customers may fail to do their part in coproducing the experience. If the system designs in customer participation and the customer might not participate, then a complete delivery system plan needs to account for this possibility.

### Adding Detail to Blueprints

Extending the simple example by incorporating all the fine points of hot dog vending would make for a more complicated but more complete process diagram. The blueprint could go into even greater detail by breaking down each step into a detailed subroutine (e.g., how long

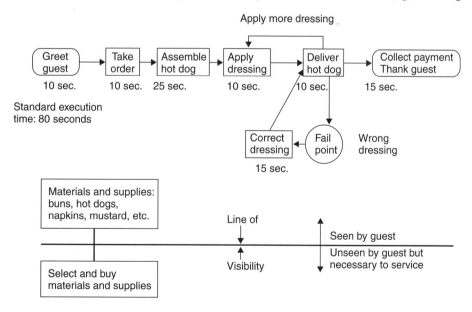

**Figure 10-2** *Blueprint for a Hot Dog Stand. (Source: Adapted from G. Lynn Shostack and Jane Kingman-Brundage. 1991. How to Design a Service, in Carole A. Congram and Margaret L. Friedman (eds.),* The AMA Handbook of Marketing for the Service Industry *(American Marketing Association), p. 244. Reprinted with permission of the American Marketing Association.)*

each hot dog should cook, ounces of condiments and their order of application, etc.). Albrecht tells the story in his book *Service America* about detailing a service blueprint for a frontline bank employee that covered *thirty-six* 11″ by 18″ pages.[7] The blueprint for the hot dog stand would become even more complex if complementary products were added, such as sub sandwiches, sodas, or ice cream desserts.

The level of detail in Albrecht's bank-employee blueprint is similar to that used to study a manufacturing process. If the organization is offering a "mass" service, the type and number of people being served may mandate extensive use of manufacturing production techniques and a "Taylorizing" of the service delivery system, whether the hospitality organization wants to or not. The need to load thousands of people a day onto a Coney Island roller coaster, serve hundreds or thousands of people a day at a McDonald's restaurant or Las Vegas gaming casino, or respond to countless phone calls at a travel agency may require that the service delivery steps be broken down into highly specialized and routinized jobs to make the process as efficient as possible, or to make the process work at all. The challenging question about those jobs is how to retain the human interaction component in the hospitality experience. The numbers of customers are so large and the service must take place so rapidly that the most personable employee will find it difficult to achieve a *wow* interaction with customers under the circumstances.

## The Universal Service Map

Figure 10-3 shows the **Universal Service Map,** a more elaborate and detailed blueprint that can be generally applied to a variety of service situations.[8] It begins, appropriately, at the point of managerial service strategy (bottom right side). In Chapter 2 on strategic planning, we talked about the importance of a customer-focused strategy, representing the managerial commitment to service excellence that drives everything the organization does, including the service delivery system. Therefore, this is the proper place to begin in reality and on our figure. A quick overview of Figure 10-3 shows that the flow of the chart is upward, with the customer on top and the management on the bottom. This arrangement is more than symbolic; it shows that the satisfied customer is the ultimate outcome of the process. All the boxes and the lines connecting them merely represent how the organization gets from the initial determination of management strategy to the final outcome of customer satisfaction.

### The Lines of Implementation and Internal Interaction

Several horizontal dotted lines divide groups of boxes. The bottom line is the *line of implementation,* which marks the structural point where management strategy gets translated into patterns of interaction between the customer and the organization. This line separates management planning from the day-to-day activities of the organization. The second line up from the bottom is the *line of internal interaction,* representing all the things that must happen inside the organization to produce the service experience. In this group of boxes are the organizational back-of-the-house functions that supply the frontline service employee with the product part of the service experience. These would include the kitchen for a restaurant, the underground trash-removal system at the Magic Kingdom, and the laundry for a hotel. The customer doesn't usually see these activities being performed, but their impact on the service experience is nonetheless important. Moving trash in the Disney theme parks is a good illustration. Since dirt, trash, and clutter interfere with the fantasy, Disney has designed a way to remove it without customers noticing. All trash produced in the Magic Kingdom is

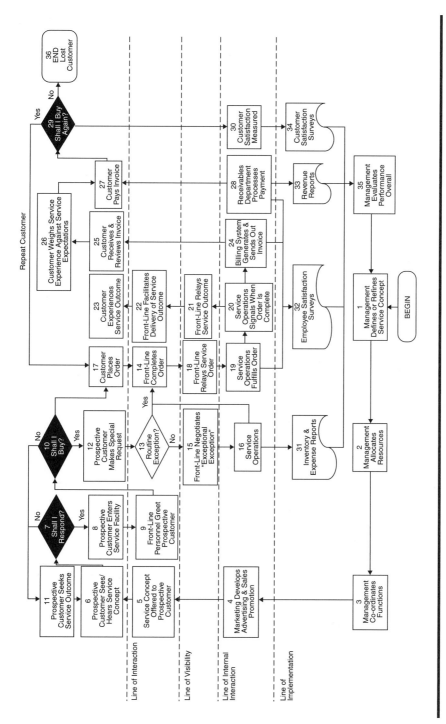

**Figure 10-3** *Universal Service Map. (Source: William J. Glynn and James G. Barnes (eds.). 1995. Understanding Services Management (West Sussex, England: John Wiley & Sons Ltd.) p. 127. © Kingman-Brundage, Inc., October 1994. Used with permission.)*

dumped into vacuum stations located strategically throughout the park. The trash is whisked away beyond sight of the customers.

### The Line of Visibility

Next is *the line of visibility.* This line separates activities that are visible to the customer from those the customer cannot see. The service employee disappears beyond this line from the view of the customer to interact with the back-of-the-house operations. After the server takes an order for the guest, she disappears from view to deliver it to the line cook in the back. Recognizing this interaction between server and cook as a category of activities is important because service failures at this point are frequent. When the server does not take the time to write down the entire order and assumes the cook will know what to do, or the convention manager forgets to tell the food and beverage department all the details about the time and length of the convention food break, problems arise. In effect, the back-of-the-house people must think of the servers as their *guests* or customers and do the best they can to serve their needs just as the front-of-the-house people serve the guests. In these interactions between servers and support staff lie many opportunities for communications problems and system breakdowns. They require as much managerial time and attention as the encounters between the guests and the front-of-the-house servers.

### The Line of Guest Interaction

Finally, the uppermost line is the line of guest interaction, also called *the line of customer interaction.* It separates those things the customer does in the service experience from those that the service employee does. These are the points of interaction between the provider and the customer at which the customer becomes, in effect, a coproducer of the service experience. It is the point where passengers respond to the flight attendant's instruction to look around and pick up all their personal belongings before leaving the plane, or where the customer drives forward to pick up the food order at the McDonald's drive-through window. The activities above this line are also the place where customers decide about the value of the experience and whether or not they will return. By noting the activities on the far right-hand side of the diagram above the line of interaction, the service manager can identify the sequence of events that influence this all-important decision process by the customer and do whatever is possible to influence the customer's decision in the positive direction.

## Fishbone Analysis

If a widespread, possibly a systemwide service delivery problem is discovered, as opposed to a more localized service failure, one way to attack it is to use cause-and-effect analysis in the form of a **fishbone diagram.** It provides a way to concentrate on the problem area and generally includes the participation of the area's employees. Although it analyzes the causes of faulty service outcomes, it can be considered as a planning strategy because its results are often used to make major changes in the delivery system.

### Midway Airlines Problem

Figure 10-4 shows an application of **fishbone analysis** to a problem at Midway Airlines: too many planes departing late.[9] That problem becomes the spine of the fish in the diagram. Then the general areas within which problems might arise that could delay flights are attached as bones to the spine. For example, "equipment" is required to get the planes off the ground on time and so becomes a potential source of delay. All of the possible contributors to an equipment failure then become bones attached to the equipment bone, and so on with each resource and potential problems with it. The potential contributors to resource failure are typically identified through group discussion with the employees involved; they should know the reasons for late departures. Midway's employees readily identified the possible trouble spots.

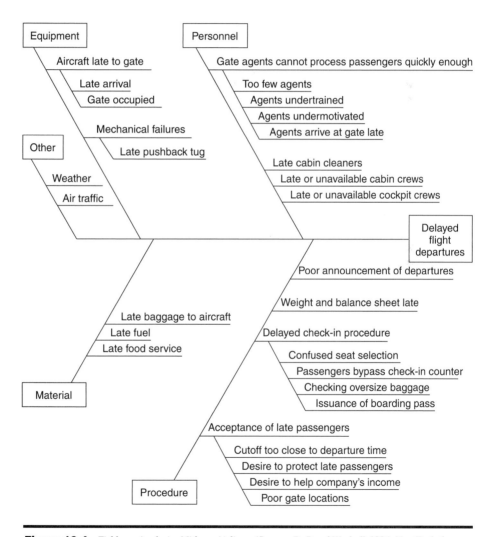

**Figure 10-4** *Fishbone Analysis: Midway Airlines. (Source: D. Daryl Wyckoff. 1984. New Tools for Achieving Service Quality.* Cornell Hotel and Restaurant Administration Quarterly *25(3):158. Reprinted with permission of* The Cornell Hotel and Restaurant Administration Quarterly. © Cornell University. All rights reserved.)

### Resource Categories

The resources required for takeoff can be categorized as equipment, personnel, material, procedures, and other. They are attached to the spine/problem. Within any one of them, a problem could arise that would cause the undesirable effect: late departures. Proceeding with the fishbone construction, the potential problems associated with each resource would then be identified, listed, and prioritized by the employee group working on this problem. This technique, known as **Pareto analysis,** calls for arranging the potential causes of the problem in their order of importance. In Table 10-1, the data representing the percentages of late flights associated with each cause are listed next to the cause in their order of importance. The Pareto analysis revealed to Midway Airlines that about 90 percent of all late take-offs were caused by only *four* of the approximately thirty possible causes. The most frequent reason for delay at all airports combined was late passengers at 53.3 percent, followed by waiting for pushback, waiting for fueling, and late weight and balance sheet. As was true of the British Airways baggage situation (the yellow and black tags), Midway was giving first-class service to the passengers who least deserved it: those who arrived late for flights.

### Airport Data

The data can also be analyzed by individual airports to see if the overall problems are the same as those found in each individual airport. As the data show, both the percentages and the reasons for delay at the Newark airport are different from those seen at the other airports. The fourth most frequent factor at Newark, "cabin cleaning and supplies," does not appear as a problem for Washington, but "late weight and balance sheet" does. By arranging the information in this way, managers looking for causes of service delivery failures have an easily used analytical tool available. For each potential failure point, they merely collect and arrange the data which the fishbone categories tell them to gather. Recognizing the problem is the first step in improving the service delivery system, but then you must know what caused the problem. You can't fix a problem if you don't know what caused it.

### No More Waiting

Once the impact of late-arriving passengers was identified, the airline decided that flights would no longer wait for them simply because they couldn't get to the airport on time. While this solution seemed to contradict the airline's commitment to service, and Midway gate agents naturally wanted to help out late-arriving passengers, the airline had clearly been denying on-time service to the many passengers who made sure to get to the airport on time. By setting up this fishbone and comparing the survey data against the key factors, the group was able to identify the problem and discover a solution that worked: don't wait on anybody. Of course, that solution caused a customer-relations problem with late arrivals, but the airline was willing to pay that price. As a matter of fact, when the word got out that Midway would not wait any more, fewer passengers arrived late. They learned to be on time or miss the flight.

The individual parts of *any* delivery system can be broken down in the same way to discover the equipment, people, procedures, material, and other factors that contribute to a service problem. Once managers measure each factor's contribution to the problem, finding a solution is relatively straightforward.

**Table 10-1** *Pareto Analysis of Flight Departure Delays*

| All Stations Except Hub | | | Newark | | | Washington (National) | | |
| --- | --- | --- | --- | --- | --- | --- | --- | --- |
| Cause of Delay | Percentage of Incidences | Cumulative Percentage | Cause of Delay | Percentage of Incidences | Cumulative Percentage | Cause of Delay | Percentage of Incidences | Cumulative Percentage |
| Late passengers | 53.3 | 53.3 | Late passengers | 23.1 | 23.1 | Late passengers | 33.3 | 33.3 |
| Waiting for pushback | 15.0 | 68.3 | Waiting for fueling | 23.1 | 46.2 | Waiting for pushback | 33.3 | 66.6 |
| Waiting for fueling | 11.3 | 79.6 | Waiting for pushback | 23.1 | 69.3 | Late weight and balance sheet | 19.0 | 85.6 |
| Late weight and balance sheet | 8.7 | 86.3 | Cabin cleaning and supplies | 15.4 | 84.7 | Waiting for fueling | 9.5 | 95.1 |

Source: D. Daryl Wyckoff. 1984. New Tools for Achieving Service Quality. *Cornell Hotel and Restaurant Administration Quarterly* 25(3):158.

## PERT/CPM

### Building a Barbecue

Let's say you want to build a backyard barbecue. You could design the barbecue with pencil and paper, go buy some bricks and mortar, go out back to dig the foundation, realize that you don't have a shovel, go buy one at the hardware store, start digging the foundation, and while you are doing that, have a chat with a neighbor who tells you that you need permission from the Neighborhood Homeowners Association before you can build a structure of that size on your property. Hospitality organizations cannot operate that way. They cannot afford to start building a hotel and then find out that the county zoning ordinance will not allow it. When the planning and delivery of the service product involve different activities, and especially when those activities recur in a repeating cycle (like planning a convention or golf tournament), a helpful technique to use is **PERT/CPM.**

### PERT/CPM Defined

The PERT/CPM planning technique, frequently used in the construction industry and the military, has many points of application in the hospitality industry as well. PERT stands for Program Evaluation Review Technique, and CPM stands for Critical-Path Method. Because these two techniques are similar, they have become merged into a single planning strategy and device with the combined PERT/CPM name. PERT/CPM offers the benefits of any good planning tool. It provides to the manager a detailed, well-organized plan combined with a control measurement process for analyzing how well the plan is being executed. PERT/CPM is useful in planning major projects such as hosting a convention, servicing an airplane, or opening a new hotel. Such activities have a beginning, an end, and a whole lot of things that must happen in between.

The steps in the process are (1) identifying the activities that must be done to complete the project, (2) determining the sequence of activities, (3) estimating how long each activity will take, (4) creating and diagramming the network of activities, and (5) finding the critical path running through the network. The successful use of the process may depend on the accuracy of the estimates made in step (3), and they are not always easy to make.

### The Diagrams

Using a PERT/CPM diagram like that seen in Figure 10-5 allows the service manager to achieve several important objectives. First, the manager gains all the usual advantages of planning. Previously unforeseen events and activities can be identified. How long something will take to do is readily estimated. Everyone involved in the project has an easily understood picture in the PERT chart that shows all the pieces of the project, the sequence in which they are laid out and must be accomplished, time estimates for finishing each project step, and the total time for completing the entire project. Finally, the PERT chart shows the items that must be done on time to get the project accomplished on time, which activities can be done at the same time as other activities, and which must happen before others. PERT/CPM can be used to plan any project that takes time; it would be hard to find any service experience that doesn't take time.

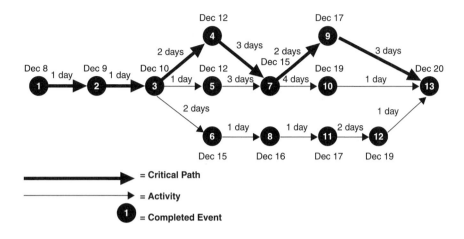

**Figure 10-5** *Simple PERT Chart.*

### Circles and Arrows

PERT/CPM diagrams are simple to create. They consist of circles or bubbles, representing *completed events,* and arrows representing the *activities that must be done* before an event can be considered completed. The arrows connect the circles, and the point of the arrow shows to which event the activity is necessary. In Figure 10-5, Event 1 must be completed before work can be begun on activities leading to completed Event 2, and the same is true of Events 2 and 3. Only after completed Event 3 occurs can work begin on Events 4, 5, and 6, which can be worked on independently of each other. Event 13 has three arrows pointing toward it, signifying that completion of Event 13 will first require completing Events 9, 10, and 12, and then completing the activities following them and leading up to Event 13. As the chart shows, Events 9, 10, and 12 themselves require that prior activities and events must be completed before their own completion. The **critical path** indicated in the chart will be explained in more detail in a moment, but it is the sequence of events that must occur on time if the project is to be completed on time. It has no "slack" in it as the other two paths do.

### Tony's Deli

Let's leave abstract events and think about the new delicatessen Tony wants to open. The final event in the sequence, the final circle on his **PERT/CPM chart,** will be "Opening Day." One activity arrow leading up to that circle might be labeled "Hold three staff training sessions." But before those training sessions can be held, several other activities and events must take place. Tony must find a place to hold training, order training materials, hire and prepare a trainer, and hire the new deli personnel. Some of those activities can be done simultaneously. Their completion might be indicated in the diagram by a circle labeled "Preparations for training sessions finished." Also included in the diagram would be estimates of how long each activity will take. Summing the activity times will give Tony a pretty good estimate of how long it will take to have a trained delicatessen staff available.

Complicated PERT/CPM networks are usually done on a computer (see example in Figure 10-6). If organizations cannot afford to do their own programming, they can use off-the-shelf PERT/CPM computer programs. The owner of a small service organization might plug in the service delivery system's essential elements, and the computer will figure out the mathematics and draw a schematic of the network.

## Building the Network

Five steps are required to build a PERT/CPM network.

### Step 1: Activity-Event Analysis

The manager defines all events that must occur for the project to be completed at all, and all activities leading up to those events. The real fruits of the planning process occur at this step. By taking the time and making the effort, the manager can detail every activity in the project and uncover every step that must be taken.

### Step 2: Activity-Event Sequencing

Once the manager has defined the activities and events that must at some time occur, they can be placed in their proper sequence, the order in which they must be done. Developing the sequence may reveal previously undiscovered or unknown events that must be scheduled. If you are describing how to tie a shoelace, you may forget event number one—that you must first *have* a shoelace—unless you take the process step by step.

### Step 3: Activity Time Estimates

The next step is for the manager to estimate how much time each activity will take so that an expected time for completing each event and the entire project can be calculated. The manager can use a simple formula to arrive at a weighted-average time estimate for each activity.

Expected time = optimistic time + 4 times most
likely time + pessimistic time / divided by 6

### Step 4: Diagramming the Project

After all the events are sequenced, the activities detailed, and the time estimates for each activity made, the pieces can be put together into the total-project diagram. As seen in Figure 10-5, each activity and event is set out in the diagrammed network along with the expected times.

### Step 5: Identifying the Critical Path

By summing up the activity times across the paths leading to the project completion, the manager can estimate the total time for completing the project and can identify the *critical path,* the CP of PERT/CPM, the sequence of activities that leaves no slack time. If these events don't happen on schedule, the project won't be finished on schedule. Other paths in

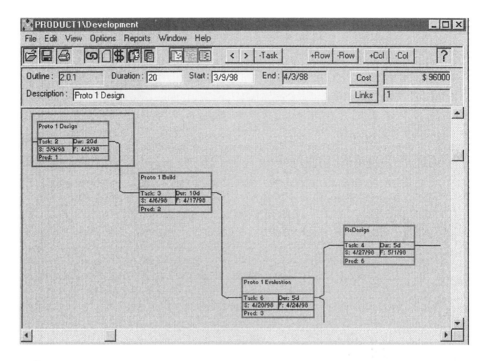

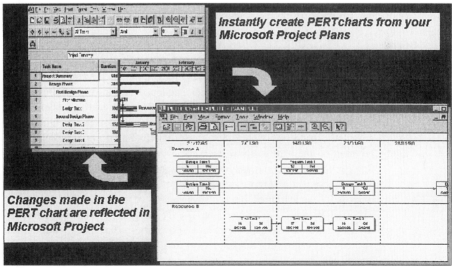

**Figure 10-6**  *On-line Computer-Generated Microsoft PERT Chart. (Screen shot reprinted by permission from Microsoft Corporation.)*

the network may have a time difference between when the events *must* happen and when they are *scheduled* to happen based on the calculation of activity times. In Figure 10-5, Event 6 must happen on December 15 or the entire project will get behind schedule, but Event 6 is scheduled for completion on December 12, so the project manager has some slack time. Even if Event 6 takes five days to complete instead of two, the delay won't affect the project completion date. Slack time also represents an opportunity to shift resources and attention away from events that finish earlier than they must and toward activities that need help.

### The Big PERT Picture

In addition to showing the critical path, the projected completion time for the project, and the complete sequencing of activities needed to get the project done, the PERT/CPM network diagram also provides a terrific visual of what is involved in the project. Using the diagram, the project manager can show everyone what the whole project looks like, what each person's part in the project is, when each activity needs to be done, which are critical, and which events precede each person's job and which events follow. Even more helpful is that the manager now has a complete model that can be used to test what might happen under a differing array of assumptions. What will happen, for example, if some of the pessimistic time estimates come true (whatever could go wrong, did go wrong)? The PERT/CPM network diagram gives the manager an easy and quick way to substitute new numbers and revise the time schedule for total project completion if necessary. Obviously, every major project involves a whole lot of uncertainties. With this tool, however, the manager can plug in the uncertainties and refigure their impact on the project if they occur.

### Holding a Convention

The PERT/CPM diagram in Figure 10-7 represents the steps necessary to prepare for and hold a convention. Convention manager Dorothy Barker went through all the steps noted above to determine the activities, their sequence, and the time estimates. Then she set up the PERT/CPM network to show the customer, the hotel staff members who will be critically involved in providing convention services, and herself all the things that must happen to complete a successful convention. This diagram can serve as a daily planning guide; it can be hung on the wall to show everyone what activities they need to accomplish each day. Since most convention managers have responsibility for more than one convention at a time, having these pictorial representations for each convention can help tremendously in keeping track of all the activities that each convention represents. A well-constructed and complete PERT/CPM chart can be used repeatedly because conventions generally have the same events and follow the same sequence of activities. The same would be true for servicing an airplane or for planning a restaurant or hotel opening or a particular cruise in a cruise ship's annual schedule.

Any time an event, process, or experience has a definable beginning and end, PERT/CPM can be used to describe and detail the sequence of activities that must occur to complete all steps on schedule. Since the activities of hospitality organizations are often sequences or processes with a beginning and an end—from cooking and serving a meal, to cleaning and preparing a room for the next day's guests, to the entire guest experience itself—the possible applications of PERT/CPM to service situations are endless and surprisingly painless.

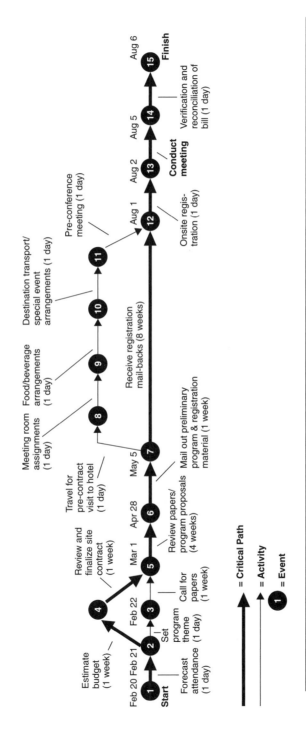

***Figure 10-7*** *PERT/CPM Chart of an Annual Convention.*

### Potential Disadvantages

The PERT/CPM process assumes that the activities leading to a project's completion are independent and can be clearly defined. That is not always the case. Also, the process depends on the accuracy of the time estimates. Since they are made by fallible human beings, they may be incorrect, and it does not take many incorrect time estimates to throw off an entire project.

## Simulations

A **simulation** is an imitation of the real thing. It may be doodled on a piece of paper with a pencil; or it may be done on a computer. Some simulations are big, like a computerized simulation of Epcot, and some are small, like a role-playing exercise at a company training session. Some simulations can even consist of professional actors simulating the guest experience to show the observing employees and managers where problems in service delivery can occur. These simulations can reveal problems that the people who work there may not have thought about. They can also improvise customer mistakes to see if the system has safeguards built in to keep the customer from failing in the experience or, if a failure does occur, to keep the customer from irreparably harming the value and quality of the experience. Organizations can use all of these simulations and more, when planning the service delivery system.

The computerized techniques are the most sophisticated; they allow incredibly detailed simulation of the service delivery system and also provide ways to measure and manipulate the system to see what might happen under different assumptions. Computers can also simulate behaviors of customers, with their infinite needs and ranges of behavior, on the receiving end of the system. The unique challenge in service delivery is that each customer is different. Because predicting exactly how any one customer will behave within the service experience is almost impossible, the opportunities for system failures are tremendous. Simulating customer behavior allows a better comprehension of how that variability in customers affects the system's ability to deliver the service at the level expected. Across the entire service experience, simulation can identify problems created by both the organization—in service design, environment, and delivery—and the customer.

### At Epcot

Simulation has been taken to the level of science at the Walt Disney World Resort, where a computerized simulation model of Epcot was used during the planning and design of the park. Different patterns of guest behavior were modeled to make decisions about park capacity and about where individual attractions, rest rooms, food-service facilities, and retail stores should be located. After the park opened, refinement and adjustment of the simulation model continued.

No one can know what any single guest might do inside the park during the course of a day. But knowledge of guest behaviors and statistical probabilities makes predicting how large groups of guests will behave a relatively simple task. Probability distributions for all possible Epcot guest behaviors were developed and then built into the model. The resulting simulation accurately reflected the movements and behavior of a day's guests as they progressed through the park. The simulation model was then used to test and optimize such planning decisions as the location, size, and capacity of the attractions, restaurants, merchandise shops, and other facilities.

### The Odyssey Restaurant Simulation

Here is a specific Epcot simulation. In the early days of the park, simulation runs were done to predict how guests would use the Odyssey Restaurant, a large fast-food facility to be built on an island in the lake between the Future World Attractions section of the park and the World Showcase section (See map on p. 94.). Other simulation runs had clearly shown that guests look for food near the exits of whatever attraction they happen to be leaving during peak mealtime periods. Since the Odyssey Restaurant was not near any attraction's exit, the model predicted that rather than go to the Odyssey, guests would instead head for fast-food locations near the Future World and World Showcase exits. The Odyssey was built on the island anyway, few guests used it, and today the facility is used for other purposes.

### Computer Simulations for All

Not every organization will have the volume of customers to justify or pay for the creation of a full-scale computer model to study the service delivery system in detail. Nonetheless, with the increasing availability of computer power in smaller, more user-friendly software packages, even Ralph's Restaurant on the corner will soon have economical access to a computerized simulation package. Already available to smaller service organizations is a computer program called a general-purpose system simulator (GPSS) on which they can simulate their delivery systems.

Many simulations are focused on modeling and predicting waiting lines or queues, which is the subject of Chapter 11.

## Cross-Functional Organizations

One final important issue in designing the service delivery system should be addressed. Thinking of the service delivery process as a system requiring the integrated, coordinated activity of people working in different departments leads to reflection on how the overall organization is designed. Is it designed so that individual departments can perform their functions smoothly, or is it designed so that the service delivery system functions smoothly? The two are not the same.

One method of organizing people and groups to enable them to work temporarily across the boundaries of functional units in which organizations are traditionally structured is the **cross-functional structure.** This term is also used to refer to an overlaying of a group or project team upon the traditional functional organizational structure to work on a task for a limited time. Traditional organizational forms are characterized by a single line of authority running from top to bottom: You report to one person; that person reports to somebody else. A cross-functional organization is characterized by multiple lines of authority: You may report to more than one person; that person may do the same. In hospitality organizations, many situations arise that call for focusing everyone's functional skills on solving a guest's problem or meeting a guest's expectation *right now.* Cross-functional structures are therefore especially useful in the hospitality industry, and in fact in any service-driven industry.

### Who's in Charge Here?

Karl Albrecht tells a story about trying to show a group of hospital managers how the cycle of service appears from the point of view of their "guests." After an excited discussion in which they defined all the tasks necessary for delivering the hospital services needed by the patient, one manager suddenly said, "But no one is in charge." In other words, because of the way the typical hospital is organized, no one person was responsible for making sure that service was smooth, seamless, and focused on the patient. Every department and every function was someone's responsibility, but no one was responsible for being sure that all the sub-services worked together for the patient's benefit. In elaborating on this point, the manager stated:

> Our hospital is organized and managed by professional specialty—by functions like nursing, housekeeping, security, pharmacy, and so on. As a result, no single person or group is really accountable for the overall success and quality of the patient's experience. The orderlies are accountable for a part of the experience, the nurses for another, the lab technicians for another and so on. There are a lot of people accountable for a part of the service cycle but no one has personal accountability for an entire cycle of service.[10]

### At the Ritz-Carlton

While discussing how the Ritz-Carlton Hotels won the Malcolm Baldrige Quality Award, Horst Schulze told about finding a cross-functional organizational solution to identify and correct system flaws. Ritz-Carlton had used guest surveys to identify 18 key guest-satisfaction measures. Ritz-Carlton hired a *process manager* for each hotel whose responsibility is to eliminate flaws and reduce work-cycle times by 50 percent in the systems that deliver the eighteen keys leading to guest satisfaction. The keys are so important that this specific person was hired to ensure that someone worried about them all the time. The Ritz-Carlton has avoided the potential limitations of the functional orientation that comes naturally to departments by authorizing the process manager to cross all functional areas to ensure that someone is focused on the hotel's guests and what satisfies them.

### Advantages and Disadvantages

To ensure that focus, other hospitality organizations use project teams, matrix structures, and other cross-functional forms. Because these forms generally involve people working under more than one line of authority, some traditional managers who believe that strict lines of authority are important have problems working with cross-functional forms. On the other hand, crossing functional areas and getting everyone focused on the guest can offer some important benefits. Table 10-2 compares the advantages and disadvantages of these organizational forms.

### The Real Boss

The main point is simple. Hospitality organizations need to use whatever organizational design best enables every unit and every person to focus on the guest's needs, wants, and expectations. Ritz-Carlton knows this, and Disney knows this. While the organization chart may show functional divisions with different people responsible for different things like maintenance, cash, and so on, everyone in these excellent hospitality organizations knows that their real boss is the guest and that their real organizational function is ensuring that the guest experience meets or exceeds the guest's expectations.

**Table 10-2** *Advantages and Disadvantages of Cross-Functional Structures*

**Advantages**

1. Create lateral communication channels that increase frequency of communication across functional areas in the organization.
2. Increase quality and quantity of information up and down the vertical hierarchy.
3. Increase flexibility in use of human expertise and capital resources.
4. Increase individual motivation, job satisfaction, commitment, and personal development.
5. Enable achievement of technical excellence more easily.

**Disadvantages**

1. Violate traditional "single line of authority" and "authority must be equal to responsibility" principles of organization.
2. Lead to ambiguity about control of resources, responsibility for technical issues, and human resources management issues.
3. Create organizational conflict between functional and project managers.
4. Create interpersonal conflict among individuals who must work together but have different backgrounds, perspectives on work, time horizons, and goals.
5. Create loss of status, insecurity for functional managers that their autonomy has been eroded.
6. More costly for organization in terms of increased overhead and staff, more meetings, delayed decisions, and more information processing.
7. More costly for individuals in terms of role ambiguity, conflict, and stress.

## Lessons Learned

1. Check for system failure (not enough elevators; too many monorail trains) before blaming people.
2. Detailed planning can avoid most service failures.
3. Plan for guest failures and how to recover from them (more on this idea in Chapter 12).
4. Design the organization itself to ensure service excellence.
5. A bad system can defeat a good employee.
6. The goal: Fail no guest; delight every guest.
7. You can't fix a problem if you don't know what caused it.
8. *Everyone* is responsible for monitoring and maintaining the quality of the service delivery system; *everyone* is responsible for avoiding service failures.

## Review Questions

1. Why is it important to check the delivery system first before checking to see whether employees are to blame for service failures?
2. Recall two different types of hospitality organizations with which you are familiar.
   A. What people and nonpeople parts of each organization's service delivery system can you see? Not see?

B. What steps does each organization in question 2A take to ensure that you can not see certain parts of the delivery system, and why does it take them?

C. Are any parts of these two delivery systems (for example, the frontline server) more important than other parts ? Or are all equally important because a service delivery system is only as strong as its weakest link?

3. If you opened a new restaurant, would you bother to blueprint your service delivery system? Why or why not?

A. If you did a blueprint, would you show it to your employees and discuss it with them, which would take time and cost money, or simply teach them their jobs on a need-to-know basis? Or would you leave it up to them whether they studied the blueprint or not?

B. The chapter referred to a service blueprint for a frontline bank employee that covered thirty-six 11″ by 18″ pages. How long would your restaurant blueprint be? Compare the relative usefulness of your blueprint with the bank-employee blueprint.

4. You have been asked to manage a local music festival.

A. How would a PERT chart help you do this?

B. What would its essential elements, the individual circles in the chart, be?

C. What would your PERT chart look like? Sketch it out, indicating the critical path.

5. Describe several situations in which hospitality managers could use cross-functional teams to improve the quality and/or value of the guest experience.

## Activities

1. Apply a PERT chart to a guest service situation in a hospitality organization with which you are familiar.

2. Blueprint the service experience provided by a hospitality organization with which you are familiar, with emphasis on the delivery system.

## Case Studies

### *Room for Improvement*

*M*onique Kazer spends quite a bit of time on the road in her job as a salesperson for a company specializing in audio-visual equipment for convention hotels and centers. She works long hours, often dines late at night, and returns to her lodging place late, sometimes after midnight. Monique is allergic to cigarette smoke, so she always requests a nonsmoking room at her hotel or motel.

Several weeks ago, tired after visiting three Newark/Jersey City/Hoboken convention hotels in one day, she arrived a few minutes after midnight at the Hospitality Inn, where she had a guaranteed reservation. The Hospitality Inn was a unit of the major chain with which her firm *did business because of the deep discounts offered. She checked in and headed for Room 315, looking forward to a hot shower and good night's sleep; tomorrow was going to be even busier than today. As always, she checked the door for a no-smoking emblem. When she entered, the smell of cigarettes or possibly cigars, mixed with air-freshener spray, almost made her sick. She began to cough, and her throat started to close up.*

*She quickly backed out, shut the door, and returned to the front desk. At least she didn't have to wait in line at that time of night, thank goodness. Desk agent Hyun Cho had a magazine open on the area beneath the counter which she used as her desk, but she was not reading it because she was obviously talking to a friend on the phone. She glanced at Monique a couple of times but continued to talk on the phone, making it clear that Monique would have to wait her turn. Ordinarily Monique would have waited a few moments, but tonight she was not in the mood so she employed her last-ditch technique for gaining attention in such a situation: She reached over the counter, took the phone out of Cho's hand, and hung it up. The service encounter went downhill from there.*

*Monique didn't even give a red-faced Hyun Cho a chance to mention the phone hang-up: "I made a reservation for a nonsmoking room, and you people put me in a room full of smoking fumes. Just change my room and we'll let it go at that."*

*Cho was a fairly conscientious night desk agent, and she had actually been talking with her babysitter, but she was still steaming from having the phone taken from her in mid-sentence. Hyun said nothing, checked the hotel records with a glance, then said to Monique: "That IS a nonsmoking room!"*

*"Check again, Ms. . . (looking at her name tag). . . . Cho, the room smells like a pre-war stag party."*

*"I don't care if it smells like hell warmed over. I don't need to check again, Ms. . . . (looking at the registration card). . . . Ka-Zer. I can read and I know my rooms and I can tell you that Room 315 is for nonsmokers." She concluded triumphantly, "We changed it over last week!"*

*Monique whispered the first curse she had uttered in a year or two, then said, "Just move me to a nonsmoking room that has been a nonsmoking room as long as you have been open."*

*"No, problem, Ms. Ka-Zer. (pause) Usually. But tonight, no can do. We're filled up."*

*Monique tried to have the room fee canceled, but Hyun refused. "If you don't show up until after midnight, it's actually the next day. No cancellations or refunds under any circumstances after midnight." She played her hole card: "Company policy." Then she added, "You ought to do something about that cough."*

*Monique left—tired, defeated, and still coughing—and headed out into the night to find another room, if she could. If not, there was always the back seat of the rented Crown Vic.*

\* \* \*

1. How would you have handled this situation if you were Monique Kazer?
2. How would you have handled this situation if you were Hyun Cho?

(Continued)

## *Room for More Improvement*

*As Monique Kazer rushed through the exit of the Hospitality Inn lobby, she almost knocked manager Roberta Morales down. Morales recognized Monique from previous visits and knew that her firm gave Hospitality Inns across the region a lot of business. Morales realized that something was wrong and suspected that the something was a service failure.*

*"I'm the inn manager. Is there something I can do for you?" she said to Monique. She heard Monique's side of the story, took her to the cocktail lounge and bought her the beverage of her choice, and asked an assistant manager to chat with Monique while she went back to the front desk. After hearing Hyun Cho's side of the story ("she yanked the phone out of my hand and slammed it down," etc.), Roberta Morales headed back to the lounge. She would speak further with Hyun Cho later on.*

\* \* \*

1. In a later chapter, you will be reading about some techniques for handling service failures. For now, what steps might you take to retain the patronage of Monique Kazer (and her entire organization)?
2. What steps would you take with regard to Hyun Cho and the failure at the front desk?
3. Using some hypothetical but realistic numbers, how much do you think it might end up costing Hospitality Inns if manager Roberta Morales is unable to recover from this failure and ends up losing the patronage of not only Monique Kazer but her entire firm?

## *Additional Readings*

Baum, Stephen H. 1990. Making Your Service Blueprint Pay Off. *Journal of Services Marketing* 4(3):45–52.

Berkley, Blair J. 1997. Designing Services with Function Analysis. *Hospitality Research Journal* 20(3):73–100.

Evans, K. R., and S. W. Brown. 1988. Strategic Options for Service Delivery Systems, in G. Frazier, ed., *Efficiency and Effectiveness in Marketing: AMA Educators' Proceedings* (Chicago: American Marketing Association), pp. 207–217.

George, William R., and Barbara E. Gibson. 1991. Blueprinting: A Tool for Managing Quality in Service, in Stephen W. Brown et al., eds., *Service Quality: Multidisciplinary and Multinational Perspectives* (Lexington, MA: Lexington Books), pp. 73–91.

Jones, P., and A. Lockwood. 1995. Hospitality Operating Systems. *International Journal of Contemporary Hospitality Management* 7(5):17–20.

Kingman-Brundage, Jane. 1989. The ABCs of Service System Blueprinting, in Mary Jo Bitner and Lawrence A. Crosby, eds., *Designing a Winning Service Strategy: 7th Annual Services Marketing Conference Proceedings* (Chicago: American Marketing Association), pp. 30–33.

Larsson, Rikard, and David E. Bowen. 1989. Organization and Customer: Managing Design and Coordination of Services. *Academy of Management Review* 14(2):213–233.

Lewis, Barbara R., and Thomas W. Entwhistle. 1990. Managing the Service Encounter: A Focus on the Employee. *International Journal of Service Industry Management* 1(3):41–52.

Lyth, D. H., and R. Johnston. 1988. *Incorporating Quality Considerations into the Design of a Customer Processing Service Operation.* Proceedings of the QIS Symposium, August (University of Karlstad, Sweden), pp. 1267–1269.

Meyer, Robert A., Deborah F. Cannon, and William E. Kent. 1996. The Fishbone (Ishikawa) Diagram: A Dynamic Learning Tool. *Hospitality and Tourism Educator* 8(1):45–47.

Nevett, W. 1985. Operations Management Perspectives and the Hospitality Industry. *International Journal of Hospitality Management* 4(4):173–178.

Shostack, G. Lynn. 1992. Understanding Services Through Blueprinting, in Teresa A. Swartz, David E. Bowen, and Stephen W. Brown, eds., *Advances in Services Marketing, and Management: Research and Practice,* Vol. 1 (Greenwich, CT: JAI Press), pp. 75–90.

Verma, Rohit, Gary M. Thompson, and Jordan J. Louviere. 1999. Configuring Service Operations in Accordance with Customer Needs and Preferences. *Journal of Service Research* 1(3):262–274.

## Notes

1. Stephen S. Tax and Stephen W. Brown. 1998. Recovering and Learning from Service Failure. *Sloan Management Review* 39(3):84.
2. Stephen S. Tax and Ian Stuart. 1997. Designing and Implementing New Services: The Challenges of Integrating Service Systems. *Journal of Retailing* 73(1):105–134.
3. Alan G. Robinson and Sam Stern. 1997. *Corporate Creativity: How Innovation and Improvement Actually Happen* (San Francisco: Berrett-Koehler Publishers), pp. 32–33.
4. Karl Albrecht. 1988. *At America's Service: How Your Company Can Join the Customer Service Revolution* (New York: Warner Books), pp. 124–125.
5. Robinson and Stern, 9–11.
6. This discussion is indebted to G. Lynn Shostack and Jane Kingman-Brundage. 1991. How to Design a Service, in Carole A. Congram and Margaret L. Friedman, eds., *The AMA Handbook of Marketing for the Service Industry* (American Marketing Association), pp. 243–261.
7. Albrecht, 89.
8. Shostack and Kingman-Brundage, 244. For more information on service blueprinting and service mapping, see: G. Lynn Shostack. 1984. Designing Services That Deliver. *Harvard Business Review* 62(1):133–139; and J. Kingman-Brundage. 1991. Technology, Design, and Service Quality. *International Journal of Service Industry Management* 2(3):47–59.
9. D. Daryl Wyckoff. 1984. New Tools for Achieving Service Quality. *Cornell Hotel and Restaurant Administration Quarterly* 25(3):89.
10. Albrecht, 38.

Chapter

**11**

# Waiting for Service

**Hospitality Principle:**

Manage the guest's wait.

*Hurry up and wait.*
—Old military saying

*"Get In Line, Brother"*
—Bluegrass gospel song

## LEARNING OBJECTIVES

After reading this chapter, you should understand:

▥ How to make any wait for service as short and pleasant as possible.
▥ How to make any wait for service *seem* short and pleasant.
▥ How to manage capacity shortages.
▥ How to manage the guest's perception of the wait.
▥ How to offset the wait's negative effects by managing the value of the experience provided to the guest.
▥ What lessons queuing theory holds for hospitality organizations.
▥ How to solve a simple waiting-line problem mathematically.

## KEY TERMS AND CONCEPTS

| | |
|---|---|
| arrival patterns | queue discipline |
| capacity day | queuing theory |
| managing the wait | single-channel waiting line |
| multichannel waiting line | waiting-line theory |
| queue | |

How long we wait, and how long we are willing to wait, are fascinating subjects. A British Airways TV commercial says we spend eight and a half weeks waiting in lines during the first thirty years of life. Parents put their children on the waiting lists for some exclusive preparatory schools before the children are born. If you want to take your own ride down the Colorado River in the Grand Canyon, rather than ride in a concession operator's raft, you will have to wait in line, at current use levels, for about twenty years.

Nobody likes to wait in line. Yet, almost every hospitality organization relies on waiting lines to match its serving capacity with the number of guests who want service. Managing the lines and how long customers have to wait in them is one of any service provider's fundamental concerns. This chapter presents some strategies for managing the *reality* and the *perception* of the guest's wait for service. These include both quantitative and perceptual strategies. The secret to managing the guest's wait effectively is to use all available techniques, in the appropriate combination, to make a seemingly endless wait acceptable and even enjoyable to the guest. Since nearly every service experience has a wait in it somewhere, **managing the wait** is sufficiently important to merit its own chapter. In some respects the wait is an inevitable part of the service experience since no organization can perfectly prepare itself to serve all guests, when they want, whatever they want (although McDonald's comes close). In another respect a wait is a service failure. Even if the wait at a popular attraction is no surprise and therefore "meets the guest's expectations," the guest doesn't like it.

## WHEN THE WAIT BEGINS

The guest experience often starts off not with a *wow* but a *wait*. The wait for service begins at the entrance to the restaurant, the busy signal on the phone, or the line in front of Space Mountain at Walt Disney World Resort. The prospective guest or customer assesses the

Space Mountain line, the number of cars in the restaurant's parking lot, or the busy signal on the phone and decides whether to walk to the next attraction, drive on to the next restaurant, hang up the phone—or to wait. What makes that guest wait or leave can be *managed*— if waiting lines are understood. If no other eating places are within eyesight, or the exceedingly hungry guest does not know what other restaurants are available nearby and doesn't want to take time to ask, or the guest is absolutely convinced that he must eat in that restaurant because the quality or uniqueness of the dining experience is said to be unsurpassed, he will probably pull into the parking lot, walk inside, and wait in line.

High expectations explain the large crowds usually standing outside an Outback Steakhouse or Cracker Barrel restaurant. The people waiting believe that the quality or the uniqueness of the dining experience will outweigh the costs to them of waiting, despite the full parking lot and the crowd standing in line outside the restaurant waiting to be served. The same high expectations can explain the lines next to Space Mountain and the other popular attractions throughout the Walt Disney World Resort. In effect, each person makes an opportunity-cost judgment. If the expected benefits of the wait outweigh the costs (boredom and impatience, to name just two) of idly standing around, then the guest will wait. If they don't, the guest will leave and go somewhere else for the service.

For those customers who cannot be served immediately but decide to wait rather than leave, how can the wait be made as short and as pleasant as possible? No matter how good the Space Mountain ride or the Cracker Barrel meal is, if the customer begins the experience angry, distressed, or unhappy about having to wait for service, that customer's expectations will be much harder to meet.

## CAPACITY AND PSYCHOLOGY: KEYS TO MANAGING LINES

Managing the wait has two major components. First is *keeping the wait as short as possible* by ensuring that the appropriate capacity has been built into the service facility to minimize the wait for the anticipated number of guests arriving at the anticipated rate. Second is ensuring that the guests who are waiting have their *psychological needs and expectations* met while they wait.

The capacity decision results from careful study of the expected demand pattern. Whether one is trying to determine how many copier machines to buy to serve a law office, how many toll booths to install on the expressway, how many phone lines to run into a travel agency, or how many blackjack tables to put in a casino, the need to make an accurate capacity estimate is the same. Management must predict three factors: *how many people* will arrive for the service, *at what rate* they will arrive, and *how long* the service will take. These three factors drive the capacity decision.

If, on every day that the organization is open for business, the same number of people were to arrive for service every day, their arrivals were evenly spaced throughout the day, and serving each person took the same length of time, the capacity decision would be easy. For example, a psychiatrist can schedule eight patients per day, schedule them to arrive on the hour, then serve each patient for forty-five minutes and use the remaining fifteen minutes to write up notes on that patient and prepare for the next. That psychiatrist has an easy capacity decision: one service facility (an office) containing one chair for the psychiatrist and one couch for the patient, plus other furnishings and equipment for one office. If the service is a guided tour through a museum, the service provider knows how long it will take, but the museum's management must predict how many people will arrive for service. If the service has a less definite beginning and ending time, like a meal or a hospital stay, both the number of persons arriving for service and the average time taken to deliver the service will have to be estimated or predicted. We will discuss several methods for making these predictions later in this chapter.

Capacity designs can affect perceptions of service quality. A restaurant with too many seats will appear empty to diners. The scarcity of other patrons may lead those who did come in and sit down to conclude that the food or service is not up to par. This assumption predisposes guests to expect a poor experience. Further, they may feel foolish for choosing a restaurant that is so obviously unpopular. The chefs and the servers have two strikes against them, just because the restaurant designers put in too many seats.

Of course, from the restaurant owner's point of view, the excess capacity costs money! Fixed costs are tied up in unused tables, silverware, equipment, rent, and so forth. Too much capacity may also mean higher variable costs as well. The manager may have to hire servers to cover the extra seats, just in case someone shows up to sit in them.

## Capacity

In an ideal world, the organization would have the exact capacity required to serve each guest immediately. Each customer for Cracker Barrel or Space Mountain would arrive just when a table or an empty car was available to provide the desired experience. Guests want that kind of service, and organizations want to provide it. Both are frequently disappointed.

### What to Do?

Because people do not arrive at service operations in neat, ordered patterns, they sometimes have to wait for service. When the organization sees that its waiting lines are becoming unacceptably long, hospitality managers face several choices:[1]

***1. Close the Doors to Further Customers.*** This choice is highly undesirable, but sometimes the movie theater manager or rock show entrepreneur must tell those waiting, "Sorry, we're full."

***2. Add Capacity.*** Because this alternative is usually expensive, organizations do not usually choose it unless they believe the high demand causing the waiting lines will continue. The organization will be particularly hesitant to add capacity if its design-day capacity is already at a high percent level, meaning that the organization is already at or below capacity most of the time. Stopgap measures for adding capacity temporarily are sometimes available. For example, employees can be asked to work overtime, a swat-team approach can be used to reassign employees from their normal areas to help unclog a service bottleneck, temporary help can be hired, or physical facilities like tents can be rented.

***3. Manage Demand.*** Simply informing guests of when the busy and slack times occur may smooth out demand. Service providers can also schedule appointments or offer inducements to customers to use capacity at nonpeak demand times. Requiring reservations at a restaurant is an example of the first method, and early-bird specials or discounts on electricity at off-peak times are examples of the second.

Reservations or appointments can be somewhat useful and even necessary when excess capacity is too expensive to lie idle, such as on an airliner, at a concert, or in an expensive restaurant. But most hospitality organizations do not have the market stature to insist that their guests make reservations, nor is the opportunity cost to the guest for not receiving the specific service at the specific time usually so great that the guest is willing to make reservations. When the airline is the only one able to fly you to Nashville at the time you need to be there, or the restaurant is the only place that you think will impress your client, only then will you bother to make a reservation and thereby help the organization efficiently manage its capacity.

Another way to manage demand is by *shifting demand.* When the wait times for popular attractions became excessive, Disney shifted demand by creating a special after-hours ticket called "Magic Kingdom's E-Ride Nights." The ticket sold for $10 and provided guests unlimited access to the nine most popular attractions for an additional three hours after the normal park close. To guarantee the guests minimal wait times on the nine attractions, the tickets sold each night were limited to a fixed number of guests and were sold in advance at the Disney resorts on a first-come, first-served basis. The actual number of tickets sold was limited to match the capacity of the nine attractions open.

The guests who paid $10 for the right to spend an extra three hours after normal closing time to ride their favorite rides as many times as they wanted to were happy and thought they got a great deal. They did not have to stand in long lines with everybody else waiting for these rides during the day. Regular daytime guests were also happier; their lines were shorter because the E-Ride Nights guests were no longer in the lines during the day. In effect, Disney expanded park capacity by shifting demand, but unlike the power company that gives customers a lower rate at off-peak times or the restaurant that offers low-cost early-bird specials, Disney was able to charge *more* and guests were happy to pay; they felt they got good value for their money.

### 4. Allow the Line to Form and Then Manage the Line by Diverting Customers.
Offer people waiting in line something else to do. Having a gift shop in a Hard Rock Cafe or Rainforest Cafe gives patrons someplace to go and something to do while they wait for the service that brought them to the organization. These diversions can become highly profitable, sometimes more profitable than the service product itself. Rainforest Cafe even calls itself "A wild place to shop and eat." An organization may go so far as to close down some available capacity to ensure that people wait long enough to become "diverted" to the gift shop, with its high-margin items for sale. Or an organization may keep a phone caller on hold longer than absolutely necessary to present a recorded message promoting other services. A related strategy is to upgrade a low-demand aspect of the organization's service to divert customers toward it and away from high-demand features. As an example, Disney upgraded The Swiss Family Tree House so that people would be willing to get out of the Space Mountain line and stand in the shorter Swiss Family Tree House line. Or entertainment can be offered to those waiting in line. Strolling bands at Disney go to the longest lines to provide diversion for those waiting. Restaurants frequently have a bar with entertainment so that guests waiting for a table can have a drink and listen to some music.

From their own daily experience, most people can cite numerous examples of organizations that allow lines to form, then manage them well or poorly.

### 5. Do Nothing.
The organization can accept the fact that it will have unhappy customers and hope that they aren't so unhappy that they vow never to return.

As an example of how one type of hospitality organization might use these options, a theme park could choose from: limit attendance by closing the park, build a new ride or expand a present ride, reenergize rides that are less preferred, and provide entertainment for the waiting lines, or simply accept higher levels of customer dissatisfaction. Customer-focused research can identify the best strategy. The goal is to find the decision that ensures customer satisfaction with the lowest capital cost. This decision allows both customers and the organization to come out ahead.

## Design Day

Whether they realize it or not, or whether they do it consciously or not, all hospitality organizations use the *design day* concept (also discussed in Chapter 2). The design day is the hypothetical day that the facility, attraction, or service was designed to handle comfortably, but not too comfortably. The design-day capacity is set to handle a predetermined amount of demand without compromising guest satisfaction. If demand is less than the design-day model, then guests are happy but the facility is underutilized. If demand exceeds the design-day capacity, then some guests will probably be unhappy. Waiting lines may form on design days, but they will not exceed the length where guests perceive a decline in the quality or value of their experience.

Benchmark organizations know just how long the lines can be and still remain within limits acceptable to guests. A major theme park might use a fifteen-minute average wait as its criterion. On the design day, it doesn't want anyone to wait longer than this average time because guest surveys have shown that the quality and value of the experience decline sharply beyond this time length. Because fifteen minutes is an average, it may take much longer to get on a popular ride. However, based on the accumulated data, a fifteen-minute average may be the best balance between having too much capacity and not enough. A truly guest-focused theme park may set its design day at a very high level, say 80 to 90 percent—meaning that supply will be adequate for demand on 80 to 90 percent of the days of the year—because it appreciates the fact that most guests have traveled a long way, have limited vacation time, and have no choice but to wait. To provide a guest experience of high quality, the organization will set the design day percentile high and built more capacity than might otherwise be practical. The cost of an unhappy guest to a major theme park that relies on return guest visits must be carefully balanced against the costs of building capacity.

## The Capacity Day

Design days are the times when capacity is the best trade-off for both the guest and the facility—not ideal for either one, but satisfactory. Many organizations also calculate and use a **capacity day,** the maximum number of customers allowed in the facility in a day or at one time. This number is often set by the fire marshal based on the number of square feet each customer must have available. The capacity day may be set by the organization itself, to represent a point beyond which overall customer dissatisfaction with crowds, lines, or delays in service is unacceptable. Hospitality organizations know that guests disappointed because they did not have the guest experience at all are preferable to dissatisfied, angry ones who did.

## QUEUING THEORY: MANAGING THE REALITY OF THE WAIT

Few organizations in any industry have the luxury of adjusting capacity quickly or managing demand by getting customers to show up when the organization wants them to, instead of when customers want to come. Most hospitality organizations must therefore rely on predicting and managing the inevitable waiting lines that are created when customers arrive looking for service.

The general problem for the organization is that adding servers costs more but reduces the wait, which improves guest-experience quality, guest satisfaction, and guest loyalty. Reducing servers saves money but increases the wait, which decreases guest-experience quality, guest satisfaction, and guest loyalty. How is the hospitality organization to find the proper cost-benefit balance?

The place to begin is in the use of **queuing theory,** sometimes called **waiting-line theory,** and the mathematical solutions this technique offers. A typical queuing-theory problem might be: If an average of forty cars per hour arrive at a drive-through window with a single server, and if it takes the server an average of two minutes to fill an order, how long does the average car spend in line? During an average hour, how many minutes will the server be working and how many minutes idle? Most applications of waiting-line theory in the hospitality industry are based on the idea that people do not arrive in neat patterns. The typical approach is to sample the arrival and service patterns of guests and use this information to simulate the distribution that best matches the reality for the particular organization's guests. A restaurant might actually count all of its guests over a period of time or sample them over a longer period using some appropriate sampling methodology and let the actual guest patterns represent the distribution of both arrival and service times.

### Characteristics of Waiting Lines

All waiting lines have three characteristics that any model must include:

*1. Arrival Patterns: The Numbers of Guests Arriving and the Manner in Which They Enter the Waiting Line.*    The arrivals could be random like patrons to a restaurant, in bulk like a bus load of tourists, or in some other distribution that is difficult to describe, like patients coming to a hospital emergency room in varying but not completely random intervals. Queue management is easiest when customer arrivals can be scheduled. Even if arrivals cannot be strictly scheduled, they can be controlled. Charging extra at popular times and offering discounts during the off season would be examples of arrival-control strategies.

*2. Queue Discipline: How the Arriving Guests Are Served.*    Options are first-come, first-served; last-come, first-served (not a formula for hospitality success), or some other set of service rules. For example, guests with reservations or wanting takeout food only may be served first, or restaurant parties of two may be served when a two-seat table is available regardless of how many parties of three or more are in line ahead of them. Guests understand such a service rule. They don't understand an implicit rule like the following, which seems to be in effect at numerous service locations: "Answer a phone call from someone sitting at home before serving the customer or guest standing right in front of you who may have traveled miles to do business with you."

The guests themselves can usually be counted on to maintain the discipline of the first-come, first-served queue. If someone breaks into the line in front of you, queue etiquette requires you to object and those in line behind you to support you. If the queue discipline in a certain grocery store line is first-come, first-served, no more than ten items, customers count each other's items and may forcefully object to a number over ten.

***3. Time for Service: How Long It Takes to Serve Guests.*** The time boundaries of some service experiences can be carefully managed, like a flight from Boston to Atlanta, or a ride in a roller coaster car. But customers in most service settings vary, voluntarily or involuntarily, in the time it takes them to receive the service. Some diners want to eat and run; others wish to savor the meal. Likewise, some hospital emergency-room patients suffer from severe wounds while others have trivial problems. The amount of time it takes to serve the different customers can be as unpredictable as the people themselves. If the waiting-line model is going to be an aid in managing the line, it must take this variation into account. Although the previous examples involve people, waiting-line theory can be applied to anything that waits in line for something to happen to it. An automobile waiting in a fully automated painting line or a meal waiting to be served is as queued up and in need of managing as the newly arriving guest at the hotel front desk.

## Line Types

In the following discussion, "channel" refers to a *server,* and "phase" refers to a *step* in the service experience once it is underway.

### Single-Channel, Single-Phase

The basic line type is the *single-channel, single-phase* queue—one server, one step. This queue type is represented as the top illustration in Figure 11-1. Mary Blaine has a one-chair hair cuttery. Customers come in, wait their turn, and have their hair cut in the single service phase. Indoor customers at some quick-serve restaurants stand in any one of several single-channel, single-phase queues. The customer looks the lines over, chooses one, stands in it waiting for service, and eventually reaches the counter to begin the single service phase. In that phase, the counter person takes the order, assembles and delivers it, and collects the money. Highway toll plazas and McDonald's counters are not the sites of multi-channel queues, even though they may have multiple servers. They consist of a group of single-channel, single-phase queues, with one server per queue.

### Single-Channel, Multiphase

The second queue type in the figure is the *single-channel, multiphase* queue, like a cafeteria line or the drive-through at a limited-menu, fast-serve facility. Essentially, it is two or more single-channel, single-phase queues in sequence. The guest waits in one queue for service from a single server, then moves on to wait in another queue for another phase of service from another single server. At a typical drive-through restaurant, customers queue up for the first phase. Each customer drives up to the order microphone, tries to understand what the person (the server, the single channel providing the first phase of service) inside the restaurant is saying, places an order (end of first phase) and then queues up again waiting to move forward to the window to receive and pay for the order (second phase, meaning

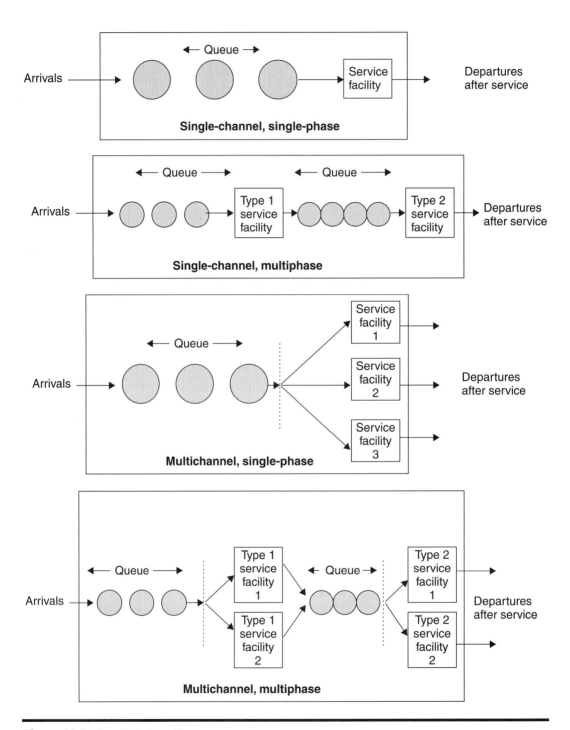

**Figure 11-1** *Some Basic Queue Types.*

another single channel for service with a single server). In this guest experience, the customer interacts with the organization twice, at two different places.

The multiphase setup did not work for Service Merchandise Company, which closed 134 stores in 1999 to avoid bankruptcy. The stores operated under a catalog-showroom concept. Customers purchased discounted items by taking a product number to a cash register and then taking a payment voucher to a warehouse counter. But customers did not like the catalog-showroom format. As a company spokesperson admitted of the format, "It kept prices down, but it didn't offer a high level of customer service. People don't want to wait in two lines."[2]

### Multichannel, Single-Phase

A third type is the *multichannel, single-phase* queue. The customer begins in a single line that then feeds into multiple channels or stations for the service, each staffed by a server. The customer waits to get to the front of the single line, then goes to the next available channel (server) for service. An example would be a bank or airline waiting line where everyone stands in a single queue, often snake-shaped to fit into available space, waiting for an open channel to any one of multiple servers. The queue discipline is to call the next person in the line to the next available teller, airline-counter attendant, telephone operator, or career counselor, who renders a single service in a single phase. The Federal Personnel Office uses this method for incoming telephone calls. The automated system tells each caller how many callers are ahead, so the caller can decide whether to wait or call back later. The single phase of service is to have a phone call answered. The multiple channels for obtaining this service are the many operators handling calls. The queue is managed by having the next available operator handle the next caller waiting in line. Many hospitality organizations find this method the most efficient way to manage their lines as it accounts well for the varying lengths of time that it takes to serve different customers. Everyone has had the experience of choosing to stand in one of several available single-channel lines—at the movie-theater refreshment stand, for example, or the hotel front desk—then watching all the other lines move much more quickly. The use of a multichannel, single-phase system eliminates this feeling of inequity or bad luck; everyone starts out in the same line.

### Multichannel, Multiphase

The last type of waiting line shown in Figure 11-1 is the most complicated to manage: the *multichannel, multiphase* queue system. Essentially, it is two or more multichannel, single-phase queues in sequence. The guest waits to get to the front of one line, then goes to the next available server. After receiving the first phase of service, the guest then gets in another line, waits to arrive at the front, then goes to the next available server/channel to receive the next phase of service. The Pepper Market, a cafeteria in Orlando's Coronado Springs Hotel, uses this pattern between its single-channel entry and exit points. At the entry point, the guest lines up to receive a "charge card" to be used at the different food stations. The guest then sees lines leading to each of several entrées and takes a place at the end of, say, the seafood line. The guest waits to become first in line, then goes to the next available seafood entrée server. The guest follows the same procedure for bread, dessert, vegetable, and so forth. The guest then gets in a checkout line and turns the charge card in to a cashier, who totals up all the purchases.

*Casual Single-Channel, Single-Phase Queue. (Used by permission from Disney Enterprises, Inc.)*

A hospitality organization will often have numerous queues linked together in various combinations. For example, a restaurant will have a line for people waiting to be seated, a wait time while the server serves other customers in a queue ahead of you before coming to take your order, a line of orders queued up for processing by the cook, a queue of servers waiting while the food is being prepared, and a line of people at the checkout. To consider just the line of people waiting to be seated, it is a multichannel, single-phase queue, if the restaurant tables are considered to be channels and being seated is considered to be a phase. Managing the wait times associated with single and multiple channels and phases is difficult, but it is critical for ensuring excellent guest service.

## Which Queue to Use?

Common sense suggests that the best queue type for an organization to use is the one that enables guests to begin receiving service as rapidly as possible. The guestologist knows that the best line type is *the one that customers prefer.* For example, they may prefer to stand in a certain type of line because they think they will be served faster, even if they won't. McDonald's believes that its several single-channel, single-phase lines serve more customers more quickly. Wendy's, Burger King, and most other quick-serve restaurants use the single-channel, multiphase queue, with customers placing an order at one location and moving to another to pick it up. At some other quick-serve restaurants and many airline counters, all customers get into one line, often a line that snakes between posts and velvet ropes. Once the customer reaches the head of the line, the customer waits to enter whichever channel leads to the next available server or attendant.

People seem to prefer the single serpentine queue, even though the length of the single line can be intimidating. They don't have to think or worry about which line to choose, or about whether to change lines if the present line seems slow or another line seems to have gotten shorter, or whether someone joining the next line over will unfairly be served more quickly. According to Burger King studies, people standing in single-channel, single-phase lines like those at McDonald's experience "tremendous stress."[3]

## Line Simulation: A Gift Shop

While a statistical distribution can be used to describe the arrival and service patterns of many standard queues, in some situations only a simulation will yield the quality of data necessary to explain and predict the reality of a particular queue. Here is how a simulation might work.

The Christmas Tree is an extremely successful Christmas-themed restaurant; their slogan, "Make every day like Christmas!" appeals to young and old. Because Christmas-related items are available in regular stores only during the holiday season, Rudolph's Gift Shop attached to the Christmas Tree does a huge business during the rest of the year. In fact, many customers come to the location to shop at Rudolph's rather than dine at the Christmas Tree.

Rudolph's has twenty checkout counters, which if fully staffed would require two people at each, for a total of forty people. If on an average day only fifty customers are typically in the shop at any one time, then full staffing of the checkout counters would be an obvious waste of money because the probability of all fifty people moving to the checkout lines at the same time is infinitely small. But if Rudolph's opens only one checkout counter, a long line will soon form. What staffing level best balances the cost of staffing Rudolph's checkouts against the cost of lost customers who vow never to return because of the long lines or lost sales as customers abandon their carts full of Christmas items and walk out?

### Observing the Flow

Over several weeks the shop manager can observe the flow of customers and time how long they are in the shop. If sufficient observations are made, the shop manager can create distributions that accurately describe customer arrival patterns, the quantity of items that they bring to the checkout stand, and their time spent in Rudolph's shopping for those items. With this information the manager can then simulate the shopping experiences of Rudolph's customers to determine how to staff the checkout counters appropriately at different times and on different days of the week. Here is how that might be done.

### Allocation Wheels

In his office, the manager could set up the two roulette wheels that appear in Figure 11-2. Spaces are allocated on the first wheel to represent, in percentage form, the time between customer arrivals at the checkout counters. From the observations already made, the shop knows that for 15 percent of their observations, the time between arrivals at checkout was zero minutes; people arrived simultaneously. For 20 percent the time between arrivals was one minute; for 25 percent, the time was two minutes; for 10 percent the time was three minutes. For another 10 percent, the time was four minutes, for 12 percent five minutes, and for 8 percent six minutes. The wheel has spaces reflecting these arrival-pattern percentages. To simulate the arrival patterns of the customers at checkout, the manager would merely spin the wheel and write on a chart the arrival interval noted in the section of the wheel when it stopped.

The second wheel in Figure 11-2 is, in similar fashion, portioned off to represent the observations about how long the customers took to go through the checkout process. This

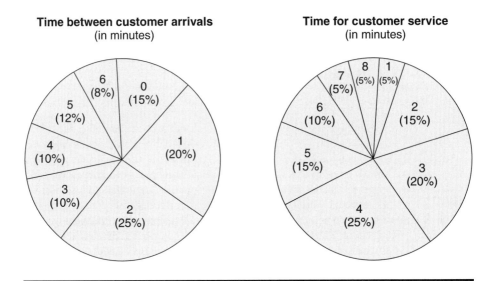

**Figure 11-2** *Wheels Representing Time between Arrivals and Time for Service at checkout.*

total would include the time to scan the purchased items, write the checks or pay cash, and wrap or bag the purchases. Since people vary in both quantity of purchases and speed of writing checks or making payment, the time for service and the proportions on the wheel representing those times would likewise vary. The observations might reveal that 5 percent of the time the transaction took one minute, 15 percent of the time two minutes, 20 percent took three minutes, 25 percent took four minutes, 15 percent took five minutes, 10 percent took six minutes, 5 percent seven minutes, and 5 percent eight minutes. This distribution is represented on the second wheel in the figure.

Now the manager can execute the simulation by spinning the first wheel to randomly determine the time between customer arrivals and spinning the second wheel to determine how long each guest took to be served once in a checkout line. By recording the numbers on a simple chart that notes the time between arrivals, times for service and, finally, the time customers were waiting, the entire day's activities can be simulated to determine the maximum, minimum, and average length of time customers waited for service plus the total waiting time for all the customers. The chart would simulate a day's activities by beginning when the shop opens and recording the arrivals throughout the day until it closes. Running this simulation many times (typically more than 100 on a computerized model) would allow the Rudolph's manager to draw some statistical conclusions about the length of waiting time, checkout capacity utilization, and the impact on waiting (and guest perception of the quality and value of the experience) that opening up more checkout stands and adding more capacity would have.

Although this is a fairly simple illustration, it does show the usefulness of determining mathematically the relationship between the service provider's capacity and the average waiting time for the guest in a way that allows the hospitality organization to find the ideal balance between the two. This same technique can be used to determine the ideal number of monorails in a theme park, toll booths on a turnpike, front-desk people in a hotel, servers and cooks in a restaurant, spaces in a parking lot, nurses in an emergency room, or any other application where an organization needs to balance the costs of providing capacity with the quality of the service experience.

Certain basic forces affect waiting lines, and they can be expressed mathematically. An explanation of the mathematics of waiting lines appears in the chapter appendix.

## Balancing Capacity and Demand

Determining the proper balance between supply and demand requires more calculations than just the basics. The gift shop in the earlier example must gather more data about customer behaviors and expectations. If, for example, it finds in interviewing or merely observing its customers that when the wait is longer than five minutes they will put down their selections and leave the shop without buying anything, then a wait longer than five minutes is unacceptable no matter what the remaining data might reveal. On the other hand, if the surveyed customers reveal strong shop loyalty, a competitive advantage for the shop because it is unique in providing holiday items throughout the year, or a clientele with a lack of anything better to do with their time in a market populated with retired or otherwise less time-sensitive customers, then the shop might choose to let the lines grow without much adjustment. The essential feature of the calculation is to determine that point beyond which the length of the wait damages the quality of the guest experience beyond the level acceptable to the guest and the organization.

Once the capacity-and-demand balance decision has been made, the organization now must plan for accommodating the inevitable lines created by uneven demand patterns. Here the challenge is to manage the wait in such a way that the guest is satisfied with it. Two major dimensions are involved. The first is the way the time spent waiting feels to the guest, and the second dimension is how to minimize the negative effects of the wait by managing the value of the experience to the guest. The organization wants each guest to conclude that the experience was well worth the wait.

## MANAGING THE PERCEPTION OF THE WAIT

Understanding what makes time fly while waiting in line is a fundamental concern for managers seeking to improve the quality of the customer wait. Guestologists have found that time flies not only when you're having fun but under other circumstances. Hospitality managers must remember that everyone is different, and these differences will influence how people feel about waiting in line. And how they *feel* about the wait is at least as important as how long the wait is.

### 1. Occupied Time Feels Shorter Than Unoccupied Time. 
If you are busy doing something while you are waiting, the time seems to go by faster. Most line waits can be made more enjoyable and made to feel less lengthy if there is something for guests to do—if they can be distracted or diverted in some way.

Disney is the master of managing time waits by giving its guests something to divert them from thinking about the wait. If the line for a particular Walt Disney World Resort attraction has become extraordinarily long, a strolling band or acrobats or some other distraction arrives to entertain and occupy the guests while they wait. For long lines, Universal Studios spaces television sets showing a video or movie. People can watch an interesting program while moving toward the entrance to the attraction.

### 2. Time Spent Waiting to Begin the Service Experience Will Feel Longer Than Time Actually Spent in the Experience Itself.

Hospitality organizations therefore try to find ways to minimize how long the wait "feels." Theme parks and other entertainment attractions may offer pre-attraction features termed the *preshow*. Guests feel in a sense that they are already in the attraction, though they are mainly still standing in line. For example, people standing in line to get into the Enchanted Tiki Room hear a caged Audio-Animatronics bird telling bad jokes. Time seems to pass more quickly for guests when they are watching a preshow or preview of the main attraction—almost as if the attraction itself has started.

The airlines send roving people down long lines waiting to check in, to begin the contact with the people that makes them feel someone is finally taking care of them. Avis rental car quickly gathers up people at the airport terminal contact point and shuttles them to an off-site facility where the line may be quite long and the wait substantial, but customers feel that Avis is at least doing *something* to take care of them. This strategy has the additional benefit of getting customers away from competing rental counters. Out at the off-site facility, they will wait longer in line because they cannot simply move to the competitor at the next counter.

Another way to spend time is to teach customers in line what they are supposed to do once they reach the actual event or attraction. The education provided during the wait time can improve or enhance the service experience and, in that way, actually becomes part of the experience. Many customers waiting in a fast-food line use the time to evaluate the menu items to select what they want. If they could walk right up to the counter, they would still need the time to review the menu options; they would then feel awkward about being at the front of a forming line unprepared to be served. Having time to stand in a line is, for these customers, an advantage.

Many restaurants give patrons standing in line a menu to look over while awaiting their table. This gives customers something to do and not only speeds up the ordering process once customers are seated but gives them the impression that the service experience has begun. Having a cocktail waitress serve waiting guests or providing a complimentary beverage if the wait is unusually long accomplishes the same purpose.

### 3. Anxious Waits Feel Longer Than More Relaxed Waits.

If people are afraid of what will happen to them once the service experience begins, the wait will seem longer. If people are sitting in an airplane that is obviously waiting for something to be fixed before it takes off, people will become quite anxious about what is wrong with the plane or what malfunction is holding it up, and the wait will feel long. If you are waiting in a hospital room, perhaps to receive the results of a diagnostic procedure, the wait will seem to drag. Sometimes, organizations want to create a little anxiety. The school principal may let the ill-behaved child waiting for punishment wait a little longer than necessary. Waiting to enter a scary ride at an amusement park will only enhance the effect of the ride.

### 4. Waits of Uncertain Length Feel Longer Than Certain Ones.

Anyone who has ever been at an airport waiting on a flight that is delayed for an unknown reason will know that such a wait feels endless. Sitting and waiting without knowing when the delay will be over causes any wait to feel much longer. Let your guests know what to expect. A time estimate can help the customer set a mental clock to let time pass more quickly until that preset time is reached. Telling phone callers how many callers are ahead of them in the phone queue serves the same purpose. Disney uses sign boards to tell guests how long before they enter the attraction from their point in line. Generally, they overestimate the time because guests are always happy when they get to the ride faster than they thought they would but never happy when they get there later. This is one reason why patients want doctors to be on time for scheduled appointments. Once the appointment time is reached, in the patient's mind it is time to be served, and any time spent after that is uncertain and long.

***5. Unexplained Waits Feel Longer Than Explained Waits.*** When you don't know what is holding up the line or causing the delay, then the wait will feel longer than if you know the reason. If traffic stops and your view ahead is blocked so you can't see why, the wait will feel long. If service is delayed, customers want to know why. Effective managers of waits will tell them or provide a visual cue that can explain the wait. For example, a line at a restaurant can be structured so customers can see that all the tables are full, or at a bank so one can see that all the tellers are busy. On the other hand, effective managers of queues will ensure that front-desk attendants or airline check-in staff doing something other than waiting on customers are kept out of sight of customers, so that they do not have to explain why their personnel are not serving customers. Restaurant managers try to keep empty tables out of sight; otherwise people queued up for a meal will think their wait does not have a legitimate explanation, and it will feel long. Restaurant guests do not buy the explanation, "That section is closed."

***6. Unfair Waits Feel Longer Than Fair Ones.*** If customers feel that the queue discipline is being consistently followed and fairly used, then the wait seems less long than it does when people are allowed to get away with cutting in line, or people are being served out of the apparent sequence of service order. Good organizations recognize this truth and manage their lines with this knowledge in mind. At times, VIP guests or some other special category of guest requires that the line discipline be broken. The layout of waiting lines into twisting maze patterns enables VIPs to be inserted subtly into line. These guests are integrated into the line flow so smoothly that those waiting do not usually notice that the discipline has been interrupted.

Organizations who for one reason or another need to break the queue discipline must find some way to communicate a reason for the apparent unfairness that customers will accept after hearing it. Time-honored reasons are "Lady with a baby!" and "Women and children first!" Passengers needing assistance go onto planes first, and nobody minds. No one complains if a disabled person goes to the front of the line. Seating a party of four at a restaurant before seating waiting parties of six or more seldom creates guest complaints or problems for the restaurant; everyone knows that almost all tables are set up for smaller parties and that some juggling must be done to accommodate the larger party.

***7. Solo Waits Feel Longer Than Group Waits.*** Waiting by yourself feels longer than waiting in a group of friends, or even a group you don't know. Organizations recognizing this perceptual issue try to organize their lines in such a way that people are grouped with other people. A double line would under this logic feel shorter than a single line, and a line structure that encourages people to interact so they feel like members of a group feels shorter than one in which the people are allowed to stay inside their own personal and highly individual spaces. In waiting-room areas, organizations can arrange the seating so as to promote interaction and a sense of being part of a group.

**8. Uncomfortable Waits Feel Longer Than Comfortable Ones.** All hospitality organizations dread seeing guests queued up in the hot sun, rain, or other uncomfortable conditions. Finding a way to keep people comfortable in outdoor queues while they wait to enter an air-conditioned environment is a real managerial challenge. Obviously, such devices as paddle fans, awnings, or artificially created shade can be useful for making the wait feel more comfortable and less lengthy.

**9. Interesting Waits Are Shorter Than Uninteresting Ones.** We have already said that occupied waits are shorter than unoccupied waits. This principle is true even if the activity in which one is occupied is only "busy work." But if you are occupied in doing something interesting while you wait, the time will seem even shorter.

**10. Happy Waits Are Shorter Than Sad Ones.** While this perhaps goes without saying in most situations, it is part of the perception of the waiting experience. Customers who are having fun, enjoying themselves, and feeling positive about the wait itself and the service experience to come will find the wait to be shorter than those who are unhappy, sullen, or feeling negative about waiting. Managers need to keep happy customers happy and make unhappy customers feel better about waiting. Using clowns is one way to turn unhappy children into happy ones. Professional comics warm up their audiences; they get them laughing during the wait, to make sure that when the television cameras come on, the guests are ready to have fun and laugh.

### The Emotional Wait State

In all of these waiting situations and especially the last one, the customer's emotional state will have a significant impact on the wait for service. Different people react differently to anxiety, uncertainty, discomfort, and other perceptual influences on the waiting time.

### Crowds and Clientele

If the waiting line being managed is large and diverse, then the "typical customer" will drive the design of the line and the associated wait. While hospitality managers should consider personality variables as much as possible in designing and managing waits, the line for large crowds must necessarily be designed to accommodate what the normal, average guest expects when entering the wait process.

If the people in line are a more select clientele with identifiable features, such as a queue at an upscale restaurant or hotel, then variability in treatment of the waiting guests may be possible and even necessary to ensure that the quality of the entire experience, including the wait, meets the guest expectations for that upscale level of service. You want to make the wait enjoyable or at least bearable, and that is harder to do with a mass-market audience than with a select, known clientele, for reasons other than the size of the mob.

### Waits in Contrast

In all of these waiting situations, the contrast effect will also influence the perception of the wait. If a customer has just had a comfortable, totally explained, predictable wait, followed by a subsequent wait that is unpredictable, anxiety producing, and of uncertain length, the second wait will seem longer than if a well-managed wait had not just occurred. Similarly, if a customer has just had a long wait, a short one will feel even shorter in contrast. If the guest has just been in a wait where employees were friendly and all servers were busy, that wait will seem shorter than a wait in which employees pay minimal attention to guests and some are engaged in activities other than serving people in line.

* * *

The key is to remember that the customer, client, or guest perceives the wait. If the objective data say the wait at your place is not too long or the wait at your company is actually shorter than it is at a competitor's, that doesn't matter to customers who think they have waited too long for your service. Customers have mental clocks in their minds that tell them when the wait is too long or just right and extremely well managed. Managing the perception is as effective a technique as managing the actual waiting time, and if the organization is particularly good at managing perceptions, it can make even very long waits acceptable and tolerable to customers.

## SERVICE VALUE AND THE WAIT

The more value the customer receives or expects to receive from the service, the more patiently the customer will wait. Since the customer defines the value of services rendered, the second major strategy for managing the perception of the wait is to manage the perceived value of the service for which the customer is waiting. This strategy can be implemented before, during, or even after the service is delivered.

### Before Service

Before receiving the service, waiting customers can be provided with information (or even with some other service) that will enhance the value of the service that motivated them to enter the queue in the first place. A hotel, for example, can enhance the perceived value of the guest experience by offering guests waiting in line some champagne or have them entertained by a chamber-music group. Such thoughtful touches not only distract and occupy the guest, they also add value to the experiences that the hotel and restaurant are selling and for which the guest must wait in line.

### During Service

During the performance of the service itself, its value (to the customer and as defined by the customer, as always) can be enhanced over the customer's expectations by a number of strategies. The organization will want to employ these strategies in any event, but the idea here is that if the service meets or exceeds expectations when the customer gets it, the wait was worth it.

In addition to providing customers with a service that is beyond their expectations in the first place, some more subtle actions can enhance the value of the service experience. Some restaurants believe in hanging signed photographs of celebrities who have eaten in the restaurant; doctors display diplomas from famous medical schools to indicate the high quality of their training. These touches tend to encourage the guest or patient to think that the meal and the medical treatment were worth the wait. As a more direct response to the wait, the server could apologize for it, which adds a personal touch that may increase the value of the experience for the guest. Hops Restaurant promises to "make a wait for your table as comfortable as possible with complimentary menu samples, beer samples, or soft drinks." These are all examples of how the value of the service to the customer can be enhanced even as it is being delivered. These enhancements all make the wait seem shorter in retrospect than it actually was; an excellent service experience diminishes the ill effects of the wait.

## After Service

After the service, the value of the experience in the eyes of customers can sometimes be enhanced, so they feel better about having taken the time to wait on the service in the first place. Although advertising is generally used to attract the attention of potential customers, people who have already purchased services are even more attentive to ads than those who have not. The ads reinforce the wisdom of not only purchasing the service but also of waiting in line to do so. Of course ads seen ahead of time can also reduce the effects of the wait while it is in progress; the ads have convinced customers that the experience will be good, so they wait more patiently. A phone call to a customer after the service experience, asking for reactions to it, can enhance the value of the experience and reduce the negative effects of the wait. Once Honda and a few other car dealers started calling up customers after they left the dealership to ask about the quality of the service experience, the other dealers had to make the calls, too. This type of personal attention after the experience can help compensate for the wait before the experience.

* * *

## Managing Waits in an Imperfect World

Managing the waiting line is a fundamental challenge for managers in the hospitality industry. The service cannot be stockpiled or inventoried, and the organization must find the right balance between having enough capacity to fill demand and having so much capacity that some sits idle most of the time. In a perfect world, the flow of customers matches the supply exactly. When one guest gets up to leave the restaurant, another walks in the door looking for lunch. When one guest finishes with the concierge, another arrives to ask a question, and so on across the entire range of services offered by organizations. In our less than perfect world, getting customers into the service setting and meeting their time expectations requires effective queue management.

## Lessons Learned

1. Manage the wait; don't just let it happen.
2. Know how long your guests are willing to wait patiently.
3. Know the psychology of managing waiting lines.
4. Use waiting-line models to understand how your queues work.
5. Try to minimize the negative effects of the wait before, during, and after the guest experience.
6. Find out how much a dissatisfied guest costs you; that will motivate you to manage the wait for your guests more carefully.

## Review Questions

1. "Just about every full-fledged guest experience has at least one wait somewhere within it." True or false?
   A. If false, name some guest experiences that do not involve a wait.
   B. Indicate some common front-of-the-house waits (as opposed to out-of-sight waits like queued up food orders) during a typical guest's experience at a casual restaurant like Bennigan's, Olive Garden, or Red Lobster. Which ones should be managed, and which ones can be left alone to take care of themselves?
   C. Indicate some common back-of-the-house waits, unseen by the guest, during a typical guest's experience at such a casual restaurant. Which ones should be managed, and which ones can be left alone to take care of themselves?
2. Think of a pleasant or enjoyable wait you have experienced within a hospitality setting. Think of an unpleasant or annoying wait.
   A. What strategies described in this chapter did the organization's managers use or fail to use that caused your wait to be one kind or the other?
   B. Did they employ any strategies not covered in the chapter?
3. What strategies are available to match the capacity of a hospitality organization with the demand for its services? Which strategies work best and under what circumstances?
4. This chapter explained how a theme park might use the design-day concept.
   A. How might the concept be used by a hotel, a restaurant, and an airline?
   B. Is the concept as applicable to those other organizations as to a theme park?
   C. If so, what are the common elements that facilitate applicability? If not, why is that?
5. Give some examples from your own experience of the different queue types in Figure 11-1. Did the queue type used seem to fit the situation? Was it readily apparent why the organization chose it? If you have to wait, which line type do you prefer and why?
6. You are the front-desk manager of a popular hotel, and you are frustrated by the number of guests you see waiting impatiently in line to check in and check out. Compare the advantages and disadvantages (and the costs and benefits, if you can) of relieving this situation by:
   A. setting up and using simulation wheels like those in Figure 11-2
   B. using some of the techniques in the chapter for managing the feel of the wait
   C. cross-training some employees so they can help out at the front desk during busy times
7. Some organizations, restaurants in particular, seem to take more interest in managing the wait in positive ways than others. How does an organization decide how much time and effort to place into managing the initial wait for service?
8. Although some academic people make a life's work out of queuing theory, many readers enjoy reading about the "psychological" methods for managing the wait more than they do studying "theory." Which is more important to managing the guest experience in hospitality organizations: the hard numbers of queuing theory or the softer psychological approach?
9. You may have heard someone say, or may have said yourself, "Whichever line I am in, the others always move faster." Can this be true?

## Activities

1. Find a situation in which a hospitality organization has found a way to control or shift guest demand. Why does the organization employ this strategy? How effective is the strategy? What incentives are offered to guests to encourage them to seek the hospitality service at one time rather than another? How profitable do you think the strategy might be?

2. Study the waiting-line situations (movies, athletic events, fast-food outlets, etc.) in which you find yourself over a period of time. Evaluate how well the lines are being managed. Which line-management strategies described in this chapter might have been used to improve these situations?

## Case Studies

### The Front Desk

*J*ane Gianini, manager at the Thusly Manor, an upscale inn and golfing resort in the North Carolina mountains, was becoming increasingly concerned about the situation at the front desk. On several occasions during the past week, she walked by the desk and saw a line of waiting guests. Several other times she walked by and saw no guests at all.

The dramatic rise in personal income and tourism during the 1990s had caused a boom in number of guests wanting to combine a stay in a fine hotel with some golfing on a beautiful hilly course. But success also brought problems for Thusly Manor, how to handle the increased numbers at the front desk among them. Gianini thought she had controlled the situation by implementing a new staffing procedure. If her calculations were correct, the new procedure should have just about eliminated both the waiting lines and the front-desk server down time. Nevertheless, she had seen guests lined up several times, and idle desk agents quite frequently.

When she first analyzed the data, she computed simple averages. To construct her present staffing schedule, she had found out how many guests arrived during each eight-hour shift on average and had divided that number by eight, to arrive at guest load per hour during a shift. She then staffed the front desk accordingly. She pulled the following data for the 8 A.M. to

**Type of Service and Percent of Service Time Used**

| Service Type | Average Service Time | Percent |
|---|---|---|
| I. Check-in/checkout | 10 minutes | 70% |
| II. Informational/misc. requests | 5 minutes | 30% |

**Frequency of Guest Arrivals at Front Desk**

| Average Time between Arrivals | Percent |
|---|---|
| 0 minutes | 30% |
| 5 minutes | 40% |
| 10 minutes | 20% |
| 20 minutes | 10% |

4 P.M. shift from her files to check on whether she had analyzed it correctly when she had set up her present system.

**1.** What was wrong with Gianini's original analysis?
**2.** How should she have analyzed this problem?

## Waiting for Gaudeaux

*G*rand Gaudeaux Cruise Lines specialized in taking passengers on luxury cruises to the Gaudeaux island chain in the Caribbean. Because of its financial success and good reputation in the industry, Grand Gaudeaux had recently been able to expand its passenger capacity by adding two brand-new, large ships to its fleet. The guest-satisfaction measurement team was meeting this morning with Steve Weitzman, CEO of Grand Gaudeaux, to discuss some surprising low guest-satisfaction ratings received from passengers on these two state-of-the-art ships. The company practice was to mail departing guests a survey about a week after their cruise, asking them a variety of questions. The recent data were troubling. Grand Gaudeaux had hoped to delight its guests by providing these new ships; instead, guests were reporting dissatisfaction.

The topic today was the dramatic downturn in the satisfaction scores. Knowing that this meeting was coming up and realizing the CEO's depth of concern, the measurement team had done some further investigation into guest opinions through a variety of means. The most interesting insight was gained from a series of focus groups in which guests from the newer, larger ships had indicated their frustration with the departure routine. It appeared that the larger the ship, the more difficult it was to get everyone ashore after the cruise ended. This long wait tended to give "cruisers" on the two newest ships an unsatisfactory last experience with Grand Gaudeaux Cruise Lines. Because of the "recency effect"—the psychological theory that the most recent events are best remembered and have greatest impact—the passenger problems in departing the ship were overshadowing the many excellent aspects of the cruise experience.

The team recognized some system solutions; for example, the port facility could be retrofitted with larger capacity to accommodate more departing passengers. Such a retrofit would involve significant expenditures. But even if the budget were available to make such improvements over the long run, the guest-satisfaction measurement team realized the acute need to improve the management of the passenger wait experience in the short run. The team knew of Weitzman's personal pride in and high hopes for the new ships. They knew he would want some answers as to what might be done to fix this source of guest dissatisfaction.

\* \* \*

If you were on the guest-satisfaction measurement team, what steps would you recommend to Weitzman?

# Appendix: *The Mathematics of Waiting Lines*

The mathematics are quite simple for a single-channel, single-phase line. An understanding of a few calculations will reveal much about the dynamics of waiting lines.

In the following example, we will use a single-channel line for a hotel's front desk, with one server/agent at the desk. We will calculate the average amount of time that a guest stands in line and stands in the system (time in line plus time being served). In addition, we will determine the idle time of the front-desk staff. These figures would be useful to a hotel manager wishing to control the waiting time for guests and to reduce the idle time for service personnel.[4]

These calculations for a single-channel, single-phase line, to illustrate the underlying principles of waiting-line management, can be done by hand. However, more complicated line systems requiring more complex formulae should be (and can easily be) analyzed by computer. Standard spreadsheet products such as Lotus and Excel have the capacity to perform such waiting-line analysis.

## *The Single-Channel, Single-Phase Case*

*The* Chelten Hotel has a simple front desk with one service station. Ben Blake, the front-office manager, has been observing the line at the front desk for several weeks. Not wanting guests to wait in line too long, he wishes to calculate the average wait in line for his guests over a one-hour period. He also wants to know how much idle time his servers will have during that hour. If front-desk agents have substantial idle time, Mr. Blake would like for them to perform some routine tasks such as sort the mail and enter charges to guest accounts.

Blake has compiled the following information for this one-hour period. For this example, we ignore variability and use averages to describe both arrival and service rates for the hotel guests:

The average time it takes to register a guest is four minutes; the hotel can register about fifteen guests per hour. This is the service rate, the units of server capacity per time period.

Ten guests are expected to arrive during the hour. This is the arrival rate.

The formulas use the following symbols:

$$\lambda = \text{arrival rate per hour (10)}$$
$$\mu = \text{service rate per hour (15)}$$

1. *Average time a guest waits in line:*

$$W_q = \lambda / \mu(\lambda - \mu) \qquad W_q = 10 / 15(15 - 10) \qquad W_q = .133 \text{ hours or 8 minutes}$$

$W_q$ means waiting time in the queue before being served. This calculation tells manager Blake that the *average* wait in the line for a guest is eight minutes. If that wait time is unacceptable to Blake, he may have to add another server.

2. *Average time spent in system:*

$$T_S = 1 / \mu - \lambda \quad T_S = 1 / 15 - 10 \quad T_S = .2 \text{ hours or 12 minutes}$$

This equation tells manager Blake that the average guest spends twelve minutes in the system, including both waiting time and service time.

3. *Average number of guests in line:*

$$L_q = \lambda^2 / \mu(\mu - \lambda) \quad L_q = 10^2 / 15(15 - 10) \quad L_q = 1.33 \text{ guests}$$

$L_q$ means the average length of the queue, in number of guests. Knowing that only 1.33 guests are in line at any one time, on average, reveals to Blake that the line's space requirements are minimal.

4. *Percent of time the server is busy:*

$$\rho = \lambda / \mu \quad \rho = 10 / 15 \quad \rho = 67\%$$

The front-desk registration procedure has one or more guests in it—either in line or being served—67 percent of the time, or about forty minutes out of every hour.

5. *Probability that there is no one in the system:*

$$\rho_0 = 1 - (\lambda/\mu) \quad \rho_0 = 1 - (10/15) \quad \rho_0 = 33\%$$

This is obviously the inverse of the previous formula. If the wait-plus-registration system has someone in it about forty minutes out of each hour, it is empty for the other twenty minutes. Blake can use this information to assign other tasks to idle servers. Now that Blake has run his calculations, the registration agents can probably look forward to an expanded job description.

## Additional Readings

Davis, M. M., and T. E. Vollmann. 1990. A Framework for Relating Waiting Time and Customer Satisfaction in a Service Operation. *Journal of Services Marketing* 4(1):61–69.

Hui, Michael K., and David K. Tse. 1996. What to Tell Consumers in Waits of Different Lengths: An Integrative Model of Service Evaluation. *Journal of Marketing* 60(2):81–90.

Katz, Karen, Blaire M. Larson, and Richard Larson. 1991. Prescription for Waiting-in-Line Blues: Entertain, Enlighten, and Engage. *Sloan Management Review* 32(4):44–53.

Laval, Bruce. 1975. Optimization of Walt Disney World Monorail System Through Computer Simulation. Proceedings 8th Annual Simulation Symposium, Tampa, FL. March 12–14:1–10.

Maister, David. 1985. The Psychology of Waiting Lines, in John Czepiel, Michael R. Solomon, and Carol F. Suprenant, eds., *The Service Encounter: Managing Employee/Customer Interaction in Service Businesses* (Lexington, MA: Lexington Books), pp. 113–124.

Taylor, Shirley. 1995. The Effects of Filled Waiting Time and Service Provider Control over the Delay on Evaluations of Service. *Journal of the Academy of Marketing Science* 23(1):38–45.

Taylor, Shirley. 1994. Waiting for Service: The Relationship Between Delays and Evaluations of Service. *Journal of Marketing* 58(2):56–69.

## Notes

1. Adapted from J. L. Heskett, W. E. Sasser, Jr., and C. W. L. Hart. 1990. *Service Breakthroughs: Changing the Rules of the Game* (New York: The Free Press), pp. 138–141.
2. Janine Young Sykes. 1999. Catalog Store to Close. *Gainesville (Florida) Sun,* February 17:9A.
3. Ibid.
4. Although the following assumptions underlie these formulas, it is not necessary to understand them to follow the discussion:
   1. Queue discipline is first-in, first-out.
   2. No balking or reneging. Customers must accept service when it is offered, and no one quits or leaves the line.
   3. Arrivals are accurately represented by a Poisson statistical distribution.
   4. Service times must follow a negative exponential Poisson distribution.
   5. Arrivals are independent.
   6. Arrival rate does not change over time.

# Fixing Service Problems

## Hospitality Principle:

Don't fail the guest twice.

*You want your customers to tell you when you've screwed up, so that you can take care of the problem and take steps to ensure that it doesn't happen again—to them, or anybody. If they don't tell you they'll just walk away shaking their heads and they'll never come back. Worse, you're likely to alienate somebody in the future by doing exactly the same thing.*

—Carl Sewell, *Customers for Life*

*Do whatever is necessary to take care of guests.*

—J. Willard Marriott, Jr., Chairman
& CEO, Marriott International, Inc.

## LEARNING OBJECTIVES

After reading this chapter, you should understand:

- How guests respond when the guest experience fails to meet their expectations.
- How organizations should respond when the experience fails to meet guest expectations.
- Why fixing service failures quickly—on the spot, if possible—is so important.
- Why positive publicity is so valuable and bad publicity so harmful.
- Why the recovery method for handling a service failure is so important.
- How to prevent, find, and recover from service failures.
- How to use the poka-yoke for avoiding problems during the service delivery process.
- How to learn from service failures.
- How guests evaluate the hospitality organization's recovery efforts.
- How to match the recovery strategy to the failure.

## KEY TERMS AND CONCEPTS

bad-mouthing
distributive fairness
evangelist
interactive fairness
poka-yoke

procedural fairness
service failure
service recovery
terrorist

## TERRORISTS AND EVANGELISTS

If your customer is irritated or angry about a **service failure,** fixing the problem is at least as important as getting it right the first time. Everyone expects that the service they've purchased will at least meet their expectations. In most cases, if that's what happens, then the customers have received what they wanted and will leave the experience satisfied. When you reserve a plane seat to New York, a dinner time at your favorite restaurant, or a hotel room at a distant location, you expect that the reservation will be honored when you arrive. Merely receiving the service that the organization is supposed to offer does not usually cause the guest to notice. What will get noticed, however, are the exceptions from what the guest expected. If these are positive exceptions, the organization creates a happy guest who remembers the *wow* experience with delight, comes back for more, and enthusiastically tells others about the great service.

In contrast are the occasions when the airline seat you reserved is gone, the restaurant didn't have your name on its reservation list, or the hotel had no rooms left when you arrived. These are the times when the organization failed to meet the guest's reasonable expectations. The guest will be dissatisfied at best. If the failure was severe enough, it turns the guest into the angry **terrorist** that every organization fears. A typical dissatisfied customer may tell eight or ten people about the problem. A terrorist may create a Web site and tell millions.

Exceeding expectations creates the apostles and **evangelists** that every organization hopes to have. Hospitality companies work hard to ensure that their guests have experiences so memorable that they can't wait to get home and tell all their friends and relatives about what a terrific time they had and how great the guest experience was. This positive word-of-mouth advertising reinforces the company's favorable public image. On the other hand, all organizations know that failures are inevitable. Consequently, like all companies that seek excellence, the good hospitality organizations work hard to identify and train their people to fix the inevitable problems. Poorly managed hospitality organizations fail to anticipate failure. They incorrectly assume that the service will always be as perfect as it was intended, the service delivery system will always be flawless, and the service providers will do their jobs exactly the way they were trained every time.

### Don't Fail Twice

Service failures can vary considerably across the dimensions of frequency, timing, and severity. A service failure can occur anytime during the single guest experience or across multiple experiences with the same organization. Since first impressions are so important, a failure occurring early may weigh more heavily than one occurring late. Big mistakes count more than little ones. The purpose of this chapter is to show the importance of fixing service failures, the reasons why failures happen, and the strategies available to recover from and avoid service failures. If the organization fails by not providing the expected guest experience in the first place, then not fixing this failure is *failing the guest twice.*

## THE IMPORTANCE OF FIXING SERVICE FAILURES

Retaining customers by providing excellent service and avoiding or fixing service failures is essential to organizational success. Frederick F. Reichheld and W. Earl Sasser, Jr., showed that if a company can reduce its rate of customer defections (leaving the organization to go to a competitor) by only 5 percent, *it can improve profits by 25 to 85 percent.*[1] Fixing service failures is clearly one of an organization's most essential activities.

When a guest has a problem, one of three outcomes usually occurs. The problem is fixed and the formerly unhappy guest leaves the experience happy; the problem isn't fixed and the unhappy guest leaves unhappy; or the organization tries to fix the problem and only succeeds in neutralizing the unhappy guest. A happy guest leaves as an apostle who spreads legends about a terrific experience. An unhappy guest may leave as a terrorist who goes and tells many others about a terrible experience. A neutralized guest may leave and forget the whole experience and probably the organization as well.

In some cases, such as total service catastrophes, neutralizing the unhappy customer is the best that the organization can hope for. If the surgeon removes the wrong leg, the TV system in the sports bar quits working during the final game of the World Series, or the restaurant meal leads to food poisoning, the best the organization can do is to neutralize the dissatisfied customer. Indeed, some organizations have developed disaster plans to prepare their employees for such situations. Airlines have emergency teams for handling crashes, theme parks have quick-response teams for accidents, and hotels have fire teams for handling evacuations in emergencies. The team's primary responsibility is to handle the emergency, to put out the fire. But the good team will also provide aid and comfort to the customers affected by the emergency, in part to restore the customer's positive perception of the organization.

### The Customer's Response to Failure

The unhappy or dissatisfied customer is the focus of the **service recovery.** An unhappy customer can do any one or a combination of three things.

### Never to Return

First, the customer can leave vowing never to return. Since this angry customer is also likely to tell others about the experience, this is the worst outcome for the organization. Here, it not only loses the future business of the dissatisfied customer, it loses the future business of all those the customer tells. The main reason for empowering servers to provide on-the-spot service recovery is to keep dissatisfied customers from leaving that way.

In a study that analyzed critical incidents during service encounters to identify the reasons for customers switching to other products or services, eight mutually exclusive reasons were identified.[2] *Core service failures* (mistakes, billing errors, service catastrophes) were the biggest reason people switched; they were mentioned by 44 percent of all respondents (noted by 11 percent as sole reason and 33 percent as one of two or more reasons). These include all critical incidents in which there were mistakes or technical failures with the service itself or delivery system. *Service delivery failures* attributable to negative employee attitudes or behaviors were the second largest category, mentioned by 34 percent of respondents. If employees were perceived as uncaring, impolite, or even rude, unresponsive or uncommunicative, unknowledgeable (as in inexperienced, untrained, inept, out of date), *they failed.* The third largest category of reasons people switched was *unsatisfactory employee response to service failure* (17 percent). When employees respond reluctantly, fail to respond with empathy or at all, or offer negative responses—for example, blaming the customer for service failure—customers understandably find those responses unsatisfactory.

Summing those percentages reveals that when customers switch from one product or service to another, they do so more than half the time because of the way they were treated or spoken to by employees. The people part of the delivery system let them down.

### Complaints

The second thing a customer can do is complain to someone in the organization. A popular book on this subject is entitled *A Complaint Is Your Friend.* Good hospitality managers know that *organizations should encourage guests to complain and thank them when they do.* A complaint is a positive opportunity for the organization. It now has the chance to make an unhappy guest happy; it can turn the lemon into lemonade. Unfortunately, only 5 to 10 percent of dissatisfied customers complain.[3] R. L. Day and E. L. Landon found that only 20 to 35 percent of people complained about the most dissatisfying consumer experience they ever had.[4] To complete the bad news, according to the research of Stephen S. Tax and Stephen W. Brown, most of the relatively few customers who do complain are dissatisfied with how companies resolve their complaints.[5] These dissatisfied customers are twice as likely to **bad-mouth** the organization as customers who are satisfied by the organization's response to service failure.[6]

If guests can be encouraged to complain, the organization gets valuable information about where problems in the guest experience are located. The customers who return to the counter with uncooked hamburgers, or tell the server about their unhappiness with the slow service, or write letters to the hotel manager describing miscellaneous dissatisfactions may help identify problems in the service, the delivery system, or the personnel. At the same time, they give the organization the opportunity to fix the problems before guests tell others about their dissatisfaction. Unfortunately, according to Tax and Brown, "most firms fail to document and categorize complaints adequately," which makes learning from mistakes more difficult.[7]

Organizations would do well to encourage guests to complain, even *teach* them how to complain if necessary, then measure and follow up on complaint resolution. Guests who suffer service failures silently are more apt to leave without returning and to bad-mouth the organization than complaining guests are.[8] British Airways found that of customers experiencing service problems, only 50 percent stayed with the airline if they did not complain to BA personnel. But a full 87 percent of those who did complain stayed and did not defect to a competitor.[9] Some companies claim even stronger results from successful complaint resolution. They believe that, on average, 70 percent of their guests will stay with the organization if a complaint is resolved in the guest's favor, and that a full 95 percent will do business again if the complaint is resolved favorably on the spot. This is why the benchmark hospitality organizations empower their frontline employees to handle many complaints personally and in whatever reasonable way they see fit, rather than seeking the manager's authorization first. As Marriott vice president Roger Dow says, "The guest-contact employee is the only one close enough to the customer to recognize and evaluate a problem and make it right for the customer and keep that customer."[10] Hart, Heskett, and Sasser agree; they say, "The surest way to recover from service mishaps is for workers on the front line to identify and solve the customer's problem."[11]

Just as handling a complaint well can be to the organization's benefit, handling it badly or not at all can hurt badly. If a dissatisfied customer complains, and then finds that the organization can't or won't fix the problem, the organization has now failed that customer twice, and everybody the customer knows is going to hear about it.

As just one example, Marriott has committed significant resources in its hotels to soliciting guest comments about the Marriott experience. Making sure no guest leaves unhappy is obviously to the organization's advantage. Marriott knows the best way to do that is to seek out its guests' complaints before they ever leave the property. The TARP Study conducted for the U.S. Office of Consumer Affairs confirms the wisdom of this approach. The data strongly suggest that customers who complain are more loyal than those who do not and, further, that having complaints satisfactorily resolved *increased* their brand loyalty.[12] These customers were happier after being dissatisfied with service than before. *Excellent organizations want their dissatisfied customers to complain.*

### Bad-Mouthing the Organization

The third thing an unhappy customer can do is to spread negative word-of-mouth about the company, telling everyone who will listen about the terrible experience.[13] If the negative experience was very expensive for the customer either financially or personally, the customer is even more likely to spread the bad word. The greater the costs to the customer, the greater the motivation to tell. If someone returns home after spending a lot of time and money flying to the Cayman Islands, staying in a hotel for a week, eating out, and paying admissions to various attractions, friends and neighbors are probably going to ask, "How was your vacation?" If it was a bad experience, the customer will make every effort to share that information with all who ask. The likelihood of anyone who listened to that person also spending the time and money to go to the Cayman Islands will be substantially diminished. Obviously, the more important the experience is to the customer, the quicker the customer will become unhappy when the experience does not meet expectations. The more unhappy a customer is, the more likely that person will complain, leave, and tell people about the experience.

## The Value of Positive Publicity: Bad-Mouth vs. *WOW*

On the other hand, the value of a wowed customer who is an apostle for the organization is considerable. Picture a family coming back home from a Caribbean island that caters to tourists. They have terrific tales to tell their friends. Their experience exceeded their expectations. To have these apostles telling everyone they know about their great vacation is very much to the Caribbean island's advantage. This positive word of mouth has great value in not only influencing others to come to the Caribbean paradise but is equally effective in blunting negative word of mouth. If a potential customer hears strong testimonials about a guest experience from three trusted friends, disregarding a complainer will be easier.

### *Credibility*

Word of mouth is important for several reasons. People who tell other people tend to be more credible than nonpersonal testimonials.[14] When your friend tells you a restaurant was bad, you no longer believe all the ads on television assuring you that the restaurant is a good place to eat. Not only is the information more credible but it tends to be more vivid. For either good or bad word of mouth, the richness of the detailed personal experience is more compelling than any commercial advertising.

### *Dollar Values*

When the lost revenue of unhappy customers who don't return is added to the lost revenue of customers who now won't come because of the negative word of mouth, the unhappy customer has created an expensive problem. Over the customer's lifetime, how much potential revenue have you lost? Carl Sewell of Sewell Cadillac in Dallas calculates that each of his customers is worth $332,000 in lifetime sales, service, and referrals.[15] The figure seems large, but it does not take many Cadillacs to add up to it. Domino's Pizza estimates that over a ten-year period a regular customer spends about $5,000.[16] Club Med has calculated that one lost customer costs the company at least $2,400.[17] Although not everyone sells Cadillacs, pizzas, or resort vacations, every hospitality organization would benefit from taking the time to calculate the value of its long-term satisfied customers. Because that value is so high, hardly any recovery effort is too extreme.

These calculations can lead to some surprisingly large numbers for even a small business. To show how a restaurant might come up with numbers like these, assume that the restaurant wows its patrons so much that they come back once a week or only once a month and spend an average of $20 each time they come in. The total value of each wowed customer's business for the next five years would be $5,200 for the weekly customer and $1,200 for the monthly customer. That's a lot of money to throw away by ignoring a complaint about a bad meal. These numbers get even bigger when the number of other people a positive word-of-mouth guest could bring to your hospitality organization is added in. If our wowed guest tells an average of five others who likewise are wowed and tell five others each, the multiplier effect is enormous. Over the estimated life of a typical customer, this can add up to many thousands of dollars in potential revenues. The point of these calculations is simple. Positive word of mouth has great value, and negative word of mouth is extremely costly.

Unhappy customers are approximately twice as likely to spread negative word of mouth as happy ones are to spread positive. Research reported by Hart, Heskett, and Sasser showed that customers who have bad experiences tell approximately eleven people; customers who have good experiences tell approximately six.[18] Word of mouth used to be one-to-one. Angry customers used to be limited to writing letters to corporate headquarters or the Better Business Bureau, putting up signs in their yard, or painting "lemon" on the car. Now for a few dollars a month, anyone with an Internet account can establish a Web site to tell the world about any offending company. In this day of instant worldwide communication, a customer can praise or complain over the Internet to millions of people. The benefits of avoiding negative word of mouth or turning it into positive are obvious.

### *Worst-Case Scenario*

When a customer is unhappy, the worst outcome for the organization is that the customer leaves vowing never to return, does not complain to the organization, switches to another service provider, and bad-mouths the organization. This dissatisfied customer has become a true terrorist for the organization. It has not only lost any future business from the customer who will never come back; it also has lost the business of the many people who will hear and be influenced by the negative word of mouth.

## How the Recovery Is Handled

The organization trying to recover from failure can impress the customer positively or negatively.[19] Research shows that for both positive and negative service recoveries how the recovery is handled is more important to the customer than the original failure.[20] Following a failure, the organization can either end up much better off or much worse off, depending on the customer's reaction to the recovery attempt. A small problem can become a big problem if the recovery effort is halfhearted or misguided. And a big problem can be turned into an example of great service when handled quickly and effectively. In one study, the researchers discovered that the most important determinant of overall customer satisfaction was their satisfaction with those responsible for dealing with failure: the claims personnel. Whether or not the organization could recover from failure also had the largest impact on intention to repatronize the organization and intention to recommend it to a friend.[21] K. D. Hoffman, Scott W. Kelley, and Holly M. Rotalsky asked a restaurant's guests to classify service failures from 1 (minor mistake) to 10 (major mistake). For example, the two most serious failures were product defects (cold, soggy, raw, burnt or spoiled food; inanimate objects in food), which were rated 6.69, and slow or unavailable service, rated 7.05. Table 12-1 shows how the restaurant responded to failure, how the guests rated the restaurant's recovery strategy from 1 (very poor) to 10 (very good), and how effective the strategy was in terms of guests indicating that they would still patronize the restaurant. Obviously, doing nothing is the worst strategy (or absence of strategy) and recovery from failure by offering free food or a discount are the best. Although the organization should always apologize for its failures, an apology alone is seldom sufficient.[22]

### *The TARP Study*

Data reported in the often-cited study done for the U.S. Office of Consumer Affairs, entitled "Consumer Complaint Handling in America" and referred to as the TARP Study, showed that customer loyalty can be increased through effective resolution of complaints. This study agrees with common sense that the way in which a service failure is handled influences the number of return visits by the customer, word of mouth, and satisfaction with the service

**Table 12-1** *Restaurant Recovery Strategies, Guest Ratings of Their Effectiveness, and Guest Repatronage Intentions*

| Recovery Strategy | Recovery Rating | Would Still Patronize |
|---|---|---|
| Free Food | 8.05 | 89.5% |
| Discount | 7.75 | 87.5 |
| Coupon | 7.00 | 40 |
| Managerial intervention | 7.00 | 99.8 |
| Replacement | 6.35 | 80.2 |
| Correction | 5.14 | 80 |
| Apology | 3.72 | 71.4 |
| Do nothing | 1.71 | 51.3 |

Source: Adapted from K. Douglas Hoffman, Scott W. Kelley, and Holly M. Rotalsky. 1995. Tracking Service Failures and Employee Recovery Efforts. *Journal of Services Marketing* 9(2):56.

experience. The influence can be positive or negative. The excellent hospitality organization does its best to ensure that the service-recovery attempt leads to a positive outcome.

### Service Recovery: A Message to Employees

Whether the organization handles service failure well or poorly has one more important outcome: It tells the employees how committed the organization is to customer satisfaction. Employees need to know that this commitment is more than a slogan. How the organization finds and fixes its service errors is a loud message to the employees about what the organization truly does believe in. Let us say that the management of Hotel A is defensive about customer complaints and keeps them secret (though employees will hear about them), resolves complaints as cheaply and quietly as possible, and seeks people to blame for the complaints. The management of Hotel B, on the other hand, aggressively seeks out and fixes service failures. It disseminates findings about complaints and failures to employees, makes quick and generous adjustments for failure, and seeks solutions rather than scapegoats. Which organization's employees will give guests better service?

## SERVICE FAILURES: WHERE AND WHY

### Where They Happen

Though some moments of truth are especially susceptible to failure, an organizational failure to meet the customer's expectations can occur just about anywhere in the guest experience. The service product may be inadequate or inappropriate or fail in some other way to meet the customer's expectations. The ordered hamburger may not look like the one advertised on TV that attracted the customer to the burger stand, or it may be uncooked, spoiled, or just not as good as the customer expected; a service failure is the result. The inanimate part of the delivery system can also fail. If the burger took an hour to get to the customer or the line at the burger stand wasn't managed properly, the system itself may have failed. The people part of the delivery system can certainly fail. If the burger-stand counter person is unfriendly, inept, poorly trained, or rude, then the experience will not likely meet the customer's expectations. Finally, there can be a failure in the environment or setting if the customer feels that the ambient temperature is too cold, the smell of food too strong, the rest rooms not clean, the parking lot unsafe, or if twisting pathways or unclear directional signs lead to the customer's becoming confused or lost. These points of possible failure all must be managed to ensure that the service experience meets and, hopefully, exceeds the customer's expectations.

## Degrees of Failure and Recovery

Service failure comes in degrees, ranging from catastrophic failures that make newspaper headlines, to insignificant slip-ups, to those failures that the customer doesn't even know about. (Scott Gross argues in his book *Positively Outrageous Service* that even here the organization should apologize.) Along this continuum are an infinite range of service errors. Since the customer defines the quality of the service experience, the customer also defines the nature and severity of the service failure. Different customers can be very unhappy or just mildly unhappy about the same failure just as different customers can be very happy or mildly happy about the same service. Some service recoveries fix the customer's problems, and other recovery efforts make things much worse. Sometimes the best a manager can do is to neutralize the angry customer.

## Customer Failure

One final source of failure is the customer. It's not always the hospitality organization's fault that the customer is unhappy. It may have done a perfect job of producing a terrific meal, but the diner simply didn't like the taste. Or the diner may have ignored the sign and set off the emergency alarm, or lost a set of keys or a child or money. Even though these problems were not created by the organization—and are beyond the organization's ability to manage no matter how much they train their people, perfect their systems, and refine their service—the organization should still address them.

The organization should also be ready to handle those failures that one guest causes for another—the diner who sneezes on another diner's food, the sports bar Red Sox fan who knocks down the Yankee fan, the inconsiderate passenger who cuts in front of others at the airline ticket counter, or loud talkers in a movie theater or concert hall. However, while doing everything in its power to rectify such situations, the hospitality organization should not admit liability for unfortunate, unavoidable occurrences that are not its fault. The Red Sox fan would probably have hit the Yankee fan in any venue.

It is simple human nature to attribute one's successes to oneself and one's failures to others. Hospitality organizations that want to keep guest-created service failures from destroying the guest experience and the guest's feelings about the organization build in strategies to help guests recover from their own failures so they can take a positive impression away from the service setting. Airlines have routines to help people who have lost their tickets complete their flights. Disney has routines to help parents who have lost their children in the parks find them again. The good organizations recognize the importance of helping guests solve the problems they create for themselves—without making them look or feel foolish or stupid while their tired children or spouse is looking on at the end of a long day in the park. They help these guests to go home happy in spite of themselves.

## DEALING WITH SERVICE FAILURES

Three major strategy types are available for dealing with service failures. First are those strategies that seek to identify potential failures before they happen. These proactive or preventive strategies are built into the design of the service and its delivery system. Other strategies focus on the service delivery process while it is happening, particularly at critical moments. Third are the outcome measures. Most of these, such as SERVQUAL, will be covered in Chapter 13. While these outcome measures enable the organization to assess overall service quality, they can also identify service failures. The information generated by outcome interviews and surveys is invaluable for developing preventive and process strategies as well. In this chapter, however, we shall focus on strategies that are not dependent upon outcome measurements or customer-satisfaction surveys.

### Preventing Service Failures

"A sandwich tossed is better than a customer lost." Arby's knows that preventing problems is easier and less costly than recovering from them. Preventive strategies are designed to avoid a service failure. As Mary Jo Bitner, Bernard H. Booms, and Lois A. Mohr put it, "The best way to ensure satisfaction . . . is not to have a failure in the first place."[23] These strategies seek to identify and fix any trouble spots before they become a problem for the customer.

#### *Forecasting and Managing Demand*

For example, if a statistical prediction of the customer demand for a theme park on a particular day indicates that the park will be full, then a preventive strategy will lead to the park's management calling in full staff, preparing extra food supplies, and having available the full capacity of each attraction. Restaurants require reservations when the anticipated demand will be great. Having a reservation system means that customers will not be disappointed when they come to the restaurant to eat. In addition, the restaurant knows the number of diners it can expect so that it can staff appropriately and have sufficient amounts of preprepared items to ensure that the eating experience is enjoyable and trouble free. If the organization plans poorly, and people have to wait too long, their perception of overall service-experience quality declines rapidly, and a service failure results. "Good dinner, fair price, but I had to wait too long; overall, I'm dissatisfied with my evening at this restaurant." Keeping the wait down avoids that type of failure.

   If the demand can be forecasted for a longer period of time, then other proactive strategies can be implemented. If demand for the next quarter or next year, for example, is expected to increase by 20 percent, then new capacity can be built, new employees hired and trained, and merchandise inventories can be increased to ensure that customers are not disappointed by long lines, unavailable souvenirs, or untrained and inadequate staff. Even if demand cannot be forecast accurately, employees can be trained to cope with major demand surges. Just as hospitals run disaster drills in conjunction with fire-and-rescue teams to prepare for unexpected, randomly occurring disasters, so can hospitality staffs be trained through practice to handle the unexpected.

#### *Quality Teams*

The popular use of quality teams is another preventive strategy. Get the people who are directly involved in the service experience together and let them identify the problems they have seen or heard about and then try to identify strategies that will prevent these problems from recurring.

### Training

Adequate training of employees before they ever get the chance to serve a customer can prevent failures. Most restaurants have extensive training for their employees before opening a new restaurant. Olive Garden, for example, has all of its employees available at least ten days before an opening to allow plenty of time to familiarize the new employees with the Olive Garden menu, standards of service, product offerings, and each other. By the time a new Olive Garden opens, the waitstaff knows the products they are serving, the system for providing the Olive Garden experience to the guest, and the other members of the restaurant team. The people who deliver any service need to know exactly what the total experience should consist of and need to be motivated to ensure that the guest experience happens the way it is supposed to, every time, for every guest.

### Simulation

Another approach to problem avoidance is to use analytical models to simulate all or part of the service delivery system or the service recovery process. Once a model, typically but not always a computerized model, is created to represent the customer/server interaction, the delivery process, or the entire guest experience, the manager and the servers can analyze a wide variety of different situations that might occur to see what impact each might have on the customer. On a simpler level, role plays and structured scenario simulations can help hospitality employees practice for all types of service failures and learn effective recovery strategies.

### Performance Standards

The organization can prevent failures by setting specific performance standards. Some are partly preventive, partly process because the employees themselves can use them to monitor their own performance levels as they go through the delivery process. Some standards are purely preventive because they can be met before customers enter the door or the park.

For example, if a restaurant has reliable predictions of how many customers come in on the different days of the week, those predictions can be used as a basis or standard for the number of salads that should be preprepared. If the prediction is correct and the standard is met, the service failure "not enough preprepared salad" should not occur. Other examples of how performance standards can prevent failures might include annual hours of training required of service personnel, number of computer terminals to be purchased to serve anticipated demand, and number of banquet tables to be set up or other facilities to be available when the organization can reasonably predict what will be needed before the service experience ever begins.

Performance standards can also be a useful indicator to guests of what service level they can expect. For example, "We will try to resolve problems of types A, B, and C within two hours; we will try to resolve problems of types D, E, and F within one week." Or "If you leave a message on our help-desk voice mail, we will call you back within one hour." Many Ritz-Carlton guests know that phone calls should be answered within three rings, and that after a guest registers a complaint, a Ritz-Carlton employee is supposed to make a follow-up call within twenty minutes to be sure the complaint has been resolved.

Of course, some of these measures overlap. For example, we shall soon discuss outcome measures. If some results of those measures are used to prevent service failures in the future, then that use becomes a preventive strategy.

### Poka-Yokes

The **poka-yoke** is a final proactive or preventive strategy for avoiding failure in the service experience and keeping it operating as flawlessly as possible. Conceived by the late Shigeo Shingo, a quality improvement leader in Japan, the basic idea is to make service quality easy to achieve and service failure difficult to achieve by inspecting the system for possible failure points and then finding or developing simple means to prevent mistakes at those points. To be sure that guests are served on a first-come, first-served basis and to discourage them from wandering all over the service setting, organizations can set up serpentine post-and-rope channels within which guests are to move forward until served. To ensure equity of service order and avoid disagreements, customers may be invited to "take a number." A surgeon's tray and a mechanic's wrench-set box may have a unique indentation for each item to ensure that no instrument is left in a patient or wrench in an engine. Shingo gave these failure-preventing devices or procedures the name *poka-yoke* (POH-kah YOH-kay), which means "mistake proofing" or "avoid mistakes" in Japanese.

***Types of Inspections.*** Shingo distinguished three types of inspection; in the services industry, they would be *successive* inspection in which the next person in the service delivery system checks the quality and accuracy of the previous person's work, *self-inspection* in which people check their own work, and *source* inspection in which potential mistakes are located at their source and fixed before they can become service errors. Poka-yokes are used mainly to prevent these mistakes. An example of successive inspection is where the food server in a restaurant checks the food order assembled by the chef before taking it out of the kitchen. An example of self-inspection is the line cook personally comparing the prepared order against a picture of what the food display should look like before putting it on the service counter. An example of source inspection is the chef monitoring the preprepared foods—such as salads or boned chicken or whatever must be assembled in advance of the rush hour—to ensure that sufficient quantities of the items are available.

***Warnings and Controls.*** Poka-yokes are either "*warnings* that signal the existence of a problem or *controls* that stop production until the problem is resolved."[24] A warning poka-yoke would be a light that flashes when the fries are ready to come out of the fryer. It signals the operator to remove the fries before they become overcooked. A control poka-yoke would be a device that turns a microwave oven off whenever the door is opened.

Warning and control poka-yokes can be of three types. *Contact* poka-yokes monitor the item's physical characteristics to determine if it is right or meets a predefined specification. Some restaurants cut their meats on scales to ensure that each cut is the right weight before cooking. The second type of poka-yoke is based on *fixed values*. McDonald's knows that a certain poundage of fries must be put in the fryer to make the fries taste the way McDonald's wants them to. So they designed a prepackaged bag containing a fixed value of potato pieces to ensure that the right quantity is placed in the fryer every time. The third type of poka-yoke is the *motion step*. It is useful in processes where an error-prone step must be completed correctly before the next step can take place. A simple example is the pop-up temperature gauge found in many turkeys. If the red button doesn't pop up, the turkey isn't done to the right temperature, and the turkey cannot move a step forward for further preparation until it does. All poka-yokes should be simple, easy to use, and inexpensive. Something can go wrong at many points in most service delivery systems, so the poka-yoke is a useful concept in providing services.

***Poka-Yokes for Customers.*** Trying to fix a problem once a customer has experienced it can lead to bad consequences for the organization, so any devices that can fail-safe the service delivery system or any part of it are extremely desirable. Customers add a further complication to the service delivery process: They are frequently right in the middle of it and often responsible for coproducing it. Poka-yokes must be included for them and for the delivery staff to prevent dangerous or unpleasant experiences.

Customers are irritated by a frequent fast-food service failure: leaving the drive-through only to find that they were served the wrong order. To avoid these failures, Burger King has installed poka-yoke video displays, called *order confirmation units,* at its drive-through windows so customers can verify the accuracy of the orders they are about to receive.

***Speed Parking.*** Here is an example of a poka-yoke designed to help customers avoid failure. The speed-parking technique, often seen at events where a lot of cars are arriving at the same time, has the cars line up and park in successive spaces under the direction of a parking attendant. Each row is filled before cars go to the next row. This parking method is fast; it keeps all cars facing the same way and in line to park in the next available space. The method has led to the creation of a poka-yoke at some theme parks and other large attractions. When guests stream into the park every morning, the parking attendant writes down the time each row is filled. When the evening comes and a family shows up lost and uncertain as to where the car might be, the attendant pulls out the poka-yoke—a list of what sections were parked at what time. The attendant asks the family about what time they arrived at the parking area, then uses the list to locate the car. The poka-yoke prevents a guest-caused failure that could have ruined the day's experience.

## Process Strategies: Monitoring the System

Process strategies for finding service failures monitor the delivery while it is taking place, while it is in process. The idea is to design mechanisms into the delivery system that will catch and fix failures before they affect the quality of the guest experience. A supervisor can monitor telephone calls, a waitperson can check the food order against what is on the plate, or a machine can control the frying time of french fries to get them perfect every time. The advantage of process controls is that they can catch errors before or as they happen, enabling prevention or immediate correction before they affect customers.

Hard Rock Cafe, for example, hires an extra person to stand at the end of the food preparation line to match the order with what's on the plate, to catch discrepancies before the guest ever sees the order. Even though the traditional job description for waitstaff includes this checking responsibility, the extra person reduces the possibility of error even further. The Opryland Hotel in Nashville cross-trains some of its employees so that they can be called upon in peak demand times when the front desk is extra busy. If the lines get too long for the regular front-desk team, this "swat team" staffs extra computers to reduce the wait for the incoming or departing guests.

THE RUSTY PELICAN

*Rusty Pelican Logo. (Courtesy of Rusty Pelican Restaurants.)*

Process standards provide employees with objective measures to monitor their own job performance while they are doing it. Specifying the maximum number of times the phone can ring before it is picked up is an example. Other illustrations include the number of times a server should revisit a table during the meal, or the number of people that can stand in line before the manager adds extra personnel to the check-in. These are all process-related measurements that allow the servers to minimize errors or catch them while the guest experience is underway.

### Rusty Pelican Standards

Restaurants know guests value prompt service. Figure 12-1 shows an example from the Rusty Pelican Restaurant specifying the steps of food and cocktail service and the standards applied to each step. Because the servers themselves determined the standards, they were eager to monitor their own performance and try to meet or surpass them. Several benefits resulted. Service quality improved, increased server productivity meant that fewer servers were needed, which increased the tip income of servers, customers (to management's surprise) were willing to pay more to receive better service, and servers identified a couple of bottlenecks—potential failure points—that interfered with prompt, reliable service. Smoothing out those points improved service quality even more.[25]

### The Complaint as a Monitoring Device

Preventive strategies can reduce the number of problems, but some will inevitably occur, and the organization cannot fix problems it doesn't know about. The research shows clearly that the most important process strategy is to get unhappy guests to complain while they are still in the guest experience. This is a more difficult challenge than one might think. While some guests are all too happy to complain, most are not. They are unwilling to take the time, or they believe that no one cares or will do anything even if they did complain, or they are too angry to say anything and just leave. *Hospitality organizations must let their guests know they are receptive to complaints.* Research on this issue has identified some important ways in which the organization can encourage its customers to complain.

## *Rusty Pelican service standards*

### Food-service standards

1. **First contact**--cocktail server speaks to customer
within two minutes of customer seating.
2. **Cocktails delivered**--beverage service at table
within four minutes of order. If no beverage order,
request for food order within four minutes of first greeting.
3. **Request for order**--within four minutes after beverage
service, customer should be asked whether he or she cares to order.
4. **Appetizers delivered**--salad, chowder, or wine delivered
within five minutes.
5. **Entrée delivered**--entrée delivered within 16 minutes of order.
6. **Dessert delivered**--dessert and coffee or after-dinner
drinks served within five minutes after plates are cleared.
7. **Check delivered**--check presented within four minutes after
dessert course or after plates are cleared if no dessert.
8. **Money picked up**--cash or credit cards picked up within
two minutes of being placed by customer on table.

### Cocktail-service standards

1. **First contact**--greeting given and cocktail order taken;
seafood bar, happy-hour specials, and wine-by-glass menus
presented within two minutes.
2. **Cocktails delivered**--cocktails delivered within five minutes
after first contact.
3. **Seafood bar delivered**--seafood bar and happy-hour specials
delivered within seven minutes of first contact; ten minutes
for cooked items.
4. **Next contact**--check for reorder of cocktail, seafood bar,
customer satisfaction, and table maintenance within five
minutes from delivery of first cocktail.

**Figure 12-1** *Service Standards at the Rusty Pelican. (Source: D. Daryl Wyckoff. 1984. New Tools for Achieving Service Quality.* Cornell Hotel and Restaurant Administration Quarterly *25(3):158. Reprinted with permission of* The Cornell Hotel and Restaurant Administration Quarterly. © *Cornell University. All rights reserved.)*

*Rusty Pelican Restaurant. (Courtesy of Rusty Pelican Restaurants.)*

### Encouraging Complaints

All service personnel should be trained to solicit complaints. Since many service problems involve server errors, getting the servers to solicit complaints about their own performance may be a challenge. The servers may see that mistakes are punished more heavily than catching errors is rewarded. Most people are less enthusiastic about admitting their mistakes than they are about sharing their successes, and the complaint strategy needs to accommodate this reality of human nature.

### Body Language as a Complaint

Service personnel can be trained to read body language for clues to an unhappy guest. If a frowning guest walks by a Disney cast member, that person is supposed to inquire as to why "the unhappy face." Taking this initiative can elicit complaints that might otherwise go unmentioned. Food-service workers, hotel front-desk agents, and other people who interact directly with guests can also be trained to recognize the signs of unhappy people. Employees must also learn how to be receptive and sympathetic to the complaint once it is elicited. Guests must perceive employees as interested and concerned. If guests do not think anyone cares, they generally won't say anything.

## Outcome Strategies

Outcome strategies identify service failures after they have occurred. It's too late this time, but maybe the problem can be fixed and future failures prevented.

### Ask

The most basic outcome strategy is simply to ask the guest. The desk agent who asks about your stay as you check out is a good example. Other more systematic illustrations would include the 800 phone numbers, the "Tell me" program at Marriott, brief questionnaires at Carl Sewell's Cadillac dealership that customers can fill out when paying their bills, and the British Airways video booths at Heathrow Airport. Organizations should make unequivocally clear to customers that they want to hear about any problems. Studies show that whether customers seek redress of a problem or simply let it go is determined by their perception of whether or not the organization really wants to hear about it and will act on it. Even customers who are reluctant to complain are more likely to do so if they perceive that something will be done about the problem.[26]

### Taking Action

Obviously, the more an organization depends on repeat business, the more critical it is for the organization to acknowledge and act on customer complaints. Some organizations report their complaint investigations back to complaining customers in detail, including information on what people were affected and what systems were changed. In that way the organization shows it is responsive to the customer's complaint and gives that person a sense of participation in the organization that may positively enhance loyalty and increase repeat visits. If the complaint shows the organization a flaw that can be corrected and if knowledge of the correction provides the customer with a sense of satisfaction for reporting the complaint, a true win-win situation results.

### Numerical Outcome Measurements

Some numerical measurements that organizations take as a matter of normal procedure can point up real and potential service failures. A standard measurement in restaurants is average check size per server per shift. Though mainly intended to measure the degree to which the servers are selling the product, it also reflects in part how well they are selling themselves to the diners. If one server or one shift is well below the average, managers will want to look into that. Other examples of numbers that reflect service failures are complaints filed at the hotel checkout, statement errors at the country club, accident rate at the theme park, and late flights at the airport.

## RECOVERING FROM SERVICE FAILURE

The organization failed. It got the guests in the door, and then it let them down. Now what? Hospitality organizations should train their employees to handle the problems when they find them. Their ability to solve problems creatively when the inevitable service failure occurs needs to be developed. Scenarios, game playing, video taping, and role playing are good ways to show them how to respond to an angry guest. Just as umpires can be trained to recognize balls and strikes through watching videos, hospitality personnel can be trained to recognize service errors and how to correct the failures they find.

## Do Something Quickly

The basic recovery principle is do something and do it quickly. Strive for *on-the-spot service recovery*. Its many benefits are one major reason why benchmark organizations empower their frontline employees to such a great extent. The one answer a guest does not want to hear is, "I'll have to ask my manager." That's why a standing guideline for *every* Disney employee is: *Provide immediate service recovery.*

Here are three of the "Ritz-Carlton Basics" that appear on the Credo Card depicted in Chapter 2, carried by every employee:

- Any employee who receives a customer complaint "owns" the complaint.
- React quickly to correct the problem immediately. Follow up with a telephone call within twenty minutes to verify that the problem has been resolved to the customer's satisfaction. Do everything you possibly can to never lose a guest.
- Every employee is empowered to resolve the problem and to prevent a repeat occurrence.

How the problem came about or who caused it does not matter. Every employee is empowered to resolve it. The company backs up that statement; each employee is authorized to spend up to $2,000 to recover from a service failure and achieve guest satisfaction.

Management must empower employees with the necessary authority, responsibility, and incentives to act and act quickly following a failure. The higher the cost of the failure to the guest in terms of money, personal reputation, or safety, the more vital it is for the organization to train the server to recognize and deal with service failures promptly, sympathetically, and effectively. Of course, empowering employees to recover from failure will not be sufficient if recovery mechanisms are not in place. If the rest of the system is in chaos, empowering the front line won't do much good.

A necessary further step is that employees should *inform their managers about system failures* even if they initiate successful recovery procedures. If they don't, the problem may recur elsewhere.

Federal Express created the Golden Falcon Award to recognize employee initiative in service recovery. Winners not only get a pin to commemorate their success but also have an article published in the company newsletter about what they did. In addition, they get a telephone call from the chief operating officer and receive a few shares of the company's stock.[27]

All hospitality personnel should be trained to apologize, ask the guests about the problem, and listen in a way that gives guests the opportunity to blow off steam. Considerable research indicates that having the chance to tell someone in authority about the service failure and the problems it created is very important in retaining the guest's future patronage. This strategy is even more effective when the organization expresses its thanks for the complaint with a tangible reward, even if it is small.[28] Many restaurants will apologize to guests who complain about a longer-than-expected wait by offering a free dessert as a small recognition of their sincere regret for disappointing the guest. Some restaurants teach their servers to give the apology and the dessert even if the guest does not complain.

### Benefits of Quick Recovery

A quick reaction to service failure has numerous benefits. Solving a problem up front instead of over time reduces the overall expense of retaining guests. The sooner the guest is satisfied, the more likely the guest will remain with the hospitality organization and the sooner will the organization benefit from the guest's repeat business. Fix their problems and most guests will come back. Fix their problems on the spot and they will almost certainly come back; they will also recommend the organization to their friends. Reward programs and incentives for employees who have done an especially good job of recovering from a service failure offer strong incentives to other employees while providing role models of the organization's commitment to service quality.

### *Ow!* to *Wow!*

A Disney saying is, "Turn tragic moments into magic moments." The best hospitality organizations view a service failure as *a great opportunity to create an unforgettable, outrageously positive response.* If Bob Smith is upset that the hotel overbooked and his room is gone by the time he arrives tired and ready for bed, the hotel cannot only walk him to a nearby hotel with the price of the room paid but might consider upgrading his room from whatever he had reserved. The guest who was denied his standard room but got a paid-for night in a VIP suite at another hotel might readily forgive the hotel that denied him his room. The organization extended its hospitality to a guest, then failed the guest. It should go the extra mile and then some to repair the damage. The right failure-recovery strategy can turn an irate guest, ready to head for the competition, into a raving evangelist.

### How Do Customers Evaluate Recovery Efforts?

Customers who have suffered a service failure and lodged a complaint want action. They use three criteria of justice to evaluate the fairness of the organization's corrective efforts: procedural, interactive, and distributive.[29] According to Tax and Brown, these three fairness dimensions explain 85 percent of the variation in customer satisfaction with how complaints are handled.[30]

### *Procedural Fairness*

**Procedural fairness** refers to whether or not the customer believes company procedures for listening to the guest's side and handling service failure are fair and not a procedural hassle full of red tape. Circuit City believes that not giving customers the best value possible is a kind of service failure, so it will pay customers a refund plus 10 percent if they show they were not given the lowest price in the area on a purchased product. Customers feel this is a fair policy. Customers also want an easy process for correcting failures. They feel that if the organization failed them, it is only fair that the organization make it easy for them to receive a just settlement. Finally, they want a procedure that gives them an opportunity to express their feelings about the failure, an opportunity to show their side of the situation.

### *Interactive Fairness*

**Interactive fairness** refers to the customer's feeling of being treated with respect and courtesy and given the opportunity to express the complaint fully. If the customer has a complaint and is denied the opportunity to state it to someone because the offending server is rude, indifferent, or uncaring, and the manager cannot be found, the customer will feel unfairly treated. A study of traffic-court offenders by Lind and Tyler revealed that many offenders whose cases were dismissed without a hearing were dissatisfied with the process and angry with the outcome, even though the dismissal was a favorable result for them.[31] Since they were denied their day in court, they were unhappy with the process. Common sense suggests and research shows that a customer who is encouraged to complain and is then treated with respect, courtesy, and given a fair settlement is more likely to repatronize the organization than one who was given a fair settlement but only with reluctance and discourtesy.[32]

### Distributive Fairness

**Distributive fairness,** or outcome fairness, is the third test that customers apply to the organization's attempts to recover from failure. What did the organization actually give or distribute to the unhappy customer as compensation for the problem? If the guest complains about a bad meal and gets only a sincere apology because that's all company policy calls for, some guests will feel unfairly treated; somehow "We're sorry" isn't enough, in the guest's judgment, to compensate for the poor meal. Once again, it all comes down to meeting the guest's expectations. The issue is difficult because each guest is different. For many guests, an apology is fair enough compensation for most service failures. For others, nothing is good enough to make up for the problem or difficulty that the service failure created for them. Finding satisfactory compensation may involve methodical trial and error on the organization's part, but the easiest way is to ask the guest.

Some research indicates that customers feel more fairly treated when organizations extend options as compensation for service failure.[33] For example, a hotel could offer a disgruntled guest a choice of either a refund or an upgrade.

## Characteristics of a Good Recovery Strategy

Hart, Heskett, and Sasser suggest that service-recovery strategies should satisfy several criteria.[34] First, they should *ensure that the failure is fixed in some positive way.* Even if the situation is a disaster, the recovery strategy should ensure that the customer's problem is addressed and, to the extent possible, fixed.

Second, recovery strategies must be *communicated clearly to the employees charged with responding to customer dissatisfaction.* The service people must know the organization expects them to find and resolve customer problems as part of their jobs.

Third, recovery strategies should be *easy for the customer to find and use.* Finally, they should be *flexible* enough to accommodate the different types of failures and the different expectations that customers have of the guest experience. The service-recovery strategy developed should always recognize that because the customer defines the quality of the service experience, the customer also defines its failures and the adequacy of the recovery strategies.

### No Better Makes It Worse

A strategy that does not improve the situation for the complaining customer is worse than useless because the organization makes plain that it can't or won't recover from failure even when informed of it. The work of Hart, Heskett, and Sasser suggests that most recovery strategies are in serious need of improvement. More than half of organizational efforts to respond to consumer complaints actually reinforce negative reactions to the service.[35] In trying to make things better, organizations may make them worse.

### Costs of Failure to Guests

One reason that customers view many recovery strategies as inadequate is that they do not really take into account all of the costs to the customer. Bad meal? Replace it. Theme park attraction broken? Give a complimentary one-day pass. Busy signal on the telephone line for airport information? Interject a recorded apology. The organization may think the relationship is back where it started. But for the customer many costs are associated with failures, and the effective organization will try to identify them and include some recognition of them in selecting the appropriate service recovery. After all, thinks the customer, the fact that the service failed is not my fault. Why should I have to wait on the side of the road for a long time because the rental car broke down? Why should I have to call back repeatedly to reservations because the airline messed up the original reservation? Why should I have to return to the restaurant because the drive-through people didn't get the order right?

### Making It Right Not Enough

Customers clearly think that when failures occur, organizations need to do more than simply make it right by replacing it or doing it over again. Of course they should do that, but they should do more. For example, if the failed meal causes the guest to be embarrassed in front of a client or boss, then the recovery strategy must not only include compensation for the meal but some consideration for the guest's emotional outlays as well. If dad tells his family about the terrific time they are all going to have at a famous resort, uses his only week of vacation to go there, and spends all the extra money he has so carefully saved, he has a lot at stake. If the experience fails somehow to meet the family's expectations, dad loses his time, his money, and his credibility with his family. The outstanding hospitality organization systematically considers how to compensate guests for losses other than financial and takes extra effort to ensure that dissatisfied guests not only have their financial losses addressed in a recovery effort but also their ego and esteem needs addressed as well. They want dad to go home a hero to his family.

### Being Wrong with Dignity

Even when the guests themselves make mistakes, good hospitality organizations help to correct them with sensitivity. That way guests leave feeling good about their overall experience and appreciating how the organization's personnel helped them redeem themselves. Imagine how depressed you would feel if you came back to the parking lot after a long day at an amusement park to find that you have lost your car keys and are locked out of your car. Then you see the park's "Auto Patrol" coming to your rescue. They even make you a new set of keys for free! Even though key problems are not its fault, the guest-oriented organization believes that the guest needs to be wrong with dignity. It knows that guests who are angry at themselves may transfer some of that anger to the organization. To overcome this very human tendency, guest-centered organizations find ways to fix problems so that angry, frustrated people leave feeling good because a bad experience has not been allowed to overshadow or cancel out all the good. By providing this high level of guest service, the hospitality organization earns the gratitude and future patronage of guests and enhances its reputation when such service successes are circulated to both external and internal customers.

## Matching the Recovery Strategy to the Failure

A customer claimed that a Starbuck's store had sold him two defective coffee makers with a total value of $500, neglected to include a promised free half-pound of coffee, and treated him rudely. The customer was not satisfied by company apologies, replacement and refund offers, and gifts. His suggested recovery strategy was that Starbuck's take out a full-page ad of apology in the *Wall Street Journal,* give him a $2,500 coffee maker, and fund a shelter for runaway children.[36]

The best recovery efforts are those that match the failure. For example, if a restaurant is out of a certain menu item, compensating the guest with a "rain check" might be appropriate. If the failure is server inattentiveness, an apology by the manager would be a more appropriate response.

Categorizing the severity and causes of service failures might be a useful way to show the type of recovery strategy that a hospitality organization should select. In Figure 12-2, the *y* or vertical axis represents the severity of the failure ranging from low to high. The horizontal axis divides service failures into those caused by the organization and those caused by the guest. When severity is high and it's the organization's fault, the proper response is the red-carpet treatment, as in the case of a sold-out hotel transporting a guest with reservations to a fully paid, upgraded room at another hotel. The organization needs to bend over backward to fix this guest's problem and should consider trying to provide a *wow* level of recovery to overcome the negative feeling the guest will have after a failure so severe. The less severe problem caused by the organization would be illustrated by a server bringing to a guest a cold food item that is supposed to be hot. The solution here is to apologize and replace the item quickly. In a more elaborate restaurant, providing a complimentary dessert might also be appropriate. McDonald's has a policy that anyone bringing a food item back to the counter with the complaint that it is cold is immediately given an apology and a replacement item with no questions asked.

The two situations where the guest caused the failure provide terrific opportunities for the organization to make guests feel positive about the experience even though they them-

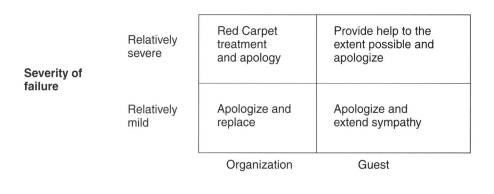

*Figure 12-2* *Matching the Recovery Strategy to the Failure.*

selves caused the failure. In a low-severity situation, a sincere apology is sufficient and will make the guest feel that the organization is taking some of the responsibility for a situation that was clearly not its fault. Indeed, some organizations will do even more, if the cost to make a guest feel better is not substantial. Many restaurants don't charge their guests for meals or items they don't like or want. Some photo developers have the same policy. The poor pictures may not be the developer's fault, but the customer feels good that the organization won't make customers pay for their own mistakes. The upper-right box represents situations where the problem is relatively severe and the guest or some external force created the problem. These are opportunities for the organization to be a hero and provide an unforgettable experience for the guest.

A Domino's delivery man showed up with pizzas at a house that was still smoldering from a devastating fire. The distraught couple standing in the front yard of their ruined house looked up at the delivery man with some annoyance, said they hadn't ordered any pizza, and wondered if the delivery person couldn't see that they were overcome by the tragedy. The delivery man responded that he knew; he had passed the house earlier, saw it burning, and had told his manager. The two decided that it would be nice to cook up some pizzas and just give them to these people in their hour of sadness. The company became a hero to the couple—customers who didn't even know they were customers.

### Service Recovery: Good Business

According to the TARP Study, companies that invested in the formation and operation of units designed to handle complaints realized returns on the investment of anywhere from 30 percent to 150 percent. These results, and the other research reported in this chapter, suggest strongly that putting money and effort into service recovery is good business.

## *Lessons Learned*

1. If the guest thinks you failed, *you failed.*
2. Fix their problems and most guests will come back; fix their problems on the spot and they will almost certainly come back.
3. Encourage guests to tell you about problems and failures; *a complaint is a gift.*
4. Train and empower your employees to find and fix failures.
5. Train your employees to listen with empathy.
6. Don't cause a service-failure problem and then fail to fix it. Don't fail the guest twice.
7. Find a fair solution, and know how guests determine what is fair.
8. Find ways to help guests fix problems *they* caused.
9. Unhappy guests will tell twice as many people about bad experiences as happy guests will tell about good experiences.
10. Even the best organizations fail a guest occasionally. Be prepared for failure; have a recovery strategy in place.
11. Find out and share with employees how much a dissatisfied guest costs you; that will show your staff the importance of recovering from service failure.
12. Empowerment works only if the system works; even an empowered employee can't recover from service failure without support from the system.

## Review Questions

1. Recall a service failure during a guest experience of your own.
   A. Describe the failure and your reaction to it.
   B. Describe the organization's response to the failure. Did your reaction seem to affect the organizational response?
   C. As a result of what happened, how do you feel about this organization now?
   D. If you were not completely satisfied, what could the organization have done to satisfy you and perhaps cause you to be even more loyal to the organization than before?
2. If you ran a hospitality organization, how would you plan to recover from failure? Would you give employees a list of common failures and their corresponding acceptable recovery strategies, or would you empower employees to use whatever recovery strategies they saw fit?
   A. Why is it important to try to fix the problem immediately?
   B. What are the characteristics of a good service recovery?
   C. One hospitality leader instructs employees to keep offering successively more significant remedies to failure until the guest smiles, then stop. Discuss this strategy.
3. Many service failures occurring during guest experiences at a hotel or at a restaurant can be predicted and fixed. Name two problems that the hotel and the restaurant probably cannot fix. What should the managers do if those failures occur?
4. Reflect on a recent hospitality experience in which you were involved, either as a guest or as an employee.
   A. What poka-yokes did you see used to fail-safe some part of the experience?
   B. Think of a new poka-yoke that might be added.
5. A guest in your organization starts an argument with another guest who has tried to cut into a waiting line.
   A. Is this a service failure? If so, who or what failed? What should you as a manager do?
   B. If, rather than starting an argument, the first guest punches the second guest, what should you as a manager do?
6. Assume that you used to work at the Rusty Pelican Restaurant but are now a hotel front-desk manager who wants to establish quantitative, measurable service standards for your employees, similar to those you used at the Rusty Pelican, regarding guest check-in and checkout.
   A. Are the situations sufficiently similar that you could effectively use similar standards?
   B. What standards would you establish?
7. Do you believe that a complaint is "a gift" from the complaining customer to the organization? If you have complained to organizations, has the reaction suggested that they believe you are presenting them with a gift?

## Activities

1. Write a letter to a local hospitality manager complaining about a dissatisfying or failed service experience you have had, the more recent the better. Describe how the organi-

zation responded to your complaint. How does the organization's recovery effort correspond to the suggestions for recovery offered in the chapter?

2. Write a letter to a local hospitality manager complimenting a service experience you have had recently. Send a carbon copy to the company president. Report back on the results. Okay to name names in this one.

3. Be on the lookout for a service failure that others are experiencing. Observe and report how the organization recovers from the failure. Evaluate the recovery strategy based on the material presented in the chapter.

4. Divide into groups. For those who have been employees, describe service failures in which you have been involved. Had you been trained in how to recover from these failures? What recovery steps did you take? Pick the best service recovery and compare with the best of other groups. What lessons can be learned from these successful recoveries?

## Case Studies

### Pizza-to-Go

*B*ob Callahan led a very hectic business life consisting of hard work, long hours, and eating on the run. Bob also liked pizza. It is therefore no surprise that he did a lot of business with his neighborhood Pizza-to-Go outlet. About once a week, just before leaving work, Bob would call PTG, order a medium thin-crust pizza with olives, sausage, and double anchovies, and pick it up on his way home. The PTG people once forgot the sausage and once put pepperoni instead of olives, but Bob forgave them and never mentioned these small slip-ups. He could do with a little less sausage in his diet, and he liked pepperoni almost as well as olives anyway. Besides, they never got the anchovies wrong, and Bob's favorite part of the entire pizza experience was the overabundance of anchovies swimming in mozzarella cheese.

Last week Bob got home from work and kicked back, ready to enjoy a beer and some pizza fixed "his way." The pizza he took out of the box was fixed somebody else's way; it was covered with olives, sausage, and what looked like a double order of onions. Bob couldn't imagine what kind of person would eat a combination like that. He called PTG immediately. The phone was answered by Vito Cifrese, who had been serving Bob regularly for about two years.

"Very sorry about that, Mr. Callahan. If you could just scrape those onions off this one time, next time you come in I'll comp you your regular order and I'll also throw in a small complimentary pizza with double anchovies for free!" Bob thought that was a pretty fair adjustment. He thanked Vito, scraped off the onions, and tried to eat the pizza. But the onion flavor remained. Bob couldn't finish the pizza; the combination of olives, sausage, and onion flavor was too much for him.

(Continued)

That all happened on an early Monday evening. On Thursday of the same week, Bob called in and ordered the usual, plus a small pizza with double anchovies. When he got to Pizza-to-Go, Vito was nowhere to be seen. Bob identified himself to the counter server who handed over the two boxes. Bob explained that both items were to be "no charge" because of an error that had been made on a previous order.

The server laughed and said, "I don't think so. Check that sign out there. This is Pizza-to-Go. Pizza-for-Free is up the street."

Bob stayed calm and asked for Vito; he could straighten this out.

"Vito quit Monday night and said he never wanted to see another pizza."

"I've gotten one or two pizzas a week from you people for the past two years. My name's Bobby Callahan. Check under my name in your database and see if Vito left any special instructions."

"What database?" said the server.

Bobby gave up. He'd find another place to do business. "I'll just take the small pizza with double anchovies."

"You don't want the big one?"

"That's right."

"Even though you called in for it? Well, we can warm it up for somebody else, I guess, if anybody else wants a weird combo like olives, sausage, and anchovies."

Bob paid without tipping, left, got home, grabbed a beer, turned on TV, kicked back, opened the box, and took out a small pizza covered with onions.

* * *

1. Was service recovery called for in this situation?
2. If so, what recovery options would you have considered?
3. What should Bob Callahan do now?

## Recovery to the Max

**B**en Sharpless, manager of the tackle store at Farney Spa and Fish Camp, had just finished explaining to new sales employee Max Gilley the importance of getting and retaining customers, recovering from service failure, and other basics of serving guests, whether they were fisherfolk who also had spa privileges or spa patrons who wanted to do a little fishing. About an hour later, Ben saw Max talking with regular customer Sally Higgins. He thought he would monitor Max's sales technique, so he moved to a spot where he could hear but not be seen.

Sally Higgins was saying,

"Max, I thought I'd fish down at the bend where you can see them feeding on the bottom."

"Ms. Higgins, you don't want to fish for those little minners. You want to put your bait about 30 feet out, where the big ones are. Here, what about this Orvis reel with the matching graphite rod and tackle box full of lures and other gadgets? I think that'll do the trick. But fishing's even better on the other side of the lake early in the morning. We've also got a fully equipped camping rig here that I can let you use, with the tent, the stove, all the supplies you could ever need.

You can camp out, turn in early, and be up and at 'em with the dawn." Ms. Higgins agreed that it was a beautiful rig. Visions of huge trout leaped in her mind. Visions of a big sale leaped in the mind of store manager Ben Sharpless.

"What kind of car do you have, Ms. Higgins? A Mercedes 300-SL, isn't it? This stuff isn't going to fit in there. We just received a special-order Land Rover with matching trailer. You'll look good in that, and you can haul all this camping and fishing equipment in the trailer with room to spare. We could let you use that for a couple of days."

Manager Sharpless was really impressed with Max's results. Max and Sally finished the paperwork, Sally Higgins left, and Sharpless went to Max Gilley to congratulate him on a big sale.

"Gilley, you're quite a salesman. I don't know if I would have loaned her all that fancy camping equipment and the Land Rover, but that Orvis rod and reel plus a fully equipped tackle box is a big sale, maybe several hundred dollars, so I guess it's worth it."

Max looked puzzled. "No, Mr. Sharpless, you got it all wrong. Ms. Higgins was just out for a walk. We started to talk, and she told me the spa was busted. Uh-oh, I says to myself. Service failure. I remembered what you told me: 'It costs several times as much to get a new guest as it does to keep a present guest, Max, so when you see any service failure, spa or fish camp, that service failure becomes yours to correct. You own that service failure until it's fixed, Max. And don't just fix it; go above and beyond. Anything we lose on that transaction will be made up in future business for the spa and fish camp. If we do lose money, what's the worst that can happen? We'll have a satisfied guest.' Wasn't that about it, Mr. Sharpless?"

Sharpless said, "Yes, Max, you learned well, but . . ."

"So I said to her, 'Since the spa is busted, why don't you go fishing?' Then I gave her the fishing tackle and the tackle box but I only loaned her the rest of the stuff. She seemed right happy, didn't she?"

Manager Sharpless sighed. "Max, if I hadn't been here, I guess you would have given her the whole darn tackle shop."

* * *

1. What do you think would have been an appropriate adjustment for this service failure? Or should a fish camp employee even be concerned about a spa service failure?
2. How can organizations encourage their employees to take ownership of service failures and try to fix them on the spot, without "giving away the store"?

## Days of Wine and Roses

Julius Mullinax was the long-time manager of the Finery Hotel, the flagship hotel of an old upscale chain. On one particular evening, a rare error had occurred in the front-desk area: a new desk agent had assigned honeymooners Harold and Sylvia Solomon to the Tweed Suite, a fully equipped executive area with computers, fax machines, and a stock market ticker, instead of to the Honeymoon Suite they had reserved. Mullinax noticed the error in time and quickly made the switch, about an hour before the newlyweds arrived. When Mullinax showed

(Continued)

the Solomons personally to their penthouse suite, they were delighted to find on the cocktail table a complimentary bottle of wine and a vase of long-stemmed roses. Manager Mullinax smiled and said, "Most lodging places try to hide their errors. The Finery feels that we should compensate our guests for our mistakes, even if they would otherwise never find out about them!" Mullinax left the Solomons too amazed to respond.

When he got back downstairs, Mullinax saw an indignant couple talking loudly with the desk agent. It seems that after checking in, George and Bobbi Hulbert had come to their room only to find that it had not been cleaned up after the previous occupants had checked out. Mullinax apologized and told them,

"If you'll just have a seat here in the lobby, we'll have that room cleaned up in five minutes." Still grumbling and complaining, the couple found a place to sit and wait. When they got to their room, there on a bedside table was a complimentary bottle of wine and a vase of lovely roses.

Upon their arrival in the Grand Rotunda of the Finery, newlyweds Miguel and Savina Rodriguez were impressed by all aspects of the hotel but especially by the kindness and Old World gentility of the elderly manager, Julius Mullinax. He insisted on showing them to their Lovebird Suite personally. Just before the elevator reached the penthouse level, the trio heard a loud snapping sound and the elevator suddenly jerked to a stop. Then it dropped several feet and stopped again with a jolt. Then, to the horror of the Rodriguez couple, the elevator compartment plunged out of control down the shaft for what seemed an eternity. The emergency system finally slowed the elevator, and it came to an uneventful halt at the main level.

Mullinax offered to try again to take them up. "Second time lucky," he chuckled. The terrified guests just stumbled out and ran to the bar for a couple of stiff ones. When they went to their room later, still shaking, there on a bedside table was a complimentary bottle of wine and a vase of lovely roses.

\* \* \*

1. What if anything was wrong with manager Mullinax's service-recovery efforts? Were any of these service recovery efforts appropriate?
2. If any efforts were inappropriate, which ones and why?
3. How does a manager determine what level of service-recovery effort to employ?

## The Hillsbrook Lodge

During the busy times of the year—ski season and the period when the leaves turned—a portion of visitors to New England bed and breakfast establishments sometimes made reservations at two or even three B&Bs. They knew that some B&Bs customarily overbooked, and these guests wanted to be sure they didn't end up after a long drive without a place to stay.

The Hillsbrook Lodge followed the practice of the other bed and breakfast places in its area. During those busy times of the year, the Lodge customarily overbooked by 10 to 15 percent. At first, lodge owners George and Audrey Spain didn't like to overbook; it seemed dishonest somehow. But the other owners were doing it, and the Hillsbrook Lodge couldn't afford to have anything less than 100 percent occupancy during the two periods of the year that enabled *them to get sufficiently ahead financially to stay open during the leaner periods. Things usually balanced themselves out; the Hillsbrook Lodge overbooked by about 15 percent, and about 15 percent of the guests usually didn't show up.*

*The B&B owners in the area had a cooperative service-recovery plan. They networked and kept in touch, so that any owners finding themselves facing guests whose reservations could not be honored could usually make a few phone calls to find another acceptable accommodation for the guests nearby. But supply and demand did not always even out, so occasionally George and Audrey were in the uncomfortable position of telling guests with reservations that not only did they themselves have no room for the guests, but neither did anyone else in the area. Guests did not usually take that news very well. But under the pressures of the next day's activities, the couple forgot these incidents quickly.*

*When the prime autumn weekend for viewing the turning of the leaves came, Audrey and George found that they were grossly overbooked. In addition to the 15 percent overbooking that they had reluctantly agreed to, they had each carelessly booked parties without the other's knowledge. So by the middle of Friday afternoon, all ten Hillsbrook rooms were taken, with several parties yet to come.*

*A fashionably dressed woman and a large man came into the Lodge, announced that they were Bruno and Sophie Tattaglia from New York, and asked to check in.*

*"Hi, Mr. and Mrs. Tattaglia. Can I call you Sophie and Bruno? Welcome to Hillsbrook Lodge! We've got a little problem. More guests showed up than we thought we were going to get, so since we operate on a first-come, first-served basis, I'm sorry to say we're filled up. But I think I can find accommodations for you at one of the other B&Bs nearby. They're all quite fine."*

*Sophie Tattaglia protested, "But we had a reservation."*

*George said, "Well, unfortunately, a reservation doesn't always equal a room on one of the busiest weekends of the year. Let me make some phone calls and see what we can do for you."*

*George found accommodations for the Tattaglias about twenty miles away. "They don't have quite the view that we do, but it's a nice place," said Audrey. The Tattaglia couple were not smiling but they seemed to accept the situation. After they left, George said to Audrey,*

*"Well, that wasn't so bad. We recovered pretty well, I thought. I hope these next people coming up the drive are as reasonable."*

*When Mr. and Mrs. Tattaglia got back to New York, they were still irritated about the Hillsbrook situation. George and Audrey Spain had thought about setting up a page on the World Wide Web to make more people aware of the Hillsbrook Lodge, but they didn't really have the time or the expertise. Mrs. Tattaglia was self-employed as a creator of Web pages. It was easy for her to set up a Web page, available to anyone in the world who had a computer and an Internet connection, describing the Tattaglia experience at the Hillsbrook Lodge, soliciting other stories of negative experiences with the Lodge, and urging potential visitors to New England not to patronize the Hillsbrook.*

\* \* \*

(Continued)

1. Overbooking is common in some parts of the hospitality and travel industry. Can you justify overbooking on ethical grounds?
2. Did the Hillsbrook Lodge have any alternatives to overbooking?
3. Once George and Audrey find out about the Hillsbrook page on the Web, can you think of any service-recovery steps they might take?

## *The Road Warriors*

*C*onsolidated Airlines has determined that business travelers account for 40 percent of its business in terms of head count but provide 72 percent of airline revenue. "Mile-collecting vacationers" make up 60 percent of head count but provide only 28 percent of revenue. The most frequent business travelers, those the airline calls "road warriors," make up only 6 percent of passengers but provide a whopping 37 percent of airline revenue.

Passenger complaints and survey results have revealed that the passengers least satisfied and most frustrated with air travel are the road warriors. The airline's best customers are most disappointed with the airline's service. That situation obviously must change.

The airline has $400 million available to improve service to passengers. How would you recommend that these funds be spent?

## Additional Readings

Anderson, Eugene W. 1998. Customer Satisfaction and Word of Mouth. *Journal of Service Research* 1(1):5–17.

Andreassen, Tor Wallin. 1999. What Drives Customer Loyalty With Complaint Resolution? *Journal of Service Research* 1(4):324–332.

Bejou, David, and Adrian Palmer. 1998. Service Failure and Loyalty: An Exploratory Empirical Study of Airline Customers. *Journal of Services Marketing* 12(1):7–22.

Bitner, Mary Jo, Bernard H. Booms, and Mary Stanfield Tetreault. 1990. The Service Encounter: Diagnosing Favorable and Unfavorable Incidents. *Journal of Marketing* 54(1):71–84.

Blackwell, Steven A., et al. 1999. The Antecedents of Customer Loyalty: An Empirical Investigation of the Role of Personal and Situational Aspects on Repurchase Decisions. *Journal of Service Research* 1(4):362–375.

Boshoff, Christo. 1999. RECOVSAT: An Instrument to Measure Satisfaction with Transaction-Specific Service Recovery. *Journal of Service Research* 1(3):236–249.

Chu, Wujin, Eitan Gerstner, and James D. Hess. 1998. Managing Dissatisfaction: How to Decrease Customer Opportunism by Partial Refunds. *Journal of Service Research* 1(2):140–154.

Chung, Beth, and K. Douglas Hoffman. 1998. Critical Incidents: Service Failures that Matter Most. *Cornell Hotel and Restaurant Administration Quarterly* 39(3):66–73.

Gilly, M. C., and B. D. Gelb. 1982. Post-Purchase Consumer-Processes and the Complaining Consumer. *Journal of Consumer Research* (9):323–328.

Goodwin, Cathy, and Ivan Ross. 1990. Consumer Evaluations of Responses to Complaints: What's Fair and Why. *Journal of Consumer Marketing* 7(2):39–47.

Johnston, Timothy C., and Molly A. Hewa. 1997. Fixing Service Failures. *Industrial Marketing Management* 26(September):467–473.

Johnston, R. 1995. Service Failure and Recovery: Impact, Attributes and Process, in T. Swartz, D. Bowen, and S. Brown, eds., *Advances in Services Marketing and Management,* Vol. 4 (Greenwich, CT: JAI Press), pp. 211–228.

Keaveney, Susan M. 1995. Customer Switching Behavior in Service Industries: An Exploratory Study. *Journal of Marketing* 59(2):71–82.

Lockwood, A. 1994. Using Service Incidents to Identify Quality Improvement Points. *International Journal of Contemporary Hospitality Management* 6(1/2):75–80.

Narayandas, Das. 1998. Measuring and Managing the Benefits of Customer Retention: An Empirical Investigation. *Journal of Service Research* 1(2):108–128.

Oliva, Terence A., Richard L. Oliver, and Ian C. MacMillian. 1992. A Catastrophe Model for Developing Service Satisfaction Strategies. *Journal of Marketing* 56(3):83–95.

R. T. Rust, B. Subramanian, and W. Wells. 1992. Making Complaints a Management Tool. *Marketing Management* 1(3):41–45.

Seiders, Kathleen, and Leonard L. Berry. 1998. Service Fairness: What It Is and Why It Matters. *Academy of Management Executive* 12(2):8–20.

Singh, Jadip. 1991. Understanding the Structure of Consumers' Satisfaction Valuations of Service Delivery. *Journal of the Academy of Marketing Science* 19(3):223–244.

Smith, Amy K., and Ruth N. Bolton. 1998. An Experimental Investigation of Customer Reactions to Service Failure and Recovery Encounters: Paradox or Peril? *Journal of Service Research* 1(1):65–81.

Stauss, Berndt, and Christian Friege. 1999. Regaining Service Customers: Costs and Benefits of Regain Management. *Journal of Service Research* 1(4):347–361.

Sundaram, D. S., Cynthia Webster, and Claudia Jurowski. 1996. Service Failure Recovery Efforts in Restaurant Dining: The Role of Criticality of Service Consumption. *Hospitality Research Journal* 20(2):137–150.

Tax, Stephen S., Stephen W. Brown, and Murali Chandrashekaran. Customer Evaluations of Service Complaint Experiences: Implications for Relationship Marketing. *Journal of Marketing* 62(2):60–76.

Tyler, T. R. 1994. Psychological Models of the Justice Motive: Antecedents of Distributive and Procedural Justice. *Journal of Personality and Social Psychology* (67):850–863.

# Notes

1. Frederick F. Reichheld and W. Earl Sasser, Jr. 1990. Zero Defections: Quality Comes to Services. *Harvard Business Review* 68(5):105–111.
2. Susan M. Keaveney. 1995. Customer Switching Behavior in Service Industries: An Exploratory Study. *Journal of Marketing* 59(2):71–82.

3. See L. Dube and M. Maute. 1996. The Antecedents of Brand Switching, Brand Loyalty and Verbal Responses to Service Failures, in T. Swartz, D. Bowen, and S. Brown, eds., *Advances in Services Marketing and Management,* Vol. 5 (Greenwich, CT: JAI Press), pp. 127–151.

4. R. L. Day and E. L. Landon. 1976. Collecting Comprehensive Complaint Data by Survey Research, in B. B. Anderson, ed., *Advances in Consumer Research,* Vol. 3 (Atlanta, GA: Association for Consumer Research), pp. 263–268.

5. Stephen S. Tax and Stephen W. Brown. 1998. Recovering and Learning from Service Failure. *Sloan Management Review* 39(3):76.

6. Jeffrey G. Blodgett, Donald H. Granbois, and Rockney G. Walters. 1993. The Effects of Perceived Justice on Complainants' Negative Word-of-Mouth Behavior and Repatronage Intentions. *Journal of Retailing* 69(4):408.

7. Tax and Brown, 83.

8. Day and Landon, 407.

9. Charles R. Weiser. 1995. Championing the Customer. *Harvard Business Review* 73(6):113.

10. Quoted in Tax and Brown, 81. For more on the importance of the front line in preventing and recovering from failure, see L. A. Schlesinger and J. L. Heskett. 1991. Breaking the Cycle of Failures in Services. *Sloan Management Review* 32(3):17–28.

11. Christopher W. L. Hart, James L. Heskett, and W. Earl Sasser, Jr. 1990. The Profitable Art of Service Recovery. *Harvard Business Review* 68(4):150.

12. Technical Assistance Research Program (TARP). 1986. *Consumer Complaint Handling in America: An Update Study* (Washington, DC: Department of Consumer Affairs). Often referred to as the TARP Study.

13. For further information on negative word of mouth, see Jagdip Singh. 1990. Voice, Exit, and Negative Word-of-Mouth Behaviors: An Investigation Across Three Service Categories. *Journal of the Academy of Marketing Science* 18(1):1–15; Marsha L. Richins. 1983. Negative Word-of-Mouth by Dissatisfied Consumers: A Pilot Study. *Journal of Marketing* 47(4):68–78; and Jeffrey G. Blodgett, Donald H. Granbois, and Rockney G. Walters. 1993. The Effects of Perceived Justice on Complainants' Negative Word-of-Mouth Behavior and Repatronage Intentions. *Journal of Retailing* 69(4):399–428.

14. Ralph L. Day. 1980. Research Perspectives on Consumer Complaining Behavior, in Charles W. Lamb and Patrick M. Dunn, eds., *Theoretical Developments in Marketing* (Chicago: American Marketing Association), pp. 211–215.

15. Carl Sewell and Paul B. Brown. 1990. *Customers for Life* (New York: Pocket Books).

16. Janelle Barlow and Claus Møller. 1996. *A Complaint Is a Gift* (San Francisco: Berrett-Koehler), p. 24.

17. Hart, Heskett, and Sasser, 151.

18. Ibid., 153.

19. See K. Douglas Hoffman, Scott W. Kelley, and Holly M. Rotalsky. 1995. Tracking Service Failures and Employee Recovery Efforts. *Journal of Services Marketing* 9(2):49–61. See also Scott W. Kelley and Mark A. Davis. 1994. Antecedents to Customer Expectations for Service Recovery. *Journal of the Academy of Marketing Sciences* 22(1):52–61; Thomas O. Jones and W. Earl Sasser, Jr. 1995. Why Satisfied Customers Defect. *Harvard Business Review* 73(6):88–99; and Richard A. Spreng, Gilbert

D. Harrell, and Robert D. Mackoy. 1995. Service Recovery: Impact on Satisfaction and Intentions. *Journal of Services Marketing* 9(1):15–23.

20. L. Berry, A. Parasuraman, and V. A. Zeithaml. 1994. Improving Service Quality in America: Lessons Learned. *Academy of Management Executive* 8(2):32–52.

21. Spreng, Harrell, and Mackoy, 18–19.

22. Hoffman, Kelley, and Rotalsky, 49–61.

23. Mary Jo Bitner, Bernard H. Booms, and Lois A. Mohr. 1994. Critical Service Encounters: The Employee's Viewpoint. *Journal of Marketing* 58(4):101.

24. Richard B. Chase and Douglas M. Stewart. 1994. Make Your Service Fail-Safe. *Sloan Management Review* 35(1):36.

25. D. Daryl Wyckoff. 1984. New Tools for Achieving Service Quality. *Cornell Hotel and Restaurant Administration Quarterly* 24(6):156.

26. Blodgett, Granbois, and Walters, 421–423.

27. J. L. Heskett, W. E. Sasser, Jr., and C. W. L. Hart. 1990. *Service Breakthroughs: Changing the Rules of the Game* (New York: The Free Press), p. 155.

28. Cathy Goodwin and Ivan Ross. 1992. Consumer Responses to Service Failures: Influence of Procedural and Interactional Fairness Perceptions. *Journal of Business Research* 25(2):160. See also Tax and Brown, 79–81.

29. Goodwin and Ross, 149–163.

30. Tax and Brown, 81.

31. E. A. Lind and Tom Tyler. 1987. *The Social Psychology of Procedural Justice* (New York: Plenum).

32. Jeffrey G. Blodgett, Kirk L. Wakefield, and James H. Barnes. 1995. The Effects of Customer Service on Consumer Complaining Behavior. *Journal of Services Marketing* 9(4):31–42.

33. Tax and Brown, 80.

34. Hart, Heskett, and Sasser, 148–156.

35. Ibid.

36. Tax and Brown, 81.

# Chapter 13

## Serving Perfectly

**Hospitality Principle:**

> *Pursue perfection relentlessly.*

*Unless you have 100% customer satisfaction—and I mean that they are excited about what you are doing—you have to improve.*

—Horst Schulze, President
The Ritz-Carlton Hotel Company, L.L.C.

Good *isn't good enough.*

—Len Berry

*Success is never final.*

—J. Willard Marriott, Jr.,
Chairman & CEO,
Marriott International, Inc.

## LEARNING OBJECTIVES

After reading this chapter, you should understand:

▦ How to measure the effectiveness of service delivery and of the overall guest experience.

▦ How to use internal methods of measuring service effectiveness, including managerial observation and employee assessment.

▦ How to acquire guest opinions of service effectiveness: comment cards, personal interviews, mail and phone surveys, and mystery shoppers.

▦ What are the costs and benefits of the different methods for acquiring guest opinions.

▦ What are the purpose, characteristics, advantages, and disadvantages of service guarantees.

▦ How to improve the experience provided to guests continuously.

## KEY TERMS AND CONCEPTS

| | |
|---|---|
| comment card | SERVQUAL |
| MBWA | structured interview |
| mystery shopper | "What gets measured gets managed." |
| service guarantee | |

All guests hope and expect to be provided with a perfect experience every time. Even though they know perfection is elusive, they hope that whatever errors happen won't affect them. All hospitality organizations face rising guest expectations and an increasing unwillingness to settle for less than guests think they paid for. This new customer activism has made service quality more important than ever as managers strive to meet both heightened customer expectations and increasing competition.

One key to creating a flawless guest experience is that the organization must know what errors are being made, what failures are occurring. If you don't know it's broken, you can hardly fix it. Consequently, measuring the quality of the guest experience is a crucial part of the hospitality organization's responsibility. Satisfied guests come back, and dissatisfied guests go somewhere else.

The best time to find out about possible service failures is before the guest leaves the service setting, while the information is still fresh in the guest's mind. Finding out on the spot also gives the organization the opportunity to recover from failure.

Accurately measuring what guests think about their restaurant meal, hotel stay, or reservation experience is a difficult challenge for hospitality organizations striving to achieve service excellence. Nevertheless, it must be done. This chapter focuses on finding out how the guest perceives the quality of the guest experience so that the hospitality manager can see, from the guest's perspective, where any problems are. After identifying problems, the best measurement devices will also show the organization where it needs to improve or change any tangible products, its service setting, its delivery system, or its personnel's skills to meet the guest's expectations. The chapter will review and evaluate the major types of quality-assessment techniques.

The critical challenge for hospitality managers seeking this information is to identify and implement the methods that best measure the quality of the experience from the guest's point of view. As we have stated throughout this text, the *guest* determines quality and value. Consequently, an acceptable experience for one guest might be a *wow* experience for another and totally unacceptable to a third. The subjective nature of the quality and value of a guest experience make identifying and implementing the appropriate measurement particularly difficult. No matter how well management planned the meal, scheduled the convention, or designed the hotel lobby, the quality of service cannot be measured until the guest experiences it.

## MEASURING GUEST SERVICE EFFECTIVENESS

A variety of methods are available to measure the quality of the guest experience. These methods differ in cost, accuracy, and degree of guest inconvenience. Measuring service quality can have many organizational benefits, but as usual the benefits must be balanced against the costs of obtaining them. The organization must balance the information needed and the extent and precision of the research expertise required to gather and interpret the information against the availability of funding. As a rule, the more accurate and precise the data, the more expensive it is to acquire.

### Managerial Observation of the Delivery Process

The simplest and least expensive technique for assessing guest service quality has already been mentioned as a failure-prevention technique: encouraging managers to keep their eyes open, especially to the interactions between employees and guests. This technique is sometimes called **MBWA,** or management by walking around. Some hospitality organizations call it "walking the front," which means observing the operation first hand, looking for problems or inefficiencies, talking to guests to assess their reactions, and relaying to frontline employees any information that might enable them to improve service quality. Managers know their own business, its goals, capabilities, and service quality standards. They know when employees deliver a high-quality experience. At their best, these observations do not inconvenience guests, and they often permit immediate correction of guest service problems. Further, managerial observation gives the boss the opportunity to reward the excellent employee and counsel an employee who might not be delivering the service as the organization wants it delivered. It also provides a modeling situation in which the supervisor observing a service failure can show the employee how to fix the problem. When managers walk the front to serve as helpers and not as spies, their presence has a favorable influence on employee attitudes and performance, and on guest satisfaction.

### *Drawbacks*

However, some managers may not have enough experience or training to fully understand what they are observing, or they may have biases which influence their objectivity. More importantly, when employees know that managers are observing the service delivery process, they invariably perform it differently. Additionally, although managerial observation may ensure the quality of the experience for a particular guest, managers can't watch every guest-employee interaction. The unobserved guest's reactions to unobserved experiences remain unknown to the manager.

### *Overcoming Drawbacks through Training*

Training hospitality managers in methods of observing guest/server interactions and measuring server performance against quality standards can eliminate both ignorance and personal bias. Unobtrusive observational techniques, random observations, and video cameras diminish employee awareness that the boss is watching. For example, many organizations tell their telephone operators and guests that all phone conversations may be "monitored for training purposes" to eliminate the observation bias by making it uncertain as to when management is actually listening in. The operators know that someone may always be listening, so they do the job by the book. Some larger companies use managers from one location to observe employees at another location for the same reason. For obvious ethical reasons, employees should be alerted that they may be monitored.

### *Internal Measures of Service Quality*

In addition to observing back-room employees producing any tangible product and servers delivering it to guests, managers of outstanding hospitality organizations develop measurements for every part of the guest experience so that they can monitor where they are failing to meet their own definition of quality service. Some standards are more or less global in the hospitality industry: twenty minutes to get a room-service breakfast, six minutes to check in, including waiting time, and less than that to get the first cup of morning coffee in the hotel restaurant.[1] Most standards are specific to the organizations deriving them and are designed to meet or beat the competition. American Airlines defines how many minutes it should take for bags to get from the stopped aircraft to the baggage-claim area. If they're not on the conveyor belts in 15 minutes, then the service-quality standard has not been met. Other organizations use number of rings for answering the phone in a guest service response area. If a reservationist, for example, hasn't picked up the phone within three rings, the service quality standard has not been met. These are service quality standards that can be developed, measured, and used as ways to ensure that the service is delivered to the customer as it should be. According to Phil Crosby in *Quality Is Free,* the price of not conforming to a quality standard can be calculated. That price is how much it costs to fix errors and failures that result from not meeting quality standards in the first place. While some may think that determining the cost of not answering the phone within three rings is impossible, quality experts like Crosby think it can and should be done.

### *Use Many Measures*

The good organizations measure quality in as many ways as they can. British Airways, for example, tracks some 350 indicators of quality, ranging from on-time performance, to aircraft cleanliness, to how much time to check in on a flight. It issues a monthly report on its key performance indicators to all its managers, who can use these internally generated indicators in conjunction with the external customer surveys to assess the quality level of their airline.[2] Both internal and external data are useful in assessing the customer's perception of the service and the technical excellence of that service. Since customers seldom see the back-of-the-house areas of the service delivery process, managers especially need to develop internal measures of performance quality in these areas.

Some of these same measures were discussed in the previous chapter on avoiding and fixing service failures. Such failures are determined and defined by the guest. If the guest thinks you failed, you failed; you didn't meet the guest's quality or value standards. To avoid failure, the organization's own service quality standards should exceed those of all but the most demanding guests. If they do, the organization's internal control measures may show that a standard has not been met, even if guests seem satisfied and no one complains. When that happens, some organizations actually apologize! They in effect say to guests, "We didn't meet our own standard of excellence tonight; next time we will, and your experience will be even better." Guests will remember that.

### Employee Assessment of Guest Experiences

Employee feedback about guest experiences should supplement managerial observation. Employees can provide input on issues such as cumbersome company policies and control procedures, managerial reporting structures, or other processes that inhibit effective service delivery. They know firsthand about organizational impediments that prevent them from delivering high-quality service.

Employee work teams and quality service circles are another source of feedback. Ritz-Carlton Hotels work teams have gathered feedback and used it to develop "zero-defect" guest service strategies. Such techniques foster an understanding and appreciation of how each employee can directly influence service quality. Employee awareness of management's strong commitment to service quality is affirmed through work teams. Using these teams requires employee training and management trust in employee judgment to correct service problems. The current employee empowerment movement discussed in Chapter 7 depends on such trust.

## SERVICE QUALITY: ASK THE GUEST

While observational methods for assessing service quality have their benefits, benchmark organizations are even more interested in hearing from guests themselves what they think about their experiences. Techniques to collect data directly from guests vary in cost, convenience, objectivity, and statistical validity. Table 13-1 provides an overview of these items and shows the advantages and disadvantages of each technique discussed in the following pages.

### Employees Survey Guests

Employees are often in an excellent position to gather guest perceptions of service quality by means of **structured interviews** or surveys. For example, a receptionist or restaurant cashier can question guests about their experience as they are leaving the hotel or restaurant. Because guests may not always be motivated to tell the whole truth, a systematic program should have questions that are professionally developed and validated to help ensure that the information gathered is both useful and accurate.

An advantage of acquiring immediate feedback is that it may allow prompt recovery from service failures. Employee training should therefore include appropriate service-recovery techniques, since research confirms that the organization benefits greatly from soliciting and resolving guest complaints. Effective hospitality managers know that recovering from service failures yields greater guest loyalty and repeat visits. In addition, because service quality information derived directly from the guest is highly believable to both employees and management, it motivates a quick recovery from service failures.

**Table 13-1**  *Techniques for Measuring Service Quality*

| Management Techniques | Advantages | Disadvantages |
|---|---|---|
| **Management Observation** | • management knows business, policies and procedures<br>• no inconvenience to customers<br>• opportunity to recover from service failure<br>• opportunity to collect detailed guest feedback<br>• opportunity to identify service problems<br>• minimal incremental cost for data gathering and documentation | • management presence may influence service providers<br>• lacks statistical validity and reliability<br>• objective observation requires specialized training<br>• employees disinclined to report problems they created |
| **Employee Feedback Programs** | • employees have knowledge of service delivery obstacles<br>• customers volunteer service experience information to employees<br>• no inconvenience to customers<br>• opportunity to recover from service failure<br>• employee empowerment improves morale<br>• opportunity to collect detailed guest feedback<br>• minimal incremental cost for data gathering and documentation | • objective observation requires specialized training<br>• employees disinclined to report problems they created<br>• lacks statistical validity and reliability |
| **Comment Cards** | • suggest that company is interested in customer opinions of service quality<br>• opportunity to recover from service failure<br>• moderate cost<br>• minimal incremental cost for data gathering and documentation | • self-selected sample of customers not statistically representative<br>• comments generally reflect extreme guest dissatisfaction or extreme satisfaction |
| **Mail Surveys** | • ability to gather representative and valid samples of targeted customers<br>• opportunity to recover from service failure<br>• customers can reflect on their service experience<br>• suggest that company is interested in customer opinions of service quality | • recollection of specific details may be inexact<br>• other service experiences may bias responses because of time lag<br>• inconvenience makes incentives for participants necessary<br>• cost to gather representative sample may be high |
| **On-Site Personal Interviews** | • opportunity to collect detailed guest feedback<br>• ability to gather representative and valid sample of targeted customers<br>• opportunity to recover from service failure<br>• suggest that company is interested in customer opinions of service quality | • may not be representative sample of guests<br>• recollection of specific service experience details may be lost<br>• other service experiences may bias responses because of time lag<br>• respondents tend to give socially desirable responses<br>• inconvenience makes incentives for participants necessary<br>• cost is moderate to high |

Source: Robert C. Ford and Susan Bach. 1997. Measuring Service Quality: Tools for Gaining the Competitive Advantage. *FIU Hospitality Review* 15(1):86–87. Reprinted with permission.

## Comment Cards

**Comment cards** are the cheapest and easiest to use of all data collection methods. If properly designed, they are easy to tally and analyze. These advantages make them attractive for gathering guest-satisfaction data, especially for smaller organizations that can not afford a quality assessment staff or consultants. Widely found throughout the hospitality industry, comment cards rely on voluntary guest participation. Guests rate the quality of the guest experience by responding to a few simple questions on a conveniently available form, typically a postcard. Guests either deposit the form in a box placed near the exit, return it directly to the service provider, or mail it to the corporate office.

What questions appear on the comment cards? The organization studies its guests to determine their expectations, then embodies those expectations in the comment card questions. If studies show a restaurant that its guests expect a friendly greeting, a properly setup table area, and overall cleanliness, its card will ask guests about those elements of the guest experience. If an organization tries to differentiate itself from similar organizations, that differentiating factor may appear on the comment card, so that the organization can gauge the success of its differentiation strategy.

### *The Olive Garden Card*

The Olive Garden comment card appears in Figure 13-1. A close look will reveal several interesting features, one being that the restaurant refers to diners not as *customers* but as *guests*. They are asked to rate all of the guest experience elements that we have been stressing. Question 3 on "first impressions" asks about the first service encounter ("Greeting") and about important environmental elements ("Table Area" and "Cleanliness"). Question 4 inquires about the quality of the service. Question 6 asks about value in the same way we have been talking about value, in terms of cost compared to quality ("How do our prices compare to the food and service?"). And because Olive Garden understands the importance of meeting the guest's expectations, guests are asked how value compared to their expectations: "about right," "lower than expected," "too high." The effectiveness of the production part of the service delivery system is explored in Question 4 ("Temperature" and "Appearance" of the tangible product) and of the people part in Question 5: "How was your server?" "Courtesy" refers, of course, to the server's general attitude during interactions with guests. "Promptness" and "Accuracy" are an evaluation of both the production and server parts of the service delivery system, since they must combine seamlessly to achieve promptness and accuracy. The Olive Garden also understands the importance of repeat business and word-of-mouth recommendations, so Questions 2 and 7 ask guests to address those issues. The back of the card has space for additional comments. If guests want to offer further opinions, they may call the Guest Relations 800 telephone number.

The Steak & Ale comment card is similar but briefer. It asks guests to rate food quality, service speed, attentiveness, cleanliness, and atmosphere as great, good, fair, or poor. The card leaves space for an open-ended statement, "As your guest, I would like to tell you . . .," and gives an 800 number. Hilton Hotels ask guests to use a scale of 1 = Low to 7 = High to rate front-desk performance, availability of luggage assistance, availability of accommodation type reserved, courtesy and efficiency of front desk at check-in and checkout, housekeeping, value of accommodations for price paid, and other areas known to be related to guest satisfaction.

## We'd like to know ...

1. *Your visit with us today:* date _____ time _____

   location/city _____

   ☐ lunch   ☐ dinner   number in party _____

   ☐ To Go!   ☐ other

2. *How often do you dine with us?*

   ☐ first time   ☐ once in a while   ☐ regularly

3. *Please rate your first impressions:*

   |             | Excellent | Very Good | Good | Fair | Poor |
   |-------------|-----------|-----------|------|------|------|
   | Greeting    |           |           |      |      |      |
   | Table area  |           |           |      |      |      |
   | Cleanliness |           |           |      |      |      |

4. *Tell us about your meal:*

   |             | Excellent | Very Good | Good | Fair | Poor |
   |-------------|-----------|-----------|------|------|------|
   | Quality     |           |           |      |      |      |
   | Temperature |           |           |      |      |      |

   Entree(s) _____

5. *How was your server?*

   |            | Excellent | Very Good | Good | Fair | Poor |
   |------------|-----------|-----------|------|------|------|
   | Courtesy   |           |           |      |      |      |
   | Promptness |           |           |      |      |      |
   | Accuracy   |           |           |      |      |      |

6. *How do our prices compare to the food and service?*

   ☐ about right   ☐ lower than expected   ☐ too high

7. *Overall, how do you feel about your visit?*

   ☐ highly satisfied   ☐ satisfied   ☐ dissatisfied

   Your name_____

   Address _____

   City_____ State_____

   Zip _____ Phone _____

   Server's name _____

*Is there anything else you would like us to know?*

_____

_____

_____

_____

_____

_____

_____

_____

_____

_____

_____

_____

_____

Your opinions will help us better serve your dining needs in the future. Please let our managers know about your visit before leaving today. If you should have any additional questions or comments, you may also contact us through Guest Relations at our home office:

The Olive Garden Guest Relations
PO Box 592037
Orlando, FL 32859-2037

**1-800-331-2729**
FAX 407/245-5189

For our hearing impaired guests, please use our telecommunications device at 1-800-443-4208 (TDD only).

**Figure 13-1**   *The Olive Garden Comment Card. (Courtesy of Darden Restaurants.)*

*The Olive Garden. (Courtesy of Darden Restaurants.)*

### Using Guest Comments

Such cards are an indication of whether the organization is meeting the general expectations of the guests who take the time to fill them out. Written comments about long waits for food, lines at the front desk, or housekeeping problems reveal the strengths and weaknesses of the service delivery system, the personnel and their training, and the service itself. Positive comments provide management with the opportunity to recognize employee excellence. This recognition reinforces the behaviors that lead to good guest service and creates role models and stories about how to provide outstanding service that other employees can use in shaping their own behavior in their jobs. Negative comments can be used in training, without mentioning specific employees, to illustrate behaviors that caused negative guest experiences. Using comment cards in these ways allows managers to train employees about how to provide excellent guest service through the voices of the guests themselves.

Comments accumulated from cards may be plotted as numerical values on bar graphs and charts that visually display how guests perceived their experience. The plots will suggest whether service failures are occurring occasionally and randomly, or whether overall service quality might be deteriorating. While guest comments and their visual representations are interesting and helpful to management, the information is not statistically valid, one reason being that the random-sample requirement of most statistical techniques is not met.

### Disadvantages

The greatest disadvantage of comment cards is that many guests ignore them and don't fill them out, so the cards received are not likely to be a true general picture of guest perceptions. Typically, only 5 percent of customers return comment cards, and they are usually either very satisfied or very dissatisfied. Managers don't even know what percentage of the delighted total or the dissatisfied total these responses represent. The other 95 percent say nothing. Were they happy, unhappy, or indifferent? You might guess indifferent, but you might be wrong. A large percentage of dissatisfied guests fill out no cards, leave quietly, and never return.

Another major disadvantage of comment cards, and in fact of many methods for acquiring feedback, is that the time lag between guest response and managerial review prevents on-the-spot correction of service gaps and failures. Once the moment of truth has passed and the angry or disappointed guest leaves after expressing negative responses on a comment card, the opportunity to recapture that guest's future business is diminished. Even worse, negative word-of-mouth advertising generated by dissatisfied guests cannot be corrected.

### *Fairfield Inns Scorecard*

Marriott's Fairfield Inns gather a greater percentage of guest responses before they leave the hotel through their Fairfield Inns Scorecard program. At checkout, guests are asked to answer several brief questions on a computer touch screen while the receptionist is processing the bill. Responding by touching a computer screen is easy and still novel enough to be fun, so most guests are willing to share their opinions about the quality of their hotel stay while the experience is fresh in their minds, instead of just the very happy or very unhappy who are motivated to return the cards.[3]

### Toll-Free 800 Numbers

Another way of measuring the quality of service is the customer-service 800 telephone number. This technique lets customers say what's on their minds 24 hours a day. Like the guest comment cards, the usefulness of the 800 number depends upon the willingness of the guests to respond, and even the convenience of this method does not guarantee a representative response from all types of guests. To improve the level of response, organizations can let callers know how they addressed caller problems and comments; callers like to know that somebody listened and did something.

## SERVICE GUARANTEES

"Satisfaction guaranteed or your money back; no questions asked." Here are some typical service guarantees.

### Amtrak's Coast Starlight Service Guarantee

If our personal service doesn't satisfy your expectations, we'll rectify the situation on the spot, guaranteed. Just notify the chief of on-board service, or the conductor, of your concern, and they will see that it is quickly taken care of.

If, in the unlikely event a problem remains, we have not earned the price of your ticket, we will issue a service credit for the full value of the one-way Coast Starlight portion of your trip.

## Suite Options Guarantee

We guarantee that your residence will be ready on the day promised with all the amenities you ordered.

We guarantee your suite will be spotlessly clean and thoroughly inspected.

We guarantee your personal satisfaction with the condition and quality of all furnishings and housewares.

We guarantee to refund your money for any item that does not meet your satisfaction.

We guarantee to do everything in our power to satisfy your special requests and make your stay exceptional.

**Service guarantees** are usually considered a marketing tool, to persuade potential guests unsure about an organization to give it a try, but they also provide a means for letting guests respond to service quality. The right to invoke a guarantee makes available to guests a strong means for telling the organization when the service delivery system is not working right. In 1989 Hampton Inn hotels were the first in the industry to offer an unconditional 100 percent satisfaction guarantee: "If you're not completely satisfied, we'll give you your night's stay for free." *Every* Hampton employee is empowered to approve this refund. To avoid abuses of the guarantee, the company keeps a database of customers who have invoked it and recommends another hotel to guests who violate the company's trust. According to Stephen Tax and Stephen Brown, the Hampton Inn organization "realized $11 million in additional revenue from the implementation of its service guarantee and scored the highest customer retention rate in the industry."[4]

## Organizational Advantages of Guarantees

As described by Chris Hart, service guarantees provide a number of important advantages to an organization.[5] If the company has a strong and well-understood service guarantee that its customers can and do readily invoke, everyone in the organization can learn much about the service delivery system from its use. Hart notes several important benefits of the guarantee in measuring and improving the effectiveness of the service delivery system:

- *The guarantee forces everyone to think about the service from the customer's point of view* since the customer decides whether or not to invoke it.
- *It pinpoints where the service failed* since the customer must give the reason for invoking the guarantee, and that reason then becomes measurement data on the service delivery system. As Chapter 12 noted, a guest complaint is a good thing for a hospitality organization that hopes to be perfect. Guarantees are an incentive to get customers to complain if their expectations (and the guarantee's terms) have not been met. These complaints help the organization to fix whatever is wrong before many more customers have problems.
- *It gets everyone to focus quickly on the problem at hand* since the costs of making good on guarantees can be quite large. Once a customer has to invoke the guarantee, the cost of the lost revenue gets management's attention directed at correcting the problem.
- *It enhances the likelihood of recovery from a service failure,* because the guest is encouraged to demand instant recovery, instead of sending in a negative guest comment card and taking the business to a competitor.
- It sends a strong message to employees and customers alike that *the organization takes its service quality seriously and will stand behind it.*

## The Good Guarantee

A good service guarantee, according to Hart, should meet several important criteria.[6] The guarantee must be:

1. *Unconditional.* The more asterisks attached to the bottom of the page, the more fine print, the less credible the guarantee will seem to both employees and customers. Few or no conditions should be required to use the guarantee.

2. *Easy to understand and communicate* both to customers who invoke it and employees who honor it. Follow the old KISS rule: Keep It Simple, Stupid. The more complicated the guarantee is, the less likely anyone will believe or use it.

3. *Focused on the customer's needs.* The guarantee should solve the customer's problems, not fit the organization's needs.

4. *A clear definition of the standard for service quality,* for everyone inside and outside the organization. If you're going to guarantee it, you'd better deliver it the way you're supposed to.

5. *Meaningful, to both the customer and the organization, in terms of what happens to both when the guarantee is invoked.* The remedy should cover the guest's dissatisfaction completely. If invoking the guarantee only partially solves the customer's problem or is of little consequence to the organization, neither the customer nor the service people will value the guarantee.

6. *Easy to use.* Invoking the guarantee and receiving its benefits should be painless for the guest. The harder a guarantee is to use, the less credible it will be, and the less likely it will help identify serious service problems. Don't ask customers to fill out a bunch of forms and talk to several different departments to have their problem solved. It wasn't their fault you messed up, so why should they have to do all the work to get it fixed?

7. *A declaration of trust* in both the customers you are trusting to use it only when they have a legitimate complaint and the employees you are trusting to correct the customer's problem quickly, fairly, and effectively without giving away the whole organization.

8. *Believable* to the customer. If customers don't believe you will really make good, then they won't use the guarantee. They think, "If it sounds too good to be true, it probably is." The classic illustration is Pizza Hut Delivery's 30-minutes-or-free guarantee, which was changed partly because people thought it was too good to be true.

## FORMAL SURVEYS

Formal survey methods can obtain guest feedback about service quality and value. While surveying is more expensive than the methods already discussed, surveys can offer statistically valid, reliable, and useful measures of guest opinion while other options cannot. Surveys can range in sophistication, precision, validity, reliability, complexity, cost, and difficulty of administration.

### Mail Surveys

Well-developed mail surveys, sent to an appropriate and willing sample, provide trustworthy information concerning guest satisfaction. Brinker International, the parent company of such restaurants as Chili's, Grady's, Romano's Macaroni Grill, and Cozymel, has developed a variation that combines the mail survey and the frequent-diner card program. The feedback advantages of the survey join with the card's promotion of guest loyalty and return visits. Once Brinker obtains basic guest demographic information on an application form for the card, it follows up with mailed surveys to guests and gains valuable feedback on eating preferences and patterns by guest category.

### Disadvantages

Organizations can use mailed surveys to their benefit, but many uncontrollable factors can influence guest responses to a mailed survey. Inaccurate and incomplete mailing lists or simple lack of interest in commenting can produce a response rate too small to provide useful information. In addition, the time lag between the experience and survey response can blur a guest's memory of details

These surveys are usually used to generate reports full of numbers. The subtleties of the guest experience and guest perceptions cannot be fully expressed numerically. Also, averages may not be sufficiently informative. If some guests remember an experience as terrific and give it a high rating while others rate it as terrible, the numerical average would suggest that guest expectations were met.

Finally, formal mail survey techniques require proper questionnaire development, validation, and data analysis, so they are expensive.

### SERVQUAL

One well-accepted technique is **SERVQUAL** (short for "service quality"), developed by A. Parasuraman and his associates. An adaptation of the SERVQUAL survey instrument, intended to evaluate service quality at Belle's Restaurant, is presented in Figure 13-2. SERVQUAL has been extensively researched to validate its psychometric properties. It measures the way customers perceive the quality of service experiences in five categories: *reliability* (the organization's ability to perform the desired service dependably, accurately, and consistently), *responsiveness* (its willingness to provide prompt service and help customers), *assurance* (employee knowledge, courtesy, and ability to convey trust), *empathy* (providing caring, individualized attention to customers), and *tangibles* (the physical facilities, equipment, and appearance of personnel).[7]

SERVQUAL also asks respondents to rate the relative importance of the five areas, so organizations can make sure they understand what matters most to customers. In each area SERVQUAL asks customers what they expected and what they actually experienced, to identify service gaps at which organizations should direct attention. Figure 13-2 shows how the items on the SERVQUAL instrument might be adapted to a restaurant situation.

The SERVQUAL instrument reflects a point we have made throughout—*the importance of the frontline server to service quality.* While tangibles refer primarily to the setting and to the physical elements of the delivery system, and reliability reflects a combination of organizational ability and server ability, the remaining three elements—responsiveness, assurance, and empathy—are almost exclusively the responsibility of the frontline server.

### SERV*OR

SERVQUAL assesses guest perceptions. The SERV*OR instrument, designed by Richard S. Lytle and colleagues, is designed to gauge *employee* perceptions of the organization's degree of service orientation.[8] Here are the scale items. They represent areas in which organiza-

**DIRECTIONS:** Listed below are five features pertaining to Belle's Restaurant and the services they offer. We would like to know how important each of these features is to *you* when you evaluate a restaurant's quality. Please allocate a total of 100 points among the five features *according to how important each feature is to you*—the more important a feature is to you, the more points you should allocate to it. Please ensure that the points you allocate to the five features add up to 100.

1.   The appearance of the restaurant's physical facilities, equipment, and personnel.
_____ points
2.   The ability of the restaurant to perform the promised service dependably and accurately.
_____ points
3.   The willingness of the restaurant to help customers and provide prompt service.
_____ points
4.   The knowledge and courtesy of the restaurant's employees and their ability to convey trust and confidence.
_____ points
5.   The caring, individualized attention the restaurant provides to its customers.
_____ points

**DIRECTIONS:** Based on your experience as a customer of restaurants, please think about the kind of restaurant that would deliver excellent service quality. Think about the kind of restaurant at which you would be pleased to eat. Please show the extent to which you think such a restaurant would possess the feature described by each statement. If you feel a feature is *not at all essential* for excellent restaurants such as the one you have in mind, circle the number "1" for *Strongly Disagree*. If you feel a feature is *absolutely essential* for excellent restaurants, circle "7" for *Strongly Agree*. If your feelings are less strong, circle one of the numbers in the middle. There are no right or wrong answers—all we are interested in is a number that truly reflects your feelings regarding restaurants that would deliver excellent service quality. **[The 22 survey items for this section are the same as those in the next section, but without any reference to Belle's Restaurant.]**

**DIRECTIONS:** The following set of statements relate to your feelings about the service at Belle's Restaurant. For each statement, please show the extent to which you believe Belle's Restaurant has the feature described by the statement. Once again, circling a "1" means that you *Strongly Disagree* that Belle's Restaurant has that feature, and circling a "7"

means that you *Strongly Agree*. You may circle any of the numbers in the middle that show how strong your feelings are. There are no right or wrong answers—all we are interested in is a number that best shows your perceptions about the service at Belle's Restaurant.
**[On the instrument itself, the five category labels (Tangibles, etc.) would be omitted.]**

**TANGIBLES**
1. Belle's Restaurant has modern-looking equipment.
2. Belle's Restaurant's physical facilities are visually appealing.
3. Belle's Restaurant's employees are neat-appearing.
4. Materials associated with the service (such as menus) are visually appealing at Belle's Restaurant.

**RELIABILITY**
5. When Belle's Restaurant promises to do something by a certain time, it does so.
6. When you have a problem, Belle's Restaurant shows sincere interest in solving it.
7. Belle's Restaurant performs the service right the first time.
8. Belle's Restaurant provides its services in the way it promises to do so.
9. Belle's Restaurant insists on error-free service performance.

**RESPONSIVENESS**
10. Employees of Belle's Restaurant tell you exactly when services will be performed.
11. Employees of Belle's Restaurant give you prompt service.
12. Employees of Belle's Restaurant are always willing to help you.
13. Employees of Belle's Restaurant are never too busy to respond to your requests.

**ASSURANCE**
14. The behavior of Belle's Restaurant employees instills confidence in customers.
15. You feel safe in going to Belle's Restaurant and doing business with them.
16. Employees of Belle's Restaurant are consistently courteous to you.
17. Employees of Belle's Restaurant have the knowledge to answer your questions.

**EMPATHY**
18. Belle's Restaurant gives you individual attention.
19. Belle's Restaurant has operating hours convenient to all its customers.
20. Belle's Restaurant has employees who give you personal attention.
21. Belle's Restaurant has your best interests at heart.
22. Employees of Belle's Restaurant try to learn your specific needs.

---

**Figure 13-2**   *Instrument for Measuring Guest Perceptions of Service Quality at Belle's Restaurant. Source: Adapted from A. Parasuraman, V. A. Zeithaml, and L. L. Berry. 1988. SERVQUAL: A Multiple-Item Scale for Measuring Consumer Perception of Service Quality.* Journal of Retailing. *64(1):38-40. Used with permission.)*

tions, according to research by this group, should concentrate if they hope to be viewed by their internal customers—the employees—as having the service orientation prerequisite for "serving perfectly":

1. customer treatment
2. employee empowerment
3. service technology
4. service-failure prevention
5. service-failure recovery
6. service standards communication
7. service vision
8. servant leadership
9. service rewards
10. service training

## Personal Interviews

Face-to-face guest interviews provide rich information when trained interviewers, able to detect nuances in responses to open-ended questions, have the opportunity to probe guests for details about their experiences. Interviewing can uncover previously unknown problems or new twists to a known problem that cannot be uncovered in a preprinted questionnaire or reflected well in numerical data. However, personal interviews are costly: interviewers must be hired and trained, interview instruments must be custom designed, and inconvenienced guests must be compensated for participating. Without incentives, most guests see little personal benefit from participating in a guest survey unless, as with the guest comment cards discussed earlier, they are either very satisfied or very dissatisfied. Finally, the most desirable time to interview guests is at the conclusion of the guest experience. Getting their attention and cooperation when they would probably prefer to leave is a challenge.

Another guest interview approach is to employ consultants or employees as "lobby lizards" who ask randomly selected guests their opinions on several key service issues. At theme parks and other attractions, teams of interviewers roam the parks seeking guest responses. These conversations enable the identification of service flaws that can be corrected while the guest is still on the property.

## Critical Incidents

Another important survey tool is the critical incident technique. Through interviews or paper-and-pencil surveys, customers are asked to identify and evaluate numerous moments—classified as dissatisfiers, neutral, or satisfiers—in their interactions with the organization. The survey lets the organization know which moments are critical to customer satisfaction, and the critical dissatisfiers can be traced back to their root causes and rectified. In one study of convention hotels, for example, conventioneers identified guest arrival, coffee break, lunch, and the conference room itself as critical incidents and factors. Once the hotel knew which incidents convention guests viewed as critical, it concentrated on making them smooth and seamless.[9]

## Focus Groups

Focus groups provide in-depth information on how guests view the service they receive. Typically, a guest focus group of six to ten guests gathers with a facilitator for several hours to discuss perceived problems and make suggestions. Marriott Corporation, for example, conducted focus groups of frequent-stay guests and incorporated their comments into the design of the Marriott Courtyard hotel model. Many organizations routinely invite guests to participate in focus groups. These guests are impressed that the company cares enough about their reactions to ask for them, and they appreciate the free return admission, complimentary dinner, or other expression of appreciation that compensates them for their time.

Focus groups are useful but also expensive, time consuming, and labor intensive, requiring as they do a group facilitator, meeting space, travel and lodging expenses for the facilitator and participants, and perhaps additional compensation to the participants. Since focus groups represent the targeted customer market, correct selection of participants is crucial in obtaining accurate information. If the customer sample is not accurate or doesn't match the desired customer profile, the resulting information can lead to inappropriate conclusions about customer experiences. A large hospitality organization can pick ideal and representative groups from its thousands of customers; an individual restaurant, hotel, or travel agency will have much greater difficulty in assembling a group that accurately represents the targeted customer profile.

## Telephone Surveys

Telephone interviews are another useful method for assessing customer perceptions of service. Car dealerships, for example, frequently use telephone interviews to measure customer satisfaction. In the hospitality industry, some tour operators phone customers to obtain feedback about a recent vacation experience while paving the way for subsequent travel arrangements.

Although telephone interviews eliminate the inconvenience to guests of gathering information while guests are still in the service location, they present other challenges. This technique also relies on retrospective information that can be blurred by the passage of time. If the service received was too brief or insignificant for guests to recall accurately, or if guests have no special motivation to participate, the information they provide is likely to be unreliable or incomplete. In addition, in this age of intense telephone solicitation, customers often regard telephone surveys as intrusions on their time and violations of their privacy. Annoyed respondents feeling resentment toward the organization for calling them at home are likely to bias the data. Red Lobster and Steak & Ale avoid some of these difficulties by building into their guest checks a code that asks every $n$th guest to call an 800 number to respond by pressing Touchtone buttons to questions about their experience at the restaurant. In return for participation, the restaurant offers coupons for free desserts or "two entrées for the price of one" on the guest's next visit. Telephone interviews in which the guest responds directly to a trained interviewer who is administering a sophisticated questionnaire are expensive. When data analysis and expert interpretation are included, the total cost for a statistically valid survey can become quite high.

## Mystery Shoppers

**Mystery shoppers** provide management with an objective snapshot of the guest experience. While posing as guests, these trained observers methodically sample the service and its delivery, take note of the environment, and then compile a systematic and detailed report of their experience. They can sample a restaurant meal, a trip on a cruise ship, or an overnight stay at a full-service resort hotel. Shopper reports generally include numerical ratings of their observations so that reactions to the guest experience can be compared over time and with other organizations. While employees usually know that their organization uses a mystery-shopper program, they don't know who the shoppers are or when they will shop. Owners of smaller organizations, such as independent restaurateurs or hoteliers, can hire an individual consultant or ask a personal friend or university class to conduct a mystery-shopper program. Larger organizations and national chains may employ a commercial service or use their own staff as shoppers.[10]

### Advantages

Since visits by mystery shoppers are unannounced, employees cannot "dress up" their performance. In addition, shoppers can be scheduled at specific times to assess the quality of service during various shifts, under diverse conditions, with different employees, and through the eyes of different types of shoppers.[11] For example, a hotel designed as a family resort employed a shopper and her children to assess the "family-friendly" factor at the property. The children said the front-desk counters were too high and prevented them from seeing what was going on. As a result, a special registration desk was installed where young guests could check in and learn about the activities available for them at the hotel.

Mystery shoppers can also observe competing organizations in a particular market and systematically gather information on their service level, facilities, prices, and special packages. Some hotels employ mystery shoppers to test the ability of their properties to respond to anticipated service problems and service delivery failures. For example, shoppers can create a problem or intensify a situation by asking certain questions or requesting unique services to assess employee responses under pressure. Mystery shoppers can also gauge the effectiveness of a particular training program by shopping at a hospitality organization before and after the training.

The American Automobile Association employs a staff of trained inspectors who indirectly act as mystery shoppers when they anonymously inspect hotels, motels, and restaurants and report their observations as a service to AAA members in their series of Tour Books. These inspectors also provide a service to the properties they visit by sharing their observations with property managers before they leave.

### Disadvantages

The main disadvantage of using a mystery shopper is the small size of the sample from which the shopper generates reports. Since anyone can have a bad day or a bad shift, a mystery shopper may base conclusions on unusual or atypical experiences. One or two observations is not a statistically valid sample of anything, but hiring enough mystery shoppers to yield a valid sample would be impractical and expensive. Further, the unique preferences, biases, or expectations of individual shoppers can unduly influence a report. Well-trained shoppers with specific information about the organization's service standards, instructions on what to observe, and guidelines for evaluating the experience avoid this pitfall.

## FINDING THE TECHNIQUE THAT FITS

Typically, **what gets measured gets managed.** But which of the measures in Table 13-1 to use? A luxury resort hotel, for example, may require more elaborate and expensive strategies to measure feedback since poor service can harm the reputation and bottom line of the hotel, the chain with which the hotel is affiliated, and the livelihood of countless employees up and down the line. The value to this hotel of finding and correcting service failures so that it can deliver the service quality its guests expect is tremendous. Failing to meet guest expectations will quickly make it and everything affiliated with it uncompetitive in a dynamic marketplace. On the other hand, a small independent restaurant whose owner loves to "interview" his patrons will probably not require sophisticated quality assessment methods.

Costs and level of expertise used to gather data also vary. An important question to ask is who should collect data: employees, consultants, or a professional survey research organization. Using employees is the least expensive alternative, but they also have the least expertise in research and may lack the communication skills to interview effectively. Consultants and survey organizations cost more but they are better able to gather and interpret more detailed, sophisticated statistical data using more sophisticated techniques. Employee-surveyors cannot measure eye-pupil dilation; professionals can.

## Your Best Evaluators: The Guests

Regardless of the evaluation technique selected to measure service quality, one thing is certain. *Guests evaluate service every time it is delivered,* forming distinct opinions about its quality and value. All hospitality organizations that aspire to excellence must constantly assess the quality of their guest experience through their guests' eyes. Most guests are happy to tell what they thought about their experience if they are asked in the right way at the right time. Telephone surveyors calling on Friday night at dinner time will get the turndown they deserve. Hospitality managers striving for excellence need to ask the right guests the right questions at the right time to obtain the information necessary to ensure service that meets and exceeds guest expectations.

## Lessons Learned

1. The quality of work and the quality of service are different; manage to achieve both.
2. If you don't measure it, you can't manage it; if you don't manage it, you can't improve it.
3. Balance the value of service information obtained from guests with the cost of obtaining it.
4. Recognize the strengths and weaknesses of available assessment techniques.
5. The more sophisticated the information needed from guests, the more expensive it is to acquire.
6. Get better or get beat.

## Review Questions

1. Is it critically important for hospitality organizations to measure guest satisfaction with service quality and value? Or is it sometimes sufficient for organizations simply to offer the best service they can and hope for the best?

2. Regarding the strengths and weaknesses of different methods for measuring service quality:
   A. What are the strengths and weaknesses of managerial observation?
   B. What are the strengths and weaknesses of guest comment cards?
   C. Why is the comment card technique used so frequently in spite of its weaknesses?
3. What provisions would you expect to find in a typical service guarantee for a restaurant?
   A. What are the advantages and disadvantages to restaurants of offering such a guarantee?
   B. How might the service guarantees of a quick-serve restaurant and a fine dining restaurant differ?
   C. Why would a hotel be more apt to use a guarantee than a restaurant, or a restaurant than a hotel? Do the restaurants with which you are familiar have guarantees?
4. What are the advantages and disadvantages to hospitality organizations of mystery shoppers? In which types of hospitality organizations do you think mystery shoppers would be most and least effective?
5. To what extent should managers use a cost/benefit analysis when trying to determine which techniques to use to measure the guest's perception of the guest experience's quality and value?

## Activities

1. Collect guest comment cards from several hospitality organizations and compare the factors about which organizations solicit comments. What conclusions can you draw? If possible, interview the managers whose organizations make the cards available to guests and ask how the managers use the results.
2. Imagine that you are a mystery shopper for a hotel. Write up a list of the activities in which you would engage, starting with deciding how long you will stay to do a thorough evaluation (24 hours? 48 hours?), then calling in to make a reservation. (What will your "number of rings" standard be? three rings? four rings?), and so forth. Will you "create a problem" just to see what happens? (For example, try to send food or wine back because you don't like it.) What evaluation system will you use for the different hotel areas? Pass/fail? An excellent-through-poor scale?
3. Go mystery shopping. If appropriate, use some of the activities from your hotel evaluation list created for question 2. Or do a quick evaluation or service audit using "the three *T*s"—Task, Treatment, Tangibles. Write up a brief description of what you found and observed on your shopping trip and send it to the manager of the service location.
4. Either in groups or individually, use Hart's criteria for a good service guarantee as presented in this chapter and create a guarantee for a real or imaginary hospitality organization.

## Case Studies

### Try Before You Buy: The Service Guarantee

**E**d Jennings had never stayed at Super 10 Suites before, but he hadn't been very satisfied with the only other lodging establishment in Grover, Montana, a regular stop in his western sales territory, so he decided to try Super 10. What persuaded him to make the switch was the guarantee of service offered by Super 10. It was basic but it offered all that Ed wanted:

"Try before you buy. We guarantee that your rooms will be cleaned, inspected and ready, with all amenities in place, or you pay nothing! No questions asked. We want you to be happy in your choice of Super 10 Suites, Grover's finest."

Ed checked in late in the evening after a hard day on the road, went to his room, and looked around. The room wasn't exactly dirty, but it wasn't exactly clean either. There were small scraps of paper on the floor, some hair in the sink, and mold in the shower. He sat down in a chair, opened the complimentary bag of pretzels, and chewed on one while he thought about whether to stay or to leave.

"Oh, well, if it doesn't get any worse than this, I guess I can take it."

Without going into all the details, it did get worse. The hot water didn't work, the bed was lumpy, and the air conditioner failed during the night. A screaming baby in the next room kept Ed awake for several hours. When Ed checked out the next day, he informed the clerk that he was exercising his service guarantee; he wasn't going to pay. Of course the clerk asked why, and Ed explained the problems he had experienced.

"Your guarantee said the room would be clean and inspected, and it was not clean. There was hair in the sink, paper scraps on the floor, and mold in the shower."

"No," said the clerk. "The guarantee says that the room will be cleaned, and it was cleaned, last week. As for inspection, I inspected it myself."

Ed said, "When you inspected it, didn't you notice the scraps, the hair, and the mold?"

"This guarantee doesn't say anything about what I noticed or didn't notice. It just says the room was inspected. And before you even ask about the amenities, that's what the pretzels are—amenities."

"All that may be true," said Ed, "but this guarantee says 'No questions asked.' "

"Didn't you see the asterisk by that? Didn't you see the fine print?" asked the clerk. "The asterisk refers to our statement at the bottom that if you ask questions, this guarantee is null and void. This other asterisk, which apparently you didn't see either, says that 'This guarantee and the terms thereof shall be valid and its terms exercisable with respect to the cost of one night's room only, with all the covenants appertaining thereunto. Management shall retain its sole and exclusive right to interpret the terms of the guarantee.' " In my opinion, and I'm the management this morning, we fulfilled our guarantee to you the guest, and then some."

(Continued)

*Ed Jennings gave it up. He had sales calls to make. Mighty tired and upset, he headed out into the day.*

\* \* \*

What was wrong with this guarantee? Indicate as many faults as you can.

## Standard Times at Happy's Restaurant

*T*he top management at Happy's Restaurants, Inc., had assigned its new Work Methods and Standards Department the task of establishing "standard times" for the chain's units. Work Methods personnel went out into the restaurants as mystery shoppers and observed operations carefully. Work Methods then reported to management that the speed and efficiency of service in virtually all of the restaurants was in need of improvement.

Laura Martin, manager of a very successful and profitable Happy's Restaurant in South Carolina, got the e-mailed memo about the new "standard times for food and cocktail service" late one afternoon. A highly experienced server herself and a respected manager, Martin just laughed at the proposed standards and set the memo aside. She thought she had noticed some mystery shoppers making secret notes, so she had expected some kind of ivory-tower memo like this. It might look good on paper, but it just couldn't be done.

Next day at the afternoon meeting, Martin told her servers: "If you hear anything about new standard times and methods for serving food and drinks, don't pay any attention. As you know, we have all committed ourselves to getting the entrées to guests within eighteen minutes of taking their orders, but our average is sixteen minutes. We've been averaging sixteen for all the years I've been here, and our comment-card results on promptness are excellent. Because you are all terrific at your jobs, I'd say fifteen minutes is the absolute best we could do. But those bozos at headquarters say the new standard is all entrées to guests within fourteen minutes of taking the order." The servers looked at each other with disbelief, then they started to laugh.

"And they also think we can have the drinks on the tables within three minutes of first guest contact." The servers just rolled their eyes and smiled. "Don't worry," said Laura Martin. "I'll straighten this out in a hurry. " Martin sent her boss an e-mail telling him that the new standards had to be a mistake because they were entirely unrealistic.

Her boss soon called her and straightened her out in a hurry: "Laura, the new standards will go into effect tomorrow. Work Methods has achieved improved results in several of our other chains already, and now all Happy's branches must conform. Sure, servers always resist at first, but they can meet the standards if you lay down the law and if they use more efficient methods."

"Maybe that's true elsewhere," said Laura, "but I know my restaurant, my kitchen staff, my servers, and my guests, and I know we can't make fourteen minutes, even with these new methods they want us to use. Things can only be done so fast."

"Martin, call a meeting of your staff, explain that the new standard times will be met, teach your people the new methods, stick to managing your unit, and leave methods and times to the Work Methods and Standards Department. That's what we pay you for, and that's what we pay them for."

Martin tried her best, but her restaurant knew how she felt about the situation. The servers at this South Carolina Happy's Restaurant failed to meet the new work standards, and the head of the Work Methods and Standards Department blamed Laura Martin. He recommended that she be moved back to her old server job or fired.

\* \* \*

1. What is the problem here?
2. Under what circumstances can such "by the minute" standards be made to work?
3. How would you determine service standards at your restaurant?

## Additional Readings

Almanza, B. A., W. Jaffe, and L. Lin. 1994. Use of the Service Attribute Matrix to Measure Consumer Satisfaction. *Hospitality Research Journal* 17(2):63–76.

Barsky, J. 1992. Customer Satisfaction in the Hotel Industry: Meaning and Measurement. *Hospitality Research Journal* 16(1):51–74.

Becker, C. 1996. Implementing the Intangibles: A Total Quality Approach for Hospitality Service Providers, in M. Olsen et al., eds., *Service Quality in Hospitality Operations* (London: Cassell): pp. 278–298.

Berry, L., A. Parasuraman, and V. A. Zeithaml. 1994. Improving Service Quality in America: Lessons Learned. *Academy of Management Executive* 8(2):32–52

Bitner, M. J., and A. R. Hubbert. 1994. Encounter Satisfaction Versus Service Quality: The Customer's Voice, in R. T. Rust and R. L. Oliver, eds. *Service Quality: New Directions in Theory and Practice* (Thousand Oaks, CA: Sage Publications), pp. 72–94.

Bojanic, D. C., and L. D. Rosen. 1994. Measuring Service Quality in Restaurants: An Application of the SERVQUAL Instrument. *Hospitality Research Journal* 18(1):3–14.

Brown, Stephen W., and Teresa A. Swartz. 1989. A Gap Analysis of Professional Service Quality. *Journal of Marketing* 53(2):92–98.

Buttle, F. 1996. SERVQUAL: Review, Critique, Research Agenda. *European Journal of Marketing* 30(1):8–32.

Cadotte, E. R., and N. Turgeon. 1988. Key Factors in Guest Satisfaction. *Cornell Hotel and Restaurant Administration Quarterly* 28(4):44–51.

Chadee, D. D., and J. Mattsson. 1996. An Empirical Assessment of Customer Satisfaction in Tourism. *Service Industries' Journal* 16(3):305–320.

Chung, Beth G. 1997. Collecting and Using Employee Feedback—An Effective Way to Understand Customers' Needs. *Cornell Hotel and Restaurant Administration Quarterly* 38(5):50–57.

Cronin, Joseph J., and Steven A. Taylor. 1994. SERVPERF Versus SERVQUAL: Reconciling Performance-Based and Perceptions-Minus-Expectations Measurement of Service Quality. *Journal of Marketing* 58(1):125–131.

Danaher, P. J., and J. Mattsson. 1994. Customer Satisfaction During the Service Delivery Process. *European Journal of Marketing* 28(5):5–16.

Ekinci, Yuksel, and Michael Riley. 1998. A Critique of the Issues and Theoretical Assumptions in Service Quality Measurement in the Lodging Industry: Time to Move the Goal-Posts? *International Journal of Hospitality Management* 17(4):349–362.

Ekinci, Yuksel, and Michael Riley. 1997. Examination of the SERVQUAL and LODGSERV Scales' Performance in the Case of Holidaymakers' Perception of Resort Hotel Service Quality. *Proceedings of the 6th Annual CHME Hospitality Research Conference* (Oxford, Brookes University, UK).

Fruchter, Gila E., and Eitan Gerstner. 1999. Selling With "Satisfaction Guaranteed." *Journal of Service Research* 1(4):300–312.

Getty, J. M., and K. N. Thompson. 1994. A Procedure for Scaling Perceptions of Lodging Quality. *Hospitality Research Journal* 18(2):75–96.

Hinkin, T. R., J. B. Tracey, and C. A. Enz. 1997. Scale Construction: Developing Reliable and Valid Measurement Instruments. *Journal of Hospitality and Tourism Research* 21(1):100–120.

Jeong, Miyoung, and Haemoon Oh. 1998. Quality Function Deployment: An Extended Framework for Service Quality and Customer Satisfaction in the Hospitality Industry. *International Journal of Hospitality Management* 17(4):375–390.

Johns, N. 1992. Quality Management in the Hospitality Industry: Definition and Specification. *International Journal of Contemporary Hospitality Management* 4(3):14–20.

Johns, N. 1992. Quality Management in the Hospitality Industry: Applications, Systems and Techniques. *International Journal of Contemporary Hospitality Management* 4(4):3–7.

Johns, N. 1993. Quality Management in the Hospitality Industry, Part 3: Recent Developments. *International Journal of Contemporary Hospitality Management* 5(1):10–15

Knutson, Bonnie, et al. 1992. Consumers' Expectations for Service Quality in Economy, Mid-price and Luxury Hotels. *Journal of Hospitality and Leisure Marketing* 1(2):27–43.

Lawrence O. Hamer, Ben Shaw-Ching Liu, and D. Sudharshan. 1999. The Effects of Intra-Encounter Changes in Expectations on Perceived Service Quality Models. *Journal of Service Research* 1(3):275–289.

LeBlanc, G. 1992. Factors Affecting Customer Evaluation of Service Quality in Travel Agencies: An Investigation of Customer Perceptions. *Journal of Travel Research* 30(4):10–16.

Lewis, R. C., and A. Pizam. 1982. The Measurement of Guest Satisfaction, in A. Pizam, R. C. Lewis, and P. Manning, eds., *The Practice of Hospitality Management* (New York: AVI Publishing), pp. 89–201.

Luchars, J. Y., and T. R. Hinkin. 1996. The Service-Quality Audit: A Hotel Case Study. *Cornell Hotel and Restaurant Administration Quarterly* 37(1):34–41.

Oh, H., and S. C. Parks. 1997. Customer Satisfaction and Service Quality: A Critical Review of the Literature and Research Implications for the Hospitality Industry. *Hospitality Research Journal* 20(3):35–64.

Parasuraman, A., V. A. Zeithaml, and L. Berry. 1991. Refinement and Reassessment of the SERVQUAL Scale. *Journal of Retailing* 67(4):420–450.

Paxson, M. Chris. 1995. Increasing Your Survey Response Rates: Practical Instructions from the Total-Design Method. *Cornell Hotel and Restaurant Administration Quarterly* 36(4):66–73.

Spreng, R. A. and R. W. Olshavski. 1993. A Desires Contingency Model of Customer Satisfaction. *Journal of the Academy of Marketing Science* 21(3):169–178.

Teas, R. K. 1993. Consumer Expectations and the Measurement of Perceived Service Quality. *Journal of Professional Services Marketing* 8(2):33–54.

Tucci, Louis A., and James Talaga. 1997. Service Guarantees and Consumers' Evaluation of Services. *Journal of Services Marketing* 11(1):10–18.

## Notes

1. Lou Cook. 1998. Mystery Shoppers: Can They Help Hotels Head Off Major Quality Problems? *Lodging* 23(8):78.
2. Steven E. Prokesch. 1995. Competing on Customer Service: An Interview with British Airways' Sir Colin Marshall. *Harvard Business Review* 73(6):101–112.
3. Stephen S. Tax and Stephen W. Brown. 1998. Recovering and Learning from Service Failure. *Sloan Management Review* 39(3):76.
4. Ibid., 75.
5. C. W. L. Hart. 1988. The Power of Unconditional Service Guarantees. *Harvard Business Review* 66(4):54–62.
6. Ibid.
7. A. Parasuraman, V. A. Zeithaml, and L. L. Berry. 1988. SERVQUAL: A Multiple-Item Scale for Measuring Consumer Perception of Service Quality. *Journal of Retailing* 64(1)12–40. Hospitality applications of SERVQUAL may be found in Bonnie Knutson, Pete Stevens, and Mark Patton. 1995. DINESERV: Measuring Service Quality in Quick Service, Casual/Theme, and Fine Dining Restaurants. *Journal of Hospitality and Leisure Marketing* 3(2):35–44; Bonnie Knutson et al. 1991. LODGSERV: A Service Quality Index for the Lodging Industry. *Hospitality Research Journal* 14(2):277–284; and Y. L. Lee and Nerilee Hing. 1995. Measuring Quality in Restaurant Operations: An Application of the SERVQUAL Instrument. *International Journal of Hospitality Management* 3(2):293–310.
8. Richard S. Lytle, Peter W. Hom, and Michael P. Mokwa. 1998. SERV*OR: A Managerial Measure of Organizational Service-Orientation. *Journal of Retailing* 74(4):455–489.
9. P. J. Danaher and J. Mattsson. 1994. Cumulative Encounter Satisfaction in the Hotel Conference Process. *International Journal of Service Industry Management* 5(4):69–80.
10. For further information about mystery shoppers, see H. Schlossberg. 1991. There's No Mystery in How to Retain Customers. *Marketing News,* January 15:10; I. Guzman. 1991. Using Shopper Studies to Evaluate Service Quality. *Marketing News,* May 9:23, 25.
11. L. Miles. 1993. Rise of the Mystery Shopper. *Marketing* (March):19. See also K. Morrall. 1994. Mystery Shopping Tests Service and Compliance. *Bank Marketing* (February):13.

Chapter

14

# Service Excellence: Leading the Way to Wow!

**Hospitality Principle:**

> Lead others to excel.

*Leaders think about empowerment, not control.*

—Warren Bennis

*If I tell you what to do, then the task is my responsibility, not yours. But if I inspire you to act on your own, the responsibility and results are yours. The difference in dedication is phenomenal.*

—Norman Brinker
Former CEO, Chili's Restaurants

## WHAT DOES THE GUEST WANT?

Guestology is simple. Study the guest, know what that person really wants and expects, and then provide it—plus a little bit more. A guestologist never stops studying the guest, using all the scientific tools available to know what that guest really wants and values. Since guests change, the study is never complete; the guest service product, the environment, and the delivery system must also change to make sure that each guest is satisfied enough to come back. Leaders of outstanding guest service organizations spend considerable time and effort studying the guest and using this information to shape their decisions on the three *S*s: *strategy, staffing,* and *systems.*

This chapter will review the book's important concepts. Then we shall conclude by showing how the leader brings it all together and makes it happen.

## STRATEGY

In this era when an amazing amount of information about guests and competition in providing services to those guests is available, only organizations that truly understand what guests want will survive and prosper. They first use this information to design a corporate strategy. They discover which of their competencies guests consider core and concentrate on making these core competencies better. They use the wants, needs, and expectations of guests to sharpen their marketing strategies, their budgeting decisions, their organizational and production systems design, and their human resource management strategy.

Southwest Airlines is an excellent example of a company that has used its understanding of the guest to discover and then provide what its passengers really want. Like most organizations, the airline originally used guest surveys to ask what guests wanted. It learned that guests wanted cheap fares, on-time performance, great meals, comfortable seats, free movies, and more. Southwest quickly recognized that, human nature being what it is, if you ask people what they want—they want everything.

Southwest realized it couldn't give its customers everything because nobody could. Gourmet meals with wine in big comfortable seats and low fares—it can't be done. So Southwest did additional research to dig deeper into guest preferences and learned that customers really wanted *low fares* and *reliable schedules* with *friendly service.* The Southwest product is now exactly what its target market wanted and, more importantly, wanted enough to pay for and return to again and again. The point is that the guestologist must dig deeper than the simple market survey of guest preferences to understand what preferences actually drive guest behavior. The organization can use the results from this deeper probing to match up the organization's core competencies and mission with what customers want. Even better for Southwest, giving guests what they want provided extra cost savings to Southwest; turning an airplane around between arrival and departure is considerably easier, faster, and cheaper without having to clean up all the mess and clutter caused by unwanted frills like food service.

### The Key Drivers

The outstanding guest service organizations have done what Southwest has done. They study their guests extensively to discover what the guests both want and value in the guest service experience and use this information to align all the elements of their corporate strategy with these expectations. On the basis of studying their targeted guest market, these organizations can identify the *key drivers* of the guest experience. Some are highly influential; some may seem relatively unimportant. Nonetheless, they all contribute to the impression that the guest takes away from the guest experience and are part of the determination of whether or not that guest will return. A trip to a theme park, or a visit to a restaurant or hotel, is a holistic experience to most people; excellent guest service organizations do the research necessary to identify all the separate components of this whole experience. Then they manage them.

### Drivers: The Basics

In a sense, these drivers can be divided into two categories. One group are those things that guests *expect* the organization to offer its guests to operate in the particular market segment. A resort hotel must have nice, clean hotel rooms with the expected amenities like shampoo and body lotion. A casual dining restaurant must have reasonably priced food, table servers, clean rest rooms, and relatively prompt service. Guests expect these characteristics *at a minimum.* These are basic expectations that the organization must meet; otherwise guests will be dissatisfied. If the organization fails habitually to meet these basic expectations, it will fail altogether. The basic characteristics are the necessary but not sufficient guest experience aspects that organizations must offer if they seek to maintain a reputation and attract the repeat business that leads to long-term success.

### Drivers: The Wows

The second category of drivers are the characteristics and qualities that make the experience memorable. These are the *wow* things that the excellent organizations provide in some or all parts of the guest experience. The organizations find a way to go beyond meeting the basic expectations with which guests arrive when they come in the door or onto the property to have a service need satisfied. The outstanding hospitality organizations provide the key factors that impel guests to return again and again, and even motivate guests to tell all their friends about these exceptional organizations.

Disney, Olive Garden, Marriott, Ritz-Carlton, and other outstanding guest service organizations continuously survey their guests to find out how well they are providing the basics that guests expect. The organization must then dig deeper to identify which factors are true keys to turning guest satisfaction into a *wow* experience.

For example, Disney knows that its guests expect transportation to be available so they can move from one part of the Walt Disney World Resort complex to another. Disney surveys its guests to be sure that they are satisfied with the transportation system. On the other hand, no one comes to the Walt Disney World Resort mainly to ride a bus, and the transportation system seldom shows up in guest surveys as a source of dissatisfaction, nor do guest opinions about the transportation system predict guest intent to revisit Disney. Even when the bus experience isn't up to the guest's level of expectation, that minor service failure shows no relation to overall satisfaction or with intent to return. Unless bus service is outrageously poor, dangerous, or grossly unsatisfactory in some other way, it has little or no impact on how guests react to the overall Disney experience. In contrast, the guest's perception of the quality of the rides and attractions, the dazzling nature of the fireworks displays, and the quality of cast member interactions with guests are highly correlated with guest satisfaction and intent to return, so they—and not bus service—become the focus of managerial concern; they are key drivers.

### Study, Study, Study

The point is that you don't know what factors in the service product, the environment, and the delivery system are the key drivers of guest satisfaction and intent to return until you carefully study all the possible drivers. Many times what management learns in such studies is a surprise because what management thought would be keys when it designed the components don't turn out to be so from the guest's point of view. This difference between what the organization delivers and what the guest expects or really wants is the service gap that Len Berry has identified, and it happens. No matter how much experience an organization has in surveying and studying guests, it will still be surprised occasionally by what guests say is really important to them.

### Accumulating Information

Excellent guest service organizations study their guests extensively and also accumulate the information they have learned about guests, individually and collectively. Computerized databases and sophisticated techniques of database analysis allow the organization to know a great deal about its guests, either as a demographic or psychographic group or as individuals. The best organizations mine these databases to dig up as much as they can about what is important to their guests so they can ensure that what is expected is provided.

### A Key Driver: Personalize

The outstanding guest service organizations that attract repeat customers have an added advantage; they can accumulate information on their frequent guests and use this information to further customize the guest experience. In other words, they know that a key driver is to *personalize* the guest experience (everyone wants to be special and treated like an individual), and intelligent use of a customer database allows the best to get better at doing these things. Customizing each guest's experience to match the guest's unique needs and expectations is becoming increasingly easy.

Ritz-Carlton is one of the best, but others are finding innovative ways to build a relationship with each customer based on powerful computer analysis of customer information. While personalizing is not easy with a high-volume, mass-produced experience like a theme-park attraction that is designed to appeal to 20,000 or more guests from all over the world every day, these data-based systems are making it easier for service settings like hotels and even restaurants to provide individualized guest interaction. Making every guest feel special is an important way for an organization to differentiate its guest experience from all others. Finding out what makes that person feel special is one role of a guestologist.

Knowing what makes each guest feel special enables organizations to add the wow factor that all guest service organizations want to provide to keep their guests coming back time and time again. The wow is the difference that the little bit more than the guest expected can make; it can turn the satisfactory experience into a memorable one and can keep the organization at the top of the customer's mind when thinking about where to go the next time that particular guest service is desired. Wows can be built into the service product, the environment, the service delivery system, or all parts of the service experience. Based on knowledge about guest likes and dislikes, the designers of the experience can build in those things they expect will give the wow. They should, however, always follow up to find out if they were successful and, if not, should try to find out where and why they failed.

### At Epcot

Wows don't have to be expensive, complicated, or elaborate, although they may be. Epcot provides good examples of a relatively inexpensive and a relatively expensive wow experience, one in the delivery system and one in the environment. The less expensive illustration is the leaping fountains next to the Imagination Pavilion. As guests exit this building, they are surprised to see a series of shooting fountains where the water appears to leap from one spot to another as if on a track. No one expects such a sight as they leave; people did not come to Epcot to see it; but when people see it they remember it and remember it as a wow.

The second, more expensive example is part of the "Honey, I Shrunk the Audience" attraction. People enter expecting a typical 3-D movie experience that will be made special because of Disney's technical and creative movie-making skills. What they don't expect but get by design is the feeling of mice running around their feet (actually, a spinning Nylon line), and a wet spray that seems to come from a sneezing dog in the movie. The guests expect the realism of 3-D but not that much, and it becomes a wow for them.

### Plan, Plan, Plan

Providing the guest with both the expected parts of the guest experience and the wow factors is the result of extensive planning. And as we know, planning starts with the guest. Capacity and location decisions, the design of personnel policies, the selection of production equipment—all must be based on the organization's best estimates of what kind of experience the guest wants, needs, and expects from the organization. If the organization's mission is to provide a theme park experience, then the first issue to resolve is where to build the physical plant and how big to build it. If the organization's mission is to build a chain of casual dining restaurants, then it must identify what food tastes, portion sizes, locations, exterior appearances, and restaurant size it should have. These decisions can be properly made if based on solid and extensive market research, and guestologists use the best data they can find to make them. While many guest service operators still base these decisions on hunches and their own personal preferences, the outstanding ones always start with the guest and make sure that every decision is based on a thorough knowledge and understanding of the guest.

### Get Constant Feedback

The good ones also know that this discovery process is never ending; they constantly seek feedback from their guests about what works and what doesn't. Guest needs, wants, and expectations change, and good organizations change with them in response to evolving guest expectations. Those organizations that constantly seek to exceed guest expectations build in their own future challenges. Today's wow is tomorrow's standard expectation for the guest who has been there and done that. The outstanding organizations are constantly seeking new ways to wow their guests, and they survey guests constantly to find out what these changing expectations are.

The Planet Hollywood in Orlando, largest in the chain, has two kitchens—one for each floor. It is therefore a nearly perfect experimental site for testing new menu items, portion sizes, and other service product features. Since the guests are typically tourists who randomly distribute themselves between the two dining levels, different menu strategies and concepts can be tried and compared to see which are best suited for the Planet Hollywood

*Orlando Planet Hollywood. (Courtesy of Planet Hollywood.)*

customer. The ability to test and compare new ideas constantly gives the food production people at Planet Hollywood a statistically valid approach to finding new ways to wow their guests. The Twilight Zone Tower of Terror at Disney-MGM Studios, which simulates a runaway elevator dropping thirteen floors, is a second illustration of how guest feedback can be used to improve guest satisfaction. While the ride as originally designed—two big drops and one little drop—was exciting, guests thought it was over too quickly. They wanted more hang time, more weightless feeling during the five-minute ride. Based on the guest feedback, Disney in 1999 introduced a new sequence with seven minor and major drops, in about the same length of time. Guests now feel that the Tower of Terror is an excellent ride, just scary enough and just long enough.

## Culture Fills the Gaps

One last issue in the strategy area is the organizational culture. Managers of outstanding hospitality organizations need to remember the importance of the organizational culture in filling in the gaps between what the organization can anticipate and train its people to deal with and the opportunities that arise in the daily encounters with a wide variety of guests. There is no way to anticipate the many different things guests will do, ask for, and expect from the service provider. The power of the culture to guide and direct employees to do the "right thing" for the guest becomes vital. Good managers know that the values, beliefs, and norms of behavior that the culture teaches its employees become critical in ensuring that the frontline employee does what the organization wants done in unplanned and unanticipated situations.

The culture must be planned and carefully thought through to ensure that the message sent to all employees is the one the organization really wants to send. An important part of

*Twilight Zone Tower of Terror. (Used by permission from Disney Enterprises, Inc.)*

any strategy is to ensure that everything that the organization and its leadership says and does is consistent with the culture it wishes to define and support. The more intangible the product, the stronger the cultural values, beliefs, and norms must be to ensure that the guest service employee provides the quality and value of guest experience that the guest expects and the organization wants to deliver.

## STAFFING

### People Make the Difference

The second *S*, staffing, has become an increasingly important factor for all guest service organizations as they realize the most effective way to differentiate themselves from their competitors is on the quality of the service encounters that the service contact personnel provide. In this day of widespread computerization and standardization, competitors can readily imitate the service product, the physical elements of the environment, and the technical aspects of the delivery system. For one service organization to duplicate the successful differentiating factor of another doesn't take very long. A chicken fajita on a taco shell that the driver can hold while driving the car is an innovation for only as long as it takes competitors to offer one-handed fajitas in their drive-throughs as well. *People*, not fajitas, make the difference. If Taco Bell has friendly servers and Burger King does not, customers will go to Taco Bell—unless they've just got to have some ground beef, or they for some reason require the ambiance of the Burger King environment, or they have an uncommon fondness for the Burger King way of producing food. For everybody else, the service people make the difference.

### Empowering the People

The challenge is to empower the server to engage each guest on a personal, individual basis while still maintaining production efficiency and consistent quality in the service delivery process. Guests enter Epcot's Spaceship Earth at a fast pace. The cast member greeting the arriving guests has just time enough to tell each guest, "Keep your arms and hands inside the car, sit down, and watch your step when entering the moving sidewalk." This encounter is highly mechanical and too short for the cast member to do much more than state this important information before the next guest arrives and needs to be reminded of the same safety precautions. Repeating their little speech feels to employees very much like working on the assembly-line job of Detroit automakers and Akron tire producers. About every six seconds a new guest, car, or tire arrives; the employee has to do or say something briefly, then the guest, car, or tire disappears down the assembly line to another worker's station. How can this job be made *fun, fair,* and *interesting?* While the Epcot workers at least have the benefit of human contact rather than contact with a tire or an auto, finding fun in the job is an effort.

Some employees in these positions figure it out and actually do have fun. They are usually the ones who were selected properly in the first place. Finding the right people for these jobs is an important responsibility of the selection process. Putting the people in these routinized jobs who are suited for them eliminates many of the problems in delivering high-quality guest experiences. Some people are just plain good at quickly establishing personal contact with guests, and they can be identified through effective selection techniques. Finding these people and training them in the basic skills necessary for effective service delivery is a key responsibility for human resource managers in hospitality organizations.

### *Server Responsibilities*

Recall that servers have three responsibilities in the guest experience: they deliver the service product (or in some cases create it on the spot), they manage the quality of the encounters or interactions between the guest and the organization, and they identify and fix the inevitable problems. Too many organizations train only for the first of these responsibilities and neglect the other two. In many instances, receiving the service product is just one element in the guest's determination of the quality and value of the guest experience. Servers must also be trained to deal effectively with the variety of personalities and concerns that different guests will bring to the guest experience.

Selection of the right person for the job starts by clearly defining what the job requires. If you want a person to be a ticket seller, then you hire a certain bundle of skills. If you want that person to be a vacation planner and also sell tickets to implement these plans, that takes an entirely different set of skills. Any job has knowledge, skills, and ability requirements; the organization's challenge is to find the "ideal employee" who fits these requirements. Such employees can and should be identified so that the employment decision can be made properly. Selecting the right people and placing them in the right jobs is one real key to ensuring the quality of the guest experience.

## Training

The second part of the staffing issue is training. The right person in the right job must be trained to do it the right way. Many jobs in the guest service industry are repetitive, simple, and boring. They also require incredible attention to detail and concentration on task performance so that the employee provides the same service experience in the same flawless way for each guest. It is easy for employee Dave Johnson to zone out, daydream, or otherwise lose interest in saying "Thank you for visiting Epcot" to the 20,000th guest. By that time his legs are tired, his attention span is short, and his interest in greeting one more person with a friendly smile and positive eye contact is about zero. Part of Dave's training should include how to cope with the nature of the job. When the encounters are short—as at a fast-food drive-through window, convention check-in, or entry point for a theme-park attraction—the training challenge is particularly difficult.

### Satisfaction from Satisfying

Similar jobs exist in the industrial sector, and job rotation, job enlargement, and job enrichment strategies have been tried with varying levels of success. The advantage guest service organizations offer to employees over most industrial settings is the guest and the positive feedback and stimulation that dealing with guests can bring. Once employees learn how to derive some sense of satisfaction out of doing something that makes a guest smile or finding ways to make a child happy, they have the ability to enjoy their jobs and something to take home and talk about that they accomplished that day. Many hospitality organizations have discovered that some of their best employees are older, retired people. They are often lonely, bored, and looking for something to do that will bring them into positive contact with other people. Hospitality jobs are especially good in providing this particular opportunity to them. Some organizations that originally recruited older people because of labor shortages have found to their pleasant surprise that older people bring an enthusiasm for service that makes them great employees.

If you just *process* people, you get discouraged and bored in many hospitality jobs. If you *engage* people, the job becomes interesting. The challenge here is the short-cycle jobs where guest contact is so fleeting that the opportunity to engage guests is nearly nonexistent. As a contrasting example, consider the waitstaff in a fine dining restaurant. With their longer time of contact, employees can use a variety of interpersonal skills to make the job personal and fun for themselves and their guests. They can interject their personalities to make the outcome a function of their own ability to provide a good guest experience. They have the time. Loading a high-volume ride at Epcot or serving a fast-food customer is a different matter and a far greater challenge for both employee and management. Guests don't have time to notice employees and their contributions to the quality of the guest experience. The level of employee engagement and subsequent satisfaction with making the difference is considerably less, and it is these jobs that create the biggest challenges for managers seeking to provide their employees with jobs that are fun, fair, and interesting. Their challenge is to find ways to give each employee the opportunity to be unique, recognized, and noticed as an individual by the guest while not compromising the speed and efficiency of the production process used to deliver the service product.

### *Trust the Technology or the People?*

Future employees will expect more job challenges and increased opportunities to be responsible for the guest encounter. Future managers will have increasingly efficient mechanized production and delivery systems available to them. Managers may have to choose between trusting these systems and trusting their employees to provide a high-quality and consistent service experience for their guests. The need to trust the employees will intensify as the competition for talented employees becomes greater. Good people want to take the responsibility, and the successful organizations will be those that find ways to preserve the quality and value of the guest experience while empowering their employees to be responsible for guest satisfaction.

## Setting the Standards

The third part of the staffing issue is the management responsibility to set performance standards and reward employees who meet them. Managers must define for the employees what their job responsibilities are, what the standards of performance are, and what management expects. These must be clearly spelled out and reinforced and rewarded by managers every day. Once a manager lets an employee provide service of less than outstanding quality, overlooks poor employee performance, or lets a "bad show" situation continue, the message goes out to everyone that managers don't always really mean what they say about providing high-quality guest service. Just as a guest has many moments of truth during the course of a single hospitality experience, employees have many moments of truth with every manager every day. What happens during these moments of truth tells the employees a great deal about what management really believes in. This is where the organizational mission statement, corporate culture, and corporate policies about guest focus become real. And just as one employee at one moment of truth can destroy the guest's perception of the entire company and what it stands for, so too can one supervisor overlooking one violation of quality standards or job performance change the way an employee looks at an organization. While most organizations have done a good job of developing selection techniques and providing the necessary job training, many fall short in the reinforcement area. When they let things slide, they miss the chance to reinforce the positive and coach away the negative aspects of employee performance.

Disney's policy of requiring its managers to be in their job areas walking the walk and talking the talk is a vital part of how the message is sent to employees that everyone is responsible for guest service, including them. This policy also builds a sense of equality among the employees in that everyone is there to serve the guest.

### At Olive Garden

Ron Magruder, former president of Olive Garden, used to tell the story about visiting some restaurants in Houston to see for himself how they were doing. He arrived at one restaurant right at the peak of the lunchtime crowd and immediately learned that the store manager was swamped. Two of her cooks had not shown up, and the restaurant was full of hungry and impatient customers. Ron, finding the manager in the kitchen trying to cook as fast as she could to keep up with orders, took off his coat, grabbed an apron, and joined her on the cook line. In the middle of this chaos, a phone call came in for the manager. It was another manager asking her if she had seen Ron yet. She tersely told the other manager not to bother her with such questions while the president of the company was working beside her at the next grill. The story got out rapidly, and there was no doubt in anyone's mind where Ron Magruder stood on customer service or what he believed in. These kinds of stories do a powerful job of reinforcing the guest service standards in organizations, and they should be told.

### Make It Fun

The last critical aspect of staffing is *fun*. Since the frontline employee is such an important part of setting the mood for the guest, and since the research shows the importance of employee attitude in determining the attitude of the guest, the guest service organization needs to find ways of ensuring that its employees are having fun doing their jobs rather than just going through the motions. While this is partly a selection issue it is also a managerial challenge to find new and exciting ways to celebrate successes and introduce a sense of fun and playfulness without letting the play get so far out of hand that it interferes with the quality or safety of the guest experience. Most people like to celebrate, and employees are no different.

### Employ the Guest

Just as organizations can benefit from thinking of their employees as customers or guests, they can also benefit from thinking of their customers as employees. This gives the organization a different way of both looking at and thinking about their customers if they define them as quasi-employees.

Customer-employees can serve several important functions. They can give helpful feedback to the organization regarding their level of satisfaction with the guest experience. In effect, they can be knowledgeable unpaid consultants. Guests are typically part of the service environment and help create the service experience for other guests. If being surrounded by other guests is an important part of each guest's experience, then how the guests are employed in helping to create each other's experience becomes an important part of the management process.

Most importantly for hospitality organizations, customers can often be allowed, encouraged, and trained to coproduce the service experience. They can actually create the salad they like at the salad bar, clean up their own trash at the quick-serve restaurant, or check themselves out of the hotel. This coproduction strategy can benefit both the customer and the hospitality organization. The organization saves on labor costs, and knowledgeable customers are likely to get the hospitality experience served "their way" because they helped to produce it. Plus, they don't have to wait for service because they're producing it themselves.

# SYSTEMS

The last *S* is all the organizational systems that support the guest experience. The best people in the world trained to perfection can't satisfy a guest if they deliver a bad product or deliver a good product late. In a huge, complex system like Walt Disney World Resort or a simple system like Ralph's Restaurant down on the corner, the whole system needs to be carefully managed so the right product is delivered to guests as they expect it to be. Guests don't care that the bed sheets are not clean yet because the laundry broke down, that the organization forgot to rotate its stock so the eggs went bad, or that the person responsible for solving their problem is on break. They just want hot, fresh, properly cooked eggs, a clean room and a comfortable bed after a tough day on the road, and someone who will respond promptly to a legitimate concern. If these things don't happen, then the production system, the support system, the information system, or the organizational system has failed, and someone had better fix it fast.

## Systems and Guestology

The most highly developed applications of guestology can be found in the systems area. Models of guest behavior in many situations can be built and used to understand and predict the ways in which the organization can satisfy the guest's expectations. Simulations are an important technique for doing this, and with the decreasing costs of computers and increasingly user-friendly software packages, simulations will become more available and relevant to all types of hospitality organizations.

Once the planning process has gotten the design right and the measurement systems are in place to get guest feedback, the stage is set to use simulations of the entire guest experience to see if it all works as a system. By knowing what guests will do, Disney can make sure that the right capacity has been built into attractions and all other features in the park, from rest rooms to telephones to merchandise outlets, to handle the number of guests expected on the design day. The design-day selection and the parameters used for the design day (such as the fifteen-minute average wait) drive the rest of the capacity decisions to ensure that the "designed" experience can be provided to the guests. Since the Disney design day is set at a high level of attendance, most guests on most days will experience a better-than-design-day experience because the lines will be shorter than designed capacity, everywhere from rest rooms to the best attractions.

## The Wait

In many hospitality organizations, the most visible part of the guest experience is *the wait for service*. The wait system, therefore, requires extra organizational time and attention to ensure that the inevitable waits are tolerable and within the limits guests will accept without becoming dissatisfied. Waiting periods are easily modeled and studied with simulation techniques and easy-to-use computer software. Everything from the number of urinals at a football stadium to the number of front-desk agents at a hotel to the number of seats on an airline route or theme park attraction can be simulated based on guest demand data. If you know how many guests are coming to your place of business and can estimate a predictable distribution to represent their arrival patterns and times for service, modeling how the waiting experience can be managed and balanced against capacity is relatively simple.

The management of waiting time is important both from the capacity standpoint and the psychological standpoint. Since few organizations can build enough capacity to serve peak demand periods, and few hospitality organizations have the ability to stockpile their mostly perishable and intangible product, managing the wait is critical for all hospitality organizations. The greater the perceived value of the guest experience, the longer the guest will wait. Again, this area is susceptible to empirical research; how long guests will wait for anything before they give up and leave can be studied, measured, and understood. Disney knows that guests are willing to wait much longer for a "thrill" ride like Space Mountain than for the Country Bear Jamboree.

\* \* \*

The management of strategy, staffing, and systems is the key to guest service excellence. They all count in creating the guest experience, and they are all related. Making any strategic change will necessarily impact the service product, the environment, and the service delivery system. It all starts with the guest.

## HOSPITALITY AND THE FUTURE

### People Making the Difference

The division between those hospitality organizations that figure out how to engage the entire employee and those who use employees only from the neck down will widen. Value added to guest experiences through the skills of employees providing them will become a more important differentiating strategy as the decreasing costs and increasingly available technology make the hospitality product and service delivery system components (except for people) increasingly easy to duplicate and emulate by all competitors. If all burgers taste alike, then the "feel-good" part of the burger service experience becomes an increasingly important part of the total. Advertising alone can't provide this difference and in fact may be counterproductive if guests don't get what the glowing ads lead them to expect. Cast members will make the difference between Disney and competing guest experiences, and the quality of cast member encounters with guests will determine whether Disney experiences are disappointing, satisfactory, or *wow,* magical-moment service experiences that build the positive word of mouth and repeat business that Disney and almost everyone else depends on in the hospitality industry. If your guests are at least 70 percent repeat customers, as is true at the Walt Disney World Resort, you must be doing something right, and if their continued repeat business is vital to your organization's survival, you had better find a way to keep doing it.

### Service or Price

Service organizations will increasingly compete on service or compete on price. A successful group of organizations in every service sector will seek to add value to each guest service experience (like a Ritz-Carlton) or seek to define value on price alone (like a Red Roof Inn). By making sure that they focus on a particular niche of the market, advertising to that niche what it will do for them and then doing it very well, these companies (like a Southwest Airlines) will thrive. The effective use of new technology and techniques in the service delivery system will allow those organizations emphasizing price as their strategy for attracting their market niche to succeed in appealing to and satisfying the price-conscious market segment. The efficient users of high technology will find ways to offer low prices and still make money. The high end of the various service markets will succeed for the same reasons. They too will use technology, but for them technology is only a means to the end of providing the maximum amount of service their guests have come to expect at a price that is reasonable for the service level. Both types of organizations will rely on technology to deliver the best value to their guests in the most efficient way. They will, consequently, make money through their efficiency where the less efficient competitor will fail. They can increasingly customize the product to each guest's expectations at the price point plus offer a little bit more as they can provide their employees with the necessary information to personalize the service in a prompt, friendly, and efficient way.

The hospitality businesses in the mass market between these two ends of the spectrum will have the most difficult challenge in the future as many are already having today. They will be challenged in offering guest services as personalized as the service-oriented firms in the marketplace have been able to offer and which guests now expect, while providing the low prices which the price-oriented firms in a competitive marketplace have also led guests to expect. This middle group of organizations seeking to serve the mass market may do neither very well. They may find themselves in the position of overpromising and underdelivering, which is not the way to have satisfied, loyal, or repeat guests.

## Keeping Promises

The excellent guest service organizations of the future will use every tool at their command to figure out what the guest wants and then provide it in a way that is consistent with the guest expectations of value and quality. If they promise a high-quality experience and friendly service, they had better provide them or the customers will not come back. Most service organizations depend on repeat business, and to fail their guests will cost them dearly in a competitive marketplace. Once you tell your customers what you will do for them, you've made a commitment and a promise. If the promise is broken or the commitment unrealized, guests will be unhappy and will tell everyone they know how unhappy they are. Few organizations can afford to break their promises, and the more a guest service organization depends upon repeat business, the less chance it can take of violating that trust. Information and opinions about service quality are freely available now and will become more so in the future. If a dissatisfied guest posts a negative comment on the Internet about your service, that comment may be readily accessible on a computer somewhere *forever.* Computers can be programmed never to forget, and the more they are involved in helping customers make selections among guest service providers, the more critical it is to avoid failing the guest. Disney now has an employee whose only job is to monitor the Disney discussion groups on the Internet to detect and hopefully correct guest complaints and false rumors that show up on this powerful communication medium. A job classification that didn't even exist ten years ago will become an increasingly important part of the organization's communication strategy as it seeks to avoid the negative word of mouth that can now travel almost instantly across cyberspace to the entire world.

### Yesterday's *Wow*

The future will be information management, people management, increasing ability to understand what each guest really wants (a "market niche of one" that allows the organization to build a relationship with each guest), and focusing on the organizational core competencies that satisfy these guest expectations. The future will also bring forth more knowledgeable customers with ever-rising expectations. The more competitors in the marketplace try to outdo each other in providing wow experiences, the more familiar these experiences will become. Yesterday's wow becomes today's expected minimal level of service. Hospitality managers will need to engage the entire organization in constantly reviewing all aspects of the guest service product, the environment, and the service delivery system to find new and, hopefully, not easily duplicated features that add the wow.

### Server-Customer Interaction

The easiest and most fruitful area in which to develop these features is in the interaction between servers and customers, where hospitality employees can make a wow experience happen. The challenge here is to empower them without jeopardizing the quality and consistency of the service product. Human error is inevitable, and the need to blend technology and people to provide a high-tech and high-touch experience of consistently high quality will be the biggest and most interesting challenge for the future guestologist.

## LEADERS AND THE FUTURE

### Leading from the Front

We conclude by stressing an idea that has been implied throughout this book: *managers must lead employees toward excellence.* The importance of the leader in hospitality organizations cannot be overemphasized. The leader is the symbol of what the organization stands for and believes. If the leader doesn't lead, all the efforts to discover the key drivers that cause the customer to seek out a particular hospitality experience, the expense of designing the service delivery system, and the effort to recruit and train the best people are wasted. Every day and in every way the leader must set the example and show all employees what their value is to the organization and to creating the hospitality experience.

Everyone wants to feel that what they do has value and meaning to a purpose larger than enriching a company's top executives and stockholders. Leaders not only inspire their employees to realize their individual worth to the organization; they also help employees see what contributions they make to the greater good by doing their jobs with excellence. Telling people how important it is that they do their jobs well is not enough. All employees must understand and believe that their contributions make a difference and that doing well whatever they do is vital.

### All Jobs and People Have Value

Many organizations make efforts in this direction but, once again and finally, few do it as well as Disney. The Disney organization has inspired its employees to believe they are responsible for creating happiness for many who need it and many who would not otherwise have it. The tremendous publicity they give to the "Give Kids the World" foundation and related ventures is not only a good thing to do but it also inspires the people inside Disney that what they do is important and has value beyond the individual jobs they perform. The company reinforces this idea with the regular use of terms related to a theatrical production, such as good show, bad show, on stage, off stage, and cast members. These terms constantly remind all employees that what they are doing has a greater purpose than merely sweeping up guest trash, working at a hamburger stand, or cleaning bathrooms. Each job has value and the person doing the job has value because of the contribution to the larger purpose. This is a vital part of inspiring people not only to do a job but to do it with pride and commitment. Obviously, not every employee or cast member will be deeply affected, but this idea is planted in so many employees' minds that it creates the strong cultural reinforcement that focuses everyone's attention on producing an "excellent show" for each guest. This is a powerful leadership technique and a valuable way to ensure that everyone stays focused on the guest.

## Leaders, Employees, Guests, and the Larger Purpose

The lessons behind these leadership techniques are simple but worth recalling at this point. Each reader of this book has aspirations to lead, or why bother studying the management of hospitality organizations? Here is a chain of relationships as conceived in the early 1990s by Walt Disney Attractions CEO Judson Green: The commitment and enthusiasm of great organizational leaders will lead to involvement and passion among organizational members.[1] Leaders find ways to provide jobs that are fun, fair, and interesting. Leaders establish a culture of guest service excellence and reinforce it by word, deed, and celebration. Leaders give value to employees by showing them they are valued for both their contributions to the organization and to the larger purpose toward which the organization aspires. Leaders have the joy and the responsibility of making it all happen: happy, motivated servers, wow guest experiences, delighted and loyal guests who return repeatedly and form the foundation of organizational business success.

We have often used Disney as the benchmark, the standard, the reference point, so it is fitting that we conclude by showing what value Disney places on its leaders. From the beginning, Disney intuitively felt that a direct relationship must exist between leadership behaviors, the cast member experience, the guest experience, and customer loyalty. Eventually the organization was able to support the intuition statistically. According to Disney executives Craig Taylor and Cindy Wheatley-Lovoy,

> We have long known that a direct, measurable relationship exists between how cast members feel about their jobs and how that gets translated into the level of service they provide. Creative, high-quality service for guests links directly to their intent to visit us again—a key part of Disney's success. . . . We can now verify statistically what we believed intuitively five years ago: There is a direct link between leadership behaviors and a quality cast experience, a quality guest experience, and our business success. The correlation is strong and specific.[2]

Taylor and Wheatley-Lovoy conclude, "In the business units in which cast members rate their leaders as outstanding in such behaviors as listening, coaching, recognition, and empowerment, the guest satisfaction ratings are the highest."[3]

## The Leader's Challenge: Blending It All Together—Seamlessly

Finally, the leader blends together the strategy, staff, and systems so that everyone knows how and why to concentrate on the guest. The strategy must be right, the staffing right, and the systems right if the combined effort is to succeed in providing the outstanding guest experience the organization is in business to provide. If the leader sees that any element is not contributing to the employee's ability to provide outstanding experiences, the leader will fix it or have it fixed. Just as the organization wants to fix any guest problem that detracts from the guest experience, the outstanding leader wants to fix any employee problem that detracts from that employee's ability to provide an outstanding guest experience.

Figure 14-1 below sums up all the elements that leaders must manage if they are to meet this challenge effectively. They must:

- Define an organizational *vision* of what guest segment is to be served and what service concept will best meet their expectations.
- Select employees with service-oriented attitudes and train them in the necessary *skills.*
- Create and make available the *incentives* that will motivate empowered employees to provide unsurpassed guest service.
- Ensure that employees have the proper *resources* to provide outstanding service.
- Design specific *delivery systems* that translate plans, employee skills, and resources into an experience that meets guest expectations and perhaps even wows the guest.
- Provide the *measurement tools* that allow employees (and coproducing guests) to see how well they are doing in providing the targeted or desired guest experience.

---

Skills + Incentives + Resources + Delivery System + Measurement − Vision
= Unfocused Employees = Unfocused Service = **Confused Guests**

Vision + Incentives + Resources + Delivery System + Measurement − Skills
= Untrained Employees = Probable Failed Service = **Disappointed Guests**

Vision + Skills + Resources + Delivery System + Measurement − Incentives
= Unmotivated Employees = Lackluster Service = **Disillusioned Guests**

Vision + Skills + Incentives + Delivery System + Measurement − Resources
= Unsupported Employees = Inadequate Service = **Complaining Guests**

Vision + Skills + Incentives + Resources + Measurement − Delivery System
=Unreliable Employees = Unreliable Service = **Unsatisfied Guests**

Vision + Skills + Incentives + Resources + Delivery System − Measurement
= Uninformed Employees = Inconsistent Service = **Unfulfilled Guests**

Vision + Skills + Incentives + Resources + Delivery System + Measurement
= **Unsurpassed Employees = Wow Service = Delighted Guests**

---

**Figure 14-1** *Leadership Keys: Achieving the Best for the Guest.*

Measurement is critical for ensuring that all the other factors are correctly focused on achieving the best for the guest. If you don't know how you're doing, you don't know if you need to do better, so you don't know how to do better. If you try to improve guest service, you don't know if you have succeeded.

The chart in Figure 14-1 shows how the guest and the guest's experience can be negatively affected when any one of these important leadership keys is missing or forgotten. Negative effects will not always occur. Just as service failures happen in the best-managed organizations, so can the frontline staff of poorly managed organizations sometimes provide successful guest experiences in spite of the organization and its faults. When one or more leadership keys are missing, however, the chances of consistent service success are reduced. The exact effect on the guest experience may not be predictable in precise terms, but it will not be a happy one.

The chart shows the effects that a missing leadership element can have on employees for a reason. Although managers will do as good a job as they can of managing the nonhuman elements, their ability to change them may be limited. If the dining room is already constructed and the kitchen equipped and set up, the manager may not be able to do much managing of the guest service environment and the mechanical parts of the delivery system. In a way this is good news; it enables managers to focus on the people part of the guest experience: the guests as part of the environment for each other, the guests as they participate in creating their own experiences, the servers as they try to contribute to outstanding experiences, the back-of-the-house employees as they provide what their internal server-guests require. These many and ever-changing elements of the guest service situation require and deserve each manager's attention; using a theme restaurant as an example, perhaps it is fortunate that the elaborate fantasy setting and the frying system don't require moment-to-moment attention as the people do.

If the organization's leaders lack an overall vision of a target market and its expectations, this lack will be communicated from the top throughout the culture and may lead to unfocused service; servers are not sure exactly what they are trying to achieve, and guests received mixed messages and inconsistent experiences. If managers put untrained people in guest contact positions, service failures and disappointed guests are probable. If incentives are lacking or inappropriate, unmotivated employees will simply go through the motions of providing lackluster service experiences. Failure to provide resource support for people in both the front and the back of the house will prohibit even a motivated and guest-focused front line from providing adequate service. Similarly, flaws in the delivery system will keep the best of personnel from providing reliably satisfactory guest experiences, much less experiences that delight; as the saying goes, "a bad system will defeat a good person every time." Finally, if levels of service quality and guest satisfaction are not measured, employees will be frustrated by not knowing whether the guest experiences they are providing are achieving the organizational service vision or not, so in a hit-or-miss fashion, they will continue to provide inconsistent service.

Only when they are all in place can the leader be effective in enabling and empowering employees. Only then can empowered employees provide the *wow* experiences that fulfill the organizational vision of providing remarkable service to delighted guests.

The leaders of each hospitality organization have an awesome responsibility and challenge. It is these people who must motivate and empower employees to do what must be done to create the guest experience with excellence. A poorly manufactured car can be recalled for a retrofit; a bad guest experience is a bad guest experience forever. A tire can be inspected many times by trained quality control engineers before it is sold; a guest experience cannot be inspected because it does not even exist for inspection before it is provided. The guest experience must be right the first time, or the server must be empowered to fix any problems on the spot.

Every manager from the chief executive officer to the frontline supervisor must ultimately make sure that all this happens, that employees feel good about what they are doing, that they convey this feeling to guests, and that guests leave knowing the experience was worth every penny paid and maybe a little bit more. Leadership makes the difference between success and failure in today's hospitality organizations, and it will make the difference in the future. This is the leadership challenge.

## IT BEGINS—AND ENDS—WITH THE GUEST

By now, you may be reciting the components of the guest experience in your sleep: service product plus service setting plus service delivery system. But isn't something or someone missing? If that is a model of the guest experience, *where is the guest?* Obviously you can't have a guest experience without a guest to experience it. That's the whole point; without the guest to initiate it, the components that the organization has assembled—the carefully designed service product, the detailed and inviting setting, the highly trained, motivated servers, and the finest back-of-the-house people and facilities—are just an experience waiting to happen. Throughout this book, we have made the point that it all starts with the guest. We think it fitting that we conclude by saying: *it all ends with the guest, too!*

## Lessons Learned

1. Train employees to think of the people in front of them as their guests.
2. Start with the guests, both external and internal.
3. Build a strong culture and sustain it with stories, deeds, and actions.
4. Manage all three parts of the guest experience.
5. Articulate a vision, transcending any single job, that gives all employees a sense of value and worth in what they do.
6. Organize, staff, train, and reward around the guest's needs.
7. If it is critical to organizational success, measure it carefully and then manage it carefully.
8. Create jobs that are fun, fair, and interesting.
9. Keep in mind the strong relationship between happy, satisfied employees and happy, satisfied guests.
10. Prevent every service failure you can, find every failure you cannot prevent, and fix every failure you find—every time and, if possible, on the spot.
11. Exceeding guest expectations today may not even meet them tomorrow.
12. Never stop teaching; inspire everyone to keep learning.

## Review Questions

1. Assume that your hospitality instructor says, "Bringing together all the principles of strategy, staffing, and systems is the job of the hospitality leader."
   A. What leader or leaders do you think the instructor is talking about?
   B. Who has greater responsibility for "bringing it all together": the hospitality organization's CEO or the local unit manager?
   C. Steak and Bake International has a well-established corporate mission, vision, and strategy. Its delivery systems are all in place, and the individual units are fully staffed. You have just been hired to manage the local Steak and Bake. Do you have responsibilities with regard to strategy, staffing, and systems other than those of a caretaker?
   D. Based on any work observations you have made or organizational experiences you have had, would you distinguish between a *leader* and a *manager?*

2. This book suggests that all people seek to be part of organizations or situations that give them a sense of being involved in and contributing to something greater than themselves. Reflect on organizations you have enjoyed being a part of or for which you have worked hard to help them succeed.
   A. Why did you enjoy them and work hard on their behalf?
   B. In your life, have you joined some organizations "to gain a sense of being involved and to contribute to something greater than yourself" and other organizations for entirely different (perhaps totally selfish or self-centered) reasons?
   C. How does all that relate to managing the guest experience in hospitality organizations?

3. Think back on hospitality organizations that you like and to which you feel loyal. What is it that they do to make you want to return and buy their services again and again? Is it that they provide the basic drivers of your satisfaction so well? Or is it that they provide some *wow* drivers in addition to the basics?

4. The book suggests that one key way to differentiate the guest experience and give it some wow is to personalize it, rather than simply "doing it by the numbers." Think about different hospitality organizations that you have patronized.
   A. Which aspects of service were "done by the numbers"?
   B. What did they do to personalize the experience for you?
   C. Could they have done more to personalize it, and if so, what?

5. Why is empowering the front line so important for hospitality organizations?
   A. Why is a strong organizational culture necessary for successful empowerment?
   B. Why are strong organizational systems necessary for successful empowerment?

6. Consider the probable growth and improvements in communications technology that will occur in coming years. How will these changes affect several different types of hospitality organizations, including hotels, restaurants, and theme parks? How might a typical hotel and restaurant make use of the Internet?

## Activities

1. Be on the lookout for service failures. Try to locate the origins of the failures within Figure 14-1.
2. Divide into groups. Describe bosses or leaders that group members have had who made you feel good about your job or activity. What did the boss or leader do to make you feel that way? Have a similar discussion about bosses or leaders who had an opposite effect on you.
3. Interview four different employees in four different jobs. How do they feel about the jobs they do? What do their leaders do to make them feel either happy or otherwise in their work?

## Case Studies

### The Penland Heights Resort

*N*estled in the mountains of western North Carolina, the luxury-level Penland Heights Resort has been family owned for generations. The employees have also been members of families who have served the guests of the Penland Heights for all those generations. They and Tom and Laura Lunsford, the owner-operators, have taken a familial pride in providing the most outstanding guest service in the Blue Ridge Mountains.

For many years, the Penland Heights was the only employer in the mountain town of Penland. Then progress began to encroach on the town, in the form of fast-food outlets, video stores, tourists, and Florida families who picked off the prime mountain locations as sites for modernistic chalets. The Penland Heights maintained its dignity and its superiority, but the employees on whom the Heights had counted for so long were getting older, and the new generation just did not seem to have the same service values as their elders. Yet, what could the Penland Heights do? Most of the young people left the area as soon as they graduated from high school. Only the younger family members of the aging employees chose to stay in Penland, to work at the Penland Heights.

Tom and Laura Lunsford dreaded the day when they and their guests would have to depend on "the new generation," and as had to happen, eventually the more youthful employees outnumbered the long-time loyal employees. The time also came that the service for which the Heights had long been famous began to slip. The senior Lunsfords felt that the new generation just did not have the service values of their older family members. The Penland management had empowered the older folks to a high degree and were happy to do so. They thought that they would have to exert much more control over their sons and daughters; otherwise the old resort would soon be on the auction block.

Their daughter Granada told them they were wrong. "These are great kids. They love this old barn of a place. Sure, their ideas . . . our ideas . . . are different from yours. But this world *and this business are different from what they were when you were younger and took over the Heights. If you give us kids a chance, we will not only hold the line; we can bring the Penland Heights back to the level of the glory days."*

* * *

1. What are the basic leadership issues in this case?
2. What leadership skills must Tom and Laura Lunsford either have or acquire to continue managing this hotel successfully under the changed social, cultural, and economic conditions of the times?
3. Do you think Tom and Laura, who are intelligent, well meaning, experienced, and highly motivated but somewhat old fashioned, are sufficiently adaptable to fit in with the "new breed" of employees? Can these old dogs learn new tricks? Or in all probability does the future of hotel leadership lie with their daughter Granada who, even though inexperienced, is more in tune with the times?

## The Hotel Kitchen

*Jean Crine, a graduate of the Culinary Institute of America, works in a hotel kitchen as a sous chef. Unlike some hotel restaurants, which seem to exist only so that their hotels can refer to themselves as "full service," this restaurant is the best in a fairly large city. Crine and a few other women hold responsible positions in the hotel, but most of the significant positions are held by men.*

*Crine shares a kitchen with the executive chef, three chefs, and two assistant chefs, all males. The atmosphere in the kitchen was very relaxed and was more social than professional until Crine was hired. When the executive chef isn't around, the other chefs tend to treat Crine like a little sister—teasing her about her clothing, her hair, her formal training (they all learned on the job), mistakes in her work, what she ate for lunch, and her lifestyle. She has expressed her annoyance at this patronizing treatment, but her irritation has only prompted an increase in the teasing.*

*On one occasion, Jean noticed an assistant chef (subordinate in organizational level to her) tossing a large salad without wearing the required rubber gloves. She politely asked him not to do so. He responded by sticking a handful of garlic dressing into her mouth. She retaliated by dumping a jar of olives on him. Some of the olive juice splashed onto a chef working on the other side of the sink. He grabbed Crine and started shaking her. She told him to remove his hands, and he yelled that no woman would tell him what to do. The assistant chef was also yelling that no woman would tell him how to toss a salad. On another occasion, one of the chefs put a picture of a woman wearing only a chef's hat on the kitchen wall. Crine asked him to remove it, but he refused. Crine spoke to the executive chef, who made the chef take the picture down. He was furious.*

*The chefs complain that Crine is outspoken, easily offended, domineering, and rebellious. They claim she is the cause of all disharmony in the kitchen and detrimental to morale and production. The executive chef has spoken severely to her about her tendency to "overreact."*

(Continued)

*Concerning the incident with the salad, Crine maintains that the assistant chef's sticking garlic dressing in her mouth was inexcusable and that her reaction was normal for any person with self-respect. She insists upon her right to be treated as a professional by her coworkers, despite their apparent feeling that women are not equal in ability to men. She feels that to tolerate treatment as an inferior in the world of high cuisine would put an end to her career.*

*Recently, Crine returned to the kitchen after a two-day absence. She remarked that it was good to see everyone again. One of the chefs replied, "Too bad the feeling isn't mutual. I wish you hadn't come back."*

\* \* \*

1. How could the organization have avoided this problem?
2. To what extent if any has Crine brought on her own difficulties? Or do you view her purely as the victim in the situation?
3. What now?

## Millionaire Hotels

*W*ilbur Beck is manager of the Major Equipment Maintenance and Engineering Group for Millionaire Hotels, a southeastern chain. Reporting to Beck are four supervisors, each responsible for a district within the southeast. Assigned to each district are a work group leader and an engineer.

Millionaire Hotels uses the PERT technique to schedule all major maintenance on hotel equipment. The process includes estimating future requirements and then ordering parts and assigning teams to the different hotels to perform the scheduled maintenance. To meet this demand, the MEM&E Group is included in the PERT chart's critical path. Therefore, all work must be done on time.

Beck has decentralized and delegated as much as he can. Within each district, the work group leader is responsible for ensuring that all schedules are met. Nelson Baldwin, supervisor of District I, has been on vacation for two weeks. A few days ago, engineer Frank Diasi came into Beck's office, stated that seven hotel engineering projects in his district were critically overdue, and said he could not possibly catch up without help. When Beck asked why the district was behind, Diasi said bluntly that work group leader Jim Clark devoted his time to "busy work" and did not do his job properly. Diasi said Clark had not performed satisfactorily at any time since his assignment to the district four months earlier.

Upon checking discreetly, Beck found that Diasi was apparently telling the truth. Everyone agreed that Clark was technically capable and personally likable, but for some reason he was not performing the duties required of his position. One employee commented that Clark did not seem to value his position very highly. Beck arranged to bail out District 1 by borrowing help from other districts, but something obviously had to be done about Clark.

When district supervisor Baldwin returned from his vacation, Beck questioned him. He said he had only recently become aware that Clark was performing poorly. He admitted that he had *not kept close track of individual performance within his district because the group as a whole had been performing fairly well; he thought district results were what counted. He asked Beck for help in determining what to do about Clark. They reviewed Clark's background together.*

*Clark is 54 years old. He came to Millionaire five years ago from another major chain. When he arrived, he and top management both anticipated that he would soon become a group manager in a position similar to Beck's. However, although he appears to be quite good technically, he simply has not lived up to expectations. For the past couple of years, he has obviously resented taking orders from younger managers. A year ago, when Clark was in another district, Beck decided that he was adequate in his present job but was not then promotable. Clark became quite angry when he heard Beck's appraisal. Since that time, his attitude has been barely acceptable.*

*\*\*\**

1. What do you suppose is wrong with Clark?
2. Who is at fault, if anyone?
3. What should be done now?

## The Management Seminar

*"I'd like to sum up what we've been talking about during this four-week management seminar,"* said Professor Stilwell to Trina Morgan and 19 other participating managers. *"Research and practical experience both show that if you give your employees the opportunity, they will get together, discuss problems, analyze alternatives, and then come up with good decisions that they will implement with enthusiasm."*

*Morgan was persuaded that group discussion and group decision making could work at Hoffman Restaurant, where she was manager. Once back at the restaurant, she called together the 30 servers and relayed this message.*

*"Our current service standards were established seven years ago. Last year we installed automated equipment in the delivery system to make your work easier, and raised your pay as a reward for work well done, but we have not changed the service standards. I am asking you to discuss the situation thoroughly and then to decide what the new standards should be in both the cocktail and food areas. I'll be back at 11 o'clock to hear what you have decided."* Morgan thought surely that the employees would set high standards and, because they had made the decision themselves, would try extra hard to achieve them.

*When Morgan returned, she listened to head server Rollie Morris, spokesman for the group: "Ms. Morgan, we appreciate your faith in us, and we are convinced that we have justified that faith by coming to the right decision. We talked it over and decided that, even with the automated equipment, which is now a part of the delivery system, the service standards are still too high. We have to just about kill ourselves to meet them, and we all go home dragging. Therefore, we unanimously agreed to abolish the standards. They make this place feel like a production line. We can deliver more wow if we are just left on our own."*

(Continued)

*The servers cheered and smiled. Morgan excused herself from the meeting, went to her office, and placed a call to Professor Stilwell.*

* * *

1. Is there a leadership problem at Hoffman Restaurant?
2. What mistakes, if any, did Trina Morgan make?
3. What will Professor Stilwell say? How will he advise Trina Morgan?
4. Do you think his advice will work?

## Additional Readings

Cichy, Ronald F., and Raymond S. Schmidgall. 1996. Leadership Qualities of Financial Executives in the U.S. Lodging Industry. *Cornell Hotel and Restaurant Administration Quarterly* 37(2):56–62.

Heifetz, Ronald A., and Donald L. Laurie. 1997. The Work of Leadership. *Harvard Business Review* 75(1):124–134.

Pittaway, Rita Carmouche, and Elizabeth Chell. 1998. The Way Forward: Leadership Research in the Hospitality Industry. *International Journal of Hospitality Management* 17(4):407–426.

Tracey, J. B., and T. R. Hinkin. 1994. Transformational Leaders in the Hospitality Industry. *Cornell Hotel and Restaurant Administration Quarterly* 35(2):18–24.

Walker, John R., and Carl G. Braunlich. 1996. Quality Leadership in the Service Industries. *Hospitality Research Journal* 19(4):155–164.

## Notes

1. In Craig R. Taylor and Cindy Wheatley-Lovoy. 1998. Leadership: Lessons From the Magic Kingdom. *Training and Development* (July):24.
2. Ibid.
3. Ibid.

# Glossary

**Action plans**—The specific plans that translate the service strategy into guides for employee activity over the coming period, usually a year.

**Advanced information system**—A system that, rather than simply providing information, is able to respond to information and choose between alternatives; see also **decision system** and **expert system.**

**Arrival patterns**—The patterns describing the number of customers arriving or entering a system in a given period of time.

**Artificial intelligence**—An advanced form of **expert system.**

**Authority-acceptance theory**—Chester Barnard's theory of what authority is and why people do or do not accept it.

**Bad-mouthing**—The spreading of negative comments and opinions about an organization by a dissatisfied customer.

**Beliefs**—A body of ideas or tenets believed to be or accepted as true.

**Benchmark organizations**—Organizations that meet and often exceed customer expectations regarding service quality and value and that have a high degree of excellence in their services, processes, and business support systems; these organizations also frequently have a world-class reputation.

**Blueprinting**—A flowchart diagram of the events and contingencies in the service process, on paper or on a computer screen, in blueprint format.

**Brainstorming**—As a qualitative forecasting tool, a method in which a group of people generate and share ideas in open discussion, often in a free-association way, about what the future may bring.

**Brand image, Brand name**—Image or name associated with a specific product, service, or organization, used to differentiate the organization's offerings so as to achieve market superiority over competitors.

**Capacity day**—The maximum number of guests allowed, by law or by the organization, in a service facility in a day or at one time, used like the **design day** to balance the costs to the organization of excess capacity and the costs to the guest (in terms of quality and value) of inadequate capacity.

**Coproduction**—The active producing or helping to produce and deliver the guest experience by guests themselves, ideally to the mutual benefit of guests and the organization.

**Comment card**—A method for obtaining guest feedback, often in the form of a postcard, enabling guests to rate the quality of the guest experience by responding to a few simple questions.

**Core competency**—A strength basic and perhaps unique to an organization.

**Cost**—The entire burden expended by a guest to receive a service, including tangible quantifiable costs (like price) and intangible nonquantifiable costs like opportunity costs of foregoing alternative opportunities, annoyance at receiving unsatisfactory service, and so forth.

**Critical path**—The sequence of activities from the start of a project to its completion having the greatest cumulative elapsed time, thereby determining how long the entire project will take.

**Critical Path Method (CPM)**—A project planning method based on the assumption that all activity times are known.

**Cross-functional organization**—A method of organizing people and groups so as to enable them to work temporarily across the boundaries or functional units in which organizations are traditionally structured; also, an overlaying of a group or project team upon the traditional functional organizational structure to work on a task for a limited time, which creates multiple lines of authority.

**Cross-selling**—Using an interaction with a guest who has come to the organization for one service as an opportunity to sell the guest another product or service.

**Culture** See **organizational culture.**

**Daily count**—A prediction arrived at by an information system after a relatively short period of time (e.g., an hour), and based on a combination of actual count, an attendance database, and knowledge of arrival-rate distributions, of how many guests will come into the service location during the whole day.

**Decision system**—An information system that, in addition to providing information, has the capability of responding to information, choosing between alternatives, and either making or helping to make a decision.

**Delphi technique**—As a qualitative forecasting tool, a rather formal process involving surveying experts to get their individual forecasts, then combining or averaging those forecasts, often followed by another round of estimates based on a sharing of the individual and combined forecasts, the goal being to arrive at a final combined forecast.

**Design day**—The day of the year which the organization assumes when determining how much capacity to design for; used to balance the costs to the organization of excess capacity and the costs to the guest (in terms of quality and value) of inadequate capacity; see also **capacity day.**

**Differentiation**—A strategy designed to create in the guest's mind desirable differences, either real or driven by marketing and advertising, between the service or product offered by the organization and other competing services and products.

**Disney "show"**—Everyone and everything that interfaces or interacts with guests on a Disney property.

**Distributive fairness**—The fairness of outcomes, organizational distributions, or compensations to guests who believe they have experienced unsatisfactory service, as determined by the guest.

**Eager factors**—The factors or elements that make an employee's job *fun,* establish the *fairness* of how the rewards are distributed, and cause the job to be *interesting* for the employee.

**Eatertainment restaurant**—A restaurant, often heavily themed, that somehow combines the provision of food and entertainment.

**Econometric models**—Elaborate mathematical descriptions of multiple and complex relationships, statistically assembled as systems of multiple regression equations; used in forecasting; see also **regression analysis.**

**Economic ordering quantity (EOQ) formula**—A formula for calculating the optimum reorder size (number of units) of an item once the reorder point is reached; designed to minimize annual order and holding costs.

**Employee development**—The use of methods designed to provide present employees with the KSAs they will need in *future* jobs and assignments.

**Empowerment**—Giving employees authority to make decisions and gain greater control over their work.

**Environment**—See **service environment.**

**Environmental assessment**—A careful examination of the present opportunities and threats in the external business environment, and forecast of the future environment, within which the organization operates to determine the impact of external factors on the organization and to discover the key drivers that will satisfy present and future guests; carried out as part of long-term strategic planning and sometimes called *the long look around.*

**Evangelist**—Extremely satisfied, delighted guest who takes every available opportunity, and often creates opportunities, to praise the organization and recommend it to friends and acquaintances.

**Expectations**—Characteristics that a guest hopes and assumes will be associated with a service experience.

**Expert system**—A sophisticated information system designed to duplicate the decision process used by an expert who gathers, organizes, and interprets information, then uses a set of decision rules to make a decision.

**External training**—Training provided for organizational members by persons or institutions outside the organization.

**Firing the guest**—A relatively recent concept involving the refusal to serve certain guests who engage in unacceptable extreme behaviors; a philosophy contrary to "the guest is always right."

**Fishbone analysis**—An approach to problem solving that involves drawing a diagram, shaped like a fishbone, of the problem and its possible causes.

**Fishbone diagram**—A diagram, shaped like a fish skeleton, used in problem solving with the problem represented by the fish spine and the possible problem areas attached to the spine.

**Focus group**—As a qualitative forecasting tool, a group of people—frequently guests—discuss with a trained group discussion leader their future hopes and expectations of the organization; often used to sound out guests about planned organizational innovations.

**Guest experience**—Defined as consisting of the service product, setting, and delivery system, it is the sum total of the experience that the guest has with the service provider on a given occasion or set of occasions; often referred to as **service experience** in other service industries.

**Guest comment card**—See **comment card.**

**Guest participation**—See **coproduction.**

**Guestologist**—A specialist in identifying how hospitality organizations can best respond to the needs, wants, and expectations of their targeted guest markets

**Guestology**—The study of guests and their behavior—their wants, needs, and expectations—with the aim of aligning the organization's strategy, staff, and systems so as to provide outstanding service to guests.

**Hospitality**—An industry consisting basically of organizations that offer guests courteous, professional food, drink, and lodging services, alone or in combination, but in an expanded definition also including theme park, gaming, cruise ship, trade show, fair, meeting planning, and convention organizations.

**Information overload**—Literally, too much information; generally referring to a tendency of information systems and their users to generate and send too much information or nonuseful information to guests and employees.

**Information system**—A system, often computerized, designed to get the right information to the right person in the right format at the right time so that it adds value to that person's decisions.

**Integrated information system**—A system designed to bring together diverse sources of organizational information to enable managerial decisions.

**Interactive fairness**—Fairness, respectfulness, and courtesy of organizational treatment during interactions regarding a service failure, as determined by the guest.

**Internal audit**—A careful examination of the organization's present internal condition, its strengths—primarily its core competencies—and weaknesses; carried out as part of long-term strategic planning and sometimes called *the searching look within.*

**Internal customer**—Persons or units within the organization that depend on and serve each other.

**Internal training**—Training provided for organizational members by persons or groups within the organization itself.

**Job content**—The tasks and procedures necessary for doing a certain job.

**Job context**—That part of the organizational mission, goals, and objectives within which the individual job fits.

**Juran's Trilogy**—Joseph Juran's model of quality: planning, control, and improvement.

**Key driver**—A primary factor within a guest experience valued highly by the guest and leading to guest satisfaction, determined by surveying and studying guests.

**KSAs**—Short for knowledge, skills, and abilities necessary to do a job.

**Lean environment**—A service setting, environment, or servicescape requiring that guests process relatively little information; used when guests are generally unfamiliar with the environment; see also **rich environment.**

**Low-price provider**—An organization that tries to compete within its market primarily by maximizing operational or production efficiencies and minimizing organizational costs so as to offer the same service as competitors at a lower price.

**Managing information**—Using information systems to get the right information to the right person in the right format at the right time.

**Managing the wait**—The organization's use of queuing theory and psychological techniques to minimize the negative impact on guests of inevitable waits.

**Market niche**—A gap in a market that an organization seeks out, focuses on, and attempts to fill to attract customers and compete successfully.

**MBWA**—Stands for *management by walking around;* managers walk around observing the operation firsthand, looking for problems or inefficiencies, talking to guests and employees, and offering suggestions; sometimes referred to as *walking the front.*

**Mission statement**—An articulation of the organization's purpose, the reason for which it was founded and for which it continues to exist; see also **vision statement.**

**Moment of truth**—A term coined by Jan Carlzon to refer to any key or crucial moment or period during a service encounter, a make-or-break moment; subsequently expanded by others to include any significant or memorable interaction point between organization and guest.

**Motivation**—The drive or compelling force that energizes people to do what they do in a given situation.

**Multichannel waiting line**—A waiting line with more than one server.

**Mystery shopper**—Hired or in-house person who poses as a guest, methodically sample the service and its delivery, observe the overall guest service operation, and then submit a report to management.

**Norms**—Standards of behavior—spoken and unspoken, obvious and subtle—that define how members (and sometimes guests) are expected to act while part of the organization.

**Organization as an information system**—The idea that the organization itself should be considered as and structured as an integrated information network or system.

**Organizational culture**—The totality of the organization's socially transmitted beliefs, values, norms, and behavior patterns.

**Organizational mission**—See **mission statement.**

**Organizational vision**—See **vision statement.**

**Pareto analysis**—A problem-solving technique based on arranging the potential causes of an organizational problem in their order of importance, from highest to lowest.

**PERT/CPM**—PERT stands for Program Evaluation Review Technique, and CPM stand for **Critical Path Method.**

**PERT/CPM Chart**—A diagram, usually used in the planning of major projects, consisting of circles representing completed events, arrows representing the activities that must be done before an event can be considered completed, and often including a **critical path** indicating the sequence of events that must occur on time if the project is to be completed on time.

**Poisson probability distribution**—A probability distribution used to describe the random arrival pattern for some waiting lines.

**Poka-yoke**—A device or procedure designed to prevent the recurrence of a defect; "mistake-proofing" in Japanese.

**Positive reinforcement**—Providing rewards to employees for organizationally approved behaviors—namely, those associated with high levels of guest satisfaction—to encourage repetition of those behaviors.

**Procedural fairness**—The fairness and straightforwardness of company procedures for handling service failure, as determined by the guest.

**Qualitative forecasting tools**—Forecasting tools that use nonquantitative, subjective information to make projections.

**Quality**—Special meaning in the hospitality field: The difference between what the guest expects and what the guest gets.

**Quantitative forecasting tools**—Forecasting tools that use quantitative, nonsubjective information or data to make projections.

**Queue**—A waiting line.

**Queue discipline**—In hospitality settings, the organization's pattern or plan for how arriving guests are served; usually first-come, first-served.

**Queuing theory**—The theory of how waiting lines behave; same as **waiting-line theory.**

**Recruitment**—The process of finding candidates with the KSAs necessary to fill organizational positions.

**Regression analysis**—Study of the statistical relationship or degree of association between two or more variables to predict a dependent variable of interest; used in forecasting.

**Rich environment**—A service setting, environment, or servicescape in which much information is available for processing by guests; used when guests are generally familiar with the environment; see also **lean environment.**

**Ritual**—A symbolic act performed to gain and maintain membership or identity within an organization.

**Role theory**—The theory of how other people or groups influence us to behave or function in particular settings or situations.

**Scenario building**—As a qualitative forecasting tool, a group of people—frequently organizational employees—assume a certain future situation or set of circumstances, then try to assess its implications for the organization; sometimes called *war gaming.*

**Selection**—The process of selecting employees to fill organizational positions from the candidates with the necessary KSAs.

**Service**—An action or performed task that takes place by direct contact between the customer or guest and representatives of the service organization.

**Service delivery system**—The human components and the physical production processes, plus the organizational and information systems, involved in delivering the service to the customer.

**Service encounter**—The actual person-to-person interaction or series of interactions between the customer and the persons delivering the service.

**Service environment**—The physical location and its characteristics within which the organization provides service to guests; same as **service setting** and **servicescape.**

**Service experience**—Same as **guest experience** but sometimes used in service industries that do not typically refer to their customers as guests.

**Service failure**—The organization's failure to deliver the promised service according to its own standards or the guest's expectations.

**Service guarantee**—An organization's written promise either to satisfy guests or to compensate them for any failure to satisfy them regarding the overall service or particular aspects of it.

**Service package**—See **service product.**

**Service product**—The entire bundle of tangibles and intangibles provided by a hospitality organization to guests during a service experience; same as **service package.**

**Service quality**—Special meaning in the services field: The difference between the service that the customer expects to get and the service that the customer actually receives.

**Service recovery**—The organization's attempt to make right or compensate for a **service failure.**

**Service setting**—The physical location and its characteristics within which the organization provides service to guests; same as **service environment** and **servicescape.**

**Service value**—The relationship of the quality of the service to its cost, or service quality divided by cost of service.

**Servicescape**—The physical location and its characteristics within which the organization provides service to guests, especially the physical aspects of the setting that contribute to the guest's overall physical "feel" of the experience; same as **service environment** and **service setting.**

**SERVQUAL**—Standing for "service quality," SERVQUAL is the best-known survey instrument within the services field; measures customer perceptions of service quality along five dimensions: reliability, responsiveness, assurance, empathy, and tangibles.

**Setting**—See **service setting.**

**Simulation**—An imitation of a real or potential problem or organizational situation.

**Single-channel waiting line**—A waiting line with only one server.

**Strategic premises**—Assumptions about the future, based on the results of forecasting, on which the organization's strategic plan is based or premised.

**Strategic plan**—The specific steps that detail how the organization intends to get from where it is to where it wishes to be in order to achieve its mission and vision.

**Structured interview: guest**—An interview conducted according to a set pattern, usually involving a standard set of professionally developed, validated questions designed to gather guest perceptions of service quality.

**Structured interview: job candidate**—A job interview conducted according to a set pattern, usually involving a standard set of questions designed to gather relevant personal and job-related data, and intended to ensure that all candidates are assessed consistently according to the same criteria.

**Symbol**—A physical object that has organizational significance or communicates an unspoken message (e.g., Mickey's ears).

**Terrorist**—Extremely dissatisfied guest who takes every available opportunity, and often creates opportunities, to bad-mouth the organization, or worse.

**Theming**—The organization and presentation of the guest experience around a unifying idea or theme, often a fantasy theme, to give guests the illusion of being in a place and time other than "the here and now"; most often used in connection with theme parks and theme restaurants.

**Time series and trend analysis**—Statistical methods for projecting past information or trends into the future; used in forecasting.

**Training methods**—Methods used to provide employees with necessary or helpful KSAs, the standard methods being classroom presentations, video, one-on-one supervised experiences, home study, and computerized presentations.

**Universal Service Map**—An elaborate and detailed **blueprint** that can be generally applied to a variety of service situations.

**Value**—Quality related to cost, or quality divided by cost.

**Values**—Preferences for certain ideas, behaviors, and outcomes over others, used and promulgated within organizations to define for members (and sometimes guests) what is right and wrong, preferred and not preferred.

**Vision statement**—An articulation of what the organization hopes to look like and be like in the future; see also **mission statement.**

**Waiting-line theory**—The theory of how waiting lines behave; same as **queuing theory.**

**Work group, work team**—A small employee group (typically under fifteen) with complementary skills committed to the achievement of a common purpose and set of specific performance goals, the members holding each other fully and jointly accountable for the team's results.

**Work team characteristics**—A set of KSAs that seem to characterize successful work teams; see Table 7-1.

**Yield management**—A technique for managing the sale of an organization's units of capacity, using forecasts based on past results, to maximize the profitability of that capacity; in other words, selling the right capacity to the right customer at the right time.

# *Appendix*

## BOOKS ON HOSPITALITY AND SERVICES

Albrecht, Karl. 1988. *At America's Service: How Corporations Can Revolutionize the Way They Treat Their Customers.* Homewood, IL: Dow Jones-Irwin.

Albrecht, Karl. 1992. *The Only Thing That Matters: Bring the Power of the Customer to the Center of Your Business.* New York: Harper Business.

Albrecht, Karl, and Lawrence J. Bradford. 1990. *The Service Advantage: How to Identify and Fulfill Customer Needs.* Homewood, IL: Dow Jones-Irwin.

Albrecht, Karl, and Ron Zemke. 1985. *Service America! Doing Business in the New Economy.* Homewood, IL: Dow Jones-Irwin.

Anton, Jon. 1996. *Customer Relationship Management: Making Hard Decisions with Soft Numbers.* Upper Saddle River, NJ: Prentice Hall.

Barlow, Janelle, and Claus Moller. 1996. *A Complaint Is a Gift: Using Customer Feedback as a Strategic Tool.* San Francisco: Berrett-Koehler.

Bateson, John E. G. 1995. *Managing Services Marketing,* 2nd ed. Fort Worth, TX: Dryden Press.

Berry, Leonard L. 1999. *Discovering the Soul of Service: The Nine Drivers of Sustainable Business Success.* New York: The Free Press.

Berry, Leonard L. 1995. *On Great Service.* New York: The Free Press.

Berry, Leonard L., and A. Parasuraman. 1991. *Marketing Services: Competing through Quality.* New York: The Free Press.

Bitner, M. J., and L. A. Crosby, eds. 1989. *Designing a Winning Service Strategy.* Chicago: American Marketing Association.

Blumberg, Donald. 1991. *Managing Service as a Strategic Profit Center.* New York: McGraw-Hill.

Bowen, David E., Richard B. Chase, and Thomas G. Cummings, eds. 1990. *Service Management Effectiveness: Balancing Strategy, Organization and Human Resources, Operations and Marketing.* San Francisco: Jossey-Bass.

Brown, Stephen W., et al., eds. 1991. *Service Quality: Multidisciplinary and Multinational Perspectives.* Lexington, MA: Lexington Books.

Collier, David A. 1994. *The Service/Quality Solution: Using Service Management to Gain Competitive Advantage.* Milwaukee: American Society for Quality Press.

Edmondson, B. 1996. *Hospitality Leadership.* Ithaca, NY: Cornell Hotel School.

Fitzsimmons, James A., and Mona J. Fitzsimmons. 1994. *Service Management for Competitive Advantage.* New York: McGraw-Hill.

Gale, Bradley T., and Robert C. Wood. 1994. *Managing Customer Value: Creating Quality and Service That Customers Can See.* New York: The Free Press.

Glynn, William, and James Barnes. 1995. *Understanding Services Management.* New York: John Wiley & Sons.

Go, F., and R. Pine. 1996. *Globalization Strategy in the Hotel Industry.* London: Routledge.

Go, F., M. Monachello, and T. Baum. 1996. *Human Resource Management in the Hospitality Industry.* New York: Wiley.

Goodman, R., Jr. 1995. *The Management of Service for the Restaurant Manager,* 2nd ed. Burr Ridge, IL: Irwin.

Gronroos, Christian. 1990. *Service Management and Marketing: Managing the Moments of Truth in Service Competition.* Lexington, MA: Lexington Books.

Gutek, Barbara A. 1995. *The Dynamics of Service: Reflections on the Changing Nature of Customer/Provider Interactions.* San Francisco: Jossey-Bass.

Harris, Elaine. 1996. *Customer Service: A Practical Approach.* Upper Saddle River, NJ: Prentice Hall.

Hayes, Bob. 1998. *Measuring Customer Satisfaction.* Milwaukee: ASQC Quality Press.

Heskett, James L. 1986. *Managing in the Service Economy.* Boston: Harvard Business School Press.

Hinton, Thomas. 1991. *The Spirit of Service: How to Create a Customer-Focused Culture.* Dubuque, IA: Kendall-Hunt.

Jones, Peter. 1993. *The International Hospitality Industry: Organizational and Operational Issues.* New York: Wiley.

Lele, Milind, and Jagdish Sheth. 1991. *The Customer Is Key.* New York: John Wiley & Sons.

Lewis, R. C., and R. E. Chambers. 1989. *Marketing Leadership in Hospitality.* New York: Van Nostrand Reinhold.

Lockwood, A., M. Baker, and A. Ghillyer. 1996. *Quality in Hospitality: Best Practice in Action.* London: Cassell.

Lovelock, Christopher H. 1992. *Managing Services: Marketing, Operations, Human Resources,* 2nd ed. Englewood Cliffs, NJ: Prentice Hall.

Marriott, J. Willard, and Kathi Ann Brown. 1997. *The Spirit to Serve: Marriott's Way.* New York: Harperbusiness.

Martin, C., A. Payne, and D. Ballantyne. 1993. *Relationship Marketing: Bringing Quality, Customer Service, and Marketing Together.* Oxford, England: Butterworth Heinemann.

McCarthy, Dennis G. 1997. *The Loyalty Link: How Loyal Employees Create Loyal Customers.* New York: John Wiley & Sons.

Mullins, L. 1992. *Hospitality Management: A Human Resources Approach.* London: Pitman.

Nebel, E. 1991. *Managing Hotels Effectively: Lessons from Outstanding General Managers.* New York: Van Nostrand Reinhold.

O'Connor, P. 1995. *Using Computers in Hospitality Management.* London: Cassell.

Olsen, M. D., E. C. Tse, and J. J. West. 1992. *Strategic Management in the Hospitality Industry.* New York: Van Nostrand Reinhold.

Palmer, Adrian. 1994. *Principles of Services Marketing.* Maidenhead, Berkshire: McGraw-Hill.

Peppers, D., and M. Rogers. 1993. *The One to One Future: Building Relationships One Customer at a Time.* New York: Currency Doubleday.

Rust, Roland T. 1994. *Service Quality: New Directions in Theory and Practice.* Thousand Oaks, CA: Sage Publications.

Teare, R., and Olsen, M. D., eds. 1992. *International Hospitality Management: Corporate Strategy in Practice.* London: Pitman.

Teare, Richard, Luiz Moutinho, and Neil Morgan, eds. 1990. *Managing and Marketing Services in the 1990s.* London: Cassell.

Technical Assistance Research Programs Institute. 1986. *Consumer Complaint Handling in America: An Update Study.* Washington, DC: Technical Assistance Research Programs Institute.

Timm, Paul. 1998. *Customer Service: Career Success through Customer Satisfaction.* Upper Saddle River, NJ: Prentice Hall.

Vavra, Terry. 1995. *After Marketing: How to Keep Customers for Life through Relationship Marketing.* Homewood, IL: Irwin Professional Publications.

Vavra, Terry. 1997. *Improving Your Measurement of Customer Satisfaction.* Milwaukee: American Society for Quality Press.

Wilson, J. R. 1994. *Word-of-Mouth Marketing.* New York: Wiley.

Zeithaml, Valarie A., A. Parasuraman, and Leonard L. Berry. 1990. *Delivering Quality Service: Balancing Customer Perceptions and Expectations.* New York: The Free Press

# Index